NOTE ON THE AUTHOR

John Maynard Keynes was born in Cambridge in 1883, son of John Neville Keynes, later registrary of the university; his mother was one of the earliest women students. Educated at Eton and King's, he passed into the Civil Service in 1906, working for over two years in the India Office. He returned to Cambridge in 1908, became a Fellow of King's in 1909 and remained so until his death.

His first entry into public affairs came with his membership of the Royal Commission on Indian Finance and Currency of 1913. Soon after the outbreak of war in 1914 he was called to the Treasury. Over the next four years his ability and his immense capacity for work took him to the top. By 1919 he was principal Treasury representative at the Peace Conference at Versailles. His passionate disagreement with decisions regarding reparations led to his resignation and the writing of *The Economic Consequences of the Peace*. From then on, Keynes was a national figure, in the centre of every economic argument and the author of countless 'Keynes plans' to solve one problem after another.

In 1936 he published the most provocative book written by any economist of his generation. *The General Theory*, as it is known to all economists, cut through all the Gordian knots of pre-Keynesian discussion of the trade cycle and propounded a new approach to the determination of the level of economic activity, the problems of employment and unemployment, the causes of inflation, the strategies of budgetary policy. Argument about the book continued until his death in 1946 and still continues today.

THE COLLECTED WRITINGS OF
JOHN MAYNARD KEYNES

Managing Editors:
Professor Austin Robinson and Professor Donald Moggridge

John Maynard Keynes (1883–1946) was without doubt one of the most influ-
ential thinkers of the twentieth century. His work revolutionised the theory
and practice of modern economics. It has had a profound impact on the
way economics is taught and written, and on economic policy, around the
world. *The Collected Writings of John Maynard Keynes*, published in full in
electronic and paperback format for the first time, makes available in thirty
volumes all of Keynes's published books and articles. This includes writings
from his time in the India Office and Treasury, correspondence in which he
developed his ideas in discussion with fellow economists and correspondence
relating to public affairs. Arguments about Keynes's work have continued
long beyond his lifetime, but his ideas remain central to any understanding of
modern economics, and a point of departure from which each new generation
of economists draws inspiration.

This volume, with its companion volume XIV, provides all the surviving letters, drafts and articles arising from Keynes's work as a monetary economist
between 1924 and 1939. It contains wherever possible both sides of all correspondence concerning his *Treatise on Money* and *General Theory*, both
before and after publication, as well as complete texts of all surviving drafts
of both works. In addition it contains important correspondence concerning
D. H. Robertson's *Banking Policy and the Price Level* and such post-*General
Theory* contributions as R. F. Harrod's first work on the theory of economic
growth. As such, it provides a remarkable chronicle of one man's intellectual
development over the quarter of a century that saw a revolution in economics.

THE COLLECTED WRITINGS OF
JOHN MAYNARD KEYNES

VOLUME XIII

THE GENERAL THEORY
AND AFTER

PART I
PREPARATION

EDITED BY
DONALD MOGGRIDGE

CAMBRIDGE UNIVERSITY PRESS

FOR THE

ROYAL ECONOMIC SOCIETY

CAMBRIDGE
UNIVERSITY PRESS

University Printing House, Cambridge CB2 8BS, United Kingdom

One Liberty Plaza, 20th Floor, New York, NY 10006, USA

477 Williamstown Road, Port Melbourne, VIC 3207, Australia

4843/24, 2nd Floor, Ansari Road, Daryaganj, Delhi - 110002, India

79 Anson Road, #06-04/06, Singapore 079906

Cambridge University Press is part of the University of Cambridge.

It furthers the University's mission by disseminating knowledge in the pursuit of education, learning and research at the highest international levels of excellence.

www.cambridge.org
Information on this title: www.cambridge.org/9781107656413

Published for the Royal Economic Society throughout the world by Cambridge University Press

This edition published 2013
3rd printing 2014

A catalogue record for this publication is available from the British Library

ISBN 978-1-107-65641-3 Paperback

CONTENTS

PART I
PREPARATION

PART II
DEFENCE AND DEVELOPMENT

GENERAL INTRODUCTION

This new standard edition of *The Collected Writings of John Maynard Keynes* forms the memorial to him of the Royal Economic Society. He devoted a very large share of his busy life to the Society. In 1911, at the age of twenty-eight, he became editor of the *Economic Journal* in succession to Edgeworth; two years later he was made secretary as well. He held these offices without intermittence until almost the end of his life. Edgeworth, it is true, returned to help him with the editorship from 1919 to 1925; MacGregor took Edgeworth's place until 1934, when Austin Robinson succeeded him and continued to assist Keynes down to 1945. But through all these years Keynes himself carried the major responsibility and made the principal decisions about the articles that were to appear in the *Economic Journal*, without any break save for one or two issues when he was seriously ill in 1937. It was only a few months before his death at Easter 1946 that he was elected president and handed over his editorship to Roy Harrod and the secretaryship to Austin Robinson.

In his dual capacity of editor and secretary Keynes played a major part in framing the policies of the Royal Economic Society. It was very largely due to him that some of the major publishing activities of the Society—Sraffa's edition of Ricardo, Stark's edition of the economic writings of Bentham, and Guillebaud's edition of Marshall, as well as a number of earlier publications in the 1930s—were initiated.

When Keynes died in 1946 it was natural that the Royal Economic Society should wish to commemorate him. It was perhaps equally natural that the Society chose to commemorate him by producing an edition of his collected works. Keynes himself had always taken a joy in fine printing, and the Society, with the help of Messrs Macmillan as publishers and the Cambridge University Press as printers, has been anxious to give Keynes's writings a permanent form that is wholly worthy of him.

The present edition will publish as much as is possible of his work in the field of economics. It will not include any private and personal correspondence or publish letters in the possession of his family. The edition is concerned, that is to say, with Keynes as an economist.

Keynes's writings fall into five broad categories. First, there are the books which he wrote and published as books. Second, there are collections of articles and pamphlets which he himself made during his lifetime (*Essays in Persuasion* and *Essays in Biography*). Third, there is a very considerable volume of published but uncollected writings—articles written for newspapers, letters to newspapers, articles in journals that have not been included in his two volumes of collections, and various pamphlets. Fourth, there are a few hitherto unpublished writings. Fifth, there is correspondence with economists and others concerned with economics or public affairs.

This series will attempt to publish a complete record of Keynes's serious writing as an economist. It is the intention to publish almost completely the whole of the first four categories listed above. The only exceptions are a few syndicated articles where Keynes wrote almost the same material for publication in different newspapers or in different countries, with minor and unimportant variations. In these cases, this series will publish one only of the variations, choosing the most interesting.

The publication of Keynes's economic correspondence must inevitably be selective. In the day of the typewriter and the filing cabinet and particularly in the case of so active and busy a man, to publish every scrap of paper that he may have dictated about some unimportant or ephemeral matter is impossible. We are aiming to collect and publish as much as possible, however, of the correspondence in which Keynes developed his own ideas in argument with his fellow economists, as well as the more significant correspondence at times when Keynes was in the middle of public affairs.

Apart from his published books, the main sources available to those preparing this series have been two. First, Keynes in his will made Richard Kahn his executor and responsible for his economic papers. They have been placed in the Marshall Library of the University of Cambridge and have been available for this edition. Until 1914 Keynes did not have a secretary and his earliest papers are in the main limited to drafts of important letters that he made in his own handwriting and retained. At that stage most of the correspondence that we possess is represented by what he received rather than by what he wrote. During the years 1914–18 and 1940–6 Keynes was serving in the Treasury. With the recent opening of the records under the thirty-year rule, many of the papers that he wrote then have become available. From 1919 onwards, throughout the rest of his life, Keynes had the help of a secretary—for many years Mrs Stevens. Thus for the last twenty-five years of his working life we have in most cases the carbon copies of his own letters as well as the originals of the letters that he received.

There were, of course, occasions during this period on which Keynes wrote himself in his own handwriting. In some of these cases, with the help of his correspondents, we have been able to collect the whole of both sides of some important interchange and we have been anxious, in justice to both correspondents, to see that both sides of the correspondence are published in full.

The second main source of information has been a group of scrapbooks kept over a very long period of years by Keynes's mother, Florence Keynes, wife of Neville Keynes. From 1919 onwards these scrapbooks contain almost the whole of Maynard Keynes's more ephemeral writing, his letters to newspapers and a great deal of material which enables one to see not only what he wrote, but the reaction of others to his writing. Without these very carefully kept scrapbooks the task of any editor or biographer of Keynes would have been immensely more difficult.

The plan of the edition, as at present intended, is this. It will total twenty-five volumes. Of these, the first eight will be Keynes's published books from *Indian Currency and Finance*, in

1913, to the *General Theory* in 1936, with the addition of his *Treatise on Probability*. There will next follow, as vols. IX and X, *Essays in Persuasion* and *Essays in Biography*, representing Keynes's own collections of articles. *Essays in Persuasion* will differ from the original printing in two respects; it will contain the full texts of the articles or pamphlets included in it and not (as in the original printing) abbreviated versions of these articles, and it will have added one or two later articles which are of exactly the same character as those included by Keynes in his original collection. In the case of *Essays in Biography*, we shall add several other biographical studies that Keynes wrote later than 1933.

There will follow four volumes, XI to XIV, of economic articles and correspondence, and one volume of social, political, and literary writings. We shall include in these volumes such part of Keynes's economic correspondence as is closely associated with the articles that are printed in them.

The further nine volumes, as we estimate at present, will deal with Keynes's *Activities* during the years from the beginning of his public life in 1905 until his death. In each of the periods into which we propose to divide this material, the volume concerned will publish his more ephemeral writings, all of it hitherto un-collected, his correspondence relating to these activities, and such other material and correspondence as is necessary to the understanding of Keynes's activities. These volumes are being edited by Elizabeth Johnson and Donald Moggridge, and it is their task to trace and interpret Keynes's activities sufficiently to make the material fully intelligible to a later generation. Until this work has progressed further, it is not possible to say with exactitude whether this material will be distributed, as we now think, over nine volumes, or whether it will need to be spread over a further volume or volumes. There will be a final volume of bibliography and index.

Those responsible for this edition have been: Lord Kahn, both as Lord Keynes's executor and as a long and intimate friend of

Lord Keynes, able to help in the interpreting of much that would otherwise be misunderstood; Sir Roy Harrod as the author of his biography; Austin Robinson as Keynes's co-editor on the *Economic Journal* and successor as secretary of the Royal Economic Society. The initial editorial tasks were carried by Elizabeth Johnson. More recently she has been joined in this responsibility by Donald Moggridge. They have been assisted at different times by Jane Thistlethwaite; Mrs McDonald, who was originally responsible for the systematic ordering of the files of the Keynes papers; Judith Masterman, who for many years worked with Mrs Johnson on the papers; and more recently by Susan Wilsher, Margaret Butler and Barbara Lowe, who prepared the index.

EDITORIAL FOREWORD

This volume, one of three dealing with Keynes's more academic writing, forms a companion volume to *A Treatise on Money* and *The General Theory of Employment, Interest and Money*. In it appear his related articles, memoranda, correspondence with other economists and what survives in the form of drafts connected with his activities as an academic monetary economist between 1924 and 1939.

The material for this volume comes from the papers he kept from the period concerned, from his published contributions to journals and books, from the correspondence retained by his contemporaries. In this connection, we should like to thank Sir Ralph Hawtrey, the late Professor Sir Dennis Robertson in his lifetime and subsequently his executor Professor S. R. Dennison, Joan Robinson, Mr P. Sraffa, Professors J. E. Meade, Sir John Hicks, B. Ohlin, F. A. von Hayek, D. G. Champernowne, W. B. Reddaway and N. Kaldor for their assistance in preparing this volume. They have provided us with correspondence and with memories that have helped to shape this material.

It has been necessary, in order to make this material intelligible to a generation which did not live through the events and may be unfamiliar with some of the personalities and issues involved, to provide a minimum of factual background. We have tried to make this background sufficient for clarity and ease of use, but neither obtrusive nor argumentative. The purpose has been to provide the material from which the reader can form his own judgment rather than to impose the judgment of the editor.

This volume differs from others in the series in one major respect. In the case of the 'circus' of Cambridge economists which discussed *A Treatise on Money* no formal written record survives. The editor, therefore, in a series of meetings, discussed the period with five of the members of the 'circus' and drafted an agreed note as to details. We hope that this record of discussions will prove useful.

No reader, we think, can fail to be impressed by the immense pains Keynes took over both *A Treatise on Money* and the *General Theory*, both in preparation and in subsequent persuasion. We suspect also that the reader will find equally impressive the trouble taken, either as editor of the *Economic Journal* or as an adviser and friend, over the work of others. Finally we suspect that this volume serves as an important record of intellectual creativity over a period of years which will interest both economists and students of the history of ideas.

NOTE TO THE READER

In this and the subsequent volume, in general all of Keynes's own writings are printed in larger type. All introductory matter and all writings by others than Keynes are printed in smaller type. The only exceptions to these general rules are that occasional quotations from a letter from Keynes to his parents or a friend used in introductory passages to clarify a situation, and draft tables of contents and the variorum of drafts of the *General Theory* in volume XIV, are printed in smaller type.

Most of Keynes's letters included in this and other volumes are reprinted from the carbon copies that remain among his papers. In most cases he has added his initials to the carbon in the familiar form in which he signed letters to all his friends. We normally have no means of knowing whether the top copy, sent to the recipients of the letter, carried a more formal signature. However, when we do, we have reprinted that signature.

Keynes in his rooms in King's 1933. Cartoon by David Low by
arrangement with the Trustees and the *Evening Standard*

Chapter 1

PROLOGUE

Although his *Tract on Monetary Reform* represents Keynes's first published work on business fluctuations, it does not represent his first work on the subject. Beyond portions of his University lectures,[1] his earliest work in this direction resulted in a paper presented to the Political Economy Club's meeting of 3 December 1913 at the Hotel Cecil in London. This paper appears to have been influenced by D. H. Robertson's fellowship dissertation submitted to Trinity College, which later appeared as *A Study of Industrial Fluctuation* in 1915,[2] for Keynes wrote to Robertson on 28 September 1913:

'Though I oughtn't to say so, I suppose, or breath[e] a word, I have been reading your Fellowship Dissertation. What a prodigious amount of work you managed to put into it, judging from the time it took me to master it. However I suppose we shall not be free to discuss it while it is still fresh in my mind, only after some months interval.

What I must say now is that your work has suggested to me what appears at first sight a superb theory about fluctuations, and I want very much to hear your opinion of it. I believe it synthesises an enormous number of your facts. I haven't nearly time enough to write it down, and am terrified lest I should forget it.'

This is surely the 'reciprocal obligation' to Robertson referred to in the passage in *A Study of Industrial Fluctuation* which mentions Keynes's paper and its importance in Robertson's thinking (page 171, footnote 2).

[1] His notes for these survive among his papers.

[2] Keynes, in fact, took an interest in Robertson's study in two capacities. First he read it, along with Professor S. J. Nicholson, when Robertson was an unsuccessful candidate for a Trinity College Fellowship in 1913. (Keynes was not, by the way, an examiner for the Cobden Prize which the same draft of the dissertation won in 1913. The examiners then were Pigou, Ashley and Kay-Shuttleworth.) Second, after Robertson had re-drafted and successfully submitted it to Trinity in 1914 (the referees were Cannan and Foxwell), Keynes read it for Macmillan as a possible publisher in May 1915. Although he told Robertson that he had recommended that Macmillan publish it 'without hesitation...as a most brilliant and important contribution to the subject', P. S. King, who with successor companies remained Robertson's publishers for the rest of his life, eventually published the book at the end of 1915, largely one suspects because Macmillan would only publish it subject to some alterations which Robertson, by then in the Army and soon to go abroad, did not have time to make.

HOW FAR ARE BANKERS RESPONSIBLE FOR THE ALTERNATIONS OF CRISIS AND DEPRESSION?

The object of this paper is partly to see what the Club thinks of a general explanation of fluctuations which is to some extent novel, and partly to discuss what sort of a depression, if any, we may now be on the brink of.

Let me take the more theoretical section first.

It can hardly be said that there is any orthodox theory of the alternations of boom and depression at the present time. But it is usual to agree that several of the explanations proffered by various authors 'have something in them', provided they be regarded as part or occasional, not as complete, explanations. Some of these theories are mainly concerned with industrial facts and considerations and some with monetary or financial considerations. I do not intend, this evening, to say anything whatever about the former.

The most ordinary theory of the way in which banking considerations come in, chiefly associated perhaps with the name of Professor Irving Fisher, is roughly as follows: Bankers find themselves with a higher ratio of cash reserves than in their opinion caution really requires. Accordingly they give more credit. This raises prices. Producers generally have a bigger volume of trade at better prices than ever they expected. They are, therefore, very ready to borrow. Bankers now raise the rate they charge for accommodation. But they do not, in general, raise it fast enough to keep pace with the growing profitableness of buying something now, with money borrowed for three months, which is going to be worth more three months hence. Gradually or suddenly bankers discover that their cash reserves have sunk to a lower ratio than is safe. Credit is sharply curtailed. Those, who have bought on the expectation of prices rising yet higher or of trade expanding yet further, find themselves out in their calculations. And a crisis or depression has arrived.

This kind of theory holds, I should say, to a great extent, the

2

academic field. I do not say that it has not sometimes been applicable to affairs or that there is not often something in it. But for my own part I have always felt it clever, rather than satisfactory. It does not seem to be laying bare fundamental things. It strikes one as diagnosing symptoms rather than causes. It is no doubt true that a crisis or depression is usually heralded by a curtailment of credit on the part of bankers. But is the explanation of this curtailment so crude and simple? It is no doubt true and ingenious and well worth pointing out that, if prices are rising at the rate of 6 per cent per annum while money can be borrowed against them at 5 per cent per annum, borrowing is more profitable than it should be. But the explanation, taken as a whole, seems to impute to bankers too great a simplicity of mind, and to assume that they are taken in, time after time, by the same very elementary train of events. Bankers think, let us suppose, that they ought to have 15 per cent of their liabilities in cash. One day they find themselves with 17 per cent and so start lending with a gay and light heart. They do not, apparently, look at their books again for many months. But when a year or two later the matter is gone into again, the bankers find to their horror that they have only 13 per cent in cash. Money is hastily called from the market, accommodation curtailed, and the papers announce next morning that the trade boom is at an end. The whole thing is based, it will be noticed, on a temporary lack of caution in bankers in the matter of the proportion of cash to liabilities.

Not only is this theory somewhat lacking in plausibility, but it cannot really be substantiated by facts. Adequate and satisfactory data of the real ratio of bankers' reserves to liabilities are not to be had. We know that at a time of crisis bankers try to reduce their liabilities and that their ratio of reserves, therefore, especially towards the end of a crisis and the middle of the depression, tends to rise. We also know that bankers' opportunities for making loans of a satisfactory character are much greater in times of boom than in times of depression and that, as a consequence, they deliberately allow their proportion of reserves to rise and fall within somewhat narrow limits. But I do not think there is much evidence that this latitude of fluctuation is great, or that a crisis is produced through the bankers' not noticing the gradual sinking of their reserves.

This, I say, is the general character of the theory of the way, in which banking is connected with crises, most in vogue in academic circles today. I wish to replace or modify it. But, first, I must digress to another theory which, while not itself correct, helps to give the clue to some useful ideas.

This theory is the theory of over-investment. Alternately, it is said, led away by excessive hopes or held back by too great fears, too great or too small a proportion of the world's reserves is fixed in the form of permanent capital improvements. In this theory, as sometimes put forward, two suggestions are made which must be erroneous. The first is that in some way more capital can be invested than there is in existence; the second is that, when there is over-investment, more investment is made than really pays; capital expenditure, that is to say, runs ahead of the opportunities of *profitable* investment. Both of these suggestions are erroneous. The first, if taken at all literally, is plainly impossible. The second is not sufficiently borne out by facts. Some investments are made foolishly in times of boom just as they are at times of depression. But the so-called periods of over-investment are often brought into being by a sudden great increase of opportunities of unusually profitable investment.

I wish to suggest or to make explicit a third, and in my opinion much more relevant, interpretation of what is or ought to be meant by over-investment. And this will bring me back to my main topic—the influence of bankers.

Of the resources of the community earned or available within a given year, a certain part is saved, a certain part spent, and a certain part is held, so far as the individual is concerned, in suspense—it is kept as free resources to be spent or saved

4

according as future circumstances may determine. The portion, thus kept in suspense, except in so far as it is hoarded—and we may practically neglect this factor so far as this country and U.S.A. are concerned—is left by individuals at their bankers. This means that the bankers have the power of determining who shall have the immediate control of the material resources corresponding to what individuals have earned and left at their bankers. If I earn £100, this means that there is £100 worth of goods corresponding, which I can have myself, if I like. If I leave the £100 with my bankers, this means, in effect, that I leave it to them temporarily to hand over to somebody else the control of material goods up to the value of £100. Now the persons to whom the bankers may thus hand over the control of the goods are divided into two classes, those who are carrying forward stocks of consumable goods or are utilising the goods in processes which rapidly yield up further stocks of consumable goods, and those who expend the goods in capital works which will not yield up at any early date consumable goods by any means equal in value to the capital which has been sunk.

Thus in any given year there are two sources from which goods (or, if you like, for it is the same thing, funds) are available for capital works—that part of the existing resources which is deliberately set aside by individuals for investment, and that fraction of the resources, which individuals hold in suspense and leave with their bankers, which bankers advance directly or indirectly for capital purposes.

Hence in any year the value of material goods actually utilised for capital works may run ahead of or fall behind the value deliberately saved, according as the advances of bankers are made, to a greater or less extent, for purposes of capital expenditure. I should say that there is a tendency to over-investment (as distinguished from over-saving) when the proportion of the funds in the hands of bankers which is fixed in permanent capital works is increasing.

Now some considerable part of the funds left with bankers

can plainly be invested in fixed forms with perfect safety. While each individual finds it convenient to keep what he has at his bankers in a liquid form, the community as a whole, relying on the law of averages, can afford to keep a smaller amount liquid than the aggregate of individual requirements.

But the important point is that if in any year the amount invested exceeds the amount saved, this establishes a scale of investment from which there must necessarily be a reaction. If the proportion advanced by bankers against fixed security increases, for the scale of investment thus established to be maintained it is necessary not merely that the proportion should be maintained at this higher level, but that it should be raised still further. A mere maintenance of the proportion at the same figure as the previous year does not permit a new investment to exceed new saving. Even if the new proportion is not itself incautious, a point must soon come when further increases are impossible.

If no one who directs capital operations could obtain funds except by inducing someone who had saved them to place them with him, clearly investment could never in any period exceed saving. The machinery of banking, however, permits this. For it is within the power of bankers to allow those who direct capital operations to encroach on the community's reserve free resources to a greater or less degree.

One of the characteristics of a boom period—I will enlarge on this again later—as distinguished from a period of depression is, I suggest, that in the former period investment exceeds saving while in the latter period investment falls short of saving. And it is the machinery of banking which makes this possible.

The set of hypothetical figures (let me emphasise the fact that they are purely hypothetical, though I have tried to make them prima facie reasonable) which I have placed in your hands illustrates how much difference to capital production a comparatively small encroachment on the community's free reserves may make.

	Units of production			Units of con- sumption	Units of saving			Units of balances left with bankers
	Agri- culture	Capital goods	Other	Total		Capitalist classes	Working classes	Total	
Period of depression	40	12	48	100	85	16	− 1	15	30
Period of boom	43	20	45	108	91	16	+ 1	17	30

	Nature of goods in the financing of which balances with bankers are employed			
	At beginning of period		At end of period	
	Capital goods	Consumption goods	Capital goods	Consumption goods
Period of depression	20	10	17	13
Period of boom	17	13	20	10

Whatever may be the quantitative importance of my theory, something of this sort must take place on some scale small or great.

I now turn, first, to the kinds of circumstances which induce bankers to allow such an encroachment or cause them to overlook it; and second, to the kinds of circumstances which bring about a reaction.

It is very difficult for bankers to know in what way those who have borrowed from them are using their funds; the security going against them does not necessarily represent the way in which they are being used. Moreover the distinction between good borrowers and bad cuts across any distinction based on the kind of way in which they are using their funds. A loan may be liquid from the point of view of an individual banker, because he knows he can get his money back if he wants, although the proceeds of it are being employed in fixed forms. And it need not

7

be to the advantage of an individual banker to discourage loans to a particular customer merely because the customer belongs to the class which is going too fast for the interests of the community.

Thus it is exceedingly difficult for a banker to know for certain when a period of over-investment is in progress; and it is not necessarily to his private advantage to discourage borrowers (provided they be sound) for capital purposes even when he does know it is in progress. His individual action cannot stay appreciably the over-investment, whilst in the meantime he is losing good business.

What are the kinds of circumstances which lead to over-investment?

A number of very profitable opportunities may offer themselves simultaneously, through an invention, for example, or the opening up of a new country.

A complex of circumstances may fill business men generally with feelings of confidence and enterprise.

A war may make a sudden and unexpected demand of great magnitude on the available supplies of capital.

Now over-investment due to any of these causes may easily conceal itself from the notice of bankers until it is too late. And this concealment is greatly facilitated by the machinery, now developed to a high pitch of perfection, by which communities and companies can spend on capital improvements in advance of making arrangements for permanent borrowing.

For example an overdraft to a municipality in good credit, which is certainly able to raise a loan when it wants to do so and which intends to raise a loan at an early date, is from the point of view of an individual banker excellently liquid business. So would be an overdraft to a very high class industrial firm to provide it with working funds for the manufacture of additional rolling stock which had been ordered by a railway company of good standing. Each of these pieces of business, taken by themselves, appear liquid; and so they are, as long as such pieces of business, taken in the aggregate, do not exceed the community's current savings. In due course the municipality and the railway company place their securities with investors; and the bank overdrafts are duly cancelled against the accounts of the investors. But if a point comes at which such pieces of business exceed in the aggregate the volume of new savings, quite a different complexion is placed on the matter. The municipality's stock is left with the underwriters, who must needs pledge the greater part of it with the banks. The railway company finds there is no market for its permanent debt and floats short-term bonds, which are not, for the most part, placed with investors but are taken up by various constituents of the money market and financed, in effect, with bank money. Thus bankers as a whole suddenly find that what looked like liquid assets has turned into assets that are very far from liquid indeed. The over-investment, which was previously latent, has become apparent, and bankers discover that too large a proportion of their assets is now represented by what are, in effect, fixed investments. The overdrafts due to particular banks are paid off, but they are replaced by security of a less satisfactory type in the hands of these or other banks.

Whether the banks are alarmed or not, their capacity for entering into new business is necessarily reduced. If a piece of business is really liquid and clears itself off, this leaves the bank free to enter immediately into another piece of business of the same kind. But if it does not clear itself off, the bank must necessarily reduce its new commitments below what they were at the corresponding period of the preceding year.

Let me summarise my argument so far. What precipitates a reduction of banking facilities and a crisis is not lack of money, that is to say of gold coins, but lack of free, uninvested capital. It is not so much the proportion of bank's commitments to its cash reserves, as the *character* of the commitments. No doubt, a tendency of the cash reserves to fall at such a time is a symptom but it is not at all a fundamental cause. Since some of the old commitments do not clear themselves off, the bank cannot enter into new business on the former side without lowering its proportion of reserves. What I mean by saying that the lack of cash, if there is a lack of it, is a symptom not a cause, is that if an unexpected supply of cash was suddenly forthcoming from somewhere [it] would in no way effect a cure. No doubt it would delay the crisis a little and would prevent things from coming to a head immediately, but it would do no real good. Prices would rise still further, the volume of banking credit required to finance a given volume of business increasing correspondingly. The over-investment would be permitted to go still further, and, when eventually a pause had to come, the position would probably be intrinsically worse than if the crisis had come sooner.

No doubt crises have come about in the past and may come about in the future merely through a temporary insufficiency of legal tender in the hands of banks. But as banking organisation is perfected and the solidarity of banking increased, it becomes easier for banks to guard against this particular type of difficulty. The modern depression in England at any rate is exceedingly unlikely to be due to this cause. It is one of my complaints against what I have described as the current theory that it suggests that this influence is still the potent and important one.

On the other hand the development of underwriting and short-term bonds and so forth tends to make, I think, the danger of over-investment greater, and makes it more likely that bankers will be unwittingly led into transforming into fixed capital too high a proportion of their assets.

Let me apply these considerations to current affairs. In the present position, as I view it, we have much more purely than on former occasions a case of over-investment free from other complications.

There is no particular evidence in any part of the world of that special kind of rashness in banking which leads to a shortage of cash. There is no great amount of speculation, except in India, in the sense of forcing up existing shares or stocks of commodities to fancy prices. There has been no important failure of harvests and no sudden calamity, causing a large unexpected demand on the world's free resources, such as the San Francisco earthquake.

But there has been, I believe, to a dangerous extent, a steady encroachment on the world's free resources; and the investment of the world's free resources in fixed capital works has been very appreciably in excess of the amount saved and deliberately set aside for such purposes.

This has not been predominantly due to rash or over-optimistic development in directions which are not really profitable or desirable in the long run. It has been due, firstly, to an erroneous supply of opportunities for investment individually of a sound and satisfactory kind. It would take me too long to go into the causes of this—settled government in other countries, great extension of borrowers supposed by the ordinary investor to be in good credit, etc.

It has been due secondly to a great extension of the facilities for spending on capital purposes in advance of making arrangements for permanent loans.

It has been due thirdly to the spending by governments on an enormous scale for military and naval purposes of funds which would have been available otherwise for saving and productive investment.

I do not see how there can possibly be any cure except a slackening of investment until saving has had time to catch up. This must necessarily be accompanied by a depression in those industries which are chiefly concerned in the production of capital goods.

If there is a bad harvest, another war, or increased expenditure by governments on military and naval purposes, I should anticipate that we may be in for a really bad depression. If not, perhaps, the necessary reaction may be taken slowly and spread over so long a period that the effect in general prosperity in industrial countries is not excessively marked.

There are, however, two dangerous elements in the situation which deserve notice—there being some connection between the two.

The first is the extreme abundance of money, in the sense not of capital but of cash. A period of depression is now associated in the public mind with a shortage of cash. This was not so in the mid nineties; but in recent times depressions have been associated with a partial breakdown of the machinery of credit and with a consequent shortage of cash. A European war apart, I do not think this is in the least degree likely to happen in the near future.

I put on one side the question whether the Bank of England has, compared with other banks, enough [gold]. But France and Russia and even Germany appear to me to have quantities of gold very great in relation to their probable needs. The gold in the American Treasury is more at the disposal of bankers than formerly. And there is quite a new factor in the situation in the form of large stocks of available gold in India and South America. A failure of the harvest in these countries may very well have the effect of throwing large quantities of gold on the London market. A surfeit of gold is, therefore, a much more real danger than a shortage. It is by a surfeit of gold that the next serious depression is likely, I believe, to be marked.

This abundance of gold leads me to my second point. It may make it even more difficult, than would otherwise be the case, to put a stop to the tendency to over-investment. This can't be done by putting a stop to new loans. For new loans are very commonly brought out for the purpose of funding debts already incurred. No useful purpose is served by deferring these. They only help to regularise the position and to make more plain how we really stand. Some loans, no doubt, are for new expenditure which will only be incurred if the loan is successfully floated. But the stopper on new expenditure by railway companies and governments and municipalities—for these are the main spenders, other borrowers hardly count in comparison—has to be put on for the most part at an earlier stage. And this is an exceedingly difficult thing to do. It will often be to the interest of an individual bank to supply such borrowers with relatively easy accommodation, when it is opposed to the interest of the financial world as a whole. There is another difficulty in the situation. There are many borrowers in the market, who have raised loans in the recent past at $3\frac{3}{4}$ to $4\frac{3}{4}$ per cent, for whom it would be worth while to pay anything from 5 to 6 per cent rather than not borrow at all. The rate at which it has been possible in the past to borrow for capital expenditure in new and developing countries has been very much below what these countries would pay rather than go without new expenditure. In technical language the demand of these borrowers is exceedingly inelastic and it is most difficult to choke them off by a slight increase of charge. On the other hand if banks and underwriters raise the rate very greatly, the value of existing stocks, of which they are large holders, is very greatly depreciated. Until lately the government of India could borrow at from $3\frac{1}{2}$ to $3\frac{3}{4}$ per cent and have been able to employ the money in ways yielding up to 5 per cent at least. Now they would have to pay 4 per cent or more. Rather than do this and depreciate their existing stock, they have largely refrained from borrowing. But it cannot be permanently worth while to refrain from paying $4\frac{3}{4}$ per cent for loans which can be used so as to yield 5 per cent; and there are other borrowers in the field less considerate to their existing stockholders.

I think bankers ought to be very severe on short-term notes and bonds; but I am doubtful how much power they really have to put a serious brake on the tendency to over-investment.

One last illustration of my theories. A great deal of rubbish appears to me to have been talked about the results of the forthcoming French loan. Large amounts of money, we are told, have been hoarded in France. French citizens are patriotic and will draw upon these hoards in order to subscribe to the loan. And the bringing out of this additional money will help to put an end to financial troubles in France and elsewhere alike. This line of thought seems [to] me to involve in an extreme degree the comparison between a shortage of free capital and a shortage of gold coins. I do not know whether these supposed hoards consist of gold or notes. If of the former, I cannot conceive what good their reappearance can do. It will merely permit a further rise of prices. This rise in the price of goods may certainly do something to check over-investment, but the temporarily increased ease of accommodation will partly counterbalance this. If, on the other hand, the hoarding is of notes, all that happens is the disclosure of the real problem. The note issue of the Bank of France falls, let us say, by £5 million, and its advances to the government are diminished by a like amount. But in so far as the loan is not immediately taken up by the public and is carried by financiers, the effect is to replace loans which look liquid by loans which look less liquid. And the effect is to reveal the seriousness of the real position. This applies equally to the other impending European loans. In so far as the loans are taken up by the public, a certain amount of deposits in banks are cancelled against the cancellation of a corresponding amount of advances. In so far as the loans have to be carried for a time by financiers, there is no cancellation and one kind of advance is merely replaced by another. The general effect is that bankers then know better than before where they are. But they are just as likely, I believe, to find that they stand worse than they had thought than they are to find that they stand better.

2 December 1913

Chapter 2

FROM THE TRACT TO
THE TREATISE

In his *Tract on Monetary Reform* (*JMK*, vol. IV), Keynes stood well within the limits of the Cambridge orthodoxy of his day in his treatment of the internal value of money, where he used a variant of the real balances quantity equation developed by Pigou from Marshall's work, and in his discussion of the external value of money or purchasing-power parity. Similarly his discussion of price fluctuations in terms of changes in real balances was Marshallian, although his policy goals of price stability, erring if necessary towards slight inflation, his preference for national management and changes in exchange rates, and his emphasis on the short run were all at odds with the tempers of Marshall and Pigou. It was in his movement from the position of the *Tract* that he was to break new ground.

Soon after the publication of the *Tract*, however, Keynes began thinking about another work on monetary theory. He appears to have started work on the book in mid-July 1924, for as late as 6 July he reported to his mother that there were 'various odds and ends which keep me from my new book which is annoying'.

From the early stages of his work on this new book, little survives beyond an extensive collection of draft tables of contents. The first of these was dated 14 July 1924.

14 July 1924

The Standard of Value

Part I   Principles of thought

Chapter I   The elements of the quantity theory defined with special reference to the U.K. and the U.S.
    1. The definition of cash—*m*—Knapp
    2. The definition of the price level—*p*
    3. The definition of purchasing power—*k* and *k'*
    4. The relation of credit to cash—*r*
Chapter II   'Managed' currency systems and 'automatic' currency systems
Chapter III   The influence of bank rate on prices

Work on the proposed book seems to have gone well during the rest of the summer of 1924, for Keynes added the following brief note at the bottom of a letter from Lydia Lopokova at Tilton to Dennis Robertson:[1]

To D. H. Robertson, 14 September 1924

Dear Dennis,

If you have nothing better to do, do come back here for a few days. We are here until the end of the month. I am working at Credit Cycle theories which I think you may like—they go half way to meet you: and would much like to talk them over.

J.M.K.

By the beginning of the Michaelmas term of 1924, the book had expanded considerably from its July origins, as the draft table of contents of 9 October indicates.

9 October 1924

The Monetary Standard

PART I   THE THEORY OF AN IDEAL STANDARD

Book I   Introduction

Chap I   The four requirements of a standard
   (i) Short-period adjustability to the fluctuations of real balances and of credit

---

[1] Lydia in the same letter referred to Keynes's progress as follows: 'Maynard develops in his mind high and low bank rate, but no one in this house has access to this particular mentality. I would feel very proud in your place.'

(ii) Intrinsic value

(iii) Long-period stability of intrinsic value

(iv) Universality or wide area of acceptability

Chap 2 The *Law* or *Equation of Money* recapitulated

Book II The analysis and the cure of the credit cycle

Chap 3 What determines the quantity and the form of bank credit

Chap 4 Prices regarded as the ratio of the supply of money credit to the supply of real credit

Chap 5 Bank rate

Chap 6 The mode by which fluctuations in the demand or supply of real credit generate price movements

Chap 7 The inevitability of the credit cycle under the pre-war gold standard

Chap 8 The control of the credit cycle by the independent control of the basis of credit and of the bank rate under an ideal standard

Chap 9 Proposals for achieving the objectives of chap 7 [*sic*] under the gold standard

Book III The intrinsic value of the monetary standard

Chap 10 The meaning and significance of 'intrinsic value'

Chap 11 The history of gold in relation to intrinsic value

Chap 12 The loss by gold of its full intrinsic value

(*a*) by its withdrawal from circulation—principle of note reserves

(*b*) by exchange standards

Chap 13 Alternative intrinsic value standards—wheat, the composite commodity or tabular standard

Chap 14 Long-period stability of intrinsic value

PART II THE PRACTICE OF AN IDEAL STANDARD
Book I The transition from gold

Chap 15

Book II The management of the new standard

Chap 16 The choice of an index number

Chap 17 The organisation of statistical knowledge

Chap 18 The instruments of control

Chap 19 The Bank of England

Book III International arrangements

Chap 20 The advantages and the dangers of an international standard

Chap 21   Arrangements between B of E and FRB
Chap 22   The forward exchanges as a means of uniting money markets
          moderately both imperial and international
Chap 23   Inter-imperial arrangements

Keynes continued working on the book throughout the autumn of 1924, as the markedly different draft contents of 30 November indicates. This particular draft is of some interest, for, before Keynes settled on calling chapter 1 'Introduction', he had thought of calling it 'A short summary of the author's theory about to be expounded' but crossed it out. A draft of this chapter survives and is printed below the table of contents of 30 November.

30 November 1924

PART I   THE THEORY OF AN IDEAL STANDARD
Book I   The analysis of the trade cycle and the theory of credit

Chap 1   Introduction
Chap 2   The meaning and significance of 'working capital'
Chap 3   Fluctuations in the demand for 'working capital' in relation to
         the trade cycle
Chap 4   The relation of the supply of 'working capital' to the banking and
         credit system
Chap 5   What determines the volumes of money credit and of real credit
         respectively created by the banks
Chap 6   Prices regarded as the ratio of the volume of money credit to the
         volume of real credit
Chap 7   Bank rate
Chap 8   The causes of the credit cycle under the pre-war gold standard,
         and its cure under an ideal standard

Book II   The monetary standard and intrinsic value (as before)
Book III   The general conditions

Chap 1   The four desiderata of an ideal standard
Chap 2   The *Law* or *Equation of Money* recapitulated

A draft of chapter 1, November 1924

A SUMMARY OF THE AUTHOR'S THEORY

I begin this book, not in the logical order, but so as to bring before the reader's mind, as soon as possible, what is most significant for my purpose.

Capital consists partly of finished goods, awaiting use or in the course of use, and partly of goods *in process*, that is in course of production. It is to the latter that I direct attention. The amount of capital, which is locked up in the form of goods in process, fluctuates from time to time in accordance with fluctuations in the activity of production.

In particular—since production takes time—an increased activity of production cannot take place without an increased supply of capital in the form of goods in process.

A supply of *new* capital, whether in the form of finished goods or of goods in process, can only come into existence in so far as those who have claims on the community's flow of income[1] are willing to *defer* their claims, i.e. out of 'savings'.

Those, who wish to get hold of claims on current income for the purpose of turning them into new capital, get into touch with those who are saving, partly directly by offering investments, and partly indirectly through the intermediary of the banks.

By an accident of our economic organisation, the fluctuating demands of industry for claims on current real income,[2] which can, by furnishing real wages to labour and in other ways, be converted into goods in process, are mainly satisfied through the banks.

Now the banks can only lend such amount of purchasing power as their customers are willing to leave them. The banks cannot, by themselves, create real purchasing power. If their

---

[1] I include in 'income' the current use or enjoyment of existing capital.

[2] It will be convenient to call claims on real income (or on real capital) 'real purchasing power' or, for short, where there is no risk of ambiguity, 'purchasing power'.

depositors diminish the real balances they hold, the banks have less purchasing power to lend. The fact, that borrowers are *more eager* and will pay a higher rate of interest for loans of purchasing power does not enable the banks to lend any more unless they can induce their depositors to keep larger real balances.

But whilst this is true of the amount of *real purchasing power* which the banks can lend, it is not true of the amount of bank money which they can lend—not, at any rate, as regards the banks taken as a whole. For when a depositor in a bank spends his deposit by buying something with it, the real purchasing power deposited with the bank will be *ipso facto* diminished by that amount, unless the person, to whom the bank money is transferred, is prepared to hold at the bank a larger real balance than before.

The amount of bank money, on the other hand, which the banks, taken as a whole, can lend, bears no direct relation to the amount of real purchasing power which their depositors are prepared to leave with them. A book-transfer from one depositor to another makes no difference to the banks,—even though this transfer may represent a diminished aggregate willingness on the part of the public to keep real purchasing power in the form of bank balances. The banks have no direct evidence when a transfer represents a diminished willingness to hold real balances and when it does not. Nor do they bother their heads to obtain indirect evidence on the matter. For their main criterion of how much to lend is a totally different one,—namely the proportion of their cash reserves to their money liabilities. If this proportion is undiminished they are content. In this event they have no motive for not creating as much bank money as before,— even though the real balances deposited with them by the public have been diminishing.

Now when the demand for circulating capital increases (for whatever reason), the pressure on the banks to meet this demand causes them either to increase the amount of bank money which they lend faster than the public are depositing purchasing power, or, at any rate, to lend as much bank money as before in spite of the fear that the public may be withdrawing purchasing power. And when the demand for circulating capital falls off, the reverse is true,—thus producing the periodic oscillation of the price level characteristic of the so-called credit cycle.

On this basis I build two sets of conclusion:—Under a credit or bank-money system, such as we have now, prices rise when the ratio of bank money to real balances increases, and prices fall when the ratio of bank money to real balances diminishes. This may come about, either by a change on the side of bank money (up or down)—which is what attention has been generally concentrated upon; or by a change on the side of real balances (down or up)—which may be just as important, particularly over short periods.

This conclusion is the same, though in different words, as the leading tenet of my *Tract on Monetary Reform*. I shall argue in this book, as I argued in that, that the general price level can be stabilised by giving the Bank of England a control over the volume of bank money created (which has to be done to some extent under *any* bank-money system), and by using this control to cause the volume of bank money to vary in the same proportion as that in which the volume of real balances varies.

My second set of conclusions, however, is new;—they seek to explain how and why, under our pre-war monetary system, fluctuations in the demand for circulating capital—however arising, and however inevitable or even desirable—tended to generate the credit cycle; how the supposed remedies which we were accustomed to apply were capable, in certain conditions, of aggravating the disease; and how the credit cycle itself, by causing, in its turn, further fluctuations in the demand for circulating capital, tended to bring about its own repetition. If this analysis of the credit cycle is correct, it makes the nature of the cure fairly obvious. Before, however, we can reach this goal, we must concentrate on a somewhat troublesome analysis.

After this has been done, there are certain other desiderata of the ideal standard to be examined. When we have established all the conditions which an ideal standard *ought* to satisfy, we are ready to proceed in Part II to practical schemes.

At this stage, Keynes was obviously satisfied with his progress, for he reported to Piero Sraffa on 30 December 1924:

> You may be interested to hear that I have now made a good start on my new book, and find that I like my underlying theory quite as well when I begin to develop it as I did at the start.

Certainly the book was coming along sufficiently well for Keynes to begin to circulate drafts of certain chapters for comment. Unfortunately none of these draft chapters survives intact beyond pencil manuscript pages of an earlier draft of what became chapter 3 of the tables of contents of 30 November 1924 and 21 March 1925. However, Dennis Robertson's comments on chapters 2 and 3 give us some idea of the trend of Keynes's and Robertson's thoughts. These chapters probably had the titles of the 30 November 1924 table of contents, which survived past Robertson's letters to the draft contents of 21 March 1925.

An early draft of chapter 3 following the contents
of 30 November 1924

WORKING CAPITAL IN SLUMPS AND BOOMS

Thus, once a slump has been allowed to develop, with prevalent unemployment and a corresponding impairment of working capital, it will be *impossible* to bring about a rapid increase of employment merely through a recovery in business sentiment or by the expenditure of public money. Such influences may raise prices, but they cannot enter a greater volume of goods into process, unless the wages fund is being adequately replenished out of current savings. It is true, as we shall see later, that rising prices may increase the flow of current savings by inflicting a levy on consumers and wage earners for the advantage of producers; and the expenditure on public works of money which has been raised by taxation may operate in the same way. But this does not alter the fact that it is only through the replenishment of working capital, by new savings becoming somehow available in liquid form, that the position can be restored. The expenditure, on the production of *fixed* capital, of public money which has been raised by borrowing, can do nothing in itself to improve matters; and it may do actual harm if it diverts existing working capital away from the production of goods in a liquid form, which unlike fixed capital will be available for the further replenishment of working capital at a later date.

The fall from boom to slump, due to an unwillingness or an inability on the part of entrepreneurs to start more goods in process by feeding income back into the machine or process, may be rapid; because any amount of goods can become available in excess of what is being fed back. But the rise from slump to boom must be more gradual; because goods can't be fed back in excess of what is becoming available. Liquid stocks, for example, can rise to any extent; but they can't fall below zero. Thus, during the period of recovery, we require not only an optimism on the part of entrepreneurs, which disposes them to start more goods into process, but also a steady accretion of current savings in liquid form to furnish the working capital which will enable them to carry their inclinations into action.

[here there is a gap of two pages in the manuscript]

Now during a boom, the stock of working capital is sufficient to employ the whole of the supply of labour at a high wage. Finally a point comes when this is no longer the case. The interruption may come for one of three reasons: (1) the goods emerging in fixed form may exceed current savings,—either because the former are increasing or the latter is diminishing; (2) the goods emerging in fixed form *plus* the addition to liquid capital may exceed current savings; or (3) the working capital required to maintain the flow of production at the same rate as before may have increased (for reasons to be explained below).

In the first and third cases the trouble arises from the supply of working capital falling below what is required to maintain productive activity at the higher level; in the second case from an unwillingness on the part of entrepreneurs to employ the working capital which is available.

In an actual crisis more than one factor may be present; and at one stage of it the demand for working capital may exceed the supply, whilst at another stage of the same crisis the supply exceeds the demand.

But we may say, broadly, that case (1) is the central characteristic of the break in a capital boom, such as the railway booms of the middle of the nineteenth century or when foreign investment has been proceeding on an excessive scale. And case (2) is the central characteristic of a crisis caused by a credit boom or by monetary deflation, where an anticipated change in the price level during the period of process indisposes entrepreneurs from activity. Case (3) covers a multitude of various circumstances which may arise,—circumstances which seldom bring about a crisis by themselves but may aggravate or precipitate other difficulties. It may be well to classify more exactly the examples of this case.

From D. H. Robertson, 27 February 1925

Dear Maynard,

Many thanks for this,—I have found it extraordinarily interesting, and await the rest eagerly.

I append 2 pages of (rather dogmatically expressed) notes.

Yours
D.H.R.

Notes on Ch. II

§1

P. 7a, line 1. After 'involves' add for clearness 'on the part of the community as a whole'.

L. 11–12. I find the phrase '*in the dark etc*' obscure. I think it confusing to suggest, as you seem to, that the 'sacrifice' connected with saving is the sacrifice made by the doers of additional work. This latter sacrifice is rewarded by wages, the former (if made voluntarily) by interest: they are distinct.
P. 8, last line. Don't you mean 'unduly large'? i.e. at the second period goods are so numerous that their marginal utility is lower than was expected. – If the flow of goods at the second period is 'unduly small', it would presumably have been smaller still if working capital had been less, i.e. there has been '*under*-saving' not '*over*-saving'.

§3

Pp. 2–3. I think it would make it easier if you stated here (as you do later on pp. 7–8) what *units* these various factors are reckoned in.
P. 7. ? Something queer still about the long sentence.
P. 8, l. 4. For 'rate' read '*total* rate' (you are skipping one stage of the argument in your recapitulation).

§4

P. 5 (2). I find this dreadfully confusing. You have defined 'intensity of employment' at any stage as 'the number of units of employment engaged on each unit of product at that stage'. Surely when trade begins to recover after a slack period, this intensity is *diminished*, owing to more economical utilisation of labour and fixed capital, i.e. fewer tons of machinery and fewer workmen are absorbed on each boot.

I should have thought it was the '*rate of turnover*' that was increased, the period of production being, as you say, correspondingly diminished:

Let T = rate of turnover, E = intensity of emp^t, P = period of prod^t, W = wage rate, C = working capital. Then $C = T \times E \times W \times \frac{1}{3}P^2$. Let there be an increase of scale of production such that if there were no speeding up T would be doubled. Then in fact T is increased (say) threefold, while E

Then we get $C_1 = 3T \times \frac{3}{4}E \times W \times \frac{1}{3} \times \dfrac{4P^2}{9}$

is reduced (say) by $\frac{1}{4}$, and P is diminished in the proportion $2T/3T$, i.e. by $\frac{1}{3}$.
$$= T \times E \times W \times \tfrac{1}{3}P^2 = C,$$
i.e. the doubled scale of output is being conducted with the old quantity of working capital.

Notes on Ch. III

§2

P. 5. I am a little uncomfortable (here and in ch. II) at the inclusion of all the earnings of fixed capital, management etc. in the 'wages bill' and therefore in working capital. The essence of the wages of labour is that they are *advanced*: while profit is only received at the time of sale, i.e. the value which it represents accrues suddenly to the goods at the last moment of the period of production,—or rather of each stage of the period of production.

P. 9, top. Since labour is more efficient in times of slump, fewer workmen are employed per boot: hence so far as this factor goes, we shd. expect production to fluctuate *less* than employment.

§3

P. 16. I take it the accurate form of this equation is $xy = pq \times (100/100 - p)$. You apply the accurate form to the calculation on p. 12 (top) and the inaccurate (p. 16) form to the calculation on p. 9, which is rather confusing. (If you apply the p. 16 form to the p. 12 illustration, you would get $p = 40$ instead of 30.)

§4

P. 7. I suspect a confusion between the entrepreneur who *buys* fixed capital and the entrepreneur who *produces* it for immediate sale. The former may be in a position to take long views, but not the latter.

Again, the fact that the latter 'cannot easily interrupt his programme of production' does not mean that investment in fixed capital won't fall off. It merely means that there will be a fall in the relative price of fixed capital goods, so that an equal or diminished amount of 'saving' (measured in wheat) will buy a larger volume of machinery. Thus there's no reason why the 'saving' available for incorporation in working capital should be reduced.

Statistically, I should have thought that even in the 1920–1 cycle, when the fluctuation of output of liquid goods was far greater than ever before, the fluctuation of the output of fixed capital was much greater than that of the output of liquid goods.

§5

P. 23, ls. 4 & 5. For 'supply' read 'demand'.? And for 'the boom' and 'the slump' read 'the outbreak of the boom' and 'the outbreak of the slump'

Your final conclusion appears to be the opposite of mine! i.e. at the crisis or top of the boom your 'working capital' is superabundant, and my 'short lacking' is deficient. But perhaps we mean the same thing, i.e. that the *goods* are abundant, but the *power and will to wait* deficient.

Keynes's own concept as to how his ideas could best be presented was still changing. By 21 March 1925 his plan was as follows:

21 March 1925

The Theory of Money with reference to the determination of the principle of an ideal standard

PART I THE THEORY OF CREDIT MONEY

Book I Working capital

Chapter 1 The relation of working capital to credit money
2 The meaning and significance of working capital
3 Fluctuations in the demand for working capital in relation to the trade cycle

Book II Money credit and real credit

Chapter 4 The nature of banking credit
5 Prices regarded as the ratio of the volume of money credit to the volume of real credit
6 What determines the volume of money credit
7 What determines the volume of real credit
8 The part played by the rate of discount

Book III The instability of price

Chapter 9 Price fluctuations initiated by changes on the side of money credit—inflation and deflation
10 Price fluctuations initiated by changes on the side of real credit —boom and slump
11 The causes of the credit cycle under the pre-war gold standard, and its cure under an ideal standard
12 The objects and methods of credit control under an ideal standard
13 A glance at international values

PART II THE THEORY OF COMMODITY MONEY

Chapter 14 The meaning and significance of 'convertibility' and 'intrinsic value'
15 The past history of gold in relation to intrinsic value
16 The present position of gold in relation to intrinsic value
17 Alternative intrinsic-value standards—wheat, the composite commodity or tabular standard
18 What should be the behaviour of the standard over long periods?

PART III CONCLUSION

Chapter 19 The four desiderata of an ideal standard

At about the same time as Robertson, Pigou (then at work on his *Industrial Fluctuations*) also appears to have seen these draft chapters. He commented in an undated letter as follows:

Dear Keynes,

Many thanks for these which I kept until my proofs came. Your point about working capital is off my lines. As I couldn't discuss it properly at this stage, I've not said anything about it. As far as I can see, it is additive to, not in conflict with, my stuff.

Yrs.

A.C.P.

By 6 April 1925, Keynes's presentation of his ideas had changed again, as this table of contents indicates.

6 April 1925

The Theory of Money with reference to the principles of an ideal standard

PART I THE THEORY OF CREDIT MONEY

Book I Money credit and real credit

Chapter I The purposes of bank deposits, i.e. of money credit
II The paradox of the 'creation' of credit
III The nature of real credit
IV The fundamental equations of money
V What determines the supply of money credit
VI What determines the supply of real credit
VII The part played by the rate of discount
VIII Price fluctuations initiated by changes on the side of money credit—inflation and deflation
IX Price fluctuations initiated by changes on the side of real credit—boom and slump

Book II The credit cycle and the trade cycle

Chapter X The function of the banks in relation to the supply of working capital
XI The meaning and significance of working capital
XII Fluctuations in the demand for working capital in relation to the trade cycle
XIII The relation of the trade cycle to the credit cycle, and the causes of the latter under the pre-war gold standard

Chapter XIV The objects and methods of credit control under an ideal
standard
XV International credit control

PART II THE THEORY OF INTRINSIC-VALUE MONEY
(as before)

Robertson's references to his conclusion and 'short lacking' in his note of
27 February (above, p. 26) point to another major Cambridge work in
monetary theory in progress during 1925, D. H. Robertson's *Banking Policy
and the Price Level* (London, 1926). In his introductory chapter, Robertson
made the following comment as to Keynes's role in the development of his
ideas (p. 5):

> I have had so many discussions with Mr J. M. Keynes on the subject-
> matter of chapters V and VI, and have rewritten them so drastically at his
> suggestion, that I think neither of us now knows how much of the ideas
> therein contained is his and how much is mine. I should like to, but
> cannot, find a form of words which would adequately express my debt
> without seeming to commit him to opinions he does not hold. I have made
> a few specific acknowledgements in footnotes; happily there is the less
> need for meticulous disentanglement as his own version of the Theory of
> Credit is to be published very soon.

We will never know the full extent of this collaboration, if only because so
much was oral and because early drafts do not survive. The letters and notes
that do survive range over chapters 5 and 6 of the book (especially the
former) and cover May to November 1925.
In the second letter, Keynes's pencil comments are reproduced as numbered
footnotes to the relevant passages.

From D. H. ROBERTSON, *Sat.* [*May 1925*]
Dear Maynard,
I wonder if you could bear to look at this again. I want specially to know
(*a*) whether Ch. III is rubbish
(*b*) whether Ch. V §6 (p. 12) can stand after the reintroduction of the gold
standard.
(*c*) whether you will pass the end of Ch. I.
Yours,
Dennis

From D. H. ROBERTSON, *Sunday* [*May 1925*]

Dear Maynard,

I hardly expect you will have patience to read this,—it is almost a second book!

It is an attempt to explain, to myself at least, why I am still inclined to go ahead and publish.

But I can't be sure yet. Thank you in any case very much for your great trouble and your candid criticism, and please don't take amiss what I say on p. 5 [below, p. 33].

Yours,

D.H.R.

To be or not to be!

I think whether the book should stand depends on five points, on all of which I still feel impenitent.

(1) Whether my distinction between 'Hoarding' and 'Forced Effective Short-Lacking'—between the 'service' of the person who keeps currency off the market and the 'service' of the person who brings it on to the market but gets less goods for it than he could have got but for something which the monetary authority has done—has validity.[1] I think it has. It is true the two things are done by the same *class of person*, namely holders of currency, but they may be done at widely different times and therefore by very different persons.

Suppose no currency but Gov^t notes: suppose in 1925 the Gov^t inflates to build a railway. By 1927 (say) the inflation is over, prices and money incomes have settled down at a higher level (any redistribution of income between classes is secondary). The community is permanently richer by a railway,[2] in which is embodied the 'Lacking' of those who, spending their notes in 1925–7, got less goods than they hoped,[3] owing to the competition of the notes spent by navvies etc. who were building the railway. Nobody would suggest in this case that in, say, 1950 the then generation of note holders were financing the railway.[4]*

The situation cannot be fundamentally altered merely because for 'Gov^t notes' we substitute 'bank-deposits', and, for 'a railway', 'circulating capital or goods in process of production'. I think my analysis (ch. v §§5–6) gives a

---

[1] Pencil comment by J.M.K. 'No—if there is no increased hoarding, there is no increased short lacking.' [2] 'and poorer by something else'.

[3] 'the navvies don't spend more (unless increased resources assumed)—they produce less'.

[4] 'just as much as the generation of debenture holders'.

* Cf. your analysis of 19th-century saving in *Ec. Consequences*.

substantially truer picture of the English or American banking systems today (please re-read carefully the middle sentences of first paragraph of §6).

It does not follow that depositors may not seriously embarrass the bank if they *change* their hoarding habits, and spend more freely. (I think I ought to give a preliminary hint of this in ch. v,—I discuss it pretty fully in vi, 4.) If they do, a Henderson or Bellerby would say, I think, that the bank ought to curtail its loans, in order to prevent the price-level rising.* I say that it may be the lesser evil for the bank to *expand* its loans, in order to keep the supply of Short Lacking intact, by forcing depositors consumers to exercise an abstinence which they no longer want to exercise,—to Lack if they will not Hoard. You would say now, I think, that there is a third way,—to tempt them to go on 'keeping real resources in the bank'. I am quite ready to be persuaded of this (subject to what I say below, head (4)), though I should call it 'tempting them to hoard so that one might not be forced into compelling them to lack'. (I think your terminology about keeping wheat in the bank is really more mystical and puzzling than mine; one doesn't keep wheat in a bank, one keeps money!)[1]

(2) Whether the assumption at certain stages of my argument that K, the proportion of Real Hoarding to income, remains unchanged, renders the whole argument so remote as to be uninteresting. I don't think so.

In ch. v I am discussing equilibrium conditions, and the assumption seems justified. In vi §§ 1-2 I am analysing a discontinuous change from one equilibrium position to another, and again the assumption seems justified.[2] I am not sure that even during the transition K necessarily diminishes for the community as a whole, for while the deposits of the old spenders fall in value, those of the new spenders (the soldiers in vi, 1) rise. But I agree that in a long-continued price rise K is certain to fall not only because (as I fully explain in vi, §§ 4 and 5) people prefer to hold goods rather than money, but also because widows etc. will be trying to escape Lacking by diminishing their hoarding rather than their consumption. This is, I confess, a new point to me, and I would like to put in a paragraph in vi, 4 to show that I recognise it.[3]

But in any case the tendency of K to fall strengthens the main argument of vi §§ 1-2, not weakens it. For it means that to keep Short Lacking up to scratch the bank must inflate *more* than if K remained constant. My argument is 'Even if K were constant, prices would have to rise: since K

---

* Cf. your *Monetary Reform*, top of p. 85 [*JMK*, vol. iv, p. 68] about using m to counteract changes in k.

[1] 'one keeps purchasing power not book entries'.   [2] 'No.'

[3] 'Most perverse. You want to increase. You say inflation impossible. If lower K, inflation diminishes it. This you say strengthens your argument because,—since inflation increases it, inflation is all the more necessary than before.'

diminishes, they must rise still more.' To make an assumption the withdrawal of which invalidates one's argument is boring: to make an assumption the withdrawal of which *reinforces* one's argument is surely a legitimate way of breaking up a very complex problem.

(3) Whether the 'real' changes which occur (harvests, inventions, etc.) are sufficiently important to induce sharp variations in the demand for Short Lacking.[1] I have no doubt of this historically, and at any rate as regards inventions I have Cassel and others on my side.

(4) Whether these sharp variations in the demand for Short Lacking have to be met mainly through the banking system. I still think they do.[2] I haven't fully got hold yet of your doctrine of attracting real resources into the banking-system by raising bank-rate, but I should think that the utmost you could do by this is to check the secondary demand in hoarding which occurs during a boom,—I don't see how you can hope actually to *increase* hoarding, which is what must be done if the bank is to compel new Lacking without a price rise. And the possibilities of 'expelling resources' if there is a real downward swing in the demand for Short Lacking seems to me still more limited.

(5) Whether, if certain real changes are strong enough to induce changes in the demand for Short Lacking (3), and therefore in the price level (4), they also 'justify' them; or whether the monetary system might be so used as to compel industry to turn the deafest possible ear to the crops or the Diesel engine. This is a function of judgment,—one aspect of the general question of stability v. progress.[3]

I feel, with Cassel, that we can't afford yet to turn a deaf ear to 'good' conditions, and that it's no use turning a deaf ear to 'bad' ones. If we can produce complete inter-local and inter-temporal crop compensation: if we could regularise the process of technical advance: well and good. Short of that, there are various devices, discussed in my ch. VII: but it would be unwise to produce artificial stagnation by monetary means; we should never have had a railway system if Hubert [Henderson] had been in power!

What we can do is to damp down secondary and unjustifiable price movements (VI, 6 sub. fin.): and I don't think any of us should often disagree in practice as to when to begin.

Conclusions

[1] I *think* the main contentions of my book are true and interesting, viz:—

(1) A banking-system which tried to provide industry with the right quantity of circulating capital and also to keep the price-level unchanged[4]

---

[1] 'No, that is not the point.' [2] 'very likely'.
[3] 'rubbish. This is assuming that inflation is the only source of saving.'
[4] 'because you have wholly ignored bank rate'.

would be faced under certain important conditions with the impossible task of reconciling two incompatible* purposes, of which the former is the more fundamental.

(2) If such a system permits the necessary price-changes, these changes set up stresses which are *not* beneficial, and which it is in the power of the bank to control by operating on the demand for circulating capital.†

Of these propositions (2) is probably of the greater practical importance; but since (1) is—in our circles—the less familiar, I am justified in emphasising it more strongly.

[2] My book is bad because it has been written in lumps when my thought was at various stages. I have missed altogether two important points, (1) the extent to which Dis-hoarding depends, not on business men trying to get out of money into goods but on widows trying to evade starvation: (2) the extent, about which I am still doubtful, to which both classes can be tempted by the bank to desist.

I can't now develop either of these points without stealing your thunder; but I should like to put in a word to show that I recognise (1).

[3] I am afraid of being swayed into publishing by the desire to avoid disappointment and loss: but I am also afraid of being swayed against publishing by my tendency to believe you are always right! Sometimes when I have stood out against this weakness, I have been justified! I think it just possible that you have reached such clear conclusions on the matters in hand, and got your own apparatus of words and thoughts for dealing with it so fixed, that you find it harder to follow the exact shades of my argument than somebody approaching it with a less committed mind, and that what seem to you howlers may be only differences of emphasis and methods of approach. In any case I feel the truth about the whole matter is so obscure and uncertain that it isn't wicked to publish what doesn't pretend to be final truth. I am so unconfident that I should always like to put at the top of everything that I write 'Nobody must believe a word of what follows'; and I think that almost *va sans dire* in books on the trade cycle, and that I would rather write a preface to that effect than not publish at all! Is that a hopeless frame of mind?

[4] If I publish, I should try to recast the phrases about depositors not doing the Lacking so as not to make them seem to imply more than they do: and I should make it clear that the 'conclusions' reached at certain stages of the argument are provisional inferences from what precedes, and may need modification in the light of what follows.

---

* I mean to add a note that under a gold standard it is given a *third* objective, which may be incompatible with both the others!

† Your contention that it is possible to operate on the *supply* would be supplementary to this, not in conflict with it.

To D. H. ROBERTSON, *28 May 1925*

Dear Dennis,

I have now read carefully the rest of the book, and also your letter, and remain just as unhappy about the whole thing as I was before. Of course, I don't think you ought to yield to my criticisms unless, or until, you are convinced by them. But I think that you ought to let some little time for reflection elapse before committing yourself, and also to get another opinion.

As regards the various points in your letter, I have something to say about several of them, but I had better limit myself to the most fundamental, because if you could convince me, or if I could convince you, about that, much of the rest would really become matters of comparative detail.

This point is the following: I am not able to accept your distinction between hoarding and forced effective short lacking. If there is no increased hoarding, then in my opinion there is no increased short lacking provided through the banking system. An act of inflation unaccompanied by any change in the amount of hoarding represents a mere transference of existing wealth without any necessary effect on the volume of consumption. You think that additional resources are released through the effect of inflation on consumption. In arguing this way I think you overlook the fact that there is no reduction of aggregate purchasing power measured in terms of real resources as a result of inflation. Let us suppose that there are £100 deposits representing 100 wheat units. Let the government, by inflation, create in its own favour an additional £10 [of] deposits. This additional demand coming on the market will have the effect of raising prices. Let us suppose that as each point is spent by the government from its new deposit prices rise 1 per cent. If the deposits in other people's hands remain the same as before in nominal value but reduced in real value, then the case might be different, but in fact *pari passu* with the government using its

34

deposits to buy something, these deposits are transferred into the pockets of the general public, so that *pari passu* with the successive 1 per cent increases of prices, the deposits of the public are increasing 1 per cent. When the government has spent its £10 the deposits of the public are £110, which have the same purchasing power in terms of wheat which their £100 had formerly. Thus there is no need for them to curtail their consumption. You seem to me to make a confusion between the permanent stock of money which the public keep and the flow of money in and out corresponding to their current income and current expenditure. An act of inflation does nothing to alter the latter. It does transfer part of the real value corresponding to the former away from the depositors into other hands. But the wealth corresponding to this is something which by hypothesis the depositors as a body never spent. What the inflation has done has been to transfer to the government the title to existing wealth to which old depositors had a title but which they would never consume so long as their hoarding remained stable. But this transfer in the ownership of existing wealth does not in any way affect the amount of available short lacking. In assuming that the public as a whole has to reduce its current consumption when inflation takes place you overlook the fact that whilst some depositors may as a result of the inflation have less real resources at the bank, other depositors have more.

I cannot help thinking that in reaching your conclusion you are partly influenced by the fact that at present there are unused resources, and you are unconsciously regarding as an argument in your favour the admitted power of inflation in some conditions to bring unused resources into use. There is also the valid argument that a transference of consumption of such a kind that productive consumption (in my sense of the word) is substituted for unproductive consumption does increase saving, and therefore short lacking. If you transfer purchasing power from retired widows to the unemployed, on condition that the unemployed work, then there is increased short lacking. But

35

that has nothing whatever to do with the banking system, and would come about whether or not we banked.

I do not know whether or not the above is clear. If not, either I must make myself clearer, or you must.

[copy unsigned]

To D. H. ROBERTSON, *31 May 1925*

Let us assume:—

(i) On the average everyone tries to keep his money deposits constant, i.e. there is no new hoarding.

(ii) On the average everyone's current money income rises in proportion to prices.

The public have £100 deposits worth 100 wheat.

The gov^t create an additional £10 and spend it.

The spending of it raises prices.

The real deposits of the public fall as prices rise but by hypothesis they try to keep their money deposits constant. As long as this remains the case, the gov^t's additional £10 remains redundant purchasing power at the initial *or at any* price level.

No position of equilibrium can be reached until someone is induced to replenish his hoard, i.e. to do *some new* hoarding out of current income. It is only when this occurs that new short lacking is provided.

This inducement to effect new hoarding comes about, in general, in one of three ways:—

(i) The *real* deposits of the public may fall to a highly inconvenient low proportion of their real income, so that they prefer to do new hoarding so as to raise them, rather than to maintain their current expenditure at its previous level.

(ii) Inflation may effect a redistribution of current real income into the hands of people whose incentive and ability to hoard is greater than those from whom it is taken.

(iii) A higher bank rate may increase the incentive to hoard.

On the other hand inflation is detrimental to hoarding in certain ways,—in particular:

(i) The expectation of higher prices which it creates diminishes the incentive to hoard.

(ii) The impoverishment of certain sections of the public diminishes their ability to hoard.

The new equilibrium of prices, as a result of a given percentage of inflation, depends upon the resultant of these forces.

(i) If the net effect of 10 per cent inflation is to cause an amount of new hoarding which is more than 10 per cent of the outstanding hoarding, prices rise less than 10 per cent;—this is an unreal case because it is not easy to see any reason why it should stimulate hoarding to such an extent.

(ii) If the net effect is to cause new hoarding equal to exactly 10 per cent of the outstanding hoarding, prices rise exactly 10 per cent;—this also is an unreal case, unless the outstanding hoarding is at its irreducible minimum which must be maintained at all costs. (I think you make this assumption at one stage.)

(iii) If the net effect is to cause new hoarding equal to less than 10 per cent of the outstanding hoarding, prices rise more than 10 per cent;—e.g. if the new hoarding is only 1 per cent of the outstanding hoarding, prices rise to 10 times their previous level, i.e. we have deposits £110 = 11 wheat units. (In this case nearly all the benefit of the £10 inflation has gone to the debtors of the bank and the gov^t has obtained by it only one wheat unit of real purchasing power.)

(iv) If *no* new hoarding is done, there is no point of equilibrium and prices rise to infinity. This happened, in the end, in Germany, Russia, etc.

Case (iii) brings out the fact that, failing case (ii), prices continue to rise until one or other of the incentives to new hoarding classified above begins to operate. In my opinion case (iii) is the normal case, i.e. any act of inflation tends to produce a rise of prices somewhat *more* than in proportion to the degree of inflation; and similarly with deflection.

What I call 'new hoarding' you call 'forced effective lacking'.[1] But though powerful motives may come into operation to promote it, it remains just as voluntary as any other form of saving; it is a result of individual decisions balancing the advantages of maintaining hoards at a given level as against those of maintaining consumption at a given level.

The theory of the causal relation between inflation and new hoarding is both new and important; and the fact that normally inflation tends to produce some new hoarding which would not otherwise have occurred is new and interesting and might, sometimes, be important. But my *caveat* about the last is that new hoarding is not the *only* form of saving—not the only source of supply of new lacking whether short or long. In so far as the new hoarding is at the expense of other investments, we lose on the savings etc.—though even in this case it *might* be useful in increasing the supply of new short lacking at the expense of that new long lacking. I think, however, that there are other and better ways of doing this.

The justification of wartime inflation seems to me to be, not so much that it causes net additional new lacking—if it does—as that it is the *quickest* way of diverting the current supply of new lacking into the gov^t's hands (ineffective, however, just in proportion as it raises prices).

The same is true in trade booms; and, therefore, probably not justified unless we are in a desperate hurry.
Conclusions:—

(i) Inflation tends to produce some amount of new hoarding— how much, it is impossible to say *a priori*.

(ii) This *may* be partly or wholly at the expense of other new investment.

(iii) If it is at the expense of other new investment, it is not useful, unless there is no other way of diverting new investment from long to short lacking.

---

[1] And since *all* hoarding has been *new* at some time or other in the past, you quite consistently reckon *all* bank deposits as the result of 'forced effective lacking' in the past.

(iv) On balance of (i), (ii) and (iii) there may quite likely be something to the credit of inflation. But this is not the whole story: and the policy of inflation cannot be recommended until we have weighed the above credit against the many familiar items to the debit of inflation.

J.M.K.

From D. H. ROBERTSON, [*June 1925*]

I think I am now convinced on the point of substance, viz. that new real Hoarding and new Short Lacking are the same (like Mrs Do-as-you-would-be-done-by and Mrs Be-done-by-as-you-did in the Water-babies!).

But I don't think the way you put it will do. For you imply that the public as a whole has a choice as to whether it will increase its *money* hoarding, and if so by how much. It hasn't. *Hoarding is by definition holding currency*: and so soon as the Gov^t has spent the new currency, the money hoarding of the public as a whole is inevitably and instantaneously increased by the full amount. Some individuals (e.g. widows) may keep their money hoards at the old level: others (e.g. traders) will find theirs increased.

Two points irrelevant to the main one, but I think important.

(1) Isn't one object of a raised-bank rate to induce traders not to cash out their gains (cf. your p. 3 bottom), but to supply for themselves some of the Short Lacking for which they have hitherto come on the bank? I.e. bank rate may help to get the increase in output financed by checking borrowers as well as by encouraging depositors. This seems to fit in both with the current, and with your new, theory of the function of bank rate.

(2) I'm not at present inclined to attach much weight to the chance of substituting short for long lacking: for it seems to me that the things I think important (e.g. railways) increase the demand for both simultaneously. But I want to think more about this.

D.H.R.

To D. H. ROBERTSON, *28 September 1925*

My dear Dennis,

I like this latest version, though God knows it is concise. I have no criticisms at all on chap. v until p. 15 is reached. I have scribbled my comments there and subsequently and in the appendix in the margin[1]—I hope intelligibly, if not explications

---

[1] These have not survived. [Ed.]

must await a *viva voce* opportunity; they are not so very fundamental this time. My general impression is that the ideas in your head are very important and very necessary to the clarification of our minds, but that, when you have got the matter *quite* straight, the whole thing can be put *much* simpler and shorter. I don't believe that so much Knappish apparatus will be necessary in the end. My only real remaining quarrel with you is hinted at in what I have scribbled on pp. 20 and 21.

L[ydia] and I are very sorry that you can't get down here. Fay and Mrs Marshall come on Wednesday; Hawtrey on Saturday for the weekend. If you happened to be in London and ask to drop in for a night, we'd be delighted to see you.

I've led such a debauched vacation in controversy and travel that I haven't made any progress with my own book. Russia is a fascinating affair—I've been trying, since I came back, to write something about it, but it's very difficult.

Ever your affectionate

J.M.K.

I thought Dobb's book[1] *very* good—rather better than you allowed in the *Nation*.

To D. H. ROBERTSON, *10 November 1925*

My dear Dennis,

I have now finished your proofs and will hand them back to you after the Tuesday Club. Perhaps we can discuss my very few outstanding points in the train on the way back.

I think that your revised chapter v is splendid,—most new and important. I think it is substantially right and at last I have no material criticism. It is the kernel and real essence of the book. Query whether you should develop somewhere its practical applications to recent events—this is the chief point I want to talk about.

[1] *Wages.*

It will be interesting to see whether anyone, and who, will when it is published see what you are driving at. You'll be lucky if you get five understanding readers within two years; after that there will be lots. Grand queries of all:—(*a*) will the Prof. understand it (*b*) will Hawtrey understand it.

Yours ever
J.M.K.

During the rest of 1925, Keynes worked only intermittently on his book. In fact, all the evidence we have of his activity, beyond a signed contract dated 28 July with Harcourt Brace for a book entitled 'The Theory of Money and Credit', is in the form of two more draft tables of contents both dating from June. Keynes's questions and comments on the first one appear as footnotes.

13 June 1925

The Theory of Money and Credit

Introduction

Chapter I   The forms of money
  II   The plan of this treatise

Book I   The theory of money

  III   Bank deposits
  IV   The fundamental equation of money
  V   The demand for purchasing power
  VI   The supply of bank money
  VII   The supply of state money
  VIII   Price changes due to changes in the supply of money—inflation and deflation;[1] and price changes due to changes in the demand for purchasing power—boom and slump

Book II   The theory of credit

Chapter IX   Money credit and real credit
  X   The function of the banks in relation to the supply of working capital

[1] ? transfer to Book III?.

30 June 1925

The Theory of Money and Credit
Introduction

[1] The original has an arrow suggesting that chapter XXII should precede chapter XX.

From the summer of 1925 to early 1926, Keynes's work on the *Treatise*
was interrupted, as he noted in his letter to Robertson (above, p. 40), by
several factors—his marriage and subsequent trip to Russia (see *JMK*,
vol. IX, 'A Short View of Russia'), controversy (see *JMK*, vol. XIX) and work
in a field that had occupied him previously in 1920, ancient history. This
last-named activity, in the form of a history of ancient monetary standards,
occupied much of the autumn and winter of 1925–6. During this period he
worked, for his own 'amusement', at a draft of up to seven chapters, five of
which survive in various forms, and discussing it with F. E. Adcock and
C. T. Seltman, two of the leading experts of the day. Seltman repeatedly
encouraged Keynes to publish his results, but all that ever appeared were a
few generalisations in chapters 1, 30 and 35 of *A Treatise on Money*. Some of
these unpublished chapters and the correspondence surrounding them—
unfortunately excluding a missing appendix entitled 'The Backwardation on
Corn in Antiquity'—appear in *JMK*, vol. XXIV.

From the spring of 1926, however, Keynes was back at work on his theory
of money and credit, as the wealth of draft tables of contents from April and
the succeeding months indicates. By the end of August 1926, calculations in
the margin of one draft table of contents, the first entitled 'A Treatise on
Money', suggest that he had written (or had worked out in some detail)
approximately 55,650 words of Book I. At the same time, Keynes was suggesting to Alfred Harcourt that the book would be published in 1927.
However, all we know of the work from this period is several more tables of
contents, the first one in proof dating from September 1927, plus diary entries
of visits from Roy Harrod, presumably followed by useful comment. Nothing
else survives.

27 April 1926

The Theory of Money and Credit
Book I   The theory of money

Chapter 5 The demand for purchasing power

    1. Investment deposits and cash deposits

    2. The effects of transference between the two

    3. The *modus operandi* of price changes

  6 The supply of bank money

  7 The supply of state money

  8 The *modus operandi* of bank rate

Book II The theory of credit (as before)

Book III The characteristics of an ideal money (as before)

26 May 1926

The Theory of Money and Credit
Book I The theory of money

Chapter 1 The forms of money

  2 The concepts of purchasing power and of price level

  3 Current money and reserve money

  4 Bank money and bank credit

    (i) Investment deposits and cash deposits

    (ii) Cash deposits and overdrafts

    (iii) Bankers' dual functions—their confusion by cranks

  5 Cash balances and real balances

    (i) The paradox of the 'creation of credit'

    (ii) The supply of cash

    (iii) The demand for general purchasing power

    (iv) Price level as the factor which brings decisions of bankers and depositors into harmony

  6 The fundamental equation of price

  7 The variability of its elements

    (i) V_1—the velocity of circulation

    (ii) V_2—the use of overdraft facilities

    (iii) V_3—the proportion of investment deposits

    (iv) T—the volume of transactions

    (v) M—the volume of total deposits or of total credits

  8 The supply of state money and methods of its management

  9 The *modus operandi* of bank rate

  10 Other than bank money

  11 International price levels

6 August 1926

The Theory of Money and Credit
Book I   The theory of money

Chapter 1   The forms of money

    2   The concepts of purchasing power and of price level

    3   Current money and reserve money

    4   Bank money and bank credit

       (i)   Investment deposits and cash deposits

       (ii)   Cash deposits and overdrafts

       (iii)   The dual functions of bankers

    5   Cash balances and real balances

       (i)   The paradox of the 'creation of credit'

       (ii)   The nature of real balances

       (iii)   Price level as the factor which brings the decisions of bankers and depositors into harmony

    6   The fundamental equation of price

       (i)   The fundamental equation

       (ii)   The price level and the volume of transactions

       (iii)   The concept of velocity of circulation

    7   The variability of its elements

       (i) M—the volume of total deposits

       (ii) V_2—the proportion of investment deposits

       (iii) E—the efficiency of the currency

31 August 1926

A Treatise on Money

[written in top right corner]

The Theory of Money and Credit
Book I   The theory of money

Chapter 1   The forms of money

    2   The definition of price level and the theory of price index numbers

       (i)   The concepts of purchasing power and of price level

       (ii)   The plurality of price levels

       (iii)   Is there an 'objective mean variation of general prices'?

       (iv)   The problem of compiling a *series* of price index numbers

       (v)   The diffusion of price levels

Chapters 3, 4, 5, 6 as before

Chapter 7 The variability of its elements in respect of the demand for purchasing power
  (i) V_2 the proportion of cash deposits
  (ii) E the efficiency of the currency

8 The variability of its elements in respect of the supply of cash
  (i) M the volume of total deposits
  (ii) The supply of state money
  (iii) Methods of managing the supply of state money

9 The *modus operandi* of bank rate
  (i) 'A higher bank rate lowers prices by checking borrowers'
  (ii) 'A higher bank rate is a result of curtailing credit'
  (iii) 'The object of a higher bank rate is to attract gold'
  (iv) The causes of bank rate summarised
  (v) The consequences of bank rate analysed
  (vi) The place of bank rate in monetary management

10 International price levels

11 Coins and notes

12 September 1926

Book II The theory of credit

Chapter I The function of the banks in relation to the supply of working capital
  (i) Money credit and real credit

II The meaning and significance of working capital

III Fluctuations in the demand for working capital

IV Stocks of commodities and the theory of speculation

V The supply of real credit
  (i) as affected by changes in the amount of purchasing power
  (ii) as affected by changes in the amount of cash

VI The variability of the demand for working capital in relation to the variability of price levels

VII The operation of the pre-war gold standard

VIII The problem of meeting the variable demand for real credit without involving a variability of price levels

23 May 1927

Book I   The theory of money

Chapter   1   The forms of money
       2   The nature of price levels
       3   Current money and reserve money
       4   Bank money and bank credit
       5   Cash balances and real balances
       6   The fundamental equations of price
       7   The elements of the fundamental equations
          (i) The velocity of circulation
          (ii) The volume of transactions
       8   (as 7)
       9   (as 8)
     10   (as 9)
     11   The regulation of note issues

Book II   The theory of price levels

Chapter   1   The theory of index numbers
       2   The diffusion of price levels
       3   The international diffusion of price levels

2 June 1927

A Treatise on Money

Book I   Introduction

Chapter   1   The forms of money
       2   The nature of price levels
          (i) The concepts of purchasing power and of price level
          (ii) The plurality of price levels
          (iii) The fundamental index numbers
          (iv) Secondary index numbers
       3   The theory of index numbers
          (i) The problem of compiling a series of price index numbers
          (ii) Is there such a thing as an 'objective mean variation of
             general prices'?
          (iii) The diffusion of price levels
       4   Current money

Book II   The theory of bank money

       5   Bank money and bank credit
          (i) Investment deposits and cash deposits

22 September 1927

A Treatise on Money
Book I Introduction
Chapter 1 The forms of money

Not until 1928 do we have any more concrete evidence of the direction of Keynes's thoughts on money. At this point, evidence is available from three sources.

First, in his preface to the 1928 edition of *Money*, D. H. Robertson indicated that the collaboration between himself and Keynes was fruitful and close, when he noted in his preface (p. ix):

My debt to Mr J. M. Keynes, already very large when the first edition of this book was published, has reached a sum which is no longer capable of expression in words. There is much in this book, especially perhaps in chapter VIII [The Question of the Cycle], which ought scarcely, even in such a book as this, to see the light of day over any other signature than his until his forthcoming work on the theory of money has been published.

Unfortunately, we have little additional evidence of Keynes's involvement in this new edition beyond a request from Robertson that he read it either before 31 August 1928 in manuscript or later in galley.

Second, there is a longish letter to Alfred Harcourt, dated 26 September 1928 in which Keynes reported:

I have devoted the whole of this summer to my Treatise on Money, thus completing four years' work on it, and have been able to make pretty good progress. I should say that four-fifths of it is now completely finished. I am hopeful that I shall have finished it before Easter [1929], and that it may be published in this country about May...

As the book has developed in my hands, it has become a much more substantial affair than, so far as I remember, I warned you of. It looks to me like exceeding 500 pages in the format which we are adopting in this country, that is to say from 170,000 to 200,000 words...

Finally, there is a previously unpublished paper on American conditions, in which Keynes adopted the mode of analysis he was then using in the *Treatise* and which he circulated for comment. The paper developed out of a discussion within the board of the National Mutual Assurance Company, of which he was chairman. Before Keynes wrote the paper, there had been a dispute with O. T. Falk as to what the Federal Reserve authorities were likely to do in response to current developments on the New York Stock Exchange, and the implications of this action for share prices and the National Mutual's American investment policy. Falk believed that there was a serious inflation in America and that the Federal Reserve would deal with the situation through a policy of tight money which would reduce share prices. If the Federal Reserve did not so act, he believed that there would be a reaction from current price levels which might be severe. In either case, Falk believed that the National Mutual should dispose of the bulk of its American securities.

In the course of the discussions, Keynes wrote two papers, dated 29 July and 1 September 1928. As they cover much the same ground, only the latter paper, which Keynes circulated to several economists, bankers and officials,[1] as well as the National Mutual board, and to which he referred in the *Treatise* (*JMK*, vol. VI, p. 170) appears here.

IS THERE INFLATION IN THE UNITED STATES?

I

Let us suppose that in 1926 *A* held common stocks worth 100 in the market. By 1928 he finds that they are worth 140 in the market. Thinking that they may be overvalued, he decides to sell them and to invest the proceeds as a time deposit which will be available to him for re-investment when, as he anticipates, the market falls. He sells them to *B*, who is of a contrary opinion and thinks the stocks cheap at 140 and worth carrying at this price on borrowed money. The 140 deposited by *A* as time deposit gets lent, directly or indirectly,[2] to *B* as call money.

The result is that time deposits are increased by 140, and loans to the stock exchange are increased by 140. Now, obviously, nobody has 'saved' this 140. Such time deposits do not represent real saving. It is not as if *A* had saved 140 out of his income and then via his bank had lent this 140 for new investments. But whilst *A* has not saved the 140, neither has his bank lent it for current expenditure or for new investment.

Now it is quite plausible to suppose that of the one billion additional loans to the stock exchange since last year, (say) half—perhaps the whole—has in the last analysis arisen in this way.

Does this constitute inflation?

[1] D. H. Robertson, R. G. Hawtrey, A. Young, C. J. Bullock, W. M. Persons, C. Snyder, Sir J. Stamp, R. McKenna, W. R. Burgess, B. Strong, Sir O. Niemeyer and Sir R. V. N. Hopkins. [Ed.]

[2] It may be that only 70 (say) will be lent directly as call money by *A*'s bank. The other 70 of call money may be forthcoming from a corporation which has made real savings out of current profits to this amount, whilst *A*'s bank buys 70 newly issued bonds which require real savings. In this case the real savings made by the corporation have found their outlet in real investment via the bank, and *A*'s deposit has reached *B* indirectly.

II

Inflation—put broadly—means that, for some reason or another, the stream of consumers' buying is increasing faster than the stream of finished goods available for them to buy, with the result that prices rise. It is not convenient to mean by it anything else. But we might give the name *latent* or *potential* inflation to a situation which is likely to lead to actual inflation if it is allowed to develop unchecked.

Now the state of affairs described above certainly does not, in itself, bring about inflation. In so far as time deposits such as A's use up reserve resources, it might be *deflationary*. But it cannot possibly in itself serve to increase the stream of buying power. The cash A has realised is immediately locked up in the loan to B.

In fact, the transaction so far is purely one between A and B. The transaction not only is in the first instance, but must remain up to its final liquidation, nothing but a bet between A and B. Either it continues indefinitely, or if it ends some day—which is more probable—it can only end in one of two ways. Either B has to recognise that he was wrong in thinking that the stocks were worth 140 and has eventually to resell them to A at (say) 120, in which case the position is liquidated with A 20 richer and B 20 poorer than before (i.e. B, having lost his bet, has to transfer to A 20 from his other assets). Or A has to recognise that he was wrong in thinking the stocks not worth 140 and has eventually to buy them back from B at (say) 160, in which case the position is liquidated with A 20 poorer and B 20 richer than before. It will be noticed that the position can be liquidated just as well by breaking A's heart as by breaking B's.

During the whole currency of the bet it adds nothing to the volume of credit available for business or new investment; though it may *take* something from the credit so available by using up reserve resources. For certain, therefore, it is not inflationary. On the contrary, unless reserve resources are appropriately increased, it is deflationary.

Does it nevertheless constitute latent or potential inflation? It might be that the strength and optimism of Wall Street would over-stimulate the new-issue market, with the result that more money would be made available for investment than corresponds to the current rate of saving. There are several things to be said about this real possibility:

(i) The stimulus to over-investment is much less than it would be if there was less difference of opinion between the *A*'s and *B*'s. In the more typical stock exchange booms of the past, bull opinion has been much more preponderant. The existence of a powerful opposition to the bull market is a moderating influence on investment. Moreover on this occasion it is impracticable to make genuine new issues (i.e. other than bonus issues or stock-splitting in respect of existing shares) *of the same kind*, namely first-class common stocks, as those of which the market quotations are running up. Anyhow, it is not happening.

(ii) The over-investment, if it is occurring, requires additional bank credit *over and above* what is being employed to finance the bull market on Wall Street—i.e. the *A–B* transactions. The larger the amount of call money used by *B*, the weaker is the evidence for over-investment. Over-investment means loans to finance new issues, new building, etc.

(iii) Subject to a certain time lag, over-investment *must* raise commodity prices because it increases the stream of buying faster than the stream of *liquid* goods available to be bought— that is the meaning of over-investment. Subject to time lag, therefore, the course of prices *proves* whether or not there is over-investment (I am assuming that there is no observable tendency for costs of production to rise).

(iv) The rate of saving in the United States (and elsewhere) is now so enormous that, over a period, under-investment is much more probable than over-investment. The difficulty will be to find an outlet for the vast investment funds coming forward—particularly if central banks resist the tendency of the rate of interest to fall.

Is there, in the light of these observations, any evidence of a tendency towards over-investment? The unusual volume of new issues in the first half of this year and the general opinion that bond houses have not been altogether successful in clearing their shelves provides some *prima facie* evidence that there might be over-investment. But, on the other hand, current savings are very large. The course of prices in the near future will give us the answer. Up to date, the figures for prices and for the volume of demand deposits, etc., do not suggest that there is over-investment.

The evidence as to prices is as follows:

Bureau of Labour wholesale		Retail food		Cost of living		Snyder's 'general' prices	
1926	100·0	1913	100	1914	100	1913	100
1927	95·4	1927	156	1927	164	1927	171
1928 (1st six months)	97·3	1928 (1st four months)	152	1928 (1st four months)	162	1928 (1st six months)	175

Thus the cost of living has been falling, as also has employment, slightly; whilst in the first half of 1928 the wholesale index has recovered half of its fall in 1927, but is still below the normal of the last five years.

The basis of credit in the shape of member bank reserve balances has moved as follows (in billion dollars):—

Daily averages

1923	1·9	1926	2·2
1924	2·0	1927	2·3
1925	2·2	1928 (6 months)	2·4

Demand deposits of all member banks have been as follows (in billion dollars):—

		Index
June 1925	16·8	88
June 1926	17·4	91
June 1927	18·5	97
June 1928	19·2	100

These figures show no more than the normal trend of most American figures, except, perhaps, for June 1926–June 1927, but during this period prices were falling.

The picture is, then, one of good, progressive trade continued with a remarkable stability of prices and credit, but accompanied, lately, by a fairly large-scale bet between A and B. There is nothing which can be called inflation yet in sight.

IV

Is the Federal Reserve Board called upon to interfere in the bet between A and B?

Only, surely, in one or other of two contingencies:

(i) If the bet were using up so much reserve balances that not enough was available for other purposes, having regard to the law;

(ii) If the high level of common stocks was stimulating over-investment in new issues.

As regards (i) the bet uses up very little reserve balances. Call money from others than banks uses more, and call money furnished by time deposits requires only 3 per cent. Thus 4 billions of call money, financed half by non-banks and half by time deposits, requires $60 million reserve balances out of a total of $2,364 million. Moreover, there is still ample legal margin to increase reserve balances. At any rate the remedy for a deficiency of credit for other purposes is for the F.R.B. not to decrease reserve balances, but to allow them to grow slightly.

(ii) brings us back to the question of whether there is evidence of over-investment. If there is, then the action of the F.R.B.

must be directed at this, rather than at the bet between A and B, though the effect of such action may be to help A against B.

The F.R.B. should be watchful for the possibility of over-investment; but it should be equally watchful for the opposite —which, over a period, is the real danger ahead of us. The real risk is not a recurrence of 1920–1, which was different in every relevant respect from the existing situation, but of 1890–6, when a prolonged slump was produced by savings finding no outlet. It would be easy for the F.R.B. to produce a business slump without intending it.

I conclude that it would be premature today to assert the existence of over-investment.

(*N.B.* The boom in real estate values is another case of a bet between A' and B' and is not in itself an over-investment— though it might be associated with over-investment in building. Nor is output in excess of demand in a particular direction—e.g. motor cars—the same thing as over-investment or requiring the same remedies. Indeed, if the motor-car industry was to find demand falling off, it would be important to stimulate demand in other directions by cheap money rather than provoke a *general* slump by dear money.)

V

What about the merits of the bet between A and B?

It follows from the above that it would be unwise to take sides on the ground of the existence of inflation and of inevitable monetary developments issuing, sooner or later, from this. It is, rather, a question as to whether or not common stocks as a class are intrinsically over-valued. *Prima facie*, judged by dividend yield and past records, they are extremely dear. Moreover, whilst it does not follow that the mere checking by the F.R.B. of a tendency towards over-investment need slump them, a real danger lies in a business depression developing as a result of the F.R.B. accidentally bringing about under-investment.

On the other hand, no one can say what level of stock prices would be justified by a falling rate of interest in combination with the popularity for investors of the stocks of the great conservatively financed and strongly entrenched semi-monopolies of the U.S.A.

For this reason one might be afraid to be *A*. Yet since at present price levels stocks would be very sensitive to a marked decline in business, one might also be afraid to be *B*. I think that the importance of call money to the stock market, except over short periods, is overestimated. I suppose it is certain that not 5 per cent of the aggregate value of common stocks is carried with call money, and perhaps not more than 2 or 3 per cent. What really matters to the stock market is how the ordinary investor is feeling about the business outlook.

I should be inclined, therefore, to predict that stocks would not slump severely (i.e. below the recent low level) unless the market was discounting a business depression. Continued monetary stringency might easily bring about such a depression, or at least the anticipation of one. But it can hardly be the intention of the F.R.B. to bring about a business depression, in order to help *A* in his bet against *B*. One would be justified in assuming that, as the autumn develops and the spring approaches, the F.R.B. will do all in its power to *avoid* a business depression.

High money rates having failed to frighten *B*, how can it be maintained that it is the duty of the Federal Reserve Board— even if it were certain that in the long run *B* has been wrong and is going to burn his fingers—to force *B* to his knees by producing the actuality of business depression?

I should have supposed that if—as seems quite likely—stocks are destined to go to a figure which is too high on any reasonable criterion, even with good trade as a permanency, they will, in due course, boil over of themselves. This would be in accordance with previous experience. The way to keep a head of steam on them and to prevent them boiling over, is to fasten down a lid on the saucepan as at present. It may be that it is call money reasonable in quantity, and price, with *A* frightened into repurchasing, perhaps against his better judgment, and nothing more to go for, which will prelude the ultimate decline.

VI

Is the current amount of member-bank borrowings from their reserve banks a good reason for deflationary measures?

The stability—allowing for trend—of the member-banks' reserve balances shows that their borrowing has not, so far, been much more than enough to balance the loss of gold and the sale of securities by the Reserve Banks. We were given to understand that both these things were more or less intentional on the part of the reserve authorities. In any case it would not be practicable, so long as the Reserve Banks' gold and securities remain at their present level, to reduce the member-bank borrowing substantially below its present figure without producing a very severe slump in current business. To reduce such borrowing by $500 million would mean that the demand deposits of the member banks would have to fall to a lower figure than for years past—to a figure which certainly would not finance the present income of the United States or anything like it.

Thus it would not be sensible to exercise pressure against the present volume of member-bank borrowing unless the reserve authorities desire either:—

(i) to reduce the present level of money incomes in the United States, and in fact the level of gold prices throughout the world,

or (ii) to recover the gold lately exported, which would probably reduce the world level of gold prices, whether they wanted it or not.

The former desire, however, there is no reason to attribute to them; and the latter is opposed to their express declarations of policy.

J. M. KEYNES

1 September 1928

59

The paper drew reactions from several of those to whom it was sent and counter-reactions from Keynes. Below are those from W. R. Burgess, C. Snyder, D. H. Robertson, C. J. Bullock, R. G. Hawtrey and Sir Josiah Stamp, as well as any surviving resulting correspondence.

From W. R. BURGESS, *20 September 1928*

Dear Mr Keynes:

Governor Strong has been laid up at his apartment almost continuously since his return and hence is not able to answer himself your note of September 6. He discussed it with me yesterday and asked me to acknowledge it for him and to tell you that he had read the memorandum with the greatest interest but has found in it so many points where he believes either your facts or your conclusions are wrong that, with his limited strength, it would be too much of a task to attempt a reply.

I wish I could escape as easily but what I shall have to say is that I must postpone a complete answer for the present. I can only say that I disagree with the conclusion but I want to take more time to give you chapter and verse for my difference of opinion. I do not think we have had a serious inflation in this country but I do think we have been in grave danger of it and have some inflation in particular directions, all of which depends upon the definition for inflation, and they are seldom obvious until after the event. I hope to have some time to discuss that later on.

Very truly yours,

W. RANDOLPH BURGESS

I have just seen Snyder's letter and memo with 98 per cent of which I agree.

From C. SNYDER, *20 September 1928*

Dear Mr Keynes,

I was very much interested in the memorandum you enclosed. It is to me a novel and, I confess, somewhat alien point of view. There does not seem a great deal of mystery in what has happened in this country in the last year or more. Owing to the abundance of credit, in excess even of what appears to be about the maximum possible growth of trade, there came a heavy expansion of bank investment amounting, for the whole country, to something like a billion and a half within a twelvemonth. This buying, of course, gave a tremendous fillip to the stock market, and there ensued a corresponding expansion of speculative loans.

The total of these loans it is difficult to estimate, since a considerable amount of borrowing on securities may be for strictly business purposes. But the total of such borrowing must now be near to 13 billions of dollars for the whole country, which, as you see, is a vastly larger sum than is represented by the so-called brokers' loans.

These security loans have had an enormous expansion in recent years, accompanying the greatest rise in stock prices which this market has ever seen, certainly since the Civil War. This has meant a corresponding expansion of growth in speculation amounting in the last twelvemonth to something like 40 per cent (share sales) on top of an already prodigious previous growth.

This latter has culminated in the wildest outbreak of speculation since 1901. And this mania has swept the whole country, penetrating even to the most distant and smaller towns. For example, we had a story one day that a single brokerage house, with a branch in Kansas City, had received from that branch alone twelve hundred separate orders in a single day. You are better fitted than I, perhaps, to estimate the effect of this upon the business morale of the country.

All this has been accompanied, partly in consequence of the abundant credit, by what appears to be, so far as the most careful estimates will show, the greatest building boom which this country has known in sixty years. Of course we may have entered the millennium; but this is always difficult to be sure of, and what we know is that a large part of this tremendous building has been purely speculative and that, so great has been the supply of credit, speculative builders have in some instances been able to mortgage hotels, apartment houses, and office buildings for more than the total cost of construction and land, so that the mortgagee holds the bag and the speculator the equity, if there is any.

Some of our shrewdest and most experienced real estate operators believe that all this has resulted in a serious inflation of real estate values, and that the recoil from this may be severe. But it is very difficult to say.

I have taken the liberty to make some comments on your memorandum, for our private use here, and I am enclosing also a couple of others which you may like to look through.[1]

So far as our interest rates are concerned, when half a billion of gold goes out our banks must, of course, find a corresponding amount to make good their deposits, or reduce their loans by from ten to twenty times this sum, which latter alternative is too drastic to think of. Hence the heavy borrowing at the Federal Reserve banks.

It seems to me that in this whole problem we have had an extraordinary and most valuable laboratory experience in the last ten years and, to my mind—perhaps I am overly optimistic—it has quite transformed the problem

[1] These are not reproduced here. [Ed.]

from a guessing game to one of definite and trustworthy measures. Of course all this is new to our economists; they do not understand it and they cannot believe it. But I think that in another ten or twenty years it will be different.

It is always a great pleasure to hear from you, and I should be very much interested to hear your further thoughts upon these matters.

Please believe me, with high regards,

Always yours,

C. SNYDER

To C. SNYDER, *2 October 1928*

Dear Mr Snyder,

Very many thanks for your most interesting letter and its enclosures. I have been spending the last four years trying to write a Treatise on Money which shall be appropriate to the problems of modern monetary systems and the credit cycle. My reflections and researches have led me to a certain extent into unfamiliar ways of looking at things. Until my book is published I cannot hope for those I am talking with on these questions to follow my line of thought—since what I say in brief almost inevitably leaves out all sorts of necessary explanations. I should, however, like to try to make a few further remarks on your communications, approaching them so far as possible from what is probably a point of view common to both of us.

Quite apart from the question as to whether or not there is or has lately been actual or potential inflation in the United States, there are, it seems to me, certain false tests of inflation which one has to beware of, as follows:—

1. You say in your paper that 'inflation is essentially a growth of bank credit at a rate faster than the growth of trade'. If after the words 'bank credit' you were to add 'used in trade', I should more or less agree with you (subject to various qualifications which it is not necessary to mention). But if you mean by bank credit the total volume of the member banks' outstanding assets, then it seems to me that an error is liable to creep in. If the extent to which the public are using the banking system, not

only for the purpose of cheque accounts, but as a means of investing their savings, is growing at a rate faster than the growth of trade, than the total volume of bank credit and that part of it which is used by the banks, directly or indirectly, for the purpose of financing securities, can (and should) also grow out of proportion to the growth of trade. If a man chooses to use some of his savings, not to buy a bond, but to make a time deposit at his bank, and if the bank then uses the time deposit to buy the bond itself, or to lend to some third party the means wherewith to carry the bond, then I see nothing inflationary in this. From the point of view of trade and prices it is what I sometimes call 'washout' credit. The mere fact that banks are standing between the owners of savings and the holders of bonds on an increasing scale has nothing inflationary in it, although the abnormal growth of such practices probably increases the precariousness of the bond and stock markets and might for this reason be regarded as a practice to be deprecated. I am hopeful that you may be sympathetic to this conclusion, because your paper of August 7 on 'Stock Market Loans and Legitimate Trade' seems to me to fall into line with it very well.

Now if this is so, it is unsafe to argue from the total values of demand and time deposits to the existence of excessive credit. As a rough test it would, I think, be much safer to take demand deposits alone as the significant test of whether or not credit is becoming dangerously expanded. Are there in fact, on this test, any noticeable signs of over-expansion?

American investors and financiers seem at the present time to be divided into two parties—those who are ready to hold bonds and stocks in spite of the general risks of the situation and expenses of borrowing; and those who think it wise to keep liquid and lend their funds to the former class. The greater the difference between the two parties, the greater will the volume of call money be. But very high call rates may so much encourage certain classes of professional financiers to keep their funds liquid in order to take advantage of these high rates, that they may actually increase the magnitude of the transactions which represent the difference of opinion between these two parties.

2. Some writers at the present time seem to argue as if the magnitude of the amount of call money used by the stock exchange is a test of the degree of the inflationary tendencies. If, for example, call money lent to the stock exchange was to fall by $800 million they would draw the conclusion that the chances of inflation were diminished. This again seems to me to be a false test. The stock exchange call money, by using up a certain amount of reserve resources, positively diminishes, other things being equal, the chances of an inflation. In so far as the abundant call money is leading to excessive new issues, then I quite agree it is a different matter.

3. Over-investment in particular directions is quite a different thing from the general over-investment which is associated with inflation. It is dangerous, therefore, to conclude that inflation is in the air because investment seems to be in danger of being overdone in particular directions. It would not follow from the fact that building had got ahead of demand, so that many new buildings were unlet, or that motor-car production had passed saturation point, so that many cars were unsold or plant going out of employment, that there was general over-investment. Indeed, these things would point to the possibility of the early development of the opposite, namely under-investment. If house building or motor-car manufacture has run ahead of demand, this will very rapidly produce a falling off in production in those particular directions, and it would be a matter of urgent public importance to find alternative outlets for current savings.

These manifestations therefore—at any rate as soon as they have come to a head—would make it important that money should be as cheap as possible, so as to encourage developments along alternative lines.

In short, the fact that houses and motors are being manufactured in excess of demand by no means proves that they are being manufactured in excess of the volume of real savings available to finance them; whereas it is the latter that one means by the general over-investment which is associated with inflation.

Leaving, then, what seem to me to be certain false tests of inflation, I come back to the test where, I feel sure, we are on common ground, namely the test of prices. We agree, I think, that if there is inflation it must show itself sooner or later in rising prices for articles of common consumption. We agree also that this is the end of a process, and that certain index numbers of sensitive articles at wholesale are an earlier indication of what is going to happen. Thus the question of fact, as distinct from the question of theory, will be settled fairly soon by the actual course which is being taken by wholesale prices. If the Federal Reserve System is primarily governed by the facts or by their anticipations of the facts on this head, the position is fairly safe. But if they pursue other criteria, such as the total volume of time and demand deposits added together, the volume of member bank borrowing, the state of Wall Street, or the volume of call money, then it seems to me that there might be a real danger of checking normal new investment so severely as to bring about by accident, some time in the first half of next year, a real setback to trade. This is the practical issue which makes all these theoretical matters so important as well as so interesting.

Two friends of mine who are associated with me in the National Mutual Assurance Company—O. T. Falk, a director, and Geoffrey Marks, the actuary and also a director—are leaving tomorrow for a visit to New York to see if they can get clearer about the situation than is possible here. I hope they may have some opportunity of a talk with you.

Yours very truly,
[copy initialled] J.M.K.

From a letter from D. H. ROBERTSON, *18 September 1928*

(3) Herewith also your memo. which I've read with much interest. My only criticism is that it is—or might be, for I haven't followed closely the arguments of your opponents—in part an ignoratio elenchi. I mean that to

hold that a central bank ought to intervene to kill a stock exchange boom doesn't seem to me to *imply* that one holds that that boom is actually causing or even threatening 'inflation' and 'over-investment'. One may merely hold that if unchecked it will lead to a collapse which, through a chain of bankruptcies, loss of confidence etc., will be very bad for business: and argue that in order to prevent that it is better to put up with the lesser evil of discouraging 'legitimate' business somewhat by keeping credit tight. Of course it might be better still to damp down the stock exchange boom *without* discouraging ordinary business: but I don't see how you're to do that until not only central banks, but ordinary banks as well, exercise more qualitative discrimination in their loans, whether by differential rates of interest or otherwise. However, that brings us back to an old hare of mine!

From C. J. BULLOCK, *22 September 1928*

My dear Keynes,

I have read with great interest your analysis of monetary conditions in the United States. The only adequate reply would be a long essay; and for this I haven't time. I wish we could sit down together this afternoon and go over it paragraph by paragraph. If we could do so, I think we should find around tea time that we had had a busy afternoon and had not completed the subject.

The first observation I will make is that your analysis of the situation, while original and penetrating, does not seem to me to take account of all the factors that would need to be taken into account before coming to a conclusion on the transaction between A and B and the attitude which the Federal Reserve authorities ought to take toward the trade they make.

For example, in the illustration with which you start, you simplify things greatly by assuming that A, when he sells his stocks to B at $140, invests the proceeds in a time deposit and then sits down on the side lines and doesn't speculate any more because he thinks the stock market is too high. Now, in fact, a great many people have sold out some stocks and gone into others.

Beside stock speculation, you need to take into account the enormous bond issues of the first six months of the present year, which jammed the market very badly by June and have been only partly relieved at this date by cessation of new issues, marking down the prices of the goods the bond dealers had on their shelves, and a strenuous summer sales campaign. Our so-called brokers' loans, as you know, include a lot of collateral loans made to bond houses concerned with new flotations.

Your letter to me was written before you could have received the Letter[1]

[1] The Weekly Letter of the Harvard Economic Society of which Bullock was president. [Ed.]

we published on September 1, in which the last four pages are devoted to a general consideration of credit expansion in the United States during the past year. When I got home from Europe, I found the conditions set forth in that Letter, and spent a good part of the month of August in making enquiries and collecting the available data. While I was at work, the Federal Reserve authorities, between the first and the middle of August, reversed their policy; and therefore we felt it necessary to point out that credit strain produced by excessive credit expansion during the past year was about to be relieved by further credit expansion, which, with the speculative fever raging unabated, might be expected to result in continued credit strain next winter, when money otherwise might be expected to get somewhat easier. The thing that impresses us is not so much the expansion that has taken place, but the insistent call for more and more credit which results from the speculative mania produced by the previous expansion. This seems to us to be producing real 'inflation', a word which up to now we have carefully refrained from using.

Gold imports in large volume would relieve the situation for a time; but, in the present temper of the speculative community and with our highly organised machinery for manufacturing and selling bonds, they would give only temporary relief. Such imports would also mean a renewal of the tremendous construction activities which characterised the first half of 1928.

Our information has been that the European central banks have balances in New York sufficient to make it unnecessary to ship much of [if?] any gold to the United States this fall. Some gold may come, but, according to this information, only to such extent as the central banks are willing to countenance. About this matter of gold movements one can never be sure in these days; but the above is the best information we can get. If your Bank, for example, wanted to raise its rate, it would of course like to see some gold exported in order to set the stage for a rate increase. But the increase would probably follow pretty quickly upon the beginning of the gold exports; and such exports would not go very far.

On your second page, in the first paragraph, you define inflation, but define it substantially as a disproportionate increase of consumers' buying which leads to a rise of prices. This seems to relate to inflation of commodity prices; and your subsequent discussion of inflation seems to come back always to commodity prices. I agree that the transaction between A and B with which you start wouldn't tend to inflate commodity prices. Nor would it make great drafts upon bank credit if A was willing to put his money into a time loan for which only a 3 per cent reserve would be required.

The sort of thing that has happened this year could be better analysed if you started with the following assumption: A has common stocks, for which he paid $100 and upon the security of which he is borrowing $50. He sells these stocks to *B* for $140; and *B* borrows $90 through a collateral loan. The result is an increase of $40 in collateral loans, since I will assume that *A* takes $50 of the money *B* pays him and pays off his loan. *A* is then left with $90, which he does not invest in a time deposit but puts out on a call loan in the stock market or uses to purchase some other stocks which he considers not so overvalued as the stock which he sold *B*. This sort of an assumption comes much nearer to describing the developments of the past year than the assumption you make.

The increase of time deposits which occurred last year was partly due to the sort of thing which your illustration takes into account; but it was also due to the conversion of demand deposits not needed for the time being for commercial purposes into time deposits bearing a higher rate of interest, a thing which banks have been encouraging because of the lower reserve requirements for time deposits. The increase of time deposits has been partly through actual saving, partly through the process you take into account in your illustration, and partly through the conversion of demand deposits of a commercial character into time deposits. The growth of time deposits of this last character constitutes an element of weakness in our situation, and is so regarded by our best bankers, who say that the reserve requirements for time deposits ought never to have been made lower than for other deposits. I don't express this as my own view, for I haven't come to any conclusion as to whether the reserve for time deposits should be fully as large as that for demand deposits; but I do know that some of the best bankers I know take this view.

The illustration that I have just given you will show you how much more I think there is in the situation than your analysis takes account of. I will also venture a few other comments.

You say, correctly enough in principle, that, if there has been over-expansion, that would show itself in the price of commodities; and your figures show that during the first half of 1928 there was no evidence of commodity price inflation. More recent price movements, especially those of the last four weeks, give a somewhat different picture; and at the present moment it would be possible to say that it is beginning to look as if the inflation of credit was affecting commodity prices, particularly the prices of those commodities used in building and in the automobile industry. I would not yet express the opinion that commodity prices are beginning to be inflated; but recent movements, if continued long enough, would lead to that result. Personally, I shall be surprised if these movements go very far this year. Most of the commodities in question are international commodities; and I doubt if, even if credit continues to expand here, its rate of increase will be enough to affect international markets greatly and produce anything that ought to be called inflation. Even so, we should not conclude that credit hasn't been inflated, or that other things, like stock prices and real estate, haven't been inflated. Since 1922 we have had peculiar conditions in the United States which have brought about a vast expansion of credit, which, for one reason or another, just hasn't affected commodity prices. I have thought that, before we got through, commodity prices would ultimately be inflated; but it hasn't happened yet. I merely make the point now that, because inflation hasn't hit commodity prices, we shouldn't argue that there hasn't been inflation in other directions.

In the next place, we think the best way to measure the expansion of bank credit is to to take the total loans and investments of the commercial banks.[1] For all member banks of the Federal Reserve System, the increase in the year ending June 30 last was somewhere between 7 and 8 per cent, which was a very large amount for a year in which the country was losing one-ninth of its effective stock of gold. All this is covered by our Letter of September 1.

Our present difficulty seems to arise from the fact that, largely as a result of the easy money policy adopted by the Federal Reserve authorities in the last half of 1927, there was let loose a speculative movement, which might have been controlled last spring (but was not, because in March the Reserve authorities stayed their hand) and might have been controlled even in August if the Reserve authorities had insisted that fall commercial require-ments should be financed largely by the liquidation of collateral loans. It would have been easier to check it last spring than it would have been in August; and it would have been easier in August than it will be next spring if the speculative movement still continues strong. At least, that is our view. Obviously the Federal Reserve authorities think they can let out some more credit this fall without having it get into speculation, and then have fall seasonal borrowings repaid next January and February, when money naturally tends to flow back to the banks. We shall see what we see.

President Lowell wrote me a letter some time ago, in which he indicated that he had before him a proposal to invite you to come here to lecture some time for a half-year. The matter has been sometimes mentioned, but never in such definite form. I hope that if you ever hear from him you will decide to come, for I am sure you would be very helpful to us, and I think you would find it an interesting experience, even in these days of partially enforced prohibition, which is more effective in academic communities than in some other places. Of course if you should come we should, in this organisation, do all that we could to make your stay pleasant.

[1] To take member bank reserves as a measurement is defective now because of the disproportionate growth of time deposits with only a 3 per cent requirement.

I got away from England as soon as possible after our conference, because Mrs Bullock and I had a lot of friends due to arrive in London about the 5th or 6th of July, and we wanted to get away before they came, because we wanted to take things easy and get a real rest. We therefore went to Paris on the 3rd of July, and stayed until the 25th, at the Hotel Westminster in the Rue de la Paix, where we had very quiet accommodations on the central courtyard and heard nothing of street noises. I had some calls to make; but I spent the mornings at the Louvre, the afternoons in bed, and in the evening we went to the theatres, the opera, or the cinema, as we elected to do each day. The weather was warm; but we had a very agreeable time and got the rest that we were looking for. Incidentally, we drank huge quantities of Vittel water, and so took a cure for rheumatism which proved remarkably efficacious.

Mrs Bullock joins me in kindest regards to Mrs Keynes and yourself.

Yours sincerely,
CHARLES J. BULLOCK

To C. J. BULLOCK, *4 October 1928*

Dear Bullock,

Very many thanks for sending me so full a commentary on my memorandum. I was particularly glad to get it because since writing my document I had of course read the Harvard Letter of September 1, and been, I confess, somewhat dismayed by it. In particular, the view which it seemed to hold that the amount of credit which could properly be created in the United States bore some definite relation to the amount of gold held by the Federal Reserve System seemed to be an abandonment of all the sort of things we have been agreeing to say for some time past. Indeed, I was very much shocked! So I am glad to have a fuller account of what lies behind it.

As you say, however, this is much too big a question to discuss satisfactorily by correspondence. I have also had some commentaries from Snyder, which cover partly the same ground as yours. So I am venturing to save myself a little time by enclosing with this a copy of my letter to him,[1] which may

[1] Above, pp. 62-5.

perhaps help a bit to bring to a head the difference of opinion between us, if there is one.

The point where we certainly agree is in finding the eventual test of over-expansion in the commodity price level; so that our difference of opinion is limited to our diagnosis of the circumstances which are liable to develop a price inflation if they are left unchecked. On the question of facts it is of course impossible to dogmatise. It seems to me to be quite reasonable to maintain that in the spring and early summer a situation was developing which, if left to itself, would probably have produced inflation. But what I am afraid of is that wrong tests will be applied in deciding how long to maintain the present dear-money policy. I cannot help feeling that the risk just now is all on the side of a business depression and a deflation rather than otherwise.

May I take just two points out of your letter for special remark.

1. In the second paragraph of your page 2,[1] where you deal with gold imports, you seem to suggest, as in the Harvard Letter, that the credit situation would be improved if gold imports were to take place. This is certainly not the test I should apply if I was aiming at a credit policy which would obviate credit cycles.

2. At the bottom of page 3[2] you take as your measure of the expansion of bank credit the total loans and investments of the commercial banks. I am not satisfied with this, for reasons which are partly explained in my letter to Snyder. For example —I take a simple case to make the theoretical point plain—if you were to save a thousand dollars out of your income and, not liking the look of things, decided not to buy a bond but to put it on time deposit with your bank; and if your bank were then to buy a bond with your thousand dollars, is the situation, in your opinion, any different, from the point of view of credit expansion, from what it would be if you had bought the bond yourself? The point is important for this reason: the Federal

[1] Above, p. 67.　　　　[2] Above, p. 69.

Reserve System cannot possibly order you to buy a bond instead of making a time deposit; all they can do is to compel the member bank to balance your time deposit by restricting its lending to some other party. But why should lending to third parties be restricted because you choose to make your investment via your bank instead of direct? Again, if a corporation puts by 100,000 dollars out of its profits to reserve, and, instead of buying a bond, lends this 100,000 dollars to the call market, attracted by the high rate obtainable, whilst the bond issuing houses, having failed to sell their bonds to the corporation, finance them with call money, why is this inflationary? It may, I entirely agree, create a dangerous bond and stock market situation. Price quotations for stocks and bonds are likely to be more stable if they are directly owned by the persons who have made the savings than if they should be owned by persons who have borrowed the savings at call or short notice. I see every reason in the world why Americans should be worried about the present speculative position. But it seems to me a mistake to conclude that this particular phenomenon is of the nature of credit expansion, meaning by credit expansion a monetary phenomenon which will result sooner or later in a rise of prices. If too prolonged an attempt is made to check the speculative position by dear money, it may very well be that the dear money, by checking new investments, will bring about a general business depression. Unless you think that at this very moment, and in the foreseeable future, new investments are being floated faster than the savings of the public can absorb them, I say that there is more risk of creating a business depression than there is necessity for avoiding a business boom.

I had had some idea of visiting America next year, and President Lowell had kindly sent me an invitation to lecture. But I am afraid that my plans are too indefinite for me to enter into any commitments, and that in any case my visit would be too short to make possible a six months' residence at Harvard, much as I should enjoy it.

We of the London & Cambridge Economic Service are very grateful to you for what you have done about the deficit which was hanging so uncomfortably about our necks.

Ever yours sincerely,
[copy initialled] J.M.K.

From C. J. BULLOCK, *25 October 1928*

My dear Keynes

I am sorry to learn from your letter of 4 October that you find it difficult to make arrangements to spend six months at Harvard either next year or some other year not too distant. In any event I hope you will plan to come to the United States at some time; and, if you do, let us know, and we can at least have a lecture from you in Cambridge and an opportunity for you to meet our organisation as well as the members of the Department of Economics.

Now, in regard to the matter about which we have been corresponding.

You appear to me to have drawn some inferences from our Letter that were not intended and perhaps not justified by the context. For example, in the first paragraph, you say the Letter seems to hold that 'the amount of credit which could properly be created in the United States bore some definite relation to the amount of gold held by the Federal Reserve System'.

If such an inference was justified, I wrote very carelessly, because that was not in my head at all. The burden of that Letter was that too much credit had been created in a year when we lost a half billion of gold, and, second, that this credit had gone largely into speculative channels and had produced excessively high money rates.

It has always been my expectation that our banking system will, like others, ultimately expand up to the limits set by law or custom; and the only questions, therefore, that I can have about expansion are the questions whether the rate is too rapid and whether the expansion takes undesirable directions.

The above will give you my point of view; and if you reread the Letter with this in mind I think you will see there is nothing in it inconsistent with the above statement, although perhaps there are some things which, without the above statement, might appear to imply something different.

As to the commodity price level being the eventual test of inflation, I don't know whether we are in agreement or not. On that point I meant to say that I still believed that, before we get through expanding credit in the

73

United States, commodity prices will show the effects. This, however, is a matter of belief. The experience of the past year makes it possible for me to conceive of such a thing as the United States reaching the limit of credit expansion without commodity prices being materially affected and purely as the result of absorption of credit by the security markets, real estate expansion, and the other things which in recent years have been willing to be inflated by cheap and abundant money. Why prices haven't been affected isn't pertinent to our present discussion, and is too long a matter to discuss by letter even if I thought that I had something new or important to say about it. Prices are continuing to move slightly upward; but they have got to continue to do that for some time before they get to the level they reached in the spring of 1923, which level we did not then think was an inflated level; and on this matter we have just got to wait and see. I shall be surprised if they don't get affected before credit expansion comes to an end; but I am not now anywhere near so sure of that as I was a year ago.

I do not see the propriety of limiting the word 'inflation' to commodity price inflation. Of course its use in economics was originally purely figurative, and I don't know now that we have any standard definitions to go by; but nothing in the etymology or history of the word 'inflation' justified us in limiting it to commodity prices. When I say this, I hasten to add that for the student of business cycles commodity price inflation has peculiar importance; but I am not today ready to say that it is the only kind of inflation that is significant.

As to time deposits, etc., and the question which you ask about the difference in the credit situation brought about by having a bank buy the bond with money that I left with it as a time deposit, I will say the following.

I would first assume that I had $1,000 in my checking account (a demand deposit requiring, in a Cambridge bank, a 10 per cent reserve). I would then assume that I changed this $1,000 into a time deposit, requiring a 3 per cent reserve. I would then assume that the bank bought a $1,000 bond. After assuming these three things, I should get as a result the fact that, by changing my deposit from a demand to a time deposit, I had reduced the bank's reserve requirements from $100 to $30, and had so given the bank $70 of free reserve with which it could expand credit.

Upon the other hand, if I had bought the bond from a bond house and then stuck it away in my tin box, I would have the bond, the bond dealer's bank would experience a $1,000 increase in its demand deposits, and my bank would lose $1,000 of demand deposits. Under such conditions there would be no $70 of reserve money released to serve as a basis for credit expansion up to the amount of $700.

74

Of course this is only one case; but it is a fairly representative case bearing on the question of whether it makes a difference whether I buy a bond and put it in my tin box or take a time deposit with the bank and let the bank purchase a bond for its portfolio.

Whether the loans and investments of member banks give a good measure of the expansion of bank credit is another question that you raise. I think they do, because they give just the same result that you would get if you took the total deposits of member banks (both demand and time deposits). I prefer to take the loans and investments as a measure of bank credit for most purposes, partly because the total which you get can be presented without going into the question of the comparative effect of demand and time deposits on the reserve position of our banks. One inevitably runs into this question the moment he attempts to measure the expansion of bank credit by total deposits.

To take demand deposits alone would seem to me to give a very bad measure of credit expansion at a time when there is proceeding, as is the case in the United States, a marked change in the proportion of time deposits.

You will see that I agree that for some purposes I should not take loans and investments, and that for the purposes for which I do use them I take them because they give the same result that total deposits would give without raising questions irrelevant for the particular purposes in question. If I were measuring credit expansion with a view to determining the relation of our gold reserve to the total amount of credit outstanding in the United States, I should take total deposits—demand and time.

I haven't covered all the questions raised by your letter; but that isn't possible if I am going to reply at any time within the next two or three weeks, which are going to be very crowded. Moreover, I am sure you didn't expect me to take up your points in all detail. The subject simply cannot be adequately covered by a letter.

We haven't changed our position about monetary policies; but we would like to see this expansion occur in helpful rather than harmful ways. Moreover, in view of gold conditions throughout the world, I should prefer to have it take place gradually and as commodity markets require it, rather than having so much of it tied up in speculation before we even know such things as how much of our present stock of gold is really 'borrowed' gold. Even on this last point, I can't go into the thing adequately, because of the limitations imposed by correspondence.

With best regards, I remain

Yours sincerely,
CHARLES J. BULLOCK

From R. G. HAWTREY, *7 October 1928*

Dear Maynard,

I was delighted to get your letter of the 21st Sept. I am glad to find you take the same sort of view as I do of Pigou's book.[1] I should not like my attack upon it to be thought unfair and uncalled for. And there is so very much to disagree with and so very little to accept!

I dare say you are right about my treatment of dealers' stocks in the trade cycle. In fact I believe I have already in some respects shifted my ground. I attach more importance than I used to to the volume of sales and to 'virtual' stocks. But I do not think these factors are separable from the amount of stocks in hand.

The sensitiveness of the dealer to the short-term rate of interest does not require a very large *amount* of stocks to be held. It is his *willingness* to hold stocks, and therefore to order more goods, that is the operative factor.

Thanks for sending me your memo., 'Is there Inflation in the U.S.?' I saw it at the Treasury before my departure, but I am glad to have a copy here.

In principle I agree with most of what you are saying. I do not think there is inflation, and I think the attempts of the Federal Reserve Banks to check speculation by means of dear money are very ill-judged. But on a point of detail, I do not quite agree as to your example of a 'bet' between A and B. At any rate I do not think the bear speculator *holding money on deposit* is at all typical. In the first place the bear speculator would not ordinarily be a bear of all securities at the same time; he could often invest in some security of which he believes the price to be favourable. Secondly most of the bears are professionals; they are brokers who are financing customers in their bull speculations, and any surplus funds go in diminution of the brokers' borrowing for that purpose. And much of the bear speculation consists simply in the brokers letting down their normal holdings of the securities they believe to be overvalued.

I should therefore dissent from that part of your argument which depends on the existence of an accumulation of stagnant time deposits as a set-off against the call loans by which the bulls are financed. It follows that I should also disagree as to the existence of a 'powerful opposition to the bull market'.

On the other hand I attach great importance to the call money 'forthcoming from a corporation which has made real savings out of current profits'. Much the greater part of the growth in brokers' loans has been in loans of this type, which do not cause inflation because they are not from

---

[1] The book in question is *Industrial Fluctuations*. The Keynes letter referred to has not survived. Hawtrey's views had recently appeared in his book *Trade and Credit*. [Ed.]

banks. In a sense these loans from corporations may be regarded as bear speculation, since the corporations prefer liquid funds to investments. But I believe the predominant motive is the desire for liquidity, not the desire to wait for a more favourable opportunity to invest. With active trade the liquidity *might* turn into inflation, but it should not be difficult for the banks to prevent this if it threatened.

[A paragraph on Harvard, where Hawtrey was Visiting Professor, is omitted here.]

Yours ever,

R. G. HAWTREY

From SIR JOSIAH STAMP, *6 October 1928*

My dear Keynes,

It was very good of you to send me your soliloquy for consideration, and I am only so sorry that I've been so long answering it...The analysis is most neatly done and I believe entirely correct. I have felt a growing suspicion for some time that the F.R.B. could not succeed, and I doubted whether they ought to. I see no proper end to this stock boom but that it should boil over naturally. But I was assured by the Chicago University Professor of Finance that there is *no* actual inflation of stock values for some time past—the leaders and favourites have gone ahead, but the total of all quoted stocks would show no advance. I have had no chance of checking this and it seemed to me *prima facie* unlikely—anyway the lesson he wanted me to know was that the advances on the minuses would have shrunk and offset the additional to the speculative leaders. But I doubt if that class of stock—rather obscure—was much held upon short money, and it is the very *fact* that stocks get mainly held in that way that induces these forward movements as favourites. This must be so if your estimate (p. 8, para. 3)[1] is correct.

On the factual point: when will the F.R.B. give it up? And will recent declarations on their side induce them to? I feel that, at the moment, no suggestion that it is *at all* uncomfortable for us would cut any ice. Only the cold logic of your note could stir them.

If you publish the note, I suggest for clarity on p. 2,[2] para. 2 define 'reserve resources' a little—it's quite clear later on but at that point a new reader may be thinking of business, not *bank*, reserves and bottom of p. 3[3] after than, [insert] 'for new objective or physical uses, such as for'.

When are you in town, that we could lunch together, and unburden our souls on the jolly old gold standard?

Yours,

J. C. STAMP

---

[1] Above, p. 58. [2] Above, p. 53. [3] Above, p. 54, line 13.

At this time, there was also another draft table of contents, dated 6 October 1928, which suggests how much the book had expanded over the previous year. In addition, just previously there is part of a note from Frank Ramsey suggesting that Keynes was still at work on his Fundamental Equation.

From a letter from F. P. RAMSEY, *3 August 1928*

I ought to have written before to say how much I enjoyed the weekend. I don't know when I've enjoyed myself so much. And how exciting your quantity equation seemed; I wish I was sufficiently used to thinking about banking to appreciate it fully and to make better criticisms. But I could see that it was a great advance.

6 October 1928

81

During 1928–9 Keynes's work on the *Treatise* also showed itself in the form of an article in the *Economic Journal* for March 1929 entitled 'The German Transfer Problem' (*JMK*, vol. XII). This article led to comments from Professor B. Ohlin and M. Jacques Rueff in the September 1929 issue of the *Journal*. In replying to these comments, Keynes made clear the connection between his article and the, as yet unfinished, *Treatise* when he noted that 'my theoretical background in approaching these problems is as yet unpublished'. He also made a point in chapter 21 of the *Treatise* (*JMK*, vol. v, p. 297) of linking what he had to say on international disequilibria to that earlier debate.

Meanwhile work continued on the *Treatise* proper. By 18 February 1929 Keynes had committed himself to publication in the autumn of 1929 and was working towards the relevant deadlines. By 2 August, when he received a second proof of the table of contents and a first proof of the preface, the first nineteen chapters, or just over 320 pages, were in page proof, while the rest of the book was finished and in draft or galley proof.

Unfortunately nothing remains of this single-volume version of the *Treatise* beyond the preface, the table of contents, a heavily re-worked first galley proof, dated 1 March 1929, of what was chapter 24 of the contents of 6 October 1928 converted to chapter 23 of the table of contents of August 1929, a second (page) proof of the same chapter, and first proofs of chapters 30 and 31, dated 16 and 27 July 1929 respectively, of the contents of August 1929.

As the first proofs of chapters 30 and 31 follow with a few minor corrections the texts of chapters 35, 36 (iv) and 38 of the finally published two-volume *Treatise*, there is little point in reprinting them here. Similarly, as the preface of August 1929 closely follows the first five paragraphs of the published preface, it needs no reprinting except for its final two sentences, which diverge from the printed version and run as follows:

Mr H. D. Henderson is always the most useful and sympathetic of critics on the plan and architecture of an argument. I owe the discovery of innumerable mistakes and muddles to Mr F. P. Ramsey, Mr P. Sraffa,[1] and Mr R. F. Kahn, all of King's College, Cambridge, and especially to Mr Kahn, whose care and acuteness have left their trace on many pages.

However, as chapter 23 disappeared in later revisions and as so little of the drafts of the *Treatise* survives, we print a variorum version of the two proofs of chapter 23. The text follows the second proof. In the footnotes,[2] we indicate all the changes which Keynes made from the first galley proof version. Following this draft chapter is the final single-volume table of contents for the *Treatise*.

A variorium of drafts of chapter 23

THE PART PLAYED BY THE BANKING SYSTEM

(i) THE DUTY OF THE BANKS TO FURNISH WORKING CAPITAL

WE are at last in a position to return to monetary problems proper, and in particular to the part played in the credit cycle by the banking system.

---

[1] Spelled 'Graffe' in the uncorrected proof. [Ed.]
[2] Keynes's original footnotes are in square brackets. [Ed.]

We have seen that a credit cycle, though it may be initiated by an investment boom in fixed capital, is likely to be accompanied sooner or later, and sometimes from the outset, by an increased demand for working capital. Now it is generally accepted in most countries that the banking system has a special responsibility to meet, so far as it can, any reasonable demands for working capital which may arise. If[1] the outside investment market for the supply of industrial capital offers facilities which are inadequate in relation to a country's normal industrial growth, as was the case, for example, in pre-war Germany, or if[1] the landlord system and the mortgage market are inadequate to provide the fixed capital of agriculture, it is true that[2] the banks may have to play an important part in mobilising the resources of their depositors to furnish fixed capital. Or, again, where the resources of the banking system are far in excess of the demands upon it for working capital—as seems to be the case in the United States today—the[3] banks are inevitably drawn, directly or indirectly, into financing fixed capital on a very large scale. Nevertheless it remains[4] a general tenet of orthodox banking, especially in Great Britain and the United States, that it is both the duty and the interest of bankers to regard the requirements of industry for the financing of working capital as the first charge on their resources, which it is their business to meet if possible. So much is this the case that we have spoken in previous chapters of the banks having a dual responsibility—the obligation[5] to provide working capital being almost as binding on them as to provide sound bank money.

There are two reasons for this. In the first place, loans for working capital are more 'liquid' in the sense that the borrower

---

[1] The word 'If' replaces 'Where' in the galley proof.
[2] The words 'it is true that' do not appear in the galley proof.
[3] In the galley proof the first part of this sentence reads 'Or, where—as seems to be the case in the United States today—the resources of the banking system are far in excess of the demands upon it for working capital . . .'
[4] The word 'remains' replaces 'is' in the galley proof.
[5] The word 'obligation' replaces 'objective' in the galley proof.

84

will be frequently turning the goods, financed by such loans, into money, so that the lender will not be 'locked up' in security which never comes on to the market as is the case with most fixed capital. In the second place, the needs of individual businesses for working capital are far[1] more variable in amount than their needs for fixed capital, and fluctuate for seasonal and other reasons, even in times of stable output when the requirements of business as a whole are averaging out. Thus the banks are able to perform a useful service by providing a pool of floating resources which can be placed at the disposal of now this business and now that. Moreover, a banker prefers for obvious business reasons a class of account which involves constant turnover and frequent transactions and combines individual variability with aggregate stability, to business which, once done, means a prolonged lock-up of the bank's resources and does not involve any further consequential transactions.

As a result of these influences, modern business and banking organisation is of such a nature that the fluctuating part of the working capital required by industry and agriculture is obtained, generally speaking, through the banks. Indeed if a business finds itself in need of additional working capital at short notice, it is usually difficult to obtain it in any other way than through a bank. Nor does the policy, especially prevalent in the United States, by which prosperous and growing businesses distribute not more than a half, or at most three-quarters of their profits and retain the balance either to reduce their normal dependence on the banks or to accumulate liquid reserves, materially diminish the dependence of business, as a whole, on the banking system for new working capital. For unless the liquid reserves of the financially stronger firms are actually held in the form of surplus stocks of those liquid goods which they will themselves require when they increase their working capital—which is seldom the case—these firms will only be able, in general, to

---

[1] The word 'far' replaces the word 'found' in the galley proof.

release even their liquid reserves by increasing the pressure on the banks from other quarters, since they must have been holding them[1] if these reserves are held in bills or in fixed deposits or otherwise[2] invested.

Now so long as stability prevails in the aggregate demand for working capital from the banks, all may be well, however much individual demands are fluctuating. But what is the position in unstable conditions when the aggregate demand for working capital itself fluctuates widely? The banks being the chief, or the only, channel through which this demand can be met, the possibility of a trade revival may wholly depend on the banks doing something to satisfy it.

But from whence are the banks to derive the additional resources which shall enable the entrepreneurs to increase their investment in working capital? For they have no direct influence either over the rate of saving or over the rate of investment in fixed capital. In a well-ordered society the maintenance of equilibrium between the amount of working capital required to maintain[3] the optimum level of employment and the supply of savings reserved against it would be secured by deliberate foresight, directed to influencing either the rate of saving or the rate of investment in other directions. When[4] there was a prospective shortage of liquid income available to be put back for the maintenance or increase of working capital, steps would be taken in good time to secure that the productive processes which were being set in motion were appropriately divided between those which would emerge in liquid form and in fixed form respectively, and, correspondingly, if a surplus was in sight. But since in fact it is the business of no one in particular to exercise this foresight, since the aggregate demands for fixed capital and for working capital are the resultants of the separate

---

[1] The words 'since they must have been holding them' replace 'directly' in the galley proof.

[2] The words 'or otherwise' replace 'indirectly' in the galley proof.

[3] The word 'maintain' replaces 'permit' in the galley proof.

[4] The word 'When' replaces 'There' in the galley proof.

decisions of many individuals each acting, generally speaking, in ignorance of the decisions of the others, and since, above all, the banks which are primarily responsible for the supply of working capital have only a remote and indirect influence over the rate of investment in fixed capital, it is not surprising that disequilibria of varying degrees of severity should occur from time to time. Hence the dilemma of the banking system as to which of its dual functions it is to subordinate to the other. Shall it assist[1] employment to recover, though this means allowing investment in working capital to outstrip the volume of savings reserved for this purpose with a resultant credit inflation? Or shall it sternly refuse reasonable demands for credit for the reasonable expansion of employment and of production, whenever the satisfaction of these demands appears to be incompatible with the stability of the price level?

For the banking system (including the central bank) holds the key—on their action in retarding or stimulating the rate of investment by their own lending and investing policy depends the equilibrium or disequilibrium between saving and investment for the community as a whole.[2]

Their[3] task is not made easier by any tendency for the income deposits or the savings deposits[4] to expand and contract (irrespective of any change in the price level)[5] at the same time as the demand for working capital is expanding or contracting. On the contrary, not only is it unlikely that these deposits[6] will spontaneously increase when the demand for[7] credit is increasing and diminish when the latter is diminishing, but the

---

[1] The word 'assist' replaces 'allow' in the galley proof.
[2] At this point in the galley proof the following title appears: (ii) THE RELATION OF THE DEMAND FOR WORKING CAPITAL TO THE SUPPLY OF REAL-CREDIT.
[3] The word 'Their' replaces 'The' in the galley proof.
[4] The words 'income deposits or the savings deposits' do not appear in the galley but replace 'amount of savings entrusted to the banks by their depositors, i.e. for the amount of real balances'.
[5] The words in brackets do not appear in the galley proof.
[6] The words 'these deposits' replace 'the variations in the amount of real balances deposited (as determined by the amount of savings deposits and the velocities of the business and income deposits)' in the galley proof.
[7] The word 'credit' is preceded by 'real' in the galley proof.

opposite is more likely to be the case. For the[1] same causes which lead the public to be eager borrowers from the banks will also cause them to be more reluctant depositors; the keenness of their need for real resources will be a motive tending towards a reduction, even at some sacrifice of convenience, in the amount of the resources which they hold in the form of money. In particular, those financially stronger firms referred to above, which keep their own liquid reserves, may have kept these partly in the form of savings deposits, which they will now withdraw. Thus simultaneously with a pressure on the banking system to increase the volume of bank money there may be an inclination on the part of the depositors towards a reduction in the volume of deposits which they are disposed to hold at a given price level.[2] Moreover, in so far as the banks endeavour to relieve the pressure on themselves by selling their investments, this will have the effect of lowering stock exchange prices, and therefore of increasing the attractiveness to the depositor, particularly to the savings depositor, of outlets for his resources other than bank deposits. Indeed the greater the efforts of the banks not to increase the volume of bank money, the greater will be the pressure on the business world to achieve the same result by the more active use of the existing volume[3] of balances.[4]

Thus whenever for whatever cause there arises a demand[5] for increased bank credit at the existing price level, forces will be set up tending *both* to increase the volume of bank money[6] *and* to decrease the volume of real balances.[7] On both counts, therefore, the price level will tend to rise. Thus it is an inherent

---

[1] At this point the following deletion from the galley proof occurs: 'stringency in the supply of working capital will itself tend to bring about some withdrawal of real balances—primarily by means of a decrease of the savings deposits and an increased velocity of the business deposits. The'

[2] The words 'deposits...price level' replace 'real balances' in the galley proof.

[3] The words 'the more...volume' replace 'bringing about the withdrawal from the banks' in the galley proof.

[4] The word 'balances' is preceded by 'real' in the galley proof.

[5] The words 'a demand' replace 'an increased demand for real credit, i.e.' in the galley proof.

[6] The words 'bank money' are written 'Bank Money' in the galley proof.

[7] The words 'real balances' are written 'Real Balances' in the galley proof.

characteristic of a modern monetary system that fluctuations in the demand for credit[1]—generally due to fluctuations in the demand for working capital—should be associated with fluctuations in the price level.

When it is said that the credit cycle is a monetary phenomenon, it is not meant that the initiating causes of the disturbance are necessarily or usually of a monetary character. If the increase in the demand for credit,[1] or the decrease in the supply of it, is due in the first instance to nothing but an actual or prospective inflation, then indeed the initiating cause is itself monetary. If the increase in the demand for credit[1] is a reaction from a previous slump which was itself the final phase of a previous credit cycle, then the initiating cause is monetary in the sense that it arose out of a previous failure to remedy a defect in the monetary machinery. But even when the initiating cause is of an entirely non-monetary character, such as wars, the variability of harvests, the progress of invention, or even Professor Pigou's somewhat mythical 'psychological errors of optimism and pessimism' on the part of the business world, it is only through the reaction of these events on the monetary machine that the credit cycle can develop.

How, then, is the banking system to avoid price fluctuations which are due, not to any wanton or avoidable inflation brought about by the banking system itself, but by a failure of equilibrium between the demands of the business world for bank credit[2] for the purposes of investment[3] and the amount of income currently saved by the depositors and available for investment through the intermediary of the banks?[4]

If the banking system is prepared, not only to refuse entirely the applications of the business world, but also drastically to cut down the accommodation which they are already giving as soon

[1] The word 'credit' is preceded by 'real' in the galley proof.
[2] The words 'bank credit' replace 'real credit' in the galley proof.
[3] The words 'for the purposes of investment' do not appear in the galley proof.
[4] The words 'income...banks' replace 'it available, as a result of the decisions of their depositors' in the galley proof.

as there are signs that their refusal to increase it is causing the diversion of existing balances,[1] they may be able to prevent prices from rising. But the result of their heroic defence of the stability of prices at all costs may be so fearful a disorganisation of the normal processes of production and employment that the net effect is much worse than if a less heroic policy had been pursued. The remedy must be sought, therefore, not in a policy designed to preserve the stability of prices without regard to the effect on the supply of credit[2] for investment in working capital,[3] but in the discovery of some means to meet the fluctuating demands for such[4] credit without causing those reactions on the stability of the price level which have been usual in past experience.

The fault of the pre-war monetary system lay in the fact that it secured neither object. It neither preserved the stability of the price level, nor did it meet successfully the fluctuating demands for working capital.[5] In fact the failure to secure the one object will often involve a failure to secure the other. For so long as the demand for working capital[5] is not met, the pressure towards instability of the price level will be almost overwhelming, unless measures are taken which are sufficiently drastic to choke[6] off this demand by destroying business confidence.

Nevertheless it must be admitted that advocates of price stability, amongst whom I number myself, have erred in the past when their words have seemed to indicate price stability as the sole objective of monetary policy to the exclusion of the right adjustment of the supply of bank credit[7] to the business world's demands for it—or at least as an objective which, if reached,

[1] The words 'the diversion of existing balances' replace 'withdrawals of real balances' in the galley proof.
[2] The word 'credit' is preceded by 'real' in the galley proof.
[3] The words 'for investment in working capital' do not appear in the galley proof.
[4] The word 'such' replaces 'real' in the galley proof.
[5] The words 'working capital' replace 'real credit' in the galley proof.
[6] The word 'choke' replaces 'hold' in the galley proof.
[7] The words 'bank credit' replace 'real credit' in the galley proof.

would necessarily involve the simultaneous attainment of all associated objectives. To speak or to write in this way is unduly to simplify the problem by overlooking the dual character of the functions of the banking system and forgetting that the purpose of monetary reform must be to reconcile the proper fulfilment of the two functions. Mr D. H. Robertson's acute and profound criticisms (in his *Banking Policy and the Price Level*), emphasising the other side of the problem, have therefore been calculated to exert a most salutary influence on contemporary thought (and have done so on mine). On the other hand, Mr Robertson, in his anxiety to emphasise the neglected aspect, seems to me, in that book, not to state the problem clearly enough as a problem of reconciliation of purposes—and, if necessary, of compromise. For, whilst price stability may be secured at the cost of not meeting adequately the demand for credit, price instability is nearly always in the actual world an indication of a failure to satisfy the demand for bank credit,[1] as well as of a failure to preserve the value of money.

Amongst modern-minded men who understand that a bank-money system must necessarily be a managed one, and know what the methods of management are, there has been an unlucky tendency to range in two opposed camps according as their fixations, moulded by reflection and experience, have become attached to the money-purveying function of banks or to their credit-purveying function. Curiously enough the stable-money party is joined to the gold-standard party in concentrating attention primarily on the money-purveying function—with the emphasis of the former on the internal price level, and of the latter on the external exchange level; whilst the modern practical banker, of the type of Mr McKenna or of the United States Federal Reserve authorities, is joined to the unorthodox,[2] such as Major Douglas and many another, in concentrating attention primarily on the credit-purveying function, with the former

[1] The words 'bank credit' replace 'real credit' in the galley proof.
[2] The word 'unorthodox' replaces 'currency agents' in the galley proof.

laying[1] the emphasis[2] on the difficulty of the task of adjusting the supply of credit, and[3] the latter on its supposed ease.

(ii) METHODS OF ADJUSTING THE SUPPLY OF WORKING CAPITAL BY MEANS OF BANKING POLICY[4]

How then ought the banking system to handle the problem of an incipient credit inflation? We have seen:

(1) that the fluctuating part of the demand for working capital is liable to fall on the banks in the shape of requests for increased loans and discounts from their customers;

(2) that these fluctuations are capable of being substantial;

(3) that if the banks try to meet an increased demand for working capital by increasing the volume of money credit, prices must rise unless there is a corresponding amount of savings not otherwise invested, which is either diverted from other purposes or represents a net increase of saving;[5] and

(4) that, so far from the savings invested through the intermediary of[6] the banks tending to increase at such a time, they are more likely to diminish unless steps are taken to the contrary.

Assuming that—for whatever reason—a substantially increased demand for working capital has fallen on the banking system, our task is now to consider what measures, wise or unwise, it lies within the power of the banks to take in order to meet it.[7]

---

[1] The words 'the former laying' do not appear in the galley proof.

[2] The words 'of the former' follow 'emphasis' in the galley proof.

[3] The word 'of' follows 'and' in the galley proof.

[4] In the galley proof the title reads:
(iii) METHODS OF INCREASING (OR DIMINISHING) THE SUPPLY OF WORKING CAPITAL THROUGH THE BANKING SYSTEM

[5] The words 'amount...increase of saving' replace 'increase of savings diverted from other purposes and entrusted to the banks by their depositors;' in the galley proof.

[6] The words 'invested through the intermediary of' replace 'entrusted to' in the galley proof.

[7] At this point the words 'The methods open to them are of two kinds:' appear in the galley proof.

Let[1] us bring our minds back to the elements of the situation. Price instability must result whenever the rates of saving and of investment part company. But it is only the existence of a currency and banking system (i.e. of money) which makes it possible that they should part company. If rates of earnings were fixed in terms of consumption goods, the phenomena which we have been analysing could not occur. In a sense, therefore, all that the banking system can do is to look to itself—to prevent itself from making mistakes and thereby causing maladjustments which, if they occur, are simply its own fault. If it care[s] to contrive to keep the market rate of interest close to the natural rate, then it will have done its duty.

But this is a jejune way of looking at the problem. In practice the duty of the banks is not so simple as this. If they limit themselves to keeping the market rate of interest close to the natural rate and disclaim all further responsibility, this is the same thing as pursuing price stability to the total neglect of credit stability; and this, we have agreed, would be an unfortunate limitation of their objective. Granted the wider objective, I make out that the methods open to them are the following:

(*a*) by restoring equilibrium between saving and investment;

(*b*) by stimulating savings;

(*c*) by changing the channels of investment;

(*d*) by attracting resources from abroad;

(*e*) by forced transferences of purchasing power.

---

[1] At this point Keynes's new copy replaces the galley proof. The galley continued:

'1. By changing the form of the already available aggregate of real bank credit (i.e. of real savings invested through the banking system);

2. By increasing the available aggregate of real bank credit—

(*a*) by attracting savings at home,

(*b*) by attracting resources from abroad,

(*c*) by transferences of purchasing power,

(*d*) by restoring equilibrium between saving and investment.'

(a) By restoring equilibrium between saving and investment

The first duty of the banking system is to make sure that there is no deflationary slack available to be taken in. It may be that a demand for additional investment springs up at a time when the existing rate of investment has been held back behind the rate of saving; so that additional resources can be made available merely by restoring equilibrium. It is true that this will—in the act of remedying a state of deflationary disequilibrium—raise prices; but it will only raise them to their proper equilibrium level with the established money rates of earnings.

Thus,[1, 2] if in the initial position the rate of investment is falling behind the rate of saving, then an expansion in the volume of credit,[3] so far from being undesirable, will be in a high degree advisable, in order to avoid forced transferences from entrepreneurs[4] to unproductive consumers.

We must not, therefore, be hasty to dub an expansion of bank lending as a credit inflation until we have first assured ourselves that it is not merely a necessary corrective for the avoidance of a credit deflation.

(b) By stimulating savings

If[5] the banks can[6] do something to increase the aggregate of current savings, they are[6] contributing to the solution of the problem both in the case where the increased investment is directed towards the production of fixed capital and in that where it is directed towards the production of consumption

---

[1] At this point the two paragraphs 'Thus...deflation' in the text are moved forward from a later galley (p. 108 after 'employment' in text).

[2] The word 'Thus' replaces 'but, if it is not the case' in the galley proof.

[3] At this point the words 'carried out just in the same way as if the second expedient above was being employed' appear in the galley proof.

[4] The words 'from entrepreneurs' appear at the end of the sentence in the galley proof.

[5] The paragraph 'If the banks...slight' in the text is moved forward from a later galley (p. 101 after 'later date' in the text).

[6] The words 'can' and 'are' replace 'could' and 'would be' in the galley proof.

goods. Unfortunately[1] the power of the banks to stimulate the rate of current savings is somewhat limited. For[2] the responsiveness of the rate of saving to the rate of interest is over short periods probably slight.[3]

They can, however, at least make sure that the rate of interest is *high enough*. As we shall see in chapter 28, the rate of interest is not always freely determined by the play of supply and demand. Thus a credit deflation, resulting from a restriction in the *volume* of credit, may sometimes be accompanied by a rate of interest which is positively too low—too low in the sense that a higher rate would stimulate saving without being deterrent to investment. In other words, the banks must make sure that the stimulus which they are offering to new savings—in particular, by the rate of interest which they offer on savings deposits—is as great as possible compatibly with the demand for purposes of investment.

(c)[4] *By changing the channels of investment*

We have under this heading to dispel illusions, more, perhaps, than to raise hopes. Practical bankers often speak as though they could increase the supply of credit for working capital at times when trade is brisk by the simple process of selling some part of their investments and replacing them by trade advances.[5] For[6] in normal times only a part[7] of the available volume of bank credit is employed in advances made for the purpose of furnishing working capital. A considerable proportion is directly invested by the banks themselves in long-dated securities and other forms

---

[1] The word 'Unfortunately' does not appear in the galley proof.
[2] The word 'For' replaces 'They can raise the rate of interest, but' in the galley proof.
[3] The following additional sentence appears in the galley proof: 'Higher bank rate is a move in the right direction from this point of view, but one from which it would not be reasonable to expect much.'
[4] In the galley proof the title reads:
I BY CHANGING THE FORM OF THE AVAILABLE AGGREGATE OF REAL BANK-CREDIT.
[5] At this point Keynes's additional copy and rearrangement of the galley proof text end, and copy from the galley proof text is resumed.
[6] The word 'For' does not appear in the galley proof.
[7] The words 'only a part' replace 'by no means the whole' in the galley proof.

representing fixed capital, and a further proportion is indirectly invested in the same forms by means of loans to individuals to enable them to carry such assets with borrowed money.[1] Thus the banks[2] can sell their investments and curtail their loans to the stock exchange and to speculators, in order to release funds for increased advances to industry.

Measures of this kind are in fact taken on a substantial scale. The statistics of the varying proportions of investments held by British banks have been given on p. 187. These figures show that the[3,4] order of magnitude of the fluctuations in the volume of investments held by the banks is comparable—at any rate over a period of two or three years—with the magnitude of the fluctuations in the demand for working capital. For example, the investments of the nine London clearing banks increased between the third quarter of 1921 and the third quarter of 1922 by £80 million, and had fallen again by £80 million by the end of 1924, and by a further £70 million by the spring of 1927. Since the banks' holdings of treasury bills were also falling during most of this period, the advances of the nine banks to their customers were in June 1927 £200 million greater than in the third quarter of 1922, although the banks' deposits were practically unchanged between the two dates.

No[5] statistics are available in Great Britain enabling a[6] distinction to be made between those advances[7] where there is a presumption that they are being employed for the purposes of working capital and those where there is a presumption that they are being employed in the stock exchange, or in mortgages, or

---

[1] In the galley proof the following sentence is inserted: 'It lies, therefore, within the power of the banks to vary the proportions of the aggregate volume of bank credit, which are employed in these different ways.'

[2] The words 'Thus the banks' replace 'Put concretely they' in the galley proof.

[3] The words 'The statistics...that the' replace 'So far as investments are concerned, statistics are available (some of which have been quoted above, p. [un-numbered]). In the case of advances, however' in the galley proof.

[4] At this point the rest of the paragraph is transposed from three paragraphs further on in the galley proof.

[5] At this point the sequence of the galley proof resumes.

[6] The word 'a' replaces 'any' in the galley.

[7] The word 'advances' replaces 'cases' in the galley proof.

in carrying other forms of fixed capital. Moreover, there is no longer the same probability as formerly[1] that the banks' holdings of bills mostly supply working capital, since the greatly increased volume of treasury bills now outstanding is a confusing item.[2] In the United States, however,[3] a determined attempt has been made to obtain the[4] statistics. The member banks are compelled to classify their advances according to the nature of the security against which they are made; and more recently the amount of the loans to brokers for stock exchange purposes has been separately published. When the latter figures have been available over a long period, they should help to clarify[5] the situation. But the fact that the way in which the proceeds of loans to individual customers are employed does not necessarily correspond to the nature of the security deposited against them still leaves an important source of confusion, for which there is at present no remedy.

However, the broad facts of the case are clear and undisputed.[6] The statistics for the United States confirm the conclusion that the total resources of the banks and their capability of varying the proportions held in different forms within this total are of sufficient magnitude to look after the whole or the greater part of the variability of the demand for working capital except in the most extreme circumstances.[7] Subject to their maintenance of an adequate proportion of more liquid assets against emergencies, all banks (except those which are specifically mortgage banks or savings banks) regard the reasonable requirements of their regular customers for advances for the conduct and development

---

[1] The words 'probability as formerly' replace 'presumption which there used to be' in the galley proof.

[2] [The British banks are beginning to publish, sporadically, various statistics bearing on both the above points, but these statistics are not yet adequate to support generalisations.]

[3] The word 'however' does not appear in the galley proof.

[4] The word 'the' does not appear in the galley proof.

[5] The words 'help to clarify' replace 'go some way towards clarifying' in the galley proof.

[6] The sentence 'The statistics...extreme circumstances' in the text is transposed. In the galley proof this appears as a paragraph after the paragraph ending 'between the two dates', which is now to be found at line 22 page 96.

[7] At this point the sequence of the galley text is resumed.

of their businesses as a first charge on their available resources—
if only for the reasons that these transactions are not only the
most remunerative in direct earning power but are also the
backbone of the typical bank's business, inasmuch as they regain
and attract the current accounts and other general banking
business of those to whom the advances are made, whereas the
purchase of an investment on the stock exchange does nothing to
attract or develop banking business proper.[1]

When, therefore, an increased demand for working capital
springs up and shows itself in increased applications to the
banks for accommodation, the banks will do their best to meet
this by changing the form of their outstanding assets mainly by
sales of some part of their investments.[2]

The question is, however, whether such action by the banks
really has the effect of influencing the course of investment
taken as a whole in the desired direction. For, unfortunately, we
cannot conclude[3] that a sufficiently elastic policy on the part of[4]
the banks in buying and selling investments would be an
adequate solution of the problem. For our analysis is not yet
finished. When a bank sells an investment in order to make an
additional advance, it does not follow that a net additional
amount of resources equal to this has been made available for
working capital.

To whom do the banks sell their investments? Broadly
speaking, there are three possible alternatives. They may sell to a
depositor to whom, at the lower price level for securities brought
about by the banks' selling, an investment has become more
attractive than before as compared with a bank deposit. They

---

[1] [Cf. Mr Stewart's evidence before the U.S. Congress Stabilization Committee (1927),
p. 765: 'The demand for credit for commercial purposes will have first call on
banking credits. For one reason, it involves the relation between the bank and the line-of-
credit customers, and, secondly, the loan usually yields a better rate of return than the
call loan.']

[2] At this point in the galley proof the two paragraphs, which are found on pages 96 and 97
in the text, occur. See above, p. 96 note 4 and p. 97 note 6.

[3] The words 'The question is...conclude' replace 'Unfortunately we cannot argue from
this' in the galley proof.

[4] The words 'on the part of' do not appear in the galley proof.

may sell to a speculator who succeeds, directly or indirectly, in borrowing back from one or other of the banks the bulk of the funds required to finance his purchase. Or they may sell (directly or indirectly) to an investor of new savings who buys a security which a bank has sold in the market in lieu of buying a new issue. Now in each of these cases the net immediate addition to the revolving fund of working capital will fall far short of the value of the investments sold by the banks. In the first case, where savings deposits are withdrawn,[1] the net result will be just the same as it would have been if the banks, instead of selling their investments, had been allowed to increase the total money volume of bank credit. In the second case, the increase in the banks' advances at the expense of their investments will not in fact represent any change in the proportions in which bank credit is employed in different forms; the intention of the banks will have been defeated. The satisfactory avoidance of this *dénouement* by some system of rationing and of refusing advances for the purpose of financing securities is impracticable for several reasons; it is difficult for the banks to know in any precise way the ultimate destination of the loans they make; any bank which discriminates too severely will be liable to lose good customers to its competitors, and almost any rule of discrimination will have an adverse effect on the conduct of regular, desirable investment business. Moreover, if the banks were to be successful in tightening up their rules so as to make them really effective, there would probably be so great a slump on the stock exchange that the banks would be unable to sell their securities at all at a reasonable price. The final objection to 'rationing' is that the sale of securities by the banks will be in fact impracticable on a large scale unless, so far from making matters more difficult for the professionals of the investment market, they are making them somewhat easier. Moreover, even if the banks were to press their securities on the market with

---

[1] The words 'where savings deposits are withdrawn' replace 'the real balances entrusted to the banks will have been diminished, and' in the galley proof.

little regard to the prices obtained, the result would only be that savings deposits would be diminished, or velocities of circulation increased,[1] so soon as securities had reached what seemed to the average depositor a bargain figure.

There remains the third alternative, namely sales to investors with new savings to invest, which would have found their outlet otherwise in new issues. We are now moving in a more promising direction. If new issues are discouraged, this will mean a diminution in the volume of new fixed capital, and they will release a greater proportion of current savings for the replenishment of working capital. But here also there is scope for disappointment. During the period of production of the new fixed capital, the new savings which are eventually to emerge in this form furnish working capital (and are no use unless they do), just as much as if they were destined to emerge in the form of available income. Thus a course of action, which discourages new issues whilst it encourages (by means of increased bank advances) the maintenance or increase of the volume of production, will in the first instance have more effect in changing the direction of productive effort than in increasing its volume. Moreover, if the impulse of expansion is towards the production of more fixed capital, no relief will be obtained in this way except by defeating the expansion, since it diminishes the amount financed by new issues as much as it increases the amount financed by the banks.

Our conclusion is, therefore, that when it is desired to increase the production of fixed capital goods, the banks can do nothing to facilitate it by changing the form of their assets. When, however, the desired[2] increase in production is of consumption goods, they can do something to substitute such production for production of fixed capital goods, but something which falls a good deal short of the amount by which they

[1] The words 'that savings deposits...increased' replace 'a loss of real balances by the banks' in the galley proof.
[2] The words 'desired increase in' replace 'increased' in the galley proof.

succeed in changing the form of their assets,[1] and only fructifies at a later date.[2]

(d) By attracting resources from abroad

There is, however, an important method of escape from these disappointing conclusions, if we are concentrating our attention on the position of a single country; and attention to this exception will allow us to discard an important unreality hitherto tacitly present in our argument, where it is a question of applying it to the actual facts. This ground of exception is to be found in the possibility of attracting additional working capital *from abroad*. Clearly this is not an expedient which can be used by all the chief trading countries of the world simultaneously. It does not, therefore, enable the world as a whole to emerge from what has been a world-wide depression. But it may be a very powerful aid towards accelerating the industrial recovery of an individual country. This may operate, not only by drawing on new savings, but also by allowing the individual country to draw on the liquid capital of the world at large. I have argued above that in the case of any single country its own liquid capital is so small a proportion of its working capital that not much relief can be expected for the latter by drawing on the former. And the same thing is true for the world as a whole. But it is not so true if we are comparing the liquid capital of the world with the working capital of a single country.

[1] The words 'and only fructifies at a later date' do not appear in the galley proof.

[2] At this point the paragraph 'If the banks...slight' on pages 94-5 appears in the galley proof. In the galley proof, two additional paragraphs appear after this paragraph which run as follows

'Where, however, it is a question of changing the direction of investment rather than of increasing its aggregate, there is more that the banks can do. In particular, by increasing the rate of interest which they allow on savings deposits, they may be able to increase materially the amount of the real balances which the public entrust to them. They might also—and do in some continental countries—offer their own short-dated negotiable notes or bonds to attract the direct investment of the new savings of the public.

In so far as these methods are successful—well and good. But in the past they have not been applied very deliberately or very strenuously; and, in so far as they have been employed, experience bears out the expectation that not a great deal, quantitatively speaking, is to be expected from them.'

The most striking recent example of the replenishment of an individual country's fund of working capital by drawing on the resources of the rest of the world has been the industrial reconstruction of Germany in 1925-7 after the stabilisation of the mark. By the end of 1924 Germany's fund of working capital had become depleted to an almost unprecedented degree; and the process of recovery might have occupied many years if she had had to depend entirely on the excess of her own savings over the output of new[1] fixed capital.

But this method has also played some part in the normal process of recovery by Great Britain from the trade depressions of the nineteenth and early twentieth centuries. The world at large can be tempted to part with some proportion of its stock of liquid capital either by the offer of an improved price or by increased pressure to repay what it owes. The period of recovery was normally characterised by both these forms of inducement or pressure. The effort to replenish working capital would be accompanied both by a rising price level and by a rising rate of discount. Thus debtor countries would be under both inducement and pressure to sell some part of their stocks of raw materials to creditor countries. The raising of bank rate by the leading creditor country in the international short-loan market would have the effect at the same time of putting pressure on the debtor countries to sell, and of supplying the necessary increase of foreign exchange to enable the creditor country to buy. As soon, however, as efforts of this kind became general to a number of countries, this particular expedient for replenishing working capital would quickly lose its virtue. Moreover, it is obvious that, unless the demands of the individual country in which the expansion begins are small in relation to the resources of the world at large, the effect of this method is to shift the incidence of the problem rather than to solve it. The effect of drawing on the normal savings of other countries will be to prepare the way for a credit inflation there also, and the drafts

---

[1] The word 'new' replaces 'additional' in the galley proof.

on their stocks of liquid capital will also produce conditions favourable to a general expansion of production. Thus, while conditions favouring a credit inflation in a particular country may sometimes be absorbed by the world at large, it may also be that they will merely be diffused.

The practical importance of this expedient arises, of course, from the fact that the most familiar of all devices for coping with an incipient credit inflation, namely raising the bank-rate, in truth largely derives its efficacy from its tendency to make good the temporary shortage of savings at home by attracting them from abroad.

The reader may, at first sight, think it somewhat paradoxical that a rise in the bank rate should be considered as a means of *increasing* the amount of bank credit available for a business expansion. He must wait for chapter 28 on 'The *Modus Operandi* of Bank Rate' for a full explanation of why this should be so. It must be sufficient to say here that a rise in bank rate serves to diminish the *net* amount of money lent to foreigners, with the result that industry at home can consume a greater quantity of goods without upsetting the price level or endangering the exchanges. If industry at home wants to borrow more, though it be at a higher rate of interest, then the higher bank rate will help it by being the instrument whereby, in effect, it is enabled to outbid foreigners for command over liquid goods.[1] When industry wants to borrow more, a higher bank rate is the instrument which allows it to do so with safety. A higher bank rate is only injurious to industry if it occurs, not in response to a tendency to more active investment at home, but as a repressive measure associated with a curtailment of the basis of credit and as part of a policy of deflation designed to crush down the existing rate of investment. In other words, a rise in bank rate, which corresponds to a rise in the 'natural' rate of interest (see chapter 28), is a means of enabling industry at home to secure resources without raising prices. It is only a rise in bank rate

[1] The words 'liquid goods' replace 'purchasing power' in the galley proof.

causing it to *exceed* the 'natural' rate of interest, which is injurious to business activity. Indeed nothing can be worse for business than a low bank rate, lower than the 'natural' rate of interest, which is kept going by means of a curtailment of the basis of credit and a rationing of bank loans—a state of affairs to which the London money market may be sometimes prone (*vide* p.   )[1].

(e) By forced transferences of purchasing power from 'unproductive' consumers

Suppose, however, that all the expedients and methods so far discussed are either unsuccessful or inadequate, and that the attempts of the banks to satisfy, nevertheless, the borrowing desires of their customers leads (inasmuch as investment is already fully equal to saving) to a credit inflation—is this no better than a confession of failure, or does it do something, though at the expense of price stability, really to satisfy the demands for additional investment? Our previous argument has demonstrated that, whilst it destroys the equilibrium of the price level, it does, in doing this, really allow some additional investment to take place.

Let us recapitulate—with additions—the modes in which a credit inflation may facilitate the transfer of purchasing power from 'unproductive' consumers to 'productive' consumers, which, as we have seen, is the necessary condition of increased employment and output.

There are two ways in which a credit inflation may increase 'productive' consumption at the expense of 'unproductive' consumption. The first way is the one which we have been considering in many previous passages, namely that by raising prices it diverts the command over available income, which would have otherwise accrued to those previously in the possession of money incomes, into the hands of entrepreneurs who have liquid goods emerging from the productive process, to

---

[1] The cross-reference was not provided by Keynes.

whom it accrues as a windfall profit on capital account; and these entrepreneurs are then in a position to place it at the disposal of a new body of 'productive' consumers. But not only do those in the possession of money incomes find that their real incomes are diminished; those who are in possession of a stock of money also discover that this stock has less than its previous real value, and may, therefore, be induced to save on a greater scale than they would otherwise, in order to make good the loss which they have involuntarily suffered in the value of their stock of money. In addition the new producers save part of their incomes to build up their income deposits.[1] This is the second way in which a credit inflation may help the situation.

Mr D. H. Robertson has called the first way 'automatic[2] lacking', and the second way 'induced lacking'. I consider that the first is the essence of a credit inflation. The second—so far as it relates to persons previously in receipt of incomes[3]—may or may not occur, and even when it occurs it may only affect the amount of saving effected through the banks and not the total amount of saving; for since the current consumption of the sufferers is already diminished to the extent of the 'automatic[2] lacking' to which they have been subjected, they are particularly unlikely at that moment to submit to a still further reduction of their current consumption, so that they will either be content with less real balances than before, thus increasing the velocity of circulation, or, if they augment their money balances, will do so at the expense of other forms of saving, perhaps, for example, by augmenting their income deposits at the expense of their savings deposits.[4]

It is important to be clear about the distinction between these two things. When a bank increases the volume of money credit to the accompaniment of a rise of prices,[5] it is evident that the

---

[1] The words 'In addition...income deposits' do not appear in the galley proof.
[2] The word 'automatic' replaces 'forced' in the galley proof.
[3] The words '—so far...incomes—' do not appear in the galley proof.
[4] [Cf. p.   above.] The cross-reference was not provided by Keynes.
[5] The words 'to the accompaniment of a rise in prices' replace 'relatively to the volume of real credit' in the galley proof.

borrower, in whose favour the additional money credit has been created, has at his command an increased purchasing power with which he can augment his fund of working capital; and this remains true even if prices rise, and however much they rise. At whose expense has this augmentation taken place? Or, in other words, whose available income has been diminished in order to supply the increased available income in the hands of the borrower? The obvious answer—but the wrong one—is to say that the transference has taken place at the expense of the depositor. It is true that the borrower, coming on to the market as an additional buyer without any diminution in the purchasing power of the existing buyers at the existing price level, raises prices. It is also true that the increase of prices diminishes the value of the depositor's deposits, i.e. of his *command* over available income. But unless we assume that the depositors as a body were about to diminish their real deposits, the increase in the price level, although it diminishes the value of the money deposits, does not for that reason necessarily diminish the consumption of the depositors. So long as depositors as a body are not drawing on their previous deposits for purposes of consumption, it is not their deposits (or the equivalent of these in available income) which they are consuming, but their *current income*. This leads us to the correct answer. What the rise of prices diminishes is the value of all current incomes payable in cash. That is to say, the *flow* of purchasing power in the hands of the rest of the community is diminished by an amount equal to the fresh purchasing power obtained by the aforesaid borrower. Even if an attempt is made to mitigate this by increasing all money incomes, the transference is not obviated. For however much money incomes all round are raised, the new loan obtained by the borrower is worth something, and to the extent of the value of this something the flow of purchasing power in the hands of the rest of the community is tapped.

To whom, on the other hand, has there accrued an increment, not of purchasing power, but of wealth corresponding to the loss of wealth of the depositors? Obviously to the *old* borrowers—i.e. to the borrowers who have borrowed at the previous lower price level and will be entitled when the time comes to repay at the new higher price level. But this transference, whilst it is a transference of wealth—not only between bank depositors and bank borrowers but between all classes of lenders and borrowers in terms of money—is not a transference of available income or one which serves in any way to augment the stock of working capital. For whilst the borrowers can repay when the due date of their loan arrives by parting with less purchasing power than what they had expected to part with, and therefore retain additional purchasing power which they may or may not employ to replenish working capital, the amount of credit[1] available in the hands of the banks, as a result of these repayments of old loans, wherewith to make new loans to business, is worth correspondingly less.[2] Thus the loss of the depositors does nothing to augment working capital; and, indeed, since there is a somewhat greater presumption that the new loans made by the banks will be used as working capital than that the windfalls accruing to the old borrowers will be so used in their entirety, the transference of wealth involved is rather more likely to diminish than otherwise the fund of working capital.

The distinction between the loss in respect of current money-income and the loss in respect of stocks of command over money partly corresponds to the distinction which we have made between currency inflation and credit inflation. Currency inflation raises the rate of money income enjoyed by the factors of production as a whole[3] just as much as it raises prices; so that in this case losses are incurred only in respect of stocks of cash. But it is the peculiarity of credit inflation that it raises prices in excess of any increase in the rates of money income enjoyed by

[1] In the galley 'credit' reads 'real-credit'.
[2] The words 'worth correspondingly less' replace 'correspondingly depleted' in the galley proof.
[3] [It may be well to repeat that throughout this argument I am not considering the question as to how price changes affect the relative remuneration of different factors of production, i.e. how far they are liable to benefit one factor at the expense of another.]

the factors of production as a whole; so that there is in this case a sacrifice of real income by the factors of production previously employed, the equivalent of which sacrifice thus becomes available to provide for additional employment.[1]

(iii) CONCLUSIONS

A maladjustment of the forces of production resulting in their partial unemployment may be due to one or other, or more than one, of several underlying causes:

(1) It may be due to a banking policy which has allowed the rate of investment to fall below the rate of savings.

(2) It may be due to relative rates of interest[2] at home and abroad, which lead to a larger scale of lending to foreigners than is suitable in the interests of the economic structure as a whole.

(3) It may be due to a wrong distribution of the available flow of investment between working capital and fixed capital.

(4) It may be due to a rate of real efficiency wages for some of the factors of production in excess of what[3] they can earn.

To cure (1) lies within the power of the banking system to a considerable extent. But the banks may need the assistance of a parallel policy by the State in the shape of direct encouragement to increased investment. How far the action of the banking system should take the form of a lower bank rate, and how far the form of an increased volume of credit, will depend on the

---

[1] At this point the paragraphs 'Thus…credit deflation' located above, page 94, appear in the galley proof. In the galley, the following additional material preceded them:

'(d) By restoring equilibrium between saving and investment

There remains one possibility still open, which is sometimes of great practical importance. We have tacitly assumed above that the savings of the country are being fully invested. If this is the case, the banks—since they can do but little to stimulate saving—can only increase the amount of real resources at the disposal of entrepreneurs operating within the country by one or other of two means—helping to withdraw real resources from investment abroad, and by forced transferences of real resources from unproductive consumers—of which the second is, if it can be avoided, an undesirable expedient.'

[2] At this point the words 'and loan facilities of differing degrees of competitive perfection for different types of investment securities' in the galley proof do not appear in the text.

[3] The word 'what' replaces 'which' in the galley proof.

state of affairs in respect of (2), which is really a branch of (1).[1]
We must postpone a detailed consideration of (2) to chapter 28.
But where, as in Great Britain, there is an element of rationing
of bank credit to home borrowers whilst the international short-
loan market runs free, it is occasionally conceivable that the
combination of a higher bank rate with an increased volume of
bank credit may be, paradoxically, the right solution.

Where (3) is the trouble, we have seen that the banks can do
something by changing the form of their assets, subject, however,
to a time-lag.

Where there is great urgency in the national interest, either to
increase the volume of a particular kind of investment at a rate
faster than resources can be diverted from other forms of
investment, or to increase the total volume of investment at a
rate faster than voluntary savings can be expected to respond to
any available stimulus, then the need for increased investment
can be met, as an emergency measure, by a deliberate credit
inflation, i.e. by an expansion of bank credit which will have the
effect of causing investment to outrun savings; though under an
international standard (e.g. gold) there will be narrow limits to
the extent to which a single country acting in isolation can move
along these lines.

Finally, if the trouble is due to an excessive rate of real
efficiency wages to some of the factors of production, then—not
unexpectedly—there is little or nothing that the banking system
can do, unless it be by engineering an inflation in the hope that[2]
this may effect[3] a reduction of *real* efficiency earnings owing to
the stickiness of *cash* efficiency earnings; and even this may be
ineffective if wages are too high relatively to wages abroad.[4]
Failing this,[5] the rate of real efficiency earnings must be reduced[6]

---

[1] The words 'which is really a branch of (1)' do not appear in the galley proof.
[2] The words 'the hope that' replace 'reliance on' in the galley proof.
[3] The words 'may effect' replace 'effecting' in the galley proof.
[4] The words 'and even...abroad' do not appear in the galley proof.
[5] The words 'Failing this' replace 'Either' in the galley proof.
[6] The words 'by manipulation of the value of money as just suggested' in the galley proof
do not appear in the text.

by the pressure of unemployment, or in some other way, or else—if a reduction of real efficiency earnings is deemed contrary to distributive justice or to the public interest—then they should be maintained by means of a subsidy which would have the effect of reducing the real efficiency wages payable by the entrepreneur whilst leaving real incomes as they were before.[1]

In any event, the solution of (4) will probably carry us outside the realm of monetary remedies. The sphere of action of the banking system is limited to the avoidance of credit deflation (and, exceptionally, to the creation of credit inflation) and the regulation of the rate of foreign lending, and, to a certain extent, to influencing the flow of investment into fixed capital and working capital respectively.

So much for the slump. When a boom is in question, there are certain further conclusions which emerge from our discussion.

In the case of a boom in fixed investment which runs ahead of saving, there is not much that the banks can do to satisfy the demand compatibly with stable prices, except by attracting resources from abroad. Either the banks must check the boom or they must be prepared to acquiesce in a rising price level. Moreover, it may be difficult for them to check it, if the forces tending towards increased fixed investment are strong, without doing harm in other directions. For the measures which they can take will only partly discriminate against production for fixed investment, and will partly discourage all types of production. If, therefore, the action of the banks to check borrowers in general also checks borrowers who would use their working capital to produce consumption goods, it will have the effect of substituting the production of fixed goods for the production of consumption goods, with the result that after an

---

[1] [Unemployment in Great Britain in 1929 was, in my judgment, attributable to an amalgam of the above causes. In so far as it was due to (4), it was probably impracticable to effect an early cure except by establishing conditions in which efficiency could increase. Thus there was nothing to be done except to press on with remedies directed to the other factors in the situation, in the hope that curing these—and time—would react favourably on (4).] This footnote did not appear in the galley.

interval equal to the production period a credit inflation will ensue in spite of all their efforts. A very strong impulse towards fixed investment may steal away resources from the production of consumption goods, in spite of the banks. And when once this has occurred, the only way of preserving the stability of prices is to curtail lending so sharply that unemployment ensues.

When, on the other hand, the boom represents a recovery from a previous slump which is highly desirable from the point of view of absorbing unemployed factors of production into employment, and is directed in due proportion to the production of consumption goods, then there is a good deal that the banks can do, given time. For if they prepare for the situation one production period beforehand by using their influence to divert resources from the production of fixed capital to that of liquid goods, then the additional working capital required to raise employment to its optimum level may be provided without any material disturbance of the price level. The practical difficulty is, of course, that in an individualist society it is difficult to induce the producers of liquid goods to increase their scale of operations until they already *see* a rising price level—nothing else will convince them that there will be a market for their increased output. Thus, in practice, the attempt to avoid inflation altogether may postpone too long the recovery from the slump, and set up a vicious circle of inactivity—each element in the circle of exchange waiting upon the others.

On the other hand, the power of the banking system to avoid a credit deflation is much greater than its[1] power to avoid an inflation—though, unfortunately, the banks'[2] inclination to do so is often correspondingly less. For they can stimulate activity both by a willingness to lend to their customers and also by the purchase of securities. Where, however, a country is a member of an international system, it may be—in particular circumstances—that an easy-money policy will have more effect in

---

[1] The word 'its' replaces 'their' in the galley proof.
[2] The words 'the banks' replace 'their' in the galley proof.

stimulating foreign lending than in stimulating home investment (cf. chapter 28 below), and will, for this reason, lead to so great a loss of gold as to be outside practical politics. Nevertheless, even in such cases where the cheap-money stimulus to investment cannot be applied, it is still[1] open to the public authorities[2] to stimulate investment by stepping[3] in with extensive programmes of public works.

It is in this power to avoid a deflation that the key to the situation lies, so far as practical policy is concerned. The kind of inflation, which may be sometimes the only way of securing the optimum of employment within a reasonable time, is never necessary except as a reaction from a preceding deflation. If only deflations were never allowed to occur, 'virtuous' inflations would never be needed; so that the banking system could use all its powers with a good conscience—even though its efforts would not quite always be crowned with complete success—against 'vicious' inflations. It is when a deflation has been allowed to develop and unemployment has ensued, that the 'virtuous' policy of allowing no corrective expansion[4] may do more harm than good.

Our argument has also served to exhibit the dangers of drastic action by the banking system, if, having failed to act in time, it thinks to remedy this by acting late. If the wages bill *minus* savings exceeds the volume of the current output of consumption goods at the pre-existing price level, there are only three ways to preserve the stability of prices—to increase savings, to reduce the rate of wages, or to reduce employment. The methods open to the banking system at this stage of the proceedings are not well calculated either to increase savings or to reduce wage rates. The only way, therefore, in which the

[1] The words 'Where, however, a country...it is still' replace 'It would have to be a very obstinate disinclination to invest on the part of entrepreneurs which could defeat a concerted effort of the banking system to prevent a credit deflation; and even then it would be' in the galley proof.

[2] At this point in the galley proof the words 'as suggested above' appear.

[3] The words 'stimulate investment by stepping' replace 'step' in the galley proof.

[4] The word 'expansion' replaces 'inflation' in the galley proof.

banking system can, acting at the last moment, preserve the stability of prices, is precipitately [to] throw out of employment an appropriate percentage of the factors of production (presently there engaged on producing fixed capital—otherwise this expedient is only temporarily effective, namely for one production period)[1]—which will do the trick of keeping prices down, but at the cost of reducing the community's real net income.

Our prime concern is, therefore, this. The most intractable troubles which a banking system has to face are generally the fruits of its own previous errors. If only our system can keep to the middle of the road, it will not need instruments, which may bend or break in the process, for getting out of ditches. Thus the continual maintenance of an equilibrium between saving and investment, subject only to rare and peculiar exceptions, should be its daily aim, and will, if successful be its greatest safeguard— the long-period stability of the standard of value being, of course, another branch[2] of policy with which we deal elsewhere.

Draft table of contents of 2 August 1929 with page references to the finest nineteen chapters of the last surviving one-volume version of the *Treatise*. 2 August 1929

Book I   The nature of money

[1] The material in brackets does not appear in the galley proof.
[2] The word 'branch' replaces the word 'brand' in the galley proof.

Book v   The management of money

Still working towards the publication date of 1 October, Keynes began proof corrections and final rewriting early in August. However, in the course of polishing he became very dissatisfied with what he had done so far and began to attempt more substantial revisions. By the end of the month, the extent of these revisions led him to write to Alfred Harcourt on 28 August:

> The rewriting of my book on which I have had to embark turns out to be somewhat drastic, so that there is now no prospect of publication before January [1930]. I am, however, clear that the rewriting is worth while and will prove a great improvement.
>
> One consequence of the re-arrangement which I am planning is that the book will probably fall very conveniently into two parts of equal

length, which I shall call 'The Pure Theory of Money' and 'The Applied Theory of Money'. I am now planning, therefore, to divide the book into two volumes under the above titles...Each of the volumes under the new plan will probably be between 300 and 330 pages...

There is very little remaining evidence as to how these major revisions took shape in detail. By 29 September, R. F. Kahn had worked his way through Keynes's new version of the fundamental equation with some enthusiasm but had little more to say, at least in letters. The more extensive correspondence on the proofs, which do not survive, dates from late 1929 and early 1930, after Keynes had delivered his 1929 lectures from the proof sheets. It appears below. (Keynes also passed proofs to Pigou, but all of his comments seem to have been oral or in the margins of the proofs.)

From D. H. ROBERTSON, *5 December 1929*

My dear Maynard,

In spite of efforts, I've left myself only $\frac{1}{2}$ an hour after all before catching the 4.42 for the 3rd day running! Which I think I can best use in setting out the chief *resistances* which I find in myself in reading the latest version.

(1) *The unique importance given to consumption index-no.* (α) I have been used to contrast Fisher's hotchpotch P with an index-number of prices of *constituents of the real national income*, including instruments,—which seems to me in a way more fundamental. But obviously yours is more suitable for your purposes: only I wasn't satisfied with the section (reference mislaid) in which you explain the possible vagaries of P'.

(β) I should have liked the analysis to be equally suitable for discussing, when it comes to vol. II, the policy of stabilising the price of effort instead of your P. As you know, I'm rather *fanatical* about this now,—and am glad to welcome the Prof in his new ed^n of *Ind[ustrial] Fluc[tuations]* as a convert. It seems to me to make the whole quantitative difference to (e.g.) the question of the adequacy of gold production. I think the terms of your equation could be so redefined as to allow for that as a possible alternative (see n. on p. 7)[1]: but I don't really expect you to think this worth while!

(2) *The nature and rôle of profits.* I'm uneasy about the definition, and detect a flavour of Catchingism about the notion that 'profits' are normally notspent, and that 'incomes' may fall short of the aggregate of sale-prices! But swallowing them as best I can, I still think I find a certain indeterminacy about the rôle of profits. They first appear as a result and bye-product of the

[1] These page references, and the galley references with the prefix o below, are to material which has not survived.

rise of P: then, though rather doubtfully, in connection with bank-rate, as a motive-force towards the excess of investment which raises P: finally in one place (p. 032) as the source out of which the income of investment is provided. The whole claim for the superiority of your equation is that it brings out the causal sequence: yet, esp. in the bank-rate chapter, I feel that the sequence is not always clear. See my notes on pp. 12, 15, 061, 113, 031, 036: to which (though I can't now remember what they are!) I have made a note that I attach importance.

(3) *Heterogeneity of investment.* I see the great gain in generality which comes if one can lump together new fixed and new working capital. But (apart from the rather shifting use of the term 'capital goods', which often seems to mean only instruments) I feel that there are places where the essential difference between f. and w. capital gives rise to latent difficulties. See notes on pp. 11 and 064. The difference is that the entrepreneur who decides that he wants more w.c. himself provides it, while the entrepreneur who decides that he wants more f.c. buys it in the market. In the case of f.c. there are 3 parties whose actions ought to be in equilibrium,—the saver, the promoter, the instrument-making-entrepreneur.—Perhaps I am wrong in finding a difficulty here,—in any case I'm not suggesting there's a deep-seated fallacy—only a complication in certain connections (esp. the stimulus given by falling bank-rate to investment) requires more elucidation.

I expect some of my notes are quite trivial and vexatious, I wrote down anything that occurred to me! I'll come at 3.0 tomorrow.

Yours

D.

J.M.K. notes, *December 1929*

Foreign investment

Like banking, the danger is for a country to lend more than its quota. Lending must coincide (1) with a desire to borrow all round, (2) a willingness to lend all round. If our quota is 125 out of 375 unsafe for us to lend more than a third of total lending.

Bank rate

When an increase in bank rate is due to an investment boom at home, it probably draws gold in the first instance because the effect on L is greater than effect on B, and thus provides necessary fodder for the price rise.

Thus in case of an investment boom in one country, the necessary cash is almost inevitably forthcoming under an automatic international system.

Labour power ? re-word index numbers.

Distinction between capital goods which have a cost of production and those which have not.

Suppose rate of interest falls.

Value of claims on future income rises.

Loan capital has no cost of production.

Natural resources.

Monopoly, good will etc. in half way position.

If rate of interest falls, investor will pay at a higher price for a house until rents fall. Thus house-building stimulated until it

. . . .

If entrepreneurs use their profits to buy investments...P' is indeterminate but not less than cost of production. If they deposit them with banks with result of increasing bull–bear position they...

P' is determined by degree of capital inflation which depends on rate of interest and bull–bear sentiment.

P'' Price of old capital determined by rate of interest *and* by expectations of *future* prices. P' will be dragged up and down by P''.

From R. F. KAHN, *17 December 1929*

My dear Mr Keynes,

I enclose the proofs. I am not sure that any of my comments are of importance, but if you have the time and feel that it is worth while, I should very much like to have an opportunity of talking about them.

There are a few general points that I should like to mention.

(1) I think I have now got my mind clear as to the necessity of separating out profits. But I am not quite confident that you sufficiently stress the distinction between profits and ordinary income: it strikes one at first rather like a conjuring trick. Are there not really two main reasons for your method of treatment?

(*a*) Profits are, in the first place, an effect rather than a cause. It would be absurd to add them to savings, because if this were done, it would be impossible for savings to fall off (assuming that no portion of profits is spent on consumption and that P' remains unchanged when savings fall off). They are, indeed, '*automatic* lacking', and as such cannot be grouped with savings.

(*b*) As a matter of practical fact, profits are not devoted, to any considerable extent, to consumption.

(2) But profits are not wholly an effect. What is done with them is of fundamental importance. If they are devoted entirely to consumption, P is infinite. But if they are devoted entirely to new investment, P' is infinite.[1] The value of P' is connected with the manner in which profits are divided between the banking system and new investment (see footnote to p. A 115 and also p. A 107).

I still feel that a few simple equations involving the elements of savings and profits that are devoted to the banking system (repayment of loans and influx to deposits) and to new investment, would make things much clearer.

(3) Would it be possible to devote a little more space to show how the intensity of the credit cycle of chap. 20 is diminished in a country that can import from abroad?

(4) I also find that insufficient space is devoted in this chapter to the slump. I note with regret the removal of the bismuth–castor oil analogy.

(5) Do you think that any attention ought to be devoted to the effect of short-period influences in the trade cycle, i.e. the effects of limited capacity and of surplus capacity on prices and profits?

(6) It has just occurred to me that a short treatment of Germany's inflation on your new lines would be very helpful. The common explanation in terms of velocity of circulation always seems very difficult to understand.

Yours sincerely,

R. F. KAHN

From D. H. ROBERTSON, *8 January 1930*

My dear Maynard,

I've been taking a holiday (from Kahn[2] and lecture-notes) over the enclosed. My goodness, how full of meat it is!—I've made some pencil scribbles, almost nothing of importance. Here are some disconnected remarks.

---

[1] At this point Keynes wrote in pencil 'No'.
[2] Robertson was reading Kahn's fellowship dissertation for King's College, Cambridge.

I'm not *quite* happy about productive consumption and the wages fund,—see p. 377.

I suspect the history in p. 372, n. is still dicky.

Did you define Liquid Capital in book III so as to include surplus stocks of half-finished goods, which is what you do in the present book? I had an idea that the original definition only included stocks of goods ready for consumption.

I suppose you will be bringing America 1925–9 up to date.—I don't know whether you will feel inclined to modify your criticisms of the F.R. system (p. 449)! It might be worth pointing out that there was a *decline* in time deposits in the second half of the boom (1928–9), owing to the substitution of loans 'for others' for 'loans on own account'

I don't feel sure the case for restriction of output below capacity is as strong as you make out (p. 389).

I've had to give up p. 388 in despair! Perhaps if I gave up 24 hours to it I could see it! I'm sure most readers will need more help.

I've been interested to turn up my own halting explanation of the gold-paradox of the nineties (*Ind. Fluc.*, p. 228): and slightly vain to see how clearly I saw in 1915 that the war was simply an ordinary investment-boom (ibid., introduction, p. ix), though, as throughout the book, I muddled up 'savings' with 'liquid goods'.

I shall have to think more about Gibson some time. I think when I went into Coates' correlation business (*Ec. Journal* 1927, p. 571), I felt there wasn't a great deal to explain: but there may be.

It will be a noble book!

Yours,

D.H.R.

From D. H. ROBERTSON, *4 March 1930*

My dear Maynard,

Proofs enclosed. I'm disappointed to find myself still full of resistances on certain points,—not, I think, on the main structure. Perhaps if I stewed in it long enough, they would vanish: but I can't now before the end of term, and I don't like to hold it up. So I'd better out with them such as they are.

I think the *origin* of them is that I still for myself do everything by dividing saving into (*a*) that done through the banking system and (*b*) that done outside, and investment into (*a*) increments of working capital (*b*) completed new machines. But of course that doesn't mean that your way of dealing with S as a whole and I as a whole isn't much superior, if it can be carried through. But at present

(1) as regards *I*. See my comments on pp. 4, 5, 8, 15, 18, which I think form a series, and I hope will make my difficulty plain. I don't know what 'investment goods' means. Sometimes, as on p. 15, the relevant distinction seems to be that between consumption goods and instrumental goods, as drawn on p. 4. But sometimes it seems to be rather that between available and non-available income, as drawn on p. 5.

(2) As regards *S*. (i) I still find myself offended by ch. x, §iii (pp. 9–10), with its suggestion that money receipts (whether 'incomes' or 'profits') must always be spent on *something*. It's so implanted in me that the troubles of e.g. the slump arise because people (whether 'profit'-receivers or others) won't buy *either* consumables *or* investments. I can see dimly that the passage at bottom of p. 13 may be designed to meet my difficulty, and perhaps if I thought long enough I might feel it did so. But §iii seems to me to raise more difficulties than it resolves.

(ii) I don't at present see how to reconcile your pp. 22–4 with my conviction that a policy of stabilising prices when efficiency increases involves forced saving, whatever its other merits. I.e. I don't in the least dispute that the final decision must be reached on a balance of considerations: but it still seems to me this particular item, for what it's worth, is on the side of labour-power-stabilisation.

I'm sorry to be so contentious. I hoped now to be able to swallow it whole!

Would rather not tackle any more proofs until after Tuesday, when I have a—still unwritten—paper to read in London: thereafter would make it a first charge.

Yours ever,

D.H.R.

From R. F. KAHN, *March 1930*

(1) (*a*) When a man saves a sum of money, he either

(i) keeps it in the bank or uses it to repay a bank loan,

or (ii) buys a new investment (i.e. a piece of capital straight from the entrepreneur who produced it),

or (iii) buys a piece of old capital or a title to capital.

Then in case (i) the saving takes place through the banking system (S_B) and case (ii) is of the S_1 type. In case (iii) we have to follow up the chain, and we shall come finally to a man who acts in accordance either with case (i) or case (ii).

(*b*) It is scarcely for me to define what I mean by the 'absence of any change of policy on the part of the banking system'. It was you who laid down the challenge when you said that the profits on the sale of consumption goods must necessarily be spent 'directly or indirectly' on new investment.

Is this the case whatever the banking system does? Suppose for instance that it maintains the same rate of interest as before, or that it maintains the former rate of increasing its loans.

(2) I recognise, of course, that if the value of investment and its cost of production are *not* equal, the profit that arises out of the deviation is just sufficient to pay for the difference (I was merely considering the condition that they *should* be equal, i.e. that the reduction in savings should be compensated, not only quantitatively, but qualitatively, by the profits on the sale of consumption goods). But here, too, the quantitative aspect seems to me important. The extent to which this profit is spent on the banking system must be equal to the extent to which the banking system pays for the increased value of investment. If the banking system refuses to increase the rate at which it increases its loans and if there is no increased incentive to savings depositors to invest their savings deposits, no autonomous capital inflation appears to be possible so long as any portion of the profit that would ensue would be devoted to the banking system. But if the whole of the profit is devoted to investment, such an autonomous change is always possible.

R.F.K.

From R. F. KAHN, *12 March 1930*

Dear Mr Keynes,

As a result of talking with Mr Robertson, I think I can make rather more vivid the point towards which I was groping on Monday. Suppose that we start from equilibrium and that there is a decrease S in the volume of saving. Let S_B come off saving that was going into the banking system and S_I off saving that was being spent on new investment. *If* the value of investment is unchanged, and if no part of profits is spent on consumption, profits $P = S = S_B + S_I$. Now in the absence of any change of policy on the part of the banking system, the value of investment *will* be unchanged if $P_I = S_I$, where P_I is the portion of profits spent on new investment and $P_B = P - P_I$ is the portion entrusted to the banking system (I am assuming the *amount* of investment to be unchanged). Thus the condition for the value of investment to be unchanged is that

$$\frac{P_I}{P_B} = \frac{S_I}{S_B}$$

Your answer would, I take it, be that *in fact* P_I/P_B is likely to be *greater* than S_I/S_B (so that the value of investment would rise)—for such reasons as that:

(1) The people who cease saving S are probably less 'bullishly', and more 'bearishly', inclined than the people to whom profits P accrue.

(2) The fact of inflation will make everybody more 'bullish'.

(3) In so far as P_B is used to repay bank loans, these loans will be renewed —so that it will be as though their profits had gone straight into the P_B category.

But I still feel that the matter cannot be entirely passed over (and I gather that Mr Robertson feels more strongly than I do).

Yours sincerely,

R. F. KAHN

From a letter to R. F. KAHN, *18 March 1930*

2. I am still not at all satisfied about 'saving through the banking system', and send you the following notes to think over before tomorrow.

(*a*) You agree that a man is saving money through the banking system when he repays a bank loan. The replacement by the bank of a loan paid off by a new loan represents the 'absence of any change of policy on the part of the banking system', but what possible difference can it make to price levels whether I buy an investment direct out of my profits or my savings, or whether I use them to repay a bank loan and the money is then lent by the bank to someone else wherewith to buy the investment?

(*b*) You purported in your previous letter, I thought, to state conditions sufficient to ensure that the value of investment is not necessarily unchanged. I pointed out in reply that even if your conditions were fulfilled the value of investment is unchanged. I do not follow what your answer is to this.

(*c*) I agree, of course, that the behaviour of the banking system taken in conjunction with all other relevant factors determines the situation. But I am unable to arrive at any simple formula connecting the change in the value of investment with the amount of saving which goes on through the banking system. My belief is that in order to get a simple formula one has to make so many artificial assumptions that the formula ceases to be of any particular interest.

But it looks as if our minds had not really met on the matter yet. I am still unable to see anything both simple and true which can be said on the matter.

Beyond these letters, nothing remains of the discussions or drafts of this period except a third galley proof of chapter 21 parts (i)–(iv) dated 4 and 7 March 1931 and a third page proof of chapter 25 dated 26 May, both of which follow the printed version except for a few stylistic corrections.

However, by this time, Keynes's public activities had brought other opportunities for comments and criticism. On 4 November 1929 Philip Snowden, the Chancellor of the Exchequer in the second Labour Government, announced the appointment of a Committee on Finance and Industry with Keynes as a member.[1] In the early stages of its deliberations, as well as later, the Committee heard Keynes present his views as to how financial policy affected price levels and how these fitted in with the Committee's terms of reference and possible Report. As the theoretical material followed the *Treatise* and as this is an example of Keynes's 'public' activities, this 'private evidence', along with Keynes's questioning of some witnesses, appears in volume XX.

This 'evidence' was circulated to R. G. Hawtrey of the Treasury as one basis for his own evidence to the Committee, along with an offer on Keynes's behalf to supply proofs of the *Treatise* as they became available.[2] This was to provide the basis for an extensive correspondence.

Keynes and Hawtrey had already discussed some of the issues later raised in the *Treatise* on 17 December 1929, when Hawtrey had presented a paper 'Money and Index Numbers'[3]. On that occasion, Keynes's comments ran as follows:

[1] The members of the Committee other than Keynes were Lord Macmillan (a Lord of Appeal in Ordinary), Sir Thomas Allen, Ernest Bevin, Lord Bradbury, R. H. Brand, Professor T. E. Gregory, L. B. Lee, C. Lubbock, Reginald McKenna, J. T. Walton Newbold, Sir Walter Raine, J. Frater Taylor and A. A. G. Tulloch. The Committee's terms of reference were 'to inquire into banking, finance and credit, paying regard to the factors both internal and international which govern their operation, and to make recommendations calculated to enable these agencies to promote the development of trade and commerce and the employment of labour'. Its report was published in July 1931.

[2] H. P. Macmillan (later Lord Macmillan) to R. G. Hawtrey, 14 March 1930. This letter was made available to us by Sir Ralph Hawtrey.

[3] *Journal of the Royal Statistical Society*, Part 1 (1930), reprinted in *The Art of Central Banking*.

FROM THE TRACT TO THE TREATISE

From (The Journal of the Royal Statistical Society), *Part I (1930)*

(MR J. M. KEYNES): I have much pleasure in moving this vote of thanks: none the less sincerely because I feel somewhat critical towards the paper. There are very few writers on monetary subjects from whom one receives more stimulus and useful suggestion than from Mr Hawtrey, and I think there are few writers on these subjects with whom I personally feel in more fundamental sympathy and agreement. The paradox is that in spite of that, I nearly always disagree in detail with what he says! Yet truly and sincerely he is one of the writers who seem to me to be most nearly on the right track! So it is in the case of this paper. I feel that he is discussing the things that matter; he is directing our minds to the true problems; and yet it is remarkable how much in detail I can find to disagree with. In particular, I am able to make very little of the first six pages. His attempt to distinguish between monetary and non-monetary causes of price fluctuation has a very ancient and distinguished lineage; it was the approach of Cournot and of Jevons, and it was to the end of his life, if not the sole approach, at least an avenue to which he attached great importance, in the mind of Edgeworth. I believe, however, it is possible to show that this is a false clue. It is not practicable when relative prices are changing to give any useful interpretation to the supposed distinction between monetary causes of change and non-monetary causes. Mr Hawtrey's own attempt appears to me to be plainly inconsistent. He tells us at the beginning—or so I understand him—that a monetary cause is a cause which tends to make all prices move equally; later on he tells us that a non-monetary cause is a cause which tends to change real costs. It is obvious that those two definitions are not comprehensive. There will be causes which are neither monetary nor non-monetary on that definition. If Mr Hawtrey had wished to be consistent he should have defined a monetary cause as a cause which tends to affect all *money costs* equally, not all *prices*, and if he had done that he would have been saying something not at all in accordance with ordinary language, because we certainly would not think of something which tended to affect all costs equally as being *par excellence* a monetary cause. I find, moreover, not very much necessary connection between this part of the paper and the second part, in which he raises for our discussion the vitally important question from the point of view of theory, as to whether it would be ideal to stabilise the purchasing power of money in terms of the articles of consumption, or whether we should stabilise the cost of human effort.

For my own part, I have come to no clear conclusion; I think that what Mr Hawtrey suggests to us has very great attractions; I believe that the idea of stabilising incomes is a fruitful one and bears a great deal of thinking about; but I suspect that the choice between the two standards ought not to be the same in all circumstances. I doubt if I should come to the same conclusion in all sets of conditions. For example, if we were living in an age when real costs were increasing—the opposite to an age of progress—I should be much more inclined to adopt his conclusion than if I were living in an age of progress in which real costs were diminishing.

Being in this doubtful state of mind, perhaps I shall be most useful if I give very briefly one or two of the arguments on the other side without implying that I necessarily disagree with the weighty reasons given by Mr Hawtrey in favour of his own conclusions.

There is first of all the point that even in an ideal state such a standard as his could not be international. That is admitted by Mr Hawtrey in the last section of his paper. Clearly real costs do not change in the same way in India, the United States and in this country. It would mean, therefore, that the standard would be changing differently in the three countries. I do not think that is necessarily an argument against Mr Hawtrey, because in the ideal state there may be much to be said for not having international standards; but when we are considering practical problems it does seem to me to be an important objection.

Then as to the *rentier*. It has often been held to have been an advantage in past history that the tendency for prices to rise on the whole has been socially expedient by reducing the claim of the *rentier* on the community. We are glad, for example, to see ancient war debts becoming a little less burdensome by the lapse of time. But whether or not we go so far as this, there is much to be said against actually *augmenting* the claim of the *rentier* in terms of goods,—which is what Mr Hawtrey's standard would do in an age of progress. Then there is what is perhaps the most important question. Would this standard, or the other, minimise social friction? I believe you have less social friction if wages on the whole tend to go up with progress than if they keep steady. I think that earners are more satisfied if, when they become more efficient, they benefit in the shape of higher wages than if they benefit by lower prices. It is purely a psychological question, but I think it is better to let wages rise slowly than to let prices decrease. That is reinforced in my opinion if one remembers that one is dealing in practice with particular cases and not with averages; for relative wages have to change from time to time, so that if the average of wages has to be stable in terms of money, individual classes of wages will have to fall. If, on the other hand, you allow the average of wages to rise slowly, the extent of such individual falls will be mitigated. Therefore, I am somewhat of the opinion that social friction would be less if you allow wages to rise slowly than if you insist on keeping wages steady and reducing prices.

Finally, Mr Hawtrey's choice of the wholesale index for his purpose strikes me as paradoxical. Whilst it might be held that the wholesale index is an approximation to a consumption index, it strikes me as the wildest paradox to suppose that it is any sort of an approximation to changes in real cost. Certainly over the last fifty years the result of stabilising the wholesale index number is the remotest that can be conceived from the process of stabilising the wages of the earners of the factors of production. The two indices have moved in opposite directions, and there is no reason of any kind for supposing that the wholesale index gives an approximation for changes in real costs.

In conclusion I should like to say that I think it most undesirable that any acute controversy should arise as to which of the two methods of stabilisation is preferable. I am inclined to believe that stabilisation is much more important over short periods than over long periods, and in short periods both methods come to much the same thing. If we have to choose between them, it is a case where I would be ready to fall in with the views of the majority. It would be a very unfortunate thing if those who are in favour of stabilising in some form or other were to fall into two camps, one of which would stabilise in terms of effort and the other in terms of commodity.

It reminds me of a story that Lord Bradbury used to tell of his intervention in a Commission on decimal coinage. When he appeared before that Commission he took up the position that of course everyone would wish to decimalise, but that the real question was whether they were going to decimalise the penny or the pound. Were they going to keep the present value of the pound and make ten farthings a hundredth part of it, or were they going to keep the present value of the penny? By that means he divided the Commission into two equal halves, and nothing was done. I should be unhappy if Mr Hawtrey were to be successful in dividing stabilisers into two equal camps. It is much more important that the notion of stabilisation should be popularised than that either one of these two methods should succeed over the other. On the whole, my preference is for stabilising commodity rather than effort; but if Mr Hawtrey obtains a great many converts to his view, I shall hush up my own opinion and join his ranks.

It was with this background that Keynes himself dispatched his first batch of proofs to Hawtrey with the following covering letter:

To R. G. HAWTREY, *23 April 1930*

My dear Ralph,

At last I am able to send you a big batch of my proofs, and am only sorry that I could not let you have them in time to read during the Easter holidays. But the printer has been rather dilatory and has now supplied stuff to me in a rush.

I am sending you the whole of the proofs from the beginning, as that will probably be the most satisfactory plan, although a good deal of the early part has no particular bearing upon the special matters which we are discussing. Some of the definitions towards the end of Book I are required later on, but the whole of Book II on index numbers is of course a separate subject. With the beginning of Book III the substantial argument begins.

In reading these proofs, will you bear the following points in mind?—

1. The book is on rather a large scale, the batch of proofs which I am now sending you representing less than a third of the whole, so that there are a good many matters very germane to the argument which will not be reached until much further on.

2. Investment, in my sense of the term, includes the fluctuations in dealers' stocks to which you attach prime importance. Thus my theory would include your theory, and is not inconsistent with it. If you are right that this is in fact the quantitatively important item, that would fit in perfectly well with my theory; though, as you will see, I differ from you on the practical judgment as to what fluctuations are of the greatest quantitative importance. The worst of it is that my full discussion of this particular matter does not come for some 200 pages further on.

3. What is vital for my theory is the change in the rate of interest. In many passages I take changes in bank rate as typical of this, or at any rate I have assumed that changes in bank rate are capable of bringing about a sufficient change in rates of interest generally. I gather that you rather question this as a statement of fact. Here again my discussion of the facts will not appear until some 300 pages later. But so far as the argument is concerned it is changes in the rate of interest which matter, and bank rate is only significant in so far as bank rate influences the rate of interest generally.

I am going back to Cambridge tomorrow, but I shall be regularly in London in the middle of the week. When you have got through this batch of stuff and possibly some more sheets which I ought to have fairly soon, will you come to dinner some evening for a discussion?

I wonder if I shall convince you! Because, although we always seem to differ on these monetary questions in discussion, I feel that ultimately I am joined in common agreement with you as against most of the rest of the world.

Yours ever,
[copy initialled] J.M.K.

Hawtrey replied on 24 April with a formal note, the only interesting part of which is the last sentence: 'I think you are right as to our fundamental agreement, but I do not yet know how important are the details and facts in regard to which we differ.'

By 30 April Hawtrey had read the first instalment of proofs 'with great interest' and was 'eager for more'. However, Keynes could only send them as fast as the printers could deal with them, sending 'a good batch' of volume II on 24 June and chapter 30 on 7 July. As Hawtrey worked through the proofs he began composing a long commentary, 'Mr Keynes's Treatise on Money', which eventually appeared as chapter VI of *The Art of Central Banking*, and a series of short proof corrections. In his letter of 5 July, Keynes began to turn his attention to Hawtrey's longer draft.

To R. G. HAWTREY, *5 July 1930*

Dear Ralph,

(1) Here are the proofs of Chapter 30. They illustrate the application of my ideas to events.

(2) Many thanks for your sheet of minor points, which I will deal with.

(3) I have your major criticisms but have not yet had time to consider them thoroughly. The preliminary points arise, however, as follows:—

(i) Could you let me have a definition of 'consumers' outlay' corresponding to the definition of 'consumers' income' which you have here given on p. 6?

(ii) On p. 7 you say that I assume in my analysis *as a rule* that there is no change in stocks of finished commodities. Could you cite cases of this? For I intended to do the opposite—that is to allow for changes of stocks *as a rule* and only to depart from this occasionally. The central analysis is meant to allow for the possibility of changes of stocks. Economy of language sometimes leads me not to mention this. But presumably your point is that my analysis is only valid as a rule on the assumption of no changes in stocks.

Yours ever,

J.M.K.

From a letter from R. G. HAWTREY, *7 July 1930*

As to the definition of consumers' outlay, there is something of the kind in paragraphs 6 to 8 of my printed statement of evidence. As an alternative I think you might take it to be the disbursements out of income deposits and out of windfalls, except that if the income deposits are replenished from other sources than income the receipts from those sources must be deducted from outgoings to arrive at outlay. As a qualification of the exception, however, I should regard an overdraft or loan not as a 'source' but as an anticipation of income.

Much difficulty arises from traders' income. At any moment the trader's net gains are partly a matter of opinion, depending on the valuation of goods not yet sold. When his unsold stocks increase, he may either value them at cost and regard himself as not yet having derived any income from them, or he may value them at market price and regard the profit included therein as applied towards the cost of holding them. In the latter alternative the profit would count both as income and as 'outlay,' the outlay being saving applied to the increase of the traders' liquid capital.

After this exchange, Hawtrey continued sending instalments of his longer criticism, but Keynes was, as yet, unprepared to discuss them as he was 'overwhelmed' with work with the Macmillan Committee, the Economic Advisory Council 'and a hundred other matters'. However, in his notes to Hawtrey, he continued to try and sort out consumers' outlay and gave reports of progress.

From a letter to R. G. HAWTREY, *11 July 1930*

P.S. Which of the possible definitions of consumer's outlay am I to take as the authentic one in considering the relationship between your theory and mine?

From a letter from R. G. HAWTREY, *16 July 1930*

As to Consumers' Outlay, the authentic definition is that in the printed statement,[1] 'what the purchasers of the final products spend out of income', with the explanations that follow it. It is, I think, substantially equivalent to that in Currency and Credit (pp. 45–6 of 3rd edition). The alternative definition given in my letter of 7 July[2] was merely intended to elucidate these other definitions and not supplant them.

From R. G. HAWTREY, *18 July 1930*

Dear Maynard,

I have been looking again at your chapter on liquid capital, and I think you have gone somewhat astray in interpreting my arguments on the subject (vol. II, pp. 131–5).

You quote from pp. 74 and 126 of *Trade and Credit*. And as it happens *each* of these passages is followed by the qualifying phrase that the reality 'is not so simple as that', which introduces an explanation of why, in the circumstances assumed, prices must rise. The explanation on p. 74 is quite perfunctory and incomplete, for there I was merely discussing the meaning of inflationism. But in the other passage, pp. 127–9, I have dealt in considerable detail with the effect of a shortage of stocks upon prices.

Yet you say that I 'seem to argue' in these passages that falling stocks are associated with falling prices.

The passage you quote from p. 156 is governed by the phrase higher up on that page, 'For the *immediate* effect of the increase in the consumers' outlay...', and is closely followed by a discussion of the effect of a shortage of stocks in raising prices after 'that stage' (p. 157).

And I attach importance to this on p. 160:

'It should be mentioned that the fluctuations in stocks do not *necessarily* always correspond with the alternations of activity and depression. Traders are *willing* to hold larger stocks at a time of activity than at a time of restricted

[1] Committee on Finance and Industry, *Minutes of Evidence*, I, 273.
[2] Above, p. 133.

134

production, and when either condition has persisted for some time, they tend to adjust their stocks by making their selling prices in the one case above and in the other below replacement value.'

Yours ever,

R. G. HAWTREY

From a letter to R. G. HAWTREY, *18 July 1930*

My attempt to explain to Pigou and Robertson[1] the difference between excess hoarding and excess saving, about which they have been making obstinate misunderstandings, has led me to what seems to be a very great improvement of exposition and some slight change of substance. So I have been drastically re-writing the chapter which deals with the fundamental equations. This looks a great deal more different from the old version than it really is. But I think it brings out much more definitely what is in my mind. I will send you the revise as soon as I have it.

To R. G. HAWTREY, *29 July 1930*

Dear Ralph,

I have been thinking about your criticisms in odd moments, though I have still not had time to get down to the matter thoroughly. But I find myself still held up by the same point of perplexity as that about which I wrote to you before. So it may save time in discussion if we make a further attempt to clear it up beforehand.

I still find myself unable to frame a clear, consistent and intelligible meaning for 'consumer's outlay' as used by you. Until I have this it is impossible to decide how fundamental our differences are. Would it be possible for you to amplify the idea for me fully? Could you express it precisely, either in terms of my notation or corresponding language of your own?

Yours ever,

[copy initialled] J.M.K.

---

[1] Records of this attempt have not survived.

PREPARATION

From R. G. HAWTREY, *1 August 1930*

Dear Maynard,

I enclose a memorandum about consumers' outlay, but I feel some difficulty in meeting your requirements in the absence of any indication of the points which are obscure to you. I do not think the subject can be fully dealt with in terms of your notation, but the following analysis may help to bridge the gulf.

Investment, I, = the excess of the consumers' income $(E+Q)$ over PR, the sale value of the consumption goods purchased by consumers. Therefore I is the total of incomes not applied to purchases for consumption.

What do the recipients do with these portions of income? They may (1) buy capital assets (e.g. houses) (2) buy participating rights in capital assets, (3) leave the money in balances, or (4) pay off overdrafts. (Payment of debts to others than banks is not a separate use, for the *creditor* must then apply the money to one of these four purposes.)

The net amount applied to buying capital assets or rights in capital assets forms, along with PR, the consumers' outlay.

This brief statement, however, must be read in connection with the memorandum.

Yours ever,

R. G. HAWTREY

CONSUMERS' OUTLAY

In Currency and Credit (p. 46) I have defined consumers' income as 'What a man has available to spend on his own needs' and consumers' outlay as 'What he so spends' (both of course being summed throughout the community). Outlay includes investment, which 'is one of the purposes on which income may be spent'.

The fundamental principle is that outlay on anything *with a view to sale* is excluded from consumers' outlay, and is classed as 'traders' turnover'. For precision this must apply not only to the outlay of traders properly so called, but to outlay by anyone on purchase with a view to sale, or on purchase with a view to a replacement of some asset sold. So far as the buying and selling of property, securities and other assets are concerned, the net cost met out of income is part of the consumers' outlay, and this applies to the trader who leaves part of his profits in his business as well as to the non-trader dealing with his private investments.

When there is on balance a net *sale* of assets, the 'diversion of capital assets to consumption' is excluded from the consumers' outlay as 'not being expenditure out of income'.

In *Currency and Credit*, p. 46, this is applied to the trader who takes more than his true net profits out of his business, but it is equally applicable to the spendthrift.

While the spendthrift's expenditure is not itself consumers' outlay, the money spent out of income by other people on buying his assets is. For him the investment market, instead of being a channel through which savings are applied to capital outlay, becomes a channel through which they are applied to consumption outlay.

The people who buy the spendthrift's assets may not pay for them out of income but may obtain bank advances for the purpose. But their borrowing merges in the indebtedness of the investment market as a whole. If the indebtedness of the investment market is increasing, that means that the outlay for which the market is a channel (capital outlay *plus* spendthrift outlay) exceeds the sums received through the net sales of securities to investors. The creation of credit reinforces the consumers' outlay with an additional outlay which is not counted as part of the consumers' outlay. To the producers this additional outlay appears as additional demand, and (subject to any change in stocks of commodities) will give rise to additional production and therefore to additional consumers' income.

This creation of credit through the investment market works ultimately in the same way as any other form of trade borrowing. Traders borrow money in order to add to their stocks of goods and the money is paid to those who participate in the production of the goods. This is an outlay, additional to the consumers' outlay, which gives rise to a corresponding addition to the consumers' income.

The consumers' outlay as a whole is spent partly (1) on goods and securities supplied *by intermediaries*, through the commodity markets and the investment market, and partly (2) on services rendered *directly* by e.g. domestic servants, and lessors of houses. So far as payments for the direct services are concerned, the consumers' outlay and the consumers' income which supplies it are equal and simultaneous. But in the case of the things supplied through intermediaries, the sums received by the market from the consumers' outlay in any period of time will not in general be exactly equal to the sums paid by the market to form the incomes of those who supply it. When the market sells more than it buys, its stocks of goods and securities are drawn upon and its cash balances are increased (or bank advances are paid off). When the market buys more than it sells, its stocks of goods and securities are added to and its cash balances are drawn upon (or bank advances increased).

Therefore the consumers' outlay over any interval of time is equal to the consumer's income *less* any addition to the market stocks of commodities and securities. ('Addition' here is of course to be taken in an algebraic sense, applicable to negative quantities.)

The distinction between goods and securities held in the market and those held by consumers is an essential one. The consumers' outlay includes those transactions which transfer the ownership of commodities or securities from the market (i.e. traders) to consumers (i.e. those who buy with a view to consuming or enjoying and not with a view to resale). In the case of a consumable commodity it is the thing itself that changes ownership, in the case of a capital asset the ownership, when it takes the form of stocks, shares, etc., may be divided, a part being held by the market and a part by consumers (i.e. investors). The change of ownership is effected not by any dealing in the capital asset itself but by the transfer of the participating rights.

To R. G. HAWTREY, *27 August 1930*

Dear Ralph,

I promised you a further letter, I think, before the end of August, and am sorry to be so late with it. I am, of course, a good deal behindhand with my schedule of work—about a fortnight as near as I can calculate, so that, although the end is now definitely in sight, I have not yet quite reached it. This means that I have not been able to give any further thought to your memorandum, so we must put off discussing it until after you are back from your holiday.

Could you now let me have back the set of proofs I sent you? The final version will shortly be available, and I naturally do not want misunderstandings to get about through uncorrected versions being in circulation. I have considerably re-written the fundamental chapter, and enclose the revised version herewith.[1] I doubt if the changes meet your particular points. They were primarily devised to meet what seemed to me misunderstandings on the part of Pigou and Robertson. But they do, I think, make my own point of view a great deal clearer than it was before.

There is also your letter of 18 July for me to answer, where you complain that I have misinterpreted you on pages 131-5 of vol. II, where I quote from your *Trade & Credit*. I have tried to make this right in the final proofs by adding the quotation to which you attach importance from your page 160 and deleting

[1] Sorry, I can't at present, as I find I have no spare copy.

138

the first 9 lines of the second paragraph of my page 132 [*JMK*, vol. VI, pp. 117–18]. It was difficult to do more, because I had to avoid upsetting the pagination.

Yours ever,

J.M.K.

In fact it was not until after publication that Keynes really got down to replying to Hawtrey's comments, which he did in a letter and long commentary on 28 November. In the commentary the passages from Hawtrey's comments which Keynes refers to are reproduced as endnotes in an Addendum beginning on page 150.

To R. G. HAWTREY, *28 November 1930*

My dear Ralph,

I have at last been able to get time for a continuous stretch of work on your notes. This is not an easy subject to discuss by word of mouth, so I thought it better to put my most important comments in writing. After you have considered these, perhaps we might meet. I am very much indebted to you for having taken such enormous trouble about it all.

Yours ever,

J. M. KEYNES

As near as I can understand your terms, their meanings are as follows:—

Consumers' income = $E + Q$, i.e. it is earnings *plus* profits in my terminology. Furthermore it is a sum of money.

Consumers' income may be used by consumers in the following ways:—

(1) In current consumption, the expense of which is, in my terminology, $P.R$

(2) In buying capital assets outright, the expense of which we will call C_1

(3) In lending money direct to traders and speculators (e.g. brokers' loans), wherewith the latter hold capital assets, the amount of which we will call C_2

(4) In increasing their bank balances, the amount of which we will call C_3.

Let us call consumers' income H_1
and consumers' outlay H_2

(where H stands for Hawtrey).
Then

$$H_1 = E + Q = P.R + C_1 + C_2 + C_3;$$

and consumers' outlay

$$H_2 = P.R + C_1.$$

At least so I understand, since 'outlay on anything with a view to sale is excluded from consumers' outlay and is classed as traders' turnover'. But at another point it appears that perhaps $H_2 = P.R + C_1 + C_2$; since an increase in traders' turnover is spoken of as involving an increase in bank credit.

Thus, if we call traders' turnover H_3, we have

$$H_1 = H_2 + H_3,$$

where H_3 is either $C_2 + C_3$ or C_3.

Now, assuming the volume of production unchanged, if H_2 increases by more than H_3 diminishes, or if H_3 increases by more than H_2 diminishes, prices must rise. More simply and with greater generality, this can be expressed by saying that if H_1 rises relatively to the volume of production, prices rise.

With less generality, we might say that if consumers' outlay increases, traders' turnover and production being unchanged, prices will rise; and again, that if traders' turnover increases, consumers' outlay and production being unchanged, prices will rise. Or, speaking broadly and without attempting complete generality, prices can only rise either if consumers' outlay increases or if traders' turnover increases.

Am I right that this is your theory?

If so, it seems to me quite true. For my second fundamental equation can be written, you will remember,

$$\Pi.O = E + (I - S).$$

Now $E + I - S = E + Q = H_1 = H_2 + H_3.$

Therefore it can be written

$$\Pi . O = H_2 + H_3 \,(= H_1),$$

from which it follows that the price level depends on the sum of consumers' outlay and traders' turnover relatively to the volume of production.

My point is that to regard $\Pi . O$ as the sum of H_2 and H_3 is not so helpful as to regard it as the sum of E and $I-S$. For it does not tell one whether the rise of prices is due to a rise in the cost of production or to a rise in profits. Yet it is essential to know this. For a rise of prices associated with a corresponding rise in the cost of production represents a position of equilibrium; whereas a rise of prices associated with a rise in profits does not. Moreover it does not bring out the relationship of profits for producers as a whole to the difference between the value of the increment of capital goods and the volume of savings (defined as I define it.)

Nevertheless I do not deny that it is sometimes helpful to regard $\Pi . O$ as the sum of H_2 and H_3. For when it is our object to raise the price level, some methods of stimulus may be chiefly calculated to increase H_2 and others chiefly calculated to increase H_3. But if we want to go a step further in our analysis of the causal train, then we shall need to know whether the increase we have brought about in H_2 and H_3 has involved an increase in E or an increase in $I-S$.

p. 3, l. 15.[1] This sentence is not true.

p. 4.[2] For the same reason I do not accept the passage beginning l. 5 and continuing to l. 7 of p. 5.

p. 6, l. 12.[3] 1st sentence of page [paragraph ?] beginning here consumers' income and outlay being sums of money by 'an equal change in the stocks of things' you mean 'an equal change in the value of stocks of things'.

p. 7.[4] As I have explained, whilst I sometimes omit references to changes in stocks of finished commodities for simplicity of exposition, I do not consider that my theory in any way requires the assumption that stocks of finished commodities are unchanged.

Your point here seems to me to be that in estimating future profits entrepreneurs lay more stress on the symptom of accumulating stocks and less on realised price falls to date, the former being an *earlier* indication of what price falls are probably going to occur. I agree of course that what matters is the *anticipated* price fall at the end of the production period, not the actual price fall to date, and that a tendency of stocks to accumulate may play an important part in determining these anticipations.

p. 7, 6 ll. from bottom.[5] I should express this by saying that the degree of departure from equilibrium represented by the change of prices which has actually occurred at any time may not, by itself, be an adequate basis for forecasting the degree of the impending departure from equilibrium. But entrepreneurs will also make mistakes (and indeed do) if they concentrate too much on the rate of accumulation of stocks and too little on prognosticating the prospective rate of investment as a whole. For it leads them to believe that they can restore equilibrium merely by curtailing output. In my analysis the significance of the accumulation of stocks is that it temporarily retards and disguises the ultimate effect on prices of a reduction in the rate of fixed investment relatively to saving. The latter calls for, and will ultimately produce, a fall in prices. Entrepreneurs can temporarily resist the full fall of prices due to this by increasing stocks, which diminishes the decline in total investment. This cannot last long, for reasons I have given. Therefore if we want a clue to the decline in fixed investment and its ultimate effects, we must watch both the actual price fall to date *and* the tendency of stocks to accumulate.

If stocks were to accumulate at a time when fixed investment was not falling off and saving was not increasing, this would cause a *rise* of prices.

p. 8, 1. 8 from bottom.[6] There would be as yet no change in prices or profits. But the accumulation of stocks would be a symptom of the factor on which I lay so much stress, namely a tendency of savings to increase relatively to fixed investment which is bound, if it continues, to produce a disequilibrium of prices and profits a little later on, because of the *impossibility* (on which I also lay great stress) of stocks continuing to accumulate to more than a very slight extent (i.e. as a percentage of annual current output).

But I emphasise that (assuming volume of production unchanged) there will not and cannot be an accumulation of stocks accompanied by a falling tendency of the price level unless fixed investment is declining relatively to saving. The latter is the fundamental factor.

As soon, however, as the volume of production begins to fall, then the decline in working capital offsets the tendency of stocks to accumulate; and the fall of prices may be greater than the decline in fixed investment relatively to saving could account for. A normal order of events is as follows:—

(1) A decline in fixed investment relatively to saving.

(2) A fall of prices, less than (1) would justify, because traders in the effort to resist the fall accumulate stocks, so that the decline in total investment is *less* than the decline in fixed investment.

(3) A fall of output, as a result of the effect of falling prices and accumulating stocks on the minds of entrepreneurs. This will probably lead to a disinvestment in working capital greater than the current increase in the accumulation of stocks, so that the decline in total investment is now *greater* than the decline in fixed investment. Consequently there is a severe fall of prices, greater than (1) would justify.

(4) This severe fall of prices greater than (1) would justify and much greater than the initial fall of prices under (2) is a function, not of a low level of output, but of a *declining* level of output. As soon, therefore, as the level of output ceases to decline further, there will be some kick-up of prices. It would lead me too far

afield to examine the causes which prevent output from declining to zero. Amongst other things one must not neglect the effect of all these events on the volume of savings.

(5) If this kick-up of prices, combined (as it sometimes is) with a low level of stocks, has the effect on the minds of entrepreneurs of causing them to increase output again, the re-investment in working capital may, so long as it is going on, offset the decline in fixed investment relatively to saving; and it may even more than offset it. Thus prices may rise to normal or even above normal.

(6) But this price level, again, is a function, not of a *high* level of output, but of a rising level. Thus as soon as output ceases to rise, we shall begin the whole story over again, unless in the meantime something has happened to restore equality between saving and new fixed investment, which, all the time, will have been the fundamental disturbing factor lurking in the background.

My feeling is that it is impossible to understand the life history of the credit cycle unless one has a formula which at each stage shows the effect on prices and profits of the volume of *total* investment relatively to saving.

p. 9, l. 12.[7] This para. may have been justified by the wording of my earlier draft. I hope I remedied this, at least in part. For I certainly agree that the volume of output depends on the anticipated price, not on the actual price, and that the volume of stocks, as well as the actual price, plays a part in fixing anticipations,—as indeed they should, since it is from these two things together (along with the volume of output if that is changing) that one can infer what changes are occurring in the underlying factor of fixed investment, which is capable of more *duration* than movements in stocks or output and is, therefore, in this sense more fundamental. For in the case of fixed investment, a low current level relatively to savings is sufficient to produce havoc,—it need not be continually declining further. But changes in stocks and output have to be continually moving ever further in the same direction, in order to produce their results; and as soon as their cumulative movement ceases and they merely remain at the high or low level which they have reached, they cease to produce their results. In particular, I argue that stocks can only change in practice within narrow limits.

p. 9.[8] The question *how much* reduction of output is caused, whether by a realised fall of price or an anticipated fall of price, is important, but not strictly a monetary problem. I have not attempted to deal with it in my book, though I have done a good deal of work at it. I am primarily concerned with what governs *prices*; though of course every conceivable factor in the situation comes in somewhere into a complete picture.

p. 10, line 6.[9] Throughout you must interpret 'a fall of prices' to mean 'a fall of prices realised or anticipated'. I have provided for this in chapter II (v).

p. 10.[10] I am dealing here with a particular course which events may take when rates of interest are raised. I did not mean to assert that this was the only conceivable course.

p. 12 (middle of the page).[11] I think that there may be an ambiguity here (and running through a great deal of your comment) as to what we mean by 'departure from equilibrium'. In this context I mean primarily 'equilibrium of prices and costs' i.e. equilibrium rewards to the entrepreneur; though I should also hold that there is not likely to be more than a transitory departure from the optimum level of output unless there is an actual or anticipated profit disequilibrium (though there always *may* be, e.g. on account of disputes as to distribution between the different factors of production).

Do you mean more all through these comments than that I have laid too much stress on realised profits in respect of the production period just ended as influencing anticipated profits in respect of the production period just beginning? I should admit that such a criticism may be fair, but it does not go very deep.

p. 13.[12] I repeat that I am not dealing with the complete set of causes which determine volume of output. For this would have led me an endlessly long journey into the theory of short-period supply and a long way from monetary theory;—though I agree that it will probably be difficult in the future to prevent monetary theory and the theory of short-period supply from running together. If I were to write the book again, I should probably attempt to probe further into the difficulties of the latter; but I have already probed far enough to know what a complicated affair it is.

As it is I have gone no further than that anticipated windfall loss or profit affects the output of entrepreneurs and their offers to the factors of production; but I have left on one side the question *how much* output is affected and also whether output can be affected in any other way.

p. 14.[13] Since $\Pi.O = E + Q = H_2 + H_3$, a change in Q *must* mean a divergence between prices and costs. A change in H_2 (i.e. in consumers' outlay) need mean no such thing. It may mean a change in E or it may be balanced by an opposite change in H_3. Thus it is erroneous to say that the cause of a divergence between prices and costs is to be found in a change in the consumers' outlay.

p. 15.[14] What this amounts to seems to me to be that the effect on prices of a change in fixed and working investment relatively to savings is apt to be temporarily mitigated and delayed by an opposite change in liquid investment, so that the change in total investment is diminished. This, as I have stated above, I accept. But I think it is only important where the changes in the other factors are quite small and for the very short period.

p. 17, middle para.[15] I do not think that I agree [with] this. It is connected with a point on an earlier page.

p. 19, middle para, last two sentences.[16] I do not see why.

p. 20.[17] The second paragraph here makes me feel, in spite of the exact understanding of many of my detailed points shown in the preceding pages, that our minds have not yet really met.

p. 22 et seq.[18] This is an old bone of contention. It is largely a question of fact, or rather of the interpretation of the evidence, and therefore does not lend itself to didactic argument.

The question is whether the amount of fluctuation in stocks due to changes in bank rate is large, fairly substantial or very small compared with the fluctuations in other forms of investment.

It is difficult or impossible to determine inductively how much of the fluctuation in stocks is attributable to changes in interest as distinct from other causes.

But I should say that the total fluctuations in stocks (as distinct from stocks which form part of working capital, i.e. are a function of the volume of output) are usually small compared with other fluctuations in investment. I have given reasons for this *passim*, but I see that I have failed to convince you.

p. 26, middle para.[19] I accept this.

p. 27, last para.[20] But this is as likely to come about through an increased preference for savings deposits compared with securities as through an increased volume of investment relatively to saving. (There is here, I think, the germ of an important difference of opinion.)

p. 29.[21] My general discussion (above) of the conception of consumers' outlay is relevant here.

p. 30, 2nd para.[22] A change in the value of investment can increase consumers' income even though there is no change in the rate of interest, no change in the supply of money and no change in velocity.

3rd para. When consumers' income is increased because Q is increased, no more money than before need have been paid out for production.

p. 31.[23] This page is also affected by the comment immediately preceding.

p. 32, 2nd para. et seq.[24] I have a good deal of sympathy with this view.

p. 33, middle of the page.[25] I do not assume that the trader maintains his expenditure on consumption unaffected by his windfall gains or losses.

p. 35, 1st sentence.[26] Is 'saving' here used in your sense or mine? It makes a good deal of difference.

p. 36, 1st sentence.[27] Not necessarily in your sense of saving.

p. 37, 3rd para.[28] Yes—this is an oversight on my part.

p. 38, last para.[29] I agree, but I meant to include this category in (*b*).

p. 39, 2nd para.[30] Yes.

p. 41, 2nd para.[31] The revival, whilst it may have been set going by cheap money, causes, when it has established itself, a change in the natural rate.

p. 43, 2nd para.[32] There will be *more* than the normal proportion of capital and labour employed at the top of the boom.

5th para.[33] No, I do not agree this.

p. 44, last para.[34] I entirely dispute this.

p. 45, 1st line.[35] Not necessarily 'isolated'. I only assume that each impulse produces its effect *pro tanto* along the lines I indicate.

p. 46, 4th para.[36] I agree. Some offset is produced for a time in this way, but the amount of 'give' is small, in my opinion.

p. 50, top.[37] That is to say, if prices are expected to fall, the natural rate falls. This consideration affects the rest of this para.

p. 53.[38] I think it is true that I have given in the chapters in question [Book III] too little prominence to the international aspect. But I wanted to split up the argument, and in these chapters I am dealing primarily, indeed almost entirely, with a closed system.

p. 55, 2nd para.[39] The answer to the concluding question is Yes.

p. 56, last para.[40] More strictly, I should have said 'relative *costs* at home and abroad, i.e. equilibrium price levels'.

p. 58, top para.[41] I agree.

p. 58, bottom.[42] As I understand your terminology:—capital outlay *plus* increase of bank balances other than traders' balances = savings. Is this right? If so, I do not understand why the maintenance of this equality should be the function of the investment market.

p. 60, last para.[43] I do not follow this. Foreign lending is always equal to the foreign balance plus gold exports.

p. 61, 3rd para.[44] No. If the foreign balance is unchanged, foreign lending can only increase if gold is exported.

If, in these pages, you mean by 'foreign lending' 'long-term foreign lending' equally I do not follow. For in that case the change in long-term foreign lending will depend on an opposite change in short-term foreign lending.

p. 62, middle para.[45] Funds flow until the rate of exchange in conjunction with the short-term rate of interest make it no longer profitable for them to flow. But the fact that an equilibrium point is sometimes reached short of gold point does not prove that a large amount of funds may not have had to move before this equilibrium is reached.

p. 62, last para.[46] I agree.

p. 63, last para. but one.[47] This seems to me to be a blunder. The transfer of funds abroad does not affect the total volume of deposits.

p. 63, last para.[48] The exchange risk applies to exactly the same extent in the case of acceptances as in the case of other instruments.

p. 65.[49] The Macmillan Committee evidence is not yet complete. But it indicates in my opinion (in spite of your memo.) that movements of short-term balances are large.

p. 66, last para.[50] That this is a purely temporary expedient, of course I agree. But it may be a very necessary one all the same. 'Short-term foreign indebtedness is the equivalent of a negative gold reserve.' I agree.

J.M.K.

PREPARATION

ADDENDUM

PASSAGES FROM R. G. HAWTREY'S COMMENTS ON THE TREATISE

¹ But so long as there is no divergence of the price of the finished product from its cost, this windfall gain or loss is offset by an equal loss or gain to the purchaser of the intermediate product.

² There may also arise the contrary case where the output of the intermediate product lags behind the sales of the finished product. I am not quite certain how to interpret Mr Keynes's fundamental equation in that case. If we suppose the price of the intermediate product to have risen above cost, and the price of the product at the next stage to be unchanged, clearly those who buy the former and sell the latter will incur a windfall loss on so much of their sales as are the equivalent of their purchases.

If they sell *more* than this, are they to be deemed to be incurring the same windfall loss on the excess? I think this is probably the right interpretation, for the quantity R of consumption goods included in output is the quantity 'purchased by consumers'.

If so, the price level of investment goods must contain the intermediate product *weighted as a negative quantity*. For example suppose that there is an output of capital goods costing £10 million a month, and that owing to a disturbance the price of these goods rises 10 per cent, so that there is a windfall gain of £1 million a month to the producers. And suppose also that the disturbance occasions an output of intermediate products exceeding what is required to keep pace with actual sales of finished products by an amount costing £5 million and sold at an advance of price of 25 per cent. Then there is a further windfall gain on the intermediate products of £1,250,000 making £2,250,000 in all. The rise in the price index of investment goods will then be 2,250,000/15,000,000 or 15 per cent.

If, on the other hand, the output of intermediate products *falls short* of what is required to keep pace with actual sales of finished products by an amount costing £5 million and sold at an advance of price of 25 per cent, then the net amount of investment costs (£10 million – £5 million) or £5 million and is priced at (£11,000,000 – £6,250,000) or £4,750,000, and there is a windfall loss of £250,000 and a fall in the price level of 5 per cent, although the prices of both finished goods and intermediate products have risen.

³ There can only be a difference between consumers' income and consumers' outlay over any period of time if there is an equal change in the stocks of things bought by consumers, i.e. finished goods and securities.

⁴ Mr Keynes assumes throughout the analysis in volume I (apart from one or two passages of secondary importance—page 174, page 288 and

pages 320–2) [*JMK*, vol. v, pp. 159, 258, 287–9] that there is no change in stocks of finished commodities. That is equivalent to assuming that the prices of finished goods are always immediately adjusted to any change in demand, so that the quantity sold remains unchanged unless and until *output* is affected. For any delay in adjusting prices will be reflected in an acceleration or retardation of sales, and therefore in a reduction or increase of stocks. It is mainly on this point that I find it necessary to differ from Mr Keynes's analysis. I believe that in practice there is always considerable delay in adjusting prices to a change in demand, and that this delay has a very special importance, because an acceleration or retardation of sales of any product tends to cause an increase or decrease in production *before* any change is made in the price to the consumer. We have here a disturbance of equilibrium independent of any change in prices, and therefore independent of the existence of windfall gain or loss or of any difference between investment and saving.

5 Thus the change of prices when it does occur is not by itself an adequate measure of the departure from equilibrium.

6 Numerical examples will make the point clearer. Suppose that consumers' income and consumers' outlay balance at £100 million a month, that the expenditure on consumption is £90 million, and that savings and investment therefore balance at £10 million a month.

Let the public start saving £15 million a month instead of £10 million. They spend only £85 million on consumption. On Mr Keynes's assumptions, the retail prices of consumption goods are forthwith reduced in just the proportion required to avoid the accumulation of any addition to stocks, that is to say, by one-eighteenth. The whole monthly output of consumption goods costing £90 million is sold for £85 million, and the producers sustain a windfall loss of £5 million a month.

In Mr Keynes's language the earnings of the community are still £100 million, although they sell their output for £95 million only, and their savings are £15 million, for the producers who suffer the windfall loss are deemed to 'save' the £5 million of their 'earnings' which they do not receive.

If, on the contrary, we assume that in the first instance the prices of consumption goods remain unchanged, the diminution of consumers' purchases by £5 million will be reflected in an accumulation of unsold stocks at the rate of £5 million a month. In that case there would be no divergence between savings and investment and no windfall loss. Mr Keynes's formula would record no disturbance of equilibrium.

Undoubtedly traders would not be willing to accumulate unsold stocks for long. But suppose that the next step is not to reduce retail prices, but to curtail orders to producers, so that the output of consumption goods is reduced by one-eighteenth. The output of consumption goods is reduced from £90 million to £85 million and earnings are reduced from £100 million to £95 million but there is still no divergence between investment and savings, and still no windfall loss. If savings continue unchanged at £15 million a month, the expenditure on consumption is reduced to £80 million a month, and the accumulation of unsold stocks still goes on.

Eventually, it is obvious, some reduction would be made in retail prices. But meanwhile there might have occurred a heavy curtailment of output. And incidentally it may be pointed out that this progressive contraction in the consumers' income could not fail to cause some falling off of savings.

⁷ Mr Keynes's formula only takes account of the reduction of prices in relation to costs, and does not recognise the possibility of a reduction of output being caused directly by a contraction of demand without an intervening fall of price.

⁸ The foregoing example starts from increased saving. Very similar results would follow from a contraction of credit, which causes a diminution of investment. Mr Keynes examines the effects of a rise in 'the interest rates effective in the market for the borrowing and lending of money for short periods' (which for convenience he calls 'bank rate') on pages 200–9 [vol. v, pp. 178–87]. He argues that 'the initial consequence of a higher bank rate will be a fall in the price of capital goods and therefore in P', the price level of new investment goods' (p. 203) [vol. v, p. 183]. The fall in price will be *followed* 'by a fall in the output of such goods' (p. 205) [vol. v, p. 184]. The decline in investment will cause a fall in the price of consumption goods, 'since there will be a reduction in the incomes of the producers of investment goods available for the purchase of liquid consumption goods'.

⁹⁺ ¹⁰ The sequence here assumed is *first* a fall of prices and *then* a contraction of output. *With that assumption* the unemployment inevitably appears as consequential upon the excess of saving over investment, for the excess of saving over investment is merely the fall of prices (relative to costs) under another name.

¹¹ Thus there may be a stage at which consumers' income and outlay have been reduced to £95 million a month, and output has been reduced in the same proportion, without any reduction in the price level. There would then be no windfall loss, and savings and investment would balance. No doubt some fall of prices would begin soon. But the fall of prices and the reduction of earnings are effects of a common cause. It may be true that the reduction of wages lags behind the fall of prices, and if so there occurs what Mr Keynes calls a windfall loss. But the windfall loss is no *adequate* measure of the departure from equilibrium. The greater the contraction of output, the less is the windfall loss.

12 Here [vol. v, pp. 235–7] Mr Keynes recognises the dual effect of 'greater ease of borrowing', an increase of output concurrent with the rise of prices and therefore not consequent upon it. But he still maintains that there is a direct effect of the rate of interest on the prices of capital goods, to which a part of the increase of production is attributable (as to this see below). And he does not bring out the fact that the increased productive activity directly due to increased borrowing facilities will make the rise of prices less than it otherwise would be.

13 Thus the discrepancy between investment and saving is not the *cause* of the divergence between prices and costs, it *is* the divergence between prices and costs. The cause of the divergence (in so far as it is monetary) is to be found in a change in demand, i.e. in the consumers' outlay.

14 If retail prices were immediately and exactly adjusted to a change in demand, there would be no change in the volume of sales. Where a trade is so organised that there is a complete differentiation of function between retailers and producers, the retailers' orders to the wholesale dealers and producers would then be precisely what they were before, and there would be no inducement for the producers to modify their prices at all. There must be *some* shrinkage of orders to bring about any reduction in wholesale prices, and the retailers cannot afford to reduce the price asked from the consumer till the wholesale price has come down. First there is a falling off of sales, then a reduction in the retailers' orders to the wholesale dealers, then a reduction of output, then a reduction of the price asked by the producer and only then a reduction of the retail price. If it were possible for producers, by cutting prices, immediately to find a price at which the demand will absorb all their output, they might be expected to do so. But there are several reasons why this cannot be done. Where retailing and producing are separate, the producer has no means of knowing how much of any price concession that he may make will be passed on to the consumer. For all he knows, the retailer may keep his price unchanged, so that the producers' concession will be a free gift to the retailer and will do nothing to stimulate demand. And this is true at each stage of manufacture. The further removed any process is from the delivery of the final product to the consumer, the smaller is the proportion of the price to the price of the final product, and the smaller is the effect of any price concession (if passed on) upon the consumers' demand. The greater the number of intervening processes and transactions, the greater the chance of the price concession being intercepted and not passed on to the consumer at all.

15 On the other hand if the wholesale price level *rises* (retail prices being unchanged) incomes of producers and wholesale dealers increase, and the retailers' sales will increase, and there is a presumption that the increase of

output will lag behind the increase of sales. There will then be an actual windfall *loss*.

[16] When a windfall loss is causing a contraction of output, there should be a rise of prices concurrently with an increase of unemployment. I know of no instance where this has ever been recorded (apart from purely seasonal movements).

[17] But whatever the best expression may be, the kind of outlay which results in the creation of an asset has a special importance in monetary theory, because it is the kind of outlay which may be financed by the creation of bank credit. 'It is uncommon for a borrower to borrow, not for any business or investment purpose, but to meet his personal expenditure on consumption; at any rate bank loans of this kind are so small a proportion of the whole that we can in general neglect them' (p. 266) [vol. v, p. 238]. It is therefore approximately true that bank credit is created for purposes of investment. Greater or less ease of borrowing affects the consumers' income and outlay, because it affects investment, and through investment affects the creation of bank credit. I have already referred to Mr Keynes's theory (p. 204) [vol. v, p. 183] that the direct effect is on the price level of capital goods, and the modified view (pp. 263–4) [vol. v, pp. 235–6] that there is concurrently a direct effect on output also.

[18] Mr Keynes quotes me as arguing that bank rate affects primarily the dealers who hold stocks of finished goods with borrowed money (pp. 193–6) [vol. v, pp. 172–5], and by way of answer relies on Tooke's 'classical refutation' of this theory. But the passage quoted from Tooke applies to 'persons who, upon imperfect information and upon insufficient grounds, or with too sanguine a view of contingencies in their favour, speculate improvidently'. Of these he says 'it is not the mere facility of borrowing or the difference between being able to discount at 3 or at 6 per cent that supplies the *motive* for purchasing or even for selling. Few persons of the description here mentioned ever speculate but upon the confident expectation of an advance of price of at least 10 per cent.' This quotation from Tooke is entirely beside the point. My argument relates not to speculators (especially not to ignorant and improvident speculators) but to regular dealers or merchants. Of the narrowness of their margins we have statistical proof. The following statistics [on p. 155], compiled by the Harvard Bureau of Business Research, are quoted in Professor M. T. Copeland's *Principles of Merchandising*. British and American income tax statistics show a somewhat higher percentage of net profit to turnover (more like 2 or 3 per cent). Possibly this is due to the inclusion of speculative gains obtained by a different type of business from those here referred to.

It seems obvious that dealers who are making a net profit of from ½ to

	Percentage of turnover		
	Gross profit	Net profit	Interest paid
Wholesale grocery			
Sales less than $500,000	11·4	0·4	1·7
Sales $500,000 to $1 million	11·5	0·5	1·7
Sales $1 million to $2 million	11·7	0·6	1·7
Sales $2 million and over	12·1	0·6	1·5
Wholesale drug business			
Under $1 million	17·2	0·7	2·4
Over $1 million	17·2	1·1	1·9
Wholesale dry goods	17·6	1·0	2·8
Wholesale automotive equipment	24·9	1·5	2·0

$1\frac{1}{2}$ per cent on their turnover, and whose interest charges amount to from $1\frac{1}{2}$ to $2\frac{3}{4}$ per cent of turnover, would be sensitive to any considerable movement in the rate of interest.

It is true that a trifling reduction in their buying prices for the goods would offset any extra charge that a high rate of interest would place upon them. But in practice the way dealers start to lower their buying prices is by restricting their purchases. And the same situation which leads them to delay purchases leads them to accelerate sales, so that the wholesale selling price tends to fall as fast as the wholesale buying price.

The same situation arises in a greater or less degree with every trader who is holding marketable assets with borrowed money. If movements in the short-term rate of interest affect the long-term rate, that is mainly because there are people carrying marketable securities with borrowed money. The stockjobber is more reluctant to extend his holding of securities if he has to pay a high rate on bank advances to carry the excess.

On the other hand where bank advances are required for working capital, i.e. for the expenses of manufacture and transport, the corresponding assets cannot be increased or decreased at will by purchase or sale in the market. The actual accrued expenses of manufacture at any time are dictated by the conditions of the business and the amount of goods in course of production. The only parts of the working capital that can easily be varied are the stocks on the one hand of materials and intermediate products, and on the other of the manufacturer's completed product. So far as these stocks are concerned, the manufacturer is really discharging the functions of a merchant and shows a merchant's sensitiveness to credit conditions. But as to the rest of his working capital he is almost entirely insensitive; the greater or less charges for bank advances are of no moment in comparison with the paramount need to keep his works employed. If he can get sufficient orders to do so, he will not refuse them on account of interest charges. On the other hand, when he cannot get sufficient orders (or effect sufficient sales to the consumer), he has the alternative of manufacturing for stock. And here the terms for bank advances will become a serious factor in his calculations. At that stage, however, other considerations enter in. The shortage of orders or of sales is itself a symptom threatening a fall of price. The banker when he charges more for advances is also probably less willing to lend. Altogether manufacturing for stock is not a very attractive expedient at a time of flagging demand.

The borrower who holds goods ready for sale and the borrower who holds marketable securities have this in common: that each can reduce his indebtedness by retarding his purchases and by accelerating his sales. But there is a difference between them. When the dealer in goods seeks to restrict his purchases, the producers of the goods immediately feel the effect in diminished orders, whereas when the dealer in securities seeks to restrict his purchases, the immediate effect is felt not by the producers of capital goods but by the promoters of capital enterprises. It is only when the promoters have responded by curtailing, withholding or postponing new issues that the producers begin to experience any diminution of orders for capital goods at all.

Now the process of discouraging new issues by raising the rate of interest is a slow one. The issue when actually made is the fruit of a long period of planning and negotiating. After a certain stage is reached, postponement (except for a short time, a matter of weeks) is likely to be a serious sacrifice.

It is, I think, a mistake to say, as Mr Keynes does in a passage quoted above, that the value of capital goods to a purchaser depends on the capitalised present value of their prospective yield at the prevailing rate of interest. For every project for capital outlay includes some expectation of profit (in the ordinary sense of net gain, not a windfall profit) over and above the yield of interest. Such a project is intended to take advantage of an opportunity for creating or extending the goodwill of a business. The promoter sees a prospect of selling the output that he anticipates.

[19] The market rate of interest does not represent the yield of a 'marginal' project *as a whole*. It represents rather the yield of the *marginal piece of equipment* included in the project. If the market rate of interest is 5 per cent, then anyone who is providing the capital for a manufacturing concern will aim at including any piece of plant of which the estimated labour-saving power (after allowing for depreciation etc.) exceeds 5 per cent of its first cost, but none of which the labour-saving power is less. It is through these decisions as to whether it is or is not worth while to install a particular kind of plant that the rate of interest ultimately equalises the demand for capital

with the supply, or in other words capital outlay with savings (in the ordinarily accepted sense).

20 It may be asked, then, how the investment market can possibly accomplish its task of equalising capital outlay with investible funds over a short period. I think the answer is to be found in the attitude of the market towards its holding of securities on the one hand and its indebtedness on the other. Whenever the market is called upon to absorb new issues in excess of the funds received from investors it suffers a net outflow of money and its indebtedness is increased. The reluctance of dealers to buy and their anxiety to sell are then reflected in a general reduction of prices of securities. But this is not the only effect. The dealers can also take steps specifically to discourage new issues. Some they may flatly refuse. Others they may accept at a high rate of commission and a low issue price, that is to say an issue price which is low even in comparison with the low prices prevailing in the market. Mr Keynes has called attention to these methods of restricting new issues (p. 204) [vol. V, p. 182], but I should say that they are far more resorted to on those occasions when the market is overburdened with unsold securities, than when the only source of trouble is a rise in the rate of short-term interest.

21 Thereupon there begins a shrinkage in the consumers' income in proportion to the decline of production, and the shrinkage of consumers' outlay (i.e. of demand) reinforces the decline of production. The vicious circle of deflation begins. It should be kept in mind that this process occurs whatever may have been the cause of the original decline in productivity. Even if that were exclusively in the production of capital goods, the ensuing shrinkage of the consumers' outlay would affect all classes of goods. Therefore the question whether it is upon investment in capital goods or in goods of all kinds that the credit contraction first takes effect is not so important as appears.

22 Provided it be understood that investment is not confined to the outlay on capital goods, it is, I think, true to say that credit contraction works by discouraging investment, and credit expansion by encouraging it. And the idea of investment is valuable in monetary theory in that an acceleration or retardation of investment causes an increase or decrease of the consumers' income whether the initiating cause be a credit movement, a change in the supply of money or a change in velocity. A 'change in investment' conveniently comprehends these ideas under a single phrase.

23 The third condition [current receipts to traders increased] means that the consumers' outlay exceeds the consumers' income, and therefore the *consumers* are drawing upon their balances. So that the conditions are really two, either there must be somewhere balances that can be spared, or balances

must be reinforced by borrowing, i.e., by a creation of bank credit. In fact the consumers' income can only be supplemented from balances to the extent that surplus balances are available or can be provided.

On the other hand as soon as the consumers' income is thus supplemented, balances are increased. In the first instance the money appears in consumers' balances, then, as consumers' outlay increases, it is passed on into traders' balances. The net amount of credit that has to be created is only the difference between what the traders pay out and what they receive from increased sales.

The initial increase in the consumers' income represents additional investment, but the increased consumers' outlay will include an increased expenditure on consumption goods, so that the net increase in investment will be something less. But it is still true that the gross amount of the traders' payments from their balances is itself all for investment.

A similar description would apply, *mutatis mutandis*, to the case where traders reduce consumers' income by paying out less money. Here either balances increase or bank credit is extinguished, the consumers' outlay falls off, and the net reduction of investment is somewhat less than the reduction in the consumers' income.

[24] When Mr Keynes says that 'in the case of saving the effect of a change in the rate of interest is direct and primary and needs no special explanation', he qualifies this statement by adding that the effect 'may often be quantitatively small in practice, especially over the short period' (p. 201) [vol. v, p. 180]. Personally I should go further and say that it is negligible, and that over a long period too it is likely to be unimportant and may even quite possibly be negative.

In my opinion the principal factor determining the amount of savings out of the consumers' outlay is the magnitude of certain classes of incomes out of which savings are chiefly made, incomes and savings being here taken in their ordinary sense. These incomes are the large and precarious incomes, that is to say, the net gain of the more important traders and in a lesser degree of the fee-paid professional men. *Small* incomes, whether from salaries and wages or from trade and professions, are not a very important source of savings, nor are *secure* incomes from rent and interest (except when they are so large that the recipients hardly know how to spend them).

[25] In reality this view of the manner in which savings are determined approximates to that of Mr Keynes. For the principal cause affecting the net gains of traders viewed as a whole is usually a rise or fall of the price level, not offset by any equivalent rise or fall of costs. By treating a windfall gain or loss arising in this way as capital and not as income, he makes the normal behaviour of the trader (or at any rate that which preserves the total

of 'savings' unchanged) to be a maintenance of his expenditure on consumption unaffected by such fluctuations in his net gains as arise from variations in the selling price of his products. A man whose net gains under monetary equilibrium are £5,000 a year, and who devotes £2,000 to his personal outlay, saves £3,000. If his net gains are increased by a windfall profit to £8,000, Mr Keynes regards the additional £3,000 as capital, and treats him as still saving only £3,000 if his personal outlay remains at £2,000. Similarly if his net gains are reduced by a windfall loss to £2,000 and he uses up the whole in personal outlay, Mr Keynes regards him as still saving £3,000.

26 Thereupon comes into play the equalising function of the investment market as an intermediary between savings and new issues.

27 Now the increase of saving will directly diminish the expenditure on consumption.

28 (It seems quite clear from the context that the word 'savings' is used here [vol. v, pp. 31–2] in its ordinary sense and not in the special sense given to it by Mr Keynes. That is to say, savings deposits may be accumulated out of windfall gains as well as out of 'earnings'.)

29 In my opinion this is erroneous. At least two of the five kinds of deposits mentioned above [and in vol. v, pp. 223–4] are likely to be subject occasionally to rapid changes. That would apply to the deposits 'attracted by the rate of interest' which might be quickly placed in securities if the rate of interest on deposit fell, and also to deposits awaiting an opportunity of being employed in the depositors' business. These latter are a very important class. It is a not uncommon practice for industrial concerns (less often for commercial concerns) so to arrange their finances that they never have to borrow from a bank. That is to say, they possess sufficient share capital and long-term loan capital to meet their maximum need for working capital. The result is that at any time when their working capital actively employed is below the maximum they have an idle cash balance, which may be large. When there is a general slackness of trade and a shrinkage of working capital, the aggregate of these balances may show a very marked rise. Deposits arising in this way are, as I understand, classed by Mr Keynes as savings deposits. Clearly they are 'not required for the purpose of current payments' (p. 36) [vol. v, p. 32].

30 They [the deposits at the end of the previous note] arise from the unwillingness of traders to buy (or produce) commodities; and they represent a 'bear' position closely analogous to that of the 'bear' investors who are unwilling to buy securities, and to whom Mr Keynes attributes the main part of the variation in savings deposits.

31 The circumstances 'which lead entrepreneurs to believe that certain

new investments will be profitable' may be classed among 'changes due to investment factors' as examples of 'a change in the natural rate occasioned by a change in the attractiveness of investment or in that of saving', quoted above. But this can hardly be said of the 'reaction stimulated by cheap money from a previous period of under-investment'. That does not arise from a change in the *natural* rate, but belongs to another class of the changes due to investment factors, 'a change in the market rate resulting from altered conditions in the loan market due to a change in monetary factors'.

32 First consider the producers working at a loss, who cease production when prices fall to normal. Does this mean that there will then be more than the normal proportion of capital and labour unemployed?

33 Secondly it is a mistake to suppose that a bear position is likely to appear among investors merely because business has become less lucrative. The bear position, the accumulation of idle money by intending investors, occurs when the investors form a less favourable opinion of the value of securities than the stockjobbers. That difference of opinion may occur at any time, and is not specially characteristic of a time of depression.

34 The investment market has no difficulty in dealing with such changes, and discharging its essential function of equalising the sales of securities to investors with the purchases of new issues from promoters. There is therefore no reason to expect that a divergence of the market rate of interest from the natural rate will ever be caused by them.

35 The prominence assigned by Mr Keynes to the 'production period' in his theory of the credit cycle depends upon the assumption of an isolated impulse.

36 This is a very desirable and proper distinction. But it does not mean that the stocks which are part of working capital are an irreducible minimum which cannot be drawn upon in any circumstances. On the contrary their essential purpose is to preserve 'continuity of production' and when needed for that purpose they are drawn upon.

37 The natural rate [of interest] is that which would cause investment and savings to be equal or in other words prices to be equal to costs. A deterrent bank rate is one which exceeds the natural rate. But when there is a deterrent rate, the price level begins to fall, and the prospect of falling prices is *itself a deterrent* on investment. Under these conditions the natural rate of interest does not secure equilibrium; the fall of prices, once started, goes on of its own momentum, and the deterrent effect upon investment can only be eliminated by the establishment of a rate *below* the natural rate. Even a rate below the natural rate, but *not sufficiently* below, will be deterrent. Thus the continuance of a deterrent bank rate does not mean the continuance of a rate above the natural rate.

38 The duration of the entire phase from the beginning of revival depended upon the progress of the gold reserves. This was really an *international* matter. Mr Keynes in my opinion gives insufficient prominence to the international aspects of the credit cycle.

39 The 'foreign balance' of a country Mr Keynes defines to be 'the balance of trade on *income* account', and the 'foreign lending' to be 'the unfavourable balance of transactions on *capital* account, i.e. the excess of the amount of our own money put at the disposal of foreigners through the net purchase by our nationals of investments situated abroad, over the corresponding amount expended by foreigners on the purchase of our investments situated at home' (pp. 131–2) [vol. v, pp. 118–19]. (It is not quite clear what is meant by 'investments' in this passage. Investment as Mr Keynes defines it is strictly confined to an increment of capital, i.e. actual goods. It is a portion of *output*. Are investments abroad to include a loan to a foreign government to meet a budget deficit and purchases of shares and other rights representing capitalised goodwill, economic rent or monopoly gains, elements of value which can never have been a part of output?)

40 Upon the position taken in these extracts I have several criticisms to make. The subject falls into two parts, (*a*) the processes affecting the foreign balance and (*b*) those affecting foreign lending.

(*a*) The amount of the foreign balance, Mr Keynes says, depends on the relative price levels at home and abroad of the goods and services which enter into international trade.

41 The decrease of purchases will be principally a decrease of imports, but there will also be a decrease of purchases of home-produced foreign trade products. The producers will endeavour to make good the loss of sales by turning to the export markets, and they may make some price concessions, but the effect, if any, on world prices is likely to be small. On the whole such price reductions as occur in foreign trade products will be small, and will tend to affect each market in which they occur *as a whole*, rather than to produce a change in relative price levels of different countries. Therefore the changes of price level that occur in the process of securing international equilibrium are mainly changes of internal price levels relative to external. Short-period equilibrium is attained by reducing or increasing consumers' income and outlay as the case may require, and so reducing or increasing the demand for foreign trade products (and particularly for imports). On the other hand *ultimate* equilibrium requires the adjustment of wages to the internal price level, and this when it occurs gives rise to a windfall gain or loss to the producers of foreign trade products, and therefore in the long run to increased or reduced productive power being applied to those products.

⁴² It is the function of the investment market to equalise capital outlay and savings (in the usual sense).

⁴³ Take the case where bank rate is lowered, and consider first the effect on long-term investment. In order that foreign lending may increase, there must be either (*a*) increased investible funds available, or (*b*) diminished investment at home or (*c*) an application to external investment of newly created bank credit. A credit expansion will, no doubt, bring about an increase in investible funds, because it will increase the consumers' income and particularly the traders' net gains. But this will only occur after an interval. And investment at home will not be diminishing but increasing, for the increase in the consumers' income and outlay will make business more profitable and will offer opportunities for extension.

⁴⁴ The increase in foreign lending really depends on the creation of bank credit in the form of bank advances for the acquisition of foreign investments.

⁴⁵ And this brings me to the other side of the question, the movement of funds seeking temporary investment. If the short-term rate of interest in any country is lower than abroad, there will be a tendency for bankers, and others with balances available for temporary investment, to place them in bills on foreign countries or on deposit abroad. But investment of this character involves an exchange risk, and in general the charge for forward exchange is at or near the level at which it counteracts the gain in interest. (No one has expounded this part of the theory of forward exchange so well as Mr Keynes.) That is not invariably so. It often happens in fact that the charge for forward exchange is less than the difference of interest so that some profit is to be made by the transfer of funds. That means either that lenders are not forthcoming to take advantage of the profit, or that there are speculators in exchange whose dealings in forward exchange more or less offset the demand of the lenders.

⁴⁶ With regard to the former alternative, it is of course obvious that the funds available for temporary investment abroad will not be unlimited. They will consist mainly (*a*) of balances forming part of traders' working capital and not immediately required in their business, and (*b*) of the assets of the banks themselves. It will only be worth while for the bigger traders to invest such balances abroad. It will not be worth while for the small man to establish relations with foreign banks or branches, and to keep himself informed about conditions abroad and the profit on small transactions would be eaten up by commissions and expenses. And even among the big men only those who can foresee that the money will not be required for their own businesses for a definite period (a month or more) will place it abroad.

⁴⁷ It should also be borne in mind that when depositors transfer funds

162

abroad the bankers who lose the deposits have to effect a corresponding contraction of their assets, and are the less able to make room for their own foreign assets.

48 There is, however, one form of international short-term investment which avoids these obstacles, and that is the acceptance on behalf of a foreign client. Low discount rates at any centre stimulate this business in competition with other centres. And as the credit instruments to which it gives rise are not drawn in foreign currencies, the banks which purchase them suffer no disturbance of their proportion of liquid assets. The character of an external investment is given to the transaction by the client's obligation to remit the means of paying the bill on maturity.

49 The migration of balances is likely to be concentrated into a short time. The prospect of profit offered by the gain of interest *minus* the charge for forward exchange will be sufficient to induce the owners of certain balances, which we may call 'susceptible' to transfer them. There is no reason why all the susceptible balances should not be transferred *at once*; presumably there is nothing to be gained by delay, and a week or two will allow time for depositors to give notice and for bankers to sell bills. If the movement is large the exchanges will reach the gold export point; then when all the susceptible balances have been transferred the exchanges will recover and a batch of less susceptible balances will seek transfer. The spot rates of exchange will gradually become more and more favourable and approach closer to the forward rates, till at last the forward discount on foreign currencies vanishes altogether. In other words, by the time all balances have been transferred, even those so reluctant that they will only move when they can guard themselves against any loss by exchange and still secure the whole gain of interest, there will no longer be any pressure on the forward exchange market at all. This process can be hastened by any increase of speculative forward purchases of foreign currencies or retarded by a decrease. It may likewise be modified by a change in the difference of short-term interest. But whether hastened or retarded it is essentially a *transitory* phase.

50 It is therefore a grave mistake to rely upon attracting foreign balances by means of a high bank rate as a feature of monetary policy, except as a purely temporary expedient. And it is also a mistake, when the circumstances require cheap money, to keep bank rate up for fear of an outflow of balances. An inflow of balances supports the exchanges and an outflow depresses them, but, once the movement is completed, the gain of balances is a source of weakness, the loss is a source of strength. The one tends to make the country a short-term debtor, the other to make it a short-term creditor. If a country is a short-term creditor, any adverse movement of the exchanges is likely to

lead to a recall of foreign credits; they, in fact, play the part of an additional gold reserve. Short-term foreign indebtedness is the equivalent of a negative gold reserve.

From R. G. HAWTREY, *6 December 1930*

Dear Maynard,

I find your memorandum very helpful towards understanding the issues between us. You will not mind if I let you have some further preliminary remarks in writing upon it, though I am afraid you have already received an excessive amount of written material from me.

(1) With regard to your interpretation of my theory (pages 1–3 of your memorandum)[1] I do not think I have ever suggested that your C_2, money 'lent direct to traders and speculators' by private individuals out of income, is to be excluded from the consumers' outlay. So long as (1) it is provided out of income, and (2) it is not placed 'on deposit' but is lent to some one other than a bank, I should treat it as an investment. Any subsequent use made of the money when the loan matures or is called up is a disposal of capital; not being out of income it is not again part of the consumers' outlay. But I do not think temporary loans made out of the consumers' income are an important matter. Most of the temporary loans from others than banks are made by industrial or commercial concerns out of their capital assets.

If C_2 drops out altogether (or rather is included in H_2 as a subsidiary part of C_1), you get $H_1 = H_2 + C_3$. The difference between consumers' income and outlay over any period is equal to the change in consumers' balances (cf. *Currency and Credit*, pages 46–7, 52, 53, 61). But you must not suppose that I rank this as a fundamental equation and a rival or alternative to your own. The equations underlying my theory you can see in *Currency and Credit*, pages 60–63, though as there formulated they do not cover all the ground by any means.

(2) I am afraid I misled you, with the use of the term 'traders' turnover' in my memorandum on consumers' outlay. I use traders' turnover to include all the receipts and disbursements of traders (producers, dealers in goods and securities, etc.), and what I meant when I referred to it was that outlay by anyone, even though not a trader, on purchase with a view to sale or to replacement of an asset sold is to be classed as part of traders' turnover. Traders' turnover is substantially equivalent to what you call the total volume of cash transactions (B on page 234 of volume I [vol. V, p. 209], and page 23 of volume II [vol. VI, p. 19]). The purchases and sales of securities and goods by individuals other than traders are a very small part of it.

[1] Above, pp. 139–41.

(3) I think an important part of the difference between us relates to the passages from which you dissent on pages 3–5 of my comments[1]. I should like to see how you arrive at the price level of investment goods in the cases where there is a decrease in working capital and liquid capital. One fault I find with your theory is that it is rigidly confined to *actual* movements of the price level, and your fundamental equations do not record tendencies which are influencing the situation before any actual price quotations are affected. The fact that the equations are based on prices of finished goods, and do not reflect adequately (and sometimes do not reflect at all) changes in the more sensitive prices of materials and intermediate products, aggravates this fault.

(4) Your answer to my arguments (page 7)[2] about a reduction or increase of stocks caused by an acceleration or retardation of sales, when prices are not adjusted to demand, is that 'what matters is the anticipated price fall at the end of the production period, not the actual price fall to date'. But till there is an *actual* price fall there is no excess of saving over investment. Consequently the excess of saving over investment cannot be the cause of the reduction of output by the entrepreneurs. The cause is to be found in the accumulating stocks which lead them to anticipate a future price fall.

And my argument goes further than that. I think you are mistaken in assuming, at any rate so far as manufacturing industry is concerned, that output is determined by anticipations of price and of profit. Output is primarily determined by the current volume of sales to the consumer. Manufacturers do not in general produce for stock to any great extent. Where there is a fully developed wholesale trade, they produce in response to orders given by the wholesalers, and the wholesalers base their orders on the retail demand. It may happen that the wholesalers' function has been absorbed on the one side by the manufacturers or on the other side by large-scale retailers. In either case output will be regulated mainly with reference to retail demand. Speculative anticipations of price movements are in general due either to conditions of supply (an alternative which for present purposes can be left out of account) or to inferences from changes already felt in consumers' demand.

A manufacturer restricts output, not because he believes that prices are about to fall, but because he cannot secure sufficient sales at the existing price of his product. He will try to get additional orders by quoting lower prices. But this is only done tentatively and gradually. And it is the price *to the consumer* that determines the ultimate volume of sales, so that the manufacturers' price concessions will not produce any appreciable effect till the retailers have passed it on.

[1] Above, pp. 141, 150.   [2] Above, pp. 141–2.

(5) The foregoing is the argument given in greater detail on pages 15–17 of my comments. It is not merely that 'the effect on prices of a change in fixed and working investment relatively to savings is apt to be temporarily mitigated and delayed by an opposite change in liquid investment' (page 11 of your memorandum), but that the *sequence* of events is different from that which your theory assumes. Nevertheless in this sentence I think I can see a real narrowing of the distance between us.

I say (page 14) that 'the discrepancy between investment and saving is not the *cause* of the divergence between prices and costs, it *is* the divergence between prices and costs'. But that does not apply to a discrepancy between 'fixed and working investment' and saving. That may occur *before* there is any divergence between prices and costs, and, if it does, there arises 'an opposite change in liquid investment'. Saving under those conditions is equal to the excess of consumers' income over consumption expenditure. Consumers' income is equal to output of consumption goods, *plus* fixed and working investment. If saving differs from fixed and working investment, consumption expenditure differs by the same amount from output of consumption goods. This difference between the output of consumption goods and the expenditure upon them is equal to the change in stocks of consumption goods.[1]

The change in stocks or in 'liquid investment' is a symptom of a loss of equilibrium. It will tend to cause a change in the price level, but it will also tend directly to cause a change in productive activity. And its efficacy in one direction will be at the expense of its efficacy in the other. In so far as there is a change in productive activity, the pressure towards a change in the price level will be diminished; in so far as there is a change in the price level the pressure towards a change in productive activity will be diminished.

In your comment upon my page 8 (pages 5–8 of your memorandum)[2] you say that, in the circumstances assumed, 'the accumulation of stocks would be a symptom of the factor on which I lay so much stress, namely a tendency of savings to increase relatively to fixed investment which is bound, if it continues, to produce a disequilibrium of prices'. I think you mean by 'fixed investment' in this passage the same thing that on page 11 you call 'fixed and working investment'. If so there is not a very wide gap between us here. You go on to indicate 'a normal order of events', starting with (1) a decline in fixed investment relative to saving, and thereafter (2) a fall of prices and an addition to stocks, followed by (3) a fall of output.

If you could agree (1) that the decline in fixed investment *may* be accompanied by no immediate fall in the prices of capital goods, (2) that the

---

[1] I have simplified this statement by disregarding the changes in stocks of intermediate products and materials.   [2] Above pp. 142–4.

addition to stocks causes a fall of output independently of the fall of prices, and (3) that the addition to stocks (or in other words insufficient sales at retail) is in general the cause of the fall of prices, I think we should be at one so far as this example is concerned.

I do not rule out an immediate fall of prices from the very beginning as an impossibility, though I think in practice it is almost invariably only *after* the market has shown a decline in sales that prices are lowered. (Prices might even have an upward momentum sufficient to keep them *rising* for a short time after demand has in reality begun to shrink.)

(6) The most important part of the difference between us is as to the causation of unemployment. By a 'departure from equilibrium' you mean a departure from 'equilibrium of prices and costs'. I include in the departure from equilibrium a drop in productive activity below normal. Throughout your references to output and employment in the *Treatise* you recognise *no* cause of unemployment except a windfall loss, actual or prospective. You exclude altogether the possibility of a decline of employment caused directly by a decline of sales.

You may say that a decline of sales and a prospective fall of prices are one and the same thing. But that is not so. It takes time for traders to decide whether a decline of sales does or does not justify a fall of price. Even when they think it does not, dealers will still restrict their orders to manufacturers *pari passu* with the decline in sales. If they anticipate a fall of price, they will restrict their orders *below* the volume of sales.

On the other hand when a *manufacturer* anticipates a fall in the price of his product, the effect, so far as his action is influenced at all, will be in the direction of *hastening* his sales, and therefore for the time being increasing productive activity. And if manufacturers in general anticipate a greater fall than dealers in general this is likely to occur. For manufacturers will make concessions on the prices they ask, and dealers will take advantage of the concessions to increase their purchases. Manufacturers will be producing more because they expect a fall of prices, and dealers will be buying more because they expect a rise.

Thus it is the *dealers'* expectations that are decisive. In the case where no dealer, wholesale or retail, intervenes between manufacturer and consumer an expectation of a fall of price will lead to a restriction of output, i.e. the dealers' standpoint will predominate in one who combines the functions of dealer and producer.

Agriculture is different from manufacturing. The agricultural producer does determine his course of action by a forecast of the future market price. That is so because he does not as a rule produce in response to an order or a forward contract.

PREPARATION

In practice of course it is likely that an expectation of a fall of prices on the part of dealers will follow hard on the heels of a shrinkage of sales, so that there will be little visible difference between your theory and mine. But, in spite of what you say in chapter 11, section v, your fundamental equation takes *no* account of a prospective fall of prices.

You try to link up the forecast of prices with the fundamental equation by saying that entrepreneurs 'forecast the relationship between saving and investment in its effect on the demand for their product'. But this does not represent what is in their minds. What each tries to forecast is the demand for his own product. Even if he is fully acquainted with your fundamental equations, he still must recognise that the demand for his product is affected by other factors than a difference between saving and investment. Apart from causes affecting his own product separately from others (which are not in point), he may anticipate changes in demand owing to income inflation or deflation.

But I do not think that traders' expectations are likely to be very much affected by the probable future monetary or credit situation. They are far more likely to judge by the day to day movements in the sales of their own products. Those day to day movements may be affected by a difference between saving and 'fixed and working investment', for that means a change in 'liquid investment'. And *expectations* of a change in liquid investment may also affect the situation (though such expectations in any one market will in general be confined to stocks of the products dealt in in the market). But liquid investment plays no part in your fundamental equations. Throughout the Treatise you refer to the difference between saving and 'investment', never to the difference between saving and 'fixed and working investment'. That is what makes your theory so rigid. It is because you leave changes in liquid investment on one side that your formula cannot take account of prospective changes of price, though you want to make it do so.

My theory does not require either *large* changes in stocks of commodities or *prolonged* intervals of unchanged prices in face of a changed volume of sales. The process may come about either quickly or slowly. My point is that the *first* result of a change in demand is a reaction upon sales, stocks and output, and only *afterwards* are prices affected. The interval may be a week or several months. Moreover the change in demand, if brought about by monetary causes or by credit regulation, is *gradual*. While it is in progress, there is a continuous effect upon sales, stocks and output, and a corresponding effect on prices which is nearly always lagging behind.

You lay stress on the unwillingness of traders to vary the amount of their stocks to any great extent. I quite agree. It is this sensitiveness of stocks that leads to changes in the volume of sales affecting output so promptly.

I have confined myself in this letter to the main theoretical questions that we shall have to consider. Other points in your memorandum I leave till we meet.

Yours ever,

R. G. HAWTREY

The written discussion surrounding the *Treatise*, at this preliminary stage, between the two men concluded with an exchange in January and February 1931 over Hawtrey's Macmillan Committee paper on regulation of the international short-term capital market (reprinted as chapter VII of *The Art of Central Banking*).

To R. G. HAWTREY, *30 January 1931*

My dear Ralph,

I have been much interested in the document which you circulated to the Macmillan Committee on my proposals for the regulation of the international short-loan market.

You set out, in a way with which I quite agree, *one* of the contingencies I had in mind. But I had also in mind what is in a sense the converse of your case.

The case you consider is the one in which a country wants to make fundamental adjustments in its domestic costs and does not wish to be hampered in doing so by short-term attraction of gold tending in the opposite of the desired direction. But there are also two other classes of cases as follows:—

(1) It may be that a country believes that its costs are in long-period equilibrium with those of the rest of the world; but that something happens, perhaps of a political character, in the outside world to cause a disturbance in the short-term rates for money elsewhere. In this case the country in question would wish to adjust itself to the new short-loan position abroad without setting in motion any force tending towards a fundamental change in costs. For the expectation would be that the necessity for such an adjustment would have disappeared before such an adjustment could have taken place. My object was to prevent temporary upsets in the international short-loan

169

market from reacting on the domestic credit situation and the volume of credit available for new enterprise. Some of the gadgets which I suggested would, as you point out, be of no particular use in the contingency you considered, but might be of utility in such a case as the above.

(2) Another class of case which might arise and one much closer in substance to the one you considered would be a situation where a country, without wishing to bring about any fundamental change in costs, wished nevertheless to nip in the bud e.g. stock exchange speculation at home or to cure stock exchange depression without wishing to attract gold in the first case or to lose it in the second, which movement would be, as in your case, of a contrary tendency to that desired. I have in mind a situation such as existed in the United States in 1928 and the first part of 1929.

I think there is immense value in your conception of an inflow of foreign short-term funds as being the equivalent to a negative gold reserve. I am making a good use of this conception in what I am now drafting for the Macmillan Committee.

Yours ever,

J. M. KEYNES

From R. G. HAWTREY, *6 February 1931*

Dear Maynard,

It is quite true that my memorandum on international short-term investment does not cover the whole ground.

With regard to causes of the types you mention (political distrust, or stock exchange speculation) it is necessary, I think, to distinguish between the cases where inflation occurs or threatens and dear money is no more than a corrective, and the cases when there is no inflationary tendency or when the dear money is more than sufficient to counteract what inflationary tendency there is.

The former class of cases is covered by my memorandum, except that I have only dealt with the steps to be taken by the country which imposes the dear money. If it regulates the forward exchange market in the appropriate manner, the others can let things be. If it does not, they could make good the omission by acting in concert. Failing concerted action, one country would still be able to check any movement of money from itself, but some or all of its neighbours might then be exposed to the contagion of dear money and might suffer a contraction of credit. If so, there would be a disturbance of underlying equilibrium to be reckoned with. In practice, however, I should expect isolated action by the Bank of England to be effective. For example, if the Bank of England wanted to maintain cheap money in face of dear money in America, and sold dollars forward, the discount on forward dollars would probably spread to all other centres. These other centres would therefore not be led by the mere fact of dear money prevailing in America to adopt dear money themselves (though they might have other reasons for doing so).

I deliberately omitted from my memorandum the problems that might arise from different central banks working at cross purposes, and trying to peg forward dealings in the same pair of currencies at inconsistent rates, because I thought that in practice the whole business of regulating forward exchange would devolve on the Bank of England.

There remains the class of cases where a country resorts to dear money in the absence of any inflationary tendency, or perhaps I should say the class of cases where dear money causes a monetary contraction when there is no such contraction and no need for it elsewhere. Under those conditions I think an attempt on the part of other countries to prevent an outflow of money by selling exchange forward might be dangerous. The effect would be to make dear money all the more effective, and so to upset underlying equilibrium between the dear-money country and the rest of the world. If the dear-money country is important enough to affect world credit conditions materially, the result will be to impose a monetary contraction on the other countries. They gain nothing by avoiding dear money in the early stages.

I should say that the right treatment in such a case is to regard the dear-money country as an enemy of the human race and to deluge it with gold till it cries for mercy.

The fact that the conditions which call for dear money are transitory is not material. The cessation of the conditions and the removal of dear money will not correct so much monetary contraction as had actually occurred.

You suggest (Vol. II, p. 326) [*JMK*, vol. VI, pp. 291–2] that in 1928/9 we could have maintained cheap money concurrently with dear money in New York if there had been a sufficient discount on forward dollars. But the real danger of the situation at that time was the credit contraction set on foot in New York. The flow of balances thither and the accompanying flow of gold tended to mitigate the contraction. And in my view much of the harm was done by the return of gold to Europe in November and December 1929, which tended to defeat the efforts of the Federal Reserve System towards credit relaxation.

Yours ever,

R. G. HAWTREY

That Keynes found his discussions with Hawtrey valuable is evident from a letter written 18 months later when Hawtrey was preparing his comments on the *Treatise* for publication in *The Art of Central Banking*.

From a letter to R. G. HAWTREY, *1 June 1932*

I have now studied your revised pages, for which many thanks. As you anticipate I really have nothing material to say. You have taken amazing pains about my book. I only wish others had taken as much trouble. And I have no complaints of misrepresentation or misunderstanding. That does not mean, of course, that I agree with the significance and emphasis of everything, but it does mean that the sort of disputes which ought to be eliminated between rational and intelligent beings have been eliminated.

As I mentioned to you, I am working it out all over again. Whilst in some respects my new version will please you no more than the old, in some respects I shall, I think, be meeting some of your points. The main respect in which you may find the exposition easier is that I now put less fundamental reliance on my conception of savings and substitute for it the conception of expenditure. Also generally speaking I do not have to deal with absolute amounts of expenditure, but with increments and decrements of expenditure. This is, so to speak, the inverse of saving, since saving is the excess of income or earnings over expenditure; but since there are two senses in which income can be used, it is much preferable to use a term about which everyone agrees. The whole thing comes out just as conveniently in terms of expenditure. The main object of my treatment, however, will be to fill in the gap of which you complain that I do not follow up the actual genesis of change and am too content with a purely formal treatment of the first and final truisms.

Of the rest of the pre-publication *Treatise* discussions, almost nothing survives. What does remain are three notes from Professor O. M. W. Sprague of Harvard University, who was in London as economic adviser to the Bank of England, and Dr W. W. Stewart, his predecessor. In the case of Stewart, we have been unable to discover any further comments or correspondence beyond a note from Keynes to Alfred Harcourt saying that if the latter desired an advance idea of the book's contents he should see Stewart in New York.

From W. W. STEWART, *7 July 1930*

My dear Keynes,

Thanks very much for the additional proofs of your book. I am taking the chapters with me to read on the boat.

We enjoyed our talks and even the evidence before the [Macmillan] committee. Our predictions are more important than our logic—and I want to keep in touch with you as matters develop and as the outlook becomes clearer.

Yours,

WALTER W. STEWART

From O. M. W. SPRAGUE, *25 June 1930*

Dear Mr Keynes,

I have read your chapter 27 with a high agreement score but have noted a few minor points which seem to me in need of correction.

On page 55, line 7[1], as I understand the paragraph, 'not' should be inserted before 'in excess of the maximum' and so forth.

On page 64 you say that the American member banks are subject by law to a weekly average reserve requirement. In fact the law only prescribes the reserve ratio, leaving to the Federal Reserve Board the particular arrangements for putting the requirement into effect. At present the reserves are computed for cities in which there are Federal Reserve Banks or branches on a semi-weekly basis; in other reserve cities on a weekly basis; and in the case of banks outside reserve cities, for semi-monthly periods.

[1] The proofs to which Sprague refers have not survived.

On page 71 I think it would strengthen your argument if it were pointed out that most central banks are tending to withdraw from the commercial banking business which formerly, in the case of the Bank of England for example, was a means of acquiring deposits, as it still is in large measure outside of Paris for the Bank of France. Of course, the more recently established central banks have in general been excluded by law from commercial banking. There is an inverse sort of window-dressing of an interesting character in countries in which banks ordinarily borrow directly from central banks. They dislike to show rediscounts when statements of condition are published and so endeavour to clean up their borrowings.

I have always been prejudiced against definite legal reserve requirements and although the case which you present is very cogent it has not yet entirely freed me from my moorings: it is not impossible that I may be convinced in the course of time.

I enjoyed greatly our discussions at the Bank the other day and very much hope occasions may frequently bring us in contact in the future.

Yours very sincerely,
O. M. W. SPRAGUE

From O. M. W. SPRAGUE, *1 July 1930*

Dear Keynes,

I enclose the duplicate proof sheets of chapter 25 of your book and take the occasion to submit a few further notes and impressions, still reserving discussion of fundamentals.

I agree with you that the use of overdrafts seems calculated to reduce to a minimum the volume of business deposits but I doubt whether the practice subjects banks to a greater contingent liability than that to which banks are subject in the United States. Practically all business concerns there secure lines of credit from banks under which they may borrow at any time on promissory notes up to an agreed-upon amount. These lines are commonly revised once a year, although of course they may be changed at any time if a bank sees reason to modify its judgment regarding the borrower. Under this method of borrowing there is of course no such exact relationship between the amount borrowed and the amount used, as is the case under the overdraft system, but the contingent liability seems to me to be entirely similar.

I am inclined to attach far more importance to business profits or to business earnings than you seem to assign to them. Take, for example, the automobile industry in the United States. It has been almost entirely built up by means of retaining earnings in the various companies. Even though the development of this particular industry may have involved losses elsewhere, as, for example, among concerns engaged in the building of horse-drawn vehicles, nevertheless it seems to me that the expansion of the automobile industry was an energising force and perhaps to the full extent of the fixed capital that it has employed. I am not prepared as yet to deduct therefrom the capital which it rendered obsolete and useless.

Your position regarding existing index numbers is one with which I heartily sympathise. Statistical labours really need the direction which can only be given by means of sound economic analysis. In particular I have long felt the need of indices that will do something towards measuring internal prices and unit costs. So much for the time being.

Sincerely yours,

O. M. W. SPRAGUE

From O. M. W. SPRAGUE, *22 July 1930*

Dear Keynes,

I have been going through much of the evidence of the witnesses before the Macmillan Committee including your own and although I have not read all of your book I have reached certain tentative conclusions which I should very much like to discuss with you.

I find myself in general agreement with your analysis of savings in relation to investment as a part of the cyclical process, but I am constantly asking myself why unbalanced relationships between the two develop. I suppose that this is because I ordinarily begin my analysis of these matters from the side of the borrower and the use which he makes of the proceeds of what he secures from the banks or the investment market: consequently I am doubtful of the outcome of special devices designed to secure a balance between savings and investments as contrasted with the outcome when such a balance is reached as an incidental result of the emergence of a balanced economic position in the industries and between countries.

I have not yet become immersed in the routine operations of the Bank and therefore any time that you might find a discussion of these matters convenient would be quite satisfactory for me, whether at my office here or at any other place that you may prefer.

Very sincerely yours,

O. M. W. SPRAGUE

Keynes finally finished the book on 14 September 1930 and wrote a characteristic note to his mother.

To F. A. KEYNES, *14 September 1930*

My dearest Mother,

This evening, at last, I have finished my book. It has occupied me seven years off and on,—and so one parts from it with mixed feelings. A relief anyhow that it hasn't dragged on into next term. Artistically it is a failure—I have changed my mind too much during the course of it for it to be a proper unity. But I think it contains an abundance of ideas and material. It is nearly twice as long as *Probability* and four times the length of my other books. It will be published on October 21 or 24.[1]

Ever your affectionate son

J.M.K.

He also must have written to Joseph Schumpeter, who replied on 18 October from Harvard.

From a letter from J. SCHUMPETER, *18 October 1930*

Just a line to congratulate you heartily on the finishing of your book. I have been[2], and shall be again, suffering enough from the weight of the labours of composing anything like a 'treatise' on money to be able to form an idea of how you must feel relieved. I do not think that any scientific book has been looked for with so universal an impatience—in our time at least—as yours is.

[1] It was published on 31 October.
[2] Schumpeter had just completed the major part of his *Das Wessen des Geldes*. This was not published until 1970.

Chapter 3

INTERLUDE

As usual, Keynes's activities during 1930 were not confined to economic theory. As noted above (p. 126), he was taking an active part in the work of the Macmillan Committee on Finance and Industry—providing by the end of the year a total of eight days of 'private' evidence, and examining witnesses. In addition, he took an active part in the work of the Economic Advisory Council which provided advice to the Prime Minister and the Cabinet on economic questions. Keynes's approach to his 'private' evidence, papers and discussions for these bodies naturally reflected his current, more abstract preoccupation with the *Treatise* and in some cases provides good glimpses into his current theoretical development, independent of the more geological *Treatise*, which shows evidence of several changes of view. As this material emanates from Keynes's public activities, it naturally appears in volume xx.

One exception to the general principle outlined above would, however, appear useful. At the time Keynes finished his *Treatise*, he was involved with Sir Josiah Stamp, Professor A. C. Pigou, Professor Lionel Robbins and Hubert Henderson as Chairman of a Committee of Economists of the Economic Advisory Council.[1] The discussions of this Committee and the papers circulated were of a somewhat different, more abstract, order from those of, say, the Economic Advisory Council Papers. Moreover, Keynes's major paper on the current economic position is of considerable interest. Dated one week after Keynes finally passed the pages of the *Treatise*, at a time when he knew of R. F. Kahn's formulation of 'the multiplier',[2] this paper provides a useful indication of Keynes's state of mind at the time he finished the *Treatise* rather than his state of mind in the *Treatise* proper. For this reason, this paper appears apart from Keynes's other, less abstract, papers for the Council (which appear in volume xx) as a brief reference point for the reader in the discussions of the *Treatise* and the road towards the *General Theory* which occupy succeeding chapters.

[1] The terms of reference of this committee were: 'To review the present economic conditions of Great Britain, to examine the causes which are responsible for it and to indicate the conditions of recovery.'
[2] Kahn was one of the secretaries of the Committee. His early formulation of the multiplier' was later circulated to the Committee.

MEMORANDUM BY MR J. M. KEYNES
TO THE COMMITTEE OF ECONOMISTS
OF THE ECONOMIC ADVISORY COUNCIL

I. Prolegomena

In the following I have endeavoured to cast what I have been trying to say into a mould which is perhaps more similar to that in which the thoughts of the other members of the Committee run. But it is not easy to do so, and since I have not had much time for reflection there are probably some mistakes in it. I plead for charity all through this document as it has been extraordinarily difficult in the time allowed to keep incidental errors of generalisation from creeping in.

1. I define 'equilibrium' real wages as those which are paid when all the factors of production are employed and entrepreneurs are securing normal returns, meaning by 'normal' returns those which leave them under no incentive either to increase or to decrease the money offers which they make to the factors of production.

2. Unless the level of money wages at home relatively to money wages abroad is such that the amount of the foreign balance (i.e. of foreign investment) *plus* the amount of home investment at the rate of interest set by world conditions (i.e., which just prevents gold movements) is at least equal to the amount of home savings, business losses will ensue. Thus there cannot be full employment unless this condition is fulfilled. The terms of trade which obtain when this condition is fulfilled I call the 'equilibrium terms of trade'.

3. Equilibrium real wages depend on:—

(*a*) the volume of physical output per head;

(*b*) the technique of industry taken in conjunction with the volume of existing capital;

(*c*) the equilibrium terms of trade.

In an international system an adverse change in the equilibrium terms of trade has exactly the same effect as a diminution in physical output per head has in a closed system, since the result is that a given quantity of effort in one country produces a smaller quantity of what is wanted.

4. Thus, when we find a condition of disequilibrium in existence, it might be due to changes under any of these three heads.

(*a*) Now, there is no evidence that real wages, at any rate up to 1929, had increased appreciably faster either than actual physical output per head or than what physical output per head would have been if all the factors of production had been employed. Any excess covered under this head is probably no more than could be covered during the short period by the amount below their normal return which entrepreneurs will accept rather than reduce output.

(*b*) This seems to me to be really a branch of (*a*) over the long period when there has been time to change the quantity and character of capital equipment. Changes under (*b*) might result, failing a compensating change in real wages, in declining output per head or more probably a smaller output per head than might have been over the long period. I see little evidence that this is a significant cause of our present troubles *at this moment*. But I find the point confusing and difficult to disentangle both from (*a*) above and from (*c*) below.

(*c*) I, therefore, attribute the major part of our troubles to the equilibrium terms of trade having turned seriously against us, without this being compensated by a reduction of money wages to correspond to the new equilibrium terms of trade.

5. When we are dealing with a closed system, it may help us to think primarily in terms of real wages. But when we come to an international system and to dealing with the equilibrium terms of trade, it appears to me that money wages at home per unit of output relatively to similar wages abroad are much more directly relevant to our problem than real wages. For example, an increase in real wages due to an increase of British money wages would, in this case, affect employment much more than,

and in a different way from, an equal increase in British real wages due to a fall (e.g.) in the price of imported foodstuffs. But we may overlook this if we concentrate too much on real wages.

6. The *actual* terms of trade today have not moved adversely to us. The fact that the money value of output per man, which was greatly depressed by the return to gold, has been tending to catch up money wages is a sign of this. So is the fact that our imports have fallen in price more than our exports and much more than our net exports, excluding imported raw material embodied in exports. These facts would be modified, but not, I should think, obliterated, if they included an allowance for the catastrophic decline in freights. Allowing for everything, the actual terms of trade have probably not changed a great deal.

The question is—by how much are the existing equilibrium terms of trade worse than the actual terms of trade? What reduction of money wages would be necessary to bring the terms of trade to equilibrium? What reduction of real wages would this entail?

There is also the question whether the long-period trend may not be such that, unless we do something about it, the equilibrium terms of trade will move further against us as time goes on.

Real wages seem to me to come in as a by-product of the remedies which we adopt to restore equilibrium. They come in at the end of the argument rather than at the beginning. That is to say, we arrive finally at a consideration—as having an important bearing on our choice between the different alternatives—as to how much each of the several expedients, both those which involve a reduction in money wages and those which do not, are calculated to reduce real wages. But the answer to this will not have much direct bearing on the question how much employment we can expect from each of the several expedients. Employment is not a function of real wages in the sense that a given degree of employment requires a determinate level of real wages, irrespective of how the employment is brought about.

Suppose that there were to be a flight from sterling and that this—over the short period at any rate—caused a violent adverse movement of the equilibrium terms of trade, but not so great a one that it could not be remedied by a sufficient reduction of money wages, which in turn would mean a reduction of real wages; and suppose that an economist were called in to diagnose the resulting unemployment; would it be useful or sensible for him to reply that the trouble was that real wages were too high? Yet, if he were in the habit of thinking of the wages question as a part of the long-period theory of distribution with the short-period theory of money and international trade in a separate compartment of his mind, this is what he might say, and, furthermore, he might be able to justify it, because it might be true that a sufficient reduction of real wages would be theoretically capable of restoring equilibrium. Moreover, *ceteris paribus* this might be the only remedy; which is another way of saying that if we cut ourselves off from all other remedies, this is the only remedy which is left.

7. For some reason we have got into the habit of assuming that changes in the terms of trade are of small significance in relation to the problems of the national economy; for example, that there never is a serious transfer problem; or, again, that the terms-of-trade argument for protection is never worth much. There must, I think, have been something in nineteenth-century conditions which made this roughly true when applied to Great Britain. But, for a variety of reasons, I am sure that this is not true today.

Nor does the fact that the effect of changes in the equilibrium terms of trade is likely to be much greater on equilibrium money wages than on equilibrium real wages help us very much; because it is precisely money wages which are sticky and difficult to move.

7a. I classify the factors determining the equilibrium terms of trade as follows:—

A. *Those affecting the magnitude of the foreign balance.*
B. *Those affecting the pressure to lend abroad.*

A. There are many reasons (leaving out the temporary aggravations of the world slump) why the terms of trade corresponding to a given magnitude of the foreign balance might move adversely to us:—

(*a*) as a result of increased tariffs abroad against our products;

(*b*) as a result of the decline of former important markets (e.g. India, China);

(*c*) as a result of the value of our monetary standard being raised relatively to monetary standards abroad without corresponding adjustments of money wages.[1]

(*d*) as a result of other countries catching us up in efficiency.

B. The pressure to lend abroad might be increased:—

(*a*) as a result of the demand schedule of borrowers abroad rising relatively to the schedule of home borrowers;

(*b*) as a result of the supply schedule of lenders at home for foreign lending falling relatively to their supply schedule for home lending.

As an example of (*a*), let us suppose that we have been saving £500 million a year and investing £300 million at home and £200 million abroad. Then if the new investments at home which are expected to yield the world rate of interest become fewer because we are an old country, or if new investments abroad are expected to yield more for reasons which do not apply at home, equilibrium may require that we should invest £200 million at home and £300 million abroad. This means that we must increase our favourable balance by £100 million. In order to do this we must cheapen our exports, i.e. alter the terms of trade to our disadvantage. Thus the effect of the incentive to lend more abroad will be to reduce equilibrium real wages.

As an example of (*b*), let us suppose that the investor feels more confidence than before in the credit or prospects of some

---

[1] I mean here that part of the consequent raising of relative gold wages which is in excess of any change in real wages relatively to output.

foreign country or set of foreign countries. He will then be more willing than before to lend unless the terms for home lending are correspondingly increased, which may be impossible having regard to the prospective yield. Or it may be that he feels less trust than before in the prospects of home investments. Again, equilibrium requires a larger favourable balance, to secure which we must cheapen our exports.

8. The terms-of-trade schedule, that is to say the terms of trade corresponding to a given value of the foreign balance, we may call 'the terms of transfer'. The degree of pressure towards foreign lending we may call 'the terms of lending'. The problem of establishing equilibrium terms of trade we may call the transfer problem (borrowing from the language of the reparations controversy). I am suggesting that the main cause of our troubles is not that British real wages have been getting ahead of British physical productivity (though they may have been getting a trifle ahead of it); but that a serious transfer problem has arisen as a result of the terms of transfer and the terms of lending both moving adversely to the equilibrium terms of trade, i.e. the foreign balance is tending to decline at a time when foreign lending is trying to increase.

The reactions of an unsolved transfer problem on domestic equilibrium may be very great, even though the deficiency of the foreign balance below equilibrium is quite a small percentage of the national income. For example, I should say that in our case the deficiency of the foreign balance cannot be above £200 million per annum at the very outside, which is only 5 per cent of the national income. Yet if—as a result of our failure to solve it otherwise than by a rate of interest punitive to home investment—the amount of home investment *plus* the amount of the foreign balance falls short of our savings by £200 million, this means that entrepreneurs will lose £200 million, which is enormous in relation to entrepreneurs' resources and must have a terrific effect in causing unemployment, and an increasing effect as times goes on.

9. In order to illustrate the horrible possibility of the transfer problem, let me offer the following caricature.

Suppose two countries England and America; labour of equal efficiency; both on the gold standard with no restrictions on foreign lending, but with strict immigration laws.

Suppose that in England savings are increasing faster than population, whilst in America population is increasing faster than savings.

Suppose that America has a tariff based on the difference between the cost of production at home and abroad, so that the tariff is raised whenever it can be proved that the difference has widened.

Suppose that the stock of gold which England is legally free to export is an insignificant fraction of America's stock of gold.

The rate of interest in England will have to rise to a level at which her savings cannot be entirely absorbed by investment. Unemployment and business losses ensue. It will become obvious that wages are too high. Wages will be reduced; whereupon the American tariff will be raised and the same situation will recur. Wages will always be too high, so long as there are any Englishmen left alive; and when the last economist expires he will at least be able to claim with his dying breath that he has always had the courage of his convictions about wages being too high and that he has always been right.

In the early stages this will be aggravated by the fact that, as a result of business losses, the confidence of the British investor in British business will be diminished; he will reckon the risks higher here than in America (quite rightly, because when everyone is dead fixed capital in England will be worth nothing); and the pressure to lend abroad will be further increased.

But there are certain mitigations which may come to the rescue. The gradually increasing impoverishment of the country will diminish saving, and the lower money wages will make us steadily more independent of imports;—a point may come, for example, if we stick to *laissez-faire* long enough, when we shall grow our own vines. Provided there is a residue of British exports (e.g. peers and old masters) which America is glad to have, and we can reduce our necessary imports *plus* our surplus savings to equality with this residue, equilibrium will be restored.

If, however, foreign lending were to be forbidden from the outset, then we might find that equilibrium real wages were even higher than they were before the story began.

The clue to the paradox is that if you bring about a situation in which entrepreneurs' returns are below what they require to keep them in business, even if they are only slightly below, you bring the whole machine to a standstill; and it may happen in an international system that even a substantial reduction of money wages in a given country will not mend matters, whilst it is theoretically possible that there is *no* reduction of money wages which will be sufficient—so long as the volume of saving, this international situation and mobility of foreign lending remain as before.

10. The remedies available to meet a transfer problem are:—

(i) To *accept* the equilibrium terms of trade and endeavour to *meet* them by reducing our money costs, i.e. our efficiency earnings in terms of money. This will only be a remedy if the foreign demand for our exports is elastic or if our preference for imports over home products is sensitive to the relative price of the two. Even if the demand for our exports is elastic rather than inelastic, it will have to be very elastic if a moderate reduction of money wages is to do the trick.

(ii) To *improve* the equilibrium terms of trade:

(*a*) by engineering a diminution of tariffs abroad;

(*b*) by imposing tariffs at home (or other forms of import restrictions);

(*c*) by raising the demand schedules of home borrowers;

(*d*) by lowering the supply schedules of home lenders for home investment.

11. Now, unless there are other serious objections to the remedies proposed, it is obviously better to recover equilibrium

by *improving* the equilibrium terms of trade than by *meeting* them. We only want to meet them by reducing money wages as a last resort and to the extent that we are unable to improve them.

Further, in so far as real wages have to be reduced, it is better, if possible, to raise prices than to reduce money wages. It is better:

(i) Because there is less social resistance to keeping money wages unchanged when cost of living rises x per cent, than to reducing money wages x per cent with prices unchanged.

(ii) Because, although a reduction of x per cent in money wages will mean a smaller reduction in real wages, this will not be believed.

(Prices of home-produced goods will not fall by as high a percentage as that in which money wages have been reduced, because these prices also include other costs and profits. Thus real wages would fall to some extent even if the working classes consumed nothing except home-produced goods; but the smaller the percentage of their consumption directed to foreign-produced goods, the smaller will be the reduction in real wages. If 10 per cent reduction in money wages means 8 per cent reduction in the prices of home-produced goods and if 90 per cent of working-class consumption is of home-produced goods, real wages will fall only 3 per cent; but if 50 per cent of such consumption is of home goods, real wages will fall nearly 6 per cent. Thus it is probable that the reduction of real wages would be substantially less than the reduction of money wages. Nevertheless, this will not be readily believed beforehand, so that the social resistance will be greater than if the same reduction of real wages were brought about by a rise of prices.)

(iii) Because the method of raising prices throws the burden over a much wider area. In particular, it throws a due share on the *rentier* class and other recipients of fixed money incomes. Thus, from the point of view both of justice and of self-interest, the trade union leaders are right in preferring a rise of prices to a reduction of money wages as a means of restoring equilibrium.

I believe it would be true to say that almost everyone would welcome a return of prices to the level of a year ago in full acknowledgment of the fact that this would raise the cost of living 5 per cent; whereas the vast majority of working-class leaders would resist a reduction of money wages.

II. My own way

1. Before proceeding to answer the questionnaire in the light of the above, I should like very briefly to substitute for the foregoing the lines along which I should analyse the problem of unemployment, if I had only myself to please.

2. I define 'primary' employment as additional employment brought about otherwise than as the result of the increased consumption of newly employed men; and 'secondary' employment as employment resulting from such increased consumption.

3. It is impossible to bring about primary employment except by increasing investment relatively to saving (using these terms as I have defined them in my book).

4. The amount of secondary employment ensuing on a given amount of primary employment does not depend on how the primary employment has been brought about.

5. We can, therefore, test the quantitative effect of an expedient on employment by its tendency to diminish the excess of saving over investment.

6. In so far as the newly employed buy foreign products with their increased incomes, this means a diminution of foreign investment. Thus the net increase of investment associated with *any* measure of bringing about primary employment will be less, so to speak, than the gross.

7. Secondary employment, whatever the character of the primary employment on which it ensues, will necessarily be associated with *some* increase (not necessarily large) in the price of home-produced goods. This will cause some substitution of home consumption of such goods for foreign consumption of them; which will be a second partial offset to the gross amount

of new investment (or diminished saving) which is the direct occasion of the primary employment.

8. Mr Kahn has produced an argument, which seems to me convincing, for supposing that in present conditions in Great Britain a given amount of primary employment gives rise to an approximately equal amount of secondary employment.

If this is correct, we may assess the existing excess of saving over investment at £187,500,000 per annum. This follows from taking our abnormal unemployment at 1,500,000 and the output corresponding to the employment of a man for a year at £250 (for 1,500,000/2 × £250 = £187,500,000). Other general considerations suggest that this is about right in order of magnitude, but perhaps a little on the high side;—if we were to take £150 million as our working figure, this might be high enough.

9. Thus if we could increase home investment by £75 million per annum and simultaneously increase the foreign balance by the same amount, we might expect to have substantially cured unemployment.[1] Put this way the problem does not sound so very formidable or impossible of accomplishment.

10. How much our methods of achieving these results would reduce real wages, it is extremely difficult to say in advance.

In so far as our methods include a reduction of money wages, real wages will be reduced by an amount depending on (a) the proportion of working-class consumption devoted to foreign goods and (b) the extent to which the price of the home goods they consume moves with money wages.

In any case, the secondary employment, to whatever remedies it is due, will cause a rise of prices in home goods which will somewhat reduce the value of a given money wage.

I would emphasise that the decrease in net foreign investment due to the newly employed consuming more foreign goods and to the rise of home prices associated with secondary employment, and also the reduction in the real value of a given money

[1] Subject to a qualification below as to what we do with the money which we no longer need to borrow for the dole.

wage due to the latter cause, will be the same *to whatever cause the increase of employment is due.*

I would emphasise this because when I was advocating government schemes of home investment, these schemes were sometimes criticised as 'inflationary' and therefore undesirable, because of the rise of home prices associated with the secondary employment ensuing on the primary employment created by the government (this is what the criticism amounted to, though it was not expressed as clearly as this). But in this sense any conceivable cause of increased employment is 'inflationary'. Even employment due to a decrease in money wages is inflationary in the sense that its secondary effects cause the prices of home-produced goods to rise relatively to the new level of money wages.

11. Please note that a reduction of saving is just as effective a remedy as an increase of investment. The worst of it is that *some* expenditure on consumption, namely when foreign goods are purchased, automatically reduces investment, because it reduces the foreign balance; in which case we are no further forward than we were. But increased consumption of home-produced goods at the expense of saving creates just as much primary employment, and consequently just as much total employment, as an equal amount of investment.

III. The questionnaire

I can make my answers to most of the questions brief, because they follow pretty clearly from what I have already written above.

I[1] (i) (a) *An increase of investment in the world at large.* This would in any case raise the world price level and bring us the

---

[1] The first part of the questionnaire ran as follows:
  'I. In what way would (a) British employment, (b) British prices, (c) British real wages, be affected by
    (i) an increase of investment (a) in the world at large, (b) in Great Britain;
    (ii) a tariff;
    (iii) a reduction of British money wages (a) all round, (b) in the relatively highly paid industries?' [Ed.]

obvious benefits due to that, including a greater demand for our goods at present prices, an increase in relative money wages abroad, and some decrease in real wages. In short, it would tend both to diminish real wages, and to turn the terms of trade in our favour, so that it would bring the actual real-wage level lower and the equilibrium real-wage level higher.

If the increase in investment was due, not wholly to a rise in the rate of interest which borrowers were willing to pay but to a fall in the market rate, it would mean a fall of the market rate in Great Britain, and consequently an increase of investment in Great Britain. This, by absorbing a larger quantity of our savings at home, would still further raise the equilibrium terms of trade and therefore the equilibrium real wage.

(i) (*b*) *An increase of investment in Great Britain.* If this was a result of a fall in the market rate of interest we have already dealt with it. If it was the result of an increase in the willingness to borrow for the purpose of investment in Great Britain (i.e. of an increase in the willingness to invest at the existing market rate), then, as before, by absorbing more of our savings at home it would raise the equilibrium terms of trade and consequently the equilibrium real wage.

(ii) *A tariff.* This would be capable of bringing assistance along several different lines.

1. In so far as it raised home prices relatively to foreign prices it would bring actual real wages nearer equilibrium real wages, but it would be wrong to assume that this is the only, or indeed the chief, way in which it would operate. A tariff which had a negligible influence on real wages would be helpful for the following reasons.

2. In so far as it enabled home products to find an outlet in foreign investment, without turning the equilibrium terms of trade against us as much as would be required by an equal increase of foreign investment due to an expansion of exports. For example, it might be easier to improve the balance of trade by £50 million by restricting the import of poultry and pig

products than it would be by increasing the volume of our staple exports by a gross amount equivalent to this after allowing for the import of raw material. The benefit of a tariff as compared with the benefit of reducing money wages, depends on the degree in which the former improved the terms of trade above the present actual terms of trade *plus* the degree in which the latter worsens the terms of trade below the present actual terms of trade. Over the short period this benefit may be very great and over a fairly long period it may be substantial.

But the benefit of a tariff as compared with the present state of affairs is much greater still. Indeed it is simply enormous. This was the point I sought to bring out in my *Manchester Guardian* letter.[1] Roughly speaking the capital wealth of the country is increased by nearly the amount of the value of the previous imports which the tariff causes to be replaced by home production; except that, where the protected article is, directly or indirectly, a raw material of an export, we must, of course, subtract the value of any resulting decline in exports.

3. In so far as a tariff reduces real wages by raising prices, it is, for the reasons given above, both a more expedient and a more just way of doing this than by a reduction of money wages.

4. In so far as it raised the spirits of business men it would increase the readiness to invest in Great Britain, thus allowing larger investment at home at the existing market rate, and thus raise the equilibrium terms of trade.

5. In so far as it facilitated the solution of the budget problem, it might have the same effect as above in increasing confidence and so improve the equilibrium terms of trade.

6. It could have no adverse effects *on employment* unless it was so ill contrived as to reduce exports more than it reduced imports.

7. It would not be more likely and would, in my opinion, be less likely than alternative remedies to provoke a subsequent

[1] Letter to the editor of the *Manchester Guardian*, 16 August 1930, entitled 'Buying a British Car', reprinted in *JMK*, vol. xx. [Ed.]

demand from trade unions for a premature increase in money wages.

8. In so far as it improved the terms of trade, it might call for a smaller reduction of real wages than alternative remedies.

In the past economists have always admitted as an academic point the terms-of-trade argument in connection with tariffs, but British economists have generally implied that in the case of Great Britain the benefit to be got from this source is small. This was probably true in the nineteenth century. It may be true today over the long period. But I think we should consider whether the terms-of-trade argument for a tariff is not today of an altogether different order of magnitude, at any rate if we are considering periods of intermediate length. One of our main problems is to secure a favourable balance of trade large enough to meet the pressure to lend abroad at existing relative rates of interest and relative attractiveness, allowing for risk, etc. There are various ways of attacking this problem. One is to subsidise home investment in some shape or form. Another is to penalise foreign lending in some shape or form. A third is to increase our exports by reducing their price. A fourth is to reduce our imports by a tariff or analogous arrangement. The orthodox advice is to employ only the third method, namely to reduce the price of our exports. But it seems to me quite uncertain whether the elasticity of demand for our exports is such that we can— except over a longish period—greatly increase their aggregate value by reducing their price. If not, then we are driven to fall back on one or more of the other expedients.

In time, no doubt, a reduction of our money wages relatively to money wages abroad would tell considerably on the demand for our exports; for it might reduce the profits of our competitors to a point at which they would be disinclined to lay down new plant. But it might be five to ten years before this had much effect. While speaking of a tariff, there are two other points worth mentioning where I, at any rate, feel that I have moved away somewhat from what I used to believe.

In the case of most manufactured articles I doubt whether today there is any great advantage to be gained by a high degree of specialisation between different countries. Any manufacturing country is probably just about as well fitted as any other to manufacture the great majority of articles. It is unlikely, for example, that there would be great advantages in all the motor-cars in the world being made in the United States, and all the tin plates being made in South Wales, and all the steel rails being made in Belgium. On the other hand, now that nearly all the manufacturing countries of the world have decided on a certain measure of self-sufficiency, a country which does not follow suit may pay a much greater price in instability than it gains through specialisation. Thus, I am not very much afraid of a tariff on manufactured articles leading to our manufacturing the wrong things. For I do not think that there are any wrong things, or at any rate not many. Here again I believe that the nineteenth-century view in favour of specialisation as against stability may have been right, at any rate for Great Britain. But today, if we take account of all sorts of familiar facts, stability may be more important, and the price we should have to pay for it as a result of diminished specialisation a far smaller price.

Let me put a concrete question to members of the Committee. Suppose it were the case that unless we had a tariff on iron and steel and motor-cars for the next five years, the motor-car industry and the heavy steel industry in this country would shrink to negligible dimensions. Would we rather see that happen than put a tariff on to protect them, assuming that the latter could be effective? I should like to know the answer of members of the Committee to this question. I am assuring common knowledge as to our capacity to make the goods in question at a real cost which is not unreasonably high. For my part, if I were to believe that these industries would be crippled without a tariff, I should regard that as a *conclusive* argument for giving them a tariff. My only reason for hesitating would be the possibility that if they were to feel the pressure of circumstances a little longer they might, after all, be able to prosper without a tariff. But many free traders seem to me to believe this sort of thing on inadequate evidence. Moreover if they were free traders, in the old sense, they would not need to bolster up their opposition to a tariff on these grounds.

There are, moreover, certain fundamental industries which I should wish to preserve, even though it was clear that we were in some measure relatively inefficient in them. I mean particularly agriculture. It seems to me worth paying a price to maintain the industry of agriculture in the country. Every other country in Europe has adopted this view. Even if it be regarded just as a luxury, are we not rich enough to afford it? At any rate, I should like to put another concrete question to members of the Committee. If they were convinced that farming would be impossible in this country on anything approaching its present scale without a tariff, however willing farmers were to change their methods and their types of production, would they be opposed to giving farmers a tariff or equivalent assistance? I would rather see a prosperous agriculture *plus* tariff log-rolling at Westminster to the extent prevailing (say) in Germany than the rural population driven to live in Birmingham making screws (and the like) with purity at Westminster at its present level.

(iii) (*a*) *Reduction of British money wages all round*. This has already been answered in effect in previous passages. The main object would be to reach down to the existing equilibrium real wage and equilibrium terms of trade rather than to raise these equilibria up, which is the main object of the other expedients.

(iii) (*b*) *Reduction of British money wages in relatively highly-paid industries*. This would have less effect in reducing real wages and less effect in improving the favourable trade balance. Its chief advantage might lie in its tending to increase investment in certain home industries and thereby raising the equilibrium terms of trade. This would also, of course, apply to an all-round reduction of British money wages, but would be of less relative importance in that case than in this case.

(iv) *Miscellaneous.* (1) We have already seen that anything which diminishes the excess of home savings over home investment tends to raise the equilibrium terms of trade. It follows, therefore, that there is a by-product of advantage from certain measures, which from every other point of view are undesirable. For example, in so far as the dole is financed by borrowing, it represents negative saving. Thus if the rate of the dole was increased to £5 a week out of the proceeds of borrowing and the whole of it spent on home-produced goods, unemployment would disappear, provided (1) that the 'genuinely seeking work' clause was strictly enforced, (2) that the newly employed factors of production spent their earnings (like the recipients of the dole) on home-produced goods, and (3) that the government spent the money previously spent on the dole on something else and the new £5 dole would in fact cost nothing. But this, after all, is only a roundabout way of saying that, subject to the above assumptions, if the government were always prepared to step in and borrow enough money and spend it on something, however unproductive, there would never be any unemployment. Nor would there be any greater reduction of real wages than if unemployment were to be cured, e.g., by a greater demand for our goods springing up abroad.

Even as it is, it is quite conceivable that a reduction of the dole would actually, apart from its psychological effect in making wage reductions easier, somewhat increase unemployment! It is the rate of accumulation of our capital wealth which such expedients would diminish, not as compared with the existing state of affairs, but as compared with other remedies. This is a reason why, even if the necessary assumptions were fulfilled, this may not be an advisable remedy! But the fact that it *is* a remedy serves to bring out the analytical point. I stress the point because I am not clear that it was fully appreciated at our last meeting.

(2) It is easy to apply the same line of argument to the possible beneficial effects on employment of a suspension of the sinking fund.

(3) An expedient which would be wasteful in conditions of equilibrium might obviously be highly profitable in existing conditions. Any form of subsidy or detriment through tariffs which did not cost more than 33 per cent of the value of the new output brought into production would pay for itself out of saving on the dole alone, without allowing for any benefit to the employed man himself (reckoning wages at £3 a week and the dole at £1 a week). In the case of some of the expedients mentioned above, the price to be paid for them would fall on the future rather than on the present. This is true of interference with the freedom of foreign lending. It is true of a tariff in so far as the objection to a tariff lies in its getting us into bad habits. Now, whilst Ramsey showed that we probably accumulated too little as it is, assuming that the future is to be reckoned equal with the present, subject to an appropriate rate of discount, I am not sure that this conclusion would hold if we assume that the progress of science, quite apart from any large accumulation of capital, will improve economic conditions at the rate of $1\frac{1}{2}$ or 2 per cent per annum for many years to come. Therefore, I would not discard an expedient which would be of material benefit over the next five years merely because it meant that our level of life twenty years hence would be a little lower than it might have been, if we had been more austere now. Moreover, too much austerity might upset the apple-cart.

(4) If a subsidy of 6 per cent on the wages bill would cure unemployment, it would pay the Treasury to grant it. For with unemployment at 18 per cent and wages three times the dole, the cost of such a subsidy would be no greater than the present cost of the dole.

Thus, if anyone thinks that a reduction of 6 per cent in wages would cure unemployment, it follows that the method of subsidy would pay for itself, as compared with going on as we are now.

Answers to II[1]

1. If we put our present abnormal unemployment at 1,500,000, I should estimate (in order of magnitude) that one-third of this is due to the world slump, five-ninths to the emergence of a transfer problem, and one-ninth to excessive real wages, in the sense of real wages running ahead of physical productivity.

2. I should guess that in order to reduce real wages all round by a given amount, it might be necessary to reduce money wages by 175 per cent of that amount. But a reduction of money wages which was concentrated on the sheltered industries would reduce real wages by a smaller amount than a similar reduction of wages concentrated on the unsheltered industries. On the other hand, a given reduction of money wages concentrated on the sheltered industries would do less to restore equilibrium than an equal reduction concentrated on the unsheltered industries.

3. I have put the amount of existing abnormal employment due to excessive real wages at one-ninth of the whole. But I am not sure that this is not too much. For in existing industries employers will sacrifice a large part of their normal return before they close down, and this probably outweighs any increase in real wages relatively to output and also any changes of technical methods of a kind adverse to wages. Thus excessive real wages are only operating at present by diminishing employment which might otherwise be offering in new and expanding industries.

4. As regards the degree of the existing excess of real wages, I should say that, if we include the reduction in the cost of living

---

[1] The second part of the questionnaire ran as follows:

'II. How much too high (in order of magnitude) are (a) real wages, (b) money wages at the existing level of world prices?

What is your estimate of the increase (a) of real wages, (b) of productivity per head since 1910–14?

If your estimate of the excess of real wages is greater than your estimate of the increase of real wages per unit of productivity, how do you explain this?' [Ed.]

since last year as amongst the effects of the world slump, it is not clear that any reduction of real wages below the level of a year ago need be necessary on this score. Broadly speaking, that is to say, I accept the verdict of the statistics. If we abstract from the special events of the last year, I should say that at the utmost a reduction of 5 per cent in average money wages sufficiently concentrated on the higher paid (relatively to 1910–14) and sheltered industries to cause a fall not exceeding 2½ per cent in average real wages would be fully sufficient to balance the increase, if any, in real wages per unit of output and changes in technical methods. And two years' normal progress might make this up.

5. As regards the amount of reduction of money wages necessary to solve the transfer problem, apart from the world slump, it is extremely difficult even to make a guess. I should certainly estimate it much higher than 5 per cent. If our trade balance is now deficient by £150 million to satisfy the pressure towards foreign lending, what all-round reduction of money wages would be necessary to expand the balance by this amount? It might easily be 20 per cent, resulting in a reduction of real wages by from 12½ to 15 per cent. The longer the period under consideration, the less it would be; but the period might have to be decidedly long before there would be any material relief from the reduction suggested above.

6. As regards the amount of reduction of money wages necessary to offset the world slump, I should doubt if any reasonably conceivable reduction would be sufficient at the present moment. I should certainly estimate it above 20 per cent;—and a reduction greater than this is not worth discussing from the practical point of view.

7. I think that the following observation is extremely important.

In minimising in the past the importance of the transfer problem, we have, I think, had in mind a situation which was changing only slowly. In this event, the amount of the necessary rate of change in money wages would be small, so that (assuming progress) the mere lapse of a little time during which money wages were not raised would be enough. Moreover, there would always be time for modifications to have their ultimate effect, before anything very dreadful happened.

The trouble today is that we are violently out of equilibrium, and that we cannot wait long enough for *laissez-faire* remedies to bring their reward. In particular, a reduction in money wages might at long last have a very beneficial effect on the value of our total exports; but it may be quite impossible for us greatly to increase our favourable balance quickly merely by reducing money wages.

I suspect, therefore, that the correct answer on austere lines is as follows: A reduction of money wages by 10 per cent will ease unemployment in five years' time. In the meanwhile you must grin and bear it.

But if you can't grin and bear it, and are prepared to have some abandonment of *laissez-faire* by tariffs, import prohibitions, subsidies, government investment and deterrents to foreign lending, then you can hope to get straight sooner. You will also be richer in the sense of owning more capital goods and foreign investments five years hence. You may, moreover, have avoided a social catastrophe. But you may also have got into bad habits and ten years hence you may be a trifle worse off than if you had been able to grin and bear it.

The worst of all, however, will be an attempt to grin and bear it which fails to last through. The risk of this is perhaps the biggest argument against the 'grin and bear it' policy.

8. It is an argument against our reducing money wages that if this helps to set [a] fashion, as it well might, world prices will never recover, and we shall be no further forward, but, on the contrary, faced with the prospect of having to repeat the process.

9. In any case, I think we should preface our report by saying that certainly any further fall in world prices and perhaps the

fall which has occurred in the last year renders all the existing international debt settlements, all internal national debt burdens, and all existing money-wage settlements seriously and perhaps disastrously inappropriate. But having said this, what are we prepared to do about it?

21 September 1930   J. M. KEYNES

Chapter 4

ARGUING OUT THE 'TREATISE'

Upon publication of the *Treatise*, Keynes received several private letters of reactions. Many of these pointed out misprints and have found use in the preparation of the new edition of volumes V and VI. Some, such as the following from Joseph Schumpeter, were more congratulatory:

From J. A. SCHUMPETER, *29 November 1930*

Dear Keynes,

Very many thanks for your work on Money just to hand which you have been so kind as to send me. I want to congratulate you most heartily on this splendid achievement. It surpasses my understanding how you have managed to accomplish it among all the multifarious calls on your time and force to which I know you are exposed. This is truly a Ricardian *tour de force*, and must cause you the most intense satisfaction. I believe it will ever stand out as a landmark in its field.

Ever yours,

JOSEPH A. SCHUMPETER

However, as this next letter from D. H. Robertson indicates, some were more critical.

From D. H. ROBERTSON, *7 January 1931*

My dear Maynard,

I was drawn away from the *Treatise* by family Christmas, and the need to construct five 20-minute B.B.C. talks on World Finance,[1] which begin tomorrow (7.25)—and which seem to have become little else than a summary of the *Treatise*! I shd. like to show you some of the later ones—about gold, Germany, etc.—before I spout them.

On the point we corresponded,—I think I should now put my objection in the form of questioning the footnote to p. 250 [*JMK*, vol. VI, p. 223],— I should have thought the banks would be doing the substitution process *anyhow*, as far as their views about the proper composition of their asset-

---

[1] The talks appeared as chapter 5 of part II of *Economic Essays and Addresses* (1931).

sheets permits: and that the possibility of re-borrowing, even at above market rate, does introduce an *additional* factor into the situation. But I may still be muddled,—it is a most perplexing subject, I think.

On the point of fact about rediscounted bills remaining on both sides of the account,—I remember being bothered about it and satisfying myself that it was so, but I can't remember from what source. But the F[ederal]. R[eserve]. Bulletin periodical figures of 'condition of all member banks' show an item called 'Bills and notes payable' or some such name, on the liabilities side, which seem to correspond closely with the Reserve Banks' figures for rediscounts.

I have read all the book once, much of it twice. It is a great achievement, marvellously full of new meat. I think the whole of Book VII, most of which is new to me, splendid. I have next to read III and IV again carefully. I am still bothered by a group of subjects connected with 'the price-level of investment', the functioning of the rate of interest, and the synthesis of the new equations with those which bring in quantity and velocity. I can't help suspecting it is still like the Book of Genesis in places,—a pre-Wicksellian E and a post-Wicksellian I, and that the latter protests too much in places, and needs a final recensor P to put him in his place. If I can make my difficulties explicit, I shall try to put them into an article eventually: but I may not be able to.—Also I believe I get more and more Hobsonian, believing that investment can be 'excessive' even if it doesn't outrun saving, and that the only way out of slumps is a drastic redistribution of leisure.

I shan't be staying in London this time, but shall be at the Tuesday Club next week

Yours,

D.

This letter from Dennis Robertson provides a useful introduction to one strand of the discussion of the *Treatise* within Cambridge. This strand involved discussions among Keynes, Robertson and Pigou.

However, at certain points, the discussions with Robertson and Pigou overlapped with those of the 'Circus' of younger Cambridge economists which met to discuss, dissect and, of course, criticise the *Treatise*. In particular, three notes by R. F. Kahn and Piero Sraffa became involved in Keynes's discussions with Robertson and Pigou. We print these notes here, with Keynes's marginal comments as footnotes. However, we leave the discussion of the circus as a whole to a later point in chapter 5 (p. 337–43).

From R. F. KAHN, *5 April 1931*

The price level of investment goods

A fundamental question that is offering considerable difficulty is how investment goods can be logically differentiated from consumption goods in regard to the manner in which their price level is determined. If the price level of consumption goods is rigidly determined by the difference between savings and cost of investment, why is not the price level of investment goods equally rigidly determined by the difference between expenditure on consumption goods and the cost of producing consumption goods?

An answer at once presents itself. The question is sensible only on the assumptions that savings are exclusively devoted to buying investment goods (new or old) and that investment goods are exclusively paid for by means of savings or out of profits. But, in fact, savings may be used to increase savings deposits and investment goods may be paid for, directly or indirectly, by increased bank loans. In actual practice this is clearly of supreme importance. But I intend to disregard it in this note. I assume some kind of a non-monetary economy in which the assumptions set out in the second sentence of this paragraph can be supposed to hold. The question then still remains.

A possible answer that suggests itself is that the whole thing depends on the assumption that profits are exclusively devoted to buying investment goods (and losses exclusively made up by selling, or restricting the purchase of investment goods). Let us test this by making the opposite assumption —that profits are exclusively devoted to buying consumption goods (and losses exclusively made up by restricting expenditure on consumption goods or by selling out stocks of them). Then if non-entrepreneurs' savings increase,[1] the price level of investment goods must necessarily rise by an equivalent amount—so that the producers of investment goods make a profit equal to this increase of savings. This profit will be exactly sufficient to set off the diminution in non-entrepreneurs' expenditure on consumption goods, and the rise in the price of investment goods does not *require* any opposite change in the price of consumption goods. But it does not follow that consumption goods continue to sell at a price equal to their cost of production. For if this price is 'above (or below) their cost of production, the resulting profit (or loss) to entrepreneurs producing' consumption goods 'necessarily provides the difference between the selling price of the' consumption goods, 'whatever this may be, and their actual cost of production'. The argument of p. 139 of the *Treatise* [*JMK*, vol. v, p. 125] is precisely reversed. It is the price level of investment goods that is now com-

[1] 'Why? I do not follow this.'

pletely determined and the price level of consumption goods that is indeterminate.

Let us now take an intermediate case where profits are devoted partly to investment goods and partly to consumption goods. Let k be the proportion of the total profits, Q, that are devoted to consumption goods. Excluding this 'negative saving' kQ, let D be the excess of cost of production of investment goods over savings. Then profit on production of consumption goods $Q_1 = kQ + D$.

In other words $k(Q_1 + Q_2) + D = Q_1$, where Q_2 is the profit on production of investment goods. If $k = 0$ (i.e. if profits are devoted entirely to investment goods), Q_1 is necessarily equal to D and Q_2 can have any value—in conformity to the exposition of the *Treatise*. (Q_1 and Q_2 can be regarded as measures of the respective price levels.)[1]

If $k = 1$ (i.e. if profits are devoted entirely to consumption goods), Q_2 is necessarily equal to $-D$ and Q_1 can have any value—in conformity with the above suggestion.

But if k lies between zero and unity (being a function of Q and nothing else), all that we can say is that if a particular value is attached to Q_1 (or Q_2), then the value of Q_2 (or Q_1) is determined by the above equation. But there is an infinite range of such possible pairs of values. And it is impossible to say *a priori* that Q_1 is any more determined than Q_2. It is possible for *either* price level to have *any* value, but not for both at the same time.

To arrive at a determinate position of equilibrium it is necessary to introduce some further factor into the problem. The argument of the *Treatise* is that there are certain *external* causes—bound up in the state of speculative sentiment—that determine the price level of investment goods. Thus if everybody is convinced that the price level of investment goods is going to be at a certain level in a month's time, this price level will be practically fixed today. This assumes (*a*) that part of the current output of investment goods can be stocked, and (*b*) that there is a stock of investment goods (e.g. ordinary shares) available for current purchase. (Assumption (*a*) is necessary if the price level is not to fall below what it will be in a month's time, assumption (*b*) if it is not to rise above that level.)

Now[2] it does not require a very strenuous leap of the imagination to make precisely the same assumptions about consumption goods. If everybody is convinced that the price level of consumption goods is going to be at a certain level in a month's time and if consumption goods can be easily

---

[1] 'No! The conclusion is that unless $Q_2 + D = 0$, Q_1 is infinite. It is obvious that in general $Q_2 + D$ will not be 0. On your assumptions, the *general* conclusion is $Q_1 = \infty$.'

[2] 'This is not an 'external' cause because it operates by altering the volume of investment. My contention is that there is no external cause affecting the price of consumption goods.'

stored and if there is a stock available to meet current requirements, this price level will be practically fixed today. (In the language of savings and investment the changes in stocks will always be such as to prevent the emergence of any difference between savings and *net* investment. But this explanation does not logically differentiate consumption goods from investment goods—the differentiation lies in the definitions in terms of which the explanation is expressed.)

It seems, therefore, not unreasonable to suggest that the difference between consumption goods and investment goods is one of degree (but, nevertheless, very enormous). There are 'external' forces operating on both price levels, but the forces that operate on the price level of investment goods are very strong and those that operate on the price level of consumption goods are very weak. The two price levels are connected together by means of the above equation, and it is not very far from the truth to say that the price level of consumption goods is determined, given a certain value of D, by the price level of investment goods, which itself is determined by 'external forces'. But, strictly speaking, the price level of consumption goods may also be dependent on 'external forces' and the price level of investment goods has to accommodate itself accordingly—though actually the amount of this accommodation will be extremely small.

This differentiation does not depend entirely on the relative weakness of the 'external forces' in the case of consumption goods. It also emerges from the fact that k (the proportion of profits that are devoted to consumption goods) is likely to be small rather than large. If k is very small, a small change in Q_1 is associated with a large charge in Q_2, and Q_1 does not differ appreciably from D unless the numerical value of Q_2 is very great. It follows on this assumption that the price level of consumption goods is the relatively rigid element in the system and the price level of investment goods the relatively fluid feature. Even if the 'external forces' were equally strong in each case, the one would be comparatively unresponsive and the other would be highly responsive. Finally, and perhaps most important of all, the actual world is not a non-monetary system of the kind that I have been assuming.

Postscript (irrelevant to the foregoing)

After proceeding in this way, I was rather horrified to discover that the equation $k(Q_1+Q_2)+D-Q_1$ would be equally true in a monetary economy. It does not depend either on the assumption that no part of profit goes to swell savings deposits or that no bank loans are utilised to purchase investment goods. In fact the relation between the two price levels persists unaltered in a monetary economy. The only difference is that there is now a further 'external force' operating on the price level of investment goods—

their price level will be higher the greater is the rate at which the banking system is making loans for the purpose of purchasing investment goods (assuming no change in 'bearishness').

That is all very well, but there still remains a difficulty. My reversal of the argument of the *Treatise* for the case where the whole of profits are devoted to consumption ($k = 1$) now leads to an absurd conclusion. It is absurd to conclude that the price level of investment goods is completely determined ($Q_2 = -D$), for it depends on the rate at which bank loans are being created for the purchase of investment goods. It may possibly be helpful if I indicate how I emerged from this difficulty.

Let B be the rate at which bank loans are being created for the purchase of new investment goods and let k' be the proportion of profits that are paid into savings deposits. Then the amount of profits that are spent on investment goods is $(1 - k - k')\, Q$.

$$\text{Then} \qquad Q_1 = kQ + D,$$
$$Q_2 = (1 - k - k')\, Q - D + B.$$

Adding
$$Q = (1 - k')\, Q + B,$$
or
$$B = k'Q.$$

In other words, the rate of expansion of bank loans is equal to the rate of increase of savings deposits.

It is, I think, now clear that it is absurd to imagine that $k = 1$. For if $k = 1$, k' is zero and Q would be infinite. It follows that if B is appreciable, the attempt to reverse the argument of the *Treatise* leads to an infinitely high price level of consumption goods.   R.F.K.

From R. F. KAHN, *17 April 1931*

It has become apparent that the general attitude set out in a note circulated a couple of weeks ago can be put in a more general way. This note confines itself to a non-monetary economy in which all money is spent either on consumption goods or on investment goods.

Let us imagine that all who are engaged in the production of consumption goods form a separate class of the community round whom a cordon can be imagined to be drawn. It is then quite clear that the rate at which money is spent by the rest of the community on consumption-good producers is equal to the rate at which consumption-good producers spend money on the rest of the community. A similar cordon can be drawn around the producers of investment goods and the same proposition will apply.

Let us now suppose that the rate of saving by some section of the community is diminished by an amount a so that the flow of money directed by this section through the consumption cordon is increased by a and the flow through the investment cordon is reduced by a.

If the price of investment goods were to remain unchanged there would be no alteration in the flow of money from the producers of investment goods to the producers of consumption goods. It follows that the expenditure of consumption-good producers on investment-good producers must increase by a, and therefore the total inflow through the investment cordon is unchanged. In other words, there is no reason for a change in the price of investment goods.

But a simple reversal of the argument leads to the conclusion that there is no reason for a change in the price of consumption goods.

There is no conflict. It *is* quite possible for the *one* price level *or* the other to remain unchanged, but not for both.

If, in the first case, the price of investment goods had gone up, their producers would have increased the expenditure on consumption goods by a corresponding amount, say b, and, in consequence, the producers of consumption goods would have increased their expenditure on investment goods, not by a, but by $a + b$. The value of b is arbitrary; but once a value has been assigned to the price of one class of goods, the price of the other class is determined.

This result is quite independent of whether or not output and employment inside each cordon is altered. R.F.K.

From PIERO SRAFFA, *9 May 1931*

(1) It is now clear that the investors' indifference curve between securities and savings deposits plays an essential rôle in the argument. The speculative element being ruled out, such a statical curve is quite conceivable. It remains to be decided whether:

(*a*) The shape of the curve is such that the elasticity of demand for securities is nearly infinite.[1] This is largely a question of fact, on which I know very little. It involves that a large proportion both of sav. deposits and of securities should be held by people who are on the margin of doubt which to prefer at the current prices; to the extent that they are held by different classes of people, with different habits etc., this is not the case.[2]

[1] 'No—very small. *Total* annual savings not above 2 per cent of capital. Fluctuation in total savings *in a year* seldom 10 per cent of total savings i.e. 0·2 of capital. Besides we are considering the interval before losers have time to make their plans. 0·02 per cent would be a high estimate I should say. Is this a *large* proportion?'

[2] 'In some crisis it may need a *largish* change of price to induce them to change. But what then?'

(b) A change in the attractiveness of securities is not accompanied by a change in the attractiveness of savings deposits.[1] But the two are likely to move together.[2] The argument in the *Treatise*, we now learn,[3] is concerned with the banks' policy toward the volume of savings deposits, and the banks' object is to maintain this volume constant. The obvious instrument at their disposal is the rate of interest allowed on savings deposits (*Treatise*, p. 143, fn. 1) [*JMK*, vol. V, p. 128 n. 1].[4] Consequently, when the excess of savings tends to raise the price of securities, the banks will reduce the interest rate on savings deposits until the relative attractiveness will be restored to the original level. The new equilibrium will be reached when the price of securities has risen in the same proportion as current savings.—No doubt it would be possible for the banks to maintain the volume of savings deposits by selling securities and cancelling an equivalent amount of business deposits. But since the banks presumably intend, by maintaining the volume of savings deposits, to prevent business deposits from filtering into, or out of, them, and thus preserve some sort of stability, I do not see why they should adopt a roundabout method which defeats their real purpose.

(2) But in criticising D.H.R., J.M.K. uses an argument by which his conclusion would be established *independently* of any indifference curve and infinite elasticity of demand. Having granted (p. 8) [below p. 229, n. 1] that an excess of savings will mean 'some increase' in the price of non-liquid assets, if the savers buy in the market before the losers have time to sell; he proceeds to argue that the increase will be purely temporary: as soon as the losers begin to sell, they will sell[5] to the same amount as the excess savers have been previously buying 'so that non-liquid assets will return back again to their previous price'.[6] Here J.M.K. has overlooked that a rise in the price of non-liquid assets means that their producers are making profits; and these profits plus exces ssavings plus current savings will be exactly sufficient to buy the current output of non-liquid assets at the enhanced price plus the assets which the losers have to sell to make good their losses (these also at an enhanced price, which simply means that they sell a smaller number than they would otherwise). This seems most orthodox Treatisism.

(3) The moral of the preceding paragraph is that whatever price level is first hit upon is a position of equilibrium, and will be maintained so long as

---

[1] 'You mean irrespective of a change in bearishness?'

[2] 'Why not previously?'

[3] Sraffa had at this time read Keynes's reply to Robertson's critical notes on the *Treatise* (below, pp. 220–9). [Ed.]

[4] 'But they don't. Nor can they adequately. If they could then price level of investments could be controlled in a way in which in fact it isn't.'

[5] '*No!!*'

[6] 'You have overlooked that when the price falls back they *lose* their profits.'

supplies are fixed, incomes are fixed, and profits are spent in the appropriate way.[1] Under these conditions the price-level does in fact depend on which of the parties is on the telephone and which is not. If this is odd, the oddity is in the assumptions as much as in the conclusion.

It is therefore all-important to determine the order in which losses and profits are made, and losses made good.

When J.M.K. asserts[2] (p. 7) [below pp. 227–8] that the excess savers must buy non-liquid assets, and the losers sell them, simultaneously, he is really asserting that deposits have an infinite velocity: for otherwise a period (however short) of time must elapse between the moment a producer receives money in payment of goods and the moment he requires that money for paying wages or interest. It is not necessary to show that in practice, since the payment has to pass through the shopkeeper and wholesaler, the period is likely to be appreciable: it is sufficient that the two things should happen one *after* the other.

Also, it is not true that in the *same* stage 'the savers find themselves with more money and the losers find themselves with less money'. If the saver does not hoard or dis-hoard, his failure to spend in consumption goods as usual must consist in his buying non-liquid assets; and when the loser finds himself with less money, the saver finds himself with only the usual money: it is the producer of non-liquid assets who finds himself, at that very moment, with more money. In the second stage, the profiteer who has no use for the additional money since he is not allowed to increase output nor wages, places it at the disposal of the loser who requires it for paying his wages.   P.S.

To P. SRAFFA, *15 May 1931*

Dear Piero,

My chief comments on your paper are the following.

1. Your 1 (*a*). I do not think that my argument involves a large proportion of savings deposits and of securities being held by people who are on the margin of doubt. I suppose that *total* annual savings are not above 2 per cent of capital. The fluctuation in total savings *in a year* would seldom be 10 per cent of total savings, i.e. 0·2 of capital. But we are considering the interval before losers have time to make their plans. So I should

---

[1] 'What does this mean?'

[2] 'I do not assert this. I say that it is a matter of indifference which happens first.'

think that 0·02 per cent would be a high estimate of the proportion of total capital held on a margin of doubt between liquid and non-liquid assets. I should call this a small rather than a large proportion. Moreover, there is in all markets a body of professionals whose business it is to be on the margin of doubt and to act quickly. For example, jobbers on the stock exchange. There are also in the case of shares, real estate, commodities, and indeed most kinds of property, buyers who are offering a price slightly different from that ruling in the market who can be induced to come in by a small change. This does not mean that circumstances may not arise when a comparatively large change of price is required to bring about the necessary transference. But that does not in the least affect the character of the argument.

2. In your 1 (*b*) why do you say 'We now learn'? There are several pages about this in the *Treatise*. In fact, the banks do not act as you suppose them to act. If they did that would simply mean that the price of securities would have to fluctuate still more, since if the banks were to raise the rate of interest allowed on savings deposits whenever the price of securities falls, this would merely mean that the price of securities would have to fall more than otherwise, unless you assume that the banks are prepared to raise the rate of interest they grant without limit, in which case there is no position of equilibrium. Also, the instrument at the disposal of the banking system to maintain the volume of savings deposits constant is certainly not a variation in the rate of interest allowed. Their method is an increase or a decrease in their assets. So my conclusion is that all this is remote from the facts, but would make no difference to the fundamental argument even if the facts were as you suppose.

3. In your (2) the crucial passage seems to be 'Here J.M.K. has overlooked that a rise in the price of non-liquid assets means that their producers are making profits; etc.'. This assumes, as did D.H.R., that the buyers of non-liquid assets must purchase *new* non-liquid assets, whereas the persons to whom they are

making offers of liquid assets in exchange for non-liquid assets are the owners of the latter, whether old or new. It is true that during the period during which the price of non-liquid assets rises, the owners of the latter have a larger capital, valued in terms of money, than they had before. But this will be exactly obliterated when the losing entrepreneurs come along with an offer of liquid assets in exchange for non-liquid assets. Unless the indifference curve has changed in the meantime, the price of non-liquid assets will return to its former figure, so that the owners of the latter, whether old or new, will have capital assets of the same money value as at the beginning of the story. It was vital to D.H.R.'s argument that the buyers of non-liquid assets should be compelled to buy newly produced non-liquid assets. Your argument seems based on the same erroneous assumption. But even if this assumption were not erroneous the argument would still be invalid for the reasons just given.

(4) In your (3) you say that 'J.M.K. asserts that the excess savers must buy non-liquid assets and the losers sell them *simultaneously*'. But I assert nothing of the kind. I say that it is a matter of indifference which happens first.

Yours ever,

[copy initialled] J.M.K.

The papers which have survived recording discussions with Robertson and Pigou open with a letter from Robertson which contained a 'document' ultimately printed in the *Economic Journal* of September 1931 under the title 'Mr Keynes' Theory of Money'.

From D. H. ROBERTSON, *2 May 1931*

My dear Maynard,

I now send you, somewhat reluctantly, this document. Reluctantly (*a*) because your very kind note about my collected works[1] is still fresh in my mind, (*b*) because even if I can't follow you in practical judgment over the tariff, I should like to have been able to subscribe to the fundamental analysis of your *Treatise* But the more I've studied it, the more obstacles I find in the way of doing so.

[1] *Economic Fragments*, (London, 1931).

Now what is to be done about publication? There may turn out to be *some* points on which I've so clearly misinterpreted you that it would be a mistake to bother the public with them. But in the main I think it is probable that if I am muddled other people are more so: and that it would be to the advantage of students to have the thing available, as a running commentary, more or less in its present form, even if there turn out to be *other* points on which, as a result of long conversations supplementing the written word, we could more or less reach agreement. Of course I would rather have it in the *Journal* than anywhere: but you will, I imagine, have Stamp in the next number and ? Pigou as well, and may not want to be overloaded. Robbins would take it for *Economica*, but understands my preference to put it in the *Journal if* you care to have it.

Your affectionate pupil,

D.H.R.

Keynes replied to Robertson's 'document' in a 9-page paper, dated 5 May 1931, which also referred to criticisms from Pigou and Sraffa. As much of this paper follows his reply to Robertson's article in the September 1931 *Economic Journal*, rather than reprint both versions, we reprint a variorum version at the end of the discussions (below, p. 219).

On the first version of Keynes's reply, R. F. Kahn commented on 7 May 1931 as follows:

From R. F. KAHN, *7 May 1931*

As from K6 [King's]

I think that as an answer to Dennis and Piero the document is admirable. I should not, however, feel it an adequate answer to the objections that I myself raised in the note that I sent you during the vacation. But Dennis and Piero do not really appreciate the nature of my objections, so this is not really a criticism of your document when regard is had to the purpose for which it was intended.

My objection is crystallised most clearly about your statement (on the top of p. 5) [below p. 225] that the price level of consumption goods depends only on the difference between savings and investment and not on the price level of investment goods. What you still appear to fail to take into consideration is that 'savings' depend on P', except in the case when *no part at all* of profits are devoted to consumption goods and when the output of investment goods is not alterable. The same point, with its end reversed, arises in connection with the last line of p. 2 [below p. 223] and the top line of p. 3 [below p. 223]

My view is that the two price levels are directly connected in the sense that if one is higher the other is also higher. It may be that under certain circumstances (i.e. those in which the volume of business deposits is independent of P and P') P' is completely determined by outside factors (the state of bearishness). But even then P *depends* on P'. Moreover in the more general case where the volume of business deposits depends on P and P' the relation between P and P' becomes even more important in *a logical sense*. It is not merely that P' depends on P because P helps to determine the volume of savings deposits, but that P and P' are related in a symmetrical manner. I venture to enclose once again my note on this point (now very antiquated) and also a subsequent one that I wrote [above pp. 203–7].

But I do not think, as I have said, that all this is in reality a criticism of the document that you have written. Such points of real criticism as I have are of a minor nature and could be neglected.

 I. P. 1, l. 18 [below p. 221]. We have come to the conclusion that this demand curve is not really a demand curve for non-liquid in terms of liquid assets (does this mean anything?) but simply a demand curve for non-liquid assets (in terms of money, *simpliciters*) by people who have the *alternative* of holding liquid assets.

 II. P. 5, l. 3 [below p. 224]. This seems to be going rather far in denying (by implication) the importance of changes in business deposits consequent on changes in the price levels and outputs.

 (The same point arises in l. 5 if the relation between P and P' is accepted.)

 III. P. 9 footnote [below p. 229, n. 7]. It really *is* going rather far, I think, to regard the possibility of a change in output as a 'special case'.

But I am afraid that this is not going to convince Dennis. His real trouble is that the very fact that prices fall means that the real value of the total money stock has increased and that the fall in prices is explained by this increase. If people took steps to prevent the real value of their hoards from increasing, prices would not fall. And anyway the main feature of the downward phase of a trade cycle is a continued increase of hoards.

Piero will be troublesome about speculators. He says that relative yields are the only things that matter—it is not a question of bearishness.

Please excuse the scribble—I am not feeling very well.

R.F.K.

Robertson replied to Keynes's papers with the following letter and a series of pencil remarks on his copy of Keynes's reply. These pencil remarks follow the variorum version of Keynes's reply as Addendum I (below, p. 236).

From D. H. ROBERTSON, *13 May 1931*

My dear Maynard,

I've now considered your typed paper. I don't find I feel I want to alter anything in mine, except a few words on p. 11 (which perhaps you could copy, and let me have the page back). But I should like to add the MS pages, which will serve to reveal how far there is really any difference between us as to what happens *after* the time-hitch. As regards the latter, I think you really give me my point on your p. 4 [below p. 224],—only to take it back again later!

As regards publication:—The Prof. and I have decided to bring out a joint book of essays in the autumn[1]—mine all monetary—in which I should like to include this. It wouldn't much matter if it didn't appear elsewhere first. It might be best if you and the Prof. had your debate à deux in the Sept. *Journal*: and you might notice mine if there was an aftermath in the Dec. number. Just as you think: only I *should* rather like to keep it as a whole as what it is—a sort of running critical commentary, avowedly rather negative and not attempting to go right to the bottom of any of the points criticised, most of which would take a volume to explain properly!

Yours
D.H.R.

From the discussion with Pigou nothing remains beyond a few fragments: a covering note by Pigou for the second draft of his criticisms, Keynes's comments on these, and a later exchange of notes. Pigou's original criticisms did not appear in the *Economic Journal* and no drafts survive.

From A. C. PIGOU, *May 1931*

Dear Keynes,

Here is the thing. 5 and 6 try to bring the issue to a head on the line you suggested in your note on my first draft.

I haven't yet fully got hold of your typescript. But, as to your comment on my criticism, I didn't mean to suggest that 'savings = addition to savings deposits' in a perfectly general way: only (1) if total deposits are fixed and (2) if the velocity of other deposits (i.e. the frequency with which they became income) is fixed.

Yours,
A.C.P.

---

[1] *Economic Essays and Addresses*, (London, 1931). Robertson did not include this article in the collection.

So far as I at present understand your typescript I should say that all the factors you speak of are relevant, but they all can be represented as acting upon my M_r and bringing about their price consequences by changing that.

To A. C. PIGOU, *11 May 1931*

A.C.P.

§4. I do not follow what this is referring to. Could you give references to the passages of mine which you have in mind and to which you take exception? So far from my being unwilling to extend my formula beyond consumption goods I have in fact done so, and devoted several pages to it.

§5. This does not bear on anything I have written, because the 'velocity of circulation' I was referring to was Fisher's velocity. If velocity is defined in your present sense, you could express your point much more briefly as follows:—

My equation runs $O . \Pi^1 = E + Q$, which I further analyse into $O . \Pi = E + I - S$. You *define* r, such that $M . r = E + Q$ (r is not, so to speak, anything which exists in nature, even to the extent that Fisher's V does, and its meaning is *solely* derived from the above equation). Consequently my $O . \Pi = E + Q$ can be re-written $O . \Pi = M . r$. Now the final conclusion of pp. 4, 5, 6, 7 seems to be merely that if O and M are unchanged, Π cannot change unless r changes correspondingly—a proposition I should not wish to deny. The actual algebra I cannot follow, because I do not understand why equation I on p. 6 holds good;— I do not see why the *total* income (in your sense) at any time should be equal to the expenditure on consumption alone at some subsequent time. Also the conclusion in the fourth line of p. 7 is odd, because apparently the price level at any time depends on what the stock of money is going to be k time-units *later*.

The advantages I claim for my equations are the following:—

(i) By analysing $M . r$ into E and Q I can distinguish between price changes due to an alteration of E and those due to changes in Q. I claim that this distinction is vital. If E increases by a

---

[1] On your first assumption of no investment, P can be substituted for Π.

given amount and at the same time Q diminishes by an equal amount, according to you nothing has happened. But according to me a vital fact is disclosed. For I distinguish between price changes which correspond to changes in cost and those which do not; whereas for you they are all the same.

(ii) I am enabled to arrive at an equation for P the price level of consumption.

(iii) I am enabled to distinguish the essentially different causes which affect P and P' respectively. This is dealt with in the paper I handed to you on Saturday.

(iv) I can show how changes in Q are related to changes in I and S. By these means I can analyse the credit cycle and the *modus operandi* of bank rate and much else. But if I lump E and Q together and simply say that changes in prices are due to changes in $E+Q$ (M and O being supposed constant), I know very little. Indeed it would be more sensible, I would suggest, to say that changes in r are caused by changes in the other factors, rather than that changes in r are the causative element, since r has no independent existence;—though why changes in r should be considered interesting in themselves I do not see. To say that changes in r are the cause is like saying that the quantity of your kitchen bill is the cause (or, if you like, a description) of what you have for lunch; and that an attempt to analyse the causes of your indigestion as being due to the distribution of your expenditure between meat and vegetables can add nothing to what is given by a knowledge of the quantity of your kitchen bill because a change in your diet will probably (except by a coincidence where the changes in your expenditure in the two directions happen to be equal and opposite) be reflected by a change in your kitchen bill. The old-fashioned quantity-theory tutor, who only looks at the quantity of the kitchen bills has, therefore, nothing to learn from the new theories about the causes of dyspepsia!

J.M.K.

From A. C. PIGOU, *May 1931*

My dear Keynes,

Thanks for your note. I had understood you to argue (1) that the prices of consumption goods were determined in one way according to one formula and the prices of production goods, your P', by an entirely different formula: and, secondly, that your formula revealed price changes that could not be revealed by the 'Cambridge equation'. Apparently you don't intend to say either of these things, but only that your formula is a variant that forms a more convenient skeleton than the Cambridge equation on which to hang a connected account of the various real causes at work. I certainly don't want to argue about that. So long as one gets at the real causes, the skeleton is of no importance: and, indeed, as I said in the *Nation*[1], that, for most purposes, your skeleton is handier and more suggestive of useful lines of approach than the other. I thought that you were claiming much more than this. But, of course, you are the person who knows what you meant; and it would be ridiculous to have a discussion as to whether or not your language was such as to make my interpretation a natural one! So, as the points left are minor ones, I don't think it would serve any purpose to print my thing. It would merely muddle people up more than they are muddled already.

Yours,

A.C.P.

To A. C. PIGOU, *15 May 1931*

My dear Pigou,

The misunderstanding has been due, I think, to your supposing that I held my equations to be in some way inconsistent with the 'Cambridge equation'. That I certainly do not. Also, the formula by which I arrive at P' is by no means fundamentally different from that by which I arrive at P. What is different is my analysis of the underlying forces determining the two. But it is evident that I have quite failed to make this as clear as I should in my book. This is one of the points I have tried to do something to clear up in the memorandum I gave you the other day.

I should like, however, to preserve your final point where you

---

[1] In his review of the *Treatise*, 'Mr. Keynes on Money', *The Nation and Athenaeum*, 24 January, 1931, pp. 554–5.

extend my equation giving the change of price when there are redundant stocks. Would not this, with a little explanation added, make an interesting note of a page or two for the *E.J.*?

Yours ever,
[copy initialled] J.M.K.

Beyond these papers, all that survives of this discussion is a letter from R. F. Kahn on the galley proofs of Keynes's Rejoinder to Robertson. Kahn's marginal comments and major textual changes resulting therefrom appear in Addendum II to the Rejoinder.

From a note from R. F. KAHN, *15 August 1931*

I enclose the proofs with some scribbled marginal comments. I feel that your reply meets the case with great adequacy, but there are three points of substance to which I would like once again to allude.

(1) If only one could discover what Dennis means by 'hoarding', most of the difficulty would be disposed of. Take his numerical example (bottom of p. 3 and top of p. 4).[1] In the example of the text it is fairly clear that it is the speculators who have hoarded the £100 (incidentally the price of machines *rises* somewhat unless the demand for them by speculators is perfectly elastic), while business deposits remain depleted by £100. But in the example of the footnote business deposits are restored to their former level and speculators disgorge the £100 'hoarded by the speculators on day 1'—'the hoard of the speculators is transferred to the bootmakers'. But why on earth should the bootmakers be regarded as hoarding if all they do is to maintain their balances at the previous level? Now I have reason to suppose that by hoarding Dennis means nothing more nor less than a change in the real value of the total stock of money. Then if the amount of money remains constant and prices fall, hoarding *ipso facto* increases. And prices cannot fall unless hoarding increases—that is a truism. I wonder if it would be advisable to challenge Dennis with this view. (The point is that unless the community *permits* the real value of its money to rise, prices cannot fall.)

(2) I do not feel that your (ii), three-quarters of the way down p. 1 [below p. 220], is a sufficient concession to the point of view—natural to those brought up on the quantity theory—that the bootmakers in Dennis' parable will *not* restore their balances to the previous level. It is only by ascribing a unique position to profits, as contrasted to other payments, that

[1] *Economic Journal*, September 1931, p. 402.

you can justify the view, which persists throughout your article, that there is no reason to expect business deposits to alter if prices alter. If business deposits do fall when prices fall (the contraction of output lends strength to this possibility), there will *pro tanto* be a tendency for P' to move in the opposite direction.

(3) I still maintain—but I fear that you have already heard me sufficiently on this point—that in ascribing P and P' to different sets of causes you are sheltering yourself behind the arbitrary asymmetry of your definition of saving. Your admission that, while P and P' are not directly related, a change in P' will react on the level of P in so far as it causes a change in 'saving' does not, it seems to me, really meet the case. If one clears the decks of your special definitions, it is surely clear that P and P' *are* directly related except in the extreme case when no part of profits is devoted to consumption. I feel that I must still maintain that the difference between the determination of P and P' lies, purely and simply, either in the fact that there exists no demand curve for consumption goods on the part of speculators (holders of liquid and non-liquid assets) or the fact that if it does exist it is relatively inelastic (in which case the difference is one of degree and not an absolute one in logic).

It was at the end of all this discussion that Keynes's rejoinder to Robertson took the form it did. Below we print a variorum of the final *Economic Journal* version and Keynes's original reply to Robertson on 5 May 1931. Robertson's marginal comments on Keynes's original reply and Kahn's detailed comments on the galley of the final version appear as Addendum I and Addendum II respectively.

From *The Economic Journal*, September 1931.

A REJOINDER

1. Since I must not occupy too much space, I will deal primarily with what appears to me to be the central difference of opinion between Mr Robertson and myself, off which most of the other fragments of contentious matter are splinters. For if we could resolve this satisfactorily, much of the rest might resolve itself. I will then treat by way of brief notes with secondary matters of which—whether or not I have expressed myself as well as I might—Mr Robertson would not, I feel, make so much, if I could convince him that the fundamentals of my position are rightly taken.

2. This central difference of opinion is as follows. Mr Robertson quotes me, correctly (p. 400) [in the *Economic Journal*, September 1931], as holding the view that if P, the price level of consumption goods, declines owing to an excess of saving over the cost of new investment, then there *need* be no counterbalancing rise in P', the price level of investment goods, 'even though there is no increase in the disposition to hoard money unspent'. Mr Robertson holds that this result cannot come about 'except as the result of an act of hoarding'. This difference of opinion is evidently a special case of a more general difference as to the character of the forces which determine the price level of investment goods. Mr Robertson is quite right that it is absolutely fundamental to my analysis to distinguish *two* factors at work, which I have christened the 'excess-savings factor' and the 'excess-bearish factor'. This is the vital matter which I have failed so far to make clear to him. I will endeavour, therefore, to re-state my position.

3.[1] There are three conceptions which need to be distinguished:

(1) The volume of savings deposits or 'inactive' deposits in the banking system, sometimes, not very conveniently, called 'hoards'.

(2) The curve, representing the relative preference of capital owners for savings deposits and other capital assets respectively (or, as I have sometimes put it, for liquid and non-liquid assets respectively),[2] in which the abscissa measures the quantity of hoards held when the price of non-liquid assets in terms of liquid assets (or hoarded money) is given by the ordinate.[3] This

---

[1] Keynes's note of 5 May 1931 began here. In what follows, differences between this and the finally printed text are noted. Keynes's footnotes in the final text appear in square brackets.

[2] The rest of this sentence does not appear in the original note. Nor do the preceding brackets.

[3] [It is assumed for the sake of simplicity that any change in the quantity of non-liquid assets during the period under consideration is small relatively to the total stock of such assets. It does not alter the character of the argument if we dispense with this limitation, but the propensity to hoard has then to be represented by a family of curves instead of by a single curve.]

curve[1] is what I have described—not very felicitously, perhaps
—as the 'state or degree of bearishness'. It might be better to
call it 'the propensity to hoard'. The meaning and significance
of this conception and its vital difference from (1)[2] is what
in my *Treatise* I have evidently failed to make sufficiently clear.
The point is that, when a capital owner is deciding whether to
prefer liquid or non-liquid assets, his final decision depends not
only on his 'state of preference', or his 'propensity to hoard', or
his 'degree of bearishness' (however one likes to put it), i.e. on
the shape of his demand[3] curve for liquid assets given the price
of non-liquid assets, but also on what the price of non-liquid
assets is. Accordingly, the amount of 'hoards' or liquid assets
which he actually holds has to be in due relation not only to[4] his
propensity to hoard, but also to[5] the price of non-liquid assets.
When a man in a given state of mind is deciding whether to hold
bank deposits or house property, his decision depends not only
on the degree of his propensity to hoard, but also on the price of
house property. His decision to hold inactive deposits is not—as
Mr Robertson almost seems to assume[6]—an absolute one
irrespective of the price of other assets. If[7] it were, it would be
impossible for the banking system to expand or contract the
volume of money by 'open market' operations; for there would
be no price at which they could find a seller or a buyer (as the
case might be) for the securities which they wished to buy or
sell.

(3) The third conception is that of a *change*[8] in 'bearishness',
as I have called it, i.e., a change in the propensity to hoard, a

[1] The word 'curve' does not appear in the original note.
[2] The rest of the sentence replaces the words 'I have evidently failed to make clear in my
"Treatise"' in the original note.
[3] The rest of the sentence replaces the words '(or indifference) curve for one in terms of the
other, but also on the relative price of the two kinds of assets' in the original note.
[4] The words 'has to be in due relation not only to' replace the words 'depends not only on'
in the original note.
[5] The word 'to' replaces the word 'on' in the original note.
[6] The words in parenthesis do not appear in the original note.
[7] The rest of this paragraph does not appear in the original note.
[8] The word 'change' is not in italics in the original note.

change in the shape of the demand curve relating the demand for liquid assets to the price of non-liquid assets.

Now (1)—namely, the amount of inactive deposits or hoards actually held—is determined by the banking system, since it is equal to the excess of the total bank money created over what is required for the active deposits. This amount by itself can give no clue to the degree of propensity to hoard or to changes in this degree. Even less can it give any clue to the excess of saving over investment. My central thesis regarding the determination of the price of non-liquid assets is that, given (a) the quantity of inactive deposits[1] offered by the banking system, and (b) the degree of propensity to hoard or state of bearishness, then the price level of non-liquid assets must be fixed at whatever figure is required to equate the quantity of hoards which the public will desire to hold at that price level with the quantity of hoards which the banking system is creating.[2] That is to say, the price of non-liquid capital assets is a function of the quantity of inactive deposits[1] in conjunction with the degree of propensity to hoard.

Accordingly, the price of non-liquid assets is not directly affected by the price of consumption goods. Indirectly, it is true, a change in the price of consumption goods will not be without reactions on the two factors which determine the price of non-liquid assets. There are two principal[3] reactions[4]—(i) a change in the price of[5] consumption goods will tend, as a rule, to cause an opposite change in the propensity to hoard, since it will make more attractive at a given price than before, relatively to the ownership of liquid assets, the ownership of instrumental capital which is useful for the production of consumption goods, and also, if it is taken as an indication of a continuing trend, the

[1] The words 'inactive deposits' replace the words 'savings deposits' in the original note.
[2] The word 'creating' replaces the words 'prepared to supply' in the original note.
[3] The words 'two principal' replace the words 'three obvious' in the original note.
[4] The word 'namely' appears at this point in the original note.
[5] The rest of (i) replaces the words 'goods entering into consumption will involve an equal change in the price of similar goods in stock, which latter form a part, though a very small part, of the total stock of non-liquid assets' in the original note.

ownership of stocks of consumption and other goods; (ii)[1] a change in the price of consumption goods may conceivably, though not necessarily, involve a change in the same direction in the volume of active deposits, with the result that, if the banking system chooses to keep *total* deposits, and not inactive[2] deposits, at a constant level, there will be a change in the opposite direction in the volume of inactive[2] deposits. (iii)[3] On the other hand, a change in the price of non-liquid assets may react on the price of consumption goods because it will cause a change in profits, which, in turn, may affect in the opposite direction the amount saved[4] by the recipients of profits.[5]

Now the tendency of (i) and (iii)[6] is to make the price of non-liquid assets move, not in the opposite, but in the *same* direction as that of consumption goods. Thus the possibility of these two reactions does not help Mr Robertson's[7] view that the price levels of consumption goods and investment goods will move in *opposite* directions—like buckets in a well. The tendency of (ii),[8] on the other hand, may be in the opposite direction; but this is likely, it seems to me, to be negligible, and to belong to the class of the innumerable small, conceivable reactions of one economic factor on another, which one generally leaves out of account, except in special cases. Moreover, it is based on the[9]

---

[1] (ii) in the text follows (iii) in the original note. (ii) in the original note ran: 'a change in the price of consumption goods will tend, as a rule, to cause an opposite change in the propensity to hoard, since it will make more attractive than before the ownership of instrumental capital which is useful for the production of consumption goods'.

[2] The word 'inactive' replaces the word 'savings' in the original note.

[3] (iii), with its associated footnotes, does not appear in the original note.

[4] [For on my definition of saving there is a decrease of saving if *any* part of increased profits is directed towards current consumption.]

[5] [And, finally, one might add, though without much relevance to the present argument, that (iv) a change in the price of consumption goods may in itself affect the amount of investment by causing changes in the amount of liquid stocks held off by the market, though this factor is not very important because it will merely diminish the magnitude of the movement of P in any direction as compared with what would happen in its absence, e.g. if all consumption goods were perishable; and (v) a change in the price of consumption goods may in itself affect the amount of saving.]

[6] '(iii)' in the text replaces '(ii)' in the original note.

[7] The words 'Mr Robertson's' replace the word 'the' in the original note.

[8] '(ii)' in the text replaces '(iii)' in the original note.

[9] The word 'the' replaces the word 'an' in the original note.

assumption that it is[1] the policy of the banking system to maintain the volume of *total* deposits unchanged,[2] whereas my argument[3] assumed that they were maintaining an unchanged policy towards the volume of inactive deposits, i.e. I was assuming that the quantity of *hoards* was unchanged.

4. Next, for my argument, which Mr Robertson contests in the latter part of his §5,[4] that an increase of saving relatively to investment does not in itself bring about any net increase in the amount of purchasing power directed to non-liquid assets. An increase of saving relatively to investment during any period means that the savers find themselves at the end of the period with an increase of wealth, which they can embark at their choice either in liquid or in non-liquid assets, whilst the producers of consumption goods find themselves with an equal decrease of wealth, which must cause them to part at their choice either with liquid or with non-liquid assets which they previously possessed. Unless the propensity to hoard of the savers is different from the propensity to hoard of the entrepreneurs—and if it is different, it will mean that there is a change of hoarding propensity[5] for the community as a whole, which change is as likely *a priori* to be in one direction as in the other—it follows that the excess of saving has *in itself*, and apart from its repercussions on the aggregate propensity to hoard,[6] no tendency to cause any change at all in the price of non-liquid assets. Nor, of course, has it any tendency to cause a change in the volume of inactive[7] deposits, except in so far as the banking system may be influenced by changes in the business deposits to fix the total deposits in such a way as to change the amount

---

[1] The words 'that it is' replace the words 'as to' in the original note.

[2] The words 'to maintain the volume of *total* deposits unchanged' replace the words 'towards the volume of *total* deposits' in the original note.

[3] The rest of the sentence replaces the words 'was concerned with their policy towards the volume of savings deposits' in the original note.

[4] The preceding clause does not appear in the original note.

[5] The words 'hoarding propensity' replace the word 'bearishness' in the original note.

[6] The words 'the aggregate propensity to hoard' replace the word 'bearishness' in the original note.

[7] The word 'inactive' replaces the word 'savings' in the original note.

of the inactive[1] deposits.[2] (Nor, equally, is a change in the propensity to hoard capable by itself, and apart from action by the banking system, of changing the volume of savings deposits— it may spend itself in a change[3] in the price of non-liquid assets.)

When, therefore,[4] I said that the price of consumption goods relatively to the cost of production depends solely on the excess of saving over investment, and that the price of investment goods depends solely on the volume of savings deposits in conjunction with the degree of bearishness (or propensity to hoard),[5] both statements were[6] formally correct. But I ought to have added, to prevent misunderstanding, that I did not mean to imply that the price of investment goods is incapable of reacting on the excess of saving over investment,[7] and hence on the price of con- sumption goods; or that the price of consumption goods is incapable of reacting on the volume of savings deposits or on the propensity to hoard,[8] and hence on the price of investment goods. I meant only that the influence of the one on the other *must*, like the influence on them of any other factor in the total

[1] The word 'inactive' replaces the word 'savings' in the original note.
[2] [This qualification does not seem to me to come to much, because one cannot say in general in which direction the business deposits will change, or how a change in them will influence the behaviour of the banking system.]
This footnote appeared as well in the original note.
[3] The word 'change' replaces the word 'fall' in the original note.
[4] The word 'therefore' does not appear in the original note.
[5] The words '(or propensity to hoard)' do not appear in the original note.
[6] The word 'were' replaces the word 'are' in the original note.
[7] [There are two principal ways in which the price of investment goods may affect the volume of saving. The first depends on the sensitiveness of the saving of the public to the *relative* price levels of investment goods and consumption goods. Do people save more when securities *[a]* are, relatively, at a bargain level, and spend more when consumable goods are at such a bargain level? The second arises when the price of investment goods is such as to bring profits or losses to the producers of such goods, and these producers are influenced by the amount of their profits and losses in deciding how much to save and how much to spend. For if an entrepreneur spends more as a *[b]* result of gaining profits, this constitutes, on my definition, a diminution of his savings.]
This footnote appears in the original note and follows it except for (*a*) the substitution of the word 'securities' in the text for the word 'investments' in the original and (*b*) the deletion of the word 'psychological' which appeared between the words 'a' and 'result' in the original.
[8] The words 'propensity to hoard' replace the words 'degree of bearishness' in the original text.

economic situation, operate *through* the excess of saving in the one case and the volume of savings deposits or the propensity to hoard[1] in the other.

5. I have found that some readers of my book have supposed[2] that an excess of saving over investment is necessarily accompanied by an equal increase of inactive deposits; so that—presumably—an excess of saving would be impossible if the banking system were[3] to behave in such a way as to keep the excess of the total deposits over the active deposits at a constant figure.[4] Their[5] interpretation of my theory seems to be this. An excess of saving is only another way of talking about an increase of inactive deposits; an increase of inactive deposits means a decrease in the velocity of circulation; thus, when I say that an excess of saving leads to a fall in the price of consumption goods, I am only repeating in a very complicated way the old story that a fall in the velocity of circulation must bring prices down, other things being equal. But, truly, this is not what I am saying.[6] The volume of inactive deposits has, in my view, no particular relation to an excess of saving, but depends on whether the banking system is creating total deposits faster than the increments can find an outlet in active deposits. Nor is there any invariable association in experience between a growth of inactive deposits and an excess of saving. During the recent boom in [the]

---

[1] The words 'propensity to hoard' replace the words 'degree of bearishness' in the original text.

[2] The words '5. I have found that some readers of my book have supposed' replace the words 'The criticisms to which the above arguments have been subjected are various: (i) A. C. P[igou]. seems to think' in the original note.

[3] The word 'were' replaces the word 'was' in the original note.

[4] At this point the original note continued: 'Surely, for a thousand reasons, this is totally false. But A.C.P. goes further. He seems to think, not only that it is true, but also that it is *my view*. I can at least affirm that this view and my view differ *toto coelo*. The volume of savings deposits has, in my view, no particular relation to an excess of saving but depends on whether the banking system is creating deposits faster than they can find an outlet in active deposits. Nor is there any invariable association in experience between a growth of savings deposits and an excess of saving. During the recent boom in [the] U.S.A. an excess of investment was accompanied by an unparalleled rate of growth of savings deposits.'

[5] The word 'their' replaces the word 'A.C.P.'s' in the original note.

[6] The rest of this paragraph does not appear in the original note at this point, as noted in footnote 4 above.

U.S.A., for example, an excess of investment was accompanied by an unparalleled rate of growth of inactive deposits.

Mr[1] Robertson's objection, though much more complicated than this, is nevertheless related, I cannot help thinking, to this point of view. He does not think that an excess of saving necessarily requires an increase of inactive deposits, or, as he would express it, an increase in hoarding.[2] But he thinks that, *unless* an excess of saving is associated with an increase in hoarding, it will mean that an increased flow of purchasing power equal to the excess saving will be directed to the purchase of investment goods. He thinks that this will involve an *equal* increase in the receipts of the producers of the current output of investment goods, so that the losses of the producers of consumption goods due to the excess saving will be balanced by profits of an *equal* amount accruing to the producers of investment goods. His argument is of such a character that if the producers of consumption goods, who are losing money, replenish their liquid assets by the sale of non-liquid assets *before* those who, saving money, use this money to buy non-liquid assets, then there will be a fall (or at any rate no rise) in the price of investment goods; but if those who are saving money 'get in first', then the opposite is the case. It would be very odd if the price level were to depend on which of the two parties was on the telephone and which was not; and this alone is enough to suggest that there must be something wrong in the argument. But let us consider it in more detail.

Let us, for the moment[3], assume with Mr Robertson[4] that the savers dispose of their savings, into liquid or non-liquid

---

[1] This paragraph, along with its associated footnote, does not appear in the original note, but replaces the following:

'(2) D.H.R[obertson]. seems to think that the validity of my argument depends on the entrepreneurs who are losing money "getting in first" on to the capital market, whereas if the excess savers get in first, something quite different happens. It would be very odd if the price level were to depend on which of the two parties was on the telephone and which was not. But I must consider the stages of the argument in more detail.'

[2] [Or does he mean by hoarding something different from an increase of inactive deposits? There are some passages in his article which suggest that perhaps he may.]

[3] The words 'for the moment' replace the words 'for the sake of argument' in the original note.   [4] The words 'with Mr Robertson' do not appear in the original note.

assets as the case may be, before the losing entrepreneurs have time to provide for their losses. (In a sense this is an impossible assumption, since in a sense the two things must take place simultaneously. The first stage must necessarily be that the savers find themselves with more money, and the losers find themselves with less money. But we will allow the savers to 'get in first' in the sense of allowing them to decide whether or not to embark this money in non-liquid assets, before the losers have time to decide whether or not to make up their cash deficiency by selling non-liquid assets.) Mr Robertson[1] seems to think that the whole of these funds, in the absence of increased hoarding, will have to be directed to the purchase of the *newly produced* non-liquid assets already on the market, and that no other assets will come on the market whatever price may be offered, so[2] that the aggregate selling price of the newly produced non-liquid assets will increase by the exact amount of the excess savings, and the resulting profits to the producers of investment goods will balance the previous losses of the producers of consumption goods.[3] But this is to mistake entirely[4] the nature of the capital market. The price of investment goods, *old and new alike*,[5] will have to rise sufficiently to induce some of[6] the existing holders, given their existing propensity to hoard,[7] to part with non-liquid assets in exchange for such part of the excess savings as, at that price, the excess savers desire to embark on the purchase of non-

[1] The words 'Mr Robertson' replace the initials 'D.H.R.' in the original note.

[2] The words 'that the whole of these funds, in the absence of increased hoardings, will have to be directed to the purchase of the *newly produced* non-liquid assets already on the market, and that no other assets will come on the market whatever price may be offered, so' replace the words 'that this will mean' in the original note.

[3] [This is, I think, a correct account of his argument on p. 401; but I am not sure whether the numerical example on p. 402 is consistent with the argument on p. 401. The latter may be, it seems to me, not 'carrying the story a little further' but a different story. In particular, it is not clear in the footnote to p. 402 why the bootmakers who end up with the same amount of money as at the beginning should be considered to be 'hoarding'.] This footnote did not appear in the original note.

[4] The word 'entirely' does not appear in the original note.

[5] The words '*old and new alike*' replace the words 'old and new together' in the original note.

[6] The words 'some of' do not appear in the original note.

[7] The words 'propensity to hoard' replace the words 'degree of bearishness' in the original note.

liquid assets. How[1] great a rise this will mean in the price of non-liquid assets will depend on the shape of the curve which measures the propensity to hoard.

But this increase will only last so long as the telephone girls, attached to the exchange to which the losing entrepreneurs belong, persist in giving them wrong numbers. As soon as they can get through,[2] they will sell non-liquid assets to the same amount as the excess savers have been previously buying them —that is, unless the hoarding propensities[3] of the savers are[4] different from the hoarding propensities of the entrepreneurs, and the effect of these sales will be to bring non-liquid assets[5] back again to their previous price. Nothing, indeed, can shake this previous price except a change in the volume of inactive[6] deposits or a change in the propensity to hoard for the community as a whole.[7] Indeed,[8] it seems to me that it would be

[1] In the original note the paragraph concluded: 'Presumably this will mean some increase in the price of non-liquid assets, how much depending on the shape of the curve.'

[2] The word 'through' replaces the words 'on to their brokers' in the original note.

[3] The words 'hoarding propensities' replace the words 'degree of bearishness' in the original note.   [4] The word 'are' replaces the word 'is' in the original note.

[5] The words 'and the effect of these sales will be to bring non-liquid assets' replace the words '—so that non-liquid assets will return' in the original note.

[6] The word 'inactive' replaces the word 'savings' in the original note.

[7] [I did not deal in my book, and I am not dealing here, with the train of events which ensues when, as a consequence of making losses, entrepreneurs reduce their output. This is a long story, though not, I think, fundamentally different, [a] which I intend to treat in detail in due course. Its only bearing on the present argument is that a change in output affects the demand for active deposits, and may therefore (according to how the banking system behaves) affect the supply of hoards.] The footnote in the original note followed this one from the text down to (a) except that the words 'in detail' followed the word 'deal'. From that point, the footnote in the original note concluded with the words 'which needs an extensive and separate treatment'.

[8] At this point the text and the original note finally diverge. The original note concluded:
'D.H.R. has, I think, a subsidiary point that the price level of new investment goods is not necessarily identical with the price level of the totality of capital assets. This is true but does not seem to me to be of any fundamental consequence. Just as there is, in any given state of bearishness, a curve of preference relating the price of total capital assets to the volume of savings deposits, so also there is a curve of preference relating the price of new investment goods to that of total capital assets; and it is reasonable to assume that the two move in the same direction though not necessarily at an equal pace.

(3) P.S[raffa].'s argument has not been reduced to writing, so that I am not so clear about what it is. I gather that it is partly concerned with the point just discussed, namely the relation between the price of new investment goods and that of the totality of non-liquid assets. It is also partly concerned with the fact that if total deposits are kept constant, changes in the volume of active deposits react on the volume of savings deposits. This has been dealt with above.'

absurd to suppose that the final result can depend on the order in which two transactions take place, which are, in the nature of the case, nearly simultaneous and each of which is as likely as the other to come first.

The essential point, which I maintain and Mr Robertson resists, is the fact that an increase of saving which is not associated with an increase of investment does not change in any way either the quantity of assets or the quantity of purchasing power, but merely transfers command over cash in the first instance, and the ownership of assets after there has been time to reduce individual cash holdings to a normal level, between one set of persons and another set, i.e. between the saving public and the disappointed entrepreneurs. Since the total amount of non-liquid assets is unchanged and the total amount of liquid assets is unchanged, nothing has happened so far (unless the new proprietors have a different hoarding propensity from the old proprietors) to cause a change in the valuation of the one in terms of the other, i.e. in the price of non-liquid assets.

I do not, by the way, understand the relevance of the quantity equation[1] with which Mr Robertson concludes his §5. We are discussing the relation between the prices of consumption goods and of investment goods—whether, assuming no change in the propensity to hoard, the one must go down when the other goes up, like buckets in a well—which he affirms and I deny. But neither of these price levels occurs in his equations, which are concerned with the price level of output as a whole and the price level of transactions.

I should like to repeat that the amount of the hoards of the public is as much outside their control as is the total quantity of money, and for the same reasons. What the state of mind of the public towards holding money, and the changes in this state of mind, determine is the price of non-liquid assets which (*cet. par.*) the creation of a given quantity of money will involve. This

[1] [In which he uses 'income' in a different sense from mine, since it is equal to income + profit in my terminology.]

is why it is so important to distinguish the forces determining the quantity of hoards (which is the affair of the bankers) from the forces determining the propensity to hoard (which is the affair of the public). The old quantity equations did not reveal this to me, and, to judge from his article, they have not revealed it to Mr Robertson, just as they did not reveal to me the way in which the relation between saving and investment influences the price level of goods passing into consumption.

6. I now turn, as briefly as I can, to Mr Robertson's other comments, beginning with his §2, where I assume that, in speaking of 'the old quantity equations', he has primarily in mind the Fisher equations.[1] I cannot admit that I have been wanting here in reasonable lucidity. I have never said that the older methods, strictly applied, would lead us to *wrong* results. My point is that they are incapable, so applied, of leading us to certain useful results. I cannot imagine why Mr Robertson should suppose that the passage he quotes from my p. 147 [*JMK*, vol. V, p. 133] is inconsistent with the Fisher equations and reduces the latter 'to the rank of untruths'. For two of the variables I mention— namely, the volume of output and the price level of output—do not occur at all in the Fisher equations, which are concerned with the volume of *transactions* and the price level of *transactions*, as I have repeatedly explained. I was trying to illustrate the point that the old quantity notions are incapable of leading us to the price level of output, by pointing out that all or any of the variables occurring in the quantity equation might be unchanged and yet the price level of output might be changed. In other words, not only does the price level of output not occur explicitly in the old quantity equation, but it is not even a function of those variables which do occur in it. Wherein does Mr Robertson's difficulty lie? For it is impossible that he can suppose that the Fisher equation purports to tell us the price level of output.

I should add that I am, avowedly, on weaker ground in the passage he quotes from Vol. II (p. 89) [*JMK*, vol. VI, p. 78]. I do

---

[1] [If not, I could, by taking up more space, adapt my argument appropriately.]

not claim to have proved inductively what I suggest may be the case; for the statistics I am using, though the best I could get, are much too dubious. For example, I agree with Mr Robertson that I would prefer a retail index to a wholesale index, if I had a retail index. But I am entitled to point out that the results, for what they are worth, are not inconsistent with my *a priori* reasoning, and may even furnish a first approximation towards measuring the potency of the forces to which I have called attention; whilst Mr Robertson, who apparently does not believe in these forces *a priori*, is equally entitled not to discard his *a priori* convictions on the strength of these statistics.

7. In §3 Mr Robertson has been wrongly instructed by Mr Golodetz. There is no difficulty in dealing with government expenditure financed out of loans, whether or not the loans are associated with the creation of new money. The only question to decide is whether a particular form of government expenditure is best regarded as investment or as negative saving. I have myself treated government expenditure on services which yield no immediate social income, as investment when it is in return for work done (e.g. war expenditure) and as negative saving otherwise (e.g. the dole). But my equation shows that it makes no immediate difference to the price level which way we regard it. I should add that the outcome depends, according to my view, on the net effect of the government's policy on the relation between savings and investment, not, as Mr Robertson suggests, on the additional quantity of money associated with this policy. So far from the equation being ill adapted to show the short-period effect of these things, it brings out clearly what nearly everyone overlooks—namely, that the short-period effect, on business profits, of the dole, if financed by borrowing, or indeed of a government deficit arising in any other way, is exactly the same (ignoring secondary repercussions) as the effect of increased investment; whilst, on the other hand, the balancing of a budget, previously unbalanced, has as disastrous a direct effect on business profits (again ignoring secondary repercussions) as that

which ensues on a decay of home investment or on a decline in exports associated with a less favourable balance of trade.

Mr Robertson's reference to the possibility of diminishing returns might be brought under the general heading of causes capable of producing spontaneous changes in efficiency earnings, to which I have devoted some pages (Vol. I, pp. 166 *et seq.*) [*JMK*, vol. V, pp. 149–53]. But in this case, as in most examples of spontaneous changes, a full discussion would soon bring one beyond the ambit of a treatise on money.

8. Mr Robertson's §4 is mainly a preamble to the more important matters which follow and with which I have endeavoured to deal above. But I must say in passing that a rise in the price of banana-cutters will not avoid any of the dire consequences predicted in my banana parable, unless it leads either to an increased output of these machines, which I have expressly excluded from my premisses (p. 176[1]) [*JMK*, vol. V, p. 158], or to diminished saving by the producers of these machines, which offsets the increased saving by the rest of the community, which again contradicts my premiss as to there being a net increment of saving. It is too much to expect of an illustration of this kind that its results should follow not only from its stated premisses, but also from their opposite.

9. The impression to which Mr Robertson has been guided, as set forth in the first paragraph of his §5, is not that which I intended. The two conceptions involved are not 'existing stock exchange securities' and 'new machines', but 'the existing stock of capital' and 'the currently produced capital'. My argument assumes that the price of both will be governed by the same influences in the sense that the purchaser of capital goods will have no prejudice for or against the new as such, though even this is not really vital to my central point; but the argument does

---

[1] [If Mr Robertson will read p. 176 again, he will see that it is not true that I tacitly assume increments of working capital to be the only form of investment. I expressly state what I assume to be happening to investment in fixed or instrumental capital. I have read Dr Hayek's article, to which Mr Robertson refers, without discovering in it anything relevant to this particular problem.]

not require that the new capital is identical with the old, either in composition or in price, in the sense that the current increment of capital is made up of different ingredients in such proportions as to be a perfect sample of the existing stock of capital. My assumption is that the forces which determine the value of the complex of newly produced capital goods relatively to the value of the existing stock of old capital goods are not relevant to the particular problem here under discussion and can be neglected. I think that Mr Robertson does not really disagree with this, and that his difficulty is again in the nature of a preamble to, and probably caused by, the very important difference of opinion, already dealt with, which is expressed in the last sentence of this paragraph.

10. Mr Robertson's comments in his §§6,7, are not of such a character that I can deal with them satisfactorily within a short compass. But, generally speaking, I agree that the passages which he criticises are not satisfactory as they stand, and ought to be rewritten. I have not made it clear what forces I am taking account of at each stage. In the passages in question I have dwelt on the effect of a change in the pure rate of interest too much in isolation, and I have not, in the passage under criticism, successfully synthesised this with the rest of my doctrine. I should add that I had in mind (e.g.) 'houses' and 'buildings' generally, or 'roads' and 'railways', as typical capital goods affected by changes in the pure rate of interest, rather than 'machines'. Mr Robertson's habitual use of 'machines' as typical capital goods, though he may intend to include 'houses' and 'roads' under this term, creates, to my mind, rather a false suggestion, because 'machines' in the natural sense of the term, i.e. 'factory equipment', which are, it is true, somewhat insensitive to changes in the pure rate of interest, are quantitatively a very trifling proportion of the total stock of capital.

11. I will consider what Mr Robertson says about nomenclature in his §8. I think I might do better than in my *Treatise*,

but it is not very easy. The last paragraph of his §8, of which I can make nothing, makes me think that he does not quite see the difficulty. For if, as he suggests, we were to define 'income' to mean 'earnings *plus* profits' ($E+Q$ in my notation) and 'saving' to mean the difference between income thus defined and expenditure on consumption ($S = E+Q-PR$), then it would follow that savings and the value of new investment would always be exactly equal (for $Q = PR+I-E$, so that $S = I$). Does Mr Robertson, in practice, mean by 'savings' exactly the same as what he means by 'the value of new investment'? I would partly defend my using the term 'savings' as I do, by my belief that the ordinary man does not attach a perfectly clear and consistent meaning to it. We do not usually regard a man as 'saving' if he refrains from spending the proceeds of an increase in the value of his securities. Mr Robertson wants to include in 'income' money profits from the price of new investment standing above its cost, but not similar profits from the price of old investment standing above its cost. I doubt if this is either convenient or instructive; for new investment, immediately it is born, flows into a pool of old investment from which it is un-differentiated. How soon must a new investment rise in price for the resulting profit to be reckoned as part of its owner's income? We have to draw a sharp line somewhere between 'income' and 'capital profits', and I have tried to draw it at the point which, after much reflection, seems to me to be the most significant.

12. When in §9 Mr Robertson says that I am right 'in laying stress on "hoarding" as a dominant feature of trade depression', he is not quoting my exact words. By 'hoarding' does he here mean (1) 'an increase of inactive deposits', or (2) 'an increased propensity to hoard', or (3) 'an excess of saving over invest-ment'? Only in cases (2) and (3) is he giving my meaning correctly. For I hold that the primary cause of trade depression is (3), aggravated at a later stage by (2). It is only in the event of efforts by the banking system to dispel the depression that (1) is

likely to result. And whilst it is true that, if the *total* quantity of money is constant, an increase in inactive deposits may, by reason of its being a reflection of a decrease in the active deposits, be a *symptom* of depression, yet action by the banking system to *decrease* the volume of inactive deposits would (*cet. par.*) aggravate the depression. Yet elsewhere Mr Robertson seems to mean by 'hoarding' case (1), in which case he is adopting the mistaken interpretation of my views which I have attributed to 'some readers' on p. 416 [above p. 226].

13. I do not doubt that I am open to much criticism for inconsistency in language and in detail. I know only too well how much better and how much more accurately the argument might be expressed. But I am sure that Mr Robertson's difficulties are mainly due, not to these imperfections, but to our minds not having met as yet on certain large issues. I have therefore endeavoured to confine myself mainly to these, because, if we could get clear about them, many of my inconsistencies, both real and apparent, would cease to be troublesome; for Mr Robertson would then readily see for himself what I meant to say or should have said consistently with my own principles.

Addendum I

D. H. ROBERTSON'S PENCIL COMMENTS ON KEYNES'S ORIGINAL NOTE OF 5 MAY 1931

page 222 line 4: 'is determined by the banking system'—'This is a half-truth,—the volume of savings deposits may alter as a result *either* of action on the part of banks *or* of action on the part of the public. That is the inconvenience of separating off s[avings]. d[eposits]. sharply from other deposits.'

page 223 lines 12–17: 'Nobody holds the view that this "will" happen,—it is a matter of finding the right explanation of its *not* happening.'

page 223 lines 17–22: 'I should have thought that the growth of savings deposits at the expense of business deposits was a feature of *prime* importance during the slump.'

page 224 line 10: 'No, of *hoarding.*'

page 224 lines 15–19: 'This is to give away your whole case,—for you apparently concede that during this "period" money stays where it is instead of changing hands once,—i.e. its v[elocity]. of c[irculation]. declines.'

page 224 lines 4-10: 'A.C.P. was analysing a state of affairs in which M remained unchanged.'

page 228 lines 2-4: 'Not very: the only reason why the price level is not infinite is because things can't happen instantaneously.'

page 228 lines 20-4: 'i.e. there *will* be an increase in savings deposits (assuming the banking system takes no action).'

page 229 footnote 1: 'There is no hint of this in the *Treatise*, I think.'

page 229 lines 6-12: 'Yes, if we are only dealing with *one act* of savings, the savings deposits of the "bears" will be reduced and we return to the old equilibrium,—with entrepreneurs so much the poorer. But if the saving is *continuous* there will be a new dose of saving to buy these entrepreneurs' securities, and then savings deposits of the "bears" will remain raised. But see my extra MS.'

page 229 footnote 8: 'I think it is fundamental.'

Addendum II

R. F. KAHN'S COMMENTS OF 15 AUGUST 1931 ON THE
GALLEY PROOF OF KEYNES'S 'REJOINDER'

page 220 lines 16-18: Keynes had written on the galley 'This is the vital matter for which I have failed so far to find an ingress to his mind.'

Kahn commented 'Is this going a little far? After all D.H.R.'s point is quite sound—what is the logical distinction between P and P'? (see (3) in my letter).'

page 222 line 24: 'Is (iii) not important?'

page 228 line 12: Kahn suggested the addition of words to the effect of 'in the absence of increased hoarding' with his phrase 'unless there is "hoarding" (see his parable of the bootmakers)' with reference to the words 'have to be'.

page 229 lines 2-3: 'But if the price level of transactions does not alter, how can the price level of output alter? Is not the point that the *volume* of transactions alters (or, alternatively, the velocity is defined in the quantity equation but not as defined by you)?'

page 233 lines 3-7: 'It seems to me very difficult to bring d[iminishing] r[eturns] under the head of these pages and I do feel that Dennis deserves credit for referring to a point that you have agreed has important bearings.'

page 233 line 27 to page 234 line 8: 'But is there not a real difficulty in the possibility of deviations between the prices of securities, (non-liquid assets?) and the price of working capital?'

page 235 lines 9–10: These ended the section in the galley. Kahn commented 'But surely Dennis is merely adopting a perfectly simple-minded and natural definition of saving—receipts minus expenditure—though it is true that it involves him in the difficulty to which you allude?'

Keynes concluded his galleys with the following paragraph: 'Mr Robertson's last paragraph of all—yes! a mere relic of Sadistic—well, not so much barbarism as puritanism. But at this point psycho-analysis must take charge and economic analysis withdraw discreetly.'

Kahn commented, 'I hope that you will decide to *omit*.'

The Robertson exchange in the *Economic Journal* led to an exchange of letters with Nicholas Kaldor, then research student at the London School of Economics.

From N. KALDOR, *19 November 1931*

Sir,

As a student of economics, may I be allowed to trespass upon your time and patience by asking you to clear up a few points in your 'Rejoinder' to Mr D. H. Robertson, in the current *Economic Journal*?

(1) On p. 418 [above p. 228], in the course of an argument which is designed to show the origin of an excess of saving over investment, the velocity of circulation remaining constant, you write: 'The price of investment goods, *old and new alike*, will have to rise sufficiently to induce some of the existing holders, given their existing propensity to hoard, to part with non-liquid assets in exchange for such part of the excess savings, as, at that price, the excess savers desire to embark on the purchase of non-liquid assets.' May I point out that in so far as the new savers (or the excess savers) keep part of their new savings in liquid form, this already implies a change in 'hoarding', i.e. in the velocity of circulation? While of course this may happen as a consequence of saving, and as such can form the basis of theory leading to a law of diminishing velocity of circulation, it cannot take place if the velocity of circulation is, *per assumptionem*, constant. In that case, the price of securities, old and new alike, must go on rising, until existing holders throw so many securities on to the market that their aggregate value equals the amount of new savings. If the existing holders desire to keep the proceeds of their securities now sold in liquid form, this again implies a change in velocity.

(2) On the same page, in the next paragraph [above p. 229], you write: 'As soon as they (i.e. the losing entrepreneurs) can get through (the telephone)

they will sell non-liquid assets to the same amount as the excess savers have been previously buying them...and the effect of these sales will be to bring non-liquid assets back again to their previous price.' May I point out, that this can only take place if the losing entrepreneurs sell securities to the whole amount with which their current receipts have diminished? In so far as these entrepreneurs will meet some part of their losses by (i) diminishing their own income, (ii) paying smaller dividends, (iii) paying lower wages, or (iv) dismissing labourers, or by any combination of these methods, there will be some rise in the price of securities (as the additional money going to buy securities and coming from the savers will be greater than the additional securities sold by the losing entrepreneurs), and consequently, *ceteris paribus*, there will be some rise in new investment. It is true, the new investment will not equal the new savings—except in the case that the losing entrepreneurs will not resort to the method of covering losses by de-cumulating capital, that is, by selling securities for consumptive purposes. In order, however, that no addition to current investment should take place it is necessary that the sale of securities for the purpose of covering losses should exactly equal the diminution of total receipts. But that is only another way of saying that no 'saving' has taken place at all: as the saving, i.e. the capital-accumulation of some has been exactly cancelled by the dis-saving, i.e. the capital decumulation (or capital consumption, if this term is preferred) of others.

The significance of this objection, which at first sight might seem a purely terminological one, is seen by showing that such a discrepancy can arise without any change in the rate of saving or in the rate of investment. Suppose (to keep to Mr Robertson's example) on one day the public switch over a streamlet of money from buying boots—not to the buying of machines, but to the buying of hats. On that day the losses of bootmakers will exactly equal the profits of the hatmakers—there will be no 'net profits' for entrepreneurs as a whole—and new equilibrium will be restored by bootmakers' contracting and hatmakers' expanding production, or by some bootmakers going over to the production of hats. But, if the bootmakers persist—instead of bearing this temporary falling-off in their income—to keep to their previous 'standard of living' by selling securities, they will bring, next day, the machine-makers into trouble. On that day some portion of the stream of money which ordinarily goes to the purchase of machines will be used in buying the securities of the bootmakers, and at the end of that day the machine-makers will find that they make losses. If the latter, following the example of the bootmakers, will also sell securities in turn, on the third day the 'depression' will be very formidable indeed: the machine-makers, or some other people producing capital goods, will experience a further diminution of their current receipts and thus aggravate the tendency to sell securities. The process is cumulative and might lead, under certain assumptions, to the destruction of the total stock of existing capital. (The velocity of circulation is assumed, of course, to remain constant, throughout the whole period.) *But the initial cause* which led to the trouble, *was not any change in the relation between savings and expenditure, or between savings and investment,* but the determination of some entrepreneurs, or we may even say, some part of the public, *to counterbalance the falling-off of their current income* (caused, in the example given, by a shift in the public demand for various goods, but it may have been caused by any other 'external' circumstance, without making any difference to the argument) *by consuming their capital,* i.e. by selling their existing property rights and thus to keep to their previous scale of expenditure, which is now greater than the value of their 'marginal product'. The only difference made by considering a change in the relation of saving and expenditure is that there will be no *net* consumption of capital: as the capital-decumulation of some is balanced by the capital-accumulation of others. (In the example given, the cumulative tendency will be averted, if the securities sold by the bootmakers be bought out of the profits of the hatmakers, in which case the only 'real' consequence will be, that the public will continue to receive more boots and less hats than it really wants to; and that the hatmakers will be 'worse-off' by the amount by which the final yield of their holdings of bootmakers' shares will fall below the amount the money would have yielded had it been invested in the hatmakers' own industries, or indeed, in anything else.)

I should be very grateful if you were kind enough to draw my attention to any flaw in my argument which you may detect, and which may render it impermissible to generalise the case considered in connection with a change in the rate of saving to the case of any other change in demand. I should not have been tempted to trouble you with the matter, but for the fact that I did not see this point considered either in Mr Robertson's or Dr Hayek's criticism; while I believe that the clearing-up of this point may render much of the difference which seems to exist between your own and Mr Robertson's and Dr Hayek's point of view, illusory.

I am, Sir,

Yours faithfully,
NICHOLAS KALDOR

To N. KALDOR, *27 November 1931*

Dear Sir,

Your letter of November 19 raises some subtle points of argument and terminology, which it would be difficult to deal with adequately within the compass of a letter. I would make, however, the following brief comments on your several points, though well aware that my inevitable brevity may prevent you from seeing my point fully.

(1) If the new savers keep part of their new savings in liquid form, this means that the liquid reserves of the losing entrepreneurs are reduced by an equal amount, so there is no change for the community, taken as a whole.

(2) I should agree that in the event of some of the contingencies that you suggest, it would make a difference; but Mr Robertson and I were dealing with a theoretical and hypothetical case of strict assumptions, and some of the contingencies you suggest are not consistent with these abstract assumptions.

(3) I am not clear that the argument of your last paragraph but one, does not involve some change in saving in the sense in which I define that. For if some part of the public were to decide, for any reason, to consume their capital, this would in itself mean a change in the rate of savings.

Yours faithfully,

J. M. KEYNES

Dear Sir,

Many thanks for your kind reply to my letter. I do not want to tax your patience any further by answering in detail the several points of your letter, some of which, as you rightfuly foretold, I was unable to understand fully. But I feel I am bound to point out that the last sentence of your reply ('if some part of the public were to decide, for any reason, to consume their capital, this would in itself mean a change in the rate of savings') does contain everything that my own argument wanted to bring out. It is just because capital consumption does imply a change in the rate of savings that I do not think the situation described by you can be regarded as an 'excess of saving over investment' or that any deficiency in the 'automatic mechanism'

241

of the system could be made responsible for such a situation. Because whatever ways of meeting a diminution in current receipts on behalf of the entrepreneurs are excluded by your theoretical assumptions,[1] it seems clear to me, that the automatic mechanism will bring about an equilibrium between savings and investment so long as the public, or some parts of the public does not spend more than it currently earns; and if it does, this always implies a consumption of capital, both from the point of view of the individual and of the community as a whole. Selling securities for consumptive purposes (as the purpose of meeting losses is by definition a consumptive purpose) is only one way—and in the modern economic system the most common way—of consuming capital. On the other hand people may be induced to consume their capital for many reasons; the fact that they make 'losses' (i.e. their current income is diminishing) is not at all a necessary condition for the emergence of this phenomenon; and I see no reason, why the case depicted by you, where the capital consumption of some is made up by the savings of the others (so that there is no net diminution of capital for the community as a whole) should be treated in any way differently from the other cases.

It seems to me that the definition in the last paragraph of your letter is contrary to the definition given in the *Treatise*, where you expressly state (Vol. I, page 139) [*JMK*, vol. V, p. 125] that any reduction in expenditure of entrepreneurs in order to cover losses constitutes positive saving; consequently capital consumed for the purpose of keeping up the entrepreneurs' 'normal' expenditure cannot possibly constitute a (negative) change in the rate of savings.

Hoping that I have not unduly troubled you,

    I am, dear Sir,

Yours sincerely,

NICHOLAS KALDOR

P.S. As regards paragraph (1) of your letter I did not say that there would be an increase in liquid assets for the community as a whole, as, clearly, this can only take place as a result of action by the banking system. But there will be an increase in 'inactive deposits' relatively to 'active deposits' which is the same thing as a change in the velocity of circulation. (As there is no reason to assume that the 'hoarding' of some will be counterbalanced by a simultaneous 'dis-hoarding' of others.)

---

[1] Such as those stated in paragraph (2) of your letter. Here I should like to point out that the question is not what is consistent or inconsistent with the assumptions in a given abstract case, but whether there can be any other way of bringing about such a discrepancy between savings and investment than that which is implied by your assumptions and which consists in consuming capital (apart, of course, from a change in velocity).

To N. KALDOR, *9 December 1931*

Dear Sir,

Yes, it is evident that the matter is too intricate to discuss by correspondence.

There are several points in your second letter which I could not accept as being really in accordance with what I am trying to say. Well, I must be more lucid next time. I am now endeavouring to express the whole thing over again more clearly and from a different angle; and in two years' time I may feel able to publish a revised and completer version.

Yours very truly,

J. M. KEYNES

Another 'review' of the *Treatise* also provoked a reply from Keynes. The review by F. A. von Hayek appeared in two instalments in *Economica* (August 1931 and February 1932). Keynes was obviously very unhappy with the August part of the review, for his copy of that issue of *Economica* is among the most heavily annotated of the surviving copies of his journals, with no less than 34 pencilled marks or comments on the 26-page review. At the end of his copy of the review, Keynes summed up his reaction by writing:

> Hayek has not read my book with that measure of 'good will' which an author is entitled to expect of a reader. Until he can do so, he will not see what I mean or know whether I am right. He evidently has a passion which leads him to pick on me, but I am left wondering what this passion is.

This feeling doubtless coloured Keynes's reply to the first part of Hayek's review, which drew a further reply from Hayek in the *Economica* for November 1931.

From Economica, *November 1931*

THE PURE THEORY OF MONEY.
A REPLY TO DR HAYEK

I

In an article recently published in *Economica* (August 1931)[1] Dr Hayek has invited me to clear up some ambiguities of termi-

---

[1] 'Reflections on the Pure Theory of Money of Mr J. M. Keynes.'

243

nology which he finds in my *Treatise on Money*, and also other matters. As he frankly says, he has found his difference with me difficult to explain. He is sure that my conclusions are wrong (though he does not clearly state which conclusions), but he finds it 'extremely difficult to demonstrate the exact point of disagreement and to state his objections'. He feels that my analysis leaves out essential things, but he declares that 'it is not at all easy to detect the flaw in the argument'. What he has done, therefore, is to pick over the precise words I have used with a view to discovering some verbal contradiction or insidious ambiguity. I think I can show that most of my alleged terminological inconsistencies are either non-existent or irrelevant to my central theme. But when I have done this (which I will attempt in some short notes at the end of this article), I feel sure that I shall have made little or no progress towards convincing Dr Hayek. For it is not really my use of language or the fact that my treatment falls far short of a complete analysis (as it certainly does) which is troubling him. It is something much more fundamental. And after reading his article carefully, I have no doubt at all what it is.

II

Dr Hayek has seriously misapprehended the character of my conclusions. He thinks that my central contention is something different from what it really is. I deduce this from two passages in his article. The first (page 290, the italics are mine) is as follows: 'The fact that more (or less) money is being invested than is being saved *is equivalent to so much money being added to (or withdrawn from) industrial circulation*, so that *the total of profits*, or the difference between the expenditure and the receipts of the entrepreneurs, which is the essential element in the second term of the fundamental equations, *will be equal to the net addition to (or subtraction from) the effective circulation*. It is here, according to Mr Keynes, that we find the monetary causes working for a change in the price level; and he considers it the main advantage of his fundamental equations that they isolate this factor.' The second passage is on page 292: 'The difference (between us) seems to lie in the fact that Mr Keynes believes that it is possible to adapt the amount of money in circulation to what is necessary for the maintenance of existing contracts without upsetting the equilibrium between saving and investing. But under the existing monetary organisation, *where all changes in the quantity of money in circulation are brought about by more or less money being lent to entrepreneurs than is being saved*,[1] any change in the circulation *must* be accompanied by a difference between saving and investing.'

These quotations may be supplemented by a passage from Dr Hayek's *Prices and Production* (page 23) where he succinctly states his own theory:

It is perfectly clear that, in order that the supply and demand for real capital should be equalised, the banks must not lend more or less than has been deposited with them as savings. *And this means naturally that they must never change the amount of their circulation.*[2] At the same time, it is no less clear that, in order that the price level may remain unchanged, the amount of money in circulation must change as the volume of production increases or decreases. The banks could *either* keep the demand for real capital within the limits set by the supply of savings, *or* keep the price level steady; but they cannot perform both functions at once.

Now the passages which I have italicised in the first of these quotations are far removed from the theory of my *Treatise on Money*. It is essential to that theory to deny these propositions —which Dr Hayek puts in *my* mouth and, to judge from the second and third quotations, believes himself. No wonder that he finds many of my conclusions inconsistent with them. So long as a problem of this major magnitude is not cleared up between us, what is the use of discussing 'irritating' terminology, which might not bother Dr Hayek at all if he were not, for these excellent other reasons, looking for trouble? Dr Hayek has missed, or at least does not discuss, the critical point at which

---

[1] My italics.　　　　　　　　[2] My italics.

our arguments part company. Having passed this by, but finding himself being led down strange and distasteful paths, he tries to prevent himself from being dragged along any further by representing the molehills in the pathway as mountains.

Dr Hayek holds himself, and implies that I also hold, that an act of monetary expansion—meaning by this a transference from the inactive deposits to the active deposits the total quantity of money being unchanged, or an increase in the total quantity of money the quantity of the inactive deposits being unchanged[1]—is not merely a possible cause of investment exceeding saving, but (1) that it is a necessary cause of this and (2) that the amount of the monetary expansion exactly measures the excess of investment over saving and hence is exactly equal to the amount of profits (in my terminology). Will Dr Hayek reconsider two matters?—(i) What passage can he quote from my *Treatise* which justifies him in attributing the above theory to me? (ii) What proof can he offer which justifies him in holding it himself?

In my *Rejoinder* to Mr D. H. Robertson, published in the *Economic Journal* for September 1931 [above pp. 129–36], I have endeavoured to re-state in a clearer way what my own theory actually is. If the total quantity of money be supposed constant, Dr Hayek's theory comes to the same thing as the theory that the excess of saving over investment is measured by the increase of the inactive deposits, which, in the above article, I have attributed to 'some readers' though I did not then know that Dr Hayek was among them.

Since Dr Hayek has not been alone amongst competent critics of my *Treatise* in falling into this misapprehension (or into some more subtle variation of it), it must be my own fault, at least in part. I suspect that it may be partly due to the fact that when I first began to work on Book III of my *Treatise* I believed something resembling this myself. My ceasing to believe it was

---

[1] This is what his words mean in the first passage quoted above, but in the passage I have quoted from *Prices and Production* Dr Hayek simplifies this (*vide* the words italicised) into an increase in the total quantity of money, but perhaps certain qualifications are to be understood.

the critical point in my own development and was the germ
from which much of my eventual theory was worked out. It is
extraordinary that I should not have made this clear, because I
was acutely conscious of the difference of general outlook which
the change of view involved; and after I had adopted this new
view, I was at great pains to bring the rest of my work into line
with it. But traces of old trains of thought are not easily
obliterated, and certain passages which I wrote some time ago,
may have been unconsciously cast into a mould less obviously
inconsistent with my own former views than they would be if I
were writing now.

Yet I doubt if it is all my fault. For anyone brought up in
the old quantity-of-money, velocity-of-circulation schools of
thought, whether it be Cambridge quantity equations or Fisher
quantity equations, this seems to be, for some obscure reason,
a difficult transition to make. Indeed I found it so myself. If
the true theory were what Dr Hayek believes it to be, the
transition would be easy. If, on the other hand, my theory is
right, not only is the angle of approach different, but it is difficult
to see just what the relationship is between the new view and
the old. Thus those who are sufficiently steeped in the old point
of view simply cannot bring themselves to believe that I am
asking them to step into a new pair of trousers, and will insist
on regarding it as nothing but an embroidered version of the
old pair which they have been wearing for years. Even so, I
could never have expected, if it had not been for more than one
experience to the contrary, that a competent economist could
read my *Treatise* carefully and leave it with the idea that it was
my view that the difference between saving and investment
could be exactly measured by changes in the quantity of money,
whether it be in the inactive circulation or the active circulation
or the total circulation, corrected or uncorrected for changes
in the velocity of circulation or the volume of output or the
number of times intermediate products change hands.

At any rate *this*—and not whether I may have used the word

'investment' in a different sense in one chapter from what I have in another—is the issue which Dr Hayek and I ought to debate. He has taken as the self-evident basis of his theory ('it is perfectly clear that' is his own phrase) a proposition which I deny. But we have not hitherto got to grips, because any denial of his own doctrine has seemed to him so unthinkable, that even thousands of words of mine directed to its refutation have been water off a duck's back, and whilst he notices that I hold conclusions inconsistent with it, he seems still unaware that I have disputed it from the outset.

The point, put very briefly, is, firstly, that money may be advanced to entrepreneurs (directly by the banks, or through the new issue market or by the sale by them of their existing assets) either to meet losses or to provide for new investment, and that statistics of the quantity of money do not enable us to distinguish between the two cases; and, secondly (to indicate a general principle by means of an illustration), that, if, desiring to be more liquid I sell Consols to my bank in exchange for a bank deposit and my bank does not choose to offset this transaction but allows its deposits to be correspondingly increased, the quantity of money is changed without anything having happened either to saving or to investment.

III

It will be worth while to pursue the matter a little further. For reading Dr Hayek's *Economica* article in the light of his book *Prices and Production*, and re-reading Mr Robertson's *Economic Journal* article in the light of Dr Hayek's two contributions, I fancy that I see at last where the stumbling-block really is. Let me try, therefore, to bring matters to an issue by stating what I believe to be Dr Hayek's fundamental theory and by explaining how, if I am right that this is what he holds, it differs from my theory. I would add that Mr Robertson's original theory was, I think, substantially the same as that which I am imputing to

Dr Hayek; though Mr Robertson may have now moved somewhat away from it.

'Voluntary' saving, according to Dr Hayek, always finds its way into investment. This is so because (in his view[1]) an increase of saving means (*cet. par.*) a net increase of purchasing power directed to the buying of what I call 'investment goods' but which Dr Hayek calls 'intermediate products' and Mr Robertson calls 'machines'.[2] It does not, however, follow from this (Dr Hayek continues) that voluntary saving and investment are always equal. For if the banking system increases the supply of money, additional funds will be available for investment in excess of the amount provided by voluntary saving, with the result that investment will exceed saving, and contrariwise if the banking system decreases the supply of money. Thus, in his view, a disequilibrium between saving and investment is *necessarily* the result of action on the part of the banking system,[3] and, if we start from a position of equilibrium, cannot possibly arise otherwise. Sometimes he assumes that the excess (or deficiency) of investment is exactly equal to the change in the quantity of money—though there are passages in his *Prices and Production* which seem to me to be inconsistent with this—in which case investment is equal to voluntary saving *plus* (or *minus*) the change in the quantity of money. Investment due to an increase in the quantity of money involves the public in a

---

[1] This is clearly assumed in pp. 45, 46, of his *Prices and Production*. Dr Hayek must have overlooked the fact that it is fundamental to my position to deny this, because, if he had noticed something so much opposed to his own theory, he must surely have criticised it. I need not pursue my reasons here, as it is precisely the same point which has been the subject of discussion between Mr Robertson and myself in the September *Economic Journal*.

[2] Dr Hayek not only implies that an increase of purchasing power directed as the result of an increase of saving to the buying of intermediate products must be spent on *newly* produced intermediate products, but also on newly produced intermediate products *which would not have been produced otherwise*. At least I cannot make sense of chapter II of his *Prices and Production* except on this assumption.

[3] It should be explained to those who have not read Dr Hayek's book that he does not regard as 'action' on the part of the banking system, i.e. as a departure by them from neutrality, changes in the quantity of money required to offset changes in the velocity of circulation or in the number of times that intermediate products change hands before reaching the consumer.

corresponding amount of what may be called 'forced' saving. Thus (to quote from Dr Hayek's *Prices and Production*, page 45) 'a transition to more or less capitalistic methods of production...may come about in one of two ways: either as a result of changes in the volume of voluntary saving (or its opposite), or as a result of a change in the quantity of money which alters the funds at the disposal of entrepreneurs for the purchase of producers' goods'. Thus it is only a departure on the part of the banking system from what Dr Hayek calls neutrality, which is capable of upsetting the equilibrium between saving and investment, and holding this view Dr Hayek naturally asks me (*Economica*, page 293): 'How can the (new) money get into circulation without creating a discrepancy between saving and investment?'

Thus Dr Hayek conceives of the flow of purchasing power as being made up of the incomes (how defined I do not know, i.e. whether equal to my E or my $E+Q$ or to neither) of the factors of production *plus* the new money[1] (if any) created by the banking system. This double stream is then divided between consumers' goods and producers' goods. If saving is increased, less purchasing power is directed towards consumers' goods with the result that their price falls. At the same time more purchasing power must be directed *pari passu* towards producers' goods with the result that—I am not sure at this point whether Dr Hayek holds that their price rises or that the quantity produced is increased or that a different kind of producers' goods is produced, but the argument of *Prices and Production*, chapter II, seems to require that there will be an output of a different kind of producers' goods.[2]

Dr Hayek concludes—and indeed it follows if one allows him his initial assumptions—that the necessary condition of

[1] Beyond what is required to offset changes in the velocity of circulation and in the number of times that intermediate products change hands.

[2] *Vide* page 45: 'A transition to more capitalistic methods of production will take place if the total demand for producers' goods (expressed in money) increases relatively to the demand for consumers' goods.'

avoiding credit cycles is for the banking system to maintain the effective quantity of money (interpreting this in Dr Hayek's quite intelligible sense) absolutely and for ever unaltered.

My analysis is quite different from this; as it necessarily must be, since, in my view, saving and investment (as I define them) can get out of gear without any change on the part of the banking system from 'neutrality' as defined by Dr Hayek, merely as a result of the public changing their rate of saving or the entrepreneurs changing their rate of investment, there being no automatic mechanism in the economic system (as Dr Hayek's view would imply there must be) to keep the two rates equal, provided that the effective quantity of money is unchanged.

As I conceive it, a changing price level—due to a change in the relation between saving and investment, costs of production being unchanged—merely *redistributes* purchasing power between those who are buying at the changed price level and those who are selling at it, as compared with what would have happened if there had not been a change in the relation between saving and investment. I am not sure that Dr Hayek sees clearly the *two* sides of the account. Has he, moreover, apprehended the significance of my equation $S + Q = I$, namely that savings *plus* profits are always exactly equal to the value of new investment? It follows from this that, if we define *income* to include profits, and savings as being the excess of income thus defined over expenditure on consumption, then savings and the value of investment are identically the same thing. He appears to conceive of savings and investment as not being identical and yet shrinks from defining them accordingly.

Dr Hayek and Mr Robertson both make use of the term 'saving' or 'voluntary saving'. But though they criticise my definition of 'saving', I am not aware that they have precisely defined it themselves. I think that it might help the debate to get on if Dr Hayek would consider exactly what he means by 'voluntary saving' on page 45 of his *Prices and Production*. It is argued that it is paradoxical on my part to exclude windfall profits and losses from my definition of income. But I suggest that it is still more paradoxical to include them in income; for in this case, given the value of the current output of investment goods, the amount of the community's income depends on how much it is saving, since any increase (or decrease) in 'voluntary' saving will have the effect of decreasing (or increasing) the community's income by an equal amount.

IV

The reader will perceive that I have been drifting into a review of Dr Hayek's *Prices and Production*. And this being so, I should like, if the editor will allow me, to consider this book a little further. The book, as it stands, seems to me to be one of the most frightful muddles I have ever read, with scarcely a sound proposition in it beginning with page 45, and yet it remains a book of some interest, which is likely to leave its mark on the mind of the reader. It is an extraordinary example of how, starting with a mistake, a remorseless logician can end up in Bedlam. Yet Dr Hayek has seen a vision, and though when he woke up he has made nonsense of his story by giving the wrong names to the objects which occur in it, his Khubla Khan is not without inspiration and must set the reader thinking with the germs of an idea in his head.

My notion of the real nature of the contribution to economic theory which Dr Hayek is making brings me back, however, to what seems to me to be the underlying cause of the second vein of discontent with myself running through Dr Hayek's *Economica* article. Dr Hayek complains that I do not myself propound any satisfactory theory of capital and interest and that I do not build on any existing theory. He means by this, I take it, the theory of capital accumulation relatively to the rate of consumption and the factors which determine the natural rate of interest. This is quite true; and I agree with Dr Hayek that a development of this theory would be highly relevant to my treatment of monetary matters and likely to throw light into dark corners. It is very possible that, looking back after a satisfactory theory has been completed, we shall see that the ideas which Böhm-Bawerk was driving at, lie at the heart of the problem and that the neglect of him by English pre-war economists was as mistaken as their neglect of Wicksell. But there is no such theory at present, and, as Dr Hayek would agree, a thorough treatment of it might lead one rather a long way from monetary theory. Nevertheless, substantially I concede Dr Hayek's point. I agree with him that a clear account of the factors determining the natural rate of interest ought to have a place in a completed *Treatise on Money*, and that it is lacking in mine: and I can only plead that I had much to say for which such a theory is not required and that my own ideas about it were still too much in embryo to deserve publication. Later on, I will endeavour to make good this deficiency.

Now it is precisely to this theory that Dr Hayek seems to me to be attempting to contribute in Lecture II of his *Prices and Production*. In this lecture he has been proceeding, so far as I can make out, on some such tacit assumption as that at every moment of time the market rate of interest is equal to what the natural rate of interest would be if the prevailing relationship of capital to consumption were to be permanent, and if entrepreneurs were acting on this latter assumption, without other errors of forecasting; and he then considers what would happen in an economic organisation satisfying the above assumption when the rate of new investment in fact fluctuates.

At least, I have found no other interpretation which makes sense of the argument, or leaves it anything but a series of baffling *non-sequiturs*. If I am wrong, I hope that some authority, such as Professor Robbins, who is confident that he understands what Dr Hayek means in pages 45–64 of his book, will act as an interpreter. If I am right, it would follow that Dr Hayek is *not* here dealing with the case, with which I was mainly preoccupied, of what happens when the market rate of interest departs from the natural rate, and that our theories occupy—as I believe they do—different *terrains*. A little consideration of his problem, however, brings out the point that the term 'natural rate of interest' is not altogether free from ambiguity. I have defined it by reference to the rate which would at any moment equalise saving and investment, after taking account of the existing psychology of the market, including errors of forecasting, and irrespective of whether or not the then prevailing rate of investment is expected to be permanent. We might call this the 'short-period' natural rate. But clearly there is also the other type, namely that envisaged by Dr Hayek, which we might call the 'long-period' natural rate. It seems to me that Dr Hayek's methods may be suitable for analysing some of the conditions which determine this 'long-period' natural rate of interest.

I am in full agreement, also, with Dr Hayek's rebuttal of John Stuart Mill's well-known dictum that 'there cannot, in short, be intrinsically a more insignificant thing, in the economy of society, than money', which he expresses admirably in the following passage from his last lecture (p. 110): 'it means also that the task of monetary theory is a much wider one than is commonly assumed; that its task is nothing less than to cover a second time the whole field which is treated by pure theory under the assumption of barter, and to investigate what changes in the conclusions of pure theory are made necessary by the introduction of indirect exchange. The first step towards a solution of this problem is to release monetary theory from the bonds which a too narrow conception of its task has created.'

V

There remain Dr Hayek's criticisms of my use of terms, on which I offer the following notes:

(1) It is not the case, as Dr Hayek alleges on the top of page 274, that I contrast with the prices paid for the factors of production only the prices of finished consumption goods.

Dr Hayek forgets that 'new investment goods' include, on my definition, unfinished consumption goods. Nevertheless, Mr Hawtrey has pointed out to me that changes in the values of unfinished goods largely cancel out in my price level of output. 'It is only,' he points out, 'in the case where the increment of investment includes some net addition to the stock of unfinished products that the price level in Mr Keynes's fundamental equations reflects the prices of unfinished products at all, and in the case where there is a net reduction in the stock of unfinished products the price level is influenced in the *contrary* direction to the prices of intermediate products. Practically we can treat Mr Keynes's price level as the price level of finished goods, subject only to a slight correction for unfinished products in certain cases.' Thus this point deserved more explanation than I gave it in my book.

(2) Is Dr Hayek's point at the bottom of page 275 and the top of page 276 that I ought to include in my Q_2 profits arising from the ownership of old capital goods which have risen in value as well as those arising from currently produced capital goods? For certain purposes I should see no objection to amalgamating the two types of profit; but for other purposes, in particular where we are dealing with the price level of output (which by its very nature distinguishes new capital from old capital) it is obviously necessary to distinguish them.

(3) It is not the case that I separate the process of the reproduction of the old capital from the addition of new capital (p. 278). I reckon the wearing out of old capital as 'disinvestment' and its replacement as 'investment', and allow for this in reaching my totals of net output and of net investment.

(4) In the first paragraph of page 279 Dr Hayek perhaps overlooks my distinction between the *cost* of investment and the *value* of investment. But both here and elsewhere (p. 281) Dr Hayek also criticises the conception of 'quantity of capital' as being invalid on the ground that the different types of specific goods constituting capital are not always identical, and when

non-identical are non-commensurable. But this is simply the same problem as that of the conception of 'price level' and the associated conception of real wages when the complex of goods refers to changes in its make-up. This I have discussed at great length in Book II of my *Treatise*, and it arises of course in all types of monetary theory alike.

(5) An examination of the context to which Dr Hayek refers in the first half of page 281 shows that the one refers to the value of current investment, and the other to the value of total investment.

(6) I confess to the verbal confusion of which Dr Hayek complains at the bottom of page 281. The object of the definition on page 130 [*JMK*, vol. v, p. 117], as can be seen from the context, is to distinguish between the *output* of consumption goods, as defined on page 127 [*JMK*, vol. v, p. 114] and, by implication, on page 135 [*JMK*, vol. v, pp. 121–2], which includes only finished consumption goods coming on the market, from the *production* of consumption goods which represents the work done during any period on goods which will eventually emerge as consumption goods. Unluckily, while I speak of the *production* of consumption goods in the first section of the paragraph in question, in the second sentence I speak of '*that* of consumption goods', not noticing that grammatically *that* refers back to the expression 'output or production', used four lines previously in connection with 'capital goods'. If Dr Hayek will read 'the production of consumption goods' (instead of 'that of consumption goods') in the second sentence of the paragraph as well as in the first sentence his mind will be at rest. This is a slip of the pen which may, I fear, have held up many readers for a moment. But that it should have left Dr Hayek in a permanent confusion as to what I mean by 'output of consumption goods' on page 135 and throughout my book is a symptom, I feel, of how thick a bank of fog still separates his mind from mine.

The exchange with Hayek in *Economica* resulted in further letters. First, there was an inconclusive series of letters between Keynes and Hayek on definitions over the months December 1931 to March 1932.

To F. A. HAYEK, *10 December 1931*

Dear Hayek,

I wonder if you could elucidate for me a little further the definition of saving which you give on page 402 of the *Economica* for November, where you say that saving consists in 'refraining from any expenditure on consumption which would be possible without diminution of the value of the existing capital'.

I should find this clearer if you could give me a formula which shows how saving is *measured*. Also, what is the difference between 'voluntary saving' and 'forced saving' in *your* terminology?

Yours sincerely,

J. M. KEYNES

From F. A. HAYEK, *15 December 1931*

Dear Keynes,

While a quite satisfactory algebraic expression of saving would be rather complicated because the concept of 'maintaining the existing capital' would make it necessary to bring in a measure of the existing capital, i.e. the average investment period, I think that for our purposes the following definition will be sufficient:

Of the total money receipts of all members of the society or the effective circulation (amount *times* velocity) M a certain proportion pM must be constantly reinvested in order to maintain the existing capital constant. $(1-p)M$ is therefore available for the purchase of consumers' goods. If $(1-p)M$ is actually spent on consumers' goods, there is no (positive or negative) saving, but if a smaller amount $(1-p-s)M$ is spent on consumers' goods, sM, the amount saved, may or may not be used to increase the total amount of new and renewed investment to $(p+s)M$, only sM being *new* investment. If sM is not used for new investment but is hoarded, the effective circulation decreases by exactly the same amount by which *new* investment falls short of saving. But if on top of the increase of investment made possible by the saving it is further increased by additional money being lent to producers to the amount of aM, then investment will exceed saving by $(p+s+a)M-(p+s)M = aM$. If, however, the new money is added at a time when only a part of the current savings isM, is being invested, then the excess of investment over saving will be only $(p+is+a)M-(p+s)M = (is+a-s)M$. It is aM or $(is+a-s)M$ which I have called 'forced savings' in contrast to sM, the voluntary saving.

I entirely agree with you that it would be better not to use the word saving in the connection with what I have called 'forced saving' but only to speak of investment in excess of saving. Unfortunately, however, the fact that you use 'saving' and 'investment' in a different sense has now made it difficult for me to adopt what is obviously the better terminology without creating confusion. It is essentially the different meaning of these concepts which is at the basis of our difference and it will be one of the main contentions of the second part of my article that while it is essential for an equilibrium that saving and investment in my sense should correspond, there seems to me to exist no reason whatever why saving and investment in your sense should correspond.

Yours sincerely,

F. A. HAYEK

To F. A. HAYEK, *16 December 1931*

Dear Hayek,

Many thanks for your letter, which makes things a good deal clearer to me.

There are, however, two expressions as to which I should like still further explanation.

When, at the beginning of your second paragraph, you spoke of 'velocity', could you give me your precise definition of this; since I reckon that there are now nine senses in which contemporary economists use this term, some of them differing but slightly and subtly from one another.

Secondly, when you speak of the existing capital being maintained constant, do you mean the money value of the existing capital, or its physical equivalent?

Yours sincerely,

J. M. KEYNES

From F. A. HAYEK, *19 December 1931*

Dear Keynes,

I have used the term 'velocity' only as a short and, as I thought, in this connection unequivocal explanation of what I meant by total effective circulation, but I do not normally work with this concept at all. My approach to the problem is rather on the lines of the cash-balances concept as developed by Mises in his *Theorie des Geldes und der Umlaufsmittel* (1912).

When I speak of maintaining capital intact I do, of course, *not* mean the money value of capital. To give an exact definition, which would hold under all circumstances, would take a great deal of space, but if we make the simplifying assumption that the total of original factors of production available remains unchanged, then it could be said that total capital, in order to remain constant, should always correspond to the product of these factors during a certain number of years, which is just another form of saying that the average period of production remains the same. My attention has just been drawn to the fact that a discussion of this problem, which on the whole agrees with my views, is given by Professor Pigou in the fourth chapter of the third edition of his *Economics of Welfare*.

Yours sincerely,

F. A. HAYEK

To F. A. HAYEK, *23 December 1931*

Dear Hayek,

Thanks for your letter of December 19. I am sorry to be so tiresome, but what I really wanted to get at was the exact significance you attach to 'effective circulation'. Do you mean by this what the Americans call the aggregate of bank debits, that is to say, turnover of cash, or do you mean something different from this?

Yours sincerely,

J. M. KEYNES

From F. A. HAYEK, *25 December 1931*

Dear Keynes,

I am sorry I have misunderstood your question. 'The total effective circulation' as I understand it and as I thought you understood it on page 393 of your *Economica* article where you speak of the 'quite intelligible

259

sense' in which I use this concept, is simply the total of all money payments effected (in cash, bank deposits, or whatever other form) during any arbitrary period of time.

Yours sincerely,

F. A. HAYEK

To F. A. HAYEK, *25 December 1931*

That is what I thought you meant and that is just my difficulty. For by the 'effective circulation M' in your first letter of Dec. 15 you seemed, judging by the context, to mean something which corresponded in some sense to what one might call 'aggregate income', which is not the same thing as aggregate money turnover. If M means money turnover, why must 'a certain proportion pM be constantly reinvested in order to maintain the existing capital constant'? I am not able to perceive any particular relation between aggregate money turnover and the amount of capital replenishment required to keep capital constant.

J.M.K.

From F. A. HAYEK, *7 January 1932*

Dear Keynes,

Returning from the meeting in Reading[1] and a few days stay in [the] country I find your letter of December 25th. The question which you put in it is, indeed, of the most central importance and if I had thought that you had any difficulties about this point I should have long ago tried to make it clearer. When, however, you wrote on p. 397 of your *Economica* article [above p. 255] that you consider the replacement of 'disinvestment' as 'investment' I thought you saw the point.

If we take a stationary society where there is no saving and no net investment (in your sense) a constant process of reproduction of existing capital will go on which is necessary in order to maintain its amount constant. In the case of circulating capital this will mean that its total amount will have to be replaced at least once during every year, and in the case of fixed capital that a certain proportion of the total existing capital which wears out during each year will have to be replaced. If we take the simplest case to which I have unfortunately confined myself too much in *Price[s] and Production*, i.e. the

---

[1] The annual conference of university teachers of Economics.

case where all the existing capital owes its existence to one of the reasons which make the existence of capital necessary, namely to the *duration of the process* of production—the other cause being the *durability of many instruments* of production—and where, therefore all capital is 'circulating capital' in the usual sense of this word—which is very misleading because this circulating capital is different from fixed capital only from the point of view of an individual and not for society as a whole—it is fairly clear that a continuous process of production requires in every stage a constant disinvestment and reinvestment so that, if we assume that goods pass from one stage of production to the next every period of time, there will be a constant stream of money directed to intermediate products which will be roughly as many times greater than the stream of money directed against consumption goods as the average number of periods of time which elapse between the application of the original factors of production and the completion of the consumption goods. (I apologise for this terrible 'German' sentence.) The proportion between the demand for consumption goods and the demand for intermediate products will however exactly correspond to the average length of the production process only on the assumption that the goods pass from one stage to the next in equal intervals corresponding to the unit period. What it will actually be depends upon the given organisation of industry, but given this organisation it will change with every change in the amount of capital existing—or, what means the same thing, the average length of the production period—and will remain different so long as the amount of capital remains at its new level (and not only so long as the amount of capital is changing).

The situation is not fundamentally different if we take the other ideal case where the existence of capital is entirely due to the other of the two causes, the durability of the instruments. If we assume that the actual process of production of the instruments as well as of the finished consumption goods takes no appreciable time so that only 'fixed' capital and no 'circulating' capital is existing, then it is again clear that, in order to maintain capital constant, such proportion of the existing machinery as wears out during a period will have to be replaced. In a stationary society this proportion will be determined by the amount of capital and its lifetime, and since the amount of capital existing at a moment of time will itself of necessity be equal to the discounted value of a year's output of consumers' goods *times* the average lifetime of the machines, the annual demand for machines will stand in a proportion to the annual output of consumers' goods which is determined by the average duration of the machines.

The problem becomes, of course, a little more complicated if one combines, as one has to do to come nearer to reality, the two factors determining the existence of capital. The simplest way out seems to me to be to reduce both factors, 'duration of the process' in the narrower sense and the duration of the instruments, to the concept of the average length of the production process in a wider sense as the common denominator. I am conscious that I have treated the durability factor lightly too in *Prices and Production*, but I did so because I hoped to make it less difficult and because I assumed a greater familiarity with Böhm-Bawerk's concepts of the average length of production than I ought obviously have done. I have, however, treated these problems at somewhat greater length in sections IX–XI of my 'Paradox of Saving'.[1]

Yours very truly,

F. A. HAYEK

To F. A. HAYEK, *12 January 1932*

Dear Hayek,

Thank you for taking so much trouble about my questions.

The point you go into was not really the one which bothered me. I quite follow the point as to the proportion of income required to make good depreciation. But incidentally in the course of what you say, you do I think make clear what assumptions underlay your conclusion.

I might put it like this. It is clear to me that in a stable society the amount required to make good depreciation is a standard proportion of the annual income. If therefore it be assumed that the cash turnover bears a fixed relation to the annual income, then I can follow that in a completely stable society, in which moreover the volume of cash turnover bears a fixed proportion to the annual income, the allowance for depreciation will bear a fixed proportion to the cash turnover. I take it from what you say that your article is intended to be subject to these assumptions.

So far so good. But I should still need to know if your definition of saving is to be of general application, what would happen in a progressive society or in a society where, e.g. new inventions are liable to cause obsolescence of existing plant (as distinct from depreciation) and where there is no stable relation-

[1] *Economica*, May 1931.

ship between cash turnover and the national income (e.g. 1931
the relationship between the two, here or in America, was widely
different from what it was in 1929).

Yours sincerely,

J. M. KEYNES

From F. A. HAYEK, *23 January 1932*

Dear Keynes,

I have had a slight attack of influenza which made me unable to do any
serious work. You will, therefore, excuse, if the answer to your last letter
has again been delayed.

If you drop the simplifying assumption of constancy of my 'coefficient of
money transactions' then, indeed, a purely monetary definition of saving
becomes impossible. In order to know what *new* investment is necessary to
offset the individual decisions of income receivers in regard to what part of
their income they spend on consumption, a rather detailed analysis of what
happens to the real structure of production in any given case becomes
necessary.

To take the case of obsolescence which you raise, i.e. losses in capital
value due to new inventions, the question how much new investment should
correspond to a given amount of saving in your sense (i.e. gross saving) can
only be answered on the basis of a quite unequivocal concept of what
constituted new investment. I suggest that it is a more satisfactory way of
approach to drop the distinction between new investment and reinvestment
in that connection entirely and to start from the proportion between consumption and total investment which would have had to exist if the structure
of production existing before that change were to be maintained permanently.
Total investment in that sense includes not only, as you seem to suggest in
your letter, the quota of income required to make good depreciation of fixed
capital, but also the constant reinvestment of all the circulating capital. And,
perhaps still more important, if the 'coefficient of money transactions'
changes it need not mean a constant money stream for investment purposes.
If any given firm which before used annually to buy a certain amount of
machines in replacement of old ones decides to produce these machines in
its own factories, the amount of money used to buy investment goods will
decrease but the total amount of investment will not have changed. In such
conditions it is impossible to measure investment in merely monetary terms
and the only measure of the amount of investment going on is the average
time for which the total of all factors of production is being invested. It is,
of course, one of the most difficult tasks of monetary theory to determine

263

what monetary changes become necessary to offset changes in the organisation of business.

The main problems, however, are two: what are the effects of changes in that proportion supposed that the money supply is so adjusted that total incomes are constant, and, secondly, what is the effect of changes in total incomes. The essential part of my theory is that it is the fluctuations in the proportions between income and total investment and the consequent changes in what I have called the structure of production which constitute the business cycle and, in particular, changes in favour of income relatively to investment which lead to a destruction of capital and a crisis. Even changes in total incomes will affect production mainly via their effect on this proportion, though in a system where prices are very rigid it will of course have serious consequences even if it would leave the proportion unchanged.

To return to the particular case of obsolescence which I set out to discuss, if in any particular industry some firms find themselves unable to earn a sufficient amortisation quota on the cost of their fixed capital because some other firms, equipped with more modern machinery undercut them—and this seems to me essentially to be what obsolescence means—the effect will be that these firms have to cut down their investment. If at the same time nobody else would invest more than is necessary to maintain his capital this would mean that the demand for investment goods would be permanently reduced to that extent. In so far as however, e.g. the firms using the new machinery are able to make new investment out of their extraordinary profits, these investments will at first be required to keep total capital constant and in this sense constitute no net addition to investment and make no increase of the total output of capital goods necessary. The output on investment goods will in this case not have changed and yet there will be no excess of saving over investment since the savings of the one group of people have been required to make up for the capital losses of another group of people. To require that in such a case production of investment goods should actually increase by the full amount of savings, as you seem to do, seem to me to invite trouble, since there is no reason why this increased proportion of investment relatively to consumption would be maintained.

I am dealing with this aspect of the problem in the second part of my 'Reflections'[1] of which I have just read the proofs.

Yours sincerely,

F. A. HAYEK

[1] 'Reflections on the Pure Theory of Money of Mr J. M. Keynes. II', *Economica*, February 1932.

To P. SRAFFA *and* R. F. KAHN, *1 February 1932*

What is the next move? I feel that the abyss yawns—and so do I. Yet I can't help feeling that there *is* something interesting in it.

J.M.K.

To F. A. HAYEK, *11 February 1932*

Dear Hayek,

I should have acknowledged before now your letter of January 23, but I have been much occupied on matters other than those of pure theory.

Your letter helps me very much towards getting at what is in your mind. I think you have now told me all that I am entitled to ask by way of correspondence. The matter could not be carried further except by an extension of your argument to a more actual case than the simplified one we have been discussing. And that is obviously a matter for a book rather than for correspondence.

But I am left with the feeling that I very seldom know, when I read your stuff, exactly what simplified assumptions you introduce or what effect it would have on the argument if these simplified assumptions were to be removed. This is more important when one is considering practical applications, than if one regards oneself as at the beginning of a long theoretical enquiry, in the earlier stages of which the use of simplified assumptions is desirable.

Going back to the point at which our correspondence started, I am left where I began, namely in doubt as to just what you mean by voluntary saving and forced saving as applied to the actual world we live in; though I think I understand now what you mean by them in certain special cases, and this of course gives me some sort of general idea as to the sort of thing you have in mind.

Many thanks for answering me so fully.

Yours sincerely,
J. M. KEYNES

To F. A. HAYEK, *29 March 1932*

Dear Hayek,

I will certainly reserve you space in this June *Journal*[1] for a reply to Sraffa[2]. But let it be no longer than it need be. It is the trouble of controversy—from an editor's point of view—that it is without end. Your MS. should reach me not later than May 1.

Having been much occupied in other directions, I have not yet studied your *Economica* article as closely as I shall. But, unless it be on one or two points which can perhaps be dealt with in isolation from the main issue, I doubt if I shall return to the charge in *Economica*. I am trying to re-shape and improve my central position, and that is probably a better way to spend one's time than in controversy.

Yours sincerely,

J. M. KEYNES

Second there were two letters from H. O. Meredith, a former Kingsman, Professor of Economics at Belfast. Unfortunately, Keynes's intervening letter does not survive.

From H. O. MEREDITH, *22 November 1931*

Dear Maynard,

I have just been reading v. Hayek in *Economica*, August, on your book. I'm afraid it's calculated to darken counsel. Making all allowances for his unfamiliarity with the machinery you employ which is (in my opinion) old fashioned...I mean particularly the device of a single production period repeating itself ad infinitum apart from the variations which it's desired to examine...I find it difficult to excuse his misunderstanding of things which you have made, I would have thought, as clear as mud—e.g. your definition of increment of investment, or again your quantitative measurement of output.

It's unfortunately true, I think, of the last fifty years that Austria has had an elaborate analysis but no machine and Cambridge a machine but an insufficiently formulated analysis. Neither Marshall nor anyone else has ever fully discussed M.'s 'paramount device of *ceteris paribus*'. Hinc, in some degree, these fears. M. had a truly English horror of selfconscious intellectual

---

[1] 'Money and Capital: A Reply', *Economic Journal*, June 1932.
[2] P. Sraffa, 'Dr. Hayek on Money and Capital', *Economic Journal*, March 1932.

processes. He liked people to go right by trained instinct and distrusted 'mere theory' in as philistine a way as any practical man. He had to find out his unfairness to Jevons and he seems never to have been really interested in the choice between alternative modes of presentation.

Perhaps the most that anyone can demand for a great work is that it should be discussed and you certainly are getting discussion. But I feel sore at finding so little in what I have read that goes beyond complaints that you have left out of your machine this or that gadget whose presence or absence could not significantly influence your conclusions. I hope you yourself feel more philosophical about these things and that however much there may be of them you won't let your own faith in your work be impaired.

I have probably said it clumsily, but it is what I wanted to say. Don't answer this: I am sure you are up to your eyes.

Yours,

H.O.M.

P.S. Can v. Hayek *really* suppose (as his plan on p. 283 suggests) that your I = total receipts of entrepreneurs expended on R and C? He has it right (on this page) in the rubric—viz. 'value of the increment of new investment goods'. And why is your 'algebra' so difficult? I am no mathematician, but I find, so far as the *algebra* goes, it's easily explained to a pass class!

From H. O. MEREDITH, *8 December 1931*

Dear Maynard,

Many thanks for the letter and for the present of your book:[1] most of it I have read, but it is good to have the stuff collected.

As to Hayek: I haven't seen the Nov. *Economica* but I took him on the August to be a pedant trained in Austrian economics and eager to show (not without some encouragement from London) that 'Codlin is the friend, not Short'![2] I.e. that your work was spoiled by being cast in the mould of Marshall instead of in that of Böhm-Bawerk.

There is this much excuse for him that Cambridge has always underrated the intellectual quality of Austrian economics, and this much excuse for Cambridge that Austrian economics have always been *pre judice* more interesting than important. Where he fails (apart from general mental limitations) is that he doesn't understand the method you are working with. You would not, I guess, find Schumpeter teaching such nonsense, because he was at pains in his youth to understand Marshall.

I had for some years past accustomed myself to think of a rise in prices as

---

[1] *Essays in Persuasion.*
[2] Charles Dickens, *The Old Curiosity Shop,* chapter XIX.

a necessary result of a rise in the ratio of industrial activity to consumables when capital is growing and its growth is not balanced by a parallel rise of saving. This is substantially your first proposition though I had never got the thing out nearly to the length to which you carry it: in particular had never caught even a glimpse of your elegant deduction in regard to profits. But I had no difficulty in fitting my mind to your machinery. Incidentally I was led by your book to re-read Wicksell for the first time for 25 years and was surprised to find how much of what happened to be my own ideas had evidently seeped through from early half comprehended reading of him. Considering the date at which he wrote what an amazing feat *Geldzins und Güterpreise* was.

I am going in Jan. to the conference of teachers of economics at Reading which seems this year to be largely concerned with your case. As least I assume that Hayek and Robertson will be definitely on it: that Shove will find it difficult to keep off it; and that W. C. Mitchell may also run into it. I hope there will be some young Cambridge present to do justice to your views. I went to Oxford last year, but it was so uncomfortable that one could not really enjoy the meetings.

Yours,

H.O.M.

Third, Keynes's dispute with Hayek provided the pretext for an article in *Economica* by Joan Robinson which attempted to elucidate and extend Keynes's exposition. Although it did not appear in *Economica* until February 1933, it was first written in the summer of 1931 and, as we shall see below (p. 342), bears an important relation to the discussions of the 'Circus' which were so important in the first steps towards the *General Theory*.

From JOAN ROBINSON, *9 April 1932*

My dear Maynard,

I hope you will like my green peas.[1] If you have any suggestions perhaps you could send this back with notes. If not send me a post card saying O.K. and I will send another copy which I have by me to *Economica*.

The argument is a bit thin in places as I have tried to make it extremely simple. In its present form I don't think it could stand up to cross examination by hostile counsel. But I didn't want to sacrifice the clarity of the outline by guarding myself at all points against crabbed objections, It's intended for

[1] Mrs Robinson's parable was set in terms of gold and green peas.

people who don't know what to think, not for the ones who have their own answer for everything.

Thanks so much for your note. I think I can have my nightmare ready by April 25.[1]

I am looking forward to hearing your lectures.

Yours,

JOAN ROBINSON

To JOAN ROBINSON, *14 April 1932*

My dear Joan,

This is excellent. The only comments I have to make do not, I think, really require that you should redraft any of it. The points are these:

1. I daresay that your calling those who sell securities in response to a change of price 'speculators' helps towards clearness. But I myself have always tried to avoid this suggestion of a separate class; since in truth all holders of securities are potential speculators in this sense, though no doubt they could be divided into two classes according as they are more or less sensitive to changes in the prices of their holdings.

2. The question as to whether the difference between consumption goods and investment goods is only a matter of degree raises various subtle questions which I will try to deal with in my lectures. But I will mention two points at once. If 'output' is defined as in my *Treatise*, there is certainly a difference in kind, because my O_1 is defined to mean the consumption goods coming on to the market, whereas O_2 means the increase in the total supplies of investment goods. So there is an asymmetry from the outset. In my new treatment, however, I am giving up this as leading to confusion, and adopting a sense of O_1 similar to that which you assume. But even so I think there remains a difference in kind, provided consumption goods are defined, as I now define them, as being goods with a negative yield (i.e. goods which have a negative yield in terms of themselves), whilst investment goods have a positive yield. But to

---

[1] An early draft of *The Theory of Imperfect Competition*.

develop the argument why, in my opinion, this involves a difference in kind, would be beyond the compass of a letter. As I have said, I do not see why you need redraft anything you have written.

3. I think you are a little hard on me as regards the assumption of constant output. It is quite true that I have not followed out the consequences of changes of output in the earlier theoretical part. I admit that this wants doing, and I shall be doing it in my lectures; though that does not absolve me from being criticised for not having done it in my *Treatise*. But in my *Treatise* itself, I have long discussions with [?of] the effects of changes in output; it is only at a particular point in the preliminary theoretical argument that I assume constant output, and I am at pains to make this absolutely clear. Surely one must be allowed at a particular stage of one's argument to make simplifying assumptions of this kind; particularly when, as you agree, the assumption in question does not make a very vital difference to the whole character of the argument. All the same, I do not ask you to make any change in what you have written.

I think that the green peas and gold parable may help people a good deal.

My own general reaction to criticisms always is that of course my treatment is obscure and sometimes inaccurate, and always incomplete, since I was tackling completely unfamiliar ground, and had not got my own mind by any means clear on all sorts of points. But the real point is not whether all this is so, as of course it is, but whether this sort of way of thinking and arguing about the subject is right. And that is what I am grateful to you for defending and expounding.

Yours ever,

[copy initialled] J.M.K.

Meanwhile, Keynes's discussions with D. H. Robertson over the subject matter of the *Treatise* continued. These were to run on in various forms until the publication of Robertson's article 'Saving and Hoarding' in the *Economic Journal* of September 1933 and Keynes's 'Mr Robertson on "Saving and Hoarding"' in the *Economic Journal* for December 1933.

These discussions ran on from Keynes's debate with Robertson in the spring and summer of 1931 (above pages 211–37). Initially, they also appear to have concerned Keynes's reply to Hayek's review, but, beyond the following letter from Robertson and the succeeding unsent reply from Keynes, nothing survives on this subject.

From D. H. ROBERTSON, *4 October 1931*

My dear Maynard,

This 3-cornered debate, all of us talking different dialects, has become so complicated that I hesitate to say whether or no you are representing me aright! For if I haven't learnt to talk the 'savings and investment' tongue, neither have I learnt to talk the 'goods of higher and lower orders' tongue of Vienna! Hayek's 'producers' goods' are different from, or rather much more comprehensive than, my 'machines' and I much prefer to deal in terms of your 'non-available output', with its two subdivisions of 'increment of fixed capital' and 'increment of working capital'.

But I think my MS enclosed [which has not survived] will show more clearly where I stand, and I still believe that in this particular matter you and I mean much the same thing. At any rate I can't make it too plain that I have never asserted that in the course of cyclical change the prices of consumption goods and of investment goods are at all likely to be found in fact moving in opposite directions. I do on the other hand think there is a good deal to be learnt from their *relative* movements in the various phases of the cycle;[1] and it's in connection with this that I suspect that Hayek, in his pp. 45 ff. and 70 ff., though I can't make sense of them as they stand, has got hold of something real, which needs to be synthesised with your and my 'wasted savings' notions in order to get a *complete* theory of fluctuations.

I find the crucial first paragraph of your p. 11,[2] in which you try to state succinctly your differences from H., hard to interpret or take sides on, because I'm uncertain whether 'investment' in lines 2 and 6 means 'volume' or value'. If I *must* try to express myself in two foreign languages at once, I think I should say that I don't think savings and *value* of investment can get out of gear without a 'departure of the banking system from neutrality', but I *do* think savings and *volume* of investment can.

[1] I.e. that a switch-over of demand from the one to the other, and the other to the one, is a cyclical and not only a long-period phenomenon: though it comes about less by individuals changing their habits than as a result of the redistribution of income between social groups.

[2] This draft has not survived, but presumably Robertson is referring to the passage on page 251 above. [Ed.]

I think, by the way, that H's charge that you use 'output of consumption goods' in different senses on p. 130 and p. 135 (Treatise) [*JMK*, vol. v, pp. 118, 121–2] is, for what it's worth, correct (cf. my note in *E.J.* p. 398).

Yours ever,

D.H.R.

To D. H. ROBERTSON, *6 October 1931* [Not sent]

My dear Dennis,

Having at last got back to Theory, I have been looking at the enclosed again. Your supplementary note, though it will be very useful to me (I am keeping a copy, if I may) from my own point of view when I am trying to rehash details, still leaves me with the strong impression that we are really at cross purposes. And for helping to clear up this sort of point, it is, if I may say to [so?], too moderate.

I think at this stage we want not to minimise all points of difference, but without maximising them to magnify them so that they become plain. For I am sure that the real trouble between us is not concerned with questions of expression or comparative detail, but is something much more important. What we are discussing is a perfectly abstract point of pure theory, though we have discussed it in terms of special examples. I shall not be happy until we have discovered exactly what the point of difference is.

Your letter concerning my note on Hayek makes me think that perhaps I may be on the right track, for in the passage you refer to, where I use the word investment, I undoubtedly mean *value* of investment, with which you disagree, and not *volume* of investment with which you agree. In other words I contend that savings and the value of investment can get out of gear without a departure of the banking system from neutrality in Hayek's sense (i.e. the gross value of money corrected for changes in Fisherine velocity of circulation, and, if you like, the number of times half-finished products change hands). I think I am on the right track because your view is quite consistent with the view you always used to hold, and which I myself held up to a moderately late date. When you were writing your *Banking Policy and the Price Level,* and we were discussing it, we both believed that inequalities between saving and investment—using those terms with the degree of vagueness with which we used them at that date—only arose as a result of what one might call an act of inflation or deflation on the part of the banking system. I worked on this basis for quite a time, but in the end I came to the conclusion that it would not do. As a result of getting what were, in my opinion, more clear definitions of saving and investment, I found that the salient phenomena could come about without any overt act on the part of the banking system. My theory as I have ultimately expressed it is the result of this change of view, and I am sure that the differences between me and you are due to the fact that you in substance still hold the old view. But I only reached my new view as the result of an attempt to handle the old view with complete thoroughness.

My treatment in the *Treatise on Money* is not as thorough as it should be, and I have been more thorough in my own reflections subsequently. But I still think it is a beginning and more thorough than what you are saying. At any rate, nothing which I have worked out since affects this particular point, though some of your other, what I regard as subsidiary points, are affected. What we have to do, it seems to me, is to get clear on this major issue. I think the most helpful way to get forward would be for you to give precise definitions of what you mean by *voluntary* savings (I do not think we differ about the meaning of investment) and also what you mean by hoarding. And finally, exactly what you mean by neutrality on the part of the banking system. Then we can consider if it is true that savings and the value of investment can only get out of gear if the banking system departs from neutrality. Assuming that one means by neutrality more or less what Hayek means—which is a perfectly intelligible notion—I maintain that on one definition of saving,

saving and the value of investment are always equal, whether the banking system is neutral or not; and that on another definition (which is my definition) they can be unequal though the banking system is neutral. I know of *no* definition on which the difference between saving and the value of investment solely depends on whether the banking system departs from neutrality.

I enclose some notes which may help.

You will have seen that I have made my references to you in my Hayek article less explicit.

Yours ever
[unsigned]

Notes attached to draft letter to D. H. Robertson 6 October 1931.

p. 3

D.H.R. has missed the vital point. The persons previously holding investment goods will only part with them *at a higher price*; and it is this higher price which constitutes the stimulus to the production of new investment goods.

It is the coming together of the ideas of the buyer of securities and of the new issuer of securities *as to price* which stimulates the new issue market and new investment.

p. 4

Do you consistently mean by 'increased hoarding' a 'decrease in the velocity of circulation'? I am not clear what kind of velocity you intend, as I do not catch the sense of 'whether as measured against things in general or as against the constituents of output'.

The discussions with D. H. Robertson began again in March 1932. Keynes began the process with a long memorandum which he sent Robertson on 22 March.

To D. H. ROBERTSON, *22 March 1932*

Dear Dennis,

I have been trying recently to avoid controversy and to get back to the beginning in restating the point of view which I seem to have put inadequately in Book Three of my *Treatise.*

Here are two instalments for your inspection, which I would be rather grateful if you would look at. The first one redefines, or defines more fully, various critical terms. The second is really addressed in the main to you, and aims at showing how my present ideas are related to the ideas which we both held, more or less, when you wrote *The Banking Policy and the Price Level.*

Yours ever,

[copy initialled] J.M.K.

NOTES ON THE DEFINITION OF SAVING

I

Let E be the amount of earnings or cost of current net output, i.e. the sum of fixed and variable costs and of entrepreneur's inducement.

Q the net profit of entrepreneurs, i.e. the amount of their actual net receipts in excess of entrepreneurs' inducement. So that $E + Q = E'$ which is total income in Hawtrey's, Hayek's and D.H.R.'s sense, and in the sense to which I have now bowed the knee.

We begin by dealing in what follows with the case where (i) O, the volume of output, (ii) E, the cost of production, (iii) the propensity of the public to hoard, i.e. its relative preference for holding its wealth in the form of money and of other assets respectively, (iv) its relative valuation of old and new assets and

(v) the quantity of inactive deposits are unchanged throughout;[1] and where the only variable items are (a) the amount of O which is consumed, (b) the amount of money which is spent on consumption.

Let F be the amount of money which is spent on consumption. We then have two alternative definitions of savings, namely $S = E - F$ and $S' = E' - F$, corresponding to the excess of earnings and the excess of income over expenditure. Now it is easily seen that S' is exactly the same thing as what in my *Treatise* I have designated I, namely the value of current investment. For $I + F$ and $E + Q$ (or E') are alternative ways of analysing the gross receipts of entrepreneurs, so that $I + F = E + Q = E'$, whence $I = E' - F = S'$. Thus the S' definition of savings works out to be identical with the value of current investment. And this is the justification for the old-fashioned 'common-sense' view that savings and investment are, necessarily and at all times, equal,—being, indeed, the same concept looked at from opposite points of view.

On the other hand the implications of this use of language are decidedly different from what 'common-sense' supposes. For S' always and necessarily accommodates itself to I. Whether I consists in housing schemes or in war finance, there need be nothing to hold us back, because I always drags S' along with it at an equal pace. S' is not the voluntary result of virtuous decisions. In fact S' is no longer the dog, which common sense believes it to be, but the tail. Not that the virtuous decisions are of no effect. But what they settle is, not the amount of saving, but the relation between the consumption price level and the cost of production,—which is not, I think, what 'common sense' supposes. In short, common sense is not really clear exactly what it means by 'saving', some of the associations and suggestions of the word being appropriate to S' and some to S.

In much of what follows I am able to argue in terms of changes

[1] The effect of keeping (iii), (iv) and (v) constant is to keep the average price of investment goods constant and to ensure $Q = Q_1$, in the notation of my *Treatise*.

in F, the amount of expenditure on consumption, where in my *Treatise* I should have spoken of S, and I can thus avoid the difficulties which many readers seem to have found in my definition of saving. This is possible because F is independent of the rival definitions of income and saving, since $E - S = E' - S' = F$. Where, however, the argument essentially depends on the absolute magnitude of Q, I have to get back to my own terminology. But for much of the argument, it is just as convenient, perhaps more so, to talk in terms of F, as to talk in terms of S. This is further facilitated if we call F the expenditure factor and $-\Delta F$ the economy factor, decreases in F representing 'economy' and *vice versa*.

Let us represent a change in investment by ΔI and the amount of economy by $-\Delta F$. Our fundamental equation can then be written

$$\Delta Q = \Delta I + \Delta F.$$

Thus the entrepreneurs' profit increases when the increase in investment is greater than the current economy and decreases when the economy is greater than the increase in investment. All the alleged ambiguous concepts—income, saving, price level, etc.—have been here eliminated. Q, I and F are all definite sums of money.

We can also write our equation $\Delta I = \Delta Q - \Delta F$, which may be read 'the increment of investment is equal to the increment of profit *plus* current economy'.

Or, looking at it again from another angle, ΔQ represents the increased amount of money which spenders have to pay, when investment is increased, for that part of their consumption which they continue to enjoy and $-\Delta F$ represents the economies which they are induced to make by the change in the situation, i.e. the diminution in the amount of money they spend on consumption. I shall try to show subsequently that in essence ΔQ corresponds to D.H.R.'s conception of 'automatic lacking', $-\Delta F$ to the idea underlying his conception of 'induced lacking' and $\Delta Q - \Delta F$ to his conception of 'imposed lacking'. And similarly ΔS and ΔQ correspond respectively to what the concepts of 'voluntary saving' and 'forced saving' are driving at. If, on the other hand, we include Q in income, then ΔQ, as well as ΔS, enters into 'voluntary saving' and into 'spontaneous lacking', with the result that the distinction between these concepts on the one hand and 'forced saving' and 'automatic lacking' on the other breaks down—so it seems to me. But I will return to this later.

II

The old 'common-sense' view not only held that savings and investment are necessarily equal (as—we have seen—*in a sense* they are), but inferred from this that therefore one need not bother. This false inference was the result of overlooking the fact that, if we define income in this way, corresponding to this sense of savings, then its amount is not independent (*cet. par.*) of the amount of the community's expenditure on goods which are consumed, i.e. is not independent of F. For if aggregate output and earnings are both unchanged, but expenditure on consumption (F) diminishes, then the aggregate income (E') of the community (being equal to $I + F$) also diminishes—*unless the effect of a reduction if [in?] F is to increase I (the value of current investment) by at least an equal amount.* Thus—ignoring for the present the words italicised—a decrease of expenditure on consumption will be associated (*cet. par.*)—partly as cause and partly as effect, as we shall see later—with a decrease in aggregate income E' of an equal amount; and consequently, in spite of the decreased expenditure on consumption, the amount of savings S' will be unaffected. Thus whilst it remains true that an increase of savings S' must increase the value of investment, it does not follow that a decreased expenditure on consumption will increase S'. The mistake of the 'common-sense' view lay not in the belief (using words as it chose to use them) that an increase of savings S' necessarily means an increase in the value of investment. The mistake lay in supposing that a decreased expenditure on consumption leads (*cet. par.*) to an increase of S'. This is why it was wrong to infer that there was no need to bother.

Not that there were not also other (though more or less connected) reasons for bothering. Even if the italicised words (to which I have still to return) were to come into operation, with the result that every change in F is offset by an equal and opposite change in I, even so it is obvious that a decrease in F does not necessarily lead to an increase of real wealth. For even if the value of current investment were to increase whenever F decreases, there would be no reason for supposing that this is also true of the amount of capital development, or volume of investment as I called it in my *Treatise*.

Finally—and above all—it is not a matter of indifference in what proportions the income E' of the community is divided between E and Q. For if Q is positive, entrepreneurs will be under a stimulus to increase output, whilst if Q is negative they will tend to decrease output. This is a good reason for wishing to split up E' into its constituents E and Q, and for 'bothering' about the effect on Q of changes in F and I'.

The two matters of primary importance to the community are the aggregate of real output and the increment of real capital. Therefore it is of great significance to show that a decreased expenditure on consumption does not necessarily lead to an increment of real capital even if aggregate real output is unchanged; whilst in practice a decreased expenditure on consumption may lead to a decreased real output (as a result of its effect on Q) and *vice versa*. Indeed it is easy to conceive circumstances in which a decreased expenditure on consumption leads to a decrease both of real output and of real investment.

III

It is now necessary to return to the words italicised and to abrogate conditions (iii), (iv) and (v) on page 1 [above pages 275–6], by means of which we prevented the price of investment goods from changing. Will every change in F be necessarily offset by an equal and opposite change in I? And if not necessarily, under what conditions?

Whatever uninstructed common sense may instinctively believe, it is impossible, once one has looked into the matter, to suppose that a change in F *necessarily* transmits itself in the shape of an equal and opposite change in I. It is easily agreed, therefore, that the policy of the banking system or the attitude of the public towards what can be vaguely summed up as 'hoarding' is capable of resulting in inequality between changes in F and I respectively. But there seems to be a good deal of doubt and controversy as to *what* behaviour of the banking system or of the public will keep $F + I$ constant or how it will alter it.

Let me try to make a complete list of the factors which might have a bearing on the matter. (I am still dealing with the case where the volume of output and the cost of production are constant.)—

1. The volume of (i) the inactive deposits, or, if you like, of 'hoards', and (ii) the active deposits and (iii) the total deposits.

2. The volume of turnover divided by the amount of (i) the active deposits, and (ii) the total deposits.

3. The volume of income (E') divided by (i) the active deposits and (ii) the total deposits.

4. The volume of earnings (E) divided by (i) the active deposits, and (ii) the total deposits.

5. The volume of 'real' deposits, active and inactive, calculated by the ratio of their money volume to the price level of (i) consumption goods, (ii) output as a whole, (iii) assets in general.

6. The cost of production (I') of capital development.

7. What I have called the 'hoarding' propensity of the public, i.e. the curve which shows at what price level assets other than inactive deposits must stand if the aggregate demand of the public for inactive deposits in preference to other kinds of assets is to add up to a given figure.

8. The relative valuation by the public of newly produced investment goods in terms of old investment goods.[1]

One of the difficulties of the situation, from the point of view of getting clear, is that modern economists may mean, apparently, by 'velocity of circulation' any of the ratios in (2) and (3) and, perhaps, (4).

Now it is my view that in practice it is generally possible, though in theory not necessarily, and indeed not invariably in practice, for the banking system to bring about any moderate change in I that it desires. If, simultaneously and apart from what the banking system is doing, there is a tendency of factors 1(ii), 2(i), (6), (7) or (8) to change, then the amount of action required on the part of the banking system to cause any given change in I will be altered.

On the other hand, if the banking system does nothing to alter [1 (iii)] and there is no change in the factors mentioned immediately above, then a change in F due to a change in the propensity to spend, i.e. in the economy factor, will have no reaction whatever on I. Thus the effect of a change in F will be to alter E' by an equal amount; in other words, the economy campaign will have had no effect whatever except to diminish the community's income (E') by the exact amount of the diminution of spending.

This follows because, unless we begin by assuming the point at issue, i.e. unless we *assume* that any change in F causes an equal and opposite change in I, a change in F leaves $E' - F$ *unchanged*, i.e. there is *no* change in the amount of income plus profit left over, after deducting expenditure on consumption, and available to come on to the investment market, and there is no reason, since the same amount of purchasing power is directed to this market as before, why investment assets should be changed in price.

---

[1] D.H.R. attributes great importance to this factor. I agree that it is necessary for completeness, otherwise, we have no sufficient link between I and factor (7). Also it may sometimes be of practical importance. But it did not occur to me to attach great *theoretical* importance to it.

It is to be noticed that if F changes and if factor (6), namely I', is unchanged, then on my theory there is *necessarily* a change in the price level of consumption goods. Consequently if factors 1(i) and 1(ii) are unchanged, factor 5(i) is necessarily altered. Thus if 5(i) is our test of the magnitude of real hoarding, it follows that *every* act of economy means, other things being equal, an increase in real hoarding. Consequently if we make the constancy of 5(i) our criterion of neutrality on the part of the banking system, then if F changes and 1(ii), 2(i), (6), (7) and (8) are unchanged, it is necessary that 1(i) should change to such an extent that 1(iii) is changed in proportion to the change in the price level of consumption goods, so as to keep 5(i) constant; and this, in the conditions assumed, will mean *some* change in I in a direction opposite to the change in F.

But, even so, there is no reason whatever to suppose that the change in I will be *equal* to the change in F. Its amount will depend on the shape of the curve in (7) and in (8), namely the relationship of the price level of new investment goods to that of the totality of investment goods.

Moreover the constancy of 5(i), i.e. no change in real hoarding, is not a sufficient condition for there to be *some* change in I in a direction opposite to the change in F. It is also necessary that (7) and (8) should be unchanged. For a suitable change in (7) and (8) is capable of precisely offsetting the change in 1(i) which is needed to compensate the effect on 5(i) of a change in F.

Anyway, factor 5(i) is a fifth wheel to the coach. For we can give a complete account of the argument without bringing it in. Indeed a reference to it only complicates the story, as it seems to me.

The same argument applies, *mutatis mutandis*, to all the other velocities of circulation, if the constancy of any one of them be taken as the criterion of neutrality. They are fifth, sixth, seventh, eighth, ninth and tenth wheels to the coach, and merely turn our Rolls into a caterpillar. All we need for our analysis are factors $1(i)$, (6), (7) and (8).

Perhaps the difference between D.H.R. and me simply boils down in the last resort to my saying that, if $1(i)$, (6), (7) and (8) are unchanged but F changes, then there is no reason to expect I to change, and to his saying that if $5(i)$, (6), (7) and (8) are unchanged but F changes and the banking system acts in such a way as to change $1(i)$ in a degree appropriate to the change in consumption price level resulting from a change in F, then there is reason to expect *some* change (but not an equal change) in I in a sense opposite to the change in F. It did not look quite like this at the outset. But if this *is* it, then there is no difference at all. For both statements are equally true.

IV

Yet I cannot help thinking that there was at one time more in it than this. For D.H.R. has never given a hint that he means by 'automatic lacking' exactly the same as what I mean by Q. Yet if he does not mean this by it, what does he mean?

I seek the interpretation by throwing my mind back to what I used to mean by 'voluntary' and 'forced' saving when I began my enquiries. The whole thing began, I think, by a consideration of what happens when a government obtains a command of purchasing power by an inflation of the volume of money. It appeared at first that the consequent rise of prices deprived the public of an amount of purchasing power equal to what the government gained. This deprivation could be called 'forced' saving; and measured in terms of money (to convert it into purchasing power is more complicated) it was equal to the increase in the volume of money. Further reflection, however, showed that, whilst the government gained purchasing power, it only gained it in the sense in which every borrower gains it; whilst it was the entrepreneurs who *gained* (in the sense of winning a net increment of assets over liability) an amount equal to what was lost by the consumers. Moreover much the same thing would occur if members of the public were to start spending their inactive deposits, thus turning them into active deposits, though in this case no corresponding benefit would accrue to the government.

Nevertheless even with this modification one found that there were what seemed, and still seem, to be insuperable difficulties in the view that the gain, to whomever accruing, was exactly equal to the amount of new money; and the whole conception was unclear.

There are two kinds of 'losses' suffered by individuals which are, or might be, relevant to the conception of 'forced' saving, as between two dates T_1 and T_2:—

(1) A reduction in the real value of deposits or other claims to money hold both at the beginning and the commencement of the period, due to the price level, which is our index of real value, rising between T_1 and T_2.

(2) A reduction in the real value of the individual's flow of money income between T_1 and T_2 due to the rising price level after allowing for any change in the amount of his money income and assuming no change in the volume of output.

Now if output is unchanged and if we mean E' by 'income', (2) adds up to zero for the community as a whole and there is no 'loss'. On the other hand, (1) is transient in the sense that a single, once-for-all reduction of type (1) is capable of maintaining a continuing loss of type (2) for those whose money incomes continue unadjusted to the higher price level. Nor is it possible to deduce either from (1) or from (2) how much command of purchasing power the Government has secured, besides which (1) has no connection at all with savings conceived of as a with-holding of income from expenditure on consumption. It is on all fours with the capital loss which individuals suffer when their securities or other capital assets fall in real value.

D.H.R. had drawn attention to a third factor, namely (3) the increase in the nominal amount of deposits held at T_2 as compared with T_1 in order to compensate for the reduction in the real value of the deposits held at T_1. But this increase in deposits bears no particular relation to *total* savings nor is it necessarily even a *part* of savings, since the increase of deposits may have been obtained partly by selling securities or other capital assets.

Thus I ceased to be able to perceive any clear relationship whatever between the quantities under (1), (2) or (3) and something which one might call 'forced' saving; and I had to seek an answer to the following questions:—

(1) Does 'forced' saving only arise (*a*) when the banking system lends money to the government or to entrepreneurs or (*b*) when the velocity of circulation is increased?

(2) Can it be regarded as a function of the amount by which prices rise or of the amount by which deposits increase or of the change in the velocity of circulation?

(3) How, in exact terms, is this amount of forced saving to be measured?

V

D.H.R. does not use the terms 'voluntary' and 'forced' saving, but speaks of spontaneous lacking, automatic lacking and induced lacking, which I will denote by L_1, L_2 and L_3 respectively. It will be convenient to consider them in the opposite order.

L_3 is equal to the reduction of current expenditure which occurs as a result of a desire to increase bank balances in order to make good a deficiency in the real value of the latter due to a rise of prices. But L_3 cannot be *equal* to the increase in bank balances, since the replenishment of bank balances by borrowing or by selling capital assets to the banks for money is *not* 'induced lacking'. Moreover for the community as a whole the increment of bank balances must be exactly equal to the amount of borrowing and sale of capital assets to the banks. Indeed there might be L_3 without any change in the aggregate of bank balances, and no L_3 in spite of a change in bank balances. Thus there is no statistical test of the amount of L_3.

L_2 occurs for any individual when, his output remaining the same, prices rise more than his income. But if we mean E' by 'income', then for the community as a whole L_2 is always zero.

D.H.R. speaks of L_1 as 'corresponding pretty well to what is ordinarily thought of as saving'. Assuming that 'income' means E', the exact truth seems to be that $L_1 + L_3 = S'$.

D.H.R.'s terminology does not provide for the case when automatic stinting causes an increase in spontaneous lacking (i.e. by entrepreneurs who are making windfall losses). Yet if we mean E' by 'income', this unavoidably occurs. Automatic stinting *necessarily* increases spontaneous lacking on the part of entrepreneurs.

If, on the other hand, we mean E by 'income', then it all becomes much simpler. There is no contradiction in assuming that L_1 is constant. We have $L_2 = Q$, $L_1 + L_3 = S$, and $L_1 + L_2 + L_3 = S + Q = S' = I$, where I is the value of the current increment of investment.

It follows, I think, that, when D.H.R. says (p. 49)[1] that 'it will be found, for instance, that the privation imposed on the public by an ordinary process of Government inflation consists partly of automatic and partly of induced lacking', this is only true if 'income' means E. For it is only true that $\Delta I = \Delta L_2 + \Delta L_3$ if $\Delta L_1 = 0$. If 'income' means E, this can be the case. But if 'income' means E', then, since L_2 is always zero for the community as a whole, we have $\Delta I = \Delta L_1 + \Delta L_3$; i.e. the privation imposed by governmental inflation ΔI would consist not of *automatic* and induced lacking, but of *spontaneous* and induced lacking. Thus my Q is intended to be a more thoroughly worked out and precisely defined version of D.H.R.'s L_2. But Q only emerges if we break up E' into E and Q and therefore involves E.

If we are to break up S into two components L_1 and L_3, then I should prefer a wider definition of L_3 without such specific

[1] Of *Banking Policy and the Price Level*. [Ed.]

reference merely to bank balances; e.g. we might define L_3 as being the amount of the change in S brought about by a change in the price level relatively to E. We should then have:— $L_1 = F(E)$; $L_2 = Q$; $L_3 = dS/dQ\,\Delta Q$. It will be noticed that $L_3 = -\Delta F$ where F is the amount of expenditure on consumption, i.e. L_3 is the same thing as what I have called the economy factor.

Hence, assuming E constant, the money value of the increment of investment, in excess of the amount of spontaneous lacking appropriate to a level of income E in equilibrium conditions, is the sum of the induced lacking $(-\Delta F)$ and the automatic lacking (Q) (as redefined above); which brings us back to the fundamental equation $\Delta I = \Delta Q - \Delta F$.

Thus if D.H.R. will allow me to reinterpret him in this way, his dictum on page 49[1] ('It will be found, for instance, that the privation imposed on the public by an ordinary process of government inflation consists partly of automatic and partly of induced lacking') is true; or, to use another phrase of his, additional government expenditure out of loan or out of inflation, superimposed on a position of equilibrium, is exactly equal to the amount of 'imposed' lacking which the consequent change in the price level of consumption goods brings with it. But if 'income' means E', then this is not true.

Now my critical departure from previous theories of 'forced' saving or of 'induced' and 'automatic' lacking lies not in my definitions (for which I claim nothing but increased precision) but in my conclusion (though this is largely due to my working out of the more precise definitions) that induced and automatic lacking are *not* simple functions of monetary factors such as the quantity of money or its velocity of circulation (although they may be influenced by monetary factors), that they can arise in other ways than as a result (to quote D.H.R.) of 'an additional daily stream of money being brought on to the market', and that, quantitatively, their amount cannot be deduced from banking

[1] Of *Banking Policy and the Price Level.* [Ed.]

statistics however complete. The simplest generalisation one can make is that, if E and L_1 are given, then the amount of the imposed lacking $(L_2 + L_3)$ varies by an amount exactly equal to the variation in the value of current investment; and the value of current investment, in its turn, depends on the amount of such investment as measured by its cost of production, on the propensity of the public to hoard, on the volume of the inactive deposits and (if one wishes to be quite complete) on the popular valuation of new investment goods relatively to old investment goods.

VI

In D.H.R.'s exposition there is an implied assumption that an inflation is likely to lead to induced lacking. So long as induced lacking is thought of in relation to the volume of money, this seems plausible. But if my redefinition of it as being the same as the economy factor is allowed, then it is more plausible to expect inflation to lead, not to an increase, but to a decrease in the economy factor.

It is true that, in so far as the public desires to keep its savings at a stable figure in terms of consumption goods it will be impelled to economise when the price of the latter rises. On the other hand, the desire to maintain a pre-established standard of life will operate—and probably more powerfully—in the opposite direction. And finally, the increase of entrepreneurs' profits (and also, quite likely, increased paper profits for all owners of equities) will essentially tend towards a decrease of economy.

Thus when a disturbance has been set up, the economy factor, (or induced lacking), so far from offsetting the effect of increased investment on profits and prices, and thus diminishing the amount of automatic lacking required, will more probably tend to aggravate it. Furthermore an increase in I' will, through its favourable effect on profits, generally diminish the propensity to hoard and thus increase I more than in proportion to I'. That is to say, the economy factor increases (and decreases) just when we don't want it to, so that given changes in investment tend to produce greater effects on Q than they would if the economy factor were constant or moved in an offsetting direction. The public tends to economise when spontaneous saving is already excessive, and to be extravagant when spontaneous saving is deficient. For these reasons a movement away from equilibrium will tend to feed on itself. The discussion of where a new resting place can be found requires, however, the abrogation of our assumption that O and E are constant, and belongs to the next chapter.

Robertson replied with an undated series of notes on Keynes's propositions.

From D. H. ROBERTSON

NOTES

1 (P. 1 note) [above pp. 275–6]. My difficulty in §§ I and II is to be sure where the change which we are studying is supposed to originate. If in a change in F, then I have no difficulty in imagining circumstances in which the price of investment goods does not matter, and Q therefore $= Q_1$. But on p. 4 [above p. 277 line 28], passage marked $+$[1], we appear to start with a change in investment, the change in F being 'induced'. Now by what mechanism—D being assumed constant—can investment increase without a rise in the price of investment goods? Since the increase of Q_1 is here pictured not as the *result* of an *increase* in F, but as the *cause* of a *decrease*, the only possible *cause* of the increase in Q_1 is a diminution in the production of consumable goods due to a transfer of the factors of production to the making of investment goods: and why should this transfer take place except under the stimulus of a rise in the price of investment goods?

Thus, if we are telling a story which starts from the end of a change in investment, the hypothesis that the price of investment goods remains unchanged seems to me inconsistent with what we know of the operation of markets and of the motives of producers; and the assumption that $Q = Q_1$ falls to the ground.

2 (P. 9) [above p. 281]. I still think that the most expressive way of describing what happens in this case is to say that an act of hoarding (or dishoarding)

---

[1] On Keynes's copy. [Ed.]

on the part of somebody takes place,—i.e. either on the part of professional holders of securities, or on the part of entrepreneurs who, with reduced incomes, insist on keeping unchanged balances.

3 (P. 10) [above p. 282]. I certainly should not hold that constancy of v(i), or even of v(ii), is a test of successful 'neutralising' action on the part of the banking system. The banking system, in my view, achieves just nothing at all in the way of 'neutralisation' by creating deposits which are spent neither on new investment goods nor on consumption goods and fail therefore to affect the price of either. This is the very point on which I have insisted in everything I've written about the subject,—and of which the U.S.A. Reconstruction Corp$^{n.}$ has been providing a new illustration.

May I assume that the normal magnitude of I is such as to make capital goods in proportion to population, so that there is no tendency for output per head to change as the result of a change in the amount of capital per head? And may I assume that there is no tendency for output per head to change for any other reason? If I may, then I should say that *in a certain sense* equilibrium is attained if the price-level of output as a whole (not the volume of money divided by this price-level) is kept constant, but that *in the full sense* equilibrium is only attained if *both* the price of consumption goods *and* the price of new investment goods is kept constant. I.e. on the assumptions named I am, as regards what I should like to know how to do, an orthodox price-stabiliser.

4 (§v). It's hopeless, I'm afraid, to try to find an exact parallelism between your concepts and those of *BP and PL*[1], for the reason that the latter were only worked out for a society of small entrepreneurs, i.e. one in which *all* incomes are immediately responsive to a rise in prices. Historically, the reason for this was that I was anxious to concentrate on unfamiliar things, and so ready to dispose summarily (on p. 21) of the effects of that redistribution of income between classes which has always been the most familiar feature of an inflation. And I think the defect has this incidental advantage, that since I haven't dealt, in my strictly analytical part, with these secondary effects at all, I haven't been under any temptation to fuse them in analysis with the primary effects, which is what (herein agreeing with Mr Edelberg!) I feel you have done.

But obviously it *is* a great shortcoming in my analysis, which I must try to remedy in any future exposition, that I haven't dealt with the general case of sticky, still less with your special case of absolutely rigid, wages etc. And as a result of reading your §v I see more clearly than I have hitherto done that the definitions and classifications of the various Lackings on p. 49 are not satisfactory for a fixed-earnings economy.

[1] *Banking Policy and the Price Level.*

(i) *Induced Lacking*. Let me first attempt a definition of Hoarding in general. A person hoards if he acts on any day in a way designed to increase the proportion of money stock to income which he finds prevailing at the beginning of the day. Now my Induced Lacking was essentially a species of Hoarding. It occurred because at certain stages of the inflation people found that their money incomes had been increased out of proportion to their money stocks, and therefore set about restoring the old proportion. But under a mobile-earnings economy these people—my entrepreneur-earners —also found that the *absolute real value* of their money stocks had been decreased by the inflation; and I was therefore led into defining I.L. on p. 49 in terms which are only applicable to people in this latter position, and which obscure the fact—which comes out better in some sentences of the math. app.—that an operation on the *proportion* money-stock/income was of the essence of I.L., as of all other types of hoarding.

Now under *your* scheme neither the money stocks nor the money incomes of *earners* are increased at all at any stage of the inflation, therefore the *proportion* money-stocks/incomes is not altered, and therefore they have no motive to perform what I must now, for the sake of clarity, label Induced Hoarding. The incomes of entrepreneurs, on the other hand, *are* increased out of proportion to their money stocks, so that they *have* a motive for performing Induced Hoarding. But, on my analysis (see arithmetical example below), the absolute real value of their money stocks is not reduced by the inflation, but left intact: therefore they do not perform Induced Lacking *as defined on p. 49*. And whatever name we choose for the activity they *do* perform, it is not clear to me that it would be natural to include it—as it *was* natural for me to include the Induced Hoarding done by my impoverished earner-entrepreneurs—under the general heading of Imposed as contrasted with Spontaneous Lacking. Thus some sort of rearrangement and re-classification of my terms seems to be needed to fit this case, and I must try to think of the most convenient one.

But the point of substance is this:—the part played under my old scheme by Induced Lacking in mitigating the rise in prices is played under yours, I think, not so much by any action the earners may take to raise the real value of their money stocks as by your assumption that entrepreneurs do not spend their windfall profits. For since the former would, under your scheme, involve also attempting to raise the proportion money-stocks/income *above its original level*, it involves something which was never contemplated in my Induced Lacking, and which is in itself, as you say, inherent [*sic*] improbable.

Hence however I rearrange my terms, it doesn't seem easy to establish a correspondence between your $-\Delta F$ and the idea lying at the back of my L_3.

(ii) *Automatic Lacking*. This is defined in *BP and PL* (p. 48), as is Lacking in general (p. 41), with reference to a man's 'current economic output'. The reason for this phrase was that, not having evolved your very convenient concept of 'non-available output', I thought it necessary, later in my analysis, to speak of those who were being paid to build up increments of working-capital as having 'income' but no 'output', and to exclude any abstinence done by them from lacking (p. 56 bottom). This no longer seems to me necessary or convenient: and under a fixed-earnings economy the phrase about 'current economic output' may carry a false suggestion that I am trying to draw a distinction between the 'true' value of a man's output and what he is paid for it if past contracts have been doctored in his favour or disfavour,—which is not what I am trying to do. Hence to fit a fixed-earnings economy I had better try to find another definition, which is not quite easy.

But in any case I am not attracted by the proposed identification of Automatic Lacking with Q/price-level. The essential difference between the two concepts can best be shown by pointing out that when an inflation stops what I mean by A.L. stops,—while your Q may go on indefinitely, even after the inflation stops, provided that earnings do not increase to catch up with the new price-level that has become established through the inflation. It is of the essence of my conception of A.L. that a man who suffers it consumes, owing to the unforeseen competition of other spenders, less than he had reason to expect,—which is not true of those who, month after month, spend an unenhanced income at an enhanced but unchanging price level.

Not everybody however of whom the above is true can be said to be performing A.L. He may have intended to diseconomise,—i.e. to consume more than his expected real income; so that while the unforeseen competition of other spenders forces him to consume less than he *intended* it does not force him to consume less than his expected real income, and he does not therefore 'lack'. My definition of A.L. (p. 45) brought out these two conditions satisfactorily for a mobile-earnings economy. For a fixed-earnings economy, I suggest provisionally to substitute 'their expected real income' for 'the value of their current output'—expected real income being defined as expected real value of expected money income. It is worth noting that A.L. is performed by entrepreneurs as well as by earners.

Perhaps I can best illustrate these points by re-telling, for a fixed-earnings economy, the early stages of my first story in *BP and PL*, App. §1. I must emphasise that what is represented as happening in period 2 is only one of the many things which *may* happen in that period: but it serves to bring out the difference, as I see it, between our concepts.

We start with a money-supply M of 1,000, of which 900 (M_A) is in the hands of earners, 100 (M_B) in the hands of entrepreneurs. K for both classes is 10, i.e., in equilibrium $E' = E'_A + E'_B = 90 + 10 = 100$. ($E'_A$ is defined as income *received by A*.)

In period 1 the Gov^t inflates (to give doles for unemployed) by adding 10 units of money to the money stream. Thus in this period $E' = E'_A + E'_B$

$= 90 + 20 = 110$. $P = \dfrac{11}{10}$. At end of period $M_A = 900$, $M_B = 110$,

$M_A/E'_A = 10$ (unchanged), $M_B/E'_B = \dfrac{11}{2}$ (decreased).

In period 2, the entrepreneurs do Induced Hoarding in order to start bringing their proportion back to 10, and to this end (acc[ording]. to the simplified hypothesis adopted in my book) withhold 10 units of money from the market,—i.e. spend 10 units less than they have received in the previous period. The Gov^t continues the inflation, adding another 10 units to the money stream. Thus in this period $E' = 110 - 10 + 10$, $E'_A = 90$, $E'_B = 20$,

$M_A = 900$, $M_B = 120$, $P = \dfrac{11}{10}$. In this second period L (my notation) $= \dfrac{I}{P}$

(your notation) $= \dfrac{10}{P}$ (money) or 11 (real). But, according to my analysis,

L is made up of $L_2 = 0$, $L_3 = \dfrac{10}{P}$. According to yours, ΔI is made up

of $\Delta Q = 10$, $-\Delta F = 0$. I.e. there is not parallelism between the concepts.

5 (P. 19) [above p. 287]. I quite agree that my treatment in *BP and PL* is likely to give an exaggerated idea of the importance of my Induced Lacking in practice. Historically I can only plead (1) that it was—it really was—your baby! (2) that I was trying to devise a state of affairs in which Pigou's proposition quoted on p. 61 ·might hold good for a time at least, (3) that I was anxious to emphasise the unfamiliar, viz. that queer things might happen *during the course* even of an inflation which ended up by leaving prices raised in proportion to the increase in the stock of money: and was therefore ready to put away into a footnote (1, p. 61) (though it's also mentioned in the text pp. 75–6) the familiar point about 'diseconomy', which had been recently exhaustively illustrated in your *Tract*.

But it is perfectly true that, even if people aim at restoring their balances to the old proportion to income, the *rate* at which they set about doing so may very well be slower than that assumed in the above story: in this case L on day 2 will consist more largely of L_2 and less largely of L_3. And it is also true that people may *not* aim at restoring their balances to the old proportion, and that the actual course of prices may be dominated by this fact. I'm therefore entirely in agreement with the general tenor of §6. (As explained earlier, I never contemplated that people would try to raise the proportion of money-stocks to income above its original level.)

6 (P. 18) [above p. 288]. I'm afraid I still think, for the reasons given in my re-rejoinder sent you, that this is mysticism, and that all such changes, however 'real' their origin, must operate through monetary channels, and leave their trace on monetary statistics.

During this period, Robertson also saw Keynes's 1932 lectures in draft and provided comments thereon. Keynes's marginal notes on Robertson's comments appear in capitals. Unfortunately Keynes's drafts do not survive.

These notes provoked additional correspondence which follows them.

From D. H. ROBERTSON, *May 1932*

NOTES

1. It is not plain to me why I is not also zero in this case,—i.e. what the nature of the supposed equilibrium is. I DON'T FOLLOW.

2. The excess of the aggregate of E' over the aggregate of F is not a correct measure of the aggregate of money-savings (to be called S'') over non-homogeneous stretch of time within which E' is changing owing to a change in the public's behaviour. To get $\Sigma S''$, we must clearly add in, for each period of time, sums held back out of income received before the period began,—or deduct sums added to expenditure within the period by depleting pre-existing balances. E.g. during period (i) we have equilibrium with $E' = E = 100$, $F = 80$, $S'' = 20$, $I' = I = 20$ (and so remains throughout). In period (ii) the public perform an act of hoarding to the extent of £10, so that we have $E' = 90$, $F = 70$, $S'' = 20 + 10 = 30$.

– 10 TO ALLOW FOR REDUCTION OF ENTREPRENEURS' SAVINGS.

In period (iii), we may suppose that the act of hoarding either (*a*) is or (*b*) is not repeated.

(*a*) People spend the whole of the income received in the preceding period. $E' = 90$, $F = 70$, $S'' = 20$. $\Sigma S''$ for the 3 periods is 70, whereas ΣS (J.M.K.'s notation) is 80, $\Sigma S'$ is 60 ($= \Sigma I$).

BUT THERE F WOULD BE 90. WE MUST THUS BE HOPELESSLY AT CROSS PURPOSES.

(*b*) People withdraw another £10.

$E' = 80$, $F = 60$, $S'' = 20 + 10 = 30$.

$\Sigma S''$ for the 3 periods is 80, whereas ΣS (J.M.K.'s notation) is 90, $\Sigma S'$ is 60 ($= \Sigma I$).

Note that in either case $\Sigma S''$ is greater than ΣI,—i.e., with this definition of money-savings, we can, if we choose, describe what has happened to the price-level etc. as being 'due to an excess of savings over investment'.

3. But cetera *aren't* paria if E' is being progressively increased, or even has been increased once for all, above its level at the period with which comparison is being made. If my income is increased from £100 to £200 the fact that my expenditure increases from £50 to £150 affords no presumption that my saving is diminished! NO, THAT IS NOT MY POINT. MY POINT IS THAT IF YOU D.H.R. WHOSE INCOME IS UNCHANGED AT £100 REDUCE YOUR EXPENDITURE BY £5 THE SUGGESTION IS THAT SAVING IS INCREASED BY £5.

4. Isn't the following a fair analogy to the argument of this whole section? 'It is an observed fact of nature that when the wind rises, the ship rolls and I am sick. The inference I can safely draw is that if I make myself sick, that will make the ship roll, and the rolling of the ship will make the wind rise.'

I see, e.g. no reason whatever why a switch-over of demand from beer to steam engines should increase the aggregate of employment. NOR DOES THIS ARGUMENT SUGGEST THAT IT WOULD.

5. ?Or if demand in general has an elasticity < 1, as seems to be true in the acute phases of a slump. NO, THIS IS A FORTIORI.

D.H.R.

D.H.R.'S NOTE 2 IS THE ESSENTIAL CLUE TO DIFFERENCE OF OPINION.

To D. H. ROBERTSON, *18 May 1932*

Dear Dennis,

In the intervals of other things I have been studying your comments on my lecture notes. But I am held up by one or two doubts or obscurities.

If I understand aright, your S'' is the excess of income in any period over expenditure in the next period. But, as before, I am uncertain exactly what you mean by an 'act of hoarding'. Can an act of hoarding take place if aggregate bank deposits remain unchanged? In short, is the amount of your 'hoarding' measured by quantity of bank deposits, or by velocity of circulation, or by some other criterion?

In the second place, do you maintain that your S'' can only differ from my S' if an act of hoarding takes place? I cannot get on in the argument unless I have a fuller account of what exactly you mean when you say that the 'Public perform an act of hoarding'.

Yours ever,

[copy initialled] J.M.K.

From D. H. ROBERTSON, *18 May 1932*

Dear Maynard,

I haven't kept a copy of my notes, which were *ad hoc*, and represented a first attempt to see how far, and how, my concepts and definitions need modification in order to make them watertight among the complexities of fixed 'earnings', security-sales, etc. But at present I don't see how to improve on the definition which I think I gave: 'A person performs an act of hoarding if he acts on any day in a way designed to raise the proportion which his money stock at the beginning of that day bears to the money income which he expects to receive on that day.' (A 'day' is, I think, really the minimum time in which a piece of money can do a job of work, i.e. no piece of money can possibly do two jobs on one day. But I'm not sure the vaguer word 'period' won't do all right in this case.)

The simplest possible case of hoarding is if I, instead of (as is my wont) buying a pair of boots a day, refrain on one day from buying a pair of boots and leave my bank balance undrawn on. This, of course, in the simplest possible case, reduces my bootmaker's income and his bank-balance. Most certainly, an act of hoarding is compatible with the aggregate of deposits remaining unchanged,—that has always been the point.

But I *think* my definition covers also the case which you invite us to consider, and in which the bootmaker, having been warned in a dream that I am not going to buy my usual pair of boots (so that they must either remain unsold or be sold cheap to someone else,—his aggregate money income being in either case reduced below normal) sells a security so as to bring his money stock at the end of the day to what it would have been if I had bought the boots as usual. But in this case it is he, not I, who performs the act of hoarding: for though he has foreknowledge that his income is going to be reduced, he insists on taking steps to preserve the same absolute money stock as before.

As to S'', I am loath to be pressed into giving a definition of 'money savings', which is a concept which I don't think I have ever used in print in connection with the analysis of cyclical disequilibria. But I do suggest that my S'' enables one, if one likes, to describe the disequilibrium by saying that 'investment exceeds savings' or vice versa, without giving such a paradoxical definition of 'savings' as S' involves. You may be able to catch me out if I say that the concept of hoarding covers all the possible causes of divergence between S' and S''; but it does seem to me at present that it covers those which we have both of us had in mind.

Yours,

D.H.R.

To D. H. ROBERTSON, *20 May 1932*

Dear Dennis,

But does not that upset my definition of income? And require some new meaning for that much abused word? On my definition of income, the bootmaker's income is not zero on the day on which he adds a pair of boots to his stocks and does not succeed in selling them. For income, as I have defined it, depends on the value of output.

Yours,

[copy initialled] J.M.K.

From D. H. ROBERTSON, *21 May 1932*

I think the arithmetic is all right.

The bootmaker's money-stock is £1000, his normal daily income £100, i.e. his proportion K is 10.

Now on a certain day I withdraw £5 from expenditure on boots, and we will assume that the bootmaker simultaneously counters (*a*) by selling his whole output of boots for £95 to other people, (*b*) by selling me a security worth £5. Then I say that he has taken an action designed to revise his proportion from 10 to 1000/95, i.e. to raise it by $\frac{1}{19}$ (or reduce the income-velocity of money by $\frac{1}{20}$): and that it is this action of his which must be held responsible for the fall of $\frac{1}{20}$ in the price of boots not being compensated for by a rise in the price of some other kind of output.

I think you were asking me to alter assumption (*a*), i.e. to suppose that the bootmaker continues to sell $\frac{19}{20}$ of his output to other people at the old price, and stores the remainder, valuing them at the old price. In this case his income, as defined by you, remains unchanged. And in this case, I admit, he does no hoarding, since his proportion remains unchanged at 10. But also in this case it is not necessary for me to show that he, or anybody else, *does* do any hoarding,—indeed, it would be very awkward if my definition led to the conclusion that they did. For in this case there is no price-fall to explain!

D.H.R.

Pencil comments of J.M.K. on the back of this note.

E' = income = value of output.

M = money balances of community.

Then any behaviour the net effect of which is to increase M/E' is an act of hoarding.

E'_1, M_1: values at time 1.

E'_2, M_2: values at time 2.

If $M_1/E'_2 > 1$ there has been hoarding.

If $M_2 > M_1$ there has been inflation (which can offset hoarding).

Let us assume M_1 constant.

To D. H. ROBERTSON, *22 May 1932*

D.H.R.

(Please return this with any comments)

Extract from your 1st note:

'During period (i) we have equilibrium with $E' = E = 100$, $F = 80$, $S'' = 20$, $I' = I = 20$. In period (ii) the public perform an act of hoarding to the extent of £10, so that we have

$$E' = 90, \ F = 70, \ S'' = 20 + 10 = 30.$$

The bootmaker's money stock is £1,000, his normal daily income £100 $^{(k\,=\,10)}$. In period (ii) his income falls to 90 and his money stock to £990 $^{(k\,=\,11)}$. By so refraining from increasing his expenditure by £90, he has raised his k from 10 to 11. Has he hoarded £90?

If so, should we not have $S'' = 20 + 10 + 90$? (Or better assume bootmakers to be half the community with money stock £500 and normal income £50, so that in period (ii) their income falls to 40 and cash to £490, and then as before.)

J.M.K.

Or re-stated as follows:

Period (i)   Bootmakers' income $E'_1 = 50$,
others' income $E'_2 = 50$.

Bootmakers' cash $M_1 = 500$
others' cash $M_2 = 500$ $\Big\}$ $k = 10$.

Bootmakers' expenditure F_1 = 40,
others' expenditure F_2 = 40.
(Investment throughout   = 20.)

Period (ii). Others reduce their expenditure on boots by 10 and add 10 to their cash, all other expenditure proceeding as before. Hence F_2 falls to 30, M_2 rises to 510, E_2' is unchanged, E_1' falls to 40, F_1 is unchanged, M_1 falls to 490. Others have hoarded 10. What have bootmakers done?

If hoarding consists in the excess of M_1 over kE_1', then they have hoarded 90, by refraining from expenditure sufficient to retain their cash in the same proportion as their income. If hoarding consists of in the excess of M_1 in period $(t+1)$ over kE_1' in period (t), then in the *third* period bootmakers hoard 90.

From D. H. ROBERTSON, *May 1932*

'A man performs an act of hoarding on any day if he acts in a way designed to increase the proportion which his money-stock at the beginning of that day bears to his expected income on that day.'

1. He is not performing such an act if his proportion is increased merely through the action of other people in preventing part of the customary stream of money from reaching him. The bootmakers therefore, in the simple case now under discussion, do not hoard on day (ii).

2. If, however, the bootmakers, foreknowing that their income on day (ii) is to be diminished, sell a security to maintain their money stock at the old level, they *do*, in accordance with the above definition, hoard.

3. Returning to case 1, there are all sorts of possibilities about what happens on day (iii).

(α) If they spend their previous day's income, in accordance with the above definition they neither hoard nor dishoard.

(β) If they try to alter the proportion which they find existing at the beginning of day (iii) back towards the proportion which existed at the beginning of day (ii), they dishoard, thereby checking the fall in prices.

(γ) If, in alarm and discouragement at the fall in prices, they try to increase their proportion even beyond the figure at which it stands at the beginning of day (iii), they hoard, thereby accentuating the fall in prices.

¶The test of the existence of hoarding or dishoarding is whether they do anything calculated to alter the average number of times which, on the preceding day, a piece of money has hit a piece of output.

                                                            D.H.R.

To D. H. ROBERTSON, *29 May 1932*

D.H.R. (please return)

I Your para. 2. If the bootmakers sell a security so as to ensure that their money stock at the end of the day shall bear the same proportion to their income of that day as it bore at the beginning of the day, are they hoarding?

II The community is composed of bootmakers and bread-makers. If both believe that their income is falling and reduce their expenditure so as to ensure that their money stock at the end of the day shall bear the same proportion to their income of that day as it bore at the beginning of the day, has anyone hoarded?

III Can prices fall if no one has hoarded?

IV If the answer is in the negative, can there be any statistical evidence of hoarding other than the fall of prices? or any statistical clue to who has hoarded? Is hoarding anything more than a subjective act of which we have no direct knowledge and which we can never know objectively except as an inference from an observed fall of prices?

J.M.K.

From D. H. ROBERTSON, *21 June 1932*

Sorry I've kept these so long—I've been under a flood of theses, exam papers, Mayweek events etc. I'm rather stale in the head and may have blundered again,—it's frightfully hard to find definitions which will cover all possible cases. I hope to return to the whole thing in the Long,—but after a detour via the theory of capital and interest!

D.H.R.

Just off to Holland for 10 days.

The answer to I and II is Yes: which shows me that I have blundered in supposing that my definition—which is, I think, all right on the supposition that people cannot react till day 2 to what has been done to them on day 1, so that 'expected income on day 2' is synonymous with 'income received on day 1'—can be extended to cover the case of foreknowledge and prophylaxis. 'A person hoards on any day, if, either by reducing his rate of expenditure or by selling securities, he acts in such a way as to contribute towards establishing at the end of the day a larger proportion between his money stock and his income than prevailed at the end of the previous day.'

This covers the cases

(i) where A initiates an economy (or bear) campaign;

(ii) where B, foreseeing such a campaign, reacts instantaneously against it (e.g. where the bootmaker, p. 1 [above p. 297], takes steps on day 2 to keep his stock at £1,000, though he knows his income is falling to £90);

(iii) where B, not having foreseen the campaign, reacts subsequently against it. (If on day 3 the bootmaker spends £90, he is not hoarding, for though he is reducing his expenditure below the £100 at which it stood on day 2, he is not doing so in such a way as to revise his proportion above 990/90.)

But you may be able to find some that it does not cover!

The essence of the matter is that he is hoarding who is contributing to decreasing 'the number of times a representative piece of money becomes income' (Pigou). I am simply trying to express that very definite and clear concept into the Petty-Marshall language of proportions.

I'm not sure if I get the point of III and IV. But so far as I can see

III Not so far as the matters here under discussion are concerned,—they can, of course, as a result of a reduction in the supply of money or increase in the rate of output of goods.

IV I don't know quite what statistical 'evidence' one can expect of the truth of any of these tautologies. But I think that 'hoarding' is a quite objective measurable thing. E.g. if the bootmaker (case iii above) spends only £80 on day 3 instead of £90, he is performing (£90/price level of day 2) units of intended real hoarding.

Isn't the concept of 'saving' in your terminology likewise simply *inferred* from the difference between the aggregate of 'normal' incomes and the aggregate of sales of consumption goods? And does it matter, provided a concept so inferred throws light on the problem of causation?

At the end of the long vacation Robertson resumed the discussions with the letter and paper printed below.

From D. H. ROBERTSON, *2 September 1932*

My dear Maynard,

The enclosed is the product of a lot of reflection. It *may* still be a muddle! But if not, I hope you'll be able to regard it as one advance towards re-agreement in substance, if not in terminology.—I return also the previous interchange, with thanks.

Are you much engaged on Tuesday afternoon? If not, may I run down[1] and

---

[1] To Tilton [Ed.].

see you on the way back from a weekend at Winchester? I could get down by the train arriving Lewes at 12.28 and must get back to Cambridge that night, as I leave shortly for the north and Ireland. There is a thing, not the enclosed, which I should rather particularly like to talk to you about first, if you are neither too busy nor too beset with guests.

A reply to Sunnyside, Winchester, would reach me up to Monday night.

Yours

D.

SOME REVISED DEFINITIONS OF
SAVING AND ALLIED CONCEPTS

§1. A person performs Lacking on any day if his consumption is less than his expected real income. His Lacking is Automatic if it is the result of Stinting, i.e. of an increase in the stream of money spent in competition with him depriving him of consumption which he would otherwise have enjoyed. (Such Stinting does not always result in Lacking as defined.) A person does *not* perform Automatic (or any other kind of) Lacking merely because, through a change in the value of money, contracts made in the past have been doctored in his disfavour.

All Lacking other than Automatic is Voluntary, and may be called Saving. It is perhaps convenient to measure Voluntary Lacking in real terms, and Saving in money ones: thus the amount of Saving done on any day is the amount of Voluntary Lacking multiplied by the expected price-level. Voluntary Lacking or Saving may be subdivided into (*a*) Induced, which is required in order to restore a proportion of money stock to money income which has been infringed as an incident of previous Automatic Lacking, (*b*) other or Spontaneous.

A person performs Hoarding on any day if he takes steps to increase the proportion of money stock to money income which he found existing at the end of the previous day. Hoarding may be measured either in real or money terms, Money Hoarding being Real Hoarding multiplied by expected price-level. All Induced Saving is necessarily Hoarding, and some Spontaneous Saving is. But not all Hoarding is Saving, since the proportion of money stock to income may be raised by turning assets into money as well as by withholding money from expenditure.

The correlative terms are Dislacking, Dissaving and Dishoarding.

§2. Applications in a society divided rigidly into (*a*) entrepreneurs with mobile incomes, (*b*) 'public' with fixed ones.

M = money stock at *end* of any day, K its period of circulation against output in terms of days, T the volume of output per circulation period, P

the price-level of output, S the total stream of money on any day devoted to the purchase of output, R money income on any day, L total Lacking done on any day, made up of L' Automatic, L'' Induced, L''' Spontaneous.

It is assumed that output is unaltered: also, for simplicity, that K is the same for both classes. The method can, I think, be easily extended to the case (presumably actual) in which $\dfrac{M}{K} = \dfrac{M_a}{K_a} + \dfrac{M_b}{K_b}$.

In equilibrium

$$S = R_a + R_b = \frac{M}{K} = P\frac{T}{K}, \text{ i.e. } P = \frac{M}{T}.$$

(1) Inflation of $\dfrac{X}{K}$ per day (to give doles to unemployable, who spend them forthwith).

$$S_1 = \frac{M+X}{K}, \quad P_1 = \frac{M+X}{T}, \quad R_{1a} = \frac{M_a+X}{K}, \quad R_{1b} = \frac{M_b}{K},$$

$$M_{1a} = M_a + \frac{X}{K}, \quad M_{1b} = M_b,$$

$$L'_{1a} = \frac{M_a}{M(1+X)}\frac{XT}{K}, \quad L'_{1b} = \frac{M_b}{M(1+X)}\frac{XT}{K}$$

(Automatic Lacking is performed by *both* classes).

The public finds no change in the proportion of money stock to income: the question of its performing Induced Lacking therefore does not arise. The entrepreneurs find their proportion raised—M_{1a} exceeds K times R_{1a} by $\dfrac{X}{K}(K-1)$. They have therefore an infinite number of alternatives about the amount, if any, of Induced Lacking which they will perform.

If they 'hoard all their profits' we get, for the next $(K-1)$ days, the exact parallel of the case taken in *BP and the PL* as the 'standard' one for a society of mobile incomes, viz. the case in which the community aim at restoring their old proportion of stock to income by economy spread over $(K-1)$ days. I.e. we have

$$S_2 = \frac{M_a+X-X}{K} + \frac{M_b}{K} + \frac{X}{K} = \frac{M+X}{K} = S_1,$$

$$P_2 = P_1, \quad L_{2b} = 0, \quad L''_{2a} = \frac{X}{K}\frac{1}{P_1}.$$

(Entrepreneurs are expecting an income of $\dfrac{M_a+X}{K}$ at a price-level P_1, while they both intend to consume, and do consume, what $\dfrac{M_a}{K}$ will buy at a price-level P_1, i.e. their 'Induced Saving' is $\frac{X}{K}$ and their 'Induced Lacking'

$\frac{X}{K}\frac{1^*}{P_1}$. The Lacking of the public is zero.)

If entrepreneurs continue to hoard their profits after the Kth day, i.e. after their proportion has reached its old value K, their lacking becomes Spontaneous. (In this case the price level will never rise above P_1.)

If entrepreneurs do not hoard all their profits, i.e. if on day 2 etc. they spend more than $\frac{M}{K}$, Automatic Lacking, *both by themselves and the public*, will

ensue. E.g. if on day 2 they spend their whole income of day 1, viz. $\frac{M_a+X}{K}$,

P_2 becomes $\frac{M+2X}{T}$, and the Total Automatic lacking done by both classes

is $\frac{X}{M+2X}\cdot\frac{T}{K}$. This shows clearly the difference between performing Automatic Lacking and suffering from past contracts having been doctored in one's disfavour.

§3 (2). An 'economy campaign' by the public, at a rate $\frac{X}{K}$ per day.

(i) Entrepreneurs leave their assets, other than money stocks, untouched.

$$S_1 = \frac{M_a}{K} + \frac{M_b-X}{K} = \frac{M-X}{K}, \quad P_1 = \frac{M-X}{T}, \quad R_{1a} = \frac{M_a-X}{K},$$

$$R_{1b} = \frac{M_b}{K}, \quad M_{1a} = M_a - \frac{X}{K},$$

which exceeds K times R_{1a} by $\frac{X}{K}(K-1)$, $M_{1b} = M_b + \frac{X}{K}$.

$$L_{1b}''' = \frac{X}{KP}, \quad L_{1b}' = -\frac{X}{KP}\frac{M_b-X}{M-X}, \quad L_{1b} = \frac{X}{KP}\frac{M_a}{M-X},$$

$$L_{1a}' = -\frac{X}{KP}\frac{M_a}{M-X}.$$

---

* This Induced Lacking by entrepreneurs *may* differ from the Induced Lacking of a whole community with mobile incomes described in *BP and PL* in that it may not be needed to restore the *absolute* real value of their money stock to its old level. Whether this absolute real value has been reduced by the events of day 1 depends on whether $[M_a+(X/K)]/P_1$ is $< M_a/P$, i.e. whether $[M_a+(X/K)T]/(M+X)$ is $< (M_aT)/M$, i.e. whether M/M_a is $< K$—which it almost certainly is in real life, but which there is no necessity in the nature of things for it to be. The fact that Induced Lacking *may* be performed by persons who find the absolute real value of their money stock increased makes it, I think, inconvenient to try to group together Automatic and Induced Lacking in a super-group Imposed Lacking, as is done in *BP* p. 49—'Imposed' is too strong a word to fit this case.

If on day 2 the entrepreneurs spend their previous day's income $\dfrac{M_a - X}{K}$, we get $S_2 = \dfrac{M - 2X}{T}$, and the price-level continues to fall under the influence of the economy campaign. Entrepreneurs are neither saving nor dissaving, neither hoarding nor dishoarding.

If however, in spite of having 'made losses', they spend the old amount $\dfrac{M_a}{K}$, they are dishoarding and dissaving an amount $\dfrac{X}{K}$. In this event we get $S_2 = S_1$, i.e. the price-level ceases falling in spite of the continuance of the economy campaign. $L_{2b} = L'''_{2b} = \dfrac{X}{KP_1}$, $L''_{2a} = -\dfrac{X}{KP_1}$,—the Dissaving of entrepreneurs is Induced because it represents an attempt to get rid of surplus money stocks.

§4 (ii). Entrepreneurs foreseeing the economy campaign and the consequent fall of P and $\dfrac{M_a}{K}$ nevertheless on day 1 spend $\dfrac{M_a}{K}$ as before and sell assets worth $\dfrac{X}{K}$ to the economising public, who buy them instead of adding to their money stocks,

$$S_1 = \frac{M - X}{K}, \quad P_1 = \frac{M - X}{T}.$$

But

$$M_{1a} = M_a - \frac{X}{K} + \frac{X}{K} = M_a, \quad M_{1b} = M_b.$$

The L_{1b}s are as in the previous case: but we now have $L'_{1a} = 0$ (entrepreneurs being gifted with prevision are not capable of suffering surprise), and instead $L'''_{1a} = -\dfrac{X}{KP_1}$ (entrepreneurs are deliberately enjoying consumption which exceeds by this amount the expected real value of their expected income).

The public have saved but not hoarded. The entrepreneurs have hoarded, for they have taken steps to make money stock bear a higher proportion to income than it previously did, viz. $\dfrac{KM_a}{M_a - X}$ instead of K. But so far from having saved, they have spontaneously dissaved $\dfrac{X}{K}$ (spontaneously dislacked $\dfrac{X}{KP_1}$).

If on day 2 they again spend $\dfrac{M_a}{K}$ and sell assets worth $\dfrac{X}{K}$ to the economising public, we have $S_2 = S_1$, $P_2 = P_1$. The stationariness of the price-level is a consequence of the fact that neither party is now hoarding or dishoarding—both are acting in such a way as to leave their proportion what it was at the end of day 1. But the entrepreneurs are again spontaneously dissaving $\frac{X}{K}$ (spontaneously dislacking $\frac{X}{KP_1}$).

At this point a further gap occurs in the Keynes–Robertson correspondence. The next item appears to be a reply by Robertson, probably in May 1933, to a note from Keynes, which has not survived, probably about an early draft of Robertson's 'Saving and Hoarding', *Economic Journal*, September 1933. Keynes's comment after (i) appears in capitals. After reading this, Robertson added the words '(Danaids' sieve)'.

From D. H. ROBERTSON [May 1933]

No!

Let $\frac{A}{n}$ be normal income of entrepreneurs.

Let $\frac{B}{n}$ be unchanging income of fixed-incomists.

Let the latter save[1] $\frac{X}{n}$ per day over a period of a year.

Then on day 1 entrepreneur income is $\frac{A-X}{n}$.

(i) If on day 2 entrepreneurs spend $\frac{A-X}{n}$ they are, in my sense, neither saving nor dissaving. Since the fixed-incomists again save $\frac{X}{n}$, entrepreneur income on day 2 is $\frac{A-2X}{n}$. And so on. Therefore, at the end of a year, fixed-incomists have saved X, entrepreneurs have saved 0, aggregate of losses has been $\frac{X}{2}(n+1)$. ENTREPRENEURS' INCOME ON DAY N IS $\frac{A}{n}-X$. THEREFORE CANNOT BE GREATER THAN REDUCTION IN DAILY INCOME. (Danaids' sieve).

(ii) If on each day from day 2 onwards entrepreneurs spend $\frac{A}{n}$, they are dissaving $\frac{X}{n}$ per day. At the end of a year, fixed-incomists have saved X,

[1] In my sense.

entrepreneurs have saved $(-X+x/n)$, total net saving has been x/n, aggregate of losses has been X. The actual course of events will be somewhere between (i) and (ii): there is no reason to suppose that (ii), or any close approximation to it, 'must necessarily' happen.

D.H.R.

Keynes replied to Robertson's note with a short note on which Robertson made ticks and marginal comments. These appear in capitals after the proposition to which they refer.

To D. H. ROBERTSON, *20 May 1933*

D.H.R.

A hoards.

Consequently B (a businessman) is in danger of suffering a reduction of cash. If B does nothing, B is not dishoarding. Presumably, therefore, if, to avoid a reduction of cash, B reduces his personal expenditure or sells a security, so as to replenish his cash above what it would otherwise be, then B is hoarding. If he sells a security to A, A's hoarding is diminished. (✓)

If he reduces his personal expenditure (which is an increase in J.M.K.'s 'saving'), some other businessmen suffer increased losses. (✓) It follows that aggregate hoarding has nothing to do with actual changes (✓) in the holding of cash, but is exactly equal to business losses $(=-Q)$ as defined by J.M.K. NO

Thus D.H.R.'s 'hoarding' is, by definition, precisely the same thing as, and exactly equal to, J.M.K.'s 'excess of saving over investment'! NO

Or, more strictly, hoarding is $-\Delta Q$ where $-\Delta Q$ is the *change* during the 'day' in the current excess of saving over investment. YES

J.M.K. means by 'saving' nothing but the sum of 'hoarding' (in D.H.R.'s sense) and investment. NO. I THINK NOT. If this is right, I see no object in D.H.R.'s 'saving' which is a fifth wheel to the coach. The only concepts we need are I (investment) and $-Q$ (losses or hoards).

Old-fashioned saving (i.e. excess of income over expenditure), which I now call 'surplus', is equal to I. J.M.K.'s 'saving' is equal to $I - Q$, D.H.R.'s 'hoarding' is equal to $-Q$. NO. What more do we want?

J.M.K.

Does this help to exhibit (incidentally) the roots of my affection for the concept $I - Q$? In *your* language, *my* savings can either be hoarded or invested; and total savings, in my language, are made up of the sum of the two employments of savings, i.e. the sum of hoarding and investment added together. SO FAR AS 'SAVINGS' *ARE* LOSSES, THEY CAN'T BE 'EMPLOYED' AT ALL,—THERE IS NOTHING TO EMPLOY! I should have no objection to this use of the term 'hoarding', once I had got used to it. The objection to it lies in the suggestion it conveys that it has something to do with actual holdings of cash. It is today, for the first time, that I discover that I have been misled by this suggestion and that hoarding can occur during a period in which *no* individual alters his holding of cash.

There is investing (agreed by both of us) and hoarding (as defined by you) and the sum of the two (which is my saving). But there is no fourth thing, such as you try to concoct by your new definition of saving.

From D. H. ROBERTSON, *23 May 1933*

A batch of entrepreneurs, trying each to increase his own money stock, succeed only in reducing, over a period of a year (consisting of n 'days'), their joint income from a rate of R per year to a rate of $R - X$ per year. I.e. the daily rate of income falls during the year by $\dfrac{X}{n}$, i.e. on each day it is lower by $\dfrac{X}{n^2}$ than on the previous day. There is no investment, and no change in the total money stock: hence the hoarding on each day equals the saving (D.H.R.) on that day, and the losses over any period of time, and therefore on any one of the D.H.R. days, equal the saving (J.M.K.) on that day.

Total hoarding or saving (D.H.R.) $= \dfrac{X}{n}$.

Total losses or saving (J.M.K.) $\quad = \dfrac{X}{n^2}(1+2+3+\ldots+n)$

$$= \frac{X}{n^2}\frac{n(n+1)}{2} = \frac{X}{2}\frac{n+1}{n}.$$

What you point out is that as n approaches infinity $\dfrac{X}{n}$ approaches o, while $\dfrac{X}{2}\dfrac{n+1}{n}$ approaches $\dfrac{X}{2}$.

This is true: but I am not clear that it invalidates the usefulness of hoarding (nor therefore of saving (D.H.R.), which is simply (so far as the present argument goes) hoarding plus investment) as a concept, if what we are concerned with is 'to analyse and arrange our material in what will turn out to be a useful way for tracing cause and effect' (*Treatise*, I, 138) [*JMK*, vol. V, p. 125]. For I feel very strongly the Hawtrey–Hansen objection that since the J.M.K. Savings *are* Losses, they are no help in elucidating a causal sequence (and to speak of them, as you do in your last note, as being 'employed' in one direction or another is meaningless, since there is nothing to employ!).

What is established is that very small doses of hoarding frequently repeated can produce large results!

Further, I do not concede that the sum of Hoarding over a period of time always approaches zero as n approaches infinity. For take the case discussed in my article, where the community consists of fixed-incomists and entrepreneurs, and the former aim at, *and succeed in*, adding to their money stocks a definite amount X in a year,—entrepreneurs spending on each day the income they received on the previous day.

However great n becomes, total hoarding remains X,—it does not tend towards zero.

Total losses or saving (J.M.K.) $= \dfrac{X}{n}(1+2+3+\ldots+n) = \dfrac{X}{2}(n+1)$,

—which increases without limit as n increases. (This, I think, is simply your principle of the Danaids' sieve.)

The inference which I tentatively draw is that my instinct has been right in following Democritus and Planck,—the ultimate units of economic time and economic change must be conceived as finite though tiny.

D.H.R.

The final stages of the Keynes–Robertson controversy over saving and hoarding had a further element in the letters. Keynes on reading Pigou's

Theory of Unemployment tried out his idea that the Professor had made a slip in analysis on Robertson in a letter dated 5 September 1933 and the discussion of this point entered future letters on 'saving and hoarding'.

To D. H. ROBERTSON, *5 September 1933*

My dear Dennis,

Have you read the Prof's book carefully? I find it most disturbing. For if I haven't completely misunderstood, it's simply nonsense from beginning to end.

My troubles began at p. 41. If dO is a firm's marginal product when employing x units of labour, W' the rate of money wages, P the price of the product and π the price of a unit of wage goods, A.C.P.'s first sentence asserts $\dfrac{PdO}{\pi} = \dfrac{W'dx}{\pi}$, which is of course, all right,—though it would seem simpler to write it $PdO = W'dx$.

He then writes real wages $= \dfrac{W'}{\pi} = F'(x)$, and, *without making any use of his first sentence* which is the fundamental postulate of employment theory, defines a thing

$$E_d = \frac{(W'/\pi)dx}{xd(W'/\pi)},$$

which he calls the elasticity of the real demand for labour; and most of the rest of the book is based on this and similar expressions.

But what bearing has E_d on the demand for labour by the firm in question? Why has it any more bearing than if π were the price of old masters? The demand for labour by that firm surely depends on the relationship between P, W' and $\dfrac{dO}{dx}$, and the value of π doesn't matter two straws.

I could understand that the *supply* of labour (assuming an increasing disutility in work) might depend on real wages. But what has it got to do with an individual firm's *demand* for labour? Moreover the same argument would prove that the volume of employment is a function of money wages only. (For put $\pi = 1$ and continue as before.)

Incidentally he asserts subsequently that E_d is necessarily negative. How does he know this? If the firm in question is producing wage goods, might not a rise in real wages increase its demand for labour?

What he calls the real demand function for labour in a particular occupation is a bogus function, in the same sense in which it would obviously be bogus if 'old masters' were substituted in the definition for 'wage goods'.

(N.B. Presumably $F'(x)$ in chapter III is the same as $F(x)$ in chapter II. Again p. 42 $\frac{\psi'(y)}{\pi}$ is the supply price of y units of a given commodity. But what is $\psi(y)$, which appears at the bottom of p. 42 and subsequently?)

Further, in chapter VIII he calculates the rate of interest *in terms of wage goods*. But this rate is of no interest or importance to a producer.

These were my first thoughts—mere perplexity at the whole argument depending on a bogus function and making no use at all of what I have called the fundamental postulate. But as I read on, it suddenly dawned upon me how the whole affair could be rationalised. *He is assuming throughout the book that the price of every individual article is fixed and constant.*

Cet. par. it is true that O, the *quantity* of a firm's output can be considered in a sense, to be a function of x alone. But A.C.P. tacitly substitutes for this the proposition that the *value* of a firm's output *in terms of wages* (i.e. P/W') is a function of x alone. This is only true if the price of this output is constant in terms of the rate of wages paid.

Going back to p. 41 his $F'(x) = \dfrac{W'}{\pi}$ and $\dfrac{Pdo}{\pi} = \dfrac{W'dx}{\pi}$, so that $F'(x) = \dfrac{P}{\pi}\dfrac{dO}{dx}$. Now O is in the short period a function of x alone but P and π are not. Thus the real wage corresponding to output O is a function not only of x but of P and of π, as indeed it is clear at first blush that it must be. Instead of $F'(x)$, he should have written $F'(x,P,\pi)$.

That this assumption underlies the whole theory becomes particularly manifest in Part II, chapter 10, where one's suspicions are at once aroused because the conclusion is obviously untrue in general, and which is a frenzied example of suppressed premisses. Here, as before, $F'(x)$ is, at the same time, the wage in terms of wage goods and the value of the marginal output in terms of wage goods, $F(x)$ being the value of total output in terms of wage goods. But obviously the value of output in terms of wage goods is a function of x and $\dfrac{P}{\pi}$, where $\dfrac{P}{\pi}$ is the *price* of output in terms of wage goods, and F cannot be treated as a function of x alone unless P and π are constant. A.C.P. is leaving out terms all the way along, and they happen to be the important terms for his discussion.

Moreover on p. 102 (§4) he is assuming that all money income is necessarily spent on the purchase of current output. This is consistent with his previous assumptions, which are, between them, a sufficient condition for unemployment to be impossible. Thus his *Theory of Unemployment* is only valid in conditions which ensure that there is no unemployment. That is how he arrives at so many results which, if there were unemployment, would be surprising.

The whole thing turns on a completely bogus use of the mathematics of a single variable. The apparatus is, from start to finish, nonsense apparatus. He arbitrarily takes two items, namely employment and real wages, out of a complex, but presumably determinate, system and then treats them, without proof or enquiry, as being analytic functions of one another. But they are not independent variables. If everything is given except real wages and employment, then neither real wages nor employment are capable of more than one value. He is discussing the fluctuations of two quantities which, on his assumptions, are both constants.

As applied to the employment offered by an individual firm, A.C.P.'s conclusions are simply wrong and absurd. As applied to aggregate employment, they are only true in the same sense that it would be true to say that the amount of employment depends on the consumption of caviare, because (*cet. par.*), both can be inferred from the community's real income. His conclusion that employment (*cet. par.*) will only improve if real wages fall is only true in the same sense that it is true (*cet. par.*) that employment will only improve if more caviare is consumed.

For heaven's sake have a good look at the work and tell me if the gist of this is right. Or am *I* talking nonsense? A.C.P. produces as great a sense of Bedlam in my mind as Hayek does. Are the undergraduates to be expected to take it seriously? What a subject! I am sending a copy of this letter to Gerald to find out what he makes of the book.   [copy unsigned]

From a letter from D. H. ROBERTSON, *15 September 1933*

I am on a brief holiday, after reporting on a great crop of theses etc... and thank God I haven't got the *Theory of Unemployment* with me: so it's no good my trying to answer your letter properly. I have always found the Prof's wage-good method hard to get into, but I *thought* I was satisfied it worked out all right. As far as I remember he draws a sharp distinction between (*A*) wage-good industries and (*B*) others. *A* is first treated as homogeneous, so that P is π and all is well. Then something is said (but I forget what!) about *A* not being in fact homogeneous. As regards (*B*) we have to conceive entrepreneurs swopping their output for wage-goods to offer to their workpeople (as they would have to do more or less if they were building a railway at the North Pole), so that both the demand for labour and the workpeople's supply price is expressible in terms of wage-goods. But I didn't *think* he assumed that the ratio of exchange between wage-goods and non-wage goods is unalterable.

As regards all incomes being spent, isn't it stated in the barter analysis (? Part I, 3) that entrepreneurs may elect to put goods into store instead of using them to hire labour with? And in the monetary part (is it Part IV?) hoarding is dealt with more or less on my lines.

But it's not much good my going on without the book to hand. What a ghastly subject it is! Here are you saying wage reductions are no good, and

Pigou saying they are a lot of good, and Walker saying they are no good at the beginning of a slump but some good at the end, and now Isles saying they are some good at the beginning but no good at the end! How I wish we could form a Cambridge front again!

From a letter from D. H. ROBERTSON, *21 September 1933*

(3) Clay's[1] enclosed *your* MS[2] with my proofs, so I forward it. I can't correct my own proof finally till I can fill in the reference to my original article. You shall have the last word, as promised! What it seems to me has happened is this. The purpose of my article was to adapt the reasoning of my *Banking Policy* in which all incomes were assumed mobile, to the world of the *Treatise on Money*, in which (1) sharp distinction was drawn between the mobile incomes of entrepreneurs and the rigid *rates* of pay of the other factors, (2) attention was concentrated on the effect of behaviour of the money streams in producing situations which would generate unemployment, but little said about the effect of the unemployment in altering the money streams: i.e. there was a tendency to treat not only the rates but the aggregates of non-entrepreneur incomes as constant. This seems to me a legitimate simplification for disentangling the *originating* causes of dis-equilibrium, and, in order to keep the discussion within reasonable limits of length, was explicitly adopted in my article. You now counter by (1) taking us back to the world from which, in order to conform to the *Treatise*, I was trying to escape, viz. a world in which the rates of pay of the whole population are mobile: (2) bringing in, in your final (1) and (2), the effects of the obliteration of some incomes by unemployment (and I suppose you would add debt repudiation), which of course I don't deny, but which don't seem to me relevant to the analysis of the originating cause of disequilibrium.

Granted *some* 'fixed' incomes are obliterated in this way, it still seems to me perfectly possible for the fixed income section of the population as a whole (what I call in my article 'the public') to save (in my sense) a large and definite sum X over a period of time in excess of investment: there is no reason to suppose that *their* aggregate income will shrink to an extent which makes it impossible for them to do this.

I really meant, before you wrote your final reply and put the thing into proof, to rewrite my rejoinder so as to bring out this point. And if you would

[1] The printers of the *Economic Journal*.

[2] 'Mr Robertson on "Saving and Hoarding" I', reprinted below pp. 327–30. Robertson's 'proof' was his reply to Keynes's criticisms which appeared in the *Economic Journal* for December 1933, under the title 'Mr Robertson on "Saving and Hoarding" III'.

accept the pencil correction now made at the beginning of §2 and rewrite your reply accordingly, I think the discussion might be made more illuminating to the reader. For as it is he will see—or ought to—that the article is dealing with one world—the world of the *Treatise*—and the interchange of rejoinders with another—the world of *Banking Policy* from which I was inviting him to depart! But if you would rather leave things as they are, I don't mind, let the reader discover for himself what has happened!

Will you however look again at your last sentence on galley 2,—'some passages seem to suggest. . .'. Does this mean passages in the article or in the rejoinder? If the latter, I suggest that it's hardly justified: for I admit in §1, para. 2, that the truth is as you say,—on the (unwarranted) assumption that there are none of those retarding forces at work the elucidation of which is an essential part of my analysis!

To D. H. ROBERTSON,[1] *26 October 1933*

My dear Dennis,

I have a shocking lot of stuff to put to you.

I. Our controversy in the Journal

I have sent on your reply to Hawtrey to him[2]. When would it suit you to have a talk with him over the week-end? If you could give him either lunch or tea on Sunday, that would not conflict with anything I have arranged.

(1) As regards your reply to me, we are I think getting very near the point when I can abolish my rejoinder and leave you with the last word. Two points, however, remain. The first one I have noted in the margin of the enclosed on page three[3].

(*a*) It appears to me that you must mean by spontaneous saving by the public something very near to, if not identical with, what I call saving in my queer sense. Indeed my saving was originally devised, as I have always believed, to meet the same need as your spontaneous saving. If so, I should agree

---

[1] The numbers and letters preceding paragraphs and sentences in this letter are those of D. H. Robertson and refer to Robertson's comments on Keynes's letter which follow this letter.

[2] R. G. Hawtrey, 'Mr Robertson on "Saving and Hoarding" II', *Economic Journal*, December 1933. Robertson's reply to this and to Keynes's note (printed below pp. 327–30) appeared in the same issue under the title 'Mr Robertson on "Saving and Hoarding" III'.

[3] The original has not survived. [Ed.]

that aggregate spontaneous saving can be a very important quantity. On the other hand, I see no connection between this and your new kind of (*b*) saving, which still remains for me a fifth wheel to the coach.

(2) The second point relates to the last paragraph on page three. I can see no connection whatever between your revised meaning of hoarding and the Marshallian K and income velocity V, and I cannot see that you have given the slightest indication of how *in general* one can be defined in terms of the other. The best you can do is to show that in the ultra-simple case when practically everything is held constant, there is an arithmetical relationship between them. That is true of almost any two factors in the economic world. If you leave this paragraph, I shall have to put in what I previously said about it.

II. My criticism of the Professor

As to the general character of what he is doing, I don't think I really differ from your explanations. (1) He is showing in what way the amount of employment is related to the real supply price of labour, *when there is full employment*, meaning by full employment that as much labour is employed as is available at the real equivalent of the existing money wage.

(2) On the second point, namely the effect on employment of altering money wages, what you now say seems to me to spoil entirely the beauty of your previous explanation, and to be something which to me is completely unconvincing. May I, to shorten the argument, put it this way? Do you agree that in the new position of short-period equilibrium, after money wages have been reduced, prices will fall in proportion to the reduction in marginal cost? You were previously arguing that this must be the tendency, and that seems to me to be absolutely right. But in the new position of short-period equilibrium, prices will fall in the same proportion as wages, with the result that entrepreneurs' income per unit of output will also have fallen in the same proportion. Thus *ceteris paribus*, we shall have equilibrium

with the same output as before, since nothing will have happened except a change in prices, the real return to everyone concerned being unchanged.

It is impossible to change anything simply by changing the general level of money wages. You can only get a change by introducing an alteration from outside in some other factor. If, for example, the fall in prices and wages leads to cheap money, that will make a difference. Or if the government has a policy of keeping aggregate money incomes constant by paying out doles equal to the difference between the actual incomes arising from output and this pre-determined figure. But in this event it is possible to get the increase of employment by cheap money, or by a dole, or whatever it is, without any reduction in money wages. Moreover, the Professor, as I understand, is strictly keeping to his *ceteris paribus* and is not introducing factors of this kind, but has simply not perceived that it is impossible to keep entrepreneurs' incomes unchanged if there is a diminution of cost at the margin. For this must have the result of causing them to lose quasi-rent all along the line.

[The rest of this letter has not survived]

From D. H. ROBERTSON, *October 1933*

I. Saving and hoarding

(1) (*a*) I'm afraid the suggested identification of my Spontaneous Saving and your 'Saving' won't do. E.g. for the Danaid case, p. 1, my S.S. over a year is $\frac{x}{n}$, while your 'Saving' is $\frac{x}{2}\frac{n+1}{n}$; for the 'standard case', p. 3, my S.S. over a year is $\frac{x}{q}$, while your 'Saving' is $\frac{x}{2}\frac{q+1}{q}$.

(*b*) Pace W. Occam, I think my Total Saving justifies itself by bringing under the same roof a number of activities which have much in common. But I *think* it has also a more utilitarian justification: for I *think* that this is the meaning of Saving which is relevant to the determination of the rate of interest on the supply side (I'm not saying—is the sole determinant of the r. of i. on the supply side, for I don't forget the banks). But I'm not prepared to develop this at present.

$$(2)\ M = KRP = \frac{RP}{V}.$$

(i) I am prepared to assert that, on the level of abstraction maintained in the *Treatise* and in my article, all the phenomena of an 'economy campaign' can be expressed verbally in terms of Hoarding and symbolically in terms of V or K. I can't understand your view that there is 'no connection whatever' between Hoarding and K (or V),—or no connection greater than that which exists between any two economic quantities—for Hoarding is now *defined* as doing certain actions which affect the proportion stock/income, or alternatively which affect V (end of §3 of my article). Indeed it is in this connection, if anywhere, that I feel Occam might have a grievance against me.

(ii) I am prepared to assert that on *any* level of abstraction all forces acting on P can be expressed in terms of M, V, or R—there is no other 'hidden factor' which doesn't find its way into the equation. But

(iii) I am not prepared to say that, if we move down to the level of abstraction in which a contraction in MV consists partly in the obliteration of incomes by unemployment and debt-repudiation, all the forces at work can conveniently be expressed verbally in the term Hoarding. Though even here I would contend that Hoarding (or alternatively a reduction of M) is *entailed by* a decision to cut down the money stream by discharging labour.

But I don't think one can be expected to move on all levels of abstraction in a single article,—which I feel to be a valid reply to your riposte as it stands. But if you really disagree with (i) above, then I think my paragraph (pruned in language if you prefer!) had better stand, with *some* riposte from you, so as to bring out the disagreement.

II. The theory of unemployment

The situation here, as regards prospect of agreement, seems really desperate!

(1) I can't make head or tail of the marked sentence![1] The formal discussion, in A.C.P.'s Part II, of the determinants of the elasticity of real demand for labour, does not require *any* assumption about *why* the price of labour falls from y to $y - \Delta y$,—e.g. whether through the fiat of an arbitration court or through the irruption of a lot of German refugees into a market so free that practically everybody available is always employed. But the fact that A.C.P. makes guesses (bad or good) about the effect on employment of a 10 per cent cut in wages in a depression indicates that even in this Part he has in mind a situation in which, at the higher wage, not everybody who would accept employment at that wage is able to find it.

And in Parts III and IV he explicitly makes the assumption that the real

[1] The sentence 'He is showing...existing money wage' in section II (1) of Keynes's letter of 28 October 1933 (above p. 316).

rate of wages is held fixed, and argues that in this event a decline in the real demand for labour will create a situation in which not everybody who would accept employment at the fixed rate of real wages will be able to find it. I.e. he seems to me throughout to be making exactly the opposite assumption to that which I understand you to attribute to him.

(2) Either I miswrote or you misread something if you thought that in my first note[1] I was arguing that in the new position of short-period equilibrium the price-level would stand below its old level in the same proportion as the wage-rate has fallen. That is exactly the view I was arguing *against*.

A.C.P.'s and my account of what happens is this. *Initially*, when the wage rate is cut, the flow of money per unit of time directed to the purchase of goods is reduced in a smaller proportion than the aggregate wage-bill, since nothing whatever has happened *so far* to reduce the aggregate of non-wage incomes. Hence the price-level falls in a smaller proportion than the wage-rate. But the marginal prime cost of the existing rate of output falls in exact proportion to the wage rate. Thus the entrepreneur is making a prime profit on the marginal unit of the existing rate of output, and the existing rate of output is not a (short-period) equilibrium one. There is an inducement to expand output until the price equals the (new) marginal cost of the (new) rate of output,—which is higher than the new marginal cost of the old rate of output because of the operation of short-period increasing cost. *This* position—and not that reached directly after the wage-cut—is the new position of equilibrium.

I don't quite understand whether (as your last letter rather suggests) you are disputing this analysis even for the simple case in which all goods are wage-goods (i.e. are consumed by both classes): or whether you are arguing that, when we differentiate between wage-goods and non-wage-goods, the analysis ceases to hold for the wage-goods. But it *does* hold for the wage-goods, on the assumption that, when wages are cut, the fraction of the—initially unchanged—total profit which is spent on wage-goods is itself unchanged. If it is this assumption which you are disputing, I can see there may be more to be said: otherwise you seem to me to be doing exactly what A.C.P. accuses 'some persons' of doing, viz. 'assuming the answer before the argument has begun'!

---

[1] This note has not survived. [Ed.]

To D. H. ROBERTSON, *1 November 1933*

D.H.R.

When the daily 'new-sense saving' of the public is $\dfrac{x}{n^2}$, my annual saving is $\dfrac{x}{2}\dfrac{n+1}{n}$ (vide your attached note, top of page 2)[1].

When the daily 'spontaneous saving' of the public is $\dfrac{x}{nq}$ you say that my annual saving is $\dfrac{x}{2}\dfrac{q+1}{q}$ (ink footnote to page 3).

What exactly is the difference between your 'spontaneous saving' and your 'new-sense saving'?

Could you, in re-writing your note, add a definition of 'spontaneous saving', which will make the reasons for the above clear?

J.M.K.

From D. H. ROBERTSON, *November 1933*

The Spontaneous Saving is that done by the public off their own bat, for reasons unknown. The Induced Saving (positive or negative) is that done by entrepreneurs with a view to restoring a proportion of money stock to income which has been disturbed by the action of others. (This distinction is, I think, already made clear in the last para. of §10 of my article.) Total Saving is the sum of Spontaneous Saving and Induced saving. Keynesian Saving is the difference between the actual income of entrepreneurs and their normal income.

In the Danaid case Induced Saving = 0, and Spontaneous Saving = Total Saving $= \dfrac{x}{n^2}$ per day $= \dfrac{x}{n}$ during the year. In the standard case (the mechanics of which are exhibited in §10 of my article for the case of inflation), Spontaneous Saving $= \dfrac{x}{nq}$ per day $= \dfrac{x}{q}$ over *the year*. On each but the first day of each of the q periods entrepreneurs spend $\dfrac{x}{nq}$ more than

---

[1] This and the succeeding reference are to Robertson's marginal comments on his own galley proofs.

their disposable income, i.e. their induced Dissaving over the year

$$= \frac{x}{nq}(K-1)q = \frac{x}{n}(K-1)$$

Therefore Total Saving over the year $= \frac{x}{q} - \frac{x}{n}(K-1) = \frac{x}{n}$. Entrepreneurs

are making losses of $\frac{x}{nq}$ on each day of the first period of K days, of $\frac{2x}{nq}$

on each day of the second, and so forth. I.e. their total losses (total Keynesian Savings) during the year are

$$\frac{Kx}{nq}(1+2\ldots+q) = \frac{Kx}{nq}\frac{q}{2}(2+q-1) = \frac{Kx}{n}\frac{q+1}{2} = \frac{x}{2}\frac{q+1}{q}.$$

D.H.R.

As Keynes also discussed Pigou's book with G. F. Shove of King's, we reprint Shove's replies as well at this point.

From G. F. SHOVE, *11 September 1933*

My dear Maynard,

I am very much interested, and rather relieved by your letter. So far I have only given A.C.P. what I call a 'first reading', i.e. have only gone through it in an armchair rather cursorily to get at the general drift of the argument. It struck me as the worst book on economics that I had read for a long time—a good deal worse than Hicks[1]. But I find it very difficult to make out what exactly he is saying and in particular what the fundamental assumptions are, and I think that this might be because of my own simplicity and lack of education. So I have suspended judgment till I have gone through it again more carefully and in detail. It is a comfort to learn from you that the fault probably does partly lie in the book and not altogether in me.

My provisional conclusion was that throughout the whole of most of Parts I, II and III he is tacitly, and I believe unconsciously, assuming that everything actually *consists of* wage goods;[2] i.e. having decided at the outset to express all prices in terms of wage goods he has glided into the assumption that all payments are made in wage goods. This would explain a number of conclusions which, as it seemed to me, are obviously not true in general, and some curious turns of expression. I had, indeed, been contemplating a note on 'Edible Currency and the New Wages-Fund Doctrine'. But I suspect that your hypothesis gets deeper and explains more. I will write again when I

---

[1] J. R. Hicks, *The Theory of Wages*. Should have reviewed this in the *Economic Journal* for June 1933.

[2] Or in tokens which can only be exchanged for them and have a constant purchasing power in terms of them.

have had time to read your letter (which I received only an hour ago) and A.C.P. more carefully.

The only thing which strikes me straight off is that A.C.P. does not *consistently* adhere to the assumption that P/π is constant since in Part II, chapter IV (p. 54) he allows for the effect of changes in a monopolist's output upon its price in terms of wage goods. But more later.

Yours
Gerald

A second assumption which I half suspected to be necessary for a good deal of his argument is that wage goods are *produced* (as well as consumed) in the uniform and constant 'packets' referred to on p. 20 §6.[1] But your hypothesis that their relative prices must be supposed constant probably does instead.

From G. F. SHOVE, *12 September 1931*

I forgot to say that my hypothesis does not fit Part II, chapter X nor any passage where the distinction between money and real wages is made. Which confirms my impression that yours is probably the right one.

G.S.

From G. F. SHOVE, *19 September 1933*

My dear Maynard,

I have now read again some of the relevant passages in the Professor's book. Not *very* carefully, because the exposition still strikes me as obscure and elliptic and I do not feel inclined to spend a vast amount of time puzzling it out. Also, as you know, I have absolutely no mathematics, so that in any case my opinion would not be worth much. But, so far as it goes, here it is. (I am not, of course, competent to judge whether A.C.P.'s mathematical expressions are justifiable, and you must excuse my own crudities and howlers in this respect.)

(1) Essentially, I cannot see any escape from your criticism. Though I don't think it can be maintained, *literally*, that the assumption of constant price ratios ('the price of every individual article is fixed and constant') is required *throughout* the book (see (3) below): and A.C.P. might conceivably put up some sort of defence for making it in the principal passage where it does seem to be required. (See (5) below.)

(2) I am still inclined to think that some parts of the argument require the assumption that all payments are made in wage goods (e.g. in particular the

[1] But possibly this only applies in places where he expressly says that for simplicity he is assuming that there is only one wage good.

thesis at the bottom of p. 155 that gratuitous transfers from the richer non-wage-earners to wage-earners of necessity reduce, *ceteris paribus*, the quantity of labour demanded at a given real wage rate). Incidentally this assumption would explain why a monopolist seeks to maximise his net revenue expressed in wage goods (p. 53), why the rate of interest is calculated in terms of wage goods (Part II, chapters V and VIII) and why in Part II, chapter III it is the real wage expressed in wage goods (not old masters) which affects employment.[1]

(3) As regards *Part II, chapter III*.

I thought at first that there was confusion here between the elasticity of demand for labour in an individual *firm* and in an *industry*. But I decided that this has been avoided. He is throughout thinking of the demand of the industry as a whole. (He claims classically that in the short period, with which he is concerned throughout, external economies are insignificant, so that the addition which an increment of labour makes to its firm's output = the addition which it makes to the total output of the industry. Hence the wage may be equated to the value of the latter.)

Nor can I see that *in this chapter* the assumption of constant price ratios is made[2] or required.

It is noticeable that in this chapter A.C.P. *avoids* saying (what would require, and be true on, this assumption) that $F(x)$ is the total value of the product or that $\psi(y)$ on p. 42 is the total value of y product or $f(y)$ total payment for supply y of material. I interpret these expressions as being simply what I call (I don't know whether rightly or wrongly) the 'integrals' of $F'(x)$, $\psi'(y)$ and $f'(y)$ i.e. to be respectively the sum of the series of marginal products over the range o to x labour, the sum of the series of demand prices for the product over the range o to y output, and the sum of the series of supply prices for the material over the range o to y supply. (That this is the right interpretation is suggested by the definition of net monopoly revenue given on p. 53, where the same notation is used. If $\psi(y)$ were total selling value of output and $f(y)$ total payment for material, he would have written $\psi(y) - f(y)$ instead of $[\psi'(y) - f'(y)] y$.)

On this interpretation, what is required *for this chapter* (Part II, chapter III) is, as it seems to me, the assumption that, in the given state of desires and technique, *the wage-rate rating in the industry does not affect prices* (i.e. price

---

[1] The assumption is not made, or purports not to be made, in Part II, chapter X. But that chapter is expressly concerned with a 'monetary economy'.

[2] A great part of the chapter is in fact concerned with the changes in the prices (in terms of wage goods) of the product and material associated with changes in the quantity of labour employed. If prices were supposed constant E_f and E_s would be infinite, the right-hand side of the 'fixed equation' (δ) at the foot of p. 44 would reduce to $1/n$, and the whole discussion from p. 43 on would be rubbish.

ratios or the relevant price ratios) *except indirectly through its effect upon (the quantity of labour unemployed in, and consequently) the output of the industry*:[1] i.e. not exactly that the price ratios are constant, but that in the given state of desires and technique, the system of prices corresponding to each given output of the industry is determinate and constant in the sense that it is independent of the wage rate ruling there. Of course, this assumption deprives the conclusions of any pretension to generality and makes them, to my mind, inapplicable to many of the most important problems encountered in practice: (it requires, I fancy, a number of conditions such as that output of the industry is a small fraction of the total income of the community, that the labour employed in it consumes only a small part of its product, that the industry employs only a small fraction of the total labour force of the community, that the wage ruling in the industry does not affect wages elsewhere, etc.). But it is less extreme than the assumption of constant price ratios, fits the context better and is more in line with the classical treatment.

(I am supposing, by the way, that in this chapter A.C.P. is contemplating changes in the wage rate in one particular industry unaccompanied by changes in rates elsewhere—except such as are consequential on changes in output—and therefore admits different wage rates in different industries. If the wage changes are supposed to be general the assumption, and indeed the whole treatment, is quite indefensible.)

(4) So far as I can see, the fatal step (which *does* require constant price ratios) of identifying the value of the addition which the marginal increment of labour makes to total output with the addition which it makes to the value of total output (i.e. equating $F(x)$ to the total value of output while at the same time equating $F'(x)$ to the wage rate)[2] is taken for the first time on p. 78 (§3): again at the bottom of p. 89: and again in the formula for money-wage rate at the bottom of p. 102 and top of p. 103. Thus the formulae for η and for E_r on p. 90 would seem to apply only on the assumption that the price of exports in terms of wage goods is constant—which is contradicted on p. 91: while on p. 103 the formulae for money-wage rate and for elasticity of the total demand for labour in the aggregate (E_r) would seem to require, in addition, that the price of home non-wage goods in terms of wage goods is constant.[3]

[1] Which means, doesn't it, that, for the purpose of studying the effect of wage changes in the industry on the employment there, your P and π may be treated as functions of x above?

[2] I still have an uneasy feeling that when *output as a whole* is under discussion there may be some simple arithmetical or mathematical justification for this: but I cannot, for the life of me, see what it is.

[3] The formula for E_r on p. 90 does not seem to require this last assumption as it stands: but if it is to be regarded as equivalent to the formula on p. 103 (as one would suppose from the remark there 'we know already'), it does. As regards the formula for η: since there is

Moreover, now that we are dealing with the general rate of wages and output as a whole, it is clearly illegitimate to assume that, in general, P/π is independent of the wage rate.

Thus I see no escape from the assumption that price ratios are constant *in these chapters* (Part II, chapters VIII, IX and X).

(5) But might not A.C.P. put up some sort of defence for making it on the following lines?

(*a*) It is clearly stated at the beginning of Part II, chapter IX (p. 89) that 'attention will be focused exclusively on the conditions that prevail in a marked industrial depression' and that in those conditions, for the reasons given on pp. 51 and 136–7, the short-period marginal cost of any individual commodity varies but little in consequence of (small) variations of output, while it has been observed elsewhere that what variation there is is upward for increases, and downward for decreases in output. And this warning must be taken to apply to chapter X also, since that is simply an application of the results of chapter IX to 'a monetary economy'.

(*b*) It is also postulated (p. 88 top) that the rate of wage must be the same in all industries: and that the wage in every industry is equal to the value of the marginal net product of labour there.

(*c*) Thus, when a small increment of labour is taken into employment it is distributed between the various industries as to keep wages equal in all of them and to make the price of every industry's product equal to its (short-period) marginal cost: and it follows from (*a*) that the marginal costs of these where output is altered will not change much as compared with each other and with those which do not expand or contract.

(*d*) Hence in an enquiry which relates only to the short period in a marked industrial depression, formulae which assume price ratios to be constant, though not strictly accurate, involve no great error.

I don't know whether there is anything in this and it would not apply to chapter VIII unless the warning on p. 89 is to be considered retrospective. Moreover, it involves, I think, the further assumption that the conditions of demand are such as to ensure that the increment of labour is so distributed among the various industries as not to involve any large increase in the quantity employed in any of them (which seems dubious if the effect on demand of the wage change is allowed for). But that is the only kind of defence I can see at present.

Yours
Gerald

here supposed to be only one kind of wage good, the formula would be all right if it were made to apply to wage goods only. But the inclusion of exports vitiates it unless the assumption that their price is constant is made,—or so it seems to me.

[There was also a brief postscript on supervision arrangements for the next term at King's.]

From G. F. SHOVE, *23 September 1933*

My dear Maynard,

After the post had gone last night, I realised that the defence with which I had tried to provide the Professor was rubbish. No doubt you saw this at once if you read it. I sent my telegram to save you the trouble of replying to it.

I had forgotten that A.C.P. is assuming all through,—and the formulae require,—that labour is the only item in (short-period) cost. Given this, if marginal cost in any industry is constant, there are no external economies, and prices are equal to marginal costs, the elasticity of demand for labour in all industries together is infinite.

I wish I could get out of the habit of thinking that there *must* be some defence for anything which the Professor says. I have spent so much time in the course of my life in abortive attempts to invent defences for him.

Yours
Gerald

From G. F. SHOVE, *22 October 1933*

My dear Maynard,

I have spent some little time this afternoon trying to see whether I could knock a hole in your refutation of the Prof.[1] I can't find a chink anywhere. I feel that it is unanswerable.

I should *like* to come to your lectures very much, because I always love hearing you expound. But I don't believe I shall be able to clear the space regularly without neglecting my own duties. So I shall be very grateful if you would let me see your stuff some time later on—though perhaps I should not have long to wait before it appears in the children's magazine.[2]

Yours
Gerald

---

[1] Presumably the refutation Keynes gave to his 1933 lectures for which Shove had seen the notes. See below p. 420.

[2] The common Cambridge nickname for *The Review of Economic Studies*, founded in 1933 by a group of younger economists.

From The Economic Journal, *December 1933*

MR ROBERTSON ON 'SAVING AND HOARDING' I

I

In his article in the *Economic Journal*, September 1933, Mr D. H. Robertson has proposed new definitions of these two terms which I should like to examine briefly.

Let us mean by current *income* the value of current output, which, I understand, is what Mr Robertson means by it. If we define savings as the excess of income during a period over expenditure on consumption during that period, it follows that savings are exactly equal to the value of output added to accumulated wealth, i.e. to investment. The sense of saving in which it is necessarily equal to investment, i.e. the excess of current income over current consumption, let us, for the present, call *surplus*. In my *Treatise on Money* I gave a definition of savings which was not the same as surplus and was, therefore, not necessarily equal to investment. Mr Robertson also feels a need for a conception of savings which is not identical with surplus and proposes one in the above article. I do not like his conception any more than he likes mine. It may, perhaps, help the reader to decide whether Mr Robertson's saving is a useful concept if I explain what appears to be its exact relation to surplus.

Let us denote surplus by S' and saving, as Mr Robertson defines it, by S.

$S'-S$, aggregated over any period of time, equals the difference between one 'day's' income at the end of the previous period and one 'day's' income at the end of the period in question. Thus its magnitude depends on how long Mr Robertson's technical 'day' is. If his day is short, e.g. a week, $S'-S$ over however long a period will always be small. For example, if incomes fall by 10 per cent during the period and the technical 'day' is a week, $S'-S$ is one tenth of a week's income. Even if a slump were to last for years and incomes were to fall to half their previous level, the total excess of saving over investment for the whole period could not in the aggregate exceed half a week's income.

Thus, the amount of saving (in his sense) depends on the length of his 'day', and the difference between investment (or surplus) and his 'saving' can never be large enough to have practical importance, unless his 'day' is a substantial period.

Furthermore, a man cannot know how much he has 'saved' during a given period in Mr Robertson's sense unless he knows how long Mr Robertson's technical 'day' is. For example, let us suppose that a man's income is falling by 1 unit a week, and that he spends during a year an amount equal to his income during that year, then if Mr Robertson's 'day' is two weeks, the man will have 'saved' 104 units, since his income in the last two weeks of the previous year was 104 units greater than his income in the last two weeks of the year in question. But if Mr Robertson's 'day' is four weeks, the man will have saved 208 units, since his income in the last four weeks of the previous year was 208 units greater than his income in the last four weeks of the year in question. Thus there is no means by which any of us can tell how much we 'saved' last year, until Mr Robertson vouchsafes to tell us the length of his technical 'day'.

So I think that for the plain man, and still more for any practical purpose, Mr Robertson's definition is, if possible, even worse than mine!

Mr Robertson's definition of his meaning of hoarding is not so clear as that of saving. If I understand the above rightly, hoarding is no longer a statistical measure of the change between a man's cash and his income. A man may increase his cash relatively to his income without hoarding, and diminish it without dishoarding. The test is whether he has 'taken steps' to increase his cash, i.e. whether his increase of cash is the result of activity or passivity on his part. In particular an entrepreneur has not dishoarded if he suffers a reduction of cash through selling his output at a lower price than he had expected.

If this interpretation is correct, Mr Robertson's present definition of hoarding has, I think, a close relation to changes in the excess of saving over investment as defined by me in my *Treatise on Money*.

For if a member of the public (*A*) hoards, some entrepreneur (*B*) is in danger of suffering a reduction of cash through not selling his output at the expected price. If *B* does nothing to redress this situation, *B* is not dishoarding. Presumably, therefore, if to avoid a reduction of cash *B* reduces his personal expenditure or sells a security, then *B* is hoarding. If he sells a security to *A*, *A*'s hoarding is thereby diminished. If he reduces his personal spending, some other entrepreneur suffers increased losses. Thus the aggregate hoarding during the period for the community as a whole has nothing to do with actual changes in the holding of cash, but is equivalent to the change in the level of business losses ($= -\Delta Q$), as defined by me. Since on my definition business losses are equal to the excess of saving over investment, *net* hoarding during the period is equal to the *change* in the excess of saving over investment during that period.

If this is correct, it would seem that Mr Robertson's definition of hoarding is an alternative way of dealing with the same order of ideas as I attempted to handle by my concept of the excess of saving over investment. I am not quite clear whether Mr Robertson's hoarding during successive periods can be aggregated over a complete period. If so, it may be that my definition of saving is equivalent to the sum of investment and of hoarding, as defined by Mr Robertson, aggregated from a base period when business profits may be considered to have been in some sense normal. If so, I feel confirmed in the view that Mr Robertson's new definition of saving is not useful. I do not think that there is any practical application for which we require any concepts other than investment and hoarding interpreted, in accordance with Mr Robertson's new definition, as a function, not of changes in cash holdings as such, but of changes in business profits and losses.

Perhaps I should add that my own use of terms today is not the same as it was when I wrote my *Treatise on Money*, and that I do not now consider my analysis in that book to be as clear or as logical as I can make it. But the question of what uses of language and modes of expression are best does not alter the essential character of the fundamental ideas which Mr Robertson and I are both trying to elucidate.

One additional, though earlier, exchange of letters concerning the *Treatise* should be printed here—that which took place with J. A. Hobson between July and November 1931. Hobson's letters of 1 July and 31 August have not survived.

To J. A. HOBSON, *24 July 1931*

Dear Hobson,

Thank you for your letter of 1 July. I am sorry not to have answered it sooner. But I have been away on a short visit to the United States and it has only recently come into my hands.

As I am not sure whether you will have kept a copy of your letter, I append it to this reply of mine so that you can refer to the passages I comment on.

Before proceeding further with the argument, we must try to clear up what may be a misunderstanding on the first page of your letter, where you say that 'there must be a body of real capital corresponding to the uninvestable savings'. I do not accept this as being true in fact or in theory;—though I am afraid it is a point which I have not made sufficiently plain. But you may conclude what is in my mind by referring again to my Banana Parable, vol. I, page 176 [*JMK*, vol. v, pp. 158–60]. In this case there is no real capital corresponding to the surplus savings. The savings of certain individuals have merely led to the fall in price of the consumable article, so that other consumers have been able to obtain and consume a larger quantity of bananas in exchange for their incomes. At the same time the producers of the bananas make a loss; and in order to meet this loss, have to transfer certain existing capital assets of theirs to those individuals who have made the savings. Thus the savings have not led to the existence of any additional real capital.

I think we must get clear about this point before going any further.

Yours sincerely,

[copy initialled] J.M.K.

P.S. I should like your original letter back with your reply.

From J. A. HOBSON, *18 August 1931*

Dear Keynes,

I have been thinking over the objection raised in your letter to the effect that I had no right to assume that there was a body of 'real savings', i.e. increases of capital goods corresponding to the uninvestable money savings.

I forgot to bring with me to Exmouth, where I am writing, your letter and book. But I have put down here a series of propositions which may go some way to reconcile our respective treatments. I hope they may at least be intelligible.

Yours sincerely,

JOHN A. HOBSON

NOTES ON OVERSAVING

1. Assume that, by spending 80 per cent of the net income in setting labour and plant to make consumption goods and 20 per cent to make more plant and other capital goods, full employment of labour and existing capital was maintained, with due regard to increasing population and a rising standard of life.

2. Next assume an accelerating production in manufacture and agriculture by improved technique and organisation (with some reduction in the rate of growth of population).

3. If, as a result of accelerating production, retail prices fell, and the same proportion (80 per cent) of the net income purchased and consumed the enlarged output, no disequilibrium need occur.

4. But if, owing to a refusal to expand consumption by full use of the 80 per cent producing power, the proportion of 'savings' grew from 20 per

cent to 30 per cent, the money savings representing this 10 per cent could not find investments that were satisfactory.

5. For the failure to buy and consume the increased output of consumption goods at the lower prices would cause a glut and a collapse of retail prices. This collapse would speedily affect the purchases from merchants and manufacturers and unemployment of capital and labour along the whole line of production would ensue.

6. There would exist large quantities of unused excessive plant and other capital goods representing past real savings, but the increase of savings due to a refusal to buy the increased output of consumption goods would not 'invest' itself in the purchase of this excessive and immutable capital.[1]

7. This refusal to raise consumption to keep pace with increasing production is seen to be the direct source of this uninvestible saving. This refusal *might* be due to sheer conservatism in standards of consumption. But it probably proceeds, in part, from a shift in the distribution of the general income favourable to saving and by enlarged company reserves and by the quasi-automatic saving of the enlarged incomes of the rich, due to the low 'utility' of further spending on their part.

8. Restriction in the supply of money, or a policy of actual inflation, altering the distribution of incomes, would doubtless aggravate this situation. But if there were no monetary trouble, this enlargement of productivity would still operate to bring about disequilibrium.[2]

To J. A. HOBSON, *28 August 1931*

Dear Hobson,

I do not think there is anything with which I disagree in your 'Notes on Over Saving', and I think that this exposition of your point of view does bring us much nearer together.

One minor point arises on your paragraph 6, namely that this should not exclude the possibility of the owners of the new savings buying the existing capital plant at a price appropriate to its value in the new conditions, though below its cost of production.

---

[1] Keynes noted in pencil at this point 'It would—at a price.'

[2] Following this passage, Keynes noted in pencil: 'This is one case. Also there is another way out besides increased consumption. If rate of interest were to fall, consumption goods the production of which used much capital would be relatively cheapened and consumption would change over to such goods, thus creating an increased demand for capital and so absorbing the extra savings.'

But my main point on these notes is that you are only contemplating one case. You are pointing to the exit of diminished savings as a remedy for the situation you are contemplating. But I suggest to you that there is also another way out besides the way of increased consumption, namely, through a fall in the rate of interest—a point which I have mentioned in previous letters. For, if the rate of interest were to fall, consumption goods, the production of which requires much capital, would be cheapened relatively to other consumption goods, with the result that consumption would change over to such goods, thus creating an increased demand for capital, and so absorbing the extra savings.

The mischief arises, to my way of thinking, when the world accepts neither exit. That is to say, when social customs, or the distribution of wealth, or other causes maintain savings at a higher level than is appropriate to the existing rate of interest, whilst at the same time the working of the monetary system prevents a fall in the rate of interest.

If you could accept this other side of the shield which I offer, as well as the face which you have stamped with your imprint, we should be at peace.

Yours sincerely,
[copy initialled] J.M.K.

To J. A. HOBSON, 2 October 1931

Dear Hobson,

Many apologies for not replying sooner to your letter of 31 August. But life has been altogether too exciting lately and I have been much preoccupied with matters not wholly theoretical.

There are only two points in your last letter on which I want to comment, as follows:—

(1) Your calculation in the middle of your page 2 that 'money savings may continue to grow faster than they can be profitably invested' would only be the case in the event of the rate of interest failing to fall fast enough; though I suppose a

point might come when the rate of interest had fallen to zero, at which point I would agree with you that my alternative exit is closed, and that your exit of more spending and less saving is the only one left. But we have not by any means reached this point yet. I think that the community can still benefit greatly from an increased stock of capital goods. That is why I continue to emphasise the rate of interest. It is the failure of the rate of interest to fall fast enough which is the root of much evil.

(2) The other point arises near the bottom of your page 3. I quite agree that real savings can exist in the shape of plant and raw materials. But in my terminology an increase in the stock of plant and raw materials is a form of investment so that in this event there is no excess saving over investment. Moreover there is no presumption that the excess of savings over fixed investment will in fact correspond to increments of working capital. In any case it would only be some part of the savings in excess of investment in fixed capital which would get embodied elsewhere. The rest would simply run to seed, and disappear in the shape of business losses. The savings of the public being [*sic*] balanced by the losses of the entrepreneurs and the community as a whole being not one penny the richer.

I return the correspondence for reference.

Yours sincerely,

J. M. KEYNES

From J. A. HOBSON, *14 October 1931*

Dear Keynes,

I expect you are up to the eyes in more practical affairs than those that have occupied our correspondence. There is, however, one crucial issue in your letter of October 2 on which I should like to comment. You say 'in my terminology an increase in the stock of plant and raw materials is a form of investment so that to this extent there is no excess saving over investment'. Now the admitted 'excess saving' consists of income paid for assistance in producing some body of 'real' income, which under a proper equilibrium it would have bought. If that real income is not plant and raw materials for enlarging the productive system, it must be final consumption goods. When a rapidly accelerating power of production operates in enlarging the supply and reducing the supply price of such goods, a 'conservatism' of the consumer may induce him to save more of his income instead of raising his standard of consumption. This refusal to buy more would account for the accumulation of excessive money savings which you hold to occur.

If this is what you hold, it is a position quite intelligible to me and perhaps true. My chief doubt is as to your correctness in saying that 'every increase of stock of plant and raw materials is a form of investment'. That would be true if all new plant and raw materials were actual 'orders' issuing from the 'reserves' of existing firms or the invested capital of new businesses. But so far as the makers of plant and raw materials are making, not to actual 'orders' but to stock in anticipation of future orders, which under conditions of depression do not fructify in actual orders, there will exist excesses of capital goods corresponding to excesses of money savings. It may be that both explanations of excessive money savings are valid.

I don't hold that an 'excess of savings over fixed investment will in fact correspond to increments of working capital'. For working capital, being in the main in bank-trader credits, will follow the increase or decrease of the productive activities of investment capital, i.e. of expanding profitable industry.

That 'the rate of interest' plays a part, sometimes an important part, I would admit, but the efficiency of its action as a stimulus or a check raises many doubts. In certain situations of boom or slump its action seems very slight and unreliable.

Don't trouble to reply. When you are a little freer, we might meet for a talk.

Yours sincerely,
J. A. HOBSON

To J. A. HOBSON, *1 November 1931*

Dear Hobson,

In reply to your letter of 14 October—I am afraid there is still a fundamental point on which our minds have not met. It is a matter on which it is extraordinarily difficult to make one's self clear, for I have had the same experience with others.

The point is that when savings exceed investment prices fall, so that that part of income which is spent buys just as much goods as would have been purchased by the whole of the income if nothing had been saved. The paradox is that saving in excess of investment involves in itself no sacrifice whatever to the standard of life of the consuming and saving class. If their income is 100 and if their saving in excess of current investment is 30, the 70 which they spend after saving 30 will buy exactly the same amount as the 100 would have bought if they had not saved at all. That is to say they have saved 30 without making any sacrifice at all in terms of consumption. On the other hand the producers have lost the 30 in question. There has been no change in the aggregate of wealth and no change in the rate of consumption, but merely a transfer of 30 units of pre-existing wealth from the producers to the savers. Obviously this cannot go on long without the producers seeking to protect themselves from such losses. Hence unemployment etc. etc.

I do not know if this makes the point any clearer. In due course I must be at pains to expound the whole matter again from the bottom upwards in a manner better calculated to catch the attention of minds habituated to other channels of thought.

Yours sincerely,
[copy initialled] J.M.K.

Chapter 5

TOWARDS THE GENERAL THEORY

It would be misleading to suppose that Keynes's activities after the publication of the *Treatise* were exclusively devoted to the defence or elucidation of his book. His Economic Advisory Council Paper (above pp. 178–200), written just after finishing the *Treatise*, indicated signs of further development. In addition, in his correspondence with Hawtrey and others Keynes made it clear that he was trying alternative lines of approach to those of the *Treatise*.

However, there was still a period of relative consolidation before Keynes began to work intensively on a new formulation of his ideas and to announce his intentions as clearly as he did in his June 1932 letter to Hawtrey (above p. 172) or his preface to the Japanese edition of the *Treatise* (*JMK*, vol. v, p. xxviii).

It was during this period of consolidation that the activities of the 'Circus' were of considerable importance. As so little documentation of its discussions survives, we print below a note on the discussions of the 'Circus' and their relationship to many of the papers in this volume.

THE CAMBRIDGE CIRCUS, 1930–1

Keynes completed his preface to the *Treatise* on 14 September 1930, the day he finished the book as a whole. The book was actually published on 31 October 1930. Within a few months of publication, however, Keynes was moving on, rethinking the fundamental equations of the *Treatise* and developing the whole apparatus of analysis out of which, over the next few years, the *General Theory* emerged. What was it that provided the impulse to this rethinking? Did it come from his own ideas and intuitions? Or did it come to him in part from external sources?

To answer this one needs to remember certain characteristics of the *Treatise* and to be aware of certain of the external sources. In the *Treatise*, the ideas implicit in *Can Lloyd George Do It?*[1] were in a secondary position—almost as a special case peculiar to an economy where international complications made it impossible, under a gold standard system, to use interest-rate policy as a means of making savings equal to investment at

---

[1] Reprinted in *Essays in Persuasion* (*JMK*, vol. IX).

normal profits [vol. V, ch. 21 (vi), vol. VI, ch. 30 (vi), ch. 36 (ii)]. Moreover, the bulk of the formal analysis of the *Treatise* placed the emphasis on changes in prices rather than output. The concern with output changes was clearly secondary.

In the process of moving changes in output to the centre of the stage which they were to occupy in the *General Theory*, thus making Keynes's general pure theory closer to his policy recommendations, three outside influences seem to have been pre-eminent: the worldwide slump after 1929, which moved the English 'local difficulties' of 1922–9 on to a broader stage, the general reception given to the *Treatise* and discussions in Cambridge during 1930–1.

Within weeks of the publication of the *Treatise*, a group of younger economists in Cambridge set to work to digest it, to understand its implicit assumptions and, inevitably, to criticise it. Practically no documentary record of their discussions remains, although a few fragments appear in this volume. This note results from an attempt, made forty years later, to pool the memories of five of the survivors—Richard Kahn, James Meade, Piero Sraffa, Joan and Austin Robinson—to supplement these fragments. It must be read with a full awareness of the fallibility of memories, particularly with regard to exact dates, over so long a period.

The 'Circus', as it was commonly called at the time, formally took place during the period January–May 1931. Initially there were informal talks in Richard Kahn's rooms in the Gibbs Building at King's. These were later expanded into what would now be called a seminar held in the Old Combination Room at Trinity. Participation was strictly by invitation.[1] Besides those named, a very small number of the ablest of the undergraduates of that generation, one or two research students and a few other members of the teaching faculty were present, at least on one or two occasions. Dennis Robertson did not wish to be deeply involved, and attended, if memories serve, on only one occasion. Keynes himself took no part in this 'seminar'. Nor, of course did Pigou, who regarded such adolescent frivolities with Olympian detachment. After each meeting of the 'Circus', Richard Kahn reported orally to Keynes in the latter's rooms in King's the subject matter of the discussions and the lines of argument. James Meade, who had just finished his undergraduate studies at Oxford, has related his impressions of the process as follows:[2]

---

[1] Those undergraduates who wished to be invited were required to satisfy an interviewing board of Austin Robinson, Richard Kahn and Piero Sraffa.

[2] P. Lambert, 'The Evolution of Keynes's Thought from the *Treatise on Money* to the *General Theory*', *Annals of Public and Co-operative Economy*, XL(3), July–September 1969, p. 250.

According to James Meade, the analogy with God in a miracle play originated with

From the point of view of a humble mortal like myself Keynes seemed to play the role of God in a morality play; he dominated the play but rarely appeared himself on the stage. Kahn was the Messenger Angel who brought messages and problems from Keynes to the 'Circus' and who went back to Heaven with the result of our deliberations.

In order to get the 'Circus' discussions into perspective, it is necessary to be fully aware of the various ingredients of thought in Cambridge during the winter and spring of 1931. But first one must have in mind that the fundamental equations of the *Treatise*, distinguishing saving on the one hand and investment on the other, did not strictly assume that a potential difference between the two would be adjusted otherwise than through a change in the prices of investment goods and/or consumption goods with consequential effects on profits. Remember the famous passage about the 'Widow's Cruse' (vol. v, p. 125).

If entrepreneurs choose to spend a portion of their profits on consumption (and there is, of course, nothing to prevent them from doing this), the effect is to *increase* the profit on the sale of liquid consumption goods by an amount exactly equal to the amount of profits which have been thus expended. This follows from our definitions, because such expenditure constitutes a diminution of saving, and therefore an increase in the difference between I' and S. Thus, however much of their profits entrepreneurs spend on consumption, the increment of wealth belonging to entrepreneurs remains the same as before. Thus profits, as a source of capital increment for entrepreneurs, are a widow's cruse which remains undepleted however much of them may be devoted to riotous living. When, on the other hand, entrepreneurs are making losses, and seek to recoup these losses by curtailing their normal expenditure on consumption, i.e. by saving more, the cruse becomes a Danaid jar which can never be filled up; for the effect of this reduced expenditure is to inflict on the producers of consumption goods a loss of an equal amount. Thus the diminution of their wealth, as a class, is as great, in spite of their savings, as it was before.

However true this was and remains in broad terms, regarded as a rigid and precise formulation of the process it was evident that the widow's cruse proposition as stated assumed a fixed national output with the whole adjustment through prices. As a 'general theory', rather than a statement of a

Mrs Meade after a weekend with Joan and Austin Robinson in 1934 during which messages from on high appeared at regular intervals and God dominated the scene without making an actual appearance. Meade related this to Professor Lambert with the remark that it was an apt description of 1931 with Richard Kahn playing the angel-messenger. Hence the quotation.

particular limiting case, it was inadequate. Towards this conclusion, and the ultimate emergence of what soon came to be known as the 'widow's cruse fallacy',[1] Richard Kahn's article on the multiplier[2] was a primary impulse. Conceived in the summer of 1930, it was in Keynes's hands in a preliminary form just before the actual publication of the *Treatise* but far too late to modify its exposition.[3] This article gave much greater precision to the line of thought that had already emerged in *Can Lloyd George Do It?*', published by Keynes and Hubert Henderson in May 1929 and in a broadcast and articles in 1931.[4]

Richard Kahn's article made it clear that the price levels of consumption goods and investment goods would be determined by their respective supply curves and by the movement along them implied by changes in national expenditure in either of these sectors. A large price increase would emerge only if the supply curve rose steeply. 'At normal times, when productive resources are fully employed, the supply of consumption goods in the short period is highly inelastic...But at times of intense depression when nearly all industries have at their disposal a large surplus of unused plant and labour, the supply curve is likely to be very elastic. The amount of secondary employment is then large and the rise of prices is small.'

Richard Kahn tried to graft his thinking about the factors that determined the size of the multiplier on to Keynes's *Treatise* system of fundamental equations. But the graft, as a gardener so often discovers, did not take and the incompatibilities became all too clear. It was only in the extreme case 'where it is not the supply of consumption goods that is completely inelastic but *total* employment is fixed, so that, if investment increases, the production of consumption goods must diminish by an equal amount,[5]...[that] Mr Keynes's equations apply in their full simplicity.' Richard Kahn went on to emphasise the unreality of this assumption in the conditions of 1931 and the

---

[1] Austin Robinson is credited with having so named it. His simple-minded example of the problems of the *Treatise* formulation was as follows: If an entrepreneur, loaded with profits, decided on his way home to have a shoe-shine, was the effect solely to raise the price of shoe-shines? Was it impossible to increase the number of shoes shone?

[2] 'The Relation of Home Investment to Unemployment', *Economic Journal*, XLI(162), June 1931.

[3] The preliminary version was refined and considerably extended in discussions in Cambridge during 1930–1. The version Keynes appears to have seen in September 1930 was solely concerned with the relation between primary and secondary employment and lacked the elegant elaboration of the later version. The Economic Advisory Council version exists in file EA/4 of the Keynes Papers.

[4] Reprinted in *Essays in Persuasion* (*JMK*, vol. IX).

[5] Thus Kahn was asserting that Keynes's *Treatise* system only held at full employment. This formulation is not to be confused with the 'Circus's' 'buckets-in-the-well fallacy', referred to by Keynes in his 1931 reply to Robertson, which implied that changes in savings caused changes in investment through their effects on the demand for securities.

high probability that 'under certain circumstances employment can be increased without any significant alteration in the difference between savings and investment'.

It was in the measurement of the cost of investment that another ingredient of the collective thinking of the 'Circus' was refined by James Meade. This became incorporated in Richard Kahn's analysis of the multiplier. Mr Meade's Relation, as it was then familiarly known, propounded that, when supply was not perfectly elastic, 'cost of investment = saving on dole + increase in excess of imports over exports + increase in unspent profits − diminution in the rate of saving due to rise in prices'.[1] The relation, Richard Kahn explained, 'could be deduced in an *a priori* kind of way by considering that money paid out by the government to the builders of roads continues to be passed on from hand to hand until it reaches one of the *culs-de-sac* indicated by the various terms on the right-hand side of the equation'.

A third strand of the formulation of the fundamental equations was attacked by Richard Kahn. In these equations, Keynes ascribed the price level of consumption goods (P) and the price level of investment goods (P') to different sets of causes. Kahn argued (above p. 219) that 'If one clears the decks of your special definitions [of income], it is surely clear that P and P' *are* directly related except in the extreme case when no part of profit is devoted to consumption.' Thus the difference between consumption goods and investment goods was only a matter of degree and Keynes's formulation of the fundamental equations implied considerable confusion. Thus another area of dissatisfaction with the *Treatise* formulation was exposed.

Thus within a short time in the winter and spring of 1931 the 'Circus' had in its hands most of the important ingredients of the system which was ultimately to appear in the *General Theory*. The apparatus lying behind the *Treatise*'s fundamental equations had ceased to be purely a system of price determination and had become a system of determination of activity and employment with possible reactions on prices. The system of expansion and contraction envisaged was a process that eliminated differences between saving and investment otherwise than through the accumulation of unspent money balances. Such concepts as the elasticity of supply of output as a whole, of consumption goods and of investment goods were also in common use.

Of course memories may be fallible. But it is possible to be reasonably certain of where the thinking of the 'Circus' stood in the summer of 1931 from

[1] This relation marked the beginnings of the idea that one could measure the multiplier not only by adding the successive doses of expenditure on consumption, but also by adding up the successive doses of non-expenditure (i.e. 'savings'). This granted, savings = initial investment. This point was made explicit by Kahn in 'The Financing of Public Works: A Note', *Economic Journal*, XLII(167), September 1932.

two pieces of evidence in addition to Kahn's multiplier article. First it was probably in the course of that summer that Joan Robinson worked out 'A Parable on Saving and Investment' that was shown to Keynes in April 1932 (above p. 268) and published in *Economica* only in February 1933.[1] In that article she records that, in regard to the widow's cruse, 'Mr Keynes has now admitted that in that passage (p. 139) [*JMK*, vol. VI, p. 125] he was tacitly assuming that output was unchanged although the price level was falling. Evidently he, like the rest of us, had been misled by his upbringing into keeping his eye on Demand and forgetting Supply.'[2] Throughout this article, Joan Robinson, while ostensibly engaged in an apologia for Keynes against a supposed Hayekian critic, in fact made embroideries, such as Kahn's point about the determination of relative prices,[3] that show the extent of her and the 'Circus's' movement away from the over-simplicities of the *Treatise*. Second, James Meade, an active participant in the discussions, returned to Oxford in the autumn of 1931 at the end of his year's visit to Trinity, Cambridge. He is cautiously confident that he took with him back to Oxford most of the essential ingredients of the subsequent system of the *General Theory*.

As noted above, Richard Kahn reported regularly to Keynes the 'Circus's' discussions, doubts, new ideas and tentative conclusions. But at the same time he took suggestions for further discussion back with him to the 'Circus'. Thus it would be wrong to think of new ideas moving only in one direction. To this stream of comment, Keynes, who had just finished a magnum opus which had occupied him for six years, might well have been unreceptive, particularly as he was deeply engrossed in matters of economic policy—drafting the Macmillan Report, working in the Economic Advisory Council and making his revenue tariff proposals public. In fact he was the opposite. He picked up the 'Circus's' ideas, sometimes only after extensive discussion,[4] incorporated them into his own thinking and went ahead. There may have been (as some members believe) a short period when the 'Circus' was slightly further on towards the *General Theory* than was Keynes. But it was a very short time. Moreover, Keynes himself appears to have been moving forward on his own lines, as the hints of equilibrium at less than full employment in his June 1931 Chicago lectures (below p. 356) and the further discussions with Richard Kahn of this idea and of the idea of a relationship between consumption and income (below pp. 373–5) indicate.[5]

[1] See Joan Robinson, *Collected Economic Papers*, vol. 1 (Oxford, 1951), p. ix.
[2] *Economica*, XIII(39), February 1933, p. 82.   [3] Ibid. pp. 81–2.
[4] See in particular Kahn's repeated attempts over relative prices (above pp. 203–7, 218–19).
[5] Keynes's analysis of over-saving in his Chicago lectures closely follows Mrs Robinson's version of the argument. See below pp. 352–8 and 'A Parable on Savings and Investment', pp. 82–3.

The speed with which Keynes began to slough off the old skin of the *Treatise* is clear in the fragments of discussion with Kahn (below pp. 373–5), in his explicit decision of early 1932, communicated to Joan Robinson (above pp. 269–70), to Ralph Hawtrey (above p. 172) and, most important, to his Japanese readers (vol. v, p. xxvii)—to rework the formulations of the *Treatise*. Certainly it is clear that before he resumed lecturing in the Easter term of 1932 he was beginning to work matters out in terms of movements of output as a whole (above pp. 145–6; below pp. 373–4) and his explicit change of lecture title from 'The Pure Theory of Money' to 'The Monetary Theory of Production' in the autumn of 1932 also indicates a change of view. The lecture notes from this term,[1] and the earliest drafts of what was to become the *General Theory* dating from this period (below pp. 381–408) all show that in less than eighteen months after publishing the *Treatise*, he was in hot pursuit of a new formulation integrating money and real variables.

In June 1931, Keynes contributed to the Harris Foundation lecture series in Chicago three lectures entitled 'An Economic Analysis of Unemployment' which although they were couched in *Treatise* terms, gave some indications of further development with their greater emphasis on movements in output (below pp. 354–6) and their hints of equilibrium at less than full employment.

From *Unemployment as a World Problem* (1931)

AN ECONOMIC ANALYSIS OF UNEMPLOYMENT

Lecture 1 *The Originating Causes of World-Unemployment*

I

We are today in the middle of the greatest economic catastrophe —the greatest catastrophe due almost entirely to economic causes—of the modern world. I am told that the view is held in Moscow that this is the last, the culminating crisis of capitalism and that our existing order of society will not survive it. Wishes are fathers to thoughts. But there is, I think, a possibility—I will not

---

[1] These lecture notes, taken by R. B. Bryce, are used below pp. 411–12, 420–21. Copies are available in the Keynes Papers.

put it higher than that—that when this crisis is looked back upon by the economic historian of the future it will be seen to mark one of the major turning-points. For it is a possibility that the duration of the slump may be much more prolonged than most people are expecting and that much will be changed, both in our ideas and in our methods, before we emerge. Not, of course, the duration of the acute phase of the slump, but that of the long, dragging conditions of semi-slump, or at least subnormal prosperity which may be expected to succeed the acute phase. Not more than a possibility, however. For I believe that our destiny is in our own hands and that we can emerge from it if only we choose—or rather if those choose who are in authority in the world.

My main theme is to be an attempt to analyse the originating causes of the slump. For unless we understand these—unless our diagnosis is correct—I do not see how we can hope to find the cure. I shall make use of my own theories of monetary causation and therefore I may, perhaps, assume implicitly some measure of familiarity with them; but I shall try not to assume so much as to embarrass those who are not acquainted with them.

I see no reason to be in the slightest degree doubtful about the initiating causes of the slump. Let us consider a brief history of events beginning about 1924 or 1925. By that time or shortly afterward the perturbations which had, perhaps inevitably, ensued on the war and the treaty of peace and the readjustments of economic relations between different countries seemed to have about run their course. Confidence was more or less restored; the mechanism of international lending was functioning freely; and while several European countries still had serious difficulties to overcome, for the world as a whole conditions seemed to be set fair. It was widely believed that the general restoration of the gold standard would complete the edifice of prosperity and that an indefinitely long period of ever-increasing economic well-being was in front of the progressive industrial nations of the world. So, apart from certain local domestic

troubles in Great Britain (and I am not dealing except incidentally with the British problem), was indeed the case for some
four or five years. Now what was the leading characteristic of
this period? Where and how were the seeds of subsequent
trouble being sown?

The leading characteristic was an extraordinary willingness to
borrow money for the purposes of new real investment at very
high rates of interest—rates of interest which were extravagantly
high on pre-war standards, rates of interest which have never in
the history of the world been earned, I should say, over a period
of years over the average of enterprise as a whole. This was a
phenomenon which was apparent not, indeed, over the whole
world but over a very large part of it.

Let us consider the United States first, because the United
States has held throughout the key position. The investment
activity in this country was something prodigious and incredible.
In the four years 1925-8 the total value of new construction in
the United States amounted to some $38,000 million. This was
—if you can credit it—at an average rate of $800 million a month
for forty-eight months consecutively. It was more than double
the amount of construction in the four years 1919-22, and, I may
add, much more than double the amount that is going on now.
Nor was this the whole of the American story. The growth of the
instalment system, which represents a sort of semi-investment,
was going on *pari passu*. And, more important still, the United
States was a free purchaser of all kinds of foreign bonds, good,
bad, and indifferent—a free lender for investment purposes, that
is to say, to the rest of the world. To an important extent the
United States was acting, in this generous foreign-loan policy, as
a conduit pipe for the savings of the more cautious Europeans,
who had less confidence in their own prosperity than America
had; so that the foreign-bond issues were often largely financed
out of short-term funds which the rest of the world was, for
considerations of safety or liquidity, depositing in New York.
But Great Britain was also lending on a substantial scale.

345

Altogether it is estimated that in 1925 the net foreign lending of capital-exporting countries amounted to about $2,300 million. Naturally the result was to facilitate investment schemes over a wide area, especially in South America. All the countries of South America found themselves in a position to finance every kind of scheme, good or bad. A comparatively small country like the republic of Colombia, to give an example, found itself able to borrow—I forget the exact figure—something approaching $200 million in New York within a brief space of time. Rates of interest were high indeed. But the lender was willing and so was the borrower. Germany, as we all know, was another country that was both able and willing to borrow on a gigantic scale; indeed, in 1925 she alone borrowed sums approaching $1,000 million.

This free borrowing was duly accompanied by capital expansion programmes. In France there was long-continued building activity; in Germany industry was reconstructed and municipal enterprise was conducted on an extravagant scale; in Spain the dictatorship embarked on enormous public works; indeed, in almost every European country a large force of labour and plant was being employed on construction, thus consuming, but not producing, consumption goods. The same was true over the whole of South America and in Australia. Even in China the prolonged civil war involved great expenditures otherwise than on producing consumption goods—which, so long as it is going on, is analytically identical with investment, even though its future fruits are less than nothing. In Russia, at the same time, immense efforts were being made to direct an unusually large proportion of the national forces to works of capital construction.

There was really only one important partial exception, namely, Great Britain. In that country investment continued throughout on a somewhat moderate scale. Road development and housing programmes did something to keep up investment. But the return to the gold standard and the relative decline of the British staple export trades seriously cut down her ability to carry on foreign investment up to anything like the same proportion of her savings as had been the case from 1900 to 1914; and for various reasons home investment was not on a sufficient scale to absorb the whole of the balance. This, I am sure, is the fundamental reason why we in Great Britain were feeling depression before the rest of the world. We were not participating in the enormous investment boom which the rest of the world was enjoying. Our savings were almost certainly in excess of our investment. In short, we were suffering a deflation.

While some part of the investment which was going on in the world at large was doubtless ill judged and unfruitful, there can, I think, be no doubt that the world was enormously enriched by the constructions of the quinquennium from 1925 to 1929; its wealth increased in these five years by as much as in any other ten or twenty years of its history. The expansion centred round building, the electrification of the world, and the associated enterprises of roads and motor cars. In those five years an appreciable change was effected in the housing, the power plant, and the transport system of a large part of the world. But it was not unduly specialised. Almost every department of capital development took its share. The capacity of the world to produce most of the staple foodstuffs and raw materials was greatly expanded; machinery and new techniques directed by science greatly increased the output of all the metals, rubber, sugar, the chief cereals, etc. The economic section of the League of Nations has published the figures. In the three years 1925–8 the output of foodstuffs and raw materials in the world as a whole increased by no less than 8 per cent and the output of manufactured goods rose by 9 per cent, that is to say, at least as fast as that of raw materials.[1] Progress was especially rapid in Europe where the increase in output was probably greater than even in North America.

Doubtless, as was inevitable in a period of such rapid change,

---

[1] I am quoting from a League of Nations' publication.

the rate of growth of some individual commodities could not always be in just the appropriate relation to that of others. But, on the whole, I see little sign of any serious want of balance such as is alleged by some authorities. The rates of growth of construction capital such as houses, of capital for manufacturing production, and of capital for raw material production; or again those of foodstuffs, of raw materials, of manufactures, of activities demanding personal services seem to me, looking back, to have been in as good a balance as one could have expected them to be. A very few more quinquennia of equal activity might, indeed, have brought us near to the economic Eldorado where all our reasonable economic needs would be satisfied.

It is not necessary for my present purpose to decide exactly how far this investment boom was inflationary in the special sense which I have given to that term—whether, in other words, it was balanced by saving or whether it was financed by surplus profits obtained by selling output at a price which was inflated above the normal costs of production. I am inclined to the view that the part played by inflation was surprisingly small, and that savings kept pace with investment to a remarkable degree. In fact, there was very little rise in the price of the commodities covered by index numbers. This does not prove that there was no inflation: first, because we have no proper consumption index numbers, so that these might, if we had them, show a different result; second, because the period was one of rapidly increasing efficiency, and it may be that while the price of many commodities was unchanged, too small a proportion of the increasing product was accruing to the factors of production and too much to the entrepreneurs, which would, according to my definition, be inflationary. Probably in some places and at some dates inflation was definitely present. But I think that the evidence suggests that savings were in fact abundantly available and were adequate to finance a very large part of the investment which was going on. This conclusion, if it is correct, will be important in the sequel.

What was it, then, that brought all this fruitful activity to a sudden termination? This brings me to the second part of my discourse.

II

It seems an extraordinary imbecility that this wonderful outburst of productive energy should be the prelude to impoverishment and depression. Some austere and puritanical souls regard it both as an inevitable and a desirable nemesis on so much over-expansion, as they call it; a nemesis on man's speculative spirit. It would, they feel, be a victory for the mammon of unrighteousness if so much prosperity was not subsequently balanced by universal bankruptcy. We need, they say, what they politely call a 'prolonged liquidation' to put us right. The liquidation, they tell us, is not yet complete. But in time it will be. And when sufficient time has elapsed for the completion of the liquidation, all will be well with us again.

I do not take this view. I find the explanation of the current business losses, of the reduction of output, and of the unemployment which necessarily ensues on this not in the high level of investment which was proceeding up to the spring of 1929, but in the subsequent cessation of this investment. I see no hope of a recovery except in a revival of the high level of investment. And I do not understand how universal bankruptcy can do any good or bring us nearer to prosperity, except in so far as it may, by some lucky chance, clear the boards for the recovery of investment.

I suggest to you, therefore, that the questions to which we have to bend our intelligences are the causes of the collapse of investment and the means of reviving investment. We cannot hope either to prophesy or to limit the duration of the slump except as the result of our understanding of these phenomena.

Looking back, it is now clear that the decline of investment began early in 1929, that it preceded (and, according to my theory, was the cause of) the decline in business profits, and that it had gathered considerable momentum prior to the Wall Street slump in the autumn of 1929.

Why did investment fall away? Probably it was due to a complex of causes.

1. Too high a rate of interest was being paid. Experience was beginning to show that borrowers could not really hope to earn on new investment the rates which they had been paying.

2. Even if some new investment could earn these high rates, in the course of time all the best propositions had got taken up, and the cream was off the business. In other words, as one would expect, the increased supply of capital goods meant that the rate of interest was due for a fall if further expansion was to be possible.

3. But just at this moment, so far from falling, the rate of interest was rising. The efforts of the Federal Reserve Banks to check the boom on Wall Street were making borrowing exceedingly dear to all kinds of borrowers.

4. A further consequence of the very dear money in the United States was to exercise a drag on the gold of the rest of the world and hence to cause a credit contraction everywhere.

5. And a third consequence was the unwillingness of American investors to buy foreign bonds since they found speculation in their own common stocks much more exciting. In 1929 net purchases of this character by the United States fell to about a quarter of what they had been in the previous year, and in 1930 they fell so low as to be negligible.

I need hardly remind you how much fixed investment fell away in the United States. If we take the familiar Dodge figures for 1925 as our index of 100, we find a fall to 88 in 1929 and to 64 in 1930, while at the present time the figures are still lower. But this falling away of fixed investment, while most marked, perhaps, in the United States, was not confined to that country. The complex of circumstances which I have outlined combined to cause a very marked diminution in the rate of investment all over the world.

Once this decline was started on a significant scale, it is exceedingly easy to see (on my way of looking at the matter) how the mere fact of a decline precipitated a further decline, for the high level of profits began to fall away, the prices of commodities inevitably declined, and these things brought with them a series of further consequences.

1. The decline in output brought a disinvestment in working capital. In the United States this was on a huge scale.

2. The decline in profit diminished the attractions of all kinds of investment.

3. The fall in prices and the cessation of lending destroyed the credit of overseas borrowers, and made borrowing dearer for them just at the moment when they needed cheaper loans if they were to continue.

This decline has continued down to the present time, and so far as fixed investment is concerned, the volume of new investment must be today, taking the world as a whole, at the lowest figure for very many years.

Here I find—and I find without any doubts or reserves whatsoever—the whole of the explanation of the present state of affairs. But there is, I am afraid you may say, one very serious gap in my argument. I have been making all through a tacit assumption. And for those who do not accept this assumption, the conclusions must be unconvincing.

My assumption is this: I have taken it for granted so far that if the volume of investment falls off, then of necessity the level of business profits falls away also. Grant me this and the rest, I think, follows. Now I believe this to be true, and I have set forth in detail the reasons for my belief in the first volume of my recently published *Treatise on Money*. But the argument is not easy, and I cannot claim that it is yet part of the accepted body of economic thought.

It will be my duty, therefore, to endeavour in my next lecture to give you an outline of this reasoning in terms as well adapted as I can find for the medium of oral exposition. I shall then, in the light of this, pass on to what I have to say of a constructive character.

Lecture 2 *The Abstract Analysis of the Slump*

I have said that it is easy on my theory of the causation of these things to see why a severe decline in the volume of investment should have produced the results that we see around us in the world today. This theory, however, will not be familiar to many of you; and I must, if my argument is to be complete and intelligible, endeavour to set forth for you at least an outline of it. You must, therefore, forgive me a somewhat abstract discussion. Those who may wish to pursue the matter further I must refer to my *Treatise on Money*. But I will try, though it be at the risk of straining your attention, to put the gist of the matter very briefly as follows.

Entrepreneurs pay out in salaries, wages, rents, and interest certain sums to the factors of production which I shall call their 'costs of production'. Some of these entrepreneurs are producing capital goods, some of them are producing consumption goods. These sums, these costs of production, represent in the aggregate the incomes of the individuals who own or are the factors of production. These individuals in their capacity of consumers expend part of these incomes on buying consumption goods from the entrepreneurs; and another part of their incomes, which part we shall call their savings, they put back, as we may express it, into the financial machine—that is to say, they deposit it with their banks or buy stock-exchange securities or real estate or repay instalments in respect of purchases previously made or the like.

At the same time the financial machine will be enabling a different set of people to order and pay for various kinds of currently produced capital goods from the entrepreneurs who produce this class of goods, such as buildings, factories, machines, equipment for transport, and public utility enterprises and the like; and the aggregate of expenditures of this kind I find it convenient to call the 'value of current investment'.

Thus there are two streams of money flowing back to the entrepreneurs, namely, that part of their incomes which the public spend on consumption and those expenditures on the purchases of capital goods which I have called the value of current investment. These two amounts added together make up the receipts or sale proceeds of the entrepreneurs.

Now the profitableness of business as a whole depends, and can depend, on nothing but the difference between the sale proceeds of the entrepreneurs and their costs of production. If more comes back to them as sale proceeds than they have expended in costs of production, it follows that they must be making a profit. And, equally, if less comes back to them than they have paid out, they must be making a loss. I am speaking all the time, remember, of entrepreneurs as a whole. As between individual entrepreneurs, some will at all times be doing better than the average and some worse.

Now for my equation, a very simple one, which gives, to my thinking, the clue to the whole business.

The costs of production of the entrepreneurs are equal to the incomes of the public. Now the incomes of the public are, obviously, equal to the sum of what they spend and of what they save. On the other hand, the sale proceeds of the entrepreneurs are equal to the sum of what the public spend on current consumption and what the financial machine is causing to be spent on current investment.

Thus the costs of the entrepreneurs are equal to what the public spend plus what they save; while the receipts of the entrepreneurs are equal to what the public spend plus the value of current investment. It follows, if you have been able to catch what I am saying, that when the value of current investment is greater than the savings of the public, the receipts of the entrepreneurs are greater than their costs, so that they make a profit; and when, on the other hand, the value of current investment is less than the savings of the public, the receipts of the entrepreneurs will be less than their costs, so that they make a loss.

353

That is my secret, the clue to the scientific explanation of booms and slumps (and of much else, as I should claim) which I offer you. For you will perceive that when the rate of current investment increases (without a corresponding change in the rate of savings) business profits increase. Moreover, the affair is cumulative. For when business profits are high, the financial machine facilitates increased orders for and purchases of capital goods, that is, it stimulates investment still further; which means that business profits are still greater; and so on. In short, a boom is in full progress. And contrariwise when investment falls off. For unless savings fall equally, which is not likely to be the case, the necessary result is that the profits of the business world fall away. This in turn reacts unfavourably on the volume of new investment; which causes a further decline in business profits. In short, a slump is upon us.

The whole matter may be summed up by saying that a boom is generated when investment exceeds saving and a slump is generated when saving exceeds investment. But behind this simplicity there lie, I am only too well aware, many complexities, many pitfalls, many opportunities for misunderstanding. You must excuse me if I slide over these, for it would take me weeks to expound them fully. Indeed, let me simplify further, for I should like for a moment to leave the variations in saving out of my argument. I shall assume that saving either varies in the wrong direction (which may, in fact, occur, especially in the early stages of the slump, since the fall in stock-exchange values as compared with the boom may by depreciating the value of people's past savings increase their desire to add to them) or is substantially unchanged, or if it varies in the right direction, so as partly to compensate changes in investment, varies insufficiently (which is likely to be the case except perhaps when the community is, toward the end of a slump, very greatly impoverished indeed). That is to say, I shall concentrate on the variability of the rate of investment. For that is, in fact, the element in the economic situation which is capable of sudden

354

and violent change. In the actual circumstances of the present hour that is the element which, according to common observation, has indeed suffered a sudden and violent change. And nothing, obviously, can restore employment which does not first restore business profits. Yet nothing, in my judgment, can restore business profits which does not first restore the volume of investment, that is to say (in other words), the volume of orders for new capital goods. (For the only theoretical alternative would be a large increase of expenditures by the public at the expense of their savings, an extravagance campaign, which at a time when everyone is nervous and uncertain and sees the value of his stocks and shares depreciating is most unlikely to occur, whether it is desirable or not.)

In the past it has been usual to believe that there was some preordained harmony by which saving and investment were necessarily equal. If we intrusted our savings to a bank, it used to be said, the bank will of course make use of them, and they will duly find their way into industry and investment. But unfortunately this is not so. I venture to say with certainty that it is not so. And it is out of the disequilibriums of savings and investment, and out of nothing else, that the fluctuations of profits, of output, and of employment are generated.

What sorts of circumstances are capable of occurring which would be of a tendency to bring the slump to an end?

It is important to notice that so long as output is declining, the effect of any decline of fixed investment is aggravated by dis-investment in working capital. But this continues only so long as output continues to decline. It ceases as soon as output ceases to decline further even though the level at which output is steady is a very low one. And as soon as output begins to recover, even though it still remains at a very low level, the tide is turned and the decline in fixed investment is partly offset by increased investment in working capital.

Now there is a reason for expecting an equilibrium point of decline to be reached. A given deficiency of investment causes a given decline of profit. A given decline of profit causes a given decline of output. Unless there is a constantly increasing deficiency of investment, there is eventually reached, therefore, a sufficiently low level of output which represents a kind of spurious equilibrium.

There is also another reason for expecting the decline to reach a stopping-point. For I must now qualify my simplifying assumption that only the rate of investment changes and that the rate of saving remains constant. At first, as I have said, the nervousness engendered by the slump may actually tend to increase saving. For saving is often effected as a safeguard against insecurity. Thus savings may decrease when stock markets are soaring and increase when they are slumping. Moreover, for the salaried and fixed-income class of the community the fall of prices will increase their margin available for saving. But as soon as output has declined heavily, strong forces will be brought into play in the direction of reducing the net volume of saving.

For one thing the unemployed will, in their effort not to allow too great a decline in their established standard of life, not only cease to save but will probably be responsible for much negative saving by living on their own previous savings and those of their friends and relations. Much more important, however, than this is likely to be the emergence of negative saving on the part of the government, whether by diminished payments to sinking funds or by actual borrowing, as is now the case in the United States. In Great Britain, for example, the dole to the unemployed, largely financed by borrowing, is now at the rate of $500 million a year—equal to about a quarter of the country's estimated rate of saving in good times. In the United States the Treasury deficit to be financed by borrowing is put at $1,000 million. These expenditures are just as good in their immediate effects on the situation as would be an equal expenditure on capital works; the only difference—and an important one enough—is that in the former cases we have nothing to show for it afterwards.

Let me illustrate this by figures for the United States which are intended to be purely illustrative, though I have chosen them so as to be, perhaps, not too remote from the facts. Let us suppose that at the end of 1928 American investment was at the rate of $10,000 million a year, while the national savings were $9,000 million. This meant, as my fundamental analysis shows, abnormal profits to American business at the rate of $1,000 million. Now let us suppose a decline in investment to $9,000 million. The exceptional profits are now obliterated. Next a further fall to $5,000 million. This means that the exceptional profits are not only obliterated, but that their place is taken by very large abnormal losses, namely, $4,000 million, so long as savings continue at $9,000 million. These developments naturally cause a steady decline in output, which aggravates the loss by bringing with it a disinvestment in working capital. Let us suppose that the disinvestment in working capital is at the rate of $1,500 million a year. As long as this is going on, the rate of net investment may fall as low as $3,500 million. This means (or would mean if other factors remained unchanged) business receipts (including agriculture, of course) of $5,500 million below normal, and output will settle down to the level which just shows a margin over prime cost even when aggregate receipts are this much short of normal. But by this time the situation itself will have bred up some remedial factors. Let us suppose that a government deficit of $1,000 million has developed and that saving by the public has fallen off by $1,000 million. Moreover, as soon as output ceases to fall further, disinvestment in working capital will cease. Thus the falling off in business receipts below normal will no longer be $5,500 million but only $2,000 million ($1,000 million relief from government deficit, $1,000 million from diminished saving, and $1,500 million from the cessation of disinvestment in working capital). This means that output is below what is justified by the new level of business receipts. Consequently it rises again. This rise means reinvestment in working capital, and business receipts may, for a time

357

and so long as this reinvestment is going on, recover almost to normal.

Nevertheless, if the nation's savings stand at $9,000 million, granted a normal level of output and employment, then, so long as the rate of long-term interest in conjunction with other factors is too high to allow of more than $5,000 million expenditure on fixed investment, a recovery staged along the foregoing lines is bound to be an illusion and a disappointment. For after it has proceeded a certain length, there is bound to be reaction and a renewed slump. Indeed, the figures accurately appropriate to the illustration may be such that the extent of the recovery will be comparatively slight.

There can, therefore, I argue, be no secure basis for a return to an equilibrium of prosperity except a recovery of fixed investment to a level commensurate with that of the national savings in prosperous times.

Lecture 3 *The Road to Recovery*

I

Whether or not my confidence is justified, I feel, then, no serious doubt or hesitation whatever as to the causes of the world slump. I trace it wholly to the breakdown of investment throughout the world. After being held by a variety of factors at a fairly high level during most of the post-war period, the volume of this investment has during the past two and a half years suffered an enormous decline—a decline not fully compensated as yet by diminished savings or by government deficits.

The problem of recovery is, therefore, a problem of re-establishing the volume of investment. The solution of this problem has two sides to it: on the one hand, a fall in the long-term rate of investment [interest?] so as to bring a new range of propositions within the practical sphere; and, on the other hand, a return of confidence to the business world so as to incline them to borrow

358

on the basis of normal expectations of the future. But the two aspects are by no means disconnected. For business confidence will not revive except with the experience of improving business profits. And, if I am right, business profits will not recover except with an increase of investment. Nevertheless the mere reaction from the bottom and the feeling that it may be no longer prudent to wait for a further fall will be likely, perhaps in the near future, to bring about some modest recovery of confidence. We need, therefore, to work meanwhile for a drastic fall in the long-term rate of interest so that full advantage may be taken of any recovery of confidence.

The problem of recovery is also, in my judgment, indissolubly bound up with the restoration of prices to a higher level, although if my theory is correct this is merely another aspect of the same phenomenon. The same events which lead to a recovery in the volume of investment will inevitably tend at the same time toward a revival of the price level. But inasmuch as the raising of prices is an essential ingredient in my policy I had better pause perhaps to offer some justification of this before I proceed to consider the ways and means by which the volume of investment and at the same time the level of prices can be raised.

Unfortunately there is not complete unanimity among the economic doctors as to the desirability of raising the general price level at this phase of the cycle. Dr Sprague, for example, in an address made recently in London which attracted much attention, declared it to be preferable that 'manufactured costs and prices should come down to equilibrium level with agricultural prices rather than that we should try to get agricultural prices up to an equilibrium level with the higher prices of manufactured goods'.

For my own part, however, I dissent very strongly from this view and I should like, if I could, to provoke vehement controversy—a real discussion of the problem—in the hope that out of the clash of minds something useful might emerge. Until we have definitely decided whether or not we should wish prices to rise we are drifting without clear intentions in a rudderless vessel.

Do we, then, want prices to rise back to a parity with what, a few months ago, we considered to be the established levels of our salaries, wages, and income generally? Or do we want to reduce our incomes to a parity with the existing level of the wholesale prices of raw commodities? Please notice that I emphasise the word 'want', for we shall confuse the argument unless we keep distinct what we want from what we think we can get. My own conclusion is that there are certain fundamental reasons of overwhelming force, quite distinct from the technical considerations tending in the same direction, which I have already indicated and to which I shall return later, for wishing prices to rise.

The first reason is on grounds of social stability and concord. Will not the social resistance to a drastic downward readjustment of salaries and wages be an ugly and a dangerous thing? I am told sometimes that these changes present comparatively little difficulty in a country such as the United States where economic rigidity has not yet set in. I find it difficult to believe this. But it is for you, not me, to say. I know that in my own country a really large cut of many wages, a cut at all of the same order of magnitude as the fall in wholesale prices, is simply an impossibility. To attempt it would be to shake the social order to its foundation. There is scarcely one responsible person in Great Britain prepared to recommend it openly. And if, for the world as a whole, such a thing could be accomplished, we should be no farther forward than if we had sought a return to equilibrium by the path of raising prices. If, under the pressure of compelling reason, we are to launch all our efforts on a crusade of unpopular public duty, let it be for larger results than this.

I have said that we should be no farther forward. But in fact even when we had accomplished the reduction of salaries and wages, we should be far worse off, for the second reason for wishing prices to rise is on grounds of social justice and expediency which have regard to the burden of indebtedness fixed in terms of money. If we reach a new equilibrium by lowering the level of salaries and wages, we increase proportionately the burden of monetary indebtedness. In doing this we should be striking at the sanctity of contract. For the burden of monetary indebtedness in the world is already so heavy that any material addition would render it intolerable. This burden takes different forms in different countries. In my own country it is the national debt raised for the purposes of the war which bulks largest. In Germany it is the weight of reparation payments fixed in terms of money. For creditor and debtor countries there is the risk of rendering the charges on the debtor countries so insupportable that they abandon a hopeless task and walk the pathway of general default. In the United States the main problem would be, I suppose, the mortgages of the farmer and loans on real estate generally. There is in fact what, in an instructive essay, Professor Alvin Johnson has called the 'farmers' indemnity'. The notion that you solve the farmers' problem by bringing down manufacturing costs so that their own produce will exchange for the same quantity of manufactured goods as formerly is to mistake the situation altogether, for you would at the same time have greatly increased the farmers' burden of mortgages which was already too high. Or take another case— loans against buildings. If the cost of new building were to fall to a parity with the price of raw materials, what would become of the security for existing loans?

Thus national debts, war debts, obligations between the creditor and debtor nations, farm mortgages, real estate mortgages—all this financial structure would be deranged by the adoption of Dr Sprague's proposal. A widespread bankruptcy, default, and repudiation of bonds would necessarily ensue. Banks would be in jeopardy. I need not continue the catalogue. And what would be the advantage of having caused so much ruin? I do not know. Dr Sprague did not tell us that.

Moreover, over and above these compelling reasons there is also the technical reason, the validity of which is not so generally recognised, which I have endeavoured to elucidate in my previous lecture. If our object is to remedy unemployment it is obvious that we must first of all make business more profitable. In other words, the problem is to cause business receipts to rise relatively to business costs. But I have already endeavoured to show that the same train of events which will lead to this desired result is also part and parcel of the causation of higher prices, and that any policy which at this stage of the credit cycle is not directed to raising prices also fails in the object of improving business profits.

The cumulative argument for wishing prices to rise appears to me, therefore, to be overwhelming, as I hope it does to you. Fortunately many if not most people agree with this view. You may feel that I have been wasting time in emphasising it. But I do not think that I have been wasting time, for while most people probably accept this view, I doubt if they feel it with sufficient intensity. I wish to take precautions beforehand against anyone asking—when I come to the second and consecutive part of my argument—whether, after all, it is so essential that prices should rise. Is it not better that liquidation should take its course? Should we not be, then, all the healthier for liquidation, which is their polite phrase for general bankruptcy, when it is complete?

II

Let us now return to our main theme. The cure of unemployment involves improving business profits. The improvement of business profits can come about only by an improvement in new investment relative to saving. An increase of investment relative to saving must also, as an inevitable by-product, bring about a rise of prices, thus ameliorating the burdens arising out of monetary indebtedness. The problem resolves itself, therefore, into the question as to what means we can adopt to increase the volume of investment, which you will remember means in my terminology the expenditure of money on the output of new capital goods of whatever kind.

When I have said this, I have, strictly speaking, said all that an economist as such is entitled to say. What remains is essentially a technical banking problem. The practical means by which investment can be increased is, or ought to be, the bankers' business, and pre-eminently the business of the central banker. But you will not consider that I have completed my task unless I give some indication of the methods which are open to the banker.

There are, in short, three lines of approach. The first line of approach is the restoration of confidence both to the lender and to the borrower. The lender must have sufficient confidence in the credit and solvency of the borrower so as not to wish to charge him a crushing addition to the pure interest charge in order to cover risk. The borrower, on the other hand, must have sufficient confidence in the business prospects to believe that he has a reasonable prospect of earning sufficient return from a new investment proposition to recover with a margin the interest which he has to bind himself to pay to the lender. Failing the restoration of confidence, we may easily have a vicious circle set up in which the rate of interest which the lender requires to cover what he considers the risks of the situation represents a higher rate than the borrower believes that he can earn.

Nevertheless, there is perhaps not a great deal that can be done deliberately to restore confidence. The turning-point may come in part from some chance and unpredictable event. But it is capable, of course, of being greatly affected by favourable international developments, as for example, an alleviation of the war debts such as Mr Hoover has lately proposed; though if he goes no farther than he has promised to go at present, the shock to confidence, long before his year of grace is out, may come perhaps just at the moment when it will interfere most with an incipient revival. In the main, however, restoration of confidence must be based, not on the vague expectations or hopes of the business world, but on a real improvement in fundamentals; in other words, on a breaking of the vicious circle. Thus if results can be achieved along the two remaining lines of approach which I have yet to mention, these favourable effects may be magnified by their reaction on the state of confidence.

The second line of approach consists in new construction programmes under the direct auspices of the government or other public authorities. Theoretically, it seems to me, there is everything to be said for action along these lines. For the government can borrow cheaply and need not be deterred by overnice calculations as to the prospective return. I have been a strong advocate of such measures in Great Britain, and I believe that they can play an extremely valuable part in breaking the vicious circle everywhere. For a government programme is calculated to improve the level of business profits and hence to increase the likelihood of private enterprise again lifting up its head. The difficulty about government programmes seems to me to be essentially a practical one. It is not easy to devise at short notice schemes which are wisely and efficiently conceived and which can be put rapidly into operation on a really large scale. Thus I applaud the idea and only hesitate to depend too much in practice on this method alone unaided by others. I am not sure that as time goes by we may not have to attempt to organise methods of direct government action along these lines more deliberately than hitherto, and that such action may play an increasingly important part in the economic life of the community.

The third line of approach consists in a reduction in the long-term rate of interest. It may be that when confidence is at its lowest ebb the rate of interest plays a comparatively small part. It may also be true that, in so far as manufacturing plants are concerned, the rate of interest is never the dominating factor. But, after all, the main volume of investment always takes the forms of housing, of public utilities and of transportation. Within these spheres the rate of interest plays, I am convinced,

a predominant part. I am ready to believe that a small change in
the rate of interest may not be sufficient. That, indeed, is why I
am pessimistic as to an early return to normal prosperity. I am
ready enough to admit that it may be extremely difficult both
to restore confidence adequately and to reduce interest rates
adequately. There will be no need to be surprised, therefore, if a
long time elapses before we have a recovery all the way back to
normal.

Nevertheless, a sufficient change in the rate of interest must
surely bring within the horizon all kinds of projects which are
out of the question at the present rate of interest. Let me quote
an example from my own country. No one believes that it will
pay to electrify the railway system of Great Britain on the basis
of borrowing at 5 per cent. At $4\frac{1}{2}$ per cent the enthusiasts believe
that it will be worth while; at 4 per cent everyone agrees it is an
open question; at $3\frac{1}{2}$ per cent it is impossible to dispute that it
will be worth while. So it must be with endless other technical
projects. Every fall in the rate of interest will bring a new range
of projects within a practical sphere. Moreover, if it be true—as
it probably is—that the demand for house room is elastic, every
significant fall in the rate of interest, by reducing the rent which
has to be charged, brings with it an additional demand for house
room.

As I look at it, indeed, the task of adjusting the long-term rate
of interest to the technical possibilities of our age so that the
demand for new capital is as nearly as possible equal to the
community's current volume of savings must be the prime
object of financial statesmanship. It may not be easy and a large
change may be needed, but there is no other way out.

Finally, how is the banking system to affect the long-term rate
of interest? For prima facie the banking system is concerned
with the short-term rate of interest rather than with the long.

In course of time I see no insuperable difficulty. There is a
normal relation between the short-term rate of interest and the
long-term, and in the long run the banking system can affect the

long-term rate by obstinately adhering to the correct policy in regard to the short-term rate. But there may also be devices for hastening the effect of the short-term rate on the long-term rate. A reduction of the long-term rate of interest amounts to the same thing as raising the price of bonds. The price of bonds amounts to the same thing as the price of non-liquid assets in terms of liquid assets. I suggest to you that there are three ways in which it is reasonable to hope to exercise an influence in this direction.

The first method is to increase the quantity of liquid assets— in other words, to increase the basis of credit by means of open-market operations, as they are usually called, on the part of the central bank. I know that this involves technical questions of some difficulty with which I must not burden this lecture. I should, however, rely confidently in due course on influencing the price of bonds by steadily supplying the market with a greater quantity of liquid assets than the market felt itself to require so that there would be a constant pressure to transform liquid assets into the more profitable non-liquid assets.

The second course is to diminish the attractions of liquid assets by lowering the rate of deposit interest. In such circumstances as the present it seems to me that the rate of interest allowed on liquid assets should be reduced as nearly as possible to the vanishing-point.

The third method is to increase the attractions of non-liquid assets, which, however, brings us back again in effect to our first remedy, namely, methods of increasing confidence.

For my own part, I should have thought it desirable to advance along all three fronts simultaneously. But the central idea that I wish to leave with you is the vital necessity for a society, living in the phase in which we are living today, to bring down the long-term rate of interest at a pace appropriate to the underlying facts. As houses and equipment of every kind increase in quantity we ought to be growing richer on the principle of compound interest. As technological changes make possible a given output of goods of every description with a diminishing quantity of human effort, again we ought to be forever increasing our level of economic well-being. But the worst of these developments is that they bring us to what may be called the dilemma of a rich country, namely, that they make it more and more difficult to find an outlet for our savings. Thus we need to pay constant conscious attention to the long-term rate of interest for fear that our vast resources may be running to waste through a failure to direct our savings into constructive uses and that this running to waste may interfere with that beneficent operation of compound interest which should, if everything was proceeding smoothly in a well-governed society, lead us within a few generations to the complete abolition of oppressive economic want.

At the same set of meetings, Keynes also took part in several seminars. He led one on 'Possibilities of Central Bank Action' in a discussion entitled 'Is it Possible for Governments and Central Banks to Do Anything on Purpose to Remedy Unemployment?' and took part in several seminars led by others. One of these discussions saw Keynes advancing ideas that were to be echoed in surviving early drafts of what was to become *The General Theory*.

The discussion in question was on the subject 'Are Wage Cuts a Remedy for Unemployment?' and was led by H. Schultz and C. Goodrich. The leaders concerned themselves with four possible combinations of circumstances: (1) Prolonged falling prices due to technological improvement; (2) Prolonged falling prices due to monetary or other causes; (3) Prolonged depression in particular industries; (4) Depression phase of business cycle. Keynes in his comments elaborated on Case 4 as follows.

From *Unemployment as a World Problem: Reports of Round Tables*, (1931) volume I.

I think that this analysis which Mr Schultz and Mr Goodrich have given us is extraordinarily good and most helpful. I have never seen it put quite so before. This division seems to be vital in the discussion of this. I have very little to add to the actual scope of this, or to criticise, but I think I have something to add, perhaps, on Case 4, which is probably the case to which the present situation most nearly belongs.

The analysis I shall like to try to outline is not merely my own; it is due to a young English economist, Mr R. F. Kahn. I should like to put his point very shortly.

In the short period to which Case 4 belongs, when there is not time for obsolescence, and in which very little new plant is being set up, we may assume that when prices fall, employers will continue to produce so long as their receipts are in excess of their prime costs. We might call the difference between their gross receipts and their prime costs their prime profit.

The amount of price fall that has to take place in order to destroy prime profit varies very widely from one industry to another. Some industries may be knocked out by a comparatively small reduction in their gross receipts—those industries where the prime cost is a very large part of the total cost, and so on down.

Now let us consider the totality of industries. You have over a short period something of the nature of a supply curve which tells you that for a given level of prime profit there will be a given level of output, that if you have a certain amount of prime profit, that would be sufficient to bring a certain quantity of potential output over the prime cost level. Every increase in aggregate prime profit will enable somebody to expand, because he will just get over the prime cost point, and every diminution will knock someone out, so if you have a supply curve which is valid over the short period only, so that for every quantity of aggregate prime profit you have a given quantity of output, you could only increase employment and output by increasing prime profit.

I have argued that the difference between the total receipts of entrepreneurs and their total output is related to the difference between what I call 'savings' and what I call 'investment'. Subject to various qualifications that I need not go into, I should say that the only way of increasing prime profit is to increase the value of investment relatively to the amount of money saving. This gives one a test as to whether a cut in wages will or will not lead to an increase in employment over the short period, on the assumption that what we are discussing is Case 4. If a reduction of wages will diminish the excess of saving, then it will increase the prime profit, and it will enable some manufacturer to increase his output.

It may be that a cut in wages will have no effect whatever on the difference between savings and investment, and it may be that it will then have an effect. Let us take first of all the case where the employer passes on the whole of the wage reduction in the price. In that case there will be a transfer of purchasing power from the wage earners to the people whose money incomes are not cut, because since wages do not take up the whole of the cost, a ten per cent reduction in wages will not cause, even if the whole of it is passed on, a ten per cent reduction in price. Therefore you will have larger purchasing power for these people whose money incomes are not cut, and smaller real incomes for everybody else whose income is cut, so you will be simply transferring purchasing power from the wage earner to the rentier class.

Are we to assume that the wage earner or the rentier is the most likely to save? Probably the rentier. If you enable him to sustain his existing standard of life by a smaller expenditure of money, there is a certain presumption that you will increase the quantity of his savings. If that happens, then pro tanto, you will be diminishing prime profit, and you will be throwing more people out of work by your reduction of wages.

Another case would be where the employer does not pass on the whole of the reduction of wages in lower prices, but is enabled for various reasons to retain more for himself. In that case there may be more of a presumption that there will be some increase in output, and there may also be the kind of result suggested by one of the speakers, namely that in certain industries the psychology of the employer may be favourably affected, and the psychology of his banker may be favourably affected. He may think that over a somewhat long period the reduction of wages works in his favour, that he is therefore a more solvent person, that it may be easier for him to borrow, and he may, in certain cases of industries, less under the weather than others, be more able and likely to expand.

In the case of the railways it might be that the railways would be more willing to spend money on renewals. That is to say, the psychological influence on the employer and on his banker, when the employer does not pass on in reduced prices all the benefit he gets from reduced wages, may tend to increase investment. Clearly that is possible. If these two pieces of analysis be put together, my conclusion would be that the effect of a reduction of wages would be determined by whether the adverse effect on saving (and by adverse effect I mean the increase of saving) would be greater or less than the increased amount of investment which might take place by the employers interpreting it, whether rightly or wrongly, as something in their favour.

On the other hand, where there is over-capacity for the time being in almost every direction, then the second favourable influence is less likely to be realised, so that at the beginning of the slump there might be more to be hoped for from wage cuts than later in the slump.

At any rate, this would offer a formula by which, theoretically, one could arrive at a conclusion as to what the result of wage cuts would be on the particular assumption of the fourth case. The net result depends upon quantities which we are not in a position to measure, but when one comes to the practical issue, I am opposed to wage cuts for a much broader ground. I agree with these arguments, but what seems to me important is a point which Mr Goodrich mentioned which I shall emphasise more than he did, that you are very much diminishing the prospect of prices returning to their former level if you cut wages, particularly if you get competitive wage cutting between different countries. If you reduce wages, that means that the equilibrium level of prices is lower than it was before, and therefore you have to have a genuine inflation, as I should understand it, a condition where employers may make abnormal profit, before you can raise prices back again to the point from which they started.

I think it is very important to get prices back to where they were in order to reduce the burden of monetary indebtedness. Getting prices back to where they started can be achieved, if there are no wage cuts, without any over-stimulus to employers which would be liable to bring about a further boom. But, if we cut wages, then we shall reach normal profits at a lower price level than the former price level, and we shall then only be able to get back, if at all, to the price level at which we started, and to restore monetary conditions to the old degree of burden by means of an inflation.

I would add, therefore, to Mr Goodrich's analysis that the bringing up of wages again could not be brought about merely by the return of the equilibrium. You would have to have a positive inflation. You would have to give employers abnormal profits before you would have over the world at large the necessary stimulus to employers to put wages back to the point from where they were brought down.

Thus there is a great deal which is indeterminate on both sides. From a practical point of view, I think one is justified in holding on to as high a level of wages as one can. For any individual country to hang behind others is difficult, therefore it is particularly objectionable to start competitive wage cutting between countries.

If we would have a period in which there was a project [prospect?] of an excessive saving for a long time to come, the reduction of wages might very well fail to bring us to equilibrium, and then you have to have further, further, and further cuts in wages. Thus there might be no equilibrium point until the burden was so intolerable that there would be a social cataclysm. There is, therefore, on general grounds of social expediency a great deal to be said for clinging to as high a wage rate as can be maintained.

MR SCHULTZ: A propos Mr Keynes's first point: I have tried to present what seems to me to be the identical argument, unfortunately before you came over here. I start with an individual firm, that is perfectly true, but in order to get the market supply curve, add the individual marginal cost curves. I have tried to indicate that when the price line cuts the marginal, or the direct cost line, the firm will go on producing.

You are talking about marginal costs. He [Kahn] is talking about prime costs.

MR SCHULTZ: I am not thinking of this as a long-run curve. I am thinking of it as a short-run reversible curve.

There is no allowance in your curve for depreciation or return to the entrepreneur.

MR SCHULTZ: I am taking the short-time point of view. I am assuming that entrepreneurs bid in the market for the factors of production, and I am assuming they are paying the market price for labour. I am including services of entrepreneurs as factors of production. The prices of all these, added up, gives me this average cost curve. I am assuming that the total cost function of the firm in question is something like this [indicating at blackboard]. This will lead to the type of analysis which I have presented.

I am distinguishing at least two cases, (1) The price line is below the lowest point on the *direct cost* curve; the business will fail. (2) The price line is above the lowest point on the direct cost curve. Direct costs will be met, and the business can continue to function until it is recapitalised.

Did you deal with my further point that you then aggregate all the curves and you can get a supply curve for industry as a whole in which the quantity of output is unequivocally related to the aggregate excess receipts over prime costs?

MR SCHULTZ: Yes. I may say that I did not develop it over here, but that is exactly what I had in mind. If we consider this, which I call the Cournot-Amoroso formula, we have this: X_1 is the output of the unit in question, and X the output of the entire industry. Eta is the elasticity of demand. I think the two analyses are practically the same.

If you then aggregate, you get a formula by which you can relate the excess of saving to the volume of investment.

MR GOODRICH: Mr Keynes, in connection with your last point, the danger of competitive wage cutting as between different nations, perhaps something further should have been said about Case 3, that in the case of the depression in the particular part of industry, what appears as a remedy from the point of view of those particular industries, countries, or parts of countries, may have certain bad consequences for the situation in general, so that one might withhold the prescription from Case 3 during the time in which the rest of industry is in Case 4.

I had that very much in mind. With our coal industry we have much reduced our costs. There were simply enormous reductions. The labour cost per ton has fallen something like thirty or forty per cent, as much as you could possibly hope for. That has plainly meant competitive wage cutting in all the European suppliers of coal. The amount of coal demanded is rather inelastic, and I think we might have been better off if we had cut wages less.

Equally in the cotton textile industry it is exceedingly doubtful whether we should get any more output, appreciably more output, if we reduce prices by cutting wages. That does not dispose of the point that the cutting of wages might be useful as a means of getting people out of the industry, but that is such a hopeless game in the middle of a depression, because where would they go? There is certainly plenty of pressure to get them out of the industry, if there were anywhere for them to go.

The 'Circus' and private discussions were moving Keynes forward from the *Treatise*, as both of the above documents suggest. One of the additional pieces from these informal discussions survives in the form of an exchange with R. F. Kahn in September 1931.

To R. F. KAHN, *20 September 1931*

When resources are fully employed, the supply schedule for goods as a whole is inelastic. Thus any new factor can only have reaction of two kinds—to cause changes in the proportionate division of output between consumption and investment goods, and to bid up (or down) the remuneration of the factors of production.

But if the cost of production is sticky or if there is already unemployment, there is a third reaction possible, namely changes in total output.

If we assume the increased output is divided between consumption and investment goods in the same proportions as the previous output and increased income divided between saving and expenditure in the same proportions as before, this introduces no new complications. The level of price and rate of profit are the same as before; and it simply means that the bidding up of the remuneration of the factors of production is associated with increasing output until maximum (or zero) output is reached.

But if each level of aggregate output has an appropriate proportion of saving to incomes attached to it, e.g. if $\dfrac{S}{E} = f(O)$ or better suppose $\dfrac{S}{E} = f_1\left(\dfrac{E}{P}\right) + f_2\left(\dfrac{Q}{P}\right)$ $[E+Q = OP]$ then points of equilibrium output can be reached which fall short of maximum and zero.

Suppose $\dfrac{dS}{dQ}$ is positive $\dfrac{dQ}{dI}$ positive

and $\dfrac{dS}{dO}$ positive dO has the same sign as Q

but $\dfrac{dQ/O\,[1]}{dO}$ negative when O is increasing, positive when O is decreasing since $\dfrac{dQ}{dS}$ is negative.

Thus if, starting with equilibrium, an increase of I makes Q positive, O increases and S increases but Q/O gradually diminishes. If Q/O reaches zero before O reaches maximum, we have 'long-period unemployment', i.e. an equilibrium position short of full employment.

[1] Not sure whether this should be $\dfrac{dQ}{dO}$, $\dfrac{dQ/O}{dO}$, or $\dfrac{dQ/OR}{dO}$.

Similarly if a decrease of I decreases Q, O decreases and S decreases with the result that Q gradually increases until it is zero, which will be likely to occur before O is zero.

J.M.K.

The only way of ensuring a maximum value for O is that $\dfrac{dI}{dO}\left(\dfrac{dI/P}{dO}\;?\right)$ should be sufficiently strongly positive when O is increasing and sufficiently strongly negative when O is decreasing. It is unlikely that this will occur without management.

The definition of Q is that $Q = 0$ when $\dfrac{dQ}{dO} = 0$ or otherwise $Q = 0$ when $\dfrac{dE}{dO} = 1$.

From R. F. KAHN, *24 September 1931*

My dear Maynard,

I must apologise for retaining the enclosed for so long. Even now I am afraid I have nothing useful to say. The difficulty is that it will take me a little time to get at home again with curly d's, and on top of that my mind is not too clear at the moment. I feel more that this new method is the right one and that the conclusions are correct, but I have not quite been able to follow the steps. If you are not needing it, would you return me the document in a few days, when I hope I shall feel competent to deal with it?

As it appears to me at the moment, the *only* condition necessary for reaching a new position of equilibrium is that S increases as E increases. But that is not quite accurate, because on top of that there is some condition necessary for equilibrium to have been possible at all i.e. that a small reduction in O (or L) will cause expenditure to increase. But I cannot see that this is the same as saying that dS/dQ $[dQ/dS?]$ has to be negative (surely not positive?). I will look into this and hope to be able to be of more assistance.

You are assuming all the time conditions of constant cost. The reward of this assumption provides, of course, a further basis for long-period unemployment, but I agree that it is best to retain the assumption for the moment.

I am sorry to be so useless.

It looks as though the exchange is beginning to slide, don't you think?

Austin [Robinson] knows absolutely nothing about Colin Clark's fears of a reduced income—they appear to be groundless.

Yours
R.F.K.

This forward movement seems to have also started to show itself in his lectures for 1931–2, which he delivered in the Easter term of 1932 and which, as noted above (p. 244), he discussed with D. H. Robertson. These had the same title, The Pure Theory of Money, as those he had delivered in the Michaelmas term of 1929. As they were beginning to cover new ground, they seem to have excited considerable comment. In addition to that with Robertson, the following exchange with Joan Robinson survives.

From JOAN ROBINSON, *May 1932*

Dear Maynard,

Austin and Kahn and I were rather worried by some points in your last lecture, and we have written some remarks[1] which perhaps you would like to see. Please forgive the somewhat dogmatic air with which we write. The upshot appears to be to strengthen your conclusions while throwing some doubt on the argument.

Yours,

JOAN ROBINSON

This was intended to be the borderline case where on your view O should be unchanged (but on ass[umption]. is increased).

On your view if $\Delta I <$ increased cost of old output O will fall. Surely this entails that if $\Delta I =$ increased cost O is unchanged? It is at this point that my argument begins.

On p. 1 I agree I have made an error tho' it does not affect the case. The cost of capital goods may go up.

JOAN

P.S. Please why are you allowed to talk about prime cost but we not allowed to talk about short period supply price?

From JOAN ROBINSON, *May 1932*

If (as we claim) the conditions laid down for the exceptional case are too strong when ΔI is all an addition to the value of C, too weak when it is all an increase in amount of C it seems natural to conclude that they are only just right for some intermediate position, and not for the whole range of intermediate positions. Therefore it seems that this particular set of conditions fail to hit the nail on the head.

[1] Not all of these have survived. [Ed.]

Keynes's note on back.

Let ΔC_1 be increased cost of consumption goods,

$\quad \Delta C_2 \quad$ increased cost of existing development,

$\quad \Delta I \quad$ cost of increased development.

Then $\Delta C_1 + \Delta C_2 > I$.

Total receipts of capital producers increased by ΔI.

Total receipts of consumption producers increased by ΔI.

$\therefore$ Total receipts increased by $2\Delta I$.

Total costs increased by $\Delta C_1 + \Delta C_2 + \Delta I$.

$\therefore Q$ falls by excess of $\Delta C_1 + \Delta C_2$ over ΔI.

From JOAN ROBINSON, *May 1932*

The Exceptional Case

When I increases ΔI is added to expenditure on consumption goods, but there is an increase in cost of the old output equal to [J.M.K. note: 'greater than'] ΔI, and this is not spent.

Let ΔI consist entirely of the cost of new capital goods, their price remaining unchanged and equal to cost. [J.M.K. note: 'No, their cost has gone up.'] Then $Q_2 = 0$. To expenditure on consumption goods and to their cost has been added I. It is therefore natural to suppose that $Q_1 = 0$ and that there is no increase in output of consumption goods. On J.M.K.'s view O should be constant $\therefore Q = 0$. *But* there has been an increase in C. Therefore a greater rise in costs than that given by the conditions of the exceptional case is necessary to keep O constant and the amount of increase necessary cannot be deduced by formal methods from the formulae. This is another case where ΔQ and ΔO do not have the same sign.

To JOAN ROBINSON, *9 May 1932*

My dear Joan,

Please don't think me too obstinate; but there have been three sorts of things at issue:—

1. First of all, I had to defend myself against charges of sheer error.

2. Then I had to revise my exposition to clear myself of just complaints of confused narration.

3. Finally there is the question which is the best of two alternative exegetical methods. Here I am open to conviction. But to be convinced I should need to see the whole theory worked out your way, and then compare it with what I am able to say in my language. I am not so familiar with your way as with my own. But my present belief is that in general, and apart possibly from the handling of certain special problems, your way would be much more difficult and cumbersome. At any rate I lack at present sufficient evidence to the contrary to induce me to scrap all my present half-forged weapons;—though that is no reason why you should not go on constructing your own.

Yours ever,
J.M.K.

From JOAN ROBINSON, *10 May 1932*

My dear Maynard,

Thanks so much for your note. You must forgive my rough manners in controversy.

I think we are now in very substantial agreement and it is idle to dispute over words. I should interpret your last lecture thus:—Let us call the nine-pins that are just not falling over the marginal entrepreneurs. Then the supply price for each output is (on your view) the average prime cost + the profit per unit just sufficient to retain the marginal entrepreneurs. There is a time element which perhaps cannot be treated on a 3rd dimension. But Time is a common enemy to us all. I believe that like the rest of us you have had your faith in supply curves shaken by Piero. But what he attacks are just the one-by-one supply curves that you regard as legitimate. His objections do not apply to the supply curve of output—but Heaven help us when he starts thinking out objections that do apply to it!

Yours,
JOAN

I think our efforts are not rival but complementary. The problem of the relationship between investment and the level of output seems to come out best our way, whereas the question of the stoppers etc. must obviously be tackled with your weapons.

J.

From JOAN ROBINSON, *11 May 1932*

My dear Maynard,

It has just occurred to me that I have been being extremely dense.

The point of our supply curve business is that it steps into what is admittedly the breach in your method, i.e. the effect on output of the redistribution of profits between industries. In the first exceptional case by saying that $\Delta Q, \Delta O$ have the same sign you are really saying (as you admit) that a ΔQ_1 has the same effect on R as an equal ΔQ_2 on C (one being $+$ and the other $-$). You are in fact taking a special case where the elasticity of supply of capital goods and of consumption goods stand in a particular relation to each other.

Our method is not obliged to confine itself to this special case, and can state the conditions in which ΔO and ΔI fail to move together, in a general way which covers your special case.

I feel very much ashamed of giving you trouble by not saying where our method dovetails into yours and allowing you to think that our tools were quite different from yours. The only difference is that you use a box spanner and we use an adjustable one.

I saw dimly all along but it only became clear to me after I had sent off my last letter.

With apologies,

JOAN

To JOAN ROBINSON, *12 May 1932*

Dear Joan,

My argument does not require that ΔQ_1 has the *same* effect on R as an equal ΔQ_2 on C. I only assume that the net effect on output is of the same sign as the change in Q.

I do not believe that your method is capable of stating in a generalised form the conditions in which ΔO and ΔI fail to move together. Indeed, it seems to me to be in the nature of things that you cannot do so, since the answer is quantitative. I do not see how you can say much more than what I say, namely that if the increment of investment causes redistribution of profit, and the net effect on the output of industries losing profit is greater than the net effect on the industries gaining profit, then the increment of investment cannot be relied on to produce

379

a net increment of output. I do not see that anything is gained in dividing industries up between those which produce capital goods and those which produce consumption goods, since there is no presumption concerning relative elasticities between the two types of industries, any more than there is in a case of a redistribution of profit between consumption industries. If one is to make a generalisation, about all one can say is that unless there is special reason to the contrary, e.g., unless the operation in question is of such a character as to bring about a drastic redistribution of existing profit, an increment in aggregate profit can reasonably be expected to produce an increment of aggregate output;—which is in substance what I have said.

You will notice further that even when one is dealing with separate industries, or separate groups of industries, my supply curve is one which relates output and profit, not one which relates output and price.

Yours,

J.M.K.

Keynes's reference to 'half-forged weapons' in his letter to Joan Robinson of 9 May certainly reflected his current position. He was, however, hard at work on refashioning his approach. In fact by 18 September 1932 he felt able to write his mother, 'I have written nearly a third of my new book on monetary theory.'

From this early period of writing during 1931–2, various fragments have survived. Of these, perhaps the most interesting are the bits and pieces from six chapters from various versions of an obviously connected treatment. The earliest of these appear to be the chapters numbered 7 to 10, beginning with one entitled 'The Monetary Theory of Production'. The two entitled 'The Parameters of a Monetary Economy' and numbered 9 and 5 in different drafts would seem to arise from slightly later work, although still before the end of 1932. In addition, the note 'Historical Retrospect' would also seem to date from this period.

Drafts of chapters 7–10 of the earliest version of what became the *General Theory*.

7. THE MONETARY THEORY OF PRODUCTION

The essence of the monetary theory of production, to which the above preliminary discussion leads us, can be expressed quite briefly, starting from the equation

$$\Delta Q = \Delta I - \Delta S,$$

or, as it may also be written

$$\Delta Q = \Delta I + \Delta F - \Delta E,$$

or $$\Delta Q = \Delta D - \Delta E$$

where Q stands for profit, I for investment, S for saving, F for spending, and D for disbursement. For these equations mean that profit (for entrepreneurs as a whole) is increasing or decreasing according as the excess of investment over saving or (which is the same thing) of disbursement over earnings is increasing or decreasing.

Now we have started with the assumption that the organisation of our society is, broadly speaking, such that entrepreneurs tend to increase or decrease their output according as their profit is increasing or decreasing. Thus we are led at once to the vital generalisation that increases and decreases in the volume of output and employment depend upon the changes in disbursement relatively to earnings (which is the alternative mode of expression I now offer to the reader as being perhaps the clearer) or in investment relatively to savings (which is the mode of expression I employed in my *Treatise on Money*). Throughout this Book we shall be engaged in developing various aspects of this central generalisation. We shall find, broadly speaking, that changes in disbursement relatively to earnings generally depend in any ordinary circumstances on the proportion of output which goes to increase capital development; with the result that the volume of employment must be expected to move in the same direction as the volume of capital development.

8. THE INSTABILITY OF A PROFIT-SEEKING
ORGANIZATION OF PRODUCTION

To fix the argument, let us take the case where there has occurred a decrease of disbursement leading to a decrease of profit. That is to say, the profits of entrepreneurs have declined below their previous level.

This does not necessarily mean that there will be immediately any significant change in the volume of output. For it might be that the receipts of every individual entrepreneur will still be in excess of the minimum receipts below which it is better worth his while to close down than to continue in production. The quantitative effect on output of a given decrease $-\Delta Q$ in the receipts of entrepreneurs will depend on:—(i) the margin between each entrepreneur's receipts and his variable costs (meaning by variable costs the costs which are a function of current output); (ii) the distribution of the total reduction $-\Delta Q$ between different entrepreneurs; and (iii) the duration of the period of diminished profit relatively to the durability of his fixed capital.

For example if $-\Delta Q$ represents 5 per cent of the receipts of entrepreneurs and is equally divided between all classes of entrepreneurs, if every entrepreneur starts with a margin of more than 5 per cent between his receipts and his prime costs, and if the duration of the decreased profit has been short, then there is no reason to expect any significant decline of output. In other words these are conditions in which there is no elasticity of short-period supply in response to a reduction in profit of less than 5 per cent.

Nevertheless, even so, an initial movement $-\Delta Q$ is likely to aggravate itself. For the reduction in entrepreneurs' profit will have a tendency to retard new capital development in respect both of value and volume, for it will not be so attractive to expand plant; and at the same time it may stimulate economy by diminishing both the expenditure of entrepreneurs whose incomes are reduced and also the expenditure of other consumers who can maintain their previous standard of life at a lower money cost. In short, the initial decline in disbursement is likely to generate, in the first instance, a further decline in disbursement, and so on until some new factor intervenes. Moreover, in actual fact it is not likely that *all* entrepreneurs will have a 5 per cent margin and, even if they have, the loss of $-\Delta Q$ will not be evenly spread, so that, though it may amount to 5 per cent of entrepreneurs' receipts on the average, it will probably come to much more than this for individual entrepreneurs. Finally, the longer the situation lasts, the larger will be the proportion of normal long-period costs which become prime costs for the purpose of calculating whether or not to reduce output.

As a net result of all these possibilities, it is, therefore, reasonable to expect that a point will be reached at which there is some elasticity of supply in response to diminished profit, the initial reduction in entrepreneurs' profit aggravating itself until, having reached an amount $-\Delta Q$, it causes a reduction $-\Delta O$ in the volume of output and a reduction $-\Delta E$ in the earnings of the factors of production, who are thrown out of work.

An initial decline in disbursement having thus brought about a decline in output, we shall find that the position is one of great instability.

For the decline in output and in earnings is quite likely to bring about a further decline in disbursement at least equal to, and perhaps even greater than, the decline in entrepreneurs' outgoings. For if nothing intervenes to stimulate fixed investment, the decline in output will, as a result of the length of the period of production, involve a decline of net investment as a result of the decreased investment in working capital; whilst the reduction in earnings may be expected to lead to some reduction in spending, so that the decline in saving may be more than is required to offset the decline in investment. It is, indeed, not difficult to conceive of instances in which spending would fall off by substantially the same amount as earnings,—e.g. if we suppose that the unemployed are maintained by the State, that the State pays for the dole by additional taxes and that the taxpayers economise by the amount of the additional taxation.[1] Or again, whilst the public may curtail their spending by a lesser amount than the decline in their earnings, the entrepreneurs on the other hand are not likely, in view of the decline in their profits, to maintain theirs at its former level; so that our condition will be satisfied in the event of the decline in entrepreneurs' expenditure being sufficient to offset the diminished margin between the earnings and the spending of the public. Let us, therefore, in order to have a simple case for the further development of our argument, assume that, on a balance of considerations relating to the reactions on investment and on spending, the amount of disbursement declines by about the same amount as the decline in earnings. Even if this were to prove to be an overstatement of what normally occurs, it will at least serve to bring out the extreme possibilities of the situation.

On this assumption, the deficiency in the profit of entrepreneurs as a whole will remain exactly the same in absolute amount as it was before. *But it will be spread over a smaller number of units of production,* as a result of a certain number having fallen out of production. Consequently the average loss will be *greater* than it was, with the result that the next most vulnerable section of entrepreneurs now falls out of production, since their receipts no longer reach the minimum required to keep them going. If, then, we maintain the same assumptions as before as to the net effect on disbursement, it follows that the receipts of the entrepreneurs who still continue to produce are yet further diminished, so that another section is impelled to close down, unless we reach a layer of entrepreneurs whose margin above prime cost is sufficient to enable them to stomach the loss; otherwise the closing down process continues without limit.

[1] If spending were to fall off by the same amount as *incomes*, the argument would be *a fortiori*; and so long as this continued to be the case, *no* equilibrium would be possible, either in the short period or in the long.

Thus if we can imagine the entrepreneurs ranged in a continuous series according to what percentage reduction in their receipts impels them to close down production, it might be that a very small diminution $-\Delta Q$ in the total receipts of entrepreneurs might by a sort of inverse tontine process gradually close down one after another of them, until production was at a total standstill. In order to produce this conclusion, however, we have had to introduce somewhat stringent assumptions. Let us consider, therefore, what emergency exits there may be in practice from so devastating a result.

The question whether entrepreneurs might obtain relief from a reduction in the rate of remuneration of the other factors of production, we postpone to the next section. The only other sources of relief would appear to be either an increase in I or a falling off in F at a slower rate than the reduction in E corresponding to the reduction in O.

Ruling out for the moment the possibility of the stimulation either of the value of investment or of the volume of capital development by the deliberate effort either of the banking system or of the government, there seems to be but little expectation of relief by way of an increase in I, since the more probable reactions happen to be in the wrong direction. Since the volume of capital development largely depends on the expectation of a satisfactory rate of entrepreneurs' profits, the experience of a steadily diminishing rate of receipts by entrepreneurs may be expected to be deterrent to development; and since the current valuation of capital goods is much influenced by the existing rate of profit, the value of investment is likely to fall off even more than the amount of development. Furthermore, during the period whilst output is being contracted there is necessarily a disinvestment in working capital. Finally, as regards the accumulation of liquid stocks of commodities, the movement will be different at different stages in the decline, increasing (and so providing some offset to the other influences) in the earlier stages before entrepreneurs have made up their minds to reduce output and are at the same time reluctant to accept current market prices for what they produce, but decreasing at later stages.

It would seem, therefore, that we have to look for first aid to changes in F relatively to changes in E. Here there is more to help, since it is natural to expect that, as the earnings of the public decline, a point will eventually be reached at which the decline in total expenditure F, of both entrepreneurs and public taken together, will cease to be so great as the decline in E. For we can, I think, be sure that sooner or later the most virtuous intentions will break down before the pressure of increasing poverty, so that savings will fall off and negative saving will begin to appear in some quarter or another to offset the effect of losses on the expenditure of entrepreneurs. Sooner or later, for example, the determination of the government to pay for the dole out of additional taxation will break down; and even if it does not, the determination of the taxpayer to economise in his personal expenditure by the full amount of the additional taxes he must pay, will weaken. Indeed the mere law of survival must tend in this direction. For communities, if any, the inborn character of which was such that they obeyed remorselessly the dictates of thrift and of 'sound finance', [would] have long ago starved to death and left no descendants!

Thus, apart from any stimulus to investment, we may reasonably rely upon a point of equilibrium being reached eventually at which $-\Delta Q$ averaged over the entrepreneurs who are still producing ceases to fall further, so that there is no reason for any further decline in output in the short period.[1] It is true that the period of sub-normal profits might be of such long duration that any degree of net loss would lead to a further decline in output. But, apart from the fact that this might mean a change in the level of entrepreneurs' inducement, it only needs a sufficient decline in economy relatively to the falling off of

[1] Though in this case, equally with the case where expenditure falls off equally with income, there can be no equilibrium in the long period, since in the long period income and earnings are equal.

earnings to furnish some point below which there will be no further fall.

Indeed once we have reached the point at which spending decreases less than earnings decrease with investment stable, the attainment of equilibrium presents no problem. For provided that spending always increases less than earnings increase and decreases less than earnings decrease, i.e. provided ΔS and ΔE have the same sign, and that investment does not change, *any* level of output is a position of stable equilibrium. For any increase of output will bring in a retarding factor, since ΔS will be positive and consequently I being assumed constant, ΔQ will be negative; whilst equally any decrease of output will bring in a stimulating factor, since ΔS will be negative and consequently ΔQ positive.

In actual fact, however, there is likely, when this point has once been reached, to be a modest kick-back in the upwards direction. For as soon as output ceases to fall further, disinvestment in working capital ceases; consequently total net investment is increased and profits improve; so that a section of entrepreneurs is brought back into production. The re-investment in working capital caused by this will then flatter the position slightly beyond its true deserts. But after minor oscillations output will finally settle down to a position of equilibrium which is stable, so long as no extraneous influence interposes to change the value of I.

The reader will notice that, apart from factors of which we have not yet taken account, there is no presumption whatever that the equilibrium output will be anywhere near the optimum output. The essence of the above process is that the real income of the community has to be forced down to a level at which the rate of saving is not so excessive relatively to investment at the current rate of interest as to produce a crescendo of business losses and the closing down of plant. Thus it is easy to conceive of a community of which the financial and economic organisation and habits of thrift are such that it cannot be trusted with a real income exceeding a certain amount; since as soon as its output rises above this figure, the increase of expenditure is not sufficient to cover the increase of cost (corresponding to the increased output) with the result that entrepreneurs' receipts fall to whatever extent is necessary to reduce output again below the critical figure.

Thus the actual level of output depends, given the habits and policies of the community in respect of saving, on their habits and policies in respect of investment. That is to say, given the response of the community's spending to changes in the levels of profits and earnings, the level of output will depend on their prevailing practices and policy in regard to the control of investment. Thus if we regard the response of individual spending to any given conditions of earnings and profits as something which is determined by nature and habit and virtually outside deliberate control at the centre, then the level of output, which will be a stable level, entirely depends on the policy of the authorities as affecting the amount of investment. An active policy of stimulating investment renders a greater volume of saving consistent with a greater volume of output. Thus it might be truer to say that the amount of saving over a period of time depends on the amount of investment, than the other way round.

It may well be that the above analysis furnishes us with a hint, and a partially correct picture, of the nature of the economic world in which we actually live. For it is probable that when the output of the community increases a point comes eventually, if not at once, when its spending F ceases to increase as rapidly as its earnings; and that, though we may contrive for a time to maintain disbursement as a whole by increasing investment as rapidly as the difference between earnings and spending rises, a critical point comes when, with our existing organisation, we cease to be able to increase investment at an adequate pace, with the result that forces come into operation which prevent a further increase of output. Nor is there any reason to suppose that the critical point represents the optimum volume of output at which, assuming an equilibrium distribution of incomes, every member of the community would prefer leisure to further opportunities to increase either consumption or saving. Thus perhaps it is only in exceptional circumstances—during a war, a boom due to a transient stimulus, or a Five Year Plan—that we are capable of raising output to its optimum point without bringing forces into operation which tend to reduce output before this optimum point has been reached. It is to be expected that in a very poor community the risk of instability, through increasing output leading to more savings than can be absorbed, is comparatively slight. Thus it is the rich Western communities of today which are the first to experience the full inconvenience of this particular factor.

We are not entitled, however, to apply this argument to the real world until we have disposed of two factors, which, in the judgment of traditional doctrine, enter in as equilibrating factors and altogether obviate the necessity of any such conclusion as that which we are propounding. The first of these is the reduction of the rate of wages; and the second is the automatic tendency in such conditions for a reduction in the rate of interest. The two are sometimes connected, because the reduced demand for money, consequent on a fall in wages, may be one of the forces relied upon to produce the reduction in the rate of interest. Nevertheless we can discuss them separately without inconvenience, dealing under the first head with the alleged effect of a reduction in the rate of wages to bring a cure by making business more profitable, and reserving for the second head any effect it may have on the rate of interest as a result of reducing the demand for money.

9 THE EFFECTS OF CHANGES IN THE
RATE OF EARNINGS

It is the almost universal conviction of entrepreneurs that the vicious circle of declining profits can be remedied by a reduction in their variable costs of production per unit of output, i.e. by what can be conveniently summed up as a reduction in efficiency wages (denoted by W_1, as in my *Treatise on Money*). They consider that this is obvious and often that it is probably the only remedy. The efficacy of this exit from the vicious circle must, therefore, now be considered.

Now the leading characteristic of this remedy, which is commonly overlooked, is that it is, taken absolutely and apart from consideration of its indirect reactions, what we may call a *competitive* remedy. That is to say, it is calculated to help any given entrepreneur who has the advantage of it, or indeed the entrepreneurs of any given group or country, provided the same advantages are not extended to *all* entrepreneurs in the closed system under examination. For the expected benefit is based on the assumption, which each entrepreneur looking only to his own affairs naturally makes, that entrepreneurs' outgoings will be diminished per unit of output without this having the effect of reducing their incomings to an equal extent. In short the supposed 'obviousness' of the efficacy of this expedient urged as an *all-round* remedy is based on the assumption that the effect of diminishing W_1 will be to increase Q and O, so that ΔQ and, therefore, $\Delta D - \Delta E$ and $\Delta I + \Delta F - \Delta E$ will in these circumstances be positive.

So far, however, from the favourable effect on ΔQ being obvious, a little reflection shows that the net effect of a reduction in W_1, whether favourable or unfavourable, can only be arrived at after an examination of the reaction of the particular type of change contemplated on ΔE, ΔI and ΔF. The only conclusion of which we can be sure from the outset is that the entrepreneurs as a body will be no further forward than they were before, unless it can be shown that a reduction in W_1 tends to increase $I - S$.

Let us, in the first instance, abstract from any resultant change in I and consider what will happen to $F - E$. With this simplification it is apparent that there will be no improvement in profit and hence no improvement in output unless the change $\Delta F - \Delta E$, resulting from the reduction in W_1, is positive.

To decide this we must first make some assumption as to the initial effect of this reduction in costs on the price level. Will competition forthwith force the entrepreneurs to reduce prices by the same amount as the reduction in costs? Or will they be able—so far as the perfection or imperfection of competition amongst producers affects them or others—to reduce prices in the first instance by a lesser amount than the reduction in costs? The latter is what they hope for and will endeavour to secure. If they are successful, then there is a redistribution of the existing real income as between entrepreneurs and earners; whilst if they are unsuccessful, then the redistribution will merely be as between rent earners and wage earners. The most general, and also the most probable, case will be that of a partial initial success by the entrepreneurs, so that there will be some redistribution of purchasing power both as between entrepreneurs and earners and also as between rent earners and wage earners. The question then is simply one of whether the redistribution of purchasing power, consequent on a reduction of W_1, is likely to affect economy favourably or unfavourably compared with its effect on earnings. Will the increase of spending by those whose purchasing power is favourably affected, minus the decrease of expenditure by those whose purchasing power is unfavourably affected, be greater or less than the reduction of earnings? Will F diminish by less or by more than E, i.e. will aggregate saving S increase or decrease on balance?

The conclusion is not arrived at so easily as in the case considered in the previous chapter where there was a reduction in E consequential on a reduction in O. For in that case there was a reduction in the real income of the community, and we could therefore infer with practical certainty that the effort to maintain the standard of life would eventually prevail over the motive to economise, in which event F would fall at a slower rate than E. But in this case, there is no aggregate reduction of real income, the real value of E' being exactly the same as before.

It follows that no general answer to our question, which will be irrespective of the circumstances of the particular case, can be given with equal certainty. But the general presumption so far (we have not yet considered the reaction on I) would seem to be adverse to the contention of the entrepreneurs that an all-round reduction in the rate of costs and earnings per unit of output is calculated to be favourable to the volume of output. For unless we beg the question by assuming an increase of output, there is bound to be a redistribution of purchasing power unfavourable to earners, even in the most favourable case in which prices are reduced by the whole amount of the reduction in unit costs (since, unless all prices have already fallen to prime cost, the percentage falls in price will be less than the percentage reduction of variable cost); and a redistribution of purchasing power, favourable to rent earners and to entrepreneurs and unfavourable to wage earners, is likely on balance to be favourable to saving.

For in the first instance the position is that wage earners are unable to maintain their previous standard of life without trenching on their savings, since prices have fallen by less than earnings; whilst rent earners and entrepreneurs will not have to spend as much as before to maintain their previous standard of life, which has now become compatible with increasing their savings. Thus there will be an increment or decrement of profit according as the former class trench on their savings more than the latter class add to theirs. It follows that the only case in which the net effect can be favourable to profit and unfavourable to saving is where the elasticity of actual consumption corresponding to a change in real income is greater for the entrepreneur and rent-earning classes than it is for the wage-earning class. And this, obviously, is improbable;—one might say very improbable!

At the best, then,—especially if fixed cost is a substantial source of income—there is a serious risk (unless we can discover a favourable reaction on I) that an all-round diminution in entrepreneurs' variable costs per unit of output may actually aggravate, rather than remedy, a subnormal level of profit which is reacting unfavourably on output. To avoid misunderstanding, I should repeat that this does not preclude the possibility of advantages from reductions in the unit cost of some entrepreneurs relatively to that of others, when the relative reductions are wisely selective on considerations of the elasticities of demand and supply for different classes of goods.

It may be worth while to point out in passing that it follows from the above (apart, as before, from reactions on investment), that government expenditure which adds to the income of the relatively poor is not only likely to be favourable to entrepreneurs during a slump when it is financed by borrowing (which is obvious), but also when it is financed out of taxation of the richer classes, since it is likely to increase the spending of the former more than it decreases the spending of the latter. The system of unemployment benefit would seem, therefore, contrary to what is sometimes supposed, to be a stabilising factor, the slump in output being likely to proceed to less extreme lengths than in the absence of such a system.

So much for the effect of a reduction in W_1 on $\Delta F - \Delta E$. What will be its reaction on ΔI? This looks at first sight more promising, but it is not simple. If ΔF is greater than ΔE, so that ΔQ increases, this may be expected to react favourably both on development and on its value, so that ΔI will increase, thus accentuating the increase in ΔQ. Apart from this, if entrepreneurs *believe* that a reduction in W_1 is in their interest, this may have a stimulating effect on ΔI, and the mere prevalence of the belief will in itself bring it partly true. On the other hand, if in fact the reduction in W_1 causes $\Delta F - \Delta E$ to be negative, the above belief, being based on precarious foundations, may collapse before its effect on ΔI has gone far enough to balance the increase in S $(= E - F)$.

Furthermore, not much effect on new investment can be expected even from greater optimism and improved confidence on the part of entrepreneurs as a result of their success in reducing unit costs, so long as output continues at a level appreciably below the capacity of the existing plant. On the other hand if the reduction in variable cost is greater than is expected to last, it is true that there may be some stimulus to take advantage of the temporary low cost to accelerate the construction of new capital.

I conclude, on the balance of considerations, that there is no presumption that an *all-round* reduction of the variable costs of production will prove favourable to the volume of employment. The plausibility of the opposite view is altogether due, I think, to a comparison between an all-round reduction, and a selective reduction or a competitive reduction;—which is very marked, since, in practice, any given reduction which is proposed nearly always presents itself as either selective or competitive. Whether a selective reduction is worth while must, of course, depend on whether it is wisely selective, which means, in the main, whether it is concentrated on industries which have high elasticities of supply and demand. And whether a competitive reduction, which would have an unfavourable effect on $F - E$ if it were applied all round, is worth while to those who initiate it, must depend on the probability that the action of the group initiating it will or will not be followed by other competitive groups.

10 THE LONG-RUN ADJUSTABILITY OF THE RATE OF INTEREST

We have argued in chapter 8 [above pp. 382–9] that a profit-seeking organisation of production is highly unstable in the sense that a movement from equilibrium tends to aggravate itself. We have argued that a point comes eventually when this ceases to be the case, namely as soon as a further reduction in earnings is attended by a less than equal reduction in disbursement. But the gravamen of our indictment lay not so much in this as in the charge that there was no guarantee that, after the progressive decline had been stayed, we could then rely on a recovery to an optimum point at which productive resources would be fully employed. It depended, we said, on the habits and policies of the community in respect of saving and investment.

Our argument was, however, an incomplete one at that stage, since we allowed for no relief from measures for the stimulation of investment. Now there are assuredly—at least so I believe—some policies aimed at stimulating investment which are capable of raising production towards the optimum point. There are also, I should admit, forces which one might fairly well call 'automatic' which operate under any normal monetary system in the direction of restoring a long-period equilibrium between saving and investment. The point upon which I cast doubt—though the contrary is generally believed—is whether these 'automatic' forces will, in the absence of deliberate management, tend to bring about not only an equilibrium between saving and investment but also an optimum level of production.

The 'automatic' forces, upon which it has been customary to rely in the long run, can be analysed—partly in repetition of what has been said already—as follows. On the one hand we have the fact that, as output, and consequently the community's real income, declines, the proportion of earnings which is saved will also decline. On the other hand as output and prices decline, the proportion of the stock of money to income will (under some, but not all, monetary systems) tend to increase. This growing relative abundance of money will, unless the general desire for liquidity relatively to income is capable of increasing without limit, lead in due course to a decline in the rate of interest. And although the decline in the rate of interest may be prevented for a time by various 'bearish' factors from exercising a favourable influence on investment, sooner or later it will do so. Thus we may expect to reach a point at which, with saving declining and investment increasing, the turn of the tide comes, whereupon the recovery will feed on itself just as the depression had fed on itself, real and money incomes will rise and savings will rise thus supporting the higher level of investment—so the argument runs—until we are back again at optimum output. It may be, if we are not careful, that the recovery will be allowed to develop into a boom with incomes continuing to rise after the optimum point of output has been reached, thus sowing the seeds of a subsequent slump; but that is another story, and it is not upon that possibility that I am depending in what follows.

The point at which I withdraw reliance upon the above course of events appears when the recovery in output leads to an increase of savings. For there is no safeguard against savings increasing faster than they can be absorbed by investment, except a monetary policy deliberately aimed at making a rate of interest sufficiently stimulating to investment; and under an 'automatic' system there is no certainty, or even possibility, of this.

Two 1932 (see above p. 380) drafts of chapters for differing arrangements of the argument of the book entitled 'The Parameters of a Monetary Economy'.

9 THE PARAMETERS OF A
MONETARY ECONOMY

Let us suppose ourselves to be in possession of all relevant knowledge concerning the behaviour of a monetary economy in different sets of hypothetical circumstances which lie within the range of practical possibility. Let us suppose a given state of affairs to exist. And let us imagine that we have been asked to explain what consequences will result to prices, output and incomes if the monetary authority decides to increase the quantity of money by a given amount. In what way will it be most instructive for us to give our explanations? For to lay down the general principles on which questions of this kind can be answered is the object of the monetary theory of production.

Deltas throughout
Work up from the quantity of money to the price level Λ
Liquidity pref. A gives us $\rho = A(M)$
Expectation of quasi-rent then gives us $P_2 = B(\rho)$
$Q_2 = L_2(P_2) \quad Q_2 = P_2 - W = P_2 - L(Q_1, Q_2)$
$Q_1 = L_1(P_1) \quad Q_1 = P_1 - W = P_1 - L(Q_1, Q_2)$
$$W = L(Q_1, Q_2)$$
Supply functions: $I' = C_2(Q_2)$, $R = C_1(Q_1)$, $O = C(Q)$, $P_1 = G(I, R)$.

(1) Quantity of money
(2) Schedules of liquidity preference
(3) Schedules of time preference
(4) Earnings reaction
(5) Supply functions
(6) The expectation of quasi-rent

5 THE PARAMETERS OF A
MONETARY ECONOMY

1. All the factors in a monetary economy which make up the total economic situation are in some degree interdependent, and react on one another. Let us, nevertheless, without implying that any one is either wholly independent of, or causally prior to, the others, endeavour to clear our minds by considering them one by one.

We have begun in the preceding chapter with the state of liquidity-preference (A) which tells us what ρ, the rate of interest exclusive of risk-allowance, will be, given to [the ?] quantity of money so that

$$\rho = A(M).[1]$$

2. The next factor to be introduced may be styled the *expected quasi-rent* (B), which is the expression of the expectation of the productivity of capital.

A capital asset will, in the course of its life, yield a certain real income of goods, services or other utilities. The money price of the real income, year by year in the future as it accrues, constitutes in Marshall's phrase its quasi-rent. In order to value a capital asset in terms of money it is necessary to have an expectation, more or less definite, as to the amounts of the prospective quasi-rents. This time series of expected quasi-rents can then be valued, after allowance for risk and doubt, by means of a comparison with the present value of a debt which would have an interest yield year by year equal to the amount of the expected quasi-rents.

Thus P_2, the price complex of capital assets, is given by the expected quasi-rent taken in conjunction with the rate of interest, being obtained by multiplying the expected quasi-rent by the number of years' purchase corresponding to the rate of interest (due allowance being, of course, made for the length of life of an asset and any prospective irregularity in the rate of receipt of quasi-rent); so that we can write

$$P_2 = B(\rho)$$

where B is the complex of expected quasi-rents and ρ the complex of rates of interest.

What economists have meant by the marginal productivity of capital—which they have seldom, if ever, defined precisely—is connected with my concept B, but is by no means identical with it. I will discuss this term in a note at the end of chapter 6.

---

[1] This, and the preceding equations, are symbolic, not objective, equations, since ρ etc. stand for a complex of numbers and are not themselves numbers.

3. The market rate of interest and the anticipated productivity of capital as expressed in expected quasi-rent, having conjoined to give us P_2, the price complex of assets, we can deduce the volume of capital development, provided that we are given the current supply schedules (C) of industries capable of producing capital goods. The reader should note that we are here interpreting P_2, not as the *average* price of assets (as in my *Treatise on Money*), but as the complex of prices of assets. For, since the supply schedules of different industries will not be the same, the same average price may lead to a different volume of investment if it is differently made up. With this proviso we may sum up the relationship between the volume of current development and the price complex for assets, as given by the current supply schedules of capital industries, by the equation

$$I' = C(P_2).$$

The average price of currently produced assets will not, of course, be the same as the average price of the total existing stock of assets, since it is unlikely that the distribution of current output between different kinds of capital goods will be in the same proportions as the stocks of the different kinds of goods. Where it is important to distinguish the price index from the price complex, we will designate the former by ΣP_2; and where it is important to distinguish the price index of currently produced assets from the price index of the stock of assets, we will designate the former by ΣP_2 and the latter by ΣP_2. There is, obviously, no necessity to distinguish between the price complex of currently produced assets and the price complex of the stock of assets.

4. We have found that the price complex of assets is given by their anticipated productivity taken in conjunction with the market rate of interest. This—I hope the reader will feel—is quite natural and as it should be. Moreover since on my view the market rate of interest is a thing in itself, dependent on liquidity preference and the quantity of money, there is no longer any

circularity[1] in this method of valuing assets, such as exists so long as the rate of interest is supposed to be in some way the same thing as, or directly arising out of, the productivity of assets.

But we still have no clue to the price complex of consumption goods, or consumables, as we may call them for short. It is here —and this the reader may find at first sight more surprising— that the state of time preference comes in for the first time, as the necessary determining factor.

For a single individual the notion of time preference is fairly clear. Given all the relevant attendant circumstances which are fixed for me by the actions of others including my income, actual and prospective, and the prices, actual and prospective, of debts, assets and consumables, it is my state of time preference which determines what part of my income I spend on consumables and what part of it I reserve. I say that this is fairly clear, since we do not have to suppose that either the amount of my income or the various relevant price levels appreciably depend on my decision. But when we try to deduce from the general state of time preference, i.e. from the complex of individual time preferences, what part of the community's aggregate income will be spent and what part will be reserved, we are soon in difficulties. For the amount of total expenditure responds immediately to the amount of total income, whilst, for the community as a whole, the amount of total income depends not less directly and immediately on the amount of total expenditure. We are, therefore, on shifting sands, and must approach our goal more circumspectly and by a different route.

We can furnish a good analogy[2] to the relation between liquidity preference and what is actually held in liquid form. In the latter case we have assumed that the public have no power to determine the available aggregate of liquid funds of money. Consequently the rate of interest has to move until the amount of money which the public desire to hold, having regard to their

---

[1] It is, I think, the failure of the attempt to avoid this circularity which makes Marshall's treatment of the rate of interest unsatisfactory. See [unnumbered] p. below.

[2] This is largely a repetition of [unnumbered] pp. above.

liquidity preferences, is equal to the amount of money which the banking system is creating. In the same way, since the amount of money reserved by the public out of their incomes must always be exactly equal to the amount of current investment, the level of prices (and hence of incomes which are equal in the aggregate to the price of output as whole) has to rise to a point at which the amount of money which the public desire to reserve, having regard to the general state of time preference, *is* equal to the amount of current investment. Thus what the general state of time preference directly determines at any moment is not the volume of investment but the *price level*, and, as we shall see, primarily the price level of consumables.

It is not necessarily the case that there is any price level at which the amount of money reserved out of income will be equal to the amount of investment. One could invent perverse systems of time preference, which would make an equilibrium of prices impossible, but there are reasons in practice why we need not fear this. The simplest condition for stable equilibrium is that when aggregate income changes, the change in aggregate expenditure should be the same in direction but smaller in absolute amount. And there are reasons for expecting that this condition will normally be satisfied. For when prices rise as a result of the economic system endeavouring to reach an equilibrium between the amount of investment and of what is reserved out of income, other fundamental factors remaining unchanged, the distribution of incomes associated with rising aggregate income will usually favour an increase in the amount reserved, inasmuch as profits are more likely than earnings to be reserved; and correspondingly when aggregate income falls. Moreover, there are further reasons which could be brought out by an examination of the actual probabilities of the case,—an examination, however, for which we need not pause in this place.

I have said above that the general stage of time preference affects *primarily* the price level of consumables. The reason for this is that the price level of assets is tied down by prospective quasi-rent, taken in conjunction with the rate of interest. It follows that time preferences can only affect the price of assets in so far as it affects one or other of these two factors; and this reaction, whilst by no means non-existent, is likely to be of a secondary character. A change in the general state of time preference, taking the form (e.g.) of an increase in the propensity to spend in any given circumstances, does not have any obvious direct effect either on prospective quasi-rent or on the rate of interest, except in so far as it changes expectations as to the price of consumables and as to the character of long-run adjustments of the rate of interest as resulting from the policy of the monetary authority or otherwise. The main reaction on the price of assets of a change in the propensity to spend is, therefore, a secondary consequence of the change, or anticipated change, in the price level of consumables. For a change in the price level of consumables will react on the expectation of quasi-rent in so far as assets are capable of yielding consumables (directly or indirectly) during the period for which the change in price is expected to last. Also a change in the prices, whether of consumables or of assets, will change the state of liquidity preference, since more money will be required for the convenient transaction of business—a matter on which we have not yet enlarged; so that the rate of interest will change, unless the monetary authority chooses to offset the change in liquidity preference by a change in the quantity of money.

Thus, given the other factors of which we have already taken account and in particular the value and volume of capital development, it is the general state of time preference (G)[1] which we need in order to fix for us P_1, the price complex of consumables, so that

$$P_1 = G(I).$$

5. This is on the assumption that there is no change in the output of consumables; and the removal of this assumption

---

[1] I omit the letters D, E and F, since they have been used already with important significations.

requires strictly that we should write in terms of simultaneous equations (just as we should strictly, since all the factors are in some measure interdependent, write the whole of this discussion in terms of multiple simultaneous equations). In the case of investment, it was reasonable (though only for short periods) to neglect the reaction of an increase in the supply of assets on the expected quasi-rent and hence on the price of assets, since, the current supply of assets being a very small proportion of the total stock, the effect of a change in the volume of current supply will also be small (unless the demand for the yield of assets is very inelastic, which there is no reason to suppose). But when we come to consumables the case is quite different, since the current supply is almost the same thing as the available supply. Hence we must bring in the supply schedule (H) of consumables, namely $R = H(P_1)$ where R is the output of consumables, and re-write our equation for P_1 as

$$P_1 = G(I, H).$$

6. In the foregoing we have assumed that the supply schedules of assets and consumables are dependent on the *prices* of the articles produced. This would be reasonable for a single industry where it can be assumed that the price of the product does not sensibly react on the cost of production. But it is not reasonable for industry as a whole, in the case of which it is more nearly accurate to think of the supply schedule as relating output to *profit*. We should, therefore, re-write the two equations which bring in the supply schedules of the two classes of output as follows:

$$I' = C'(Q_2)$$
$$R = H'(Q_1),$$

where I' is the volume of development, and Q_2 and Q_1 are the complex of profits on the production of different kinds of assets and consumables respectively, given P_2 and P_1 and other relevant circumstances.

Total output (O) is equal to the sum of I' and R, so that[1]

$$O = C'(Q_2) + G'(Q_1),$$

which we may also write

$$O = \mathcal{J}(Q),$$

where Q is the complex of profits on all classes of output and $\mathcal{J}$ is the supply schedule relating output as a whole to the complex of profits.

Now the determination of O is, in a sense, our goal. For the maintenance of O at an optimum level should be one of the twin objects of the management of an economic system (the other object being the maintenance of an optimum distribution of income).

7. We are now ready to complete the circle of our analysis and to remind ourselves of the ultimate interdependence of the various factors which we have been analysing.

We have already mentioned that the state of liquidity preference partly depends on the price level. But it is obvious that it also depends—amongst other things which have to be enumerated in detail when the analysis of liquidity preference, or the demand for money as it might otherwise be expressed, is the special topic of our enquiry—upon the volume of output.

Thus finally we have

$$A = K(O,P)$$

or, perhaps better, $\qquad A = K(E,Q)$

where E is the complex of earnings and Q the complex of profits.

8. The above discussion yields us what I would dub the four parameters of a monetary economy,—namely the quantity of money and the three fundamental factors of market psychology or, if you like, of the prevailing attitude to the future, as expressed in the state of liquidity preference, in the expectation

---

[1] Keynes originally drafted this chapter using different notation and did not replace G' with H' at this point in his revisions.

of quasi-rent, and in the rate of time preference. These parameters themselves are not entirely independent of one another and the schedules expressing them should be stated, strictly, in the form of simultaneous equations. But for purposes of analysis they are as distinct from one another as economic factors ever are. Incidentally they yield between them the price complexes of the three classes of purchasable things, namely of debts, of assets and of consumables; and—whilst we had better repeat once more that there is some measure of interdependence between all the elements of an economic system—there is significance in the statements that, given the quantity of money, the price of debts (i.e. the rate of interest) is primarily determined by the state of liquidity preference; that, given the rate of interest, the price of assets is primarily determined by the expectation of quasi-rent; and that, given the price of assets, the price of consumables is primarily determined by the state of time preference.

The task of the monetary authority is to adjust to the best of its ability the quantity of money to changes in the other parameters, so as to maintain, as nearly as possible, an optimum level of output. We shall see in the sequel that the optimum level of output depends on the maintenance of an optimum level of investment, so that we can re-express the task of the monetary authority as being to maintain a rate of interest which leads to an optimum level of investment. This is, however, a case where success will feed on itself. For the more successful the monetary authority is expected to be, the less violent will be the fluctuations in the prevailing attitude to the future as measured by the other three parameters, and consequently the easier the task of the monetary authority and the greater the likelihood of its success.

A note, probably written in 1932, giving an historical, retrospective, view of certain opinions.

HISTORICAL RETROSPECT

The orthodox equilibrium theory of economics has assumed, or has at least not denied, that there are natural forces tending to bring the volume of the community's output, and hence its real income, back to the optimum level whenever temporary forces have led it to depart from this level. But we have seen in the preceding chapters that the equilibrium level towards which output tends to return after temporary disturbances is not necessarily the optimum level, but depends on the strength of the forces in the community which tend towards saving.

Now orthodox theory in modern times has always concentrated on the importance of saving as a means of making a community wealthy, though it is evident that this cannot be so unless an increase of saving leads to an increase of investment.

But uninstructed public opinion and the common sense of the business world have always tended to support policies which are seen, when analysed, to be directed towards increasing investment or even, in some cases, towards diminishing saving. On these matters economists have seldom succeeded in convincing the public. Their failure to do so, and the deep-rooted suspicions as to their competence which their unsuccessful attempts have aroused, are, I think, at the bottom of the explanation of the low standing of economists regarded as practical experts and the unwillingness of statesmen and business men to accept their advice. For it now seems to me that the economists, in their devotion to a theory of self-adjusting equilibrium, have been, on the whole, wrong in their practical advice and that the instincts of practical men have been, on the whole, the sounder.

There are three leading examples of popular beliefs in favour of policies, which are seen on analysis to increase $I - S$, as being 'good for trade', i.e. as tending towards optimum output.

(1) Mercantilist and protectionist policies as tending to increase foreign investment by improving the balance of trade;

(2) Anti-usury laws and principles and cheap-money policies as tending to increase home investment by lowering the rate of interest;

(3) Expenditure as being a thing in itself 'good for trade' by diminishing the excess of S over I.

For a modern community one may say that it is a normal thing, except at times of war and at the height of booms, for output to be below the optimum level. Hence the justification of these 'popular' policies. For, after all, the maintenance of output, and hence of real income, at the optimum level, in the sense of everyone being able to obtain as much employment as he desires for a reward equal to the real wage he would get with output in equilibrium at an optimum level, should be the primary object of policy. The community is entitled to decide for itself in what proportions it desires to divide the results of its efforts between present consumption and future consumption. Moreover saving itself is most likely to be spontaneously greater when output, and hence real income, is at its optimum. Thus so far from its being true that, if we look after saving, output and investment will look after themselves, the opposite is more nearly true, namely that, if we look after investment, output and saving will look after themselves. For it is frequently the case in practice that a deliberate increase in saving will diminish investment and hence output (with, ultimately, a reaction on saving); whereas a deliberate increase in investment will increase output and hence saving. Indeed, whenever output is below the optimum level, i.e. whenever there is involuntary unemployment, we may be sure that an increase in investment will, so to speak, 'finance itself', partly by absorbing savings which were previously wasted in financing debts and losses, and partly by increasing savings as a result of increasing real income.

The idea of a monetary theory of production seems to have played an important role during 1932–3 in Keynes's movement from the *Treatise* to the *General Theory*. Keynes himself certainly made something of the idea when in late 1932 he devoted his contribution to a *Festschrift* for Professor A. Spiethoff to the subject.

From *Der Stand und die nächste Zunkunft der konjunkturforschung: Festschrift für Arthur Spiethoff* (1933).

A MONETARY THEORY OF PRODUCTION

In my opinion the main reason why the problem of crises is unsolved, or at any rate why this theory is so unsatisfactory, is to be found in the lack of what might be termed a *monetary theory of production*.

The distinction which is normally made between a barter economy and a monetary economy depends upon the employment of money as a convenient means of effecting exchanges— as an instrument of great convenience, but transitory and neutral in its effect. It is regarded as a mere link between cloth and wheat, or between the day's labour spent on building the canoe and the day's labour spent on harvesting the crop. It is not supposed to affect the essential nature of the transaction from being, in the minds of those making it, one between real things, or to modify the motives and decisions of the parties to it. Money, that is to say, is employed, but is treated as being in some sense *neutral*.

That, however, is not the distinction which I have in mind when I say that we lack a monetary theory of production. An economy, which uses money but uses it merely as a neutral link between transactions in real things and real assets and does not allow it to enter into motives or decisions, might be called—for want of a better name—a *real-exchange economy*. The theory which I desiderate would deal, in contradistinction to this, with an economy in which money plays a part of its own and affects motives and decisions and is, in short, one of the operative factors in the situation, so that the course of events cannot be predicted, either in the long period or in the short, without a knowledge of the behaviour of money between the first state and the last. And it is this which we ought to mean when we speak of a *monetary economy*.

Most treatises on the principles of economics are concerned mainly, if not entirely, with a real-exchange economy; and—which is more peculiar—the same thing is also largely true of most treatises on the theory of money. In particular, Marshall's *Principles of Economics* is avowedly concerned with a real-exchange economy; and so, I think, is by far the greater part of the treatises of Professor Pigou—to name those English works on which I have been brought up and with which I am most familiar. But the same thing is also true of the dominant systematic treatises in other languages and countries.

Marshall expressly states (*Principles*, pp. 61, 62) that he is dealing with *relative* exchange values. The proposition that the prices of a ton of lead and a ton of tin are £15 and £90 means no more to him in this context than that the value of a ton of tin in terms of lead is six tons (along with a number of other similar propositions). 'We may throughout this volume', he explains, 'neglect possible changes in the general purchasing power of money. Thus the price of anything will be taken as representative of its exchange value relatively to *things* in general' (my italics). He quotes Cournot to the effect that 'we get the same sort of convenience from assuming the existence of a standard of uniform purchasing power by which to measure value, that astronomers do by assuming that there is a "mean sun" which crosses the meridian at uniform intervals, so that the clock can keep pace with it; whereas the actual sun crosses the meridian sometimes before and sometimes after noon as shown by the clock'. In short, though money is present and is made use of for convenience, it may be considered to cancel out for the purposes of most of the general conclusions of the *Principles*. Or if we turn to the writings of Professor Pigou, the assumptions of a real-exchange economy appear most characteristically in his taking as his normal case that in which the shape of the supply schedule of labour in terms of real wages is virtually independent of changes in the value of money.

The divergence between the real-exchange economics and my desired monetary economics is, however, most marked and perhaps most important when we come to the discussion of the rate of interest and to the relation between the volume of output and the amount of expenditure.

Everyone would, of course, agree that it is in a monetary economy in my sense of the term that we actually live. Professor Pigou knows as well as anyone that wages are in fact sticky in terms of money. Marshall was perfectly aware that the existence of debts gives a high degree of practical importance to changes in the value of money. Nevertheless it is my belief that the far-reaching and in some respects fundamental differences between the conclusions of a monetary economy and those of the more simplified real-exchange economy have been greatly underestimated by the exponents of the traditional economics; with the result that the machinery of thought with which real-exchange economics has equipped the minds of practitioners in the world of affairs, and also of economists themselves, has led in practice to many erroneous conclusions and policies. The idea that it is comparatively easy to adapt the hypothetical conclusions of a real wage economics to the real world of monetary economics is a mistake. It is extraordinarily difficult to make the adaptation, and perhaps impossible without the aid of a developed theory of monetary economics.

One of the chief causes of confusion lies in the fact that the assumptions of the real-exchange economy have been tacit, and you will search treatises on real-exchange economics in vain for any express statement of the simplifications introduced or for the relationship of its hypothetical conclusions to the facts of the real world. We are not told what conditions have to be fulfilled if money is to be neutral. Nor is it easy to supply the gap. Now the conditions required for the 'neutrality' of money, in the sense in which this is assumed in—again to take this book as a leading example—Marshall's *Principles of Economics*, are, I suspect, precisely the same as those which will insure that crises *do not occur*. If this is true, the real-exchange economics, on which most of us have been brought up and with the conclusions of which our minds are deeply impregnated, though a valuable abstraction in itself and perfectly valid as an intellectual conception, is a singularly blunt weapon for dealing with the problem of booms and depressions. For it has assumed away the very matter under investigation.

Even if the above is in some respects an overstatement, it contains, I believe, the clue to our difficulties. This is not the same thing as to say that the problem of booms and depressions is a purely monetary problem. For this statement is generally meant to imply that a complete solution is to be found in banking policy. I am saying that booms and depressions are phenomena peculiar to an economy in which—in some significant sense which I am not attempting to define precisely in this place— money is not neutral.

Accordingly I believe that the next task is to work out in some detail a monetary theory of production, to supplement the real-exchange theories which we already possess. At any rate that is the task on which I am now occupying myself, in some confidence that I am not wasting my time.

Keynes also emphasised this complex of ideas when he entitled his course of lectures in the Michaelmas terms of 1932 and 1933 'The Monetary Theory of Production', thus breaking with the title he had used since 1929–30, 'The Pure Theory of Money' In his first lecture under this new title on 10 October 1932, Keynes made it clear that this change of title did signify a change in attitude and that he was at the beginning of a new book.[1]

[1] The comments dealing with Keynes's Cambridge lectures of 1932–4 depend heavily on the notes of R. B. Bryce who attended the lectures in each of those years and has kindly allowed us to consult his notes. The notes for 1933 and 1934 are supplemented by those of B. Thring and D. G. Champernowne.

In the lectures for 1932, Keynes developed the distinction between a neutral economy, which paralleled the real-exchange economy of the Spiethoff *Festschrift*, and a monetary economy. He placed particular emphasis on the idea that in a monetary economy short-period supply prices of factors of production did not all behave in the manner characteristic of machines, falling away quickly in periods of over supply. He believed such price adjustments might be possible in a 'communist' state or a slave economy, but not in his monetary economy.

Keynes then moved into a discussion of a model in which changes in output depended on changes in the relationship between disbursement and earnings, where disbursement was equal to investment plus spending (profits being a residual). The model did not contain a multiplier in any explicit sense, but it did have the idea of liquidity preference. Keynes distinguished liquidity preference from the state of bearishness of the *Treatise* by stating that the latter idea muddled up assets and debts against money while the former concentrated on debts and money alone. The model also had asset values determined by the stream of prospective quasi-rents and the rate of interest, the latter being the upshot of liquidity preference. Thus the volume of investment was a function of prospective quasi-rents, the rate of interest and the cost of production of capital goods. In such a system, Keynes believed there was no long-period tendency towards full employment as there was in a neutral economy. The lectures concluded with a discussion of the parameters of a monetary economy (above p. 397) and a discussion of precursors of his ideas.

Between his 1932 and 1933 lectures stands Keynes's pamphlet *The Means to Prosperity* (*JMK*, vol. IX, part VII). This first appeared as four articles in *The Times* between 13 and 16 March 1933 and soon after in pamphlet form. The American edition of the pamphlet, reprinted in volume IX, also incorporated material from Keynes's article 'The Multiplier' which appeared in the *New Statesman* of 1 April 1933.

During the period surrounding the pamphlet, Richard Kahn was in America and the following fragments of letters between Keynes and Kahn give some idea of how matters were moving.[1]

From a letter from R. F. KAHN *from Chicago, 20 January 1933*

The figures are really beautiful. I had completely missed the possibility of confirming the thing in this simple way. I do feel that the point ought to be

---

[1] Keynes's letter to Kahn of 1 January has disappeared. Thus we have only Kahn's reaction.

brought to the notice of the public. If you find an opportunity of doing so you might point out that today the ratio is greater than two because (*a*) supply is more elastic when depression is severe, (*b*) the dole is largely financed out of taxation rather than borrowing.

If you applied the same calculation to 1932 you would expect a big discrepancy owing to economy, public and private. (You are assuming a constant propensity to save on the part of individuals and the state.) Some time I must try to arrive at a guess of the effect of (i) reduced state expenditures (on e.g. teachers' salaries), (ii) increased state taxation. It would be very difficult and it would, by the nature of the case, be impossible to establish any universal ratios.

From a letter to R. F. KAHN, *29 January 1933*

Colin [Clark] was delighted with the multiplier for secondary employment, but I tell him that all it does is to increase slightly my confidence in the accuracy of his statistics. He has further elaborated...[his calculations] but I tell him not to overcook it because, if he succeeds in making the actual and computed curves identical, I shall distrust his statistics again, since I know for certain that the multiplier is not always 2. We shall not know until the Budget whether the dole is really being paid out of taxation, but if it is, this must, as you say, have appreciably raised the multiplier from what it was.

From a letter to R. F. KAHN, *24 March 1933*

I am now engaged in trying to write out for *The Times* or alternatively for *The New Station*[1] a really detailed, but nevertheless popular, account of the relation between primary and secondary employment. I hope I don't make any bloomers, —I wish you were here to look over my shoulder.

From a letter to R. F. KAHN, *30 March 1933*

...I enclose a copy of my final article [in *The Times*]; also one in *The New Station* on the multiplier, which I hope will meet

---

[1] The Cambridge nickname for the recently amalgamated *New Statesman and Nation*.

with your approval. I have, I think, found rather a simple way of putting it all.

From a letter from R. F. KAHN *from New York, 30 March 1933*

Thank you so much for the typewritten version and the subsequent pages from 'The Times'. Apart from everything else, the exposition of 'secondary employment' is beautiful. Curiously enough, I had been grappling for something of the same sort in my Cincinnati speech (see March *Proceedings of American Statistical Association*),[1] even going so far as to use the word 'leakage'.

The Means to Prosperity gave rise to correspondence with Professor L. F. Giblin of the University of Melbourne. Giblin, an old Kingsman, had come close to the concept of the multiplier in his inaugural lecture in 1929.

From L. F. GIBLIN, *21 September 1933*

Dear Keynes,

Thanks for the American edition of *Means to Prosperity* which arrived last week. I was very interested in the additional matter and thought the new discussion helped the case considerably. But the new arithmetic I found difficult. I looked up the N.S. and S. [*sic.*] article of April 1 (which I had missed) and found the same difficulty there, but not protruded quite so aggressively. There was no adverse comment from correspondents in the following numbers, and it seems absurd for me at this distance of time and place to object to what has passed without comment in England. In any case, you must have had comments from U.S. before this. However, to be on the safe side, I am sending you my comments and will cable[2] the two important corrections I think should be made.

'Important' is rather overstating it, as the alterations I suggest do not affect the argument. But any substantial numerical slip does in practice prejudice a case.

The first page of the attached comments contains all that I am seriously worried about; pages 2 and 3 are my own guesses at the thing and page 4 is just straining at the meaning of words.

---

[1] 'Public Works and Inflation', *Bulletin of the American Statistical Association, Supplement*, March 1933. [Ed.]
[2] The cable has not survived.

Glad to hear of David Garnett alighting casually in your fields. It looks, for one thing, as if there had been 'an addition to British income' in this particular case.

Yours faithfully

L. F. GIBLIN

The Means to Prosperity (American Edition)

On page 8, last para [*JMK*, vol. IX, p. 342], it is said:—

'The primary expenditure of an additional £100 can be divided into two parts. The first part...does not become income in the hands of an Englishman.'

On page 10, first para [vol. IX, p. 343], it is estimated that 70 per cent becomes additional home income. Therefore (page 10 last para) the primary effect of expenditure of £100 is £70, and the total effect £70 $(1 + \frac{1}{2} + \frac{1}{4} + \ldots)$ = £140. The multiplier is therefore 1·4 and not 2.

On page 11, second para [vol. IX, p. 344], 60 per cent is assumed for each of the two proportions. Additional income is therefore £60 $\{1 + 0\cdot36 + (0\cdot36)^2 + \ldots\}$ = £93 and multiplier is 0·93, not 1½.

On page 12 [vol. IX, pp. 344–5] it is said:—

'I will base my estimates on these figures which also lead to a multiplier of 2.' These figures appear (not quite grammatically) to be 66 and 75 per cent. For these, £100 expenditure gives additional income: £66 $(1 + \frac{1}{2} + \frac{1}{4} \ldots)$ = £132. Multiplier is 1·32, not 2.

On page 13 [vol. IX, p. 345] the fourth line should read:—

'The total increase in incomes...will be £66 $(1 + \frac{1}{2} + \frac{1}{4} + \ldots)$ = £132', not £200.

In the following pages £132 should replace £200 in relevant places.

If I am right in these comments, it looks as if the American text might have been the result of a dovetailing of two possible statements on the subject, in one of which the whole of the original expenditure is assumed to go immediately into British income. (I have at times made similar computations here, e.g. on the total increase in income following from a given increase in export production.) This assumption would be approximately true for certain kinds of loan expenditure, e.g. on a certain kind of road or on reservoirs, on the conditions you postulate,—

(1) that the dole is paid out of taxes,

(2) that unused reserves are ample, and

(3) that there is no appreciable allowance to be made for depletion of stocks.

This assumption (of all primary expenditure becoming additional British income) would also be true if money were borrowed to relieve the taxpayer without any decrease in public expenditure.

I think something is lost in persuasiveness and accuracy by making the statement too general. If we call the two proportions p and q,—p equal to the proportion of expenditure going into home income, and q equal to the proportion of income going into expenditure, the p for primary expenditure might usefully be distinguished from the p for secondary effects; and possibly the q also. Obviously the first p would vary greatly with the object of borrowing. If to relieve the taxpayer, p might nearly equal 1; and also for certain public works. Under the assumptions of the previous paragraph, the first p would only deviate appreciably from 1 when a considerable proportion of primary expenditure was for imports, and I expect that public works could be found where imported material, such as timber or rubber, absorbed half the expenditure, and reduced the first p to $\frac{1}{2}$. The p's after the first would be approximately constant (call them p'). In the case of most public works, the secondary expenditure would be predominantly working-class expenditure, and the general proportion of imports to national income should give a higher limit to the deduction necessary, so that p' could be safely put at $\frac{4}{5}$. Loans in relief of income tax would imply greater expenditure on imports, but still p' would be close to $\frac{4}{5}$, and a general value, p' equal to $\frac{4}{5}$, would be near enough for all kinds of loan expenditure.

There would be similar variations in the q's. For most public works expenditure I should expect the first q to be nearly 1, and that it could be safely put at 0·9, which could stand also for subsequent q's. Loans for the relief of income tax would have a very different first q, at which I could not make a guess. It would depend on the hoarding prevalent in higher incomes, and might easily be down to 0·5, though of course it would improve as the whole plan became effective. Subsequent q's would not be very different from the public works q's, and might approach 0·9 from below. I think then that the results of loan expenditure might be stated with greater accuracy and force for the majority of public works, for which the first p could be put equal to 1, subsequent p's equal to $\frac{4}{5}$, and all q's at 0·9. As $0·9 \times \frac{4}{5}$ equals 0·6, the increase of incomes for £100 of primary expenditure would be

$$\pounds 100\,(1+0·6+0·36+\ldots) = \pounds 250.$$

It could then be explained that other types of loan expenditure would give less additional income, according to various circumstances, with a lower limit of perhaps

$$\pounds 50\,(1+0·6+0·36+\ldots) = \pounds 125.$$

But the £50 is arbitrary,—I cannot make a reasoned shot at it.

I might add that there is a small discrepancy in the English edition where (page 13, line 4 [vol. IX, p. 346, n. 4]) it is written:— 'However to be on the safe side, let us, *as before*, take the multiplier as 1½.' Actually (page 12, line 6 [vol. IX, p. 34, n. 1]) you have 'Let us, in order to give ourselves a further margin of safety, base our argument on the figure of £150', which implies a multiplier of 1¼, not 1½.

On page 13, third para [vol. IX, p. 345], it is estimated that:—'Two thirds of the *increased* income, i.e. £44, will accrue to men previously supported by the dole.'

This *should* mean that incomes of men on the dole are increased by £44, but the implications of this are contradicted by the initial assumption of an increase in incomes of only £66 from £100 expenditure.

If income of dole-men is increased by £44, then on the estimates of £130 for average wages and £50 for the cost of the dole, a dole-man will be employed for x years, where $44 + 50x = 130x$ and $x = 0.55$. The dole replaced will be $0.55 \times £50 = £27.5$. Income of dole-men will be £44 + £27.5 = £71.5. With secondary efforts a dole-man will be employed for $0.55 (1 + \frac{1}{2} + \frac{1}{4} \ldots) = 1.1$ years, and relief to budget will be £55.

<u>*but*</u>, primary additional income to dole-men = £44
primary additional income to taxpayer = £27.5
Total = £71.5

So additional income is £71.5 plus other increases in income, profits etc., which is inconsistent with total primary increase of income of £66.

The third para of page 13 must then be taken to mean that men previously on the dole will receive £44 income at first impact *in place of* about £17 received from the dole.

We have then:—

Increased income to dole-men £44 − £17 = £27
Increased income to taxpayer = £17
Other increased income = £22
Total = £66

It would then I think be clearer to state page 13 para 3 somewhat in this way:—

'I consider...safe to assume that £44 out of every £100 of initial expenditure would be paid to men previously on the dole replacing the dole for the corresponding period which would be about one third of a year with average wages at 50s. a week.'

From L. F. GIBLIN, *22 September 1933*

Dear Keynes,

I must apologise for having sent off to you yesterday,—thinking the mail closed then,—a hasty and ill-considered screed on the 'Multiplier'. It was done hurriedly in broken time and I should not have sent it off without more deliberation. A number of points in it dissatisfied me when I read it through last night: I will burden you only with a couple.

1. My suggestion that working-class expenditure would have less than the average of imports (bottom of page 2) was rotten,—simply a blind assumption of Australian conditions. I have not attempted an estimate,—which no doubt has been made,—but I should guess 40 per cent imports in wages at 50s. a week, and a much lower figure for income tax incomes. I should be inclined to reduce my p' on this account.

2. In case of loans for relief of income tax, if you count the income tax relieved as additional income, a large proportion say 50 per cent *might* not be spent, and total additional income would be of the form

$$£100 + \tfrac{2}{3}(£50)(1 + \tfrac{1}{2} + \tfrac{1}{4} +) = 167.$$

But incomes could not be increased by primary expenditure, for *income tax assessment*,—and the proportion of additional income going into revenue should, I fancy, be modified in this case. But I have not thought this out clearly.

Yours faithfully,
L. F. GIBLIN

A point I meant to raise in connection with (1): In Australia we *must* take proportion of (imports + *exportable goods consumed*) to income spent, in reckoning p.—I am not clear how far the same applies to England.

To L. F. GIBLIN, *27 October 1933*

My dear Giblin,

Thank you very much for your communication about that additional chapter in the *Means to Prosperity*. From several of your minor points I do not dissent, and will pay attention to them if I ever come to re-write it. But your major criticism as to the amount of the multiplier seems to me to be wrong.

The point is that in estimating on page 8 that £200 of primary expenditure will provide one man-year of primary employment, I have already allowed for the fact that some of the £200 primary expenditure will not become income in the hands of an Englishman. The others whose authority I quote for the £200 were not concerned with refinements of this kind, and intended that as their estimate of total primary expenditure leading to one man-year of primary employment. That is why on page 10 I do not have to multiply the whole result by 0·7 in arriving at the multiplier for total employment.

Pages 2 and 3 of your typewritten letter are very interesting, but go rather beyond what I was attempting in this short pamphlet. I was aiming, so to speak, not at giving the best possible estimate, but at giving an estimate which I believed to be on the safe side in Great Britain. When I come to write on the multiplier in my next book, I shall try to deal very thoroughly with the principles on which one should try to arrive at the best possible estimate.

Yours sincerely,
[copy initialled] J.M.K.

At the same time as he was working up his articles for *The Times*, Keynes was also preparing his *Essays in Biography* (*JMK*, vol. x) for publication. This process largely involved minor adjustments to previously published material, but in the case of his essay on Malthus, it meant an extensive reworking of a paper read to the Cambridge Political Economy Club in 1922 in the light of the current redevelopment of his ideas. This entailed the inclusion of the material on Malthus and Ricardo.[1] Thus, with *The Means to Prosperity*, the essay on Malthus marks an important stage on the way to the *General Theory*.

During the rest of 1933, Keynes was at work on his book, but almost no material survives to indicate where he was at any particular time. In fact, the only discussion note surviving is a brief postcard from Keynes to Joan Robinson, dated 8 May 1933.

To JOAN ROBINSON, *8 May 1933*

Quite right—bearishness may lower the short-term rate. But I think I make it clearer in my exposition.

J.M.K.

[1] For a complete discussion of the alterations see the footnote to page 71 of vol. x.

During the summer of 1933, with stocks of *A Treatise on Money* running low, Keynes told Daniel Macmillan that he wanted to pull himself together 'to make the small number of corrections I propose before reprinting'. However, before the stock of volume I ran out, Keynes had not done any corrections, and he thus ordered an uncorrected reprint. The same occurred with volume II, though it also needed correcting in February 1934. Keynes's reason for his decision was put to Daniel Macmillan as follows on 17 August 1933:

> I have been working at my next contribution to monetary theory, which will probably appear, I hope, some time in the first half of next year. In view of this I have not been wanting to spend time revising my *Treatise on Money*, even in minor particulars, and am anxious to put off doing so until after my next book has appeared.

Again in the Michaelmas term of 1933, Keynes lectured under the title 'The Monetary Theory of Production'. However, he had changed the contents of his lectures considerably from the previous year.

First he began his lectures by distinguishing between the classical theory and his approach. He suggested that the determination of the volume of employed resources was relatively neglected by classical theorists as compared with the theory of value. Keynes then went on to deal with the two fundamental postulates of classical economics broadly along the lines of chapter 2 of the *General Theory* and built up to the definition of involuntary unemployment of that chapter. In his second lecture he went into a discussion of Pigou's *Theory of Unemployment* along the lines of his letters to Robertson and Shove (above pp. 310–13). In that lecture he dealt with the distinction between the neutral economy of the classical economists and the money wage or entrepreneur economy, as he now called the real world, briefly alluding to the realisation problem of Marx. In his third lecture he dealt with the two salient characteristics of an entrepreneur economy: (*a*) that firms taken as a whole cannot protect themselves as a whole by producing more of this and less of that—when effective demand is low someone must lose; (*b*) that firms cannot protect themselves by revising their contracts with factors of production, for this will only help incidentally through indirect effects on other factors. All this was really by way of introduction for Keynes, who then turned to definitions and the construction of his own aggregate model, dealing in terms of expected values. Having thus defined income, investment, savings and the like for the purposes of his model, Keynes then went on to deal with relationships between and determinants of the size of crucial variables. In the course of these he clearly identified his marginal propensity to consume and the multiplier. He also worked in investment as being determined by expected quasi-rents and the rate of interest and tied the rate of interest down through liquidity preference with its analogues to the transactions, precautionary and speculative motives, linking commodities and equities together. After adding in a variable he referred to as 'the state of the news' he believed that he had isolated the crucial variables in the system, and he ended his lectures with some long-term speculations as to the rate of interest compatible with full employment.

In December 1933, the first surviving complete table of contents to Keynes's new book was available.

[Plan in a bundle of papers dated December 1933]

The General Theory of Employment

BOOK IV THE THEORY OF PRICES

Work continued into 1934. On 29 March, Keynes wrote to Joan Robinson:

> I am going through a stiff week's supervision from R.F.K. on my M.S. He is a marvellous critic and suggester and improver—there never was anyone in the history of the world to whom it was so helpful to submit one's stuff.

Four days earlier, he had reported to his mother that the book 'was now nearing completion'.

On 13 April, Keynes wrote to Richard Kahn, and gave a progress report:

From a letter to R. F. KAHN, *13 April 1934*

I have been making rather extensive changes in the early chapters of my book, to a considerable extent consequential on a simple and obvious, but beautiful and important (I think) precise definition of what is meant by effective demand:—

Let W be the marginal prime cost of production when output is O.

Let P be the expected selling price of this output.

Then OP is effective demand.

The fundamental assumption of the classical theory, 'supply creates its own demand', is that $OW = OP$ *whatever* the level of O, so that effective demand is incapable of setting a limit to employment which consequently depends on the relation between marginal product in wage-good industries and marginal disutility of employment. On *my* theory $OW \neq OP$ for *all* values of O, and entrepreneurs have to choose a value of O for which it *is* equal;—otherwise the equality of price and marginal prime cost is infringed. This is the real starting point of everything.

The overall position on the development of the *General Theory* by mid-1934 is best indicated by three documents. First, we have another table of contents, which dates from well before the first proof version of 11 October 1934 and onwards. For this table of contents, we have drafts of chapters 6–12. As chapter 12 follows the final printed version with very few changes, we deal with it in the Appendix to volume XIV which lists differences between the various proofs and drafts and the final printed version. However, as the other chapters are significantly different from the final version and the various proofs, we print them in as full a state as they survive.

The General Theory of Employment, Interest and Money

Drafts of chapters 6–11 following the mid-1934 table of contents.

6 EFFECTIVE DEMAND AND INCOME

I

There are, then, two fundamental quantities, if we follow our present line of analysis; namely the expectation of the sale proceeds of the current output of finished goods which leads to the decision to use capital equipment to produce the goods, and the actual value of the sale proceeds which is realised when the goods in question are finished. The former is what matters if we wish to know what determines the volume of employment, and the latter if we wish to know the actual profits of the entrepreneur; though the influences of the two overlap, since production is a continuous process and expectation is gradually modified, largely in the light of the current level of profits.

Which of these two quantities do we have in mind when we speak of the *income* of the community? In common parlance the term *income* is somewhat vague and we do not clearly know; but I should say that we incline to the latter, since we certainly mean by profits what the entrepreneur succeeds in making and not what he hopes to make and we are disposed to identify his income with his profits. On the other hand, the *real* income of the community obviously depends, given its capital equipment, on the volume of its employment;—that is to say, it depends on the expectation, and not on the realisation, of the sale proceeds.

In my *Treatise on Money* I took as my meaning of *income*, not the expectations which led to the current employment of the capital equipment actually in use, but the expectations which would have led to the original erection as well as the current employment of the equipment actually in use. I shifted subsequently to making income mean the expected sale proceeds of current output. There is much to be said for this procedure from certain points of view. But finally I have come to the conclusion that the use of language, which is most convenient on a balance of considerations and involves the least departure from current usage, is to call the actual sale proceeds *income* and the present value of the expected sale proceeds *effective demand*. Thus it is the present value of the expectation of income which constitutes the effective demand; and it is the effective demand which is the incentive to the employment of equipment and labour. The difference between the two we shall call *entrepreneur's windfall*—profit or loss, as the case may be; so that the excess of income over effective demand is entrepreneur's windfall profit.

The following notation will be used.

Y for *Y*ncome

D for effective *D*emand

F for entrepreneur's wind*f*all

These expressions are in terms of money. Income and effective demand in terms of the wage unit will be written Y_w and D_w.

The *quasi-rent* (Q) from a given output of finished goods we have already defined in chapter 4 as being the excess of the expected sale proceeds of the goods over their prime cost (NW).[1] Thus the sum of the quasi-rent and prime cost of a given output is equal to the effective demand for it, i.e. $D = Q + NW$, which may also be written $D_w = Q_w + N$.

II

Now, a firm's capital equipment being given, there is, each day, the question of the train of employment to be set going that day which will maximise the firm's quasi-rent. Under normal assumptions of competition etc. the condition of maximum quasi-rent will be satisfied by a volume of employment such that the prime cost of the marginal employment will be equal to the expected sale proceeds of the resulting increment of product. For the sake of simplicity and clearness of exposition, we shall, therefore, assume in what follows that we are dealing with this case; though a complete exposition (which would lead us beyond our present subject) must, of course, take account of, and adapt the argument to, the well-known exceptions to it. We shall assume, that is to say, that employment will be carried to a point at which $\Delta D_w = \Delta N$, and that $\dfrac{d D_w}{d N}$ is the real wage.

Furthermore, in the normal case we must assume decreasing returns for a given capital equipment. This condition is usually defined in terms of output; but interpreted in terms of our units it means that, as N increases, the increase in N will be less [more?] than the increase in D_w, i.e. that $\dfrac{d D_w}{d N}$ (which measures the real wage) decreases with N.

Now so long as ΔD_w is greater than ΔN it will pay the entrepreneurs to increase their demand for employment; and so long as $\dfrac{d D_w}{d N}$ is greater than the marginal disutility of labour it

---

[1] We are here identifying prime cost with labour cost which is not strictly correct, but is, I think, a legitimate simplification of this stage of the argument.

will pay workers to increase their offer of employment. Thus the volume of employment can come to equilibrium either because ΔD_w would be less than ΔN if employment were to be further increased, or because no more labour is forthcoming at a real wage not greater than $\frac{d\,D_w}{d\,N}$. The reader will remember that according to the classical theory, $\Delta D_w = \Delta N$ for *all* values of N, so that the volume of employment always comes to equilibrium at the point at which $\frac{d\,D_w}{d\,N}$ is equal to the marginal disutility of labour. We, however, are envisaging the possibility that in general ΔD_w is *not* equal to ΔN, so that a limit may be set to a further increase of employment by the fact that for the values of N in excess of a certain figure ΔD_w would be *less* than ΔN.

Thus the innovation of the present theory is, at this stage, purely negative. Its significance will depend on our establishing our contention that there is, in general, only one level of output at which equality holds between marginal prime cost and the anticipated price, so that under competition the aim of maximising profit will cause entrepreneurs to choose that level of employment for which this equality holds. Only if the equality held good, as the classical theory assumes, for all levels of output, would it be true that there is nothing to check the increase of employment except an inability on the part of entrepreneurs to obtain the services of a greater quantity of the factors of production; which would mean (for reasons discussed already) that entrepreneurs would choose that level of output for which the marginal product of a unit of labour has a value equal to the marginal disutility of a unit of labour.

The above is, of course, subject to the qualification that different classes of enterprise do not, in fact, respond equally in the degree in which they modify the employment they offer to equal changes in the effective demand for their product, since they are not all working under the same conditions of supply. Thus the same aggregate effective demand may correspond to different levels of employment according to the way in which it is distributed between different classes of enterprise. This will be a matter for subsequent discussion, which I mention at once only to avoid premature criticism. But at the present stage of the argument I shall abstract from it and assume that all firms have similar employment functions, so that aggregate employment is a simple function of the aggregate effective demand measured in terms of the wage unit.

7 CONSUMPTION GOODS AND INVESTMENT GOODS

We have mentioned in passing that, whilst all production is with a view to consumption, finished goods fall into two classes according as the effective demand for them depends predominantly on expectations of consumers' demand or partly on expectations of consumers' demand and partly on another factor conveniently summed up as the rate of interest.

The precise meaning of the rate of interest will be examined in [a later] chapter. But there is no risk of misunderstanding if we distinguish at once between those decisions to produce a finished product which depend on an expectation of consumers' demands at a date so near at hand that interest charges cannot materially affect the value at the dates when the prime costs are to be incurred (to be called the 'present value') of the prospective sale proceeds from the ultimate consumer, and those which depend (directly or indirectly) on an expectation of consumers' demand at a date sufficiently far off for these charges to be significant.

We define *consumption goods*, therefore, as goods the effective demand for which depends on expectations as to the expenditures of ultimate consumers at a near date; and *investment goods* as goods the effective demand for which depends on expectations as to the expenditures of ultimate consumers at a date sufficiently remote for interest charges to be significant.

In the standard case, in which the rate of interest is zero,

428

there is for any given article an optimum interval between the average date of import and the date of consumption, at which costs will be at a minimum;—a shorter process of production will be less efficient technically, whilst a longer process will also be less efficient by reason (e.g.) of storage costs and deterioration. If, however, the rate of interest exceeds zero, a new element of cost will be introduced which increases with the length of the process, so that the optimum interval will be shortened, whilst at the same time the supply of the article will have to be curtailed until the effective demand per unit has increased sufficiently to cover the increased cost—a cost which will be increased both by the interest charges and also by the diminished efficiency of the shorter method of production. If, moreover, the rate of interest is negative, it will be profitable to produce now for further categories of prospective consumers' demand which otherwise would fall, even with a zero rate of interest, short of the cost.

Now whether prospective consumers' demand is or is not translated into current effective demand depends partly on the price which consumers are expected to pay for a given article at the date at which the demand is to be satisfied, partly on the degree of probability attaching to the expectation, and partly on the rate of interest at which the future sale proceeds have to be discounted when comparing them with present costs. Prospective demand will be catered for, i.e. will become effective up to the point at which the price consumers are expected to pay, discounted for risk and interest, is equal to the marginal prime cost of the output in question.

Thus an increment of employment will not be undertaken unless it is expected to be accompanied by an increment of consumers' demand at such dates that, discounted for risk and interest, there is an increment of effective demand at least equal to the marginal prime cost of the increment of employment.

This is probably not the clearest approach to the fundamental idea of this book; but it may help the reader in the long run if we approach it gradually and from various angles as opportunity offers. If, however, he finds the above perplexing, let him pass on. The strict purpose of this chapter is limited to dividing finished goods into the two categories of consumption goods and investment goods. Consumption goods, we should add, do not cease to be consumption goods on the above definition merely because they fail, through miscalculation, to be consumed at the intended date and are temporarily added to stock for consumption at a later date;—consumption goods are those with the decision to produce which considerations of the rate of interest did not significantly enter.

Unless we are to limit consumption goods to services directly rendered to a consumer, it is evident that the distinction between consumption goods and investment goods is a matter of degree. There is, in a sense, an arbitrary element in fixing the precise point of division. Into which category does a motor car fall? Into which does a house fall? I should reckon a motor car as a consumption good and a house as an investment good. But if we apply our line of division consistently, no theoretical confusion will ensue from the fact that others might draw the line of division differently.

8 INVESTMENT AND SAVING

The capital wealth of the community consists in the provision for future consumption already made in the shape of natural resources, the capital equipment of finished goods, and the stock of unfinished goods in process. Its content is perpetually shifting. Some part of current employment is directed towards increasing provision for the future, and some part of current consumption exhausts a provision previously made. Its current valuation is also shifting in accordance with the shift of expectation.

It is obvious, therefore, that an attempt at a quantitative comparison of the eventual real capital after the elapse of an interval of time with the initial real capital, in order to discover by what *net* amount it has been increased or diminished, would involve a problem insoluble except in special cases, of the quantitative comparison of non-homogeneous items.

The following quantities, however, can be calculated unequivocally:—

(1) The value of the goods newly finished during a specified interval of time, which we will call a year, and retained as part of the capital stock to provide for future consumption together with the excess in the value of the eventual working capital over the value of the initial working capital, which we shall call the current *gross investment* and designate by I.

(2) The value of the aggregate initial equipment of natural resources and finished goods together with the working capital in the shape of unfinished goods, taken at the prices ruling at the beginning of the year, which we shall call the *initial capital assets* and designate by A_1.

(3) The value of the aggregate eventual equipment of natural resources and finished goods together with the working capital in the shape of unfinished goods, taken at the prices ruling at the end of the year, which we shall call the *eventual capital assets* and designate by A_2.

The difference between A_1 and A_2 will be due to three factors, namely: (i) the amount of gross investment during the period; (ii) the wastage of initial capital through its fruition in facilitating production during the period whether for consumption or investment, and (iii) the change in the value of capital existing both at the beginning and at the end of the period due to a shift in expectation. I doubt if there is any strict statistical method for distinguishing between (ii) and (iii), though it might be possible to do so by means of some hypothetical calculation. But whilst it would be necessary to make this calculation, if we have to distinguish between something which we could call the current *net* investment of the period due to the excess of current gross investment over capital wastage and what we might call the capital windfall gain or loss of the period due to a shift of expectation, the distinction is not strictly required for our present purpose. If, nevertheless, for some purpose of statistical or historical description, we wish to speak of *net* current investment after allowing for wastage as distinct from changes in the value of capital due to causes other than wastage, the most convenient course may be, I think, to regard each finished capital asset as having a rate of wastage allowance attached to it at the beginning of its life sufficient to account for its initial cost over the course of its existence, and unalterable subsequently by reason of its premature obsolescence or temporary disuse, or changes in its value. This may seem rather artificial, but it has the advantage not only that it is additive from one period to the next, but that the wastage allowance gradually wipes off capital windfall, which will, on the above definition, always be zero in the long period. The matter is, in any case, merely one of accounting or descriptive convenience.

It is more important, before we pass on, to point out a certain element of weakness in our definition of gross investment as given above, namely that the gross investment during $n_1 + n_2$ days regarded as a single unit may be, for either of two reasons, unequal to the gross investment during the first n_1 days *plus* the gross investment during the ensuing n_2 days, regarded as two separate units. For a product finished during the first n_1 days and used up during the ensuing n_2 days drops out of the first calculation but not out of the second; whilst a change occurring in the second part of the period in the value of a product finished but not used in the first part drops out of the second calculation but not out of the first. For this reason, it was necessary, if our definition was to be free from this difficulty, that we should define investment with reference to specific intervals of time which we call years. Thus the gross investment over two years must be calculated by adding together the result of separate calculations for each of the years and not as the result of a single calculation for the two years taken together. It has, therefore, this element of arbitrariness in it, analogous to the arbitrariness of the distinctions between finished goods and unfinished goods and between consumption goods and investment goods, as already made.

All these arbitrary distinctions, however, are only arbitrary in a highly *a priori* sense. For from another point of view they are not arbitrary at all, but are made (like many similar distinctions in economics) so as to correspond to our actual psychology and ways of behaving and deciding and to enable us to answer the concrete questions which are likely to be asked. If we had reason to expect that a different set of lines of division would be more appropriate to our psychology of behaviour and decision, we should have to draw them differently. But the nature of the reasoning would be the same. Our analysis remains logically sound if it applies unequivocally wherever we draw our lines of division provided we draw them consistently. Moreover *none* of these quasi-arbitrary lines of division are relevant to the operative cause-factor, i.e. to effective demand. The magnitude of effective demand, which is what matters, is the same wherever the above lines of division are drawn. We are, in the above, in the realm of *ex post facto* results, of which the only importance (in our present context) lies in their influence on subsequent decisions. Our reason for bringing in actual gross investment is because the actual rate of current gross investment, calculated in some such way as the above, is an important influence in practice on the current expectation of the prospective rate of gross investment in the near future.

Having made these distinctions as clearly and as emphatically as we can, we shall in what follows frequently drop the distinction between 'gross investment' and 'effective demand based on an expectation of gross investment', leaving the reader to supply the more exact phrase himself if he desires and supplying it ourselves where there is an ambiguity. And similarly as regards the distinction between the expected consumption and the actual consumption. We shall, indeed, designate the two constituents of effective demand as effective investment demand and effective consumption demand. But I hope that it will not lead to misunderstanding if we often drop into the less cumbrous expressions and, indeed, go one step further, speaking of 'investment' *sans phrase* where we mean 'gross investment'.

The reader should not overlook the fact that in the above definition I have included in actual investment the investment of working capital due to an increase in the unfinished consumption goods in process whereas when we are dealing with expectation the increased production on consumption goods is attributed to effective consumption demand and not to effective investment demand. Thus, when we are using our shortened phraseology, employment directed to increasing the stock of unfinished consumption goods is reckoned as due to consumption and not to investment. In any case, I now consider that in my *Treatise on Money* I overestimated, as a result of the insufficient attention given in that book to the distinction between actual and anticipated demand, the importance of transitional changes in the stock of unfinished consumption goods. For actual consumers' demand, which arises out of an unforeseen increase in the current volume of employment, will mainly spend itself in the absorption of floating stocks, which is a form of disinvestment and an entrepreneur's windfall,[1] and will not be much reflected in a further effective demand associated with secondary increase in current employment. In so far as the depletion of stocks leads to a subsequent activity to replenish them up to a normal level, the employment thus caused is properly attributed to investment, since normal stocks fall under the description of investment goods.

.   .   .   .

[Pages 8 and 9 of the original draft have not survived]

Thus capital wastage which is not currently repaired or replaced only matters in so far as it influences what individuals choose to regard as the 'sinking fund' appropriate to it during the period, meaning by this the sum which they feel impelled to

---

[1] It is true that this temporary entrepreneur's windfall may often prove misleading in practice and be a fruitful source of subsequent miscalculation.

434

set aside out of the sale proceeds of output as not available on principles of sound finance for expenditure on current consumption. In other words, depreciation allowances made and regarded as a part of gross saving, which we must now proceed to define. Gross investment, which includes replacements and repairs as well as new investment but ignores capital wastage which is not replaced, and gross saving, which includes sinking funds set aside now to provide whether at once or subsequently for capital wastage, are the fundamental quantities.

III

There can be no doubt as to what we ordinarily mean by the amount of an individual's savings over any period, namely the difference between his current income and his current consumption; and there is no reason why we should depart from this usage for the purposes of theoretical analysis or when we extend the term from individual saving to aggregate saving. Since, therefore, our definition of *saving* must correspond to our definition of *income*, the only doubt about the meaning of saving flows from the doubt about the meaning of income.

So far as the labour or prime factors of production are concerned, there is no serious ambiguity as to what we mean by their earnings or income. But we have seen that in defining the money income of entrepreneurs and capitalists there is more difficulty. Three alternatives present themselves. We might mean by their income the inducement in the shape of long-period expectation which led them to set up the existing capital equipment. Or we might mean the inducement in the shape of short-period expectation which leads them to employ their capital equipment for the particular output which constitutes the real income of the period. Or we might mean (in some sense) the realised sale proceeds from this particular output.

In my *Treatise on Money* I defined income in a manner which approximated to the first[1] of these three senses. This use of terms

---

[1] Not quite, because I defined income as the inducement which would now be required in order that the equipment now in use should be created if it did not already exist.

was received, however, with reluctance or misunderstanding by many readers; and, apart from this, I am now satisfied, as I have explained above, that the advantage lies with the third of the above senses for *income*, whilst availing ourselves of the expression *effective demand* for the second of them.

Thus, as a corollary of my definition of gross income, I now define *gross saving*, whether for an individual or for the community, as a whole, as the excess of gross income over consumption. If we denote saving by S and consumption by C, it follows that $S = Y - C$.

In truth, however, the conception of *saving* will no longer play the important part in our present argument which it played in my *Treatise on Money*. For the same ideas can be more conveniently handled by means of the inverse of saving; namely *consumption*. However we may prefer to define income, the sum of saving and consumption must be taken as equal to income. Thus it comes essentially to the same thing to take *income* and *consumption* as our fundamental quantities, as to take *income* and *saving*.

Readers, however, who have accustomed themselves to the definitions of my *Treatise on Money*, must be warned of a confusing consequence of the change in terms now introduced. In that book an important rôle was played by the *difference* between investment and saving. But with our new definitions saving and investment will always, and necessarily, be *equal*. It may be useful, therefore, at this stage to link up the old argument with the new. According to the present argument, the volume of employment (and consequently of output and real income) is fixed by the entrepreneur under the notion of seeking to maximise his quasi-rent. The volume of employment which will maximise his quasi-rent depends on the schedule of effective demand,—which, again, depends on the entrepreneur's expectations of the sum of the sale proceeds resulting from consumption and investment respectively on various hypotheses. In my *Treatise on Money* the concept of changes in the excess of investment over saving as there defined was a way of handling changes in quasi-rent, or rather, since I did not in that book distinguish clearly between expected and realised results[1]—in entrepreneurs' profits. I there argued that change in the excess of investment over saving was the motive force governing change in the volume of output. Thus the new argument, though (as I now think) it was made more accurate and instructive, is no more than a development of the old.

Expressed in the language of my *Treatise on Money*, it would run:—the expectation of an increased excess of investment over saving, given the former volume of employment and output, will induce entrepreneurs to increase the volume of employment and output. Both arguments depend on the discovery, if it can be called such, that an increase in the sum of consumption and investment will be associated with an increase in entrepreneurs' profit and that the expectation of an increase in entrepreneurs' profit will be associated with a higher level of employment and output. The significance of both lies in their attempt to show that the volume of employment is determined by the efforts of the entrepreneurs to maximise the excess of investment over saving as defined in my *Treatise on Money*.

IV

As in the case of investment, it is again gross saving, not net saving, that matters; i.e. the saving, corresponding to the gross investment which is an ingredient in effective demand, must include what entrepreneurs choose to set aside as depreciation allowances and capital sinking funds and the like. This may be a serious factor in the situation in a non-static economy during a period which immediately succeeds a lively burst of investment in long-lived capital. For even if our estimate of net saving falls to zero, there may still be a large amount of gross saving which

---

[1] My method then was to regard the current realised profit as determining the current expectation of profit.

can only be absorbed by new investment, as distinct from repairs and replacements; since, although the previous investment is wearing out with time, the date has not yet arrived for spending anything approaching the correct depreciation allowance on actual repairs and renewals. This, again, is a reason why a burst of investment is likely to be succeeded by a slump unless corrective measures are taken, since the depreciation allowances and sinking funds brought into existence by the burst of investment lead to a large augmentation of gross saving which cannot readily be matched by an equally great gross investment, and this forces incomes down until it is offset by negative saving in some other direction. Sinking funds are apt to withdraw expenditure from consumption long before the demand for expenditure on replacements (which they are anticipating) comes into play; i.e. they diminish current effective demand and only increase effective demand in the year in which the replacement is actually made. In a static society this would average itself out. But not so in the world in which we live.

For example, in Great Britain at the present time (1934) the substantial amount of housebuilding and of investment by local authorities and public boards in the previous decade has led, in accordance with the principles of 'sound' finance, to an amount of sinking funds being set up far in excess of any present requirements for expenditure on repairs and renewals; with the result that even if net private saving were to sink to zero, it would be a severe task to restore full employment in the face of this heavy volume of statutory saving by public and semi-public authorities, entirely dissociated from any corresponding new investment.

Consumption—to repeat the obvious again—is the sole end and object of all economic activity. Opportunities for employment are necessarily limited by the extent of effective demand. Effective demand can be derived only from present consumption or from present provision for future consumption. The consumption for which we can profitably provide in advance cannot be pushed indefinitely into the future. We cannot provide for future consumption by financial expedients but only by current physical output. In so far as our social and business organisation separates financial provision for the future from physical provision for the future so that efforts to secure the former do not necessarily carry the latter with them, financial prudence will be liable to destroy effective demand and thus impair well-being, as there are many examples to testify. The greater, moreover, the consumption for which we have provided in advance, the more difficult it is to find something further to provide for in advance, and the greater our dependence on present consumption as a source of effective demand. Yet the larger our incomes, the stronger, unfortunately, is our propensity to withhold our income from present consumption. So, failing some novel expedient, there is, as we shall see, no answer to the riddle, except that there must be sufficient unemployment to keep us so poor that we are disinclined to set aside more gross savings than the equivalent of the physical provision for future consumption (including replacements) which it pays to produce today.

9 THE FUNCTIONS RELATING TO EMPLOYMENT, CONSUMPTION AND INVESTMENT

Effective demand is made up of the sum of two factors based respectively on the expectation of what is going to be consumed and on the expectation of what is going to be invested. But the effective demand determines the volume of employment, and the expectations of consumption and investment are themselves not independent of the volume of employment. Thus the demand which is actually effective can only be arrived at by considering the functional relationship between different levels of effective demand and the corresponding quantities of employment to which they would lead; and, on the other hand, the functional

439

relationships between different quantities of employment are the corresponding volumes of consumption and of investment.

The first of these functional relationships I shall call the employment function and we shall study it in detail in [a later] chapter. Here it must be sufficient to mention it. $D_w = F(N)$ is the employment function, where an effective demand equal to D_w leads to N units of labour being employed.

The second and third functional relationships I shall call the propensities to spend and to invest; and of these we shall begin the study in the next two chapters, though we shall have to break off the discussion of the latter before we have got very far, in order to undertake a long but necessary digression on the theory of the rate of interest.

In defining these functions we have to decide which of the factors determining the actual consumption and investment in various hypothetical sets of circumstances we are to regard as constituting the propensity itself, and which to treat as the variables of the functional propensity. The choice must depend, of course, upon which factors we shall usually be regarding as variable in our subsequent analysis; though we shall not in any way be precluded from regarding the propensity itself as subject to change.

I propose to regard the available skill and quantity of labour, the available technique and quantity of equipment, the disutility of labour, suspension and risk, the sound [?social] and economic structure including the forces (other than our variable set forth below) which determine the distribution of income, and the motives affecting the readiness to consume which I shall distinguish in chapter 10 under the category 'subjective', as being the factors which constitute the propensities themselves; and to regard as the variables of these functions (*a*) the actual quantity of employment, (*b*) the rate of interest, and (*c*) the state of confidence or long-term expectation of quasi-rent. Of these we have defined (*a*) already whilst (*b*) and (*c*) will be introduced in chapter 11 and further discussed in Book III.

Subject to these explanations, the propensity to consume may be expressed by the functional relationship

$$C_w = f_1(N, r, E)$$

which means that C_w will be the amount of consumption measured in wage units when real income is what results from an amount of employment N, and when r is the rate of interest and E the state of long-term expectation. This could equally well be written

$$C = Wf_1(N, r, E),$$

where C is the consumption measured in money and W is the wage unit measurement in money. It follows that a change in the amount of consumption measured in wage units can only be due to a change either in the propensity to spend, or in the quantity of employment, or in the rate of interest, or in the state of long-term expectation.

Similarly, the propensity to invest is expressed by the functional relationship

$$I_w = f_2(N, r, E),$$

which means that a volume of employment N, a rate of interest r, and a long-term expectation E will lead to an amount of gross investment of a value I_w measured in wage units. This expression could be written equally well in the form

$$I = Wf_2(N, r, E),$$

where I is the amount of investment measured in money. We shall argue in what follows that, given the propensities to spend and to invest, consumption will depend mainly on N and investment mainly on r and E. Thus the simplified expressions

$$C_w = f_1(N) \text{ and } I_w = f_2(r, E)$$

may sometimes be legitimate.

Both C_w and I_w are to be interpreted in this context in terms of expectation, i.e. as the expected rates of consumption and investment. Hence it follows that $D_w = C_w + I_w$. Thus the level of employment, given the propensities to spend and to invest, is given by the value of N which satisfies the equation

$$F(N) = f_1(N, r, E) + f_2(N, r, E).$$

10 THE PROPENSITY TO SPEND

Although the analysis of the subjective factors which determine the propensity to spend itself raises no point of novelty, it will be useful, with a view to the subsequent argument, to remind ourselves of what they are. But it may be sufficient if we give a catalogue of what are usually the more important, without enlarging on them at any length.

There are, in general, eight main motives or objects of a subjective character which lead individuals to refrain from spending out of their incomes:—

(i) To build up a reserve against unforeseen contingencies;

(ii) To provide for an anticipated future relation between the income and the needs of the individual or his family different from that which exists in the present, as, for example, in relation to old age, family education, or the maintenance of dependants;

(iii) To enjoy interest and appreciation, i.e. because a larger real consumption at a later date is preferred to a smaller immediate consumption;

(iv) To enjoy a gradually increasing expenditure, since it gratifies a common instinct to look forward to a gradually improving standard of life rather than the contrary, even though the capacity for enjoyment may be diminishing;

(v) To enjoy a sense of independence and the power to do things, though without a clear idea or definite intention of specific action;

. . . .

[Page 2 of the original has not survived.]

increasing income, which, incidentally, will protect the management from criticism, since increasing income due to accumulation is seldom distinguished from increasing income due to efficiency;

(iv) The motive of financial prudence and the anxiety to be 'on the right side' by discharging debt and writing off the cost of assets ahead of, rather than behind, the actual rate of wastage and obsolescence.

Since, moreover, it is the *gross* rate of saving which is relevant, we have to add to the above motives, both in the case of individuals and of institutions, the object of making financial provision against the gradual wastage and obsolescence of existing assets. The strength of this motive, apart from its prudential aspects, will mainly depend on the quantity and character of the capital equipment. But it will also depend in some degree on the degree to which this equipment is being *used*, i.e. some part of it is a function of the quantity of employment. It is a question, therefore, whether to include saving of this kind in the propensity to save itself as being a characteristic of the general economic environment which we are taking as given, or whether to regard it as saving which depends on the variable N. Perhaps the most convenient course is to regard normal financial provision for wastage and obsolescence as influencing the propensity itself, reckoning any excess or deficiency from normal associated with fluctuations in employment as positive or negative saving (as the case may be) depending on the variable N.

Corresponding to these motives favouring positive saving, there are also operative at times motives which lead to negative saving. Several of the motives towards positive saving catalogued above as affecting individuals have their intended counterpart in negative saving at a later date, as, for example, with saving to provide for family needs or old age. In circumstances in which the habit of purchasing annuities prevails negative saving of this type may be important. On the other hand, an increased purchasing of annuities as a result of a fall in the rate of interest must be regarded, not as a change of propensity, but as a change depending on the variable r. Death duties, which are not made good out of income, represent negative saving, (but *not* negative investment or a reduction of the national wealth as often stated in popular controversy) if the state spends the proceeds as revenue.

Now the strength of all these motives will vary enormously according to the institutions and organisations of the economic society which we presume, according to habits formed by race, education, convention, religion and current morals, according to present hopes, according to the scale and technique of capital equipment, and according to the prevailing distribution of wealth and the established standards of life. In the argument of this book, however, we shall not concern ourselves, except in occasional digressions, with the results of far-reaching social changes or with the slow effects of secular progress. We shall, that is to say, take as given the main background of subjective motives to saving and to consumption respectively, which determine the propensity to spend, and consider the effect of changes in certain other factors regarded as variables in this context, which affect the amount which the community actually spends without there having been any change in the propensity to spend.

II

The 'objective' or variable factors of which we have to take account are, mainly, (*a*) the quantity of employment N as determining the aggregate current rate of real income, (*b*) the rate of interest r, (*c*) the state of 'confidence' or long-term expectation E.

Not only is the first of these influences the most important in itself, being in the short period much more variable than the second, but it is the relevant influence if we are considering what changes in saving will be appreciable *cet. par.* with a given change in employment.

444

For a man is disposed, as a rule, to save more, as his real income increases. This is especially the case if we have short periods in view (as in the case of the so-called cyclical fluctuations of employment during which habits, as distinct from more permanent psychological propensities, are not given time enough to adapt themselves to changed objective circumstances). For a man's habitual standard of life usually has the first claim on his income, and he is apt to save the difference which discovers itself between his actual income and the expense of his habitual standard; or, if he does adjust his expenditure to changes in his income, he will over short periods do so imperfectly. Thus a rising income will often be accompanied by decreased saving, on a greater scale at first than subsequently.

Apart from short-period *changes* in the level of income, it is also obvious that a higher absolute level of real income will be favourable, as a rule, to saving. For the satisfaction of the immediate primary needs of a man and his family is usually a stronger motive than the motives towards accumulation, which only acquire effective sway when a margin of comfort has been attained. These reasons will lead, as a rule, to a greater *proportion* of income being saved, as real income increases. But whether or not a greater proportion is saved, we can take it as a fundamental psychological rule of any modern community that, when its real income is increased, it will not increase its consumption by an equal *absolute* amount, unless a large and unusual change is occurring at the same time in other factors. We shall find, indeed, in Book IV that the stability of the economic system essentially depends on this rule prevailing in practice. This means, in terms of functional relationship

$$C_w f_1(N), \text{ that } \Delta C_w < [\Delta] N, \text{ or } \frac{d f_1(N)}{d N} < 1.$$

A decline in the level of employment is likely, if it goes far, to produce negative saving not only by individuals and institutions using up the financial reserves which they have accumulated in

445

better times, but also by the government, which will be liable, willingly or unwillingly, to run into a budgetary deficit or will provide unemployment relief, for example, out of borrowed money.

Thus, when employment falls to a low level, spending will decline by a smaller amount than that by which income has declined, by reason both of the habitual behaviour of individuals and also of the probable policy of governments; and this—as we shall see—is the explanation why a new position of equilibrium can usually be reached within a modest range of fluctuation. Otherwise a fall of income, once started, might proceed to extreme lengths.

The influence on the distribution of wealth, and through this on spending, of the more or less permanent solid structure of the community has been taken into account in the propensity to spend itself. But in so far as fluctuations in the quantity of employment or in the rate of interest have short-period effects on distribution, we must remember that, for much the same reasons as those which apply in the case of changes in the aggregate of real income, a more unequal distribution of this aggregate will be unfavourable to spending and a more equal distribution favourable. I doubt, however, if this factor is important in practice. For there is a certain amount of evidence available which suggests that the distribution of current income between the different factors is often surprisingly stable. If a more careful statistical enquiry were to confirm this, it would indicate that the employment function tends to approximate to a straight line drawn at a constant angle, which on the basis of the figures I have seen would be in the neighbourhood of $45°$, between the axes of the quantity of employment and the effective demand measured in wage units; since these would be a nearly constant ratio ($= D/NW$) between ΔD and $\Delta N, W$, i.e. between ΔD_w and ΔN.[1]

---

[1] So far as the long period is concerned, this may reflect the fact that for more than a hundred years past the long-term rate of interest has fluctuated round a stable level. (Cf.

The influence on spending of the second factor, namely, changes in the rate of interest, is open to more doubt. For the classical theory of the rate of interest, which was based on the idea that the rate of interest was the prime factor which brought the supply and demand for savings into equilibrium, it would be convenient to suppose that expenditure or consumption is *cet. par.* negatively sensitive to changes in the rate of interest, so that any rise in the rate of interest would appreciably diminish consumption. It has long been recognised, however, that the total effect of changes in the rate of interest on present consumption is complex and indeterminate, being dependent on conflicting tendencies, since some of the subjective motives towards saving will be more easily satisfied if the rate of interest rises whilst others will be weakened. Over a long period substantial changes in the rate of interest probably tend to modify social habits considerably, thus affecting the actual propensity to spend,—though in which direction it would be hard to say, except in the light of actual experience. The usual type of short-period fluctuation in the rate of interest is not likely, however, to have much *direct* influence on spending either way. There are not many people who will alter their way of living because the rate of interest has fallen from 5 to 4 per cent. Indirectly there may be more effects, though not all in the same direction. Perhaps the most important influence on expenditure operating through changes in the rate of interest depends on the effect of these changes on the appreciation or depreciation in the price of securities and other assets. For it would not be reasonable for a man to keep his capital and his income in quite separate compartments of his consciousness. If he is enjoying a windfall increment in the value of his capital, it is natural that his motives towards current spending should be strengthened; and

the figures given in my *Treatise on Money*, vol. 2, pp. 198–201 [*JMK*, vol. VI, pp. 178–80].) But in the short period the comparative stability, if it really exists, must reflect a tendency for *average* real prime cost to increase at about the same rate as output, as supply equipment is gradually brought into use. The question needs, however, more consideration than I can give it here.

weakened if he is suffering capital losses. Apart from this last factor, the main conclusion suggested by experience is, I think, that the short-period influence of the rate of interest on individual spending out of a given income is secondary and relatively unimportant, except, perhaps, where unusually large changes are in question.

The third variable, namely that of long-term expectation, which has, as we shall find, an important influence on invest-ment, need scarcely be taken into account separately from the rate of interest in its influence on expenditure. Much of what we have just said about the effect of changes in the rate of interest applies to changes in the state of long-term expectation. In particular it is their influence in raising or lowering the values of securities and other assets which chiefly affects the rate of expenditure.

III

We are left, therefore, with the conclusion that changes in the rate of spending on consumption (measured in wage units) mainly depend on changes in the rate at which income (also measured in wage units) is being earned. That is to say, there will, as a rule, be no serious error in assuming

$$\Delta C_w = \frac{df}{dn} \Delta N.$$

This means no more, however, than that the *direct* influence of changes in the rate of interest on consumption is small, not that the total influence is small. Quite the contrary. For aggregate saving must be equal to aggregate investment; [a] rise in the rate of interest (unless it is offset by an opposite change in long-term expectation) will diminish investment; hence a rise in the rate of interest will decrease incomes to a level at which saving is decreased in the same measure as investment; which means that incomes will decrease by a *greater* absolute amount than investment; so that, when the rate of interest rises, the rate of consumption must decrease. We can be sure, therefore, that if a rise in the rate of interest causes investment to decrease, both saving and consumption will also decrease, on a balance of consideration.

Thus, whilst it may be the case that a rise in the rate of interest might cause individuals to save more *out of a given income*, we can be quite sure that a rise in the rate of interest (assuming no favourable change in long-term expectation) will decrease the actual aggregate of individual savings. The same line of argument can even tell us by how much a rise in the rate of interest will *cet. par.* decrease incomes. For incomes will have to fall (or be redistributed) by just that amount which is required, with the existing individual propensities to spend, to decrease savings by the same amount by which the rise in the rate of interest will, in the existing propensity to invest (*vide infra*), decrease investment.

The rise in the rate of interest might induce us to save more, *if* our incomes were unchanged. But if the higher rate of interest retards investment, our incomes will not, and cannot, be unchanged. They must necessarily fall until the declining capacity to save has sufficiently offset the stimulus to save given by the higher rate of interest. The more virtuous we are, the more determinedly thrifty, the more obstinately orthodox in our national and personal finance, the more our incomes will have to fall when interest rises or long-term expectation continues adverse. Obstinacy can bring only a penalty and no reward. For bow the knee we must. It is a *logical* necessity.

Thus, after all, the actual rates of aggregate saving and spending do not depend on precaution, foresight, calculation, improvement, independence, enterprise, pride or avarice. Virtue and vice play no part. It all depends on whether the rate of interest is or is not favourable to investment, after taking account of our long-term expectations.[1]

[1] In one or two sentences of this chapter we have tacitly anticipated ideas which will be introduced in the next chapter.

II THE PROPENSITY TO INVEST

We have seen in the preceding chapter that in any given set of circumstances the amount of consumption expenditure at each level of employment is mainly determined by the current propensity to spend. But the actual consumption is not determined until the level of employment is ascertained; and for this we must show what determines the rate of gross investment, a matter upon which, so far, we have no sufficient light. As soon as we know the rate of investment, however, the propensity to spend will tell us what level of employment will be consistent with this rate of investment; for the level of employment at which entrepreneurs will aim will be that level which, with the given propensity to spend, will lead to an expected excess of income over expenditure equal to the given rate of investment.

It is usually supposed that the motive to invest mainly depends on the rate of interest; but upon what the rate of interest itself depends is more obscure. I will discuss this motive in Book III. But meanwhile it will help the discussion forward if we begin it here, starting, so to speak, from the other end.

The motive to invest will obviously depend—to begin our analysis at its obvious beginning—upon whether the producers of investment goods expect to be able to sell their finished output at a satisfactory margin over its prime cost. In accordance, that is to say, with our general principles (and subject to the usual qualifications), the output of investment goods will depend on the effective demand for them taken in conjunction with their conditions of supply.

When a man buys an investment or capital asset, what is it that he is buying? The answer is that he is buying the right to the series of prospective quasi-rents, which he expects to obtain from selling its output after deducting the running expenses of obtaining that output; the prospective quasi-rents being the anticipated series of annuities representing the expected excess of sale proceeds over prime cost during the life of the asset.

Upon what will these expectations be based? Upon prospective estimates of four factors:—(i) the scarcity or abundance of the type of asset in question, i.e. the supply of assets capable of rendering similar or equivalent service, (ii) the strength of the demand for its product compared with the demand for other things, (iii) the state of effective demand during the life of the assets, taken in conjunction with the shape of the supply function of the asset's product, and (iv) changes in the wage unit during the life of the asset. If, as in our present context, we are concerned with the quasi-rents of assets generally rather than with the quasi-rents of particular assets, we can substitute for (ii) the demand for goods and services, in the provision of which the services of capital play a relatively large part. Similarly we can substitute for (i) the scarcity or abundance of assets in general, i.e. of capital, relatively to output as a whole. We might also sum up (i) and (ii) and one aspect of (iii) as the prospective marginal physical productivity of capital in terms of goods in general; whilst another aspect of (iii) and (iv) can be summed up as the prospective value of money. At any rate, the four factors taken together determine an anticipated annual yield in terms of money over a series of years.

This answers our question. The purchaser of an investment is buying the prospect of a series of annuities over a term of years. The four factors which determine this prospect constitute what in chapter 9 we have called the *state of long-term expectation* (how long depending, of course, on the life of the asset) and have been denoted by E.

But whilst this tells us what the purchaser of an investment is buying it does not tell us the present value of what he is buying, i.e. what it will be reasonable for him to pay for it, cash down. Yet it is the purchaser's estimate of its present value which determines the effective demand for the investment, and is, consequently, what we need to know in our present context.

It is here that the rate of interest comes in. The series of annuities in prospect can be compared, after allowance for risk, with the series of annuities over a similar term which could be obtained by lending out a sum of money at interest. It follows that the present value of the prospective quasi-rents which an asset will yield during its life is determined by, and is equal to, the sum of money which could be lent out at interest with equal risk to produce an equivalent annual yield. To be quite accurate, the prospective quasi-rents of an asset during the course of its life constitute a series of fluctuating annuities; but if we are given the complex of rates of interest at which money can be lent for various periods, it is a matter of simple arithmetic to calculate the present value of this series of fluctuating annuities.

To sum up:—if Q_r is the prospective quasi-rent from an asset at time r and d_r is the present value of £1 deferred r years, then $\Sigma Q_r d_r$ is the present value of an asset summed over its effective life. The series Q_r, which can be called the prospective yield of the investment, depends on the state of long-term expectation E; whilst the series d_r is given by the rate of interest. The two together determine the schedule of effective demand for investment; and, finally, the supply from this for investment goods fixes the amount of employment which will be actually directed towards investment corresponding to any given effective demand.

Let the reader note that this method of valuation offers us no means, merely by knowing an asset's prospective yield, with an allowance for risk, to deduce either the rate of interest or the present value of the asset. We must, from some other source, ascertain the rate of interest, and only then can we value the asset by 'capitalising' its prospective quasi-rents. The marginal physical productivity of the investment in terms of goods in general together with the value of money over the relevant period will determine the yield of the investment; but the present value of this yield will depend on the rate of interest.

In a realistic study the effects of these two factors naturally run together. But in our theoretical analysis we shall do well to separate them. The state of long-term expectation which determines the prospective yield of an investment will be examined, therefore, in the next chapter; whilst the more fundamental problem of the rate of interest will be considered in Book III. Only at the conclusion of Book III, when we have finished our study of the rate of interest, will it be possible to take a comprehensive view of the propensity to invest in its actual complexity.

II

We have seen that a new investment has a prospective yield in the sense of a series of annuities or quasi-rents $Q_1, Q_2 \ldots$, which it is hoped to gain from it on the successive occasions of using it over the course of its life. Given this series of annuities (and assuming, so as to avoid unnecessary complications, that the prospective yield will accrue at an even rate over the life of the investment) there is some rate of interest on the basis of which the present value of the series of annuities will be equal to the supply price of the investment. The rate thus arrived at we may call *the marginal yield (or efficiency) of capital.*

It follows, of course, that new investment will be pushed to the point beyond which the marginal yield of capital would fall short of the current rate of interest. For this point determines the margin of profitability between the alternatives of using money to purchase an investment and of lending it at interest. Thus the existence of the alternative use for money of lending it at interest has the effect of keeping capital goods sufficiently scarce to ensure that their marginal yield does not fall below the rate of interest.

For this reason it is much preferable to speak of capital as having a quasi-rent depending on its marginal yield than as being *productive*. The only reason why an asset yields up during its life services having an aggregate value greater than its supply

453

price is because it is *scarce*; and it is scarce because of the competition of the rate of interest.[1]

I sympathise, therefore, with the pre-classical doctrine that everything is *produced* by labour, aided by what used to be called art and is now called technique, by natural resources which are free or cost a rent according to their scarcity or abundance, and by the results of past labour, embodied in investments, which also command a price according to their scarcity or abundance. In so far as we can identify prime costs with labour costs, the modern doctrine according to which price tends to equal marginal prime cost is, in a sense, a return to the old conception of the wage unit as the ultimate standard of value. It is preferable to regard labour, including, of course, the personal services of the entrepreneur and his assistants, as the sole factor of production, operating in a given environment of technique, natural resources, capital equipment and effective demand.

To pursue the question further at this point would anticipate unduly the subject of [a later] chapter. Before leaving, however, this part of our analysis into the nature of investment, I should like to emphasise again that it is the scarcity of capital which is the essential reason why it has a yield. It is true that some lengthy or roundabout processes are efficient. But so are some short processes. Lengthy processes are not efficient because they are lengthy, any more than short processes are efficient because they are short. Some lengthy processes would be very inefficient, for there are such things as spoiling or wasting with time.[2] With a given labour force there is a definite limit to the quantity of labour embodied in roundabout processes which can be used to advantage. Apart from many other considerations, there must be a due proportion between the amount of labour employed in making machines and the amount employed in using them. The

---

[1] The conditions in which the rate of interest is a necessary deterrent will be distinguished in Book III from those in which it is an unnecessary deterrent,—the distinction depending upon whether the current rate of interest is above or below the rate which is compatible with full employment.

[2] Cf. Marshall's note on Böhm-Bawerk, *Principles*, p. 583.

ultimate quantity of value will not increase indefinitely, relatively to the quantity of labour employed, as the processes adopted become more and more roundabout.

Moreover there are all sorts of reasons why various kinds of services and facilities are scarce and therefore expensive relatively to the quantity of labour involved (measured, let us say, in time-effort). For example, smelly processes command a higher reward, because people will not undertake them unless they do. So do risky processes. But we do not go about saying that smelly or risky processes are efficient as such, or that the smellier or riskier we make them the more efficient they will be. Indeed, quite the contrary. Other things being equal, a process is inefficient by reason of its being smelly or risky. And so with a lengthy process. An invention is efficient if it is able to shorten the process by which a given amount of labour produces a given amount of product. Not all labour is accomplished in equally agreeable attendant circumstances; and conditions of equilibrium require that articles produced in less agreeable attendant circumstances (characterised by smelliness, risk or the lapse of time) must be kept sufficiently scarce to command a higher price.

In considering, therefore, why capital assets normally produce in the course of their life aggregate quasi-rents greater than their original supply price, the essential question for enquiry is why such assets are so scarce that the demand for them, at a price spread over their life equal to their cost of production, is greater than their supply.

The answer usually given is to the effect that the aggregate quantity of assets (or capital) must in equilibrium be kept down to a sufficiently low figure to prevent its marginal efficiency from falling below the marginal disutility of 'waiting'. But the marginal disutility of 'waiting' depends on the aggregate of employment (subject to certain qualifications already mentioned which we need not stop to repeat). If aggregate employment has stood for a long time past at or near full employment, then there is a sense in which it is legitimate to say that the scarcity of capital is due to the disutility of 'waiting'. If, on the other hand, the supply of capital has been kept below its potential level by aggregate employment falling, often or chronically, below full employment, then it is more instructive to attribute the scarcity of capital primarily to the factors which have caused chronic unemployment, namely—if the analysis of this book is correct— to the rate of interest having been too high, having regard to the existing propensity to invest, to allow an amount of investment which is consistent, having regard to the existing propensity to save, with full employment.

In such circumstances, therefore, it is reasonable to maintain that it is the rate of interest which has kept the quantity of capital in check. In any case, if the propensity to spend is always such as to afford some margin of savings when employment is full, and if the rate of interest is kept low enough to allow full employment for a sufficient length of time, the quantity of capital must eventually increase up to a point where its marginal efficiency is tending to zero; i.e. capital would cease to be scarce. The question why capital is scarce is, therefore, best regarded as being, in the long run, the same question as why the rate of interest exceeds zero.

Another indication of Keynes's position in the middle of 1934 comes from his visit to the United States. In the course of his visit in May and June Keynes set out 'a brief economic analysis of the American situation for my own satisfaction' and gave a paper based on it to the American Political Economy Club on 6 June 1934. The members of this club included R. M. McIver, W. C. Mitchell, J. M. Clark, A. D. Gayer, J. Angell, J. Schumpeter, A. A. Berle, A. H. Hansen. As the first draft of this paper antedated his visit to Washington, Keynes may also have used it in his discussions with officials he met there, as well as those he saw in New York.[1]

[1] The people involved may have been, if one follows Keynes's list of appointments: H. Feis, J. B. Eastman, R. Tugwell, W. W. Rieffler, G. Terborgh, L. Beam, E. Meyer, C. Snyder.

5 June 1934

I. THE THEORY OF EFFECTIVE DEMAND

In a given situation output and employment cannot increase unless entrepreneurs anticipate an increased effective demand and prepare to meet it. A false expectation will obviously improve matters for a short time, and indeed go a short way to justify itself. Nevertheless, unless the expectation is in fact soundly based, it will soon be revised. We can therefore, for practical purposes, concentrate on expectations of changes in effective demand which are soundly based.

To fix our ideas let us consider the case of increasing effective demand, leaving the converse case on one side. Increased effective demand can only be *initiated* in one or other of three ways.

(1) A greater readiness of the public to spend on consumption out of a given income. This may be called an *increased propensity to consume* and must be distinguished from an increased actual consumption consequent on an increased income. An increased propensity to consume means an increased consumption out of a given income.

(2) From what may be called an *increased propensity to invest*. This might be caused either by an improvement of confidence in regard to future returns on investments, or by a lower rate of interest which induces an increased expenditure on building up capital assets, or by governmental loan expenditure.

(3) From an increase in working capital in anticipation of increased consumers' demand.

The third of these need not be considered separately since it is simply a factor which intensifies the effects of either of the other two during the period in which a community is moving from a lower scale of output to a higher scale of output. When the higher scale has been reached and no further increase is in prospect, this factor ceases to operate, since it is the *increment* of working capital in passing from one scale of output to another

457

which matters, not merely a higher absolute volume of working capital after it has been attained.

Now in the United States at the present time little is to be hoped on the first head as an initiating impulse, though it might well be that an initial success in raising production to a higher level would have the effect of increasing the propensity to consume, first of all by removing intangible fears which inhibit consumption, and partly (after an interval of time) because debts incurred during the slump would have been sufficiently cleared up.

Thus, the first impulse must come from an increased propensity to invest. It is convenient to include under this head any expenditure by the government, financed not out of taxation, but by borrowing, whether the expenditure is to build up capital assets or merely for relief purposes. It would, however, come to the same thing if we were to include increased relief expenditure under the heading of an increased propensity to consume. It is purely a matter of words and classification, but I believe that the course of convenience lies in treating all governmental loan expenditure as being equivalent to investment,—at least when we are considering short-run effects.

The evidence seems to show that investment through private agencies has not increased, and may even have declined, since the present administration came into office. We have, therefore, to concentrate on the statistics of governmental loan expenditure if we are to ascertain whether effective demand is tending to increase. Strictly speaking, these statistics should, of course, also cover state and local loan expenditure, as well as the expenditure of the central government. If these statistics are lacking, our conclusions must be subject to a corresponding margin of error. But I am told that for the period since July last total loan expenditures not financed by advances from the federal government have been so small as not to affect the picture.

The first datum, therefore, in investigating the present situation, is the monthly figure of governmental loan expenditure; corrected, so far as possible, by any available figures or impressions as to local governmental loan expenditure or investment by private enterprise or changes in the propensity to consume.

II. THE PRINCIPLE OF THE MULTIPLIER

The importance of governmental loan expenditure as an initiating factor flows from the fact that the train of events does not stop there. The initial increase in effective demand thus set up spreads itself in gradually widening circles, so that the total eventual increase in effective demand resulting from a given rate of governmental loan expenditure may be several times as great as the volume of the initiating factor itself. The factor relating the magnitude of the two is what I call the *multiplier*.

Now it is evident that if we were accustomed to spend on consumption the *whole* of any increment of income, the multiplier would become, in the course of time, indefinitely great. For let us suppose governmental loan expenditure of $100 million in the first month, continuing at the same monthly rate indefinitely. Assuming for convenience that the time lag between the expenditure of an increment of individual income and its re-expenditure on consumption by those who sell to the first recipients of the new incomes is about a month, in the second month the increase of effective demand would be $100 million in respect of the re-expenditure of the previous month's increment of income, plus $100 million from the current loan expenditure, making $200 million in all. Similarly, in the third month, the figure would be $300 million and in the fourth month $400 million etc. That is to say, an increment of $100 million a month in the *rate* of loan expenditure would, if it were continued indefinitely, lead under the above hypothesis to an increment of effective demand gradually increasing without limit.

In practice, however, there are many reasons why the multiplier is very much lower than has been assumed in the above example. When the incomes of individuals and corpora-

459

tions making up the community are increased, it is an invariable psychological rule that they do not in fact spend the whole of it on increased consumption. It is safe to say that when incomes are increased the absolute amount saved is also increased, though not necessarily in proportion. After a slump, moreover, a large subtraction is necessary on account of the fact that an employed man does not increase his consumption by the whole amount of his wages. He was previously kept alive by public relief or by living on his own saving, or by sponging on his friends, or by getting into debt with tradesmen. Thus, if a man previously out of work obtains productive employment at a wage of $20 a week, he is very far from increasing his consumption by $20 and it is only the excess of his consumption when at work over what he and his family consumed when he was out of work, which enters into the multiplier.

There are further many other subtractions to be made. For example, some of the expenditure would be directed toward imported goods (in the case of Great Britain this is of course large, since we import most of our food). Such expenditure will increase effective demand in the world as a whole, but not in the particular country under observation. It is also quite likely that governmental loan expenditure will divert resources which would otherwise have been employed by private enterprise— though only to a slight extent until full employment is being approached.

Thus on each occasion of re-expenditure a certain percentage of the previous expenditure does not take effect in increasing effective demand, so that the force of the multiplier gradually wears itself out and aggregates to a moderate finite figure instead of being indefinitely large as we first suppose.

It is, indeed, only by rather rash guesswork that one can arrive at the final figure of what the multiplier is likely to be. My own belief is, however, that whilst accuracy is unobtainable in the present state of our statistics, one can make a fairly reliable shot at the order of magnitude. In the case of Great Britain I have studied the matter as carefully as the nature of the data permits. I am clear that the multiplier cannot be less than 2, meaning by this that each month's governmental loan expenditure will cause an additional secondary expenditure of equal amount, not wholly in the next month, but in the course of subsequent months as a whole. This is a very conservative estimate and the figure might be as high as 3, though the actual figure will of course depend upon the particular circumstances of the moment.

In the United States I should suppose that the multiplier must be higher than in Great Britain, partly because relief expenditure is not on such a generous scale as in Great Britain in relation to normal income (more like a third in U.S.A. as compared with nearly a half in Great Britain), so that the increase in effective demand which results from putting a man to work at a normal wage is greater in the United States than in Great Britain; and partly because the subtraction in respect of expenditure on imported goods is much less. On the other hand, the tendency of corporations to save increased profit instead of distributing it to shareholders to be expended by them is probably greater in the United States. On a balance of considerations I should be extremely surprised if the multiplier in the United States is less than 3, and it is probably appreciably higher.

It must be understood that I mean by this not that effective demand will be increased forthwith by three times the amount of the loan expenditure, but that governmental loan expenditure of $1·00 in a given month will cause an increase in effective demand of, say $3·00, spread over the ensuing months. That is to say, continuing governmental loan expenditure at the rate of $1·00 a month will, after a due interval, increase the national income by $3·00 a month, which increase will be maintained so long as the loan expenditure continues or is replaced by private investment. The effect of the multiplier is gradual and cumulative, and probably does not reach its peak for at least a year. Thus, governmental loan expenditure of $1 million a day continued for 365 days is much greater in its effect on the daily rate of effective demand on the 365th day than a similar expenditure continued only for 30 days on the daily effective demand at the end of that period.

It should be noticed that we are measuring effective demand *in terms of money*. Thus increased effective demand does not mean that production will increase in the same proportion. If there were full employment, increased governmental loan expenditure would be purely inflationary and would simply spend itself in higher prices without increasing production. When, however, there are surplus unemployed resources of labour and equipment, the effect of increasing effective demand is partly to increase output and employment and partly to raise prices. The proportion between the two effects will depend upon the elasticity of supply and the tendency of costs to rise with increasing output. So long as the labour and capital equipment of the country are greatly underemployed, the effect will be mainly seen in increased employment. After the bottlenecks are being reached by reason of certain key specialised resources being fully employed, the effects will spend themselves to a greater extent in raising prices. When a point has been reached at which the whole of the labour and capital equipment of the community are employed, further increases in effective demand would have no effect whatever except to raise prices without limit. A situation of true inflation will have been reached, and the precepts of 'sound' finance will have at last become valid.

III. PRELIMINARY DATA FOR THE APPLICATION OF THE ABOVE PRINCIPLES TO THE UNITED STATES IN 1934

Many data are lacking for estimating the changes in effective demand for recent months. This is particularly the case if we desire to make an absolute comparison with dates some time back. I am of the opinion, however, that there is a basis of comparison over recent periods. For the big variables have been governmental loan expenditure, working capital (meaning by this unfinished goods in process) and inventories (meaning by this more or less finished goods in stock). As to the first of these, broad conclusions can be reached. Changes in the index of production are fairly good indicators of the second; leaving only the third to be guessed on the basis of general impression. Construction contracts financed otherwise than by the Government have not been large enough at any recent date to enter materially into the picture; I am told that the same is true of state and local expenditure financed by loans exclusive of those advanced by the federal government.

The best method of proceeding, therefore, appears to be first of all to estimate the figure of true governmental loan expenditure month by month and then to compare the magnitude of this with the observed results in terms of production, employment and income as indicated by the available statistics.

After consulting with those who are in the best position to advise me, I have come to the conclusion that the safest method to estimate monthly governmental loan expenditure is the following:

1. To ignore receipts and expenditures within the normal budget since these will approximately balance over the year as a total.

2. To regard as true governmental loan expenditure the outgoings of C.W.A., P.W.A., the Federal Emergency Relief Organisation and various miscellaneous emergency outgoings of the same character;—in fact the aggregate of the emergency expenditure as shown in the monthly accounts of the Treasury, exclusive of the expenditures of the Reconstruction Finance Corporation, other than for relief.

3. To add to the total reached under '2', 50 per cent of the non-relief expenditures of the Reconstruction Finance Corporation. A small part of these expenditures do indeed represent direct expenditure by government but the major part is in the

nature of refinancing money paid out to various institutes and individuals. Some part of it will be used by the latter to get themselves more liquid, and part for new expenditure. For the earlier months when the bulk of the loans were to banks, the best guess might be different. But for recent months perhaps the R.F.C. outgoings might be regarded as causing an immediate increase of effective demand of half their amount. I believe, however, that for the last six months a somewhat different guess would not greatly affect the result.

4. To add (or subtract) from the above the excess of A.A.A. payments to farmers over receipts from processing taxes. These two are expected to balance approximately over a period of time, but temporarily they may move widely apart. Up to date processing taxes have substantially exceeded outgoings. I am told that from now on this tendency will be reserved and that when a position of equilibrium has been reached, payments to farmers will as a rule exceed the receipts from processing taxes.

5. To take a three months' moving average of the total last arrived at.

The result is as follows:

Up to September 1933 the figure was running at about $100 million monthly or, say, 3 per cent of the national income. Since then the figures are as follows:

	Three months' moving average ($ million)	Actual for month ($ million)
October 1933	123	156
November 1933	158	212
December 1933	231	325
January 1934	369	569
February 1934	422	373
March 1934	435	363
April 1934	345	310
May 1934	311	260

Thus the economic situation in the period since October has had the benefit of increased governmental loan expenditure at a rate equivalent to about 9 per cent of the national income, whilst the substitution of a rising index of production for a falling index means that there was also a substantial increase of working capital during that period. As regards inventories, I am not in a position to make a good guess. It would seem natural to suppose that they were at a high figure in July and August, fell off during the rest of the year, rose again during the late winter and early spring and may still be rising now.

The average monthly governmental loan expenditure in the first five months of 1934 is about $380 million or about 11 per cent of the national income.

If the multiplier is 3, we should expect that the effect of the above increased expenditure would be to increase incomes by 24 per cent (8 × 3), if it is continued for a sufficient period; whilst a multiplier of 4 would give 32 per cent. In fact the expenditure has not yet continued long enough to get the full benefit of the multiplier, whilst the multiplier has probably been much less than its eventual figure during the early months, owing to the tendency to use the initial increment of income to pay back debts of various kinds.[1] Thus, on balance, one would expect the effect on the national income, from what has happened to date, to be much less than its eventual effect after governmental loan expenditure had continued for the rest of the year on the same scale. On the other hand, the effect of the multiplier has undoubtedly been temporarily accentuated by the growth of working capital and inventories. This factor may become weaker as time goes on.

Let us now compare the above hypothetical conclusions with the actual change in production, income and employment.

Between March 1933 and July of the same year, the Federal Reserve Adjusted Index of Production rose sharply from 59 to 100. The experts of the Federal Reserve Board tell me that this index has recently been a little unsatisfactory in that it has tended to exaggerate the extent of movements being based on certain specially sensitive items. Thus the figure of 100 over-

---

[1] My final conclusion was that the multiplier may have been as low as 2 for the earlier increments of income as such large amounts have been used to repay debts both by corporations and by individuals.

states what happened. Nevertheless, it is clear that there was an enormous expansion. This however, had no sound basis except in business optimism. During that period the administration had done nothing but make a little progress towards liquefying the bank situation. This would prevent the position from getting worse and even make it a little better, but it would certainly not justify such a leap forward in the index of production. Thus actual effective demand fell short of anticipations and the subsequent period had to experience the force, not only of revised expectations, but also of the absorption of the excessive inventories produced during the period of optimism; for so far there had been no increase in investment either through governmental or through private agencies. The low point of the reaction seems to have been reached last November when the index of production had fallen from 100 to 72. In subsequent months it has climbed steadily as follows: November, 72; December, 75; January 1934, 78; February, 81; March, 84; April, 85; and it is likely that when the May figure is available it will not be materially different from the figure of March and April. It will be seen that this expansion coincides with the period of governmental loan expenditures and an actual increase in effective demand. It may well be that once again business optimism has gone a little ahead of the facts and that by May the effective demand, though increased, has been over-estimated. Probably this is a small factor as compared with last year. From the period, therefore, from November to April—and May could be substituted for April without much inaccuracy—the index of production rose 18 per cent. As already explained, this probably a little over-states the truth but not much. During the same period payrolls increased by 17 per cent, adjusted sales of department stores by 17 per cent, employment by 15 per cent and car loadings, if we substitute comparison between October and March for one between November and April which looks misleading, also by 16 per cent. It seems therefore fairly safe to say that the volume of industrial and mining production increased 15 per cent, whilst the Bureau of Labor index suggests that prices rose 3 per cent, making a total increase in industrial income of 18 per cent. Other items making up the national income have not increased so much. I have as yet no comprehensive figures for the aggregate result such as I hope to get. Meanwhile I am inclined to think that national income in the aggregate increased during this period by about 15 per cent.

Having regard to the various cross-currents and the short length of time which has elapsed since the level of governmental loan expenditure commenced, I consider this conclusion reasonably concordant with our previous hypothetical results.

Now let us endeavour to glance into the future.

So far as I can ascertain governmental loan expenditure will not increase and may diminish in June and July below the May level. Having regard, however, to the likelihood of agricultural relief and to the fact that in June the A.A.A. may be paying farmers in respect to hog products much in excess of their receipts from processing taxes, I am now inclined to think that the aggregate will not fall below and may even slightly exceed the May level.[1] In August and September P.W.A. expenditure should be increased and those months [are] likely to show a better total. It is as yet too soon to make predictions for the later months of the year, which will largely depend on decisions not yet taken.

Thus I should expect the three months moving average to be not far from the May figure during June and July but more likely to fall short of it than to exceed it, rising again after that date at least to the April level. Against this the aggregate of effective demand will probably have to contend with some seasonal recession, with some absorption of inventories produced during the spring and with no further material increase in working capital in place of a rapidly increasing working capital figure. It is a precarious matter to sum up the net result. I

[1] My final conclusion was that the June three months moving average would closely approximate to the May figure.

should say that the country is already in the middle of a minor recession, which is likely to carry the national income in June and July 3 per cent, and perhaps 5 per cent below the May level, but after that there should be a recovery. If the monthly average of government disbursements could be raised to $400 million I should have no doubt whatever that there would be a substantial recovery by the autumn. On the other hand, if these disbursements should fall away to say $200 million it is even more certain that there should be a serious relapse.

I am almost prepared to prophesy an autumn recovery. I should not be surprised to see it carry through fairly well into the spring, apart from seasonal factors. The real doubt in my mind relates to the later period. Sooner or later government expenditures are pretty certain to sag away; but the hope would be that normal business investment would be ready to take their place before that happens. To estimate the likelihood of this happening and to suggest means of securing it, would take me beyond the field of this paper. At present it is obvious that nothing is to be hoped from business. The widespread lack of confidence, the high rate of interest to those who wish to borrow and the high relative cost of durable goods, stand in the way.

The object of this memorandum is, however, not to make forecasts but to provide a theoretical background against which to judge the course of events as further information becomes available. My main purpose is to refute the prevailing idea that governmental loan expenditure is on so small a scale as to be a minor factor in the situation. I am sure that it will be a dominant factor over the ensuing months. The whole progress of events will be governed by the figure of governmental loan expenditure. The difference between $200 million a month and $400 million a month will be the difference between depression and recovery.

[There then followed a series of statistical tables providing the raw data which he had used in his calculations. These are not reproduced here.]

Finally, by mid-1934, one suspects that Keynes began to think seriously of a preface. One early fragment of what must have been a preface survives. It is of interest for its discussion of the role of controversy in economics.

In some respects this is a very controversial book. There are many passages in which I attack with vehemence the views of others, and it is unlikely that I shall escape reprisals. I should, therefore, like to say a little of what experience and reflection have led me to feel about controversy between economists.

It is notorious that controversy in economics is peculiarly provocative of irritation. The two teachers under whom I was first brought up in the subject, Marshall and Prof. Pigou, have both held that controversy in our subject is unsatisfactory and distasteful and should be strongly deprecated. Marshall himself would practise elaborate arts of composition to avoid it, and, being not less easily provoked than other men, the needful self-control would bring him near to bursting point when he was, nevertheless, subjected to criticism. On the other hand, controversy may assist progress and be healthy in spite of being disagreeable; whilst the avoidance of it may allow the charlatan, who is commoner in economics than in the exact or natural sciences, to flourish unrebutted. Are Marshall and Prof. Pigou right? Should we compose our books as though we were the only students of the subject in the world and remain as silent under criticism as if we were deaf? Or should we go at it hammer and tongs? My own answer is equivocal.

There is a great deal to be said in favour of the attitude of Marshall and Prof. Pigou. When we write economic theory, we write in a quasi-formal style; and there can be no doubt, in spite of the disadvantages, that this is our best available means of conveying our thoughts to one another. But when an economist writes in a quasi-formal style, he is composing neither a document verbally complete and exact so as to be capable of a strict legal interpretation, nor a logically complete proof. Whilst it is his duty to make his premises and his use of terms as clear as he can, he never states all his premises and his definitions are not perfectly clear-cut. He never mentions all the qualifications necessary to his conclusions. He has no means of stating, once and for all, the precise level of abstraction on which he is moving, and he does not move on the same level all the time. It is, I think, of the essential nature of economic exposition that it gives, not a complete statement, which, even if it were possible, would be prolix and complicated to the point of obscurity but a sample statement, so to speak, out of all the things which could be said, intended to suggest to the reader the whole bundle of associated ideas, so that, if he catches the bundle, he will not in the least be confused or impeded by the technical incompleteness of the mere words which the author has written down, taken by themselves.

This means, on the one hand, that an economic writer requires from his reader much goodwill and intelligence and a large measure of co-operation; and, on the other hand, that there are a thousand futile, yet verbally legitimate, objections which an objector can raise. In economics you cannot *convict* your opponent of error; you can only *convince* him of it. And, even if you are right, you cannot convince him, if there is a defect in your own powers of persuasion and exposition or if his head is already so filled with contrary notions that he cannot catch the clues to your thought which you are trying to throw to him.

The result is that much criticism, which has verbal justification in what the author has written, is nevertheless altogether futile and maddeningly irritating; for it merely indicates that the minds of author and reader have failed to meet. This is the type of controversy, common enough even amongst the most distinguished exponents of the subject, which merits the full disfavour of Marshall and Prof. Pigou. But, of course, this does not mean that all criticism is futile, and it is dangerous, I think, to be too wary of it. Moreover a candid author surely enjoys criticism which comes from a thorough understanding of his thesis. There is no greater satisfaction than in the exchanging of ideas between minds which have truly met, leading to further discoveries and a shift of view in response to difficulties and objections.

I ask forgiveness, therefore, if I have failed in the necessary goodwill and intellectual sympathy when I criticise; and to those minds to which, for whatever reasons, my ideas do not find an easy entry, I offer the assurance in advance that they will not find it difficult, where the country to be traversed is so extensive and complicated, to discover reasons which will seem to them adequate, for refusing to follow. Time rather than controversy (I agree with my mentors) will sort out the true from the false.

After his return from America in June, Keynes remained hard at work at the book. From this period of summer revisions, we have revisions of chapters 8 and 9 of the spring table of contents and first versions of what were to become chapters 4, 5 and 11 of the completed book. As the last three bear a close relation to the final proofs, they are not reprinted here, but are dealt with in the Appendix to volume XIV. The first two are reprinted below.

Drafts of chapters 8, and 9 of the draft of the *General Theory* for the summer of 1934.

8 INVESTMENT AND SAVING

I

The capital wealth of the community consists in the provision for future consumption already made in the shape of natural resources, of the equipment of capital goods, and of the stock of consumption goods and of unfinished goods in process. Its content is perpetually shifting. Some part of current employment is directed towards increasing provision for the future, and some part of the current consumption exhausts a provision previously made. Its current valuation is also shifting in accordance with the shift of expectation. It is obvious, therefore, that an attempt at a quantitative comparison of the eventual real capital after the elapse of an interval of time with the initial real capital, in order to discover by what *net* amount it has been increased or diminished, would involve a problem, insoluble except in special cases, of the quantitative comparison of non-homogeneous items.

It follows, however, from what we have already explained, that it is *not* this more or less incalculable net increment of the community's wealth that we mean by *investment*. By current investment we mean that part of current income which is not consumed. We began with the gross sale proceeds of current output in the shape of newly finished goods and services (which includes the current series of such things as houses), after deduction, of course, of the outgoings of one entrepreneur to another. We then deducted user cost from this to give us the measure of current income. If from current income we then deduct the value of what is consumed so as to give us the value of that part of current output which is neither consumed nor required to make good user cost, we are left with the measure of current investment.

Thus current investment includes the selling value of the output of currently finished capital goods, of consumption goods added to stock and of unfinished goods in process, after deduction of the user cost of the initial stock of capital goods, consumption goods and unfinished goods which have been used up during the period. Since the user cost which is deducted may be greater than the value of the new investment goods, it is conceivable that current investment may be negative.

Effective demand, however, is gross of user cost, being equal to the gross proceeds of current output, i.e. to consumption *plus* investment *plus* the user cost of current output.

The fact that it is the *gross* value of output which constitutes effective demand is a matter of great practical importance. Owing to the postponement of repairs and replacements and the gradual absorption of stocks during a slump current investment can easily decline to a figure little, if at all, above zero, in spite of the output of newly finished investment goods remaining quite appreciable. It is the practicability of not making good user cost, i.e. of making a financial but not a physical provision for it, which helps to explain the violence of the fluctuations; whilst, on the other hand, it is the impracticability of continuing this course indefinitely which is a potent factor in bringing about an eventual recovery.

That user cost has to be added to income to yield effective demand is brought out forcibly and naturally in Mr Colin Clark's 'National Income, 1924–1931'; since, as soon as he gets down to the statistical facts, it is the gross value of output, i.e. effective demand which inevitably emerges as the relevant factor. He also shows what a large part user cost normally is, of the value of new investment goods. For example, he estimates that in Great Britain, over the years 1928–1931,[1] the gross value of new investment output, user cost and current investment were as follows:

	1928	1929	1930	1931
		(£ million)		
Gross investment output	791	731	620	482
User cost[2]	433	435	437	439
Current investment	358	296	183	43

. . . .

[Pages 4–7 of the original have not survived.]

III

User cost has been *debited* to the output of new investment goods; that is to say, current investment is reckoned after deduction of user cost from the value of the output of new

---

[1] Op. cit. pp. 117 and 138.

[2] Mr Clark calls this 'the value of physical wastage of old capital'. He does not enter in detail into the problems of obsolescence etc. But his method of calculation indicates, I think, that what he is aiming at roughly corresponds to what I mean by 'user cost'. If not, the above figures must be amended accordingly.

investment goods. If, however, entrepreneurs choose to set aside in respect of depreciation allowances, capital sinking funds and the like a sum greater than the user cost, this excess must be *credited* to current saving. Thus capital losses in excess of user cost come into the picture in so far as these influence what individuals choose to regard as the 'sinking fund' appropriate to the period, meaning by this the sum which they feel impelled to set aside out of the sale proceeds of output as not available, on principles of sound finance, for expenditure on current consumption. In other words, depreciation allowances must be regarded as a part of saving. Investment includes replacements and repairs in excess of user cost as well as new investment, which includes sinking funds in excess of user cost set aside now to provide, whether at once or subsequently, for capital losses.

The fact that the whole of the financial provision, which entrepreneurs see fit to set aside against capital wastage and losses, has either to be taken off investment or added on to saving may be a serious factor in the situation in a non-static economy during a period which immediately succeeds a lively burst of investment in long-lived capital. For even if private saving falls to zero, there may still be a large amount of financial provision by entrepreneurs which can only be absorbed by new investment; since, although the existing capital equipment is wearing out with time, the date has not yet arrived for spending on actual repairs and renewals anything approaching the full financial provision which is being set aside. Thus a burst of investment is likely to be succeeded by a slump unless there are offsetting factors, since the user cost and the additional depreciation allowances and sinking funds ensuing on the burst of investment lead to a large augmentation either of disinvestment in respect of user cost or of saving by entrepreneurs which cannot readily be matched by a sufficient output of new investment goods: and this forces incomes down until it is offset by negative saving in some other directions. Sinking funds, whether or not they are in excess of user cost, are apt to withdraw expenditure from consumption long before the demand for expenditure on replacements (which they are anticipating) comes into play; i.e. they diminish current effective demand and only increase effective demand in the year in which the replacement is actually made. In a static society this would average itself out. But not so in the world in which we live.

For example, in Great Britain at the present time (1934) the substantial amount of housebuilding and of other new investments since the war has led to an amount of sinking funds being set up far in excess of any present requirements for expenditure on repairs and renewals, a tendency which has been accentuated where the investment has been made by local authorities and public boards, by the principles of 'sound' finance which often require sinking funds much in excess of actual user cost; with the result that even if private saving were to sink to zero, it would be a severe task to restore full employment in the face of this heavy volume of statutory saving by public and semi-public authorities, entirely dissociated from any corresponding new investment.

Consumption—to repeat the obvious again—is the sole end and object of all economic activity. Opportunities for employment are necessarily limited by the extent of effective demand. Effective demand can be derived only from present consumption or from present provision for future consumption. The consumption for which we can profitably provide in advance cannot be pushed indefinitely into the future. We cannot as a community provide for future consumption by financial expedients but only by current physical output. In so far as our social and business organisation separates financial provision for the future from physical provision for the future so that efforts to secure the former do not necessarily carry the latter with them, financial prudence will be liable to destroy effective demand and thus impair well-being, as there are many examples to testify. The greater, moreover, the consumption for which we have provided in advance, the more difficult it is to find something

475

further to provide for in advance, and the greater our dependence on present consumption as a source of effective demand. Yet the larger our incomes, the stronger, unfortunately, is our propensity to withhold our income from present consumption. So, failing some novel expedient, there is, as we shall see, no answer to the riddle, except that there must be sufficient unemployment to keep us so poor that we are disinclined to set aside more savings than the equivalent of the physical provision for future consumption which it pays to produce today.

IV

We have defined income as equal to the sum of investment and of consumption; and we have defined saving as equal to the excess of income over consumption. It follows that, for the community as a whole, investment and saving are necessarily, and by definition, equal. There can be no escape from this conclusion—which, after all, is in full harmony with common sense and the common usage of the world—unless we so define income[1] that it is not equal to the sum of investment and of consumption, or so define saving that it is not equal to the excess of income over consumption.[2]

[1] In my *Treatise on Money* I deliberately defined income so that it was *not* equal to the sum of investment and consumption. For I excluded from income a quantity which I there called profits (namely the excess of the actual return to the entrepreneur over the quasi-rent which would have led him to erect the amount of equipment actually in use); whereas this quantity, being a part of entrepreneurs' profits (as defined in this book), is a part of investment *plus* consumption. I recognise, however (vide, e.g. *Treatise on Money*, vol. I, p. 140 [*JMK*, vol. V, pp. 126–8], and also *passim*) that investment *plus* profits (as there defined) was necessarily equal to saving. Thus the above is a change of terminology and not a change of view.

[2] Mr Robertson has maintained a difference between saving and investment by defining today's income as being equal to *yesterday*'s consumption plus investment, so that today's saving, in his sense, is equal to yesterday's investment *plus* the excess of yesterday's consumption over today's consumption. Thus his saving exceeds his investment by the excess of yesterday's income (in my sense) over today's income; and when he says that there is an excess of saving over investment, he means literally the same thing as I mean when I say that income is falling and the excess of saving in his sense is exactly equal to the decline of income in my sense. If it were true that current expectations were always determined by yesterday's realised results, today's effective demand would be equal to yesterday's income. Thus I interpret Mr Robertson's method as an alternative attempt to

But we must not proceed from this inevitable equality to the plausible inference, which has been commonly drawn from it, that, when an individual saves, he necessarily increases investment by an equal amount. It is true that when an individual saves, he increases his own wealth. But the conclusion that he also increases aggregate wealth fails to allow for the fact that an act of individual saving may react on someone else's savings and hence on someone else's wealth. Indeed, *cet. par.* it is certain that individual saving will have this effect, except in so far as it causes a corresponding increase of investment to occur *pari passu.*

For if the increased saving is foreseen, the profits, which would have been earned otherwise from the same production of consumption goods as before, will decline by the amount of the increase;

.   .   .   .

[Pages 14–17 of the original have not survived.]

V

It follows from the above that we can analyse the transactions of the entrepreneurs either from the standpoint of their outgoings or from that of their incomings. They sell their output for $C + I + U$, made up of C from what is consumed, I from what is invested and U from what is used up.[1] Their own return Q is the excess of these sale proceeds over E, their outgoings to the other factors of production. Thus $C + I + U = E + Q$.

We have, similarly, a double analysis of the transactions of the public, first in their capacity as earners and recipients of income and secondly in their capacity as spenders for consumption and as savers for accumulation. Their aggregate income Y is made up of the income of the earners E and the income of the entre-

mine (being, perhaps, a first approximation to it) to make the same distinction, so vital for causal analysis, that I have tried to make by the contrast between effective demand and income. *Vide* Mr Robertson's article 'Saving and Hoarding' (*Economic Journal*, September 1933, p. 399) and the discussion between Mr Robertson, Mr Hawtrey and myself (*Economic Journal*, December 1933, p. 658).

[1] I am here ignoring the distinction between expectation and realised results.

preneurs $Q - U$; and they spend their income on current consumption C or retain it as savings S for the acquisition of capital assets of some kind or another. Thus

$$E + Q - U = Y = C + S.$$

We have, therefore, the following equalities by definition:

$$C + I = E + Q = Y + U = C + S.$$

VI

Is there any significant meaning in the phrase 'forced saving'?

In my *Treatise on Money* (vol. I, p. 171 footnote) [*JMK*, vol. v, p. 154 footnote] I gave some references to earlier uses of this phrase and suggested that they bore some affinity to the difference between investment and 'saving' in the sense in which I there used the latter term. I am no longer confident that there was in fact so much affinity as I then supposed. But, in any case, it is certain that 'forced saving' or analogous phrases employed more recently (e.g. by Professor Hayek or Professor Robbins) have no definite relation to the difference between investment and 'saving' in the sense intended in my *Treatise on Money*. For whilst it is not possible to say exactly what these authors mean by this term, it is evident that 'forced saving' in their sense is a phenomenon which results directly from, and is measured by, changes in the quantity of money or bank credit.

Changes in the quantity of money can, of course, in so far as they lead to price changes, cause transferences of purchasing power (or wealth) from one group in the community to another, and this (as Mr Robertson was the first to show) may react on the amounts which certain individuals choose to save. Also, if the volume of output changes, as a result of changes in the quantity of money, the proportions of the total product going to the entrepreneur and to the prime cost factors respectively with [will?] shift in the favour of the one or the other according to the elasticity of supply, and this, in turn, may affect the volume of saving both because incomes are greater and also because they are differently distributed. But such changes in the amounts saved are no more 'forced savings' than any other changes in the saving of individuals due to change in their circumstances. Moreover, as we shall see, the amount of the change in aggregate saving which results from a given change in the quantity of money is highly variable and depends on many other factors.

If, however, 'forced saving' is intended to mean the change in aggregate saving due to a change in the quantity of money, we must be told whether the *existing* rate of saving is always taken as the base; and if not, what the base is. The most reasonable definition along these lines is, perhaps, the following:—Forced saving is the excess of actual saving over what would be saved if the quantity of money were such as to maintain equality between the 'natural' rate of interest and the market rate. But even when we have reached this degree of precision, different writers mean different things by the 'natural' rate of interest.

When I wrote my *Treatise on Money*, I believed, in common with those who speak of 'forced saving', that there was a unique 'natural' rate of interest. But as we shall find in Book III this is not the case. There is, in my sense of this term, a 'natural' rate of interest corresponding to every hypothetical level of employment. Thus 'forced saving', according to the definition suggested above, still has no defined meaning, until we have specified what 'natural' rate of interest we have in mind. If we select (as would be reasonable) the natural rate of interest which corresponds to full employment, the above definition becomes:—'Forced saving is the excess of actual saving over what could be saved if the quantity of money were such as to maintain full employment.' This definition would make good sense, but a sense in which a forced excess of saving would be a very rare, perhaps a non-existent phenomenon and a forced deficiency of saving the usual state of affairs. It is, however, impracticable to give a clear account of a term which is probably not clear even in the minds of those who use it.

9 THE FUNCTIONS RELATING EMPLOYMENT TO THE INDEPENDENT VARIABLES OF THE SYSTEM

We have now reached the point where we must distinguish between what we assume as given, which factors we take as the independent variables of our system and which as the dependent variables.

I propose to regard as given the existing skill and quantity of labour available, the existing technique and quantity of equipment, the tastes of the consumer and the disutility of different intensities of labour, and of the activities of supervision and organisation, and the social structure including the forces, other than our variables set forth below, which determine the distribution of the national income.

Our independent variables (at this stage) are the propensity to spend, the marginal efficiency of capital and the rate of interest —three terms which have still to be defined.

Our dependent variables are the volume of employment and the national income (or national dividend) measured in wage units.[1] These two dependent units, however, really come to the same thing, as we shall see in a moment, though it is sometimes convenient to speak in terms of one and sometimes in terms of the other.

The factors, which we have taken as given, partly contribute towards determining our independent variables (which are not, so to speak, our ultimate atomic independent elements), but not completely. For example, we shall see that the marginal efficiency of capital depends partly on the given factors and partly on what we shall call the state of long-term expectation which cannot be

---

[1] 'Wages' in this context includes, strictly speaking, whatever enters into prime cost. We are assuming that we have some unit of the effort expended in producing current output and that the wage unit is equal to the marginal product of this unit of effort. I have suggested above ([unnumbered] p.) that different kinds of effort should be weighted in proportion to their remuneration per unit of time, the basic unit of effort being the effort of the lowest paid labour per unit of time. See [unnumbered] p. above.

inferred from the given factors. But there are certain other relevant derivatives which the given factors determine completely, so that we can treat these derivatives as being given. In particular, the given factors allow us to infer what level of national income measured in terms of wage units will correspond to any given level of employment. Within the economic framework, that is to say, which we are taking as given, the national income depends on the volume of employment, i.e. on the quantity of effort currently devoted to production, in the sense that there is a uniform correlation between the two. Furthermore, they allow us to infer the shape of what we shall call the employment functions for different types of products;—that is to say, the quantity of employment which will be devoted to production corresponding to any given level of effective demand measured in terms of wage units, the employment functions embodying the factors arising out of the physical conditions of supply.[1] Finally they furnish us with the supply function of labour (or effort);—that is to say, they tell us the maximum quantity of effort which will be available in response to any given wage unit. Thus, using the above terms, the law of diminishing return in the short period from the application of an increasing number of units of effort to a given equipment etc. means that the wage unit diminishes as employment increases; and the law of the increasing disutility of effort means that the maximum quantity of effort available for employment diminishes as the wage unit diminishes.

I have said that the three variables named above are our independent variables at this stage of the argument. But since they are not the ultimate short-term variables, we may hope to carry our analysis to a further point subsequently. Even at this stage, however, there is much to be said for regarding the motives affecting the readiness to consume, which I shall distinguish in chapter 10 under the category 'subjective', as

[1] We are ignoring at this stage certain complications which arise when the employment functions of different products have different [elasticities] within the relevant range of employment. See [an unnumbered] chapter below.

amongst the given factors of the system; since they are of a kind which as a rule (though not invariably) are unlikely to change materially within a short period of time. In this case we are left with the *two* independent variables, the marginal efficiency of capital and the rate of interest. When, however, we have carried our analysis further, we shall find that the marginal efficiency of capital depends partly on the given factors and partly on what we shall call the state of long-term expectation; whilst the rate of interest will be found to depend partly on what we shall call the state of liquidity preference and partly on the quantity of money measured in terms of wage units.

Thus eventually our independent variables will prove to be (1) the state of long-term expectation, (2) the state of liquidity preference and (3) the quantity of money measured in terms of wage units. This means that, if we take as given the factors catalogued above including the subjective factors which determine the propensity to spend, the national income (or dividend) and the quantity of employment will depend on the values assumed by the above three variables. In some contexts, however, it may be advisable to include the propensity to spend amongst the variables of the system rather than amongst the factors taken as given.

The last sentence of the previous paragraph calls attention to the importance of our emphasising that the division of the determinants of the economic system into the two groups of given factors and independent variables is, from any absolute standpoint, quite arbitrary. The division is made entirely on the basis of experience, so as to correspond to the factors, changes in which are seen to be so slow or so comparatively irrelevant as to have only a small and comparatively negligible short-term influence on our *quaesitum*, and to those, changes in which are found in practice to exercise a dominant influence on our *quaesitum*. Our object in this context is to discover what determines at any time the national income or dividend of a given economic system and (which is the same thing) its employment; which means in a study so complex as economics, in which we cannot hope to make completely accurate generalisations, the factors in which the changes *mainly* determine our *quaesitum*. Thus we begin our theoretical study with the conclusion derived from experience that changes in effective demand are what matters and we then proceed to analyse, again interspersing our logic with practical judgments based on experience, what can best be regarded as the variables chiefly significant in changing effective demand. Our final task, perhaps, is to select those variables which can be deliberately controlled or managed by central authority in the kind of system in which we actually live.

II

We can express the above symbolically as follows:—

(i) $N_1 = F_1(C_w)$ and $N_2 = F_2(I_w)$ are the employment functions for consumption and investment goods respectively where effective demands C_W and I_W for the two classes of goods lead to volumes of employment N_1 and N_2 respectively on producing them.

(ii) $C_w = Q_1(N, r, e)$ is the propensity to spend where an aggregate employment N, a rate of interest r, and a marginal efficiency of capital e lead to an effective demand C_w for consumption goods.

(iii) $I_w = Q_2(N, r, e)$ is the propensity to invest where N, r and e lead to an effective demand I_w for investment goods.[1]

Since $N = N_1 + N_2$, the volume of employment N will be determined by the equation

$$N = F_1\{Q_1(N, r, e)\} + F_2\{Q_2(N, r, e)\},$$

which may be written

$$N = f_1(N, r, e) + f_2(N, r, e).$$

We shall argue subsequently that both r and e are comparatively unimportant to C_w, so that $N_1 = f_1(N)$ approximately;

---

[1] If W is the money wage and C and I the effective demands in terms of money we have of course, $C = WQ_1(N,r,e)$ and $I = WQ_2(N,r,e)$.

also that N has not much bearing on I_w. Hence for practical purposes we can usually think in terms of the simplified equation

$$N = f_1(N) + f_2(r, e).$$

Thus since the functions F_1, F_2 and Q_2 depend on the given factors, the volume of employment N is determined when we know Q_1 the propensity to spend, r the rate of interest and e the marginal efficiency of capital;—to the further definition of which three terms we must now proceed.

The above equation is subject, of course, to the limitation that N cannot exceed full employment, since when that point is reached we can no longer make the assumption, tacitly introduced above, that the productive processes for consumption and investment goods respectively do not compete with one another for resources. It is possible, indeed, that these processes may begin to compete for resources before full employment is reached. Nor would it be difficult to make our notation take account of this. But it is not necessary with schematic equations such as the above, the only purpose of which is to elucidate general ideas.

By 7 September 1934, after a long visit from R. F. Kahn, during which, as Keynes told his mother, 'as usual he was extraordinarily helpful', Keynes wrote to Daniel Macmillan of his new book. By 13 September, he had sent the first three chapters to the printers with instructions that they should be returned in time for him to use them as texts for his lectures, now entitled 'The General Theory of Employment'.

Meanwhile, work continued on later chapters. On 18 September, he reported to Kahn:

I'm working fairly hard and have found out one or two interesting novelties. In particular, I think I've solved the riddle of how to define *income* in some sort of a *net* sense—and it comes out very near to the money value of the Prof's national dividend. The deduction from the gross sales proceeds of the output of a given equipment necessary to yield income is that part of the quasi-rent which is necessary to induce the entrepreneur not to leave his equipment idle. This works just as well when the initial equipment is a half-finished machine or a ton of copper. In other words the appropriate depreciation allowance is the sacrifice involved in using the equipment as compared with postponing its use, as estimated by the entrepreneur himself. I haven't as yet thought this through to the end, but it looks to me promising. It's only paradoxical where the equipment is highly perishable by the mere lapse of a short period of time—e.g. a bottle of port just ready to drink and no good next year.

On 27 September he gave Kahn a further report.

I am getting towards the end of the re-writing which you led me into and will show you the new way for dealing with net income in detail next term. It is clumsy in some ways but the best I have done yet.

In his lectures during the Michaelmas term, Keynes basically took his students through chapters 2–14 of the first proof version of the *General Theory*, following the text sufficiently carefully that the notes we have examined pick up quoted almost word for word, such as the references to Queen Elizabeth and Queen Victoria on page 40 of the final text. For this reason, we shall not deal with the lectures at any length and leave the reader to follow their drift in the proof changes in the appendix.

During this term, Keynes gave a public broadcast in a series entitled 'Poverty in Plenty' reflecting his current state of mind. This broadcast was reprinted in *The Listener* and, in a revised form, in the *New Republic*. The *Listener* version, which appears below, contains references to the views of other participants in the series.

The other lectures in the series were published in a volume *Poverty in Plenty* during 1935. However, Keynes refused to allow the inclusion of his talk on the grounds that 'the informal talk and the written book are totally different mediums for expressing one's ideas and should not be confused and identified' and that the idea of subsequent publication is 'likely to work to the disadvantage of the spoken word'.

From THE LISTENER, *21 November 1934*

POVERTY IN PLENTY: IS THE ECONOMIC SYSTEM SELF-ADJUSTING?

If we consider what has been said in these talks so far, it is clear, I think, that there is one point about which we all agree—a point which was rightly emphasised by Mr Henderson. The point is this. Whatever may be the best remedy for poverty in plenty, we must reject all those alleged remedies which consist, in substance, of getting rid of the plenty. It may be true, for various reasons, that, as the potential plenty increases, the problem of getting the fruits of it distributed to the great body of consumers will present increasing difficulties. But it is to the analysis and solution of these difficulties that we must direct our minds. To seek an escape by making the productive machine less productive must be wrong. I often find myself in favour of measures to restrict output as a temporary palliative or to meet an emergency. But the temper of mind which turns too easily to restriction is dangerous. For it has nothing useful to contribute to the permanent solution.

But this is another way of saying that we must not regard the conditions of supply—that is to say, our facilities to produce—as being the fundamental source of our troubles. And, if this is agreed, it seems to follow that it is the conditions of demand which our diagnosis must search and probe for the explanation. Indeed, it is, I think, fair to say that all the contributors to these talks meet to this extent on common ground. If you will examine carefully what they have told you, you will find that each one of them finds the major part of his explanation in some factor which relates to the conditions of demand. But though we, your mentors, all start out in the same direction, we soon part company into two main groups. And even within each group every one of us has a somewhat different explanation of what is wrong with demand, and, consequently, a different idea of the right remedy. Between us, perhaps, we shall succeed in giving you a fair sample of the competing opinions of the contemporary world.

I have said that we fall into two main groups. What is it that makes the cleavage which thus divides us? On the one side are those who believe that the existing economic system is, in the long run, a self-adjusting system, though with creaks and groans and jerks, and interrupted by time lags, outside interference and

486

mistakes. Of those who adhere, broadly speaking, to this school of thought, Mr Henderson lays stress on the increased difficulty of *rapid* self-adjustment to change, rightly attaching importance to the greater loss and delay involved in a change-over from one type of production to another—when changes in technique or in tastes make this necessary—in an environment where population and markets are no longer expanding rapidly; whilst Mr Brand stresses the growing tendency for outside interference to hinder the processes of self-adjustment; and Professor Robbins, to judge from his syllabus, stresses the effect of business mistakes under the influence of the uncertainty and the false expectations due to the faults of post-war monetary systems. These authorities do not, of course, believe that the system is automatically or immediately self-adjusting. But they do believe that it has an inherent tendency towards self-adjustment, if it is not interfered with and if the action of change and chance is not too rapid.

On the other side of the gulf are those who reject the idea that the existing economic system is, in any significant sense, self-adjusting. They believe that the failure of effective demand to reach the full potentialities of supply, in spite of human psychological demand being immensely far from satisfied for the vast majority of individuals, is due to much more fundamental causes. Dr Dalton stresses the great inequality of incomes which causes a separation between the power to consume and the desire to consume. Mr Hobson believes that the great resources at the disposal of the entrepreneur are a chronic cause of his setting up plant capable of producing more than the limited resources of the consumer can absorb. Mr Orage demanded a method of increasing consumer power so as to overcome the difficulties pointed out by Dr Dalton and Mr Hobson. Mrs Wootton, who is to contribute to this series next week, calls for planning, although she only half-rejects the theory of self-adjustment, having not yet reached, one feels, a synthesis satisfactory to herself between her intellectual theory and her spiritual home.

The gulf between these two schools of thought is deeper, I believe, than most of those on either side of it are aware of. On which side does the essential truth lie? That is the vital question for us to solve. That is the overshadowing problem of which these talks should make you clearly conscious, if they are to serve their purpose.

I can scarcely begin here to give you the reasons for what I believe to be the right answer. But I can tell you on which side of the gulf I myself stand; and I can give you a brief indication of what has to be settled before either school can thoroughly dispose of its adversary.

The strength of the self-adjusting school depends on its having behind it almost the whole body of organised economic thinking and doctrine of the last hundred years. This is a formidable power. It is the product of acute minds and has persuaded and convinced the great majority of the intelligent and disinterested persons who have studied it. It has vast prestige and a more far-reaching influence than is obvious. For it lies behind the education and the habitual modes of thought, not only of economists, but of bankers and business men and civil servants and politicians of all parties. The essential elements in it are fervently accepted by Marxists. Indeed, Marxism is a highly plausible inference from the Ricardian economics, that capitalistic individualism cannot possibly work in practice. So much so, that, if Ricardian economics were to fall, an essential prop to the intellectual foundations of Marxism would fall with it.

Thus, if the heretics on the other side of the gulf are to demolish the forces of nineteenth-century orthodoxy—and I include Marxism in orthodoxy equally with *laissez-faire*, these two being the nineteenth-century twins of Say and Ricardo— they must attack them in their citadel. No successful attack has yet been made. The heretics of today are the descendants of a long line of heretics who, overwhelmed but never extinguished, have survived as isolated groups of cranks. They are deeply dissatisfied. They believe that common observation is enough to show that facts do not conform to the orthodox reasoning. They propose remedies prompted by instinct, by flair, by practical good sense, by experience of the world—half-right, most of them, and half-wrong. Contemporary discontents have given them a volume of popular support and an opportunity for propagating their ideas such as they have not had for several generations. But they have made no impression on the citadel. Indeed, many of them themselves accept the orthodox premises; and it is only because their flair is stronger than their logic that they do not accept its conclusions.

Now *I* range myself with the heretics. I believe their flair and their instinct move them towards the right conclusion. But I was brought up in the citadel and I recognise its power and might. A large part of the established body of economic doctrine I cannot but accept as broadly correct. I do not doubt it. For me, therefore, it is impossible to rest satisfied until I can put my finger on the flaw in that part of the orthodox reasoning which leads to the conclusions which for various reasons seem to me to be inacceptable. I believe that I am on my way to do so. There is, I am convinced, a fatal flaw in that part of the orthodox reasoning which deals with the theory of what determines the level of effective demand and the volume of aggregate employment; the flaw being largely due to the failure of the classical doctrine to develop a satisfactory theory of the rate of interest.

Put very briefly, the point is something like this. Any individual, if he finds himself with a certain income, will, according to his habits, his tastes and his motives towards prudence, spend a portion of it on consumption and the rest he will save. If his income increases, he will almost certainly consume more than before but it is highly probable that he will also save more. That is to say, he will not increase his consumption by the full amount of the increase in his income. Thus if a given national income is less equally divided, or, if the national income increases so that individual incomes are greater than before, the gap between total incomes and the total expenditure on consumption is likely to widen. But incomes can only be generated by producing goods for consumption or by producing goods for use as capital. Thus the gap between total incomes and expenditure on consumption *cannot* be greater than the amount of new capital which it is thought worth while to produce. Consequently, our habit of withholding from consumption an increasing sum as our incomes increase means that it is impossible for our incomes to increase unless either we change our habits so as to consume more or the business world calculates that it is worth while to produce more capital goods. For, failing both these alternatives, the increased employment and output, by which alone increased incomes can be generated, will prove unprofitable and will not persist.

Now the school which believes in self-adjustment is, in fact, assuming that the rate of interest adjusts itself more or less automatically, so as to encourage just the right amount of production of capital goods to keep our incomes at the maximum level which our energies and our organisation and our knowledge of how to produce efficiently are capable of providing. This is, however, pure assumption. There is no theoretical reason for believing it to be true. A very moderate amount of observation of the facts, unclouded by preconceptions, is sufficient to show that they do not bear it out. Those standing on my side of the gulf, whom I have ventured to describe as half-right and half-wrong, have perceived this; and they conclude that the only remedy is for us to change the distribution of wealth and modify our habits in such a way as to increase our propensity to spend our incomes on current consumption. I agree with them in thinking that this would be a remedy. But I disagree with them when they go further and argue that it is the only remedy. For there is an alternative, namely, to increase the output of capital goods by reducing the rate of interest and in other ways.

When the rate of interest has fallen to a very low figure and has remained there sufficiently long to show that there is no further capital construction worth doing even at that low rate, then I should agree that the facts point to the necessity of drastic social changes directed towards increasing consumption. For it would be clear that we already had as great a stock of capital as we could usefully employ.

Even as things are, there is a strong presumption that a greater equality of incomes would lead to increased employment and greater aggregate income. But hitherto the rate of interest has been too high to allow us to have all the capital goods, particularly houses, which would be useful to us. Thus, at present, it is important to maintain a careful balance between stimulating consumption and stimulating investment. Economic welfare and social well-being will be increased in the long run by a policy which tends to make capital goods so abundant, that the reward which can be gained from owning them falls to so modest a figure as to be no longer a serious burden on anyone. The right course is to get rid of the scarcity of capital goods—which will rid us at the same time of most of the evils of capitalism—whilst also moving in the direction of increasing the share of income falling to those whose economic welfare will gain most by their having the chance to consume more.

None of this, however, will happen by itself or of its own accord. The system is not self-adjusting, and, without purposive direction, it is incapable of translating our actual poverty into our potential plenty.

To develop so fundamental a matter any further than this would obviously lead us far beyond the opportunities of this brief talk. I will add no more than this: if the basic system of thought on which Mr Henderson, Mr Brand and Professor Robbins rely is, in its essentials, unassailable, then there is no escape from their broad conclusions, namely, that whilst there are increasingly perplexing problems and plenty of opportunities to make disastrous mistakes, yet nevertheless we must keep our heads and depend on the ultimate soundness of the traditional teaching—the proposals of the heretics, however plausible and even advantageous in the short run, being essentially superficial and ultimately dangerous. Only if they are successfully attacked in the citadel can we reasonably ask them to look at the problem in a radically new way.

Meanwhile I hope we shall await, with what patience we can command, a successful outcome of the great activity of thought amongst economists today—a fever of activity such as has not been known for a century. We are, in my very confident belief—a belief, I fear, shared by few, either on the right or on the left—at one of those uncommon junctures of human affairs where we can be saved by the solution of an intellectual problem, and in no other way. If we know the whole truth already, we shall not succeed indefinitely in avoiding a clash of human passions seeking an escape from the intolerable. But I have a better hope.

Meanwhile, it is not unlikely that English principles of compromise will mitigate the evils of the situation by leading statesmen and administrators to temper the worst consequences of the errors of the teaching in which they have been brought up by doing things which are quite inconsistent with their own principles, in practice neither orthodox nor heretic, of which some signs are already manifest.

With the beginning of the year 1935, Keynes set out his view of his new book in a letter to G. B. Shaw, which grew out of the Stalin–Shaw–Wells–Keynes controversy in the *New Statesman* (*JMK*, vol. XXIV). The full letter appears in that context, but the following passages are of interest as an indication of Keynes's state of mind at the beginning of what was to be a year of controversy with economists:

From a letter to GEORGE BERNARD SHAW *1 January 1935*

To understand *my* state of mind, however, you have to know that I believe myself to be writing a book on economic theory which will largely revolutionise—not, I suppose, at once but in the course of the next ten years—the way the world thinks about economic problems. When my new theory has been duly assimilated and mixed with politics and feelings and passions, I can't predict what the final upshot will be in its effect on action and affairs. But there will be a great change, and, in particular, the Ricardian foundations of Marxism will be knocked away.

I can't expect you, or anyone else, to believe this at the present stage. But for myself I don't merely hope what I say, in my own mind I'm quite sure.

The first economist outside his immediate circle to whom Keynes showed the first proofs was D. H. Robertson, and the following correspondence ensued. In this and later correspondence concerning the *General Theory*, the references in square brackets are to the variorum guide to the drafts of the *General Theory* which appears as an appendix to volume XIV and to the final text reprinted as Volume VII.

From D. H. ROBERTSON, *January 1935*

A stationary community consists of a baker, a miller, a farmer and an ironmonger, each with attached workpeople.

The baker receives £400 weekly from sale of bread, pays £100 wages (including his own profit), pays £33⅓ to ironmonger for repair of ovens, pays £266⅔ to miller for flour.

The miller receives £266⅔, pays £100 wages, pays £33⅓ to ironmonger for repair of machinery, pays £133⅓ to farmer for wheat.

The farmer receives £133⅓, pays £100 wages, pays £33⅓ to ironmonger for repair of ploughs.

The ironmonger receives £100, pays £100 wages.

Income is £400. What is gross investment, and what is effective demand?

Is gross investment £100 (paid for maintenance of fixed capital), or is it this *plus* (£266⅔ + £133⅓) paid for maintenance of working capital, i.e. £500 in all? And is effective demand therefore £500 or £900?

The definitions suggest the former[1] answer, for as far as I can see no distinction is formally drawn between maintenance of fixed and maintenance of working capital. Yet I can hardly believe this is intended, for if it is, 'gross investment' is of course enormously more than (e.g.) Clark's estimate quoted on p. 74. (Cf. Marshall's guess, *Principles* p. 592, that gross investment, so defined, is ¼ of national *wealth*.)

[1] For 'former' J.M.K. wrote 'latter?' in pencil. [Ed.]

To D. H. ROBERTSON, *29 January 1935*

Dear Dennis,

Unfortunately I have no text (you have one and the printer the other). The following is the best I can do out of my head— but I think it is right.

(1) In two respects you don't give me enough data.

(i) Let us assume, in addition to your assumptions, that, if the ovens, machinery and ploughs had not been used, £10 would have been spent in maintaining them, and (so as to keep to the simplest case) that the result of this would have been to make them just as good at the end of the period as in the case where they are used and have £100 spent on them.

(ii) Was it necessary to spend the whole of the £100 for the sake of bread? I.e. does the whole of this sum enter into the supply price of the bread in the sense that if it were not spent, the supply of bread could not have been provided for £400? In other words, were the ovens being repaired wholly for the sake of the bread or partly for the sake of the future of the ovens?

Let us take two cases (*a*) where the whole of the £100 enters into the supply price of the bread, (*b*) where £60 only enters into the price of the bread and the other £40 need not have been spent except with a view to the future of the ovens.

You are tacitly taking case (*a*). For in case (*b*) the price of the bread is £360 (not £400).

In case (*a*)

$$B = 0,\ B' = 10,\ C = C',\ A = 400,$$

so that $U = (C' - B') - (C - B) = -10$

and $Y = A + B - U = 410$ (*not* 400).

Effective demand $D = Y' + U'$ (where Y' and U' are the expectation of Y and U)

$\qquad = 410 - 10$ (assuming $Y = Y'$ and $U = U'$)

$\qquad = 400$ (N.B. It is effective demand (not income) which is equal to 400)

and gross investment $I = 0$.

This is the answer in the particular case you put to me.

In case (*b*)

$$B = 40, B' = 10, C = C', A = 360, U = 30,$$

so that $Y = 370$,

$$D = 400 \text{ (as before)},$$

and $I = 40$.

(For in the special case when newly finished output A includes *no* investment goods, gross investment $I = B$.)

(2) The question whether the maintenance of working capital is part of gross investment is the same as the question where we draw the line between A and B. It is similar to the question whether the cost of oiling the machine is part of A or part of B. The answer makes no difference to effective demand but it does make a difference (as you point out) to gross investment, and also to income.

I give the criterion, I think, at the bottom of the first galley or top of the second of chapter 6 [vol. XIV p. 401]. It depends, as just pointed out, on whether the expense enters into the supply price of the bread. Gross investment does not include that part of repairs and maintenance which enters into the supply price of the current output of consumption goods. The bread could certainly not have been made without the flour; so that the cost of the flour is part of A. How far the repairs and maintenance are for the sake of the bread and how far for the future of the ovens and machinery is more difficult but can be answered by the above criterion.

(3) But the main point I would urge is that all this is *not* fundamental. *Being clear* is fundamental, but the choice of definitions of income and investment is not. That is why (perhaps wrongly) I have not elaborated them more. Very likely it would help to put in an example (such as the above).

But if you prefer any other definitions of income, gross investment and user cost, take them. Provided your definition of net investment (i.e. excess of gross investment over user cost) differs from mine by the same quantity as that by which your definition of income differs from mine, the argument of the rest of my book will proceed undisturbed; always provided that we agree about the measure of consumption and that income is equal to consumption plus net investment.

I give my own special definitions of Y, I and U not, so to speak, because I love them for their own sake or because they are important, but because they illustrate what concepts are involved in a clear view of the problem.

Let $Y_K U_K I_K D_K$ be my definitions and $Y_D U_D I_D D_D$ be your definitions. Then provided we agree (1) about the value of consumption C and (2) that income is the sum of consumption and net investment, it follows that

$$Y_K - I_K + U_K = Y_D - I_D + U_D (= C),$$

so that $$Y_K - Y_D = I_K - I_D = U_D - U_K;$$

and it is, therefore, still the case that $D_K = D_D$, i.e. effective demand (the fundamental concept) is unchanged and the argument proceeds as before. *Any* definitions of Y, I and U which are subject to the above conditions will do equally well. D is what matters and it is about the value of D that, I claim, there can be no room for difference of opinion.

But you have convinced me that more explanation is required. I shall re-write the passages in question.

Yours ever,

J.M.K.

From D. H. ROBERTSON, *3 February 1935*

My dear Maynard,

I've now made a wad of notes on chs. 1–18 of your book. Ch. 19 (essential properties of interest and money) I've read several times but not assimilated: perhaps I shall find in the end that it contains the key to some of my earlier perplexities. But as I've got rather behindhand with the events of this last week, and have various extraneous lectures etc. hanging over me, I think I'd better try to get my reflections on 1–18 into order this weekend, for what they're worth, and to keep 19 a bit longer.

I've found it extremely hard to see the wood for the trees, or to make up my mind where I stand about the whole thing. Some points (e.g. ch. 13) are obviously superb, in your old philosopho-economic manner: but you won't want it to be judged by them. I've tried in what follows to arrange my notes so as (I) to bring out my reactions to what I take to be your main propositions, (II) to add a collection of comments on points of detail, (III) to add a commentary on your commentary on Marshall.

Yours,

D.H.R.

I'm afraid some of the papers have fetched loose from their moorings. My references are to pencil page-numbers, not galleys.

P.S. I think I had better keep ch. 18 as well, as it's closely bound up with 19.

I. *Main propositions*

(I) '*Progressive expansions and contractions of aggregate money income' involving progressive expansions and contractions of output and employment, occur in the real world.*' This is common ground to everybody, so the interest centres on the machinery. As to this,

(i) I'm afraid I haven't altered my view that equations of the type of those on p. 63 [vol. XIV p. 424] are unsuitable for application to heterogeneous slices of time within which income is changing, because they obscure the time element. (I never liked Kahn's s[hort]. p[eriod]. method in his public works article: but it did at least allow *time* (though unspecified in amount) for the 'savings', corresponding to an act of investment financed (e.g.) by new bank money, to be elicited: whereas now, since there is no limit to the shortness of the time over which we are at liberty to apply your equations, they are simultaneous and identical.) It seems to me that the rehabilitation of the Grand Tautology takes us all back to pre-Withers, pre-Wicksell days, and obscures instead of clarifying what happens when an act of investment takes place. But you have made up your mind on this! so more important is

(ii) I am still uncertain what the lynch-pin of your new mechanism is. On pp. 19–21 [vol. XIV pp. 370–72] everything is made to turn on the difference between D, the sum for which output can actually be sold, and D', the sum for which it was expected it would be sold: and all the crimes of 'classical' economists are put down to their ignoring the possibility of this difference (which incidentally I don't think they ever have done!).

But on p. 23 [vol. XIV p. 373] D is quietly in a footnote defined in terms of expectations, as it is on p. 63 [vol. XIV p. 424]. The difference between D and

D', on which everything was to turn, has become obliterated, and D' is never heard of again.[1]

Is then the lynch-pin to be found in the difference between D and Y? That is suggested in the footnote to p. 67 [vol. XIV p. 427, n. 3], where this difference is said to be 'vital for causal analysis'. Now the difference between D and Y (p. 63 [vol. XIV p. 424]) consists partly in D (since the death of D') containing an element of expectation,[2] and partly in it containing an element of user cost. I gather from pp. 44–5 [vol. XIV p. 397] that the former element of difference is not held to be fundamental. Is it ever (up to the end of ch. 19) explained in the text *how* the latter element of difference gives rise to trouble?

I had better append here my difficulties about user cost. It is evident from your letter that I was on a completely wrong track about it. For I thought that, in my example and accepting your additional assumption that if no bread had been produced £10 would have been spent on maintenance of machines, user cost was £90, viz. the difference between what, with a given output, *has* to be spent on maintenance in order to keep the machinery up to scratch,[3] and *what would have* had to be spent for this purpose if there would be no output. For I thought that the essence of the story was that user cost enters into short-period supply price,—that your doctrine was an elaboration of Marshall's doctrine that 'extra wear and tear of machinery' does so enter. And if Colin Clark is evaluating the output of investment goods, surely he will include the whole £100 worth of new screws, spare parts etc. in his catalogue,—I don't see how he can help doing so.

But now I find (case (*b*), p. 2 of your letter) [above p. 494] that it is only that part of maintenance expenses which is *not* 'gross investment', and has no connection with user cost—viz. the £60 spent in maintaining equipment 'for sake of the bread'—that enters into short-period supply price (? or long period either).

If this is right, surely it ought to be explained (*a*) that there is no connection between the whole story of user cost and Marshall's proposition that wear-and-tear of machinery enters into short-period supply price,—for we are certainly led to suppose such a connection (p. 55, n. 1 [vol. XIV p. 411, n. 6]): (*b*) that an inventory of the net output of the construction industries, such as I take Clark and Kuznets to be compiling, will be (ignoring changes in working capital) considerably greater not merely than net investment but also than gross investment,—e.g. in case (*b*) it will be £100, not £40.

You will see that I am in a muddle about all this: and I'm not really

---

[1] At some stage this paragraph was crossed out in pencil. [Ed.]
[2] This being so, may not 'actually' be deleted on p. 19, line 8 [vol. XIV, p. 370].
[3] 'Scratch $= C = C'$.'

consoled by your concession that it's all a matter of taste and doesn't really matter to the argument: for what seems to conflict with the note on p. 55 [vol. XIV p. 411] already quoted, where the difference between D and Y seems to have taken the place vacated by the extinct difference between S and I and the extinct difference between D and D' as *the* thing of crucial importance.

(II) '*Under some conditions, authority should promote the expansion of aggregate money income by measures, e.g. open-market purchases, designed to lower the rate of interest.*' This is common ground to everybody except the extreme Hayekians,—e.g. it would, I think, be accepted by Haberler and Hansen, as well as by N. Chamberlain and M. Norman. Your chs. 14 and 17 contain a great deal of valuable argument bearing on it, worked out by means of the valuable concept of the liquidity function. I think there is little if anything *said* in these chapters with which I disagree: but I feel I should like to add that in the long run and in most communities the most important force modifying the average liquidity function for the whole community is a change in the propensity to spend on the part of the ordinary population, who do not swing about between money and debts (or assets), but having scratched together a little money look for an asset (or debt) to buy with it. I agree that in a country with a highly organised capital market a moderate increase in humdrum saving-and-investing[1] of this kind may be thwarted in its effectiveness on the rate of interest by a shift along the liquidity-curve of existing more-or-less professional holders of securities. But if the change in saving is large compared with the professional market, this change in saving will work its effect.

Am I still allowed to believe that if, of two communities similar in their general economic conditions, the inhabitants of A are in the habit of devoting $\frac{1}{6}$ of their income to the purchase of securities, and the inhabitants of B $\frac{1}{10}$, the rate of interest will be lower in the former? I *do* believe it, and I think it is compatible with the doctrine of liquidity-function, provided the latter is correctly formulated and kept in its proper place. But I think such fundamental truths are apt to be obscured by statements such as 'the rate of interest is a function of the amount of money'.

? Incidentally, to the extent that 'money' includes deposit accounts bearing interest, the theory becomes not a theory of the rate of interest but of the gap between different rates of interest, viz. the yield on Gov^t securities and the interest on bank deposits. I'm not sure even current accounts and notes aren't best regarded as bearing interest which is handed back to the bank in payment for services.

[1] In the everyday sense.

(III) '*The conditions alluded to in II are chronic and endemic in the modern world.*' I take this proposition to be the real *differentia* of the book, marking it off from your own *Treatise* as well as from most of the other literature of disequilibrium, which runs, as the *Treatise* did, in terms of fluctuations around a norm and not of chronic failure to get up to a norm. I don't see much in pre-war history to persuade me of its then truth, and incline to think that if the 19th cent. economists *had* discovered it, they would have discovered what was then a mare's nest. But I'm certainly not able to reject it *a priori* as an interpretation of the present and the probable future. I'm impressed by the evidence of slumpiness in the American boom, and by the difficulties created by certain modern changes not directly connected with the rate of interest,—the slackening of population growth, the ending of the era of geographical exploration, the tendency (cf. McKenna's speech)[1] for big combines not to come to the banks for working capital coupled with the unwillingness of the banks to provide fixed capital. And I must suspend judgment till I've got further with the interest chapter. (But incidentally one of your most impressive arguments so far for the importance of 'wasted saving', p. 75 [vol. XIV p. 438], is perfectly compatible with, and indeed requires, the ordinary view of the slump as a reaction from a preceding boom.)

(IV) Part I contains a proposition about unemployment which I don't feel sure that I've yet understood. Is it this? 'The usual condition of industry is as follows:—the money value of the marginal product of employed labour and the wage being (say) £3, large numbers of workpeople are known by employers to be available for employment at (say) £2: yet none of them finds employment, since (apart altogether from defects in organisation, in the mobility of labour etc.) monetary conditions are such that if one more man were employed, the money value of the marginal product of labour would collapse to zero.'

If this *is* the proposition, it seems to me highly implausible. Detailed comments on this part follow, pp. 6–7 [below p. 501].

II. *Detailed comments*

P. 3 [vol. XIV p. 353]. Has 'classical' theory, in *any* sense, ever tried to apply the notion of *marginal* disutility in connection with the *numbers* of workpeople? It seems to me appropriate in connection with the amount of work done by an individual, but not in connection with numbers,—no-one surely has ever suggested that the 101st man is to be conceived of as naturally lazier than the 100th man! However, I don't think the substance of your argument would be much affected if the word were omitted.

[1] To the share holders of the Midland Bank, 24 January 1935. [Ed.]

P. 7. Middle paragraph [vol. xiv pp. 357–8; *General Theory*, pp. 9–10]: that 'the productivity of the economic machine' is high does not prove that the marginal productivity of labour is high.—'Truculence' seems to me an *ignoratio elenchi*! Nobody has called it 'truculent' to try to maintain money wages when prices are falling, only at the worst pigheaded. See the very temperate statement of Robbins, *Great Depression*, pp. 82–3.

'As a rule, more labour....' I don't know what the second half of this sentence means. It *appears* to mean 'The offer of a lower wage will elicit a larger total supply of labour than does the offer of a higher wage', i.e. the supply curve of labour is 'backward-rising'. There is some plausibility in this as regards the short-period reactions of an individual in respect of hours or intensity of work, but none, surely, as regards numbers.—But perhaps the sentence means something different.[1]

Surely all that the fall in money wages, when it does occur, proves is that people *are* capable, in the light of experience, of revising their collective judgments about the disutility of labour, bringing the collective judgment into closer harmony with that which individuals have already made.

P. 9 [*General Theory*, p. 12]. 'For it is far from being consistent....' All this seems to me a complete misunderstanding,—possibly having its roots in your use of the word 'classical'. I suppose there *might* be some reason for expecting a strict Ricardian to hold the views attributed to 'classical theory', if he bothered himself about short-period problems at all: but there is none, surely, for expecting any post-Jevonian to do so. Why should one be expected to hold that short-period equilibrium, any more than long-period equilibrium, is established as it were instantaneously and by magic? What one might be expected to hold, and does hold, is that if a gap appears between market demand price and marginal prime cost for the existing level of output, output will be altered until, at its new level, market demand price and marginal prime cost are again in equality.

P. 10. Line 4 [*General Theory*, p. 12]. ... 'the proposition that labour is always in a position to determine what real wage shall correspond to full employment'. I can't see at all what this proposition means![2] In any case, I don't think it is plain whether it is being put forward as another heresy of the classical school, or as something which you yourself maintain.

Pp. 11–12 [vol. xiv pp. 364–5; *General Theory*, pp. 13–14]. I am not persuaded that all this is good history or working-class psychology. What about the big series of strikes in 1910–12 for higher money wages in face of the rising

---

[1] At some stage the last four sentences of this paragraph were crossed out in pencil and the word 'yet' added between the words 'don't' and 'know' in the first sentence. [Ed.]

[2] 'I am in a position to determine what real wage shall correspond to the maximum of employment which corresponds to a real wage of 10 loaves.' I *can't* make sense of this!

cost of living? Were the railwaymen really only thinking of their position *relatively* to the coal miners and vice versa?—I should have thought that custom, the novelty and unreliability of index numbers etc. were quite sufficient reasons for the admitted tendency of workpeople (and others) to think, within limits, in terms of money,—which, I agree, is a most fortunate fact for enabling recovery from depression.

P. 33 [vol. XIV pp. 386–8; *General Theory*, pp. 41–2]. Surely the theoretical difficulty, viz. that, as the aggregate to be measured changes, its composition also usually changes, is just the same in the case of labour as in the case of commodities,—and in *both* cases there are devices for evading or minimising it, e.g. by reweighting the components in accordance with the relative expenditure on them.

Further, from a *causal* point of view, the employment function is not a primary thing but is the resultant of the entrepreneur's expectation of the public's demand for output and[1] his knowledge of the function relating output to employment. However, if it is thus recognised to be both a short-circuit and—in the last resort—imprecise like any other index number, I don't object to it!

P. 38. line 11 [vol. XIV p. 392]. Short-term expectation is surely very much concerned with estimating the prospective demand for *intermediate* capital goods, e.g. bricks and pig-iron, which are seldom produced 'to order'.

P. 55, note; last sentence [vol. XIV p. 412 n. 1]. Surely, as argued by you earlier, there are plenty of other reasons besides non-homogeneity of equipment for the existence of increasing short-period marginal costs.

Pp. 59–60 [vol. XIV p. 419–20]. There seems to me no doubt that Marshall's quasi-rent is *net*. (i) The footnote which you say has disappeared is still present in the 8th edn,—on p. 426, where it is pointed out truly that this meaning is required in order to give a true analogy with the rent of land,—'wear-&-tear' income on machinery corresponding to *royalty* not to rent. (ii) The passage which you quote (middle of p. 60 [vol. XIV p. 420, n.]) from the note in *Principles* p. 424 seems to me to prove exactly the opposite of what you say: the present value of a machine = the discounted sum of future gross yields minus the discounted sum of future maintenance expenses: hence if we say, as Marshall does, that it is the discounted sum of future quasi-rents, that implies that by a quasi-rent we mean gross yield minus maintenance expenses.

P. 67, note [vol. XIV p. 427 n. 3]. I don't *quite* agree that 'when I say that there is an excess of saving over investment I mean literally the same thing you mean when you say that income is falling'. I intend to make a statement about the *cause* of that happening which we both now describe

---

[1] At some point, the preceding ten words were crossed out in pencil. [Ed.]

as income falling.—No doubt this is a question of 'the meaning of meaning'.

P. 75 [vol. XIV p. 438]. I don't see why it should be said that entrepreneurs' saving 'determines' private saving any more than vice versa. For (using your terminology) attempted saving by individuals will in certain circumstances reduce the incomes and savings of companies as well as of other individuals.

P. 97 [*General Theory*, p. 135]. Why Q's not P's? If you are going to define the m.e. of capital as a percentage of supply price of the asset, and compare it with the rate of interest, it is surely *net* yields which you must take. If you take Q's, the proper basis of comparison would not be with the rate of interest as ordinarily understood, but with an annuity extinguished at the same date as the machine is expected to expire. Cf. my note on your pp. 59–60.

Pp. 103–4 [vol. XIV p. 463; *General Theory*, pp. 142–3]. I have several distinct comments on this.

(i) The most fundamental is that you seem to me to be completely mis-representing poor old Fisher, whose argument is *not* that it is the rise in the rate of interest that creates windfall gains (thereby stimulating output) but the *failure of the rate of interest to rise enough* that does this. See P[*urchasing*]. P[*ower*]. of Money p. 60, where the order of events is given: (1) Prices rise: (2) 'the rate of interest rises, *but not sufficiently*' (my italics): (3) entrepreneurs are bucked up and borrow more. So on p. 232 'the adjustment of the rate of interest compensates to some extent, *but not nearly enough* (my italics), for the fluctuations in the value of money'. So he means *exactly* what you mean when you say 'the stimulus to output depends on the m.e. of capital rising relatively to the rate of interest'.

(ii) You object to the[1] theory so stated (*a*) that if the price rise is not foreseen it will have no effect on current activity, (*b*) that if it *is* foreseen, prices will rise *now*, so that there will be no prospective windfall profits: hence lenders will not be able to extort from borrowers even that partial compensation which Fisher says they do tend to succeed in extorting.

To this I reply (*a*) There will be no effect on activity *now*: but the emergence of windfall profit *now* will tend to stimulate activity in the future, on your principle that expectations are influenced largely by recently realised results. (*b*) This might be true if all 'activity' consisted of dealing, and (virtually) all costs consisted therefore of the purchase of goods physically identical with those subsequently sold. But the most important forms of activity consist in growing and making: and it is notorious that the wages and salaries which farmers and manufacturers have to pay do *not* rise in proportion to expected rises in the prices of the products which they sell.

---

[1] Or do you endorse it? You seem to me to do both.

Hence the prospects of windfall gain *do* arise. It was part of the purpose of Adarkar's and my notes[1] to make plain that the capital gain which in these circumstances Fisher says that the entrepreneur working with borrowed money will make at the expense of his creditor is simply a ghost or reflection of the income-gain which he makes at the expense of his workpeople etc. If by a speedy rise in wages etc. the latter is prevented, the former will be prevented too: and the lender, as you say, will have to sit down under the diminution in real value of his money loan. But experience shows that things do not happen so.

(iii) The last par. on p. 104 seems a non sequitur to your own argument. You have *denied* above that a *rise* in the rate of interest *stimulates* output: yet now you say that by a 'similar' process an (expected) *fall* in the rate of interest does tend to *check* output. There is no parallel to the reasoning of this paragraph in the preceding paragraphs: the proper parallel would be 'Although a rise in the rate of interest does not itself stimulate output, an *expected* rise in the rate may indirectly raise the m.e. of capital and stimulate output, because it means that equipment produced now will compete on favourable terms with equipment which will be produced later on.'

Pp. 145–6 [vol. xiv p. 487; *General Theory*, p. 193]. I can't make much of Hansen's remark, but I don't think these pages are at all a fair account of Hayek's own exposition (*Prices and Production*, 1st edn. pp. 68–75, new edn. pp. 73–85). In his own queer language he is saying that the fall in the rate of interest will so much increase the demand price for machines (in spite of the fall in the price of their products) as to make it profitable to produce more machines. He explicitly says (2nd edn. p. 74) that in a period of transition the price margins and the amounts paid as interest do *not* coincide, and that the relation between them is one of the main objects of investigation.

Your real case against H. is that he oughtn't to assume that the increase in saving will in all circumstances lower the rate of interest: but instead of making it you set up to be knocked down a proposition which he expressly disowns!

III. *Marshalliana*

I am *very* much out of sympathy with your treatment of what you call the classical and I call the modern economists! (Since I have never read Ricardo, I leave him out.)

P. 21 [*General Theory*, p. 32]. What are Marshall's descriptions of the credit cycle in *Principles* pp. 709–11 and *M[oney]. C[redit]. and C[ommerce]*.

[1] B. R. Adarkar, 'Fisher's Real Rate Doctrine', *Economic Journal*, June 1934 and D. H. Robertson, 'Industrial Fluctuation and the Natural Rate of Interest', *Economic Journal*, December 1934. [Ed.]

pp. 249–51 but studies of the fluctuations in 'effective demand'? E.g. from the former 'But though men have the power to purchase they may not choose to use it': from the latter 'Thus the desire to buy and the willingness to pay increased prices grow together:...there is a general rise in the incomes of those engaged in trade: they spend freely, increase the demand for goods and raise prices still higher'.

What is the whole monetary part of Pigou's *Industrial Fluctuations*, and of his *Theory of Unemployment*, but a study of the movements of 'effective demand'?

You never, I think, quote from the works of either of these authors dealing with the problems which you are discussing, but only from their works avowedly dealing with the broad problems of general equilibrium. The whole thing seems to me rather like criticising a work on the general astronomy of the solar system because it does not contain a theory of tides.

But granted that you are justified in doing this, and accepting your own repeated assurance that your *only* complaint against M. is that he assumes constant (not necessarily, in any ordinary sense, full) employment, you nevertheless seem to me to give the impression that you hold him guilty of 'errors' and 'mistakes', of obscurity and circular reasoning, *on his own ground*, and thus to make the nature of your charge extraordinarily obscure.[1]

I concede at once that M. is fluid in his use of the word capital (and I like Cassel's distinction between 'real capital' and 'capital-disposal', which I always use in lectures etc.). But I don't think this ever gives rise to ambiguity, certainly not in the passage in *Pr[inciples]*. 313 quoted on your p. 145 [vol. XIV p. 483] in conjunction with a definition of capital given hundreds of pages earlier. This page of yours *does* seem to me *very* captious!

Apart from this purely verbal point, M's argument seems to me quite clear and uncircular.[2] The process to which you object at the bottom of p. 138 [below p. 477; *General Theory*, p. 184] is simply the ordinary process of the theory of value. To the individual buyer of tea the price is the given thing, and the quantity bought dependent on it: but looking at it from the outside we see that the price itself is dependent on the aggregate demand schedules of buyers, taken in conjunction with the quantity available in the market. —M's warning against circularity, quoted by you on p. 101 [vol. XIV pp. 461–2; *General Theory*, pp. 139–40], seems to me simply the familiar reminder, which he constantly makes also à propos of the general theory of value and

---

[1] I think it contributes to the obscurity that the charge, and the quotations supporting it, are spread over 3 chapters, 12, 15, 16. Could it be re-arranged so to make it continuous?

[2] N.B. your first wad of quotation on p. 141 [vol. XIV p. 479] is from VI, 2, not VI, 6: on p. 143 I have marked a place where the wording has been altered in later editions,—not I think for the better.

of the theory of wages, 'don't be carried away by Jevons and the Austrians into forgetting the influence of cost of production'.—I agree that strictly the words 'taken in conjunction with the rate of interest' ought to be added where you say (p. 143 [vol. XIV p. 481]) they ought: but it is so obvious from the previous sentence that they are understood that I shouldn't have thought that any reader had ever had any difficulty in supplying them, or that their omission could possibly be taken to imply a sense of circular sin!

Is this all just Marshallolatry on my part? I really don't think so, for unlike you (p. 53 [*sic*], n. [vol. XIV p. 463, *General Theory*, p. 140]) I find his theory of wages *less* satisfactory than his theory of interest, and have criticised it quite strongly in my 'Wage-grumbles'!

From D. H. ROBERTSON, *10 February 1935*

My dear Maynard,

Here are your chs. 18 and 19, each with a wad of comments.

I'm afraid you'll feel the general tenor of my comments (which seem almost to have reached the dimensions of a book) rather hostile. And I'm the more sorry for that in that I don't think I'm unsympathetic to what I feel to be the newest and practically the most important thing which you are saying,—viz. that in the post-war world there have been certain long-term depressive influences at work of a kind which most critics hitherto have regarded as purely slump-phenomena, explicable in terms of the events of a preceding boom. I *don't* think there is much reason for supposing this to have been true pre-war: and I think it is early to judge whether it is going to be true in the future, i.e. how far it is a strictly-post-war phase and how far a rich-20th-century phase. But I'm far from certain it isn't the latter: and if it turns out to be, I may often be found agreeing with you in practice on the need for Gov^t work programmes,[1]—even for Gesellian taxing schemes and what not. On the other hand a large part of your theoretical structure is still to me almost complete mumbo-jumbo! You will probably conclude that this is due to ossification—or at least excessive conservatism—of mind: and it *may* be so. But I do feel pretty sure there are a number of things on which there is a need for a good deal more clarification,—in particular

(1) What is the keystone of the new arch,—D versus D', or D versus Y, or what?

(2) Why the difference in approach to the various own-rates of interest in ch. 19? (See my long note.)

[1] ? But if they are going *chronic*, one will have to give up financing them by interest-bearing loans, and substitute direct 'inflation'.

(3) What exactly *is* the proposition about wages and employment in Book I?

Many thanks for letting me see it.

Yours ever—in spite of these bites at the hand that fed me—

D.H.R.

Chapter 18

Bottom of p. 87, middle of 88 [vol. XIV p. 491; *General Theory*, pp. 211, 213]— the terminology has become a little confusing, 'investment' and 'investments' being now used to denote not a process but concrete assets. The 'producers of new investments' (i.e. of new assets, e.g. machines) do not as a rule desire a *yield* at all, but a *price*: and all depends on whether or not the demand price for such assets rises through the released stream of money demand being switched—directly or indirectly—on to them. If it does, that is the same thing as saying the rate of interest is reduced,—a given 'prospective yield' becomes capitalised at a larger number of years' purchase. But I quite agree that it may *not*.

Bottom of 88, top of 89 [vol. XIV p. 492; *General Theory*, pp. 213–4]. I find this muddling. There is no *opposition* between 'productivity' and 'scarcity'. Things have value not simply because they're uncommon, but because they're uncommon relatively to the demand for them, which in the case of factors of production depends on their productivity, conceived as a schedule.

P. 90 [vol. XIV p. 493, *General Theory*, pp. 215–6]. While holding no particular brief for the Austrian jargon, I can't help feeling that in your criticism of it you are thinking too much of what you and I have called the 'period of production',—viz. the 'working capital' period, with fixed instruments given. I would heartily agree that improvements in efficiency tend to *shorten this* period, e.g. by making it possible to sow 2 crops a year, to reduce inventories etc. But if by 'starting up input' one means, as the Austrians mean, mining the ore which is going to make the machines which make the.....reaping machines to harvest the crops, then it is surely a different story.

P. 90, last par. but 1 [vol. XIV p. 494; *General Theory*, p. 216]. Interest is here regarded in a new way, viz. as (partly, at any rate) consisting of the cost of bringing together borrowers (presumably distress-borrowers, for with the m.p. of capital-disposal at zero, there will be no others) and lenders. It is without doubt highly desirable that these costs should be reduced to a minimum: but so far as they are irreducible, is there anything uneconomic in the use of capital-disposal being restricted to these employments in which its yield will cover these costs? The situation you depict seems to be one in which the community has carried 'rationalisation' too far, and needs to retrace its steps, e.g. by employing orchestras in cafés instead of radio-gramophones.

P. 92, last par. but 1 [vol. XIV p. 496; *General Theory*, pp. 220–1]. Is the antithesis between instrumental goods and consumption goods, or between consumption-goods (e.g. electric current) which at present embody much waiting and consumption-goods (e.g. handmade furniture) which embody little? If it is the latter, then the proposition seems to be right,—the price of electric current will fall relatively to that of handmade chairs. But what proposition, if any, are you making about the price of instrumental goods,—that it will fall to zero, or that it will fall to equality with their labour cost? The latter is presumably correct, and that may not in all cases mean a great fall below present levels, for some instrumental goods are made mainly by labour. It is the price of *house-room per week* that will fall spectacularly, not the price of *houses*.—I expect this is what you are saying, but the antithesis seems to me queerly phrased.

Chapter 19[1]

I find this chapter extremely interesting and intriguing, and am far from having arrived at a clear view of it, in spite of numerous readings.

Here are some of my difficulties,—of which (3) is the centre.

(1) On p. 4 you seem to me to be answering your own previous objection to the 'Fisher' doctrine, i.e. you are stating that, if the money price of wheat is expected to be higher a year hence, the money cost of the human-and-material plant required now in order to put wheat on the market a year hence will not necessarily rise in the same proportion, or at all. Hence a windfall profit will emerge for creditor-entrepreneurs, as Fisher states, unless the money rate of interest is pushed up.—Since I agree with your own refutation of your previous refutation of Fisher, this note is not a criticism!

(2) I find great difficulty in attaching sense to the house own-rate of interest (p. 5). For houses yield, not little houses, but a flow of house-room: and I thought we were all agreed that we can't evaluate the value of a house in terms of house-room unless we know the *money* rate of interest.

May I therefore, to bring out my essential difficulty, take *wheat* as a thing with a positive own-rate,—as exemplified, e.g., in India, where a large part of short-term agricultural lending is done in wheat (or other grains) at high positive rates of interest? And let me take *apples* as representative of things which are liable to heavy deterioration, so that the own-rate is likely to be negative.

(3) What now seems to emerge is that, in spite of the disparagement of

---

[1] The relevant draft of this chapter has not survived. [Ed.]

'productivity' in the preceding chapter, your *generalised* theory of interest on p. 5 is an almost pure productivity theory. It is because wheat is productive in terms of itself that the ryot is able to offer an own-rate of interest on wheat borrowed to be repaid after harvest (the sentence marked on p. 5 seems to make it clear that you regard your house-rate as dependent on productivity though as I say I don't properly understand the concept). And it is because apples are negatively productive in terms of themselves—i.e. by the end of the year 100 tons of apples will have become (e.g.) 80 tons unless heavy costs are incurred to prevent it—that a borrower would only offer a negative own-rate of interest on apples.

Now why, why, why should poor old Money be alone excluded from the generalised theory, and nothing said about its productivity in terms of itself when discussing the forces which determine the own-rate of interest which borrowers will offer for its use? Surely at this time of day you will not reply with Aristotle that money is barren? For people borrow money in order to part with it for commodities and services, and to sell the product resulting from messing about with those commodities and services, thereby obtaining more money than they borrowed. Money—generalised purchasing power— is every bit as productive as specific commodities, and it is monstrous in discussing its own-rate to omit all mention of the thing—productivity, positive or negative—which in your theory dominates every other own-rate.

It is true that you permit one link between the generalised theory and the money theory, viz. liquidity-virtue. You rightly suggest that if it is thought especially safe or respectable to be an owner of wheat or apples, that will restrict the supply of wheat or apples offered on the loan-market, thus making the positive own-rate of wheat greater and the negative own-rate of apples less than would otherwise be the case. And you rightly say that this consideration is sometimes of specially great importance in the case of money. But this is a force acting on the *supply* side of the loan-market, and does not justify the suppression of productivity, which is a force acting on the demand side. People do not *borrow* money in order to be liquid,—the 'liquidity' obtained by holding a *borrowed* bank balance is an extremely meretricious form of liquidity!

In the case of every commodity except money you allow us to conceive of a loan-market, with various forces—*imprimis* productivity—acting on the demand side, and various other forces—*imprimis* presumably power and will to defer consumption, but secondarily also liquidity-virtue of the commodity in question—on the supply side. In the case of money only you adopt an entirely different method of approach, and the whole thing is boiled down to liquidity-virtue. Thus the difference which emerges between money and other things has been implicit from the start in your method of approach!

(4) The statement that own-rates of interest tend to fall with an increase in output of the commodity in question strikes me as ambiguous. If the increase in output is expected to continue, own-rates will surely tend to *rise*: if wheat is going to become more and more abundant in each successive year, ryots will offer continuously larger and larger bundles of wheat-next-year in exchange for a given amount of wheat-now. If the increase in output supposed on p. 5 is of this kind, q surely will be *rising* and a_1 thereupon *falling*. It is an increase in output *now relatively* to output in the future that causes q to fall and a_1 to rise. Perhaps this is what is meant: but I find the whole passage very difficult to follow. The main reason why, if wheat prices have fallen, production (whether or not they're expected to rise again in the more or less remote future) will be curtailed is that costs, including interest, are fixed in terms of money: and if either money interest or any other money cost is reduced, output will tend to expand again!

(5) On the other hand I agree almost completely with the listing of the peculiarities which make money an awkward customer on pp. 10–17, and do not think they have been so clearly stated before. But it seems to me that it would be equally valid, and somewhat more general, to list them as forces tending to maintain its *exchange value* rather than its own rate of interest. E.g. in the rule-proving exception of the gold-mining country (p. 11 top), relief is obtained not solely or perhaps mainly through the money rate of interest falling, but also through the direct expenditure of the increased incomes of the gold-miners.

I agree with the qualified benediction of Silvio on p. 15!

(6) Pp. 18.1–18.5. I'm afraid these pages have broken me completely. (i) I can't see why one should be specially anxious to hold the thing *in terms of which* contracts are fixed,—one wants to hold the thing *by means of which* contracts have to be fulfilled. As long as money remains the means of payment (and if it isn't that, what is it?) one will want to hold money, not wheat, even though the amount of money that one will be called on to pay (e.g. in pre-war tithe) is made to vary with the price of wheat. (ii) I don't know what 'marginal efficiency' means when suddenly used of a consumable good such as wheat,—it has always previously been used of fixed capital. (iii) I can't, though probably ought to be able to, follow the crucial argument marked on 18.3, and I plead for it to be expanded (and for the last sentence of the page to be rewritten?). (iv) I can't see that my expectation that, if the prices of commodities fall, money wages will not be substantially reduced depends on my knowledge that, in the said state of affairs, the supply of money will not be easily increased. If I had reason to know that the supply of money *would* be easily increased, my expectation that money wages would be reduced would be, if anything, still more tenuous. The argument

seems to me to have got the wrong way round, somehow. (v) In the conclusion, p. 18.4, there seems to me a confusion between money wage-rates being altered and the supply of money being altered. What was wrong in the German inflation was not that wage-rates were put up when prices rose, but that though money was declining in value the supply of money was enormously increased (money was given a reverse or negative 'elasticity of production'). It would have helped to *preserve* stability if wage rates had been put up more in the American expansion of the 20s, because it would have prevented the emergence of windfall profits.

(7) P. 20. The argument seems to me *exactly* the wrong way round. It is because people do *not* regard Gov^t securities as having liquidity-virtue compared with money that the money rate of interest remains high. If people came to regard them as having high liquidity-virtue the money rate of interest would fall. So, in a society in which land is regarded as having high liquidity-virtue and is at the same time almost the only thing one can buy, the money rate of interest will *pro tanto* tend to be *low*.

(In India, where the mere ownership of land has vast social value, the yields on mortgages are greatly below the yields on other agricultural debts. Well-intentioned efforts in some provinces to prevent peasants by law from alienating their land have *raised* the current rate of interest.)

Keynes replied to Robertson's criticisms later in February only to be countered by Robertson.

To D. H. ROBERTSON, *20 February 1935*

Dear Dennis,

Here are my comments. I return yours and also the original text for reference. I would be grateful if I could have your comments back again sometime (I have a copy of my own), since there are several points which I shall want to work through with the text at leisure when I am engaged in revision.

Yours ever,
[copy initialled] J.M.K.

COMMENTS ON D.H.R.'S CRITICISMS

I

You say that the first proposition you write down 'is common ground to everybody'. But in truth it is the opposite of my main contention, which is that progressive expansions and contractions of output and employment involve progressive expansions and contractions of aggregate money income, and not the other way round. This inversion is, I think, rather important as differentiating the two points of view.

The difference between D and Y is introduced in order to deal with the time element (as I point out below the difference between D and Y has nothing to do with your point (ii)). So long as one attempts to argue in terms of actual income time-element difficulties certainly arise. But it is of the nature of expectation that it takes account of the time element.

The grand tautology has either to be accepted or disposed of. I think it is important because it clears away lots of very subtle muddles which seem to take almost everyone in. They think they can use the terms with their natural senses and yet escape the tautology. One might call $2 + 2 = 4$ a grand tautology. Indeed it is, but that would not dispose of it.

(ii) The difference between D and D' has nothing whatever to do with expectation. Indeed you point out that I several times mention this. You seem to have been deceived by my not expressly putting in certain words on page 19. In the first paragraph of II on p.19 [vol. XIV, p. 370] the words 'it is expected that' should be inserted where I have now inserted them in this text.[1] That you should have supposed the distinction between D and D' has anything to do with the distinction between expected and realised results means, I think, that all this passage has wholly slipped you by. The distinction between these symbols is as follows:

D is the sale proceeds for which it is expected that the output from employing N men can be *sold*.

They did not remain there in later drafts. [Ed.]

D' is the sale proceeds the expectation of which will cause the output from employing N men to be *produced*. It is simply the age-old supply function.

The classical (or Pigouvian) theory believes that N men will be employed where N is such that when N men are employed the marginal output of wage goods has a utility equal to the marginal disutility of labour. This overlooks the possibility that the value of N to which this leads would result in a value of D *less* than D', so that if this number of men were employed, entrepreneurs would be working at a loss. That is to say, they do not envisage the possibility of D and D' being unequal.

I argue that there is only one value of N for which $D = D'$ and that this may have a lower value than the N given by the classical theory. In this case actual employment is given by the lower value. The main object of the first part of my book is to show what governs effective demand, i.e. what governs the shape of the functional equation $D = f(N)$.

The employment function $D' = F(N)$ can be derived from the ordinary supply function, or rather from the family of ordinary supply functions corresponding to different hypotheses.

My theory is that the actual level of employment is not given by the classical theory as above, i.e. by the equality which causes marginal output etc. but by that value of N for which $D = D'$, i.e. for which $f(N) = F(N)$.

When once it is admitted that D and D' are *not* equal for *all* values of N, this is obvious. So I do not continue to argue it. Nor do I spend much time on D', except for some embroideries at a later stage, since it is only a re-concoction of our old friend the supply function. Virtually the whole of the rest of that part of my book in your hands is, therefore, directed to discovering what determines D, the level of effective demand. Definitions occupy rather more space than they should, namely the whole of Book II. But Books III and IV are strictly devoted to the matter in hand, namely the determination of D. With this the substance of my theory is complete.

The employment function is *frequently* heard of again. It runs through the whole book, though it is true that its theoretical side is only developed in detail in a later chapter than those you have. For I make the volume of output essentially depend on the conditions of demand and supply. The notion that supply is never heard of again suggests that you think that I, like yourself, throw over all my fundamental economic principles when I come to study fluctuations!

User cost

Yes, the essence of the story *is* that user cost enters into supply price. But it is, of course, *marginal* user cost, not total user cost which enters into the supply price. In your example, output consists of one object only, namely bread, since you have taken gross investment to be zero. But if, as in my modification of your example, you suppose that output consists of two objects, the bread, and the capital goods corresponding to some gross investment, I am only saying that the user cost of producing these capital goods does not enter into the supply price of the bread, any more than the user cost of producing beer enters into the supply price of bread. But, of course, the marginal user cost of producing bread does enter into the supply price of bread. By, however, taking a peculiar limiting case where $B = 0$, you have introduced a tacit assumption that in that case U is zero at the margin, and have thus misled yourself. For U is zero at the margin, if B is constant whatever the output of bread; and your example suggests that $B = 0$ whatever the output of bread, i.e. is constant.

One can put it thus (in the case we are taking where $C = C'$):
$U = B - B'$ and B' is independent of output so that $\dfrac{dU}{dO} = \dfrac{dB}{dO}$.
Hence if B varies with the output of bread, marginal user cost ΔU is not zero and enters into the supply price of bread.

II

When you say that liquidity preference probably depends mainly on changes in the propensity to spend and regard this chiefly as a difference in emphasis from my view, it is again evident that we are hopelessly at cross purposes. For one of my main points is precisely that changes in the propensity to spend are in themselves (as distinct from their possible repercussions on output) wholly and of logical necessity irrelevant to liquidity preference.

In the example you give of two communities devoting one-fifth and one-tenth of their incomes to the purchase of securities, you are certainly not entitled, on my view, to say that the rate of interest will be lower in the former;—unless indeed you include in 'their general economic conditions' an assumption that employment is the same under both and that the monetary authorities in the two are under some compulsion to establish such respective rates of interest as shall insure this result. For, if you mean by 'general economic conditions' the same technique, existing equipment, population and individual psychological propensities, apart from the question of the proportion of income devoted to the purchase of securities, then it is impossible to infer from the data you give what the relative rates of interest would be. All one can say is that if the rate of interest is not lower in the former, the amount of unemployment will be greater.

You are in effect saying that, if a community which had the one-tenth habit changes to the one-fifth habit, the rate of interest will necessarily fall (you do not say how much it will fall, e.g. whether it will fall sufficiently to maintain employment at its previous figure). I say that the rate of interest is governed by other factors; though, of course, the change in habit will have repercussions on these other factors, the net effect of which cannot be predicted without knowledge of the particular circumstances.

III

This does not arise in a way in which we can discuss it until we are nearer together as to what I am saying. I feel that we cannot really get to grips until you differ from me either much more or much less.

IV

No, this is not my proposition. I state (page 6 and top of page 7) that the opposite of it 'so far from being a mere possibility is frequently the case'. Obviously in the case you suggest the cheaper workers would be taken on and the dearer ones become unemployed in their place. I state what I believe to be the classical or Pigouvian theory on pages 3 and 5. Do you dispute the accuracy of this? If so, what is their theory?

My point is that, given the equipment and technique of production (i.e. the supply function), the amount of employment will depend on the *demand*; and that if there is increased demand, leading to more output and therefore to a lower marginal productivity of labour and therefore to a lower real wage, this will not, in general, be interfered with by labour withdrawing its services. Therefore, it is essential to discover what determines demand. This, I repeat, is my real subject matter. My solution, put in a sentence, is that, given the propensity to spend, demand is a function of the amount of investment.

Detailed comments

Page 7. Perhaps I should have said 'the *marginal* productivity of the machine', and in the second passage you refer to 'more labour *than is now employed*'. But isn't this obvious?

Page 9. I certainly had Jevons and Marshall, and not Ricardo, in mind. For it is they who taught us that 'prices are governed by marginal prime cost in terms of money'.

Page 10. Perhaps I should have written, 'Labour is always in a position to determine its own real wage *by accepting a change in its money wage*', adding the words underlined.[1]

Page 32. The employment function is independent of the entrepreneur's expectation of demand in the same sense that the ordinary supply function is independent of the demand.

Pages 59–60. This is an interesting interpretation of Marshall which had not occurred to me. For it is not easy to see how the present value of a machine can be made to equal a sum of discounted future net yields, unless the machine is immortal. I have always regarded the series of quasi-rents as a *finite* series, the number of terms depending on the life of the machine. How, for example, would you apply your interpretation to a machine with a life of ten years? Does the present value of such a machine partly depend on the rate of interest twenty years hence?

Page 67. Could you elaborate this? What *is* 'the statement about the cause' which you intend to make?

Page 75. I agree that the word 'private' should be deleted.

Page 87[2]. Demand will only be switched on to them if *either* the expectation of prospective yield is increased *or* the rate of interest is decreased. But, in the latter case, it is not 'the same thing as saying the rate of interest is reduced';—it is a *result* of the rate of interest being reduced.

Page 90. God knows what the Austrians mean by 'period of production'. Nothing, in my opinion. *Vide* Knight's article in the forthcoming March *E.J.*[3]

Page 91. Yes, there is something uneconomic. For the costs in question do not correspond to any social cost.

Page 92. Yes, I am saying that the capital price of instrumental goods will be, as it is now, what they cost to produce. But their net quasi-rent, i.e. the price of their services after making good wastage etc. will approximate to zero.

[1] At this point, Robertson added the following: 'It is not this proposition but the *next* which puzzles me.' [Ed.]

[2] The next four references refer to Robertson's comments of 10 February on chapter 18, where the 'page' references actually refer to galleys. [Ed.]

[3] F. H. Knight, 'Professor Hayek and the Theory of Investment', *Economic Journal*, March 1935. [Ed.]

Page 97. Yes, you are right that I mean annuities, i.e. rates of interest for limited terms, not rates of interest for a perpetual annuity.

Pages 103–4. Fisher, of course, holds that inflationary measures are favourable to output and, though I state the matter rather differently, I am, of course, in agreement with him about this. But I have always interpreted his special theory of appreciation and interest as being something quite apart from his general doctrine as to the advantages of inflation. In the passage you criticise I was thinking of the Fisher doctrine of appreciation and interest as being on the following lines:

A lender has £100 worth 100 units of goods and is willing to lend for a year at 5 per cent. Something then happens to cause him to expect £100 to be worth 98 units of goods a year hence. He is then, according to Fisher, only willing to lend at some higher figure than the 5 per cent; theoretically 7 per cent, but in fact he will not get back all the depreciation since he is not backing a certainty, and perhaps 6 per cent will be the rate. Now, as against this, my contention is that the expectation of a change in price has *no* effect on the rate of interest, since it leaves unchanged the relative attractions of cash and loans. Are you denying this? Do you think that an expectation of higher prices in future causes the rate of interest to rise?

I agree that in other contexts Fisher in effect assumes that an expectation of higher prices causes the marginal efficiency of capital to rise. And this, of course, I agree with. My point is that it has been very common hitherto to confuse the proposition that the marginal efficiency of capital is greater with the proposition that the rate of interest is greater. It looks to me as if *you* may still be holding that an increase in the marginal efficiency of capital, whilst not quite the same thing as a rise in the rate of interest, necessarily involves it. For otherwise you must agree with me in accepting one half of the Fisher doctrine and denying the other half.

In your (ii) we are partly in agreement. For you are here

giving reasons for my conclusion that in the circumstances supposed the marginal efficiency of capital will rise. But my essential point is that, whether *or not* there is a speedy rise in wages, the lender will have to sit down under the diminution in the real value of his money or money loan.

(iv) There is no difference here from what I say, but I agree that it is more symmetrical to state my point in terms of a rise rather than a fall. I will re-write it. This passage was interpolated afterwards and does not, as printed, run comfortably for a reader who has been thinking up to this point in terms of a rise.

Pages 145–6. Thanks for the reference to Hayek which I will study. I do not doubt that Hayek says somewhere the opposite to what I am here attributing to him. But this is a passage which I have not yet checked up or traced down the passages for which I am relying on my memory. I think that the doctrine I am quoting begins with Mises, is to be found sporadically in Hayek and much more specifically in Robbins. It is from them that Hansen has got it.

Chapter 19. This is too long a story for correspondence. I admit the obscurity of this chapter. A time may come when I am, so to speak, sufficiently familiar with my own ideas to make it easier. But at present I doubt if the chapter is any use except to someone who has entered into, and is sympathetic with, the ideas in previous chapters; to which it has, I think, to be regarded as posterior. For it is far easier to argue the ideas involved in the much simpler way in which they arise in the chapter on liquidity preference.

Marshalliana

I will consider all this carefully, but at present I can make very little of it. For, on the one hand, you say that you are quite satisfied with Marshall's theory of the rate of interest; whilst, on the other hand, you have no adverse comments to make on the main substance of mine. But, whichever is right, there can be no possible doubt that they are totally different.

This brings me to the main impression with which your criticisms leave me. I feel that you must, as said above, either differ from me much more or much less. You make no frontal attack on any of my main points. Yet there is not really a single point of importance where I have succeeded in making you change your mind. I am baffled by your practice of reading into everything I write something not very incompatible with what you already believe.

The explanation is to be found, I think, where you say that a large part of my theoretical structure is to you almost complete mumbo-jumbo. For this book is a purely theoretical work, *not* a collection of wisecracks. *Everything* turns on the mumbo-jumbo and so long as that is still obscure to you our minds have not really met.

From D. H. ROBERTSON, *11 March 1935*

My dear Maynard,

I've spent a good many hours this weekend over your comments,—but haven't managed to cover anything like the whole ground, and I expect that it *will* be best that in the main I should wait now till I can see the completed work with a fresh eye. But I hope you'll bear with me if I try, in as brief a compass as possible, (1) to re-state some of my perplexities about Book I, (2) to deal with rising-prices and the rate of interest.

Yours ever,

D.H.R.

I. Book I

Text, p. 19 [vol. XIV, p. 370].

(1) I can see that I have been stupid[1] over D'. But what puzzles me now is that you now seem to me to be saying that Marshall, Pigou, etc. deny that conditions ever exist when in industry as a whole sales receipts are less than costs + expected profits, i.e. in effect deny that general industrial depression can exist. I don't think you *can* be saying this, and I must have somehow misunderstood again. But I *do* think there is excuse for confusion when you try to bring down two such different fowl as Say and Pigou with the same barrel: Pigou, *Ind[ustrial]*. *Fluc[tuations]*. p. 84 strongly attacks the

---

[1] In 1949 while going through these papers, Robertson added the following: 'But fancy labelling a supply curve D'?' [Ed.]

'confusing suggestion which would make it appear that *generalised* errors of forecast are in the nature of things impossible' because, as is alleged 'increased outputs—created in error—constitute increased reciprocal demand for one another'.

(2) I still can't grasp the second half of the sentence on text p. 7 near bottom [vol. XIV, p. 358; *General Theory*, p. 10] which begins 'As a rule, more labour. . .'. It now *seems* to me to mean 'if effective demand increases, more people will be drawn into employment, accepting, if necessary, a lower money wage than now prevails in order to obtain employment'. But it can't mean this, for (*a*) experience suggests that if e. d. increases money wages will, if anything, tend to rise, (*b*) if it *did* mean this it would confirm my attempt in notes p. 4 [above p. 500] to formulate your proposition about employment, which you say is wrong. Incidentally, I can't see that what you say on text 6 and top of 7 [vol. XIV, pp. 356–7; *General Theory*, pp. 8–9] is in any way the 'opposite' of the proposition which I have tried to father on you! But my chief trouble is that the proposition which you substitute for the bastard (Comments p. 7 [above p. 501]) seems to me simply a re-statement of what is common ground (see e.g. Pigou, *Ind. Fluc.* 308 and *T[heory]. of U[nemployment]*. 293–7), viz. that, owing to the tendency of workpeople to think in money, rising prices tend to draw into employment persons who would otherwise have stood out of employment. But I suspect you to be *also* making, or leading up to, another proposition which I *don't* believe, viz. that in a closed system it is impossible, by reducing money wages to reduce real wages.

So I am left, as usual, neither agreeing nor disagreeing as much as you would wish!

II. *Rising prices and interest*

(1) The rate of interest is the price of the use of loanable funds: hence any cause which raises the curve of expected marginal productivity of loanable funds will tend to raise the rate of interest, through increasing the competition of borrowers to obtain the use of loanable funds. (The yield on old bonds must conform, with lags and modifications, to other interest-rates,—see *Treatise on Money*, II, 354–5 [*JHT*, vol. VI, pp. 344–5].)

(2) One such cause is an expected rise in product-prices which is not accompanied by a corresponding rise in labour etc. costs. (Thus I *do* agree with Fisher, *Th[eory]. of Interest*, p. 410, that in such conditions '[businessmen's] willingness to borrow will itself tend to raise interest'.)

(3) Ignorance on the part of lenders will prevent the rise in the rate of interest from being as great as it would be if the two sides of the market were equal in foresight and lenders therefore in a position to take full advantage of the enhanced demand for their wares.

(4) The rise in the rate of interest will be damped down by the tendency of the owners of stores of money (*a*) as *interest* rises, to take money out of store and lend it thus increasing the supply of loanable funds, (*b*) as *prices* rise, to take money out of store and invest it themselves in labour or commodities instead of adding to the demand for loanable funds for those purposes. Experience seems to show that these counteracting forces are unable in the end to prevent the rate of interest from rising. (In my analysis, both (*a*) and (*b*) appear as causes diminishing K.)

You seem to me to be saying that your liquidity-analysis proves that (unless the supply of money is curtailed) the rate of interest *cannot* rise, and that my propositions 1–3, however plausible and universally believed, must simply be dismissed as irrelevant. I do not think so. If I am right about the facts, and the rate of interest *does* rise, this *does* mean that if we examine the position at any moment your liquidity-curve will be found lying at a higher level than at the start. But is not this because you have chosen to express in money terms the preferences of people about holding money, while I have chosen to express them in real terms? That people are now ready, with an enhanced rate of interest, to hold the old quantity of money (even perhaps in practice an increased quantity) is not really strange, since it is compatible with their holding in the form of money a diminished quantity of real value.

I will try at leisure to think the whole question through again: but my present feeling is that my 'real' method (learnt at your knee!) helps me to account for a well-established fact, while your present 'money' method leads you to deny it!

To D. H. ROBERTSON, *14 March 1935*

My dear Dennis,

Yes, I think that we had better break off the discussion at this point. There is, however, one passage in your latest notes which possibly brings things to a head.

The first of your three propositions is the following, 'The rate of interest is the price of the use of loanable funds, hence any cause which raises the curve of expected marginal productivity of loanable funds will tend to raise the rate of interest through increasing the competition of borrowers to obtain the use of loanable funds.' You say this is 'plausible and universally believed'. If you were to substitute 'almost universally' I should agree. But it is precisely this proposition which I am denying. What bothers me is not so much that I should have failed to convince you that it is false, as that I should have apparently failed to convey to you that I deny it! However, I will try to be clearer if I can when I get back again to proof sheets[1].

Yours ever,
J. M. KEYNES

There the correspondence rested until just before the *General Theory* was published. In October 1935, Keynes wrote to Robertson as follows:

To D. H. ROBERTSON, *10 October 1935*

My dear Dennis,

How are you and what have you been doing in the vacation? I, as you may suppose, have been plugging away at the proofs. It seemed to me better to send you nothing more until I had reached a more advanced stage. I am now practically finished, and am sending my galleys to the printers to be paged. I should rather like to send you the page proofs as they come along, but do not feel under any obligation to make any comments. You will find that there are considerable alterations from the text you saw, and I think that the great majority of the passages you specially commented upon have been modified, but whether you will be satisfied by the modifications is another matter.

One point of detail. You criticised me for tackling Pigou and Marshall on the basis of their writings on value rather than their writings on fluctuations. I did not do this on purpose, but simply through an inability to discover anything relevant in their

---

[1] At the foot of his copy of this letter, Robertson added the following note to Richard Kahn on 9 November 1947: 'But *did* he ever mean to deny this? Do *you* mean to deny it? The "tendency" will only fail to eventuate in an *actual* rise in the rate of interest (1) if the supply of money is perfectly elastic, which he surely did not believe that it *was* in England in the 1930s though he may have thought that it *might* be, or (2) if the interest-elasticity of liquidity preference is infinite, of which he "knows no example hitherto" (*GTE* p. 207).

But even if one or other of these phenomena prevents the tendency from being effective in raising the rate of interest, they do not prevent it from existing. Why should he have wanted to deny its existence?'

writings on fluctuations. I have now made the omission good in the case of Pigou's *Theory of Unemployment* by devoting a lengthy appendix to this work in detail. But I have still failed to find anything relevant to the matters I discuss in his *Industrial Fluctuations*. You are more learned in that than I am, so, if you can easily direct me to a passage, I will be grateful.

Yours ever,
[copy initialled] J.M.K.

From D. H. ROBERTSON, *11 October 1935*

My dear Maynard,

Many thanks for your letter. Yes I am reasonably well, and had some very good holiday walking in Scotland,—and a look-in on Tyneside on the way south under the aegis of Leslie Runciman.

I have the draft of Bonavia's book on Transport[1], and should like to bring it round and talk about it during the weekend if I may.

I am glad yours is so well forward. I don't know *what* to say about seeing it again. In a way I feel I would rather wait now until I can see it all at once, and refer backward and forward, rather than in lumps: and in vacation rather than in term, so that I can wallow uninterruptedly. If you think I could be any use at this stage in suggesting purely verbal changes, let me be so: otherwise I believe that the chances of my coming to a right judgment about it will be better if I wait till it is in covers and till I am quit in December of lectures, boards, College councils, theatrical management and what not.

I think I think that pretty well the whole of *Industrial Fluctuations*, being a study of the variations in Effective Demand, is relevant to your theme: and especially those chapters, say I, 13, 16 and 17, and II, 7, which bear on the determination of the rate of interest under dynamic conditions. But I expect you will reply that that is because I still haven't grasped what your theme is!

I wish I were persuaded that economic sanctions will do the trick! I can't help fearing it will still come to a head-on choice between letting the Duce get away with it and using the British navy to deny him the Canal.

I will ring up some time tomorrow.

Yours,
D.H.R.

---

[1] One of the Cambridge Economic Handbooks. [Ed.]

During the winter and spring of 1935, work continued to go ahead. On 15 January, Keynes reported to R. F. Kahn:

I have done two more chapters for you, if you have time to look at them. Between them they cover the ground of the philosophical chapter, ninety per cent re-written. I rather want to know what you think of my latest concerning the fundamental characteristics of interest which has been considerably remodelled and is, I think, rather beautiful, if it is correct.

Similarly on 26 March he reported to Kahn:

I have now finished a full-dress critique of the Prof. to go in as an appendix to the chapter on changes in money wages. It will need your very close eye to make sure that I have not anywhere misunderstood him or misrepresented him. The stuff he writes seems to me the most extra-ordinary in some ways in the history of the subject. But it has a dreadful fascination for me, and I cannot leave it alone.

The major surviving written discussions of the book in draft really date from early June 1935 when Keynes sent galley proofs to R. F. Harrod, R. G. Hawtrey, Richard Kahn and Joan Robinson. The set of galleys sent comprised chapters 1–25 of the following table of contents:

June 1935 table of contents

The General Theory of Employment, Interest and Money

BOOK I INTRODUCTION

BOOK II DEFINITIONS AND IDEAS

BOOK III THE PROPENSITY TO CONSUME

In dealing with this correspondence and the associated marginal comments on the galleys, we will treat each correspondent in turn completely—beginning with R. F. Harrod.

To R. F. HARROD, *5 June 1935*

My dear Roy,

I am sending you at last galley proofs of almost the whole of my book. From the table of contents which I am also enclosing, you will see that you have here the whole thing with the exception of the three concluding chapters.

The copy is a spare one and there is no reason why you

should not scribble in the margins any comments which occur to you. I am extremely anxious to know how it strikes you.

The different sections are in different states of revision, and you will find various internal inconsistencies which will have to be put right. Broadly speaking, the first six chapters and the last six are in a later stage of revision than the intermediate ones.

Yours ever,

J. M. KEYNES

From R. F. HARROD, *31 July 1935*

Dear Maynard,

I have read with great interest to the end of Bk II. The enclosed are merely some jottings on particular points. But I am not sending back the galleys, as I shall probably want to re-read, when I have finished the whole of what I have. I can't yet make any sensible general remarks. I am enjoying it very much.

Yours,

ROY

Galley 3. 2nd postulate [vol. XIV pp. 353–4; *General Theory*, pp. 5–6].

I do not find this very crucial section altogether clearly expressed. As it is so important, I do suggest re-drafting.

You are really dealing with 3 sorts of unemployment. 1. What I will call frictional unemployment, allowed for in classical theory and described by you down to the words 'in addition'. 2. Voluntary unemployment—at least you say 'it cannot be described as involuntary', which according to classical theory is all the unemployment there is besides the frictional. This you deal with from the words 'in addition' to the end of that para. 3. Involuntary unemployment (in *addition* to the frictional) to be defined by you later.

I don't think this threefold division comes out clearly. Nor is it plain what you mean when you say that unemployment (II) 'cannot be described as involuntary'. I think it is a great pity to introduce a reference to 'involuntary unemployment', which is carefully defined later, by a side-wind. (Frictional unemployment (I) is also in a sense involuntary.)

Moreover when you say 'subject to these admittedly important qualifications', you are *really*, but not explicitly or clearly referring back to matters mentioned before the words 'in addition'. For the unemployment due to the cause mentioned after these words is not a qualification but is precisely that determined by the classical postulates themselves. What *follows* explains how much unemployment of the kind referred to in the 'in addition' sentence there will be according to classical theory.

Galley 5 [vol. XIV p. 357; *General Theory*, p. 9]. I find the *2nd para.* obscure. 'At variance with the facts' suggests dogmatism in rather a challenging way. I don't see that you would lose anything by omitting this. I *think* I see what you mean, but it seems to me that it might give a critical reader opportunity for cavilling.

Galley 7. III para. 3 [vol. XIV p. 364; *General Theory*, p. 14]. I agree with the general drift of this section. But the para. 3 is a howling paradox in its present form, unless you insert some such words at the end of line 1 as '*albeit unconsciously*'. Industrial struggles are clearly not *consciously* struggles about the sharing between particular trades of a given average wage. Every labour man would repudiate this violently.

The industrial struggles are almost always *intended* to strike at capitalists not fellow workers. And if there is no strike against rising prices, that may be because it is thought (even if wrongly) that the whole community (including capitalists) is in the same boat. I press this point because I do think it important in this book that you should avoid *un-necessary* paradox.

Galley 13. IV paras 2 and 4 [vol. XIV p. 375]. Ambiguous expressions: 'D_1 will increase by less than the increase in D.' 'The D_1 part of D will increase more slowly than D.' What you mean is that the arithmetic addition to D_1 is less than the arithmetic addition to D (I believe). But your expressions, especially the second, might be interpreted as 'the proportionate increase in D_1 (which starts, of course, by being smaller than D) will be less than the proportional increase of D' (and this, tho' it may be true, is, I believe going rather further than you intend).

Galley 20. End of ch. 4 [vol. XIV p. 387]. D should surely read D' to be in conformity with the notation in ch. 3 (II).

Furthermore, while I agree that you can treat the matter perfectly well by relating supply price directly to N rather than output, I find this explanation very difficult to understand. What is the good of talking about it unless you can evaluate it in principle? But if you do, you introduce units of output.

Actually I cannot follow your last sentence—this may be mere stupidity—but I do suggest it is rather difficult and *un-necessary*. What I cannot directly follow is that $D' = F(N)/\phi(N)$ is the ordinary supply curve.

Galley 25. Last para. [vol. XIV pp. 401–2]. Ought not the word 'consumable' to come in before 'goods'? You remember that some newly finished goods are capital equipment (cf. def. galley 23, 2nd para. [vol. XIV p. 395]). These are surely included in C.

TOWARDS THE GENERAL THEORY

Galley 26. 2nd para. [vol. XIV p. 462]. The words in brackets 'hereafter defined as prime costs'. Can't you drop these and leave prime costs till you come to define them? There is the grammatical difficulty that it is not perfectly clear that they refer, as I take it they must, to 'the current outgoings of entrepreneurs' and not to the 'balance of the current outgoings of entrepreneurs'. And there is the further point of substance that while the outgoings of entrepreneurs in the aggregate *may* (but see below) be regarded as equivalent to prime costs, they are certainly not necessarily the prime costs of the goods which the particular entrepreneurs produce. And this bracket confuses by suggesting that you wish them to be.

Moreover 'current outgoings of entrepreneurs' is *not* equal to but probably greater than prime costs as defined in II below, for some of those outgoings are in fact the *profits* of other entrepreneurs.

I am awfully sorry that you have had to define prime costs as not including user costs (user cost v[ery]. interesting!), because your definition cuts across the established usage as I understand it of the recent voluminous literature on imperfect competition. But I suppose it is inevitable! I should have liked you to use for *your* prime costs some such expression as 'prime factor costs'.

Galley 29 [vol. XIV p. 412, n. 1]. I don't care for your last sentence in footnote 2, because it neglects the analysis of imperfect competition so laboriously achieved by many (including your Joan Robinson!). Quasi-rent is, to put it briefly, the excess of prime cost over marginal revenue (= marginal cost) × no. of units produced. The absurdity to which you refer just doesn't arise. (And in the exceptional case of perfect competition it is expected that marginal wage cost > than av[erage]. wage cost.) Many of the younger generation have become keen on and familiar with these concepts and would regard your note as *ignoratio elenchi*!

Galley 35. footnote [vol. XIV p. 427, n. 3]. Words 'in my sense' in brackets. It should be made plain that the reference is to the sense of *this* volume, as in the text to which the footnote refers you have been discussing the *Treatise* sense.

Galley 35. I, last para. but I [vol. XIV p. 428.]. A little more than half way down. 'Without retaining anything in exchange'. This suggests a gift and is confusing. I suggest instead 'and reduces the total of his assets by that amount'.

At the end of I I have the feeling that you ought to deal *explicitly* with how the creation and cancellation of credit by banks fits in with this analysis, as this has been the subject of such keen debate and confusing misunderstanding. (Having read to end of Bk II I still feel this.)

Galley 39. 1st sentence of 1st new para. [vol. XIV p. 437]. Meaning plain but

18 529 KEA

wording needs revision? for 'every net investment' the 'aggregate of net investment'?

Line 17 of this paragraph [vol. XIV p. 437]. Ought not the words ' + prime' to go in after user? On the other hand from footnote 1 I gather that in speaking of *gross* incomes of firms you have already deducted prime costs. This seems odd. Have you done this consistently?

Last word of this para. 'saving'. This refers to S_2? Ought you not to add 'by private individuals'?

From R. F. HARROD, *1 August 1935*

Dear Maynard,

I now come to a point which I think is of considerable importance and I should like you to give it your earnest attention. I have been reading Bks III and IV as far as ch. 16, and I think your positive doctrine excellent and important and a great contribution, to which I can subscribe.

But in your critical part I think you have fallen into what I can only characterise as a confusion, and while there are only one or two passages which, if I am right, *need* to be corrected, I feel it has made you quite un-necessarily critical of Marshall and others. The error, as I conceive it, stands out most clearly in the last sentence of the 2nd para. on galley 64 [vol. XIV pp. 470–71; *General Theory*, p. 165, last sentence]; 'whilst the notion that the rate of interest...whatever the rate of interest'. The view that I object to lies in the argument that *because* saving must always and necessarily equal net investment (which I accept) there is 'no sense' in the view that interest is a price which equates the demand for saving in the shape of investment to the supply which results from the community's propensity to save. Now I come on to your positive doctrine presently. What I am concerned to contend now is that the discovery that saving necessarily equals investment has no relevance to the sensibleness or otherwise of the doctrine referred to above. (Of course in that doctrine the demand for saving must be conceived not as an absolute amount of investment but as a schedule by which the amount of investment is related to various rates of interest.) This doctrine makes perfectly good sense, but is open to the charge of being incorrect. I find no sense in saying that this doctrine makes no sense *because* in this case supply is always and necessarily equal to demand.

Take the case of supply and demand as applied to commodities. It is true that in certain cases there may be disequilibrium between supply and demand in the sense of production exceeding or falling short of consumption, the balance being absorbed in or released from stocks. Price movements may be thought of as bringing production into equality with consumption. But there are commodities in which production must always and necessarily be equal to consumption. And no one has thought of saying that the laws of supply and demand make no sense because of that. Take the number of private German lessons given in London. Here production is always and necessarily equal to consumption. That cannot be doubted. Yet there is also in this case no reason to doubt that the price of a German lesson is determined by the supply and demand functions in the ordinary way. It seems to me that the discovery that saving = investment has deceived you into thinking you could derive from that an argument in favour of your general attack on the classical explanation of the rate of interest which is specious and indeed invalid.

In order to give you pause for thought, I should like to add that this was the most criticised part of your address in Oxford,[1] in which you brought out this argument. Frankly it convinced no one.

It seems to me you give the case away so far as that argument is concerned, when you say, as I think you do somewhere—I fear I haven't noted the place, but perhaps I shall find it again—that this classical doctrine would be all right if there was some *other* mechanism always ensuring a full employment position. Yet even in those circumstances it would still be true that saving necessarily equals investment. So it isn't *that* truth which invalidates the classical position. That seems to be right. If there was and it was known that there would continue to be full employment, the classical theory would come into its own again modified by something about liquidity preference.

By bringing in this as it seems to me quite invalid argument you will distract attention from the valid arguments you adduce for your position. I have referred to the passage in para. 2 of ch. 14. The second para. on galley 70 [vol. XIV p. 475; *General Theory*, p. 177, second full paragraph] wants re-modelling. And I dare say there are other passages: I will small-tooth-comb it for them once I know that you agree to the principle.

The notion that price is determined by supply and demand always rests on a *cet. par.* assumption: e.g. that there are no price changes of other things or that they are irrelevant. What you seem to me to have shown is that there are changes in other things which are so relevant and of such overpowering importance, that the old s. and d. analysis had better be put away. You have incidentally shown also that we know very little about the supply schedule of saving, i.e. amount of saving considered as a function of the rate of interest *cet. par.* which includes level of income being given. You have further shown

---

[1] Keynes spoke to the Oxford economists in February 1935 on the marginal efficiency of capital and the rate of interest. [Ed.]

that the level of income has an over-riding importance in determining the amount of saving (= amount of investment). You have further shown that the level of income is linked in a roundabout way (and ∴ the level of saving in a still more roundabout way) to the rate of interest. And this in such a way that the level of income and the rate of interest are indeterminate unless you bring in another equation, which you do in fact, viz. the liquidity preference schedule. To say that in the special circumstances of this particular field of exchange the ordinary supply and demand functions are no use, because the quantity is functionally linked to another variable outside the factors usually considered in supply and demand analysis (viz. total income) is very different from saying (and this is what I object to) that the supply and demand functions can in principle give no solution because in this case supply necessarily equals demand.

Note. What I mean by ordinary supply and demand functions is this. Supply function relates amount people choose to save (= amount invested) to the rate of interest. Demand function relates quantity of new investment undertaken (= amount saved) to rate of interest. In both cases *cet. par. Ceteris* includes level of income. Now you are perfectly justified in saying that the amount of saving is so clearly related to the level of income that to cover the level of income by the *cet. par.* clause is to refuse to examine the problem. But when you do examine the functional relation all sorts of funny things (including the very important one that variations in the propensity to save may be offset by variations in the level of income in such wise that they have no effect on the rate of interest) appear. But you are *not* justified in denying to classical theory a logical and water-tight view, albeit one which neglected the most important features in the situation. And in your best passages where you relate the classical doctrine to the economics of full employment you don't deny this.

I won't write more until I hear how you react to this. But I would like to write a good deal more if I hear that you don't react, because I feel that the matter is very important.

Yours,

ROY

I transcribe some more notes on minor points.

Galley 43, ch. 10, para. 1 [vol. XIV p. 444]. Would you, please, resist (i) (ii) and (iii) after the three words 'partly', as these 3 governing factors turn out to have an importance in the subsequent text which the reader doesn't realise they will when reading—and so he has to refer back and make it out for himself.

Galley 50, para. 3, 2nd sentence [vol. XIV p. 461; *General Theory*, pp. 135–6]. 'The greatest...efficiency of capital.' This is extraordinarily obscure where it stands and is, I suggest, un-necessary, as the point is covered lower down.

Galley 51, II, para. 2 [*General Theory*, p. 138, first paragraph]. I have noted: 'If the product is homogeneous I don't see where the difficulty lies.'

Galley 52, top [vol. XIV p. 462; *General Theory*, p. 139, top]. I have noted:— 'But you yourself say that the rate of interest = current marginal efficiency of capital.'

Galley 52, 2nd complete para. *General Theory*, p. 140]. Ref. to Marshall in first line. I have noted:— 'In this traditional theory agrees. Where it differs from you is in finding the other determinant required in your (ii) and (iii) of ch. 10.'

Galley 54, fragment of para. at top [*General Theory*, p. 143, last sentence of first full paragraph]. I have noted:— 'But isn't this if foreseen reflected in the current rate of interest, and, if not foreseen, impotent?'

Galley 54, IV, 2nd para. end [*General Theory*, p. 145, last two sentences of part paragraph at top]. I have noted:— 'But there is a risk here even if a favourable change is equally likely.'

Galley 61 [*General Theory*, p. 160 top]. Does fortnightly settlement—but you know all about this!—really work this way? I had heard that the daily settlement of N.Y. had universalised and regularised trading on margins which our fortnightly settlement makes it possible for many speculators to avoid, so that our system really made for less speculation.

Galley 64, line 9 [vol. XIV p. 470; *General Theory*, p. 165]. Something wrong.

Para. 2, early part [vol. XIV p. 470], I have noted:— 'But of course modern classical theory combines these.'

Later part. I have expanded my differences of opinion in enclosed letter.   R.F.H.

From R. F. HARROD, *1 August 1935*

Dear Maynard,

You may wonder why I lay such stress on a point that merely concerns formal proof rather than the conclusions reached. I am thinking of the effectiveness of your work. Its effectiveness is diminished if you try to eradicate very deep-rooted habits of thought *unnecessarily*. One of these is the supply and demand analysis. I am not merely thinking of the aged and fossilised, but of the younger generation who have been thinking perhaps only for a few years but very hard about these topics. It is doing great violence to their fundamental groundwork of thought, if you tell them that two independent demand and supply functions won't jointly determine price and quantity. Tell them that there may be more than one solution. Tell them that we don't know the supply function. Tell them that the *ceteris paribus* clause is inadmissible and that we can discover more important functional relationships governing price and quantity in this case which render the s. and d. analysis nugatory. But don't impugn that analysis itself.

The fact that saving is only another aspect of investment makes it *worse* not *better*. If there were two separate things, saving and investment, then it is clear that the two equations will not determine both. But with one thing, then if you allowed the *cet. par.* clause which you rightly do not, it would be quite logical and sensible to approach it in the classical way.

Yours,

ROY

From R. F. HARROD, *3 August 1935*

Dear Maynard,

I have now read about two-thirds of what I have. I hope not only to finish but to re-read. My main feeling is this—that I think your own theory is a construction of durability and elegance. I am entirely with you and feel the matter is of great importance. I am not nearly so convinced by the critical parts generally. I am sure that your best point is where you say that the classical theory assumes full employment or a given level of income or something like that. I am inclined to think that the keystone of this edifice is the quantity theory of money in its crude form, which fixes the general price level, and allows money wage reductions to be real wage reductions, and prevents saving from re-altering the general price level. What I feel on the other hand about some of your guerilla skirmishing is that you haven't always explored the precise implications of the theories as closely as their authors, you see clearly their defect from your point of view, but are too ready to attack their self-consistency. In fine, my view, for what it is worth, is that in your final revision you would do well to reduce rather than to amplify the destructive parts, when in doubt.

My other personal impression is, quite between ourselves, that the new book will be understood by almost as many people as understood the *Treatise*. That is perhaps inevitable. It means that still another work, a Manual of Elements, will be wanted. I am afraid my notes have been very scrappy so far. I take my mother and the proofs to Cornwall tomorrow and hope to brood upon them there.

Yours,

ROY

TOWARDS THE GENERAL THEORY

From R. F. HARROD, *6 August 1935*

Dear Maynard,

Herewith some more occasional notes. I have finished the first reading of what you sent me, and am really impressed with its power and convincingness. Do you want my copy back at once? Or may I keep it a little longer?—so that I may look it over and see how the various things fit together.

Yours,

ROY

Galley 52 [vol. XIV pp. 461–3; *General Theory*, pp. 139–41]. On re-reading I again feel that you do less than justice to Marshall (and the traditional view). I don't think he failed to appreciate the distinctness of the concepts of marginal efficiency of capital and the rate of interest. He knew that there was a schedule of marginal efficiencies, and he thought that interest was determined by this and the schedule of the propensity to save. Now you use both these schedules—but to determine the level of income, the relevance of whose variations in this nexus he did not appreciate.

I don't like your last para. of II on Galley 52 both because I think it is wrong, in the sense that it seeks to attribute some dubiety and fluctuation of view to Marshall which is not there and also because this line of attack is likely to lead to barren controversy—defence of the orthodox view against an unjustified attack—which may detract attention from your essential point and lead to much waste of words and thoughts.

Personally I don't think this II is necessary. But I especially dislike the last para. of it.

Your position is clear. The two schedules supposed to determine the rate of interest by classical theory, in fact determine the level of income of which it gives no satisfactory account, while the rate of interest is determined by the schedule of liquidity preference and the quantity of liquid medium. What do you gain by attributing a logical defect to the traditional view, when all you need to attribute is incorrectness?

Galley 64. 2nd para. last sentence [vol. XIV p. 470; *General Theory*, p. 165]. This embodies the crux of what I object to. Especially the words 'makes no sense'. You are saying that if the amount of something produced necessarily equals the amount consumed it makes no sense to say that a price brings demand into equality with supply. And that, I am confident, won't do.

I don't believe you *can* dispose of the traditional theory until you have stated your view. And I suggest deletion of words from 'Broadly speaking...' to end of I. Anyhow the statement that traditional answers follow two lines is quite obsolete, because for decades all decent economists have held that both lines, viz. supply and demand, are necessary to the determination of the rate of interest. *Both* lines are present in Böhm-Bawerk, Cassel, Marshall, etc.

Suppose after equilibrium the marginal efficiency of capital rises. Orthodox theory says that the rate of interest will rise to limit investment and encourage saving. Namely ordinary supply and demand analysis. There is a new marginal efficiency of capital curve which intersects the propensity to save schedule higher and farther to the right. *Your* answer to this is no—the rate of interest is determined by liquidity preference and the quantity of money, both of which may be unchanged and ∴ the rate of interest will not necessarily rise. What happens? Total income is increased by the extra investment operating through the multiplier, until—in the mathematical not temporal sense of until—with the old rate of interest and the existing propensity to save, saving is up by the same amount as investment. Your own doctrine as to what determines the rate of interest is necessary in order to rebut the orthodox view, which cannot be rejected out of hand like this.

You seem to me to be on quite sure ground in your criticism of classical theory on galley 65, para. 1 [vol. XIV p. 471; *General Theory*, p. 166, last paragraph].

The hour is late and I won't attempt to grapple with ch. 15 now, but I will let you have my reflections tomorrow.

I feel that the only way I could possibly be of any assistance is not in the elaboration of your own view, but in endeavouring to restrain you in your criticisms. I feel that you have been thinking so much about your own views that you are inclined to do less than justice to the existing doctrines. Yet it is these very existing doctrines that have been intensively chewed upon by the economists who are not path-breakers, but none the less endowed with some intellectual power. They have pondered on them again and again from many points of view, lectured on them, taught them, considered many possible lines of attack and defence, and finally embraced and endorsed them, and here you come rushing in and in the most airy way accuse them of logical inconsistency and suggest that they haven't thought much about them. Suppose your reasons in the constructive and critical parts were equally good, you would have a far greater chance of carrying conviction in the former because your adversaries have not had years of thought in which to prepare an answer. But I don't think they are equally good,—and for the same reason—namely that your years of thought have been mainly given to the constructive part.

Now from the practical point of view I do think it very important that you should not light-heartedly ride roughshod over cherished convictions unless you are certain and doubly certain that you are right. And for your argument you don't need to do so! What I think is important from the point of view of the effect and influence of the work is that you should minimise and not maximise the amount of generally accepted doctrine that your views entail the scrapping of. A general holocaust is more exciting. But anything you write now has such immense relevance that you no longer require these artificial stimulants to secure attention. Everyone will be all attention in any case. Don't go out of your way to provoke dogged resistance on the part of professional economists! Well, I shall come on to ch. 15 tomorrow in my most critical mood.

R.F.H.

To R. F. HARROD, *9 August 1935*

My dear Roy,

Thank you very much indeed for taking so much trouble. I have not dealt with nearly all your points as yet, since I am taking them in their turn when I come to revise the chapters in question. It is too disturbing to turn one's mind on to all of them at once. So far they have been of great benefit.

In particular I have adopted your suggestion about reclassifying the different types of unemployment. I think this has led to a vast improvement. One way and another I have re-written the first three chapters on so large a scale that I am getting another galley proof which I hope to send you early next week. So put off your re-reading until this is in your hands. I have also adopted your suggestion about using the term 'marginal factor cost'. Like you I do very much dislike excluding user cost from prime cost, and had been casting round for an alternative term without success. Your 'factor cost' is just right, I think. The chapters dealing with income, user cost and the rest of the definitions I have also dealt with very drastically, and have managed to delete about half of it altogether. I have felt that these chapters were a great drag on getting to the real business, and would perplex the reader quite unnecessarily with a lot of points which do not really matter to my proper theme. But it is only now, after an interval, that I have been able to perceive which parts can be thrown into the waste paper basket—and thank God they are considerable. I think all this will now read much simpler and more convincing. What I have to say is not really so terribly complicated; but there is some evil genius which sits at the elbow of every economist, forcing him into all sorts of contorted and unnecessary complications.

The only points so far where I do not accept your criticisms are:

1. Galley 20, end of chapter 4 [above p. 528]. I do not agree that my method does not avoid units or aggregate output. The whole of your comment here indicates I think that you have not got me. I have, however, re-written this in the light of what seems to me to be your misunderstanding.

2. I am bothered about your comment of galley 29 [above p. 529] which I enclose herewith. This does not matter, since I have managed to delete the whole of the chapter dealing with quasi-rent. But surely one means by quasi-rent the excess price over *average* cost, multiplied by the number of units?

There remain your comments about my criticism of the classical theory of the rate of interest as distinguished from my own theory. I have not really got to this yet, and have only glanced at your notes without comparing them with my own text. But my first reaction here is one of disagreement. I still maintain that there is 'no sense' in the view that interest is a price which equates saving and investment; or at any rate that if one could invent a sense for it, it would be quite remote from anything intended by the classical theorists. Perhaps the clue is to be found where you allege that I am doing great violence to the accepted and familiar when I maintain that 'two independent demand and supply functions won't jointly determine price and quantities', for my whole point is that the functions in question are *not independent*. To my way of thinking, to say that the rate of interest equates saving and investment is just like saying that market price is fixed as that value which ensures that the sum which the purchaser pays shall be exactly equal to the sum which the vendor receives. However, I will recur to this matter in its proper place, and will certainly be at pains to make the matter clearer and more cogent if I can.

Yours ever,

J. M. KEYNES

From R. F. HARROD, *as from Sennen Cove near Land's End, 12 August 1935*

Dear Maynard,

I move to the above address on 16 August and shall be there for about a week.

I am very glad to hear of your simplification of the chapters dealing with user cost, income etc. because, tho' very interesting, they did provide a curious stumbling block for the average educated reader or the journalist-economist, which coming at an early stage would limit the appeal of your book.

Prime factor cost. One small point. You say you are adopting my suggestion of 'marginal factor cost'. But I expect this is a mistake for what I did suggest, viz. prime factor cost (which can of course be further divided into marginal and average): I had in mind almost a hyphen between prime and factor. Prime costs proper, viz. those which can be avoided by not under-taking output in the short period, divide into prime-factor costs, viz. those involved in employing concurrently ultimate factors of production, labour, short loans etc. and user costs, or supplementary factor costs, viz. those involved in using machinery,—generally, the products of prime factors employed in the past. They are prime costs because they can be avoided by not using the machinery, but they are not prime-factor costs because they do not involve the concurrent employment of ultimate factors of production (and aren't necessarily paid out to anyone as income).

Marginal revenue. I have appended another note to my original note on galley 29.[1]

[1] (Above p. 529). The additional note runs as follows: 'Quasi-rent *is* the (excess of price over av. cost) × by number of units. I assumed in this note that you were in your text assuming that av. prime cost = marg. prime cost. For if marg. cost > av. prime, no difficulty arises about quasi-rent for (apart from question of marg. revenue differing from price) we have a quasi-rent equal to (marg. cost – av. cost) × no. of units. Where then marg. cost > av. prime your absurdity does not occur. But I was taking the case, more difficult from the old fashioned point of view, in which marg. prime $\neq$ av. prime. This difficulty is overcome by the doctrine of imperfect competition in which marg. prime = marg. revenue, and in which even if marg. prime $\neq$ av. prime, there is still a quasi-rent due to the excess of price over marg. revenue.

'So that, tho' what you say about user cost is true and important, I don't think it necessary to explain the existence of quasi-rent, *even in the case favourable to your argument*, in which av. prime = marg. prime.'

539

Saving and investment. A few words about the equation of saving and investment. I agree that there is no sense in saying that interest equates S to I in sense that if rate of interest were different there would be an excess of S over I or of I over S. But I hold there is sense in saying that interest equates the demand for investment to the supply of saving. And I also hold that the fact that S must be equal to I does not in itself invalidate the proposition that interest is the price which makes them equal. I further hold that if there was some other mechanism for securing constancy of income, which the *old* classical doctrine assumes (i.e. it implicitly assumes constancy of income and does not envisage the rate of interest as the mechanism for keeping incomes constant) then the classical doctrine that it is the rate of interest which equates the propensity to invest to the propensity to save would not only make sense but also be true.

Where anyhow I am sure you must be on insecure ground is when you say that the fact that S must be equal to I invalidates the notion that the rate of interest equates the propensity to save to the propensity to invest. The price of a German lesson does not ensure merely that the amount spent on such lessons is equal to the amount received by teachers: for that would be true if the lessons were compulsorily ordained by the state and the fees were compulsory like unemployment insurance payments. No: the price of the lessons ensures that the amount of lessons which people freely choose to take is equal to the amount that they freely choose to give, and this equation of supply to demand by price is possible, in spite of the fact that the amount of lessons given must necessarily be equal to the amount received.

The essence of your point I feel to be that the *cet. par.* clause of the supply and demand analysis, which in this case includes the level of income, is *invalid*. The classical theory ∴ is invalid but not nonsense.

Yours,

ROY

To R. F. HARROD, *14 August 1935*

Dear Roy,

Prime Factor Cost

I mean here I think the same that you mean. But it did not seem to me necessary to put 'prime' in front of 'factor'. I was considering prime cost as made up of user cost and factor cost, each of the constituents and also the sum of the two being, of course, further divided into marginal and average. I do not see that it is necessary to subdivide supplementary costs into supplementary factor costs and something else. Thus, I mean by factor costs those current disbursements to the factors of production which could be avoided by not using the machinery. However, it would be very easy to make any further subdivision you like if there were any occasion for it. I will deal with your other point later.

Yours ever,

J. M. KEYNES

Do I ever affirm or deny that 'the propensity to save has to be equated to the propensity to invest' or words to that effect? If so, I should not in a revised draft. The propensity to save is a schedule or function, not a quantity at all, namely the function relating different levels of net income to the amounts saved at each level. The inducement to invest (I no longer speak of a 'propensity' to invest) is the relation between the schedule of marginal efficiency of capital and a given rate of interest. A change in the rate of interest will change both the propensity to save and the inducement to invest; but there is no sense in which it can be said to *equate* them. If we take everything else as given, the rate of interest determines the equilibrium level of income at which consumption *plus* investment provides the amount of employment, the supply price of the output of which is equal to that level of income. But if entrepreneurs make mistakes and offer a different level of employment, saving and investment will still be equal.

One can (as assumed [above p. 520]) only invent a meaning for the classical ideas, if one assumes that income and employment *cannot change*. On this assumption the rate of interest causes the propensity to save and the inducement to invest to change in such a way relative to one another that income and employment are always the same whatever the rate of interest. In this case one can abolish the function 'propensity to save' and introduce a new one, namely the curve which intersects the family 'of propensities to save' corresponding to different rates of interest at the point of each corresponding to the unchangeable volume of income. This is the classical supply curve of savings. But if income and employment are capable of changing, there is no longer any such thing.

However, I will try to render matters clearer when I get to redrafting that chapter.

J.M.K.

To R. F. HARROD, *17 August 1935*

My dear Roy,

Here are the last two chapters of my book (I've already sent you chapter 25, haven't I?). They are unread and unrevised in proof. But chapter 26 is too long, I think, and wants a little cutting. In chapter 27 the *emphasis* hasn't worked out as I intended, and it will need some re-consideration.

Yours ever,

J.M.K.

From R. F. HARROD, *from Sennen Cove, 19 August 1935*

Dear Maynard,

Your last chapters have just arrived. We intend to return to London on Thursday the 22nd. But our plans are not rigidly fixed, so would you write to Christ Church, which always has the proper instructions about forwarding.

I thought the revised draft of Book I very clear and good. I have made one or two further notes on it, which I enclose.

With regard to interest and the classical theory, I will try to isolate the offending phrases or sentences and let you have them.

I have just discovered Angus Davidson, who lives in a very small village here remote from the world.

Yours,

ROY

2nd draft [Keynes's marginal comments appear as footnotes. No copies of the relevant drafts survive.]

Ch. 1. line 5. I should *like* you to say instead of 'Classical Theory of Economics'—'Classical Theory of the Subject'. It is less tremendous, but, I feel, a more accurate description of what you have done, and ∴ desirable. The rest of the chapter would follow on quite logically.

Galley 7. III, 2nd sentence. To make the final 'it' grammatical, don't you want 'who consent to a reduction of money wages' instead of 'who weaken to their demand for m-w'?

Galley 8. IV. Def. in italics. I *prefer* your former definition. It seems to me clearer; also I think it is better because it does not bring in demand.

With the classical notion of a continuous supply curve, the proposition that any fall in real wages would lead to a withdrawal of labour is tantamount to saying that at the existing wage no more labour will be forthcoming. You have made the requisite breach with classical theory by pointing out that at the existing real wage and even at a lower one more labour is available than employed. I think the introduction of demand is confusing at this point.[1]

Galley 12. (I ought to have mentioned this before.) 4th paragraph. 'If this were true. . .' I find this sentence awfully difficult. Take the words '. . .will no longer be accompanied by any increase of output'. Don't you have to add at existing money-wage rates? But what does Say's Law say about that? It does not preclude the screwing up of output by inducing more labour by offering higher rates: Z will still be equal to D. Does output as a whole ever cease to have *some* elasticity?[2] Anyhow not till long after the 'full employment' of your former definition has been reached.[3]

The most that I can make of this reasoning is the following:—

Any increase of demand makes its own supply: there is no such thing as unemployment due to deficient aggregate demand. Competition will $\therefore$ induce entrepreneurs to expand *without limit*. *But* they will not expand if so doing puts them at a competitive disadvantage; this can only happen if in endeavouring to expand they have to offer higher prices to attract factors from each other. But so long as there is involuntary unemployment, they will not have to do this. $\therefore$ if there is involuntary unemployment there is no obstacle to expansion. $\therefore$ Say's Law provides for employment in your sense.

Is this a correct interpretation? Perhaps I have missed some point. I confess I can make nothing of a state in which output is absolutely inelastic.[4]

But I am not sure that the argument as I have set it out is absolutely watertight, because tho' diminishing returns is no obstacle to a general expansion, demand price always being equal to cost, however high, yet it might provide a force keeping *competitors* in check, one entrepreneur being in a position in which he cannot expand owing to increasing costs unless the others do.

I am in agreement with the concluding sentences of this paragraph.

[1] It is rather confusing but it is not *correct* without it.
[2] Yes.　　　　　　　　[3] No.
[4] Quantity theory of money in full control.

543

Galley 13. III, line 7, 'costs'. This must be 'prices of factors'. Surely you don't want to assume here (in contradiction to preceding pages) that costs per unit of output are constant in ordinary sense?[1] Yet from your footnote (1) I judge that you do. Such does violence to the general picture you have given on preceding pages where you suppose increased costs, and also is in direct contradiction to (b) below, for by it the m.p. of labour is the same for every value of N.[2]

If you make the change suggested, footnote (1) must go.

Reference to the temporary assumption at the top of galley 14 suggests that you do mean what I mean. It was your footnote (1) that put me out and it must surely be a slip.[3]

Galley 14a. 1st full paragraph. Steeped as I am in the mutual determinacy of the classical system, I very much dislike the first two sentences. I dare say you won't agree! They seem to be over-dogmatic, and I don't believe in the last resort that pure theory *can* yield a causal proposition of this kind! What I should like would be in place of 'real wages' in line 2, 'marginal disutility of labour measured in real terms', and in place of the 2nd sentence a statement to the effect that the prop. to con. and the rate of new inv. are uniformly related to a given level of employment and that in turn to a given level of real wages.

From R. F. HARROD, *21 August 1935*

Having re-read ch. 15 I am more depressed about it than I was before, when in the first flush of enthusiasm I was ready to swallow anything.

Let me make this preliminary point. I don't for a moment believe that the authors to whom you refer conceived the possibility of saving being anything else than equal to investment. The *in*equality between saving and investment was a newfangled idea propounded by you in the *Treatise* and since taken up by others and mis-applied. So that when you argue that once we see that saving must be equal to investment, this argument falls, they would reply that they had always supposed that saving must be equal to investment and that that was the basis of their argument. You rightly say that $S = I$ corresponds to the truism that sales = purchases. But what is it that compels sales to be equal to purchases, when everyone is perfectly free to sell or not to sell and to buy or not to buy? The traditional answer is price, which in the case of $S = I$ is the rate of interest. (The parallel between $S(= I)$ and commodities which cannot be put to stock is complete. And the existence of stocks is not of the essence of supply and demand analysis but a complicating factor.)

[1] Yes.　　[2] Footnote deleted.　　[3] Yes.

I agree with your para. on galley 70 [vol. XIV p. 475; *General Theory*, p. 177], beginning 'Certainly the ordinary man...'. He thinks an increased propensity to save will lower the rate of interest. The next point you *ought* to go on to (vide your nonsense paragraph beginning 'Now the analysis...') is that the rate of interest may not fall because there is another variable in the situation, viz. the level of income. The increased propensity to save *may*, instead of lowering the rate of interest, merely lower the level of income by reducing the multiplier, and establish a new equilibrium with the *old* rate of interest and less employment.

Now you should go on to say that not only *may* this be so, but in certain circumstances it *must* be so, viz. if there is no change in the liquidity preference schedule or the quantity of money. Q.E.D.

The classical school went wrong, one, because they did not perceive that there was another dependent variable in the situation, viz. the level of income, and, two, because they did not appreciate that there are other forces which if unchanged would compel the rate of interest to be what it is, and thus, so to say, compel the change in the situation to act not on the rate of interest but on the other dependent variable, viz. the level of income.

Then you can come back to your delusion of the 'ordinary man, banker, civil servant' etc. (vide para. 1 on galley 70) and point out that when an individual performs an act of saving there may be no net addition to aggregate saving (and in certain circs. there can be none) because his particular saving may merely act on the multiplier and not on the rate of interest (and in certain circs. must do so).

In the bottom para. of 70 [vol. XIV, p. 476] when you say that saving and investment are twin determinates, you are in perfect agreement with the classical system. Only the classical system made them determined by something different. For the classical school they were determined by the marginal efficiency of capital and the propensity to save, for you by the same marginal efficiency of capital, but on the other side by the rate of interest, which for you is determined by something quite different. But the propensity to save comes into your system too, but in a different way, viz. in determining the value of the multiplier.

I can't follow the paragraphs beginning 'The second approach of the classical theory...' [vol. XIV p. 476] because I only know of one approach in any reasonably modern theory—tho' with troublesome terminological wrangling.

The last two paras. of the ch. [vol. XIV pp. 477–8; *General Theory*, pp. 184–5] seem to me to be O.K.

N.B. I can't help thinking that the doctrine of the multiplier ought to be explicitly set forth somewhere here rather than later.

Where the classical school undoubtedly begins to get into difficulties is when in their *monetary* department they begin to discuss the effect of the rate of interest on the level of activity. Because once they begin to do this, they recognise the level of income to be a variable (whereas it is essential to their pure theory of interest to assume it constant) and they recognise some kind of nexus between interest and the level of income. This however is a development which takes place in the department of money and may be held to undermine their general theory; but this is no excuse for attacking the general theory as inconsistent or confused on its own premises.

I send off these notes as I write them.

R.F.H.

From R. F. HARROD, *22 August 1935*

Ch. 16

It follows from what I said about ch.15 that I am not happy about ch. 16. But I don't want to worry you too much about it. I feel that you have made your main point of departure from the classical position—viz. the introduction of variations in total income as a relevant factor in this connection—abundantly clear in other places. This chapter seems to seek to go further and to convict the classical economists of confusion or circularity within the limitations of their own premises. This attempt is not essential for your purpose. And if not essential I should have thought it had much better be left out. For it is clearly impossible to give a satisfactory criticism of this kind on the basis of short passages torn from their context. Such a criticism is *bound* to *seem* unfair and I believe it is unfair. If you are merely making the same point at length that they did not consider variations of income as having the significance that you attach to them, chapter and verse are not necessary—no one will dispute your thesis. That you have done more than this I remain profoundly unconvinced. And controversy of this kind lends itself to such easy refutation by reference to other isolated passages. A storm of dust is raised—for what purpose? I will give two examples of what I mean by unfairness and then desist.

Galley 73, footnotes 3 and 4 [vol. XIV pp. 479, n. 3; 480, n. 1]. Reading forward from the sentence to which footnote 3 is attached, it seems clear that M[arshall]. is thinking of the extra work as due 'to an extensive increase in the demand for capital', which is precisely in your words a rise in the marginal efficiency of capital.

If this is so footnotes 3 and 4 both become irrelevant. You have given your own good reasons in another place for supposing that a rise in the m. e. of cap. won't cause a rise in the rate of interest. Nothing is gained by making a long quotation merely to repeat that point here.

546

Galley 74, 1st full para. [vol. XIV p. 481]. But it is abundantly clear that M[arshall]. does mean 'taken in conjunction with the rate of interest'—a rate determined for him by conditions surrounding the new marginal investments. I don't see a shadow of evidence that M[arshall]. 'is aware that his argument is becoming circular' or that it is becoming circular. The rate of interest, which we require to know in order to assess the value of risky capital, = the marginal efficiency of the new investment. The marginal efficiency of the new investment depends on the amount of new investment undertaken. What determines that amount? According to M[arshall]. there will be that amount which makes the m. e. of cap. equal to the marginal disutility of saving (from an income taken as constant). This is not your view I grant, but there is nothing circular in it.

Galley 82, 1st line [vol. XIV p. 488]. A small point. Ought the words 'the actual value of' to be inserted before $L_2(r)$? I am not quite clear whether this is what you mean or hold that the function itself may change, since at the end of the para. you suggest the possibility of the increase of money changing r but not M_2, which would imply an offsetting change in the function.

Galley 84 [vol. XIV p. 489; *General Theory*, pp. 205–7]. Aren't the thoughts expounded here worthy of being brought into greater prominence (e.g. at the end of the book) as suggesting an instrument of public policy? I mean that the banks should name a minimum price at which they severally or acting through some cartel organisation would be prepared to buy govt. obligations.

R.F.H.

To R. F. HARROD, *27 August 1935*

My dear Roy,

Here is a copy of the remaining chapter 25 which you have not already had.

I am still too much engrossed in re-writing the earlier chapters to have given as close an attention as I wish to all you have written me about chapters 14, 15 and 16. But I have now read what you say carefully enough to feel fairly convinced as to the broad position.

It is, I am sure, a big question of substance, not of manners or controversial fairness. If you are right as to what I have established, it is certain that you are also right that a good many of my criticisms need reconsideration. But I am still of the opinion that if my constructive sections are correct, my critical sections are more than justified. And I think that your acceptance of my constructive parts can only be partial if you do not accept my critical sections.

I will, of course, go carefully through your detailed points and be careful not to make criticisms of which I do not feel doubly sure. But the general effect of your reaction, apart from making me realise that I must re-write all this drastically if I am to make myself clear, is to make me feel that my assault on the classical school ought to be intensified rather than abated. My motive is, of course, not in order to get read. But it may be needed in order to get understood. I am frightfully afraid of the tendency, of which I see some signs in you, to appear to accept my constructive part and to find some accommodation between this and deeply cherished views which would in fact only be possible if my constructive part has been partially misunderstood. That is to say, I expect a great deal of what I write to be water off a duck's back. I am certain that it will be water off a duck's back unless I am sufficiently strong in my criticism to force the classicals to make rejoinders. I *want*, so to speak, to raise a dust; because it is only out of the controversy that will arise that what I am saying will get understood. Take your own case (on the assumption that I am right). If I had left out all the parts you object to about the classical school, you would have simply told me that you were largely in sympathy and liked it. But my attack on the classical school has brought to a head the fact that I have only half shifted you away from it. Your preoccupation with the old beliefs—and much more so in the case of most other people—would prevent you from seeing the half of what I am saying unless I moved to the attack.

But all this, of course, brings us back to the point as to whether I am right and in particular as to what it is which I accuse you of not having seen.

Let me take one or two passages from your script which I had better quote since I think you have no copy. You say, 'I do not think Marshall failed to appreciate the distinctness of the concepts of marginal efficiency of capital and the rate of interest. He knew that there was a schedule of marginal efficiencies and he thought that interest was determined by this and the schedule of propensity to save. Now you use both these schedules, but to determine the level of income, the relevance of whose variations in this nexus he did not appreciate.' To deal with a minor point first, I think this is overstating a great deal the clearness of Marshall's thought, since it overlooks the fact that my definition of marginal efficiency of capital is quite different from anything to be found in his work or in that of any other classical economist (except for a passage which he makes little subsequent use of in Irving Fisher's latest book). I emphasise this, because the discovery of the definition of marginal efficiency of capital looks very slight and scarcely more than formal, yet in my own progress of thought it was absolutely vital. Let us, however, assume that you are rightly interpreting Marshall. What the above passage then comes to is what you emphasise in numerous other places, namely, that my discovery consists in showing that the classical theory forgets the part played by changes in the level of income, but that this omission can be repaired, and we are then left with the rate of interest determining at what point, so to speak, the schedule of the propensity to save cuts the schedule of marginal efficiencies. This appears to be a view to which I have converted you and which you think to be my view. If this was true, then the modification called for in the classical theory would be much milder than that which I appear to demand. But the fact is that the above is not my view as to what happens—far from it, and it is to that substantial point that we have to direct our minds.

I shall try to re-write the chapters in question so as to make it more clear what it is I am saying. I can scarcely hope to achieve this in a letter. But I must obviously give a few indications of what it is I am driving at.

In the first place the statement that the classical theory would hold if incomes were constant needs a good deal of elaboration before it is intelligible. Obviously by *income* you cannot mean *money income*. If, on the other hand, you were to mean *employ-ment* being constant you would be more on the right track, but still the conditions would not be sufficient.

The main point is, however, that my theory is essentially not a theory that the rate of interest is the factor which, allowing for changes in the level of income, brings the propensity to save into equilibrium with the inducement to invest. My theory is that the rate of interest is the price which brings the demand for liquidity into equilibrium with the amount of liquidity available. It has nothing whatever to do with saving. You say in one passage that I am doing great violence to the fundamental ground-work of thought in getting rid of supply and demand analysis. But I am doing no such thing. I am substituting demand and supply analysis for liquidity instead of that for savings. Marshall you say 'thought interest was determined by the schedule of marginal efficiencies and the schedule of the propensity to save'; he forgot that incomes could change. I am saying something totally different from this when I say that interest is determined by the demand and supply for liquidity. You imply in passage after passage that, if the schedule of marginal efficiencies is known and if the propensity to save is known, the rate of interest can be deduced. But my whole point is that it cannot be deduced from these factors and has to be found from a different source. This is where your ingenious analogy of the private German lessons fails. You say quite correctly that the price of the lesson equates the propensity to give German lessons with the marginal efficiency of German lessons. In the case you have chosen price does play that function. But suppose that whenever the price of a German lesson went down the demand schedule also shifted its position, the whole thing would have no meaning. You get your point of equilibrium because the demand and supply schedules for German lessons do not shift their position whenever the price changes. If for any price whatever the demand and supply schedules shifted so that they intersected at the point in question, clearly they would not be determined by the price. Now it is the characteristic of the demand and supply schedules for savings that they have this unfortunate characteristic. In truth there are no such things as these schedules. They are completely bogus. Without bringing in liquidity preference the position of equilibrium is entirely indeterminate, and any method, such as the classical one, which endeavours to arrive at the rate of interest without bringing in liquidity preference is bound to be circular in the worst possible sense of the word.

I fancy that the misunderstanding partly comes from the fact that, although you have lately accepted the view that saving and investment are equal, you still think of them as being different things; whereas I regard them as being merely different names for the same phenomenon looked at from different points of view. Saving is a name given to a certain quantity looked at as the excess of income over consumption. Investment is the name given to the same quantity regarded as the constituent of income other than consumption. The demand for German lessons is quite a different thing from the supply of German lessons even though the two may be equal. But saving and investment are the *same* thing. It is vital for the application of the supply and demand analysis with interest as the equilibrating factor that interest should cause saving to increase and investment to diminish, as the classicals all believe. But if the rate of interest operates on the amount of saving in the same direction as on the amount of investment; if, that is to say, a rise in the rate of interest necessarily diminishes saving, then the independence of the two things necessary to allow interest to be an equilibrating factor is non-existent.

I can scarcely expect you to be much impressed by all this rigmarole, and you must wait for my revised version where I shall try to be more convincing. But my own firm conviction is that your mind is still half in the classical world, and that you ought to be accusing me, not of bad manners, but of faulty theory.

What you say about the last chapter but one is somewhat connected with this. It is certainly not my object in this chapter unduly to depreciate the classical school, and I will see if I can put in a passage to make that clear. What I want is to do justice to schools of thought which the classicals have treated as imbecile for the last hundred years and, above all, to show that I am not really being so great an innovator, except as against the classical school, but have important predecessors and am returning to an age-long tradition of common sense. It would help me if you were to mark passages which you especially object to, or which you think could be curtailed. I should certainly like to reduce the space given to the mercantilists, but feel that I must give chapter and verse. I cannot but think, however, that you would feel rather differently about this chapter if I were able to convince you that the classical theory of the rate of interest has to be discarded in toto, and is incapable of rehabilitation in any shape or form.

Yours ever,

J.M.K.

P.S. Will you ponder the following propositions:

1. Saving and investment are merely alternative names for the difference between income and consumption.

2. The supply curve of savings and the demand curve for investments have no determinate point of intersection, since they lie along one another in all conditions throughout the whole of their length. This applies equally in equilibrium or in disequilibrium. There are no conceivable circumstances in which the one curve does not occupy the same situation as the other throughout its length;—provided, of course, the same conditions, whatever conditions are assumed, are taken as applying to both alike.

3. The propensity to save and the schedule of marginal efficiencies are two curves which do not intersect anywhere, because they are not *in pari materia* and do not relate to the same variables. The propensity to save is a curve which relates the amount of investment to the amount of income. The schedule of the marginal efficiencies of capital is a curve which relates the

amount of investment to the rate of interest. There is no sense in which they can be said to intersect.

What then remains? What are the demand and supply (other than those for liquidity) which the rate of interest is in certain hypothetical positions supposed to equilibrate?

I have rewritten effective demand, income, and user cost radically.

From R. F. HARROD, *30 August 1935*

Dear Maynard,

No, no; you do me throughout great injustice. I have understood you much better than you think. You say that I think you mean as follows:—'we are left then with the rate of interest determining at what point, so to speak, the schedule of the propensity to save cuts the schedule of marginal efficiencies'. You suggest that I think you keep the twin classical determinates and shove in the rate of interest (itself determined otherwise). But that is not at all what I take your view to be.

Your view, as I understand it is *broadly* this:—

Volume of investment determined by	⌈marginal efficiency of capital schedule ⌊rate of interest
Rate of interest determined by	⌈liquidity preference schedule ⌊quantity of money
Volume of employment determined by	⌈volume of investment ⌊multiplier
Value of multiplier determined by	propensity to save

I think that you are saying—and rightly—that the inclusion of dependent variability of level of income necessitates radical re-construction on above lines.

None the less I hold that if you assumed income constant, classical view makes perfectly *good sense*. It may be open to criticism on minor points, but it is not nonsense.

To quote from your letter 'You say I am doing great violence to the fundamental ground-work of thought in getting rid of supply and demand analysis.' I am not suggesting that you are getting rid of it in your *own* analysis. On the contrary you use it in the determination of employment, for instance. What I am objecting to you is your *criticism* (of the classical position) which implies that such an analysis doesn't make sense.

You write 'you imply in passage after passage that if the schedule of marg. eff. is known and if the propensity to save is known, the rate of interest can be deduced'. I never suggest that it *can* be so deduced, but only that it *would* be so deducible if the level (and distribution among different income levels) of income were constant. You go on 'But suppose that whenever the price of a German lesson went down the demand schedule also shifted its position, the whole thing would have no meaning.' I agree entirely. That is precisely your point. The supply schedule of saving, according to you, moves automatically and necessarily to the right when the rate of interest goes down, and if the supply schedule (and not the supply) is a function of the price, the supply and demand analysis won't apply in that particular place. But that is no excuse for saying (as you have done) that the classical economists who assumed that the supply *schedule* could be treated as a constant, *were not making sense* when they said that the rate of interest was determined by supply and demand of saving.

'Any method which endeavours to arrive at the rate of interest without bringing in liquidity preference is bound to be circular in the worst possible sense of the word.' Yes, if income is variable. No, if income is constant. But, you say, income *is* variable. Granted. That brings us back to the old point:— they were wrong to take it as constant, but having made that mistake their argument was quite logical.

'Although you have lately accepted the view that S and I are equal, you still think of them [as] being different things.' No; I always thought they were equal and the same thing. I always explained to students that they appeared unequal in the *Treatise*, because of a special and peculiar definition of income. At my *first* reading of Hayek I noticed that he was assuming the possibility of inequality without accepting some arbitrary definition such as yours to allow that possibility.

'The demand for German lessons is a different thing from the supply even though the two may be equal. But saving and investment are the same thing.' A German lesson is a German lesson. The demand schedule for saving is a different thing from the propensity to save. (Now don't accuse me of saying here that interest is determined by them. I merely re-iterate that thinking saving the same as investment doesn't itself make nonsense of the view that the amount of it is determined by different things: a demand schedule and a supply schedule.)

'Without bringing in liquidity preference the position of equilibrium is entirely indeterminate.' I agree. And when I am seduced by the view that you give liquidity preference too much work, the view that I would then fall back on is that equilib. *is* indeterminate!

Only in one sentence explaining your constructive view do you seem to me to go too far. You say 'the rate of interest has nothing to do with saving'.

This does seem rather extreme and isn't necessary. You don't need to deny that the rate of interest has some effect on the amount of any given income saved. All this would mean would be that the value of the multiplier is a function of, among other things, the rate of interest.

'The supply curve of savings and the demand curve for investment have no determinate point of intersection, since they lie along one another throughout their whole length.' Certainly: at least on one def. of supply curve of saving. But generally when you draw a supply curve $x = f(y)$, it is assumed that you are treating x as a function of a single variable, price, and other things including income were equal. That is the classical supply curve. To relate the classical supply curve to yours, you would have to draw a family of classical supply curves corresponding to different levels of income and to show that the value of each corresponding to a given rate of interest was identical with that of the demand curve, owing to the operation of the multiplier affecting the level of income. The value (x) of demand for each different value of y (interest) makes (via the multiplier) income and that when you draw the classical supply curve for that level of income (i.e. schedule of saving propensity at various interest rates at that level of income) the value (x) of this supply curve for the value of y used in computing that level of income is identical with the value (x) of the demand curve. I have tried to put this in other words again in note at end.

'The propensity to save and the schedule of marg. efficiencies are two curves which do not intersect anywhere because they are not *in pari materia*.' Agreed.

Mercantilist chapter. I appreciate what you say about returning to age-long tradition of common sense. But the common sense was embodied in a hopelessly confused notion of economic system as a whole. I think you are inclined to rationalise isolated pieces of common sense too much, and to suggest that they were part of a coherent system of thought. It is that suggestion which seems to me to give the impression of the hopeless sterility of economics, swaying to and fro between two schools. Unfortunately I have sent back that chapter which was a later proof.

Now: to sum up, I don't know if I have said enough to convince you that I do understand the broad outline of your system (if I do!). Anyhow your representation of the way in which I took it was quite wrong. I think that I am well placed, because I have thought a great deal about the implications of the *Treatise*, having lectured on it etc. and I have heard some of your views in advance. What I fear is that less well-placed readers may not understand so much; and that the dust you want to raise will obscure the view of your central points. If the economists who read your book don't take the essential points, the outlook is bad. There is a limit to what the human mind can assimilate. Most of the readers won't have the time or opportunity or assimilative powers of grasping the points raised in subsequent controversies.

What is important for the initial understanding, which is so much to be desired, is that their minds should be strongly directed on to your essential points. You present them with the most attractive kind of red-herring, namely controversial attacks on certain authors and about subjects they know well. The mind likes to take refuge from the un-familiar (your views which you want to put across) with the familiar (what exactly did Marshall mean in such and such a passage). And I don't think you lead them pleasantly from the familiar to the unfamiliar, because I think your criticisms are much too cursory and, I am bound to say again, unjust. .'. I think the tactics suggested in your letter *mistaken*.

I don't know if you feel that anything is to be gained by oral discussion! A viva voce eliciting how far I have understood or misunderstood your position might determine what weight should be attached to my objections. I am scheduled to sail for Ireland on Tuesday night, though that fixture is not absolutely rigid. I shall remain there about 10 days.

Yours,

ROY

Your really important and effective criticism of the classical view occurs in Book I. It is implicit in the classical view that any given level of output is uniquely correlated with a given level of *real* wages (by princs. of dim. returns and increasing disutility of work). Once you knock that on the head, as you do most effectively, the level of output is either indeterminate or has to be determined by some new equation not provided for in the classical system. Thus the way is clear for a radical reconstruction. Your new equation is the liquidity preference schedule. (This does not of course directly determine the level of output but does so in the roundabout way described on page 1 of this letter.) No further criticism of the classical system is required. All your subsequent criticism is fussy, irrelevant, dubious, hair-splitting and hair-raising.

Note to p. 4 [above p. 555]

Let y_1, y_2 etc. be rates of interest and Y_1, Y_2 etc. incomes corresponding to them (Y_1 being derived from y_1 via marginal efficiency of cap. and the multiplier). For each value of Y draw classical supply curves, of which *each* curve shows amount of saving corresponding to various values of y at a given level of Y. Then according to you it will be found that the value of y at which the curve appropriate to income Y_r intersects the demand curve is in fact y_r, where y_r represents any given rate of interest whatever. The so-called supply curve in the passage from your letter which I have quoted is the locus of points on the classical supply curves for that value of y corresponding to the level of income on the assumption of which each was drawn.

To R. F. HARROD, *10 September 1935*

My dear Roy,

I absolve you completely of misunderstanding my theory. It could not be stated better than on the first page of your letter. Also I think the construction in the note, of which I attach a copy to remind you of it, is both correct and very useful as a help to exposition, and I shall like to appropriate it. But what you say seems to me to fail either as a statement of what the classical theory says or as a justification of its subject to special assumptions. I make a great distinction between the classical theory of employment, which does make perfect sense and works all right on certain special assumptions, and the classical theory of the rate of interest which makes no sense on any assumptions whatever. I have now thought about the matter enough (having reached these chapters in my revision) to express myself more clearly.

Let me start out from your note which I understand as follows:—

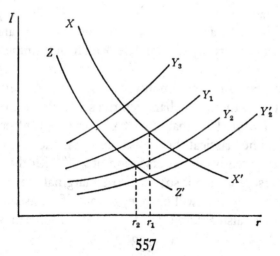

r the rate of interest is measured horizontally, the quantity of investment (or saving) vertically. XX' is the schedule of the marginal efficiency of capital showing how much investment will take place at each rate of interest. The curves Y_1, Y_2, Y_3 show the relation between the propensity to save and the rate of interest, assuming successively that income is Y_1, Y_2, Y_3. Now you argue that, *if* income is Y_1, the rate of interest is given by the intersection of the Y_1 saving curve with XX', the schedule of the marginal efficiency of capital; and that *this* is the classical theory of the rate of interest.

I will return to this in a moment. But, first of all, I should like to point out that what the diagram does show (and most elegantly) is the relation between the rate of interest and the level of income, given the schedule of the marginal efficiency of capital and the propensity to consume.

The reason that this is *not* a theory of the rate of interest in any circumstances is that the assumption of a fixed income Y_1 is too all-embracing and does not allow for those things to vary which the classical theory assumes to vary. For, if either the propensity to save or the marginal efficiency curve changes, the level of income changes; so that the assumption of a given level of income involves us in assuming that neither of the classical theory's own chosen variables is capable of change,—unless there are changes in certain other factors which happen by a miracle to be such as to leave income unchanged (and in this case it is the nature of the miracle which determines the rate of interest).

Take the case most commonly contemplated by the classical theory in which there is a change in the schedule of the marginal efficiency of capital so that the XX' curve is replaced by the curve ZZ'. The classical theory assumes that the rate of interest will then be given by the intersection of ZZ' with the Y_1 curve. But, of course, this is not so; for if the marginal efficiency curve shifts, income *cet. par.* will change, so that, if we assume income fixed, we must also assume that the marginal efficiency curve is fixed. The only circumstance in which a change in the marginal efficiency curve can leave income unchanged (assuming that the propensity to save does not change), is in the event of liquidity preference happening to change by just the amount necessary to balance the change in the marginal efficiency curve. But in this event it would still be the change in liquidity preference which was determining the rate of interest.

The question whether or not the real wage is equal to the marginal disutility of labour *does* depend on whether or not there is full employment. But no similar reconciliation is possible between the theory that the rate of interest depends on the intersection of the propensity to consume with the schedule of the marginal efficiency of capital, and the theory that it depends on liquidity preference. The fault of the classical theory lies, not in its limiting its terrain by assuming constant income, but in its failing to see that, if either of its own variables (namely propensity to save and schedule of marginal efficiency of capital) change, income must also *cet. par.* change; so that its tool breaks in its hand and it doesn't know and can't tell us what will happen to the rate of interest, when either of its own variables changes.

I say, therefore, that it is *nonsense* to assume at the same time that income is constant and that the propensity to save and the schedule of the marginal efficiency of capital are variable.

Look through again my various quotations from classical economists and tell me which of them is not nonsense.

I shall be here from Sept. 22 at least up to the end of the month. Will you come down for a night or two after you are back from Ireland?[1] It is probable that by then I shall have finished re-writing the chapters dealing with rate of interest.

Yours ever,

J. M. KEYNES

[1] Anytime from Sept. 27 to Oct. 5.

You will see that I have, in a sense, shifted my ground in the above. I have gained a great deal from your hard knocks, and would like some more. Since I wrote the above I have finished my redraft of the relevant chapter and it should be back from the printer if you can come as above.

From R. F. HARROD, *20 September 1935*

Dear Maynard,

By all means use my construction of a family of classical supply curves if you feel so disposed.

To return to your point that the classical theory doesn't make sense. You write: 'the assumption of a fixed income is too all-embracing and does not allow for those things to vary which the classical theory assumes to vary. For, if either the propensity to save or the marginal efficiency curve changes, the level of income changes.' Yes, according to you; not necessarily according to the classical theory. And if it does change, it does not do so by the *right* amount for *your* theory. *Take an increased propensity to save.* Why will income vary? The level of income, remember, is uniquely determined by the marginal disutility of labour and its marginal productivity. Which of these varies? If the rate of interest falls, as classical theory supposes it to do, then the productivity curve moves to the right—future product being discounted at a lower rate—and income goes *up*! An increase in the marg. eff. of capital might also cause income to go up (e.g. if due to an invention making *both* labour and capital more effective, or to the opening of a new foreign market). But there is no guarantee in classical theory that it will go up by the right amount to make a rise in the rate of interest un-necessary. So that tho' income can't be taken as constant in the face of these changes, the variations in it induced by variations in the propensity to save or m. e. of cap. are not according to classical theory of the order of magnitude you require for your theory.

Return to the increased propensity to save. The classical theorists supposed a fall in the rate of interest. A pure miracle, say you, with your liquidity preference in mind. You claim that income will fall sufficiently to reduce saving to the level at which it stood before the change in propensity and so allow equilibrium with the old rate of interest. But doesn't this fall in income look a little like a miracle? With the level of income uniquely determined by the labour disutility and productivity functions it is not only a miracle but an impossibility. By your employment theory, (viz. disutility of labour determining only maximum level of income), you make appropriate variations of income a *possibility*. By your theory that interest is otherwise determined, viz. by liquidity preference, you make it a *necessity*.

What I think is that you are apt to forget the position before your own mind began to work along these lines. I also think that, while your definition of the marginal efficiency of capital is one of the most brilliant and important parts of the book, you are wrong in supposing that the idea (tho' in a vaguer and cruder form) was not present in the classical writers. You get it in Marshall's review of Jevons (1871)!

I don't find the long passage from Marshall (ch. 16) nonsense. I find it harder to understand some of your criticisms. I cannot find any confusion between interest and quasi-rent. According to both him and you, the current rate of interest = the marginal efficiency of capital. But whereas according to you the rate of interest is independently determined, according to him the two unknowns, amount of investment and rate of interest, are jointly determined by the marginal efficiency of capital schedule and the propensity to save (from a level of income taken as given). The value of capital other than that involved in the current marginal investment is determined by the quasi-rent *and* the rate of interest. Subject to the ordinary difficulties of expressing any of these things in language, the M[arshall]. passage seems to me crystal clear and your criticism in the text comparatively difficult to follow.

What I don't like about the chapter is the implied allegation that Marshall's system of thought was fundamentally confused, whereas I believe the confusion to be due to your failure to think yourself back into the system of thought you have abandoned. But for those who are still in it, I believe your chapter will seem captious and lacking in comprehension.

I should be delighted to come for a night one day next week.

Yours,
ROY

To R. F. HARROD, *25 September 1935*

My dear Roy,

I am content! If the classical theory could not be made, even by you, to make more coherent sense than that, it does not deserve very many compliments. However, you must see my re-draft. I am hopeful it may content you and, if it doesn't, I must see what further I can do.

One obstacle, by the way, to your attempted rationalisation arises out of the attitude of the classical school when they reach volume 2 on the subject of money. Marshall believed that an increase in the quantity of money tended to reduce the rate of interest. How would you make this fit in?

It would be very nice if you could come to Tilton this week-end, the 28th. We may, perhaps, be in London from September 30 to October 2, though we shall be back again in Tilton in the last part of that week.

Yours ever,
[copy initialled] J.M.K.

From R. F. HARROD, *27 September 1935*

Dear Maynard,

I quite agree with your point about vol. 2 on money. That is the little cloud in the sky which is destined (with the aid of your magic) to engulf the whole country.

I don't think you find it in the old economics. Your passage from Ricardo is the direct contradiction. I should guess that old Cannan (who never got beyond 1848) would strenuously deny it. Marshall, if I remember right, was saying in 1888 that an increase of money would *raise* the money but lower the real rate of interest.

How does it fit in? It is a monetary *friction* (and ∴ presumably of short-period importance only!). When you consider the system in real terms it simply is not there. And this is where you come in with overwhelming force. The monetary phenomenon can't be so dismissed. For the labour disutility function which is on any theory of fundamental importance to the theory of unemployment, is essentially expressible in monetary terms. To get back to real terms, you would have to assume that the real labour disutility schedule altered whenever there was a change in the price level. Such an analysis is clearly analogous to the Ptolemaic epicycles and must be dismissed.

That is, I think that if you choose your ground well, as you have done in Bk I, you have a superb case. And I deplore all the more attacks from ill-chosen ground, as those of ch. 16 appear to me to be.

Yours,
ROY

Galley 79. (iii), 2nd para. [vol. XIV p. 487; *General Theory*, p. 196]. I have noted:— 'Isn't there a latent contradiction here?' I should have thought that if cash can only be borrowed at a high rate, that would strengthen the motive for holding cash. Instead of investing a surplus, you refrain from doing so in order not to have to borrow on overdraft later. With given liquidity requirements, then, the higher the overdraft rate the higher the rate earnable by lending must be to overcome liquidity preference. Later you say if bank charges were avoided, this *strengthens* the motive for holding cash. But surely a high overdraft rate has the same effect as bank charges.

It is quite true that you wouldn't borrow money in order to hold it as cash, if the rate for borrowing is high. But people don't borrow in order to hold cash, they borrow in order to *avoid* holding cash at some immediately antecedent or subsequent time.

Galley 88. last words of last para. but one before II [vol. XIV p. 491; *General*

Theory, p. 213]. I was rather uneasy about these. I have noted against the words 'diminish the sum':—'But unless it increases this sum by ΔS, it must bid up the price of bonds, unless we revert to the argument of the Treatise, which hasn't figured previously in these pages, that there will simultaneously be Δ(entrepreneurial dissaving) $= \Delta S$.'

First para. of II. I have noted 'obscure'.

On II generally (galleys 88–90 [vol. XIV pp. 491–4; *General Theory*, pp. 213–17]) I have noted:—'This section important and interesting in its positive doctrine. Doubtful of validity and relevance of critical strain.'

Galley 112. footnote 1 [below p. 509; *General Theory*, p. 283]. I have noted:—'Might we have a proviso for imperfect competition?'

And at the end of first complete paragraph [vol. XIV p. 509; *General Theory*, p. 283, bottom] 'Thus the limiting case $e_{or} = 1$.' I have noted:—'Why is this the limiting case? What about decreasing costs?'

Galley 114. 1st paragraph, 1st sentence [vol. XIV p. 509; *General Theory*, p. 287, second paragraph] seems to me a little unkind and sweeping. 'Only' is so very strong. I have written the suggestion:—'It is in this connection that I find the principal significance of the conception...'

Galley 115. 3rd line [vol. XIV p. 510; *General Theory*, p. 289, first paragraph]. In previous passages you have used language to which the following would be an equivalent here:—'though at a real wage equal to or less than the existing one'.

Galley 115. (2) line 4 [vol. XIV p. 510]. I have noted:—'I am not quite clear how you use marginal prime cost here; I *hope* you have used it to *include* user cost, for that is the usage I like.' But if so, your original definition of prime cost required the amendment I suggested in loco.

Galley 120. 5th para. line 2 [vol. XIV p. 456; *General Theory*, p. 120, fourth paragraph]. Against the words general principle I have noted:—'viz. the general principle referred to in the last sentence. That this is so is not quite clear from the language. The reader might take it to refer to the general principle of the multiplier itself, in which case the meaning would be reversed.'

Galley 121. just before IV '(say 5 per cent)' [vol. XIV p. 457; *General Theory*, p. 122]. I have noted:—'So low? cf. Kuznets & Clark, sup.'

Galley 125. 2nd whole paragraph [vol. XIV p. 458; *General Theory*, p. 130, second paragraph]. I have noted:—'Does this mean scrapping entirely the view that increased gold production tends to diminish the value of gold?'

Galley 130. 1st whole para. line 11 [vol. XIV p. 509; *General Theory*, p. 265, first full paragraph]. After 'so' insert 'low'.

Galley 133. appendix on Pigou. I don't apply my general remarks on your critical parts to this, which I think is splendid!

R.F.H.

From R. F. HARROD, *8 October 1935*

Dear Maynard,

A letter from Dennis [Robertson] suggested this thought to me, which seems to me to be clearer than anything I have seen expressed so far.

Banks have two functions, one concerned with the circulating medium one with lending. After much controversy it has been well established—despite Cannan and the banks—that the banks can *create* money. With that the conclusion has been allowed to slip through unchallenged that they can also create new lending. Whereas in fact in the sphere of lending what Cannan and the bankers say is right—they can only lend what is lent to them. They are irretrievable middlemen. Is that a clear statement of the position?

Yours,

ROY

To R. F. HARROD, *9 October 1935*

Dear Roy,

I think your argument stops too soon. It may be an inconvenient use of words to say that banks create lending. But they cause lending to come into existence, which would not be there otherwise, by modifying the terms of lending. That is to say, when the conditions exist which tend towards an increase in the quantity of money, the banks bring about the requisite increase of lending by modifying the terms on which lending happens. In other words, by decreasing the liquidity premium (or increasing it, as the case may be) they appropriately augment the demand for money. The amount of lending is a function of the terms of lending and is obviously not absolute.

Yours ever,

[copy initialled] J.M.K.

From R. F. HARROD, *10 October 1935*

Dear Maynard,

Sorry. I can't have made clear what I was driving at. The banks as you say by decreasing liquidity preference bring down the terms of lending and so cause there to be more lending than there would otherwise be. My point was that they can't swell the total of lending *from their own sources*. For their lendings are always equal to their borrowings. I now think that the main source of the muddle of the 'constant money' theorists is that they imagine that the banks can create additional lending out of nothing as they *can* create additional money. This is linked with the idea of investment being greater than saving etc.

I haven't got a point to argue. This merely assists *me* to see more clearly the point at which the Hayekian school has gone off the lines.

Yours,
ROY

Keynes's discussions of the subject matter of the *General Theory* with R. G. Hawtrey appear to have started in March 1935 during a visit by Hawtrey to Cambridge. This led to the following exchange of letters.

From R. G. HAWTREY, *12 March 1935*

Dear Maynard,

Is the following a correct version of your argument that savings and capital outlay must always be equal?

If an excess of capital outlay is assumed, say £10 million, then additional incomes to the amount of £10 million will be generated by this outlay. If any assumed portion, say £1 million, is saved, and the balance of £9 million is spent on consumption then a *further* £9 million of income will be generated. Thus if one-tenth of every income be assumed to be saved, the income generated will be: £10 million + £9 million + £8 million +,... The sum of this series is £100 million, out of which the saving will be £10 million. That the additional capital outlay must be accompanied by an equal amount of additional saving would be a valid inference if incomes were generated *simultaneously* with the capital outlay.

That would be so if additional demand were immediately met from additional production, i.e. if there were never any change in stocks of commodities. But the possibility of drawing on stocks allows an interval, which may be considerable, between the generating of incomes by capital outlay and the resulting increase in production and further increase in incomes and saving. During that interval there *will* be a discrepancy between capital outlay and savings.

Nor is it necessarily true even that there will be a *tendency* for savings to catch up capital outlay. The expansion of demand for consumers' goods is likely to lead to additional capital outlay, and there is no certainty that this will not exceed the additional savings. The re-establishment of equilibrium

565

is likely to depend on the positive action of the investment market (with or without pressure from the banks) to adjust capital outlay to savings.

I think you argued that, even if for a time goods are sold from stock and not replaced by new production, the sellers of the goods will then be holding the proceeds of sale idle and these will constitute 'savings'. But even if the proceeds of sale are not used to pay off bank advances, but remain as idle balances, these idle balances are not 'savings', because they are not put by out of *income*. A man who sells off an extra £1,000 of income which he can save. He transforms £1,000 of working capital or liquid capital into money, and the money (apart from any that he may draw out on account of his own profit) remains as part of the capital of his business.

Yours ever,
RALPH HAWTREY

To R. G. HAWTREY, *14 March 1935*

My dear Ralph,

I think I had better wait until I can send you my proofs rather than attempt to say in a letter exactly what I do mean;— particularly as I shall probably add a passage dealing with your specific point in the appropriate context.

There is, however, one point where there is some misunderstanding. I do not maintain that the proceeds of sale of goods previously in stock constitute *savings*. On my use of terms they are negative investment, since my investment is your capital outlay minus or plus changes in stocks. What I did say was that the proceeds of sales of stocks were available to *finance* new capital outlay in your sense just as much as savings would be.

Yours ever,
J. M. KEYNES

On 12 June, Keynes laid the basis for discussion in earnest.

To R. G. HAWTREY, *12 June 1935*

Dear Ralph,

I at last enclose for your inspection the galley proofs of the greater part of my book. From the table of contents which I also enclose you will see that you have here the whole thing with the exception of the three last chapters.

This copy is a spare one and there is no reason why you should not scribble any comments in the margin. I am extremely anxious to know how it strikes you.

The different sections are in different states of revision and you will find various internal inconsistencies which will have to be put right. Broadly speaking, the first six chapters and the last six are in a later stage of revision than the intermediate ones.

Many congratulations on your election as a Fellow of the British Academy. If, however, I am by misadventure mentioning this too soon, delete the words.

Yours ever,

J. M. KEYNES

Late in June, Hawtrey sent Keynes a series of comments on chapters 1–24, which formed the basis for a long series of discussions in the period after 1 September 1935.

From R. G. HAWTREY, *June 1935*

GENERAL THEORY OF EMPLOYMENT, INTEREST AND MONEY

Comments on chapters 1 to 24

'*Effective demand*' (chapter 3, II, p. 11 [below p. 370])

Presumably the definition of effective demand as 'the sum for which the current output can actually be sold' is to be amended, for it is the phrase immediately below, 'the sum for which it is expected that this output can be sold', which represents the usage adopted in subsequent passages (with a few exceptions).

It seems to me quite impossible to adopt a numerical expression for the total *expected* demand for goods. There will, no doubt, be some producers who may be said to have a numerically measurable expectation. Some of them may be producing a known daily output in expectation of selling at the market price or possibly under contracts at known prices. But even in such cases these prices do not represent the demand for the output. For the total demand will be the proceeds of sale *at retail*, and in general the retailer will not make any definite estimate of those proceeds, he will order from the manufacturer an amount which he thinks he can sell at the current price in a reasonable time. But a 'reasonable' time will be an interval quite indefinite within fairly wide limits. A retailer who makes a practice of ordering twelve dozen at a time of hats of a certain pattern may find that he sometimes sells them in two months and sometimes in four. If he finds his actual sales increase to a rate of, say, nine dozen in a month he will very likely double his order. But he will make no definite estimate of his future rate of sales. Nor will he mind much if he takes three months or even four to sell the twenty-four dozen.

There are some goods and services which do not pass through retailers' hands. A railway will maintain a certain establishment corresponding to an expectation of traffic. But a decision to increase or decrease the establishment will never be based on a *precise* estimate of future traffic. Action will be taken when *at least* a certain change in traffic is anticipated, the possibility of a greater change being fully recognised but not acted on.

And even if traders are deemed all to make precise forecasts of demand, are they to be supposed to make these forecasts all for the same period of time? If not, how are the forecasts to be added up into a significant total?

Thus effective demand in the sense of total expected demand for output per unit of time is a fiction. Nor does it seem to be a very useful fiction. It enables you to associate the number employed, N, with the quantity, D, but it does not throw any fresh light on the motives which actually determine N.

And if you are going to employ the concept of expected demand it seems to me very undesirable to use the phrase, 'effective' demand, which other people invariably use to mean actual demand.

In chapter 7 you define Y' (the income contained in D, the effective demand) as 'the short-period expectation which would lead to the use of the equipment' (p. 32 [vol. XIV p. 422]). That is different from the short-period expectation which actually exists. This is one of the less fully revised chapters, and perhaps the foregoing phrase is to be altered to that which appears at the top of p. 33 [vol. XIV p. 423], 'which leads to the decision to use existing capital equipment to produce this output' (i.e. to use the equipment only to the extent that it is actually being used).

But that is not quite the same thing as the actual short-period expectation.

The passage in chapter 5 (I) (pp. 21–2 [vol. XIV pp. 391–3; *General Theory*, pp. 48–50]) supposes discrepancies to exist between the actual state of expectation at any moment and the volume of employment at that moment, which may differ from 'the long-period employment corresponding to the existing state of expectation'.

If 'the economic machine is occupied at any given time with a number of overlapping activities the existence of which is due to various past states of expectation' (p. 22 [*General Theory*, p. 50]), then the existing output corresponds not to the existing state of expectation but to these various past states.

The definition, if it is to be retained, ought to be cleared up.

Long-term expectation

If there are difficulties about adding up short-term expectations of demand into a numerical total, they are moderate in comparison with those of applying that process to long-term expectations.

$Y''(= P'' + E'')$ is 'the long-period expectation which would have led to new investment in the equipment' (p. 32 [vol. XIV p. 422]). It is not a total of any set of actual expectations, but of the purely hypothetical expectations which would have evoked the new investment. These expectations may differ widely from those which were entertained when the investment in the equipment actually occurred. Moreover the expectations on which investment is based are not concerned with anything but the prospective yield or profit: they may include a forecast of the other constituents of demand, E, but they need not.

You identify Y'', the income of long-period expectation, with income as used in the *Treatise on Money*. But that is a mistake. Normal profit, as defined in the *Treatise*, corresponds sufficiently closely with P''. But the other constituents of income are actual incomes, with no reference to expectations at all.

Finished and unfinished goods

The distinction on p. 23 [vol. XIV p. 396; *General Theory*, pp. 50–1] is somewhat obscure. Goods are divided into two categories, consumption goods, 'which are expected to pass into consumption when they are finished', and capital goods, 'the effective demand for which depends on long-term expectations of consumers' demand'. But raw materials and intermediate products are to be classed as 'finished'. These therefore are not 'consumption goods'. But in many cases the demand for them will not be the subject of long-term expectations. It would seem for example that wheat is a 'finished product'.

User cost

I understand user cost (p. 26 [vol. XIV p. 402]) to be that part of depreciation which arises from the equipment *being used*, to the exclusion of the loss of value (whether from deterioration or from obsolescence or any other cause) which would equally occur if it were not used. It is therefore so much of depreciation as is included in prime costs (taken in the usual significance), and omits so much as is included in overhead costs. The distinction is interesting and for some purposes important, but it is not clear why it should be made for the purpose of defining income. In the calculations of prospective yield actually made by promoters of new enterprises allowance is invariably made for depreciation as a whole and not only for user cost. This may involve highly conjectural estimates of the rate of obsolescence, but those estimates are in fact made, and there is no reason to suppose that they tend to be excessive. When in chapter 7 [vol. XIV p. 422] an expression is introduced for prospective yield on the basis of an allowance for user cost only, this does not represent the expectation on which investment in new enterprises is actually based. And I note that in chapter 12, III [*General Theory*, p. 141], you find fault with those who neglect the competitive effect of 'inventions and new technique in estimating the marginal efficiency of capital'.

So far as income itself is concerned, and its derivative saving, it is quite rightly pointed out in chapter 6 (v) [vol. XIV p. 415] that the precise definition of depreciation does not matter, but in the definition of prospective yield it is essential to employ whatever measure of depreciation is actually in practice used.

In the definition of user cost (pp. 25–6 [vol. XIV p. 402]) the hypothetical value, $C' - B'$, of the capital equipment as it would have been if not used is to be arrived at by deducting the cost not only of maintenance but of 'improvement'. To what extent is the 'improvement' to involve scrapping? For a piece of plant scrapped before it is worn out the user cost is reduced to nil, or at any rate to something less than it would have been if the plant had been scrapped only on account of wear and deterioration.

Quasi-rent

It seems a mistake to attribute a new and unaccustomed meaning to this term. As used by Marshall, and by most other economists, it means a transitory gain made through the temporary scarcity of some factor of production, e.g. a limited amount of plant or a limited supply of skilled labour available for meeting an unexpectedly increased demand. If the return from an investment actually earned is to be called profit, why not call the expected profit the expected profit? The terms net and gross can be used to distinguish whether depreciation is or is not deducted.

Investment

Is it really necessary to use the term 'investment' for the increment of wealth? It is seriously misleading. The increment of wealth is composed of: (1) the cost of new instrumental goods; (2) any designed increment (or decrement) of working capital; (3) any undesigned increment (or decrement) of unsold goods.

When you discuss the motives and tendencies by which investment is determined, you neglect (3) altogether, and you do not seem to have much regard to (2).

In chapter 8 (1) [vol. xiv p. 428] you discuss 'the prevalence of the idea that saving and net investment, taken in their straightforward sense, can differ from one another'. But the straightforward sense of 'investment' undoubtedly excludes the undesigned increment of unsold goods, and consequently it can differ from saving. And in chapter 15 (p. 70) [vol. xiv pp. 475–6] you attribute to the 'traditional theory' the view that the 'output of capital' may differ from saving, and then proceed to identify 'output of capital' with 'investment', i.e. the increment of wealth. I doubt whether any economist except yourself would use the expression 'output of capital' to include the involuntary accumulation of unsold goods.

Once you have established the fact that the increment of wealth is, in consequence of your definition, identically equal to saving, there is no further need to refer to the matter. And I note that you yourself use the term 'investment' in a different sense later on (chapter 13, vi [vol. xiv p. 468; *General Theory*, pp. 158–60]).

Colin Clark

The figures for gross investment output quoted in the table in chapter 9 (p. 40 [vol. xiv p. 440]) include *external* investment. This should I think be deducted. And Colin Clark has now abandoned the figures you quote for maintenance and depreciation.

Marginal efficiency of capital

Marginal efficiency of 'an investment or capital asset' is defined (chapter 12, 1 [*General Theory*, p. 135]) in terms of 'prospective yield'. But prospective yield is defined (chapter 7, 1 [vol. xiv p. 419]) in terms of *profit*, and is only applicable to a going concern, that is to say, to an assemblage of plant organised for production. Profit, as you define it, includes interest, but it also includes the remuneration of the entrepreneur. Consequently it ought not to enter into a calculation of the yield of capital as such.

For the purposes of the classical theory of interest you require the prospective yield not of an enterprise or going concern, but of each *separate instrument* included in the plant. The prospective yield of an instrument is to be measured by its cost-saving capacity. In any plant there will be some instruments so indispensable that their cost-saving capacity may correspond to a yield of thousands per cent. There will be others less essential, but still with a yield many times the rate of interest. But there may also be instruments at or near the margin, which it will only just be worth while to use, and which might involve a loss if the rate of interest were substantially higher.

The point at which the marginal efficiency of capital assets makes itself felt is in the decision as to how highly capitalised each separate concern shall be, how deep its equipment shall penetrate along the scale of falling prospective yields.

In the case of those durable consumers' goods which you include in investment the calculation of marginal efficiency must likewise be applied to each separate piece of equipment. But here the prospective yield will not be wholly in terms of labour-saving capacity; it will be partly, perhaps principally, in terms of enjoyment.

To complete your theory of marginal efficiency, you must apply it also to working capital. There will be for any concern a necessary minimum of working capital which would be employed whatever the rate of interest might be, and there will be a further stock held not for necessity but for convenience. Your theory of investment is expressed entirely in terms of long-period expectation and prospective yield. In the *Treatise on Money* you at any rate thought it worth while to say something about the relation of the rate of interest and of credit facilities to working capital and stocks of goods. You now simply leave it out.

You define the marginal efficiency of a capital asset as the rate of discount which would make the present value of its prospective yield just equal to its supply price, and then you define the current marginal efficiency of capital as 'the greatest of these marginal efficiencies'. Surely you should say 'least' instead of greatest. If the rate of interest is 4 per cent, it is not worth while to produce any capital assets with a marginal efficiency of less than 4 per cent, while many may exist and may still be coming into existence with a much higher yield.

And is it not a mistake to call the yield of all capital assets alike their 'marginal' efficiency? 'Marginal' here seems to have no significance at all, and might be confined to the case which is marginal in the accepted sense.

Classical theory of interest

You say in chapter 15 (p. 71 [vol. XIV p. 477]) that in equilibrium the rate of interest will be equal to the marginal efficiency of capital, but that 'to make this into a theory of the rate of interest or to derive the rate of interest from it involves a circular argument'. For we must already know the scale of current investment, and therefore the rate of interest, before we can know the marginal efficiency of capital.

But that is not so. The marginal efficiency of capital at any time is the lowest yield of any capital asset which is being produced. If you ask why none is being produced with a lower yield, the answer may be that *hitherto* the rate of interest has not been low enough to make it worth while. But whatever the cause, the marginal efficiency of capital at any moment is a matter of fact. If the rate of interest differs from the marginal efficiency of capital, there results disequilibrium in the form of a tendency to accelerate or retard the output of capital. The disequilibrium, along with the tendency, might persist for a considerable time. But that is a question of dynamics, while the classical theory is one of statics.

The classical theory does not involve any assumption as to the volume of employment.

Liquidity preference

You say that the motive for holding any money in excess of what is needed for transactions and for precaution is the risk of loss involved in investment, in consequence of uncertainty as to the future rate of interest (chapter 14, II, p. 66 [vol. XIV p. 472; *General Theory*, pp. 168–9]). A man holds cash in preference to investments when he fears a capital loss on realisation so heavy as to offset the gain from the receipt of interest. (I think your formula $\Sigma p_{rr} d_n$ requires revision, but I will not go into that.)

This tendency is the foundation of your whole theory. You regard it as the dominant factor relating the supply of money to the state of employment, prices, etc.

I need hardly say I would not deny the existence of that tendency. It may well acquire importance at a time when there is some force at work (e.g. open market purchases by banks on an exceptional scale) which forces up the prices of fixed-interest securities to what the ordinary business man regards as an artificial and precarious level. But this is a very rare state of things. It has probably existed in a greater or less degree in England and America since 1932. Possibly it occurred once before in the middle of the 'nineties. But I do not think there is any trace of it at any other time. From 1818 to 1889 the fluctuations in the prices of fixed-interest securities were never great enough to induce investors to take serious precautions against a capital loss. It must be remembered that, to be effective, the risk of loss must be heavy enough to offset the gain from the receipt of interest.

You point out quite rightly that the tendency to prefer cash depends on a difference of opinion among investors. If all took the same view of the future rate of interest, that view would necessarily be reflected in the present rate of interest. When the banks are induced to buy securities on a large scale by motives quite different from those of an ordinary investor, this difference of opinion may occur. But hardly otherwise. I do not think the stock market in England or America or anywhere else takes a very lively interest in the long-term rate of interest as such, except when there is a threat of war. People are much more concerned with the value of shares, and in the value of shares of the speculative type the rate of interest is usually only a minor factor. The investor is willing to accept the judgment of the market on the price of gilt-edged securities without question.

Even if the tendency to prefer cash to investments does acquire importance at certain times, it cannot be assumed that it acquires such outstanding importance as to govern the monetary situation. You do not argue that it does; you simply omit to mention other factors.

Chapter 19

The discussion of the relation of 'own-rates' of interest to the marginal efficiency of capital is brilliant and original. But do you not require to distinguish between the two principal factors determining forward rates, (1) carrying costs, and (2) the prospect of increased or diminished supply? The discussion as it stands is concerned mainly with (1) to the exclusion of (2).

In the case of carrying costs, the general principle is, I think, that it is a disadvantage to become a forward seller or debtor of a commodity and an advantage to become a forward buyer or creditor. If it is the practice for those who borrow for the acquisition of capital equipment to become debtors in terms of a commodity, the creditors will be given the advantages of the forward buyer. But if the volume of such obligations becomes large relatively to the stock of the commodity, the advantage of the forward buyer becomes very much diluted. In fact a 'credit system' will develop in which the available stock of the commodity will be accumulated in the hands of a group of dealers (corresponding to the bankers) on whom the debtors will be able to draw. Since the dealers will be both creditors and debtors and can make a profit out of the business, the introduction of a credit system will practically eliminate carrying costs. High carrying costs do undoubtedly militate against the use of a commodity as money, but, *once it is so used*, the carrying costs do not appreciably affect the rate of interest.

On the other hand the rate of interest is very much affected by prospective plenty or scarcity of the medium in which it is calculated. This is the Irving Fisher principle of appreciation and interest, which you refer to in chapter 12.

With regard to your criticisms in that passage, I do not think the 'dilemma' (p. 53 [*General Theory*, p. 142]) is a real one. According to Irving Fisher the change in the value of money is only operative so far as it is foreseen. But that does not mean that the prices of existing goods will rise to the anticipated future level. For the advantages of holding money and holding goods are equalised *by the rate of interest itself*. If prices are expected to rise by 2 per cent in six months, and the rate of interest would otherwise be 3 per cent, then the rate of interest should rise to 7 per cent, and the six months forward prices of all commodities should be 2 per cent higher.

In chapter 13, on long-term expectation, you do not distinguish between the state of mind of the promoter of a capital enterprise and that of the purchaser of shares. It is usual for a very limited number of promoters to start an enterprise to take advantage of some new opening. They include people of technical knowledge and skill, who expect to make a 'profit' over and above interest at the market rate on the capital equipment they install. Very often they hope for an abnormal profit (a quasi-rent in Marshall's sense) but a normal profit, if the prospect is sufficiently sure, will do.

In the majority of cases there is no public issue of shares till a going concern has been created, and the prospect of profit, having become much more definite, can be capitalised in the price of the shares. Even when the public issue is made, it is common for the promoters to retain control, or at any rate to continue responsible for management and policy, and for the raising of fresh capital from the market when required.

I should say that the promoter's activities are usually governed by the prospect of *selling* his product. Either he thinks the time has come for an extension of an existing enterprise in an industry where demand is expanding and straining capacity, or he has hopes from some new departure. Having decided to start his venture, he must raise funds for the requisite capital equipment, and it is at that stage that the marginal efficiency of capital has to be taken into account. He has the choice of employing more labour and less capital or less labour and more capital. This is entirely a question of costs. He will keep down costs in order to keep up profits. Once committed to the venture he is committed to the costs, and his choice as between capital and labour at the margin is not very speculative in character. What is speculative is the margin of profit which depends on his forecast of demand.

The promoters may get shares on special terms, and may choose to realise a capital gain on at any rate a part of their holding. But I should say that it is exceptional for them to clear out altogether. If the concern has a speculative character, gambling in the shares may go on on a large scale, but that need not affect the operations of the promoters who are responsible for the 'investment' in the sense of the creation of a capital enterprise, except that when new capital has to be raised the state of the market in the shares becomes important.

Of course there are some enterprises that are floated from the very beginning by a public issue, particularly for exploiting some new invention or newly discovered natural resources. But there must still be promoters to take the initiative and to be responsible for the whole business of planning, organisation and management.

It is in the minds of promoters, not in those of purchasers of shares, that are to be found the long-term expectations upon which the volume of capital outlay depends.

To R. G. HAWTREY, *4 September 1935*

My dear Ralph,

I have been dealing with your notes on my book pari passu with re-writing the corresponding chapters; with the result that I am by no means at the end of them. I have, however, completed my re-writing of the first three books, namely chapters 1–11, and have, therefore, carefully considered your notes up to that point.

My re-writing has been so drastic that it is no longer much worth while to deal with your criticisms seriatim. How you will consider that I have disposed of them by my revision I cannot say. Several have, I think, been fully disposed of. But there are others which perhaps reach down to deeper differences of opinion.

I should mention that a number of your criticisms I do accept and have done my best to meet them. One or two points, not of the first importance, where I do not agree are as follows:—

1. You are not right, I think, as to the meaning attached to quasi-rent by Marshall and his followers. Quasi-rent as used by him does not mean a transitory gain made through a temporary scarcity factor, but the total return during any period whether

normal or abnormal from the possession of capital equipment or the like.

2. I understand your reason for excluding an undesigned increment of unsold goods from the definition of investment. But I cannot agree that your meaning of investment thus arrived at is 'the straightforward sense' in which it has commonly been used. Not that you are not perfectly entitled to define investment in this way;—you will see what I have said about this definition in my revised books.

3. You say that Colin Clark has now abandoned the figures I quote for maintenance and depreciation. I was not aware of this. Do you remember where he has stated this? Has he given revised figures?—However, there is no need for me to bother you about this. I can write to him direct.

Generally speaking, my revision has been aimed at simplification. Your criticisms have made it evident that I have raised a good many complications and difficulties which, whether right or wrong, were quite unnecessary to my thesis, and I have been trying to clear these up anyway. I will write to you again about your notes subsequent to chapter 11 later on.

Yours ever,

[copy initialled] J.M.K.

From R. G. HAWTREY, *18 September 1935*

Dear Maynard,

Thanks for your letter of 4 September. I shall be deeply interested to see your revised version. Meanwhile, here are some further remarks on the three points you specifically refer to:—

(1) *Quasi-rent.* I agree I was wrong in regarding 'temporary scarcity' as essential to Marshall's conception. But I still think that your use of the term differs essentially from his. He applied it to the receipts of *any* group of productive agents whose behaviour bears an analogy to the Ricardian theory of rent. That is to say, whenever a market is governed by the circumstances of the least favourably placed agent and the receipts of any other agent correspond to its differential advantage, you have in the latter an example of a quasi-rent.

Over short periods the receipts from the possession of capital equipment may behave as a quasi-rent in this sense. But there are other instances, such as the rent of skill of workmen in a favourable market.

If you simply identify quasi-rent with the yield of a capital asset over any period, long or short, you are losing sight of the essential characteristic of Marshall's concept, for over a period long enough for markets to be affected by a fresh supply of capital equipment the yield approximates to a normal profit, and the analogy with the Ricardian rent disappears. It is a mistake to apply the term quasi-rent *unconditionally* to any class of receipts; it is an attribute which may attach to various economic quantities according to circumstances.

(2) *Investment*. You do not agree that the term investment in 'the straightforward sense' excludes an undesigned increment of unsold goods. Logically I think you could make out a good case. Ordinarily, investment means the acquisition of rights in enterprises. You transfer the application of the term from the enterprises to their assets. This modification once admitted, it seems reasonable to say that the assets may include not only fixed and necessary working capital, but stocks of goods in whatever circumstances acquired.

That would be all right were it not that the term investment does irresistibly suggest to the mind of the economist or the business man investment in capital goods. Comments that have been made on your *Treatise* are themselves demonstration enough. And you yourself are not exempt from this weakness.

You showed it in the *Treatise* when you described the 'decision' to which investment was due. And now you show it again. In chapter 3 (IV) [vol. XIV p. 375] you divide the effective demand, D, into D_1, the expected consumption, and D_2, the expected investment. D_1, you say, is a function of N, where $D_1 = F(N)$. But D_2 'depends on quite different factors, which we shall subsequently sum up as the marginal efficiency of capital and the rate of interest. For the amount of new investment will depend on what investments are expected to be profitable...' Not at all. The amount of new investment depends on the excess of income over D_1. Do you mean that the *expectations* of the producers of investment goods will be governed by the marginal efficiency of capital and the rate of interest, although the actual amount of investment will not? Surely not.

In chapter 5 (I) [vol. XIV p. 392; *General Theory*, pp. 46–7] you distinguish between long-term expectation, which 'is concerned with investment' and short-term expectation, which 'is mainly concerned with estimating the prospective demand for consumption goods'. But clearly long-term expectation is concerned not with 'investment' but with capital goods.

Again in chapter 8 (III) [vol. XIV pp. 432–3] you introduce your explanation of how an act of individual saving may react on someone else's savings, by saying 'it is certain that individual saving must have this effect, except in so far as it causes a corresponding increase of investment to occur *pari passu*'. But of course with your definition, the increase in investment and the increase in savings are inseparable. In the passage immediately following you seem to regard the adjustment of investment to saving as a process *occupying time*.

In chapter 11 (II) [vol. XIV p. 453] you argue that 'a rise in the rate of interest...will diminish investment; hence a rise in the rate of interest must similarly have the effect of reducing income to a level at which saving is decreased in the same measure as investment'. Now of course I should not dispute the practical conclusion that when investment is diminished by a rise in the rate of interest, incomes are reduced. But the argument is wrongly expressed. What is immediately diminished by the rise in the rate of interest is not investment but capital outlay. So long as saving remains undiminished, the excess of saving over capital outlay is covered by the increment of unsold goods. It is the unwillingness of traders to accumulate unsold goods that leads to restriction of output and a fall in incomes.

In some passages (chapter 7 (I) [vol. XIV p. 418] and chapter 12 (I) [*General Theory*, p. 135]) you refer not to investment but to 'an' investment. What is the relation of an investment to investment? Investment is the *difference* between two quantities of wealth per unit of time, output and consumption. Output is composed of items, individual products. But can an individual product be an investment? In chapter 12 you refer to 'an investment or a capital asset' as if they were more or less the same thing. Even if investment were composed of nothing but capital goods, I do not think you could properly regard it as made up of a number of separate investments each consisting in the production of a capital good. For these items make a gross total, from which you must deduct replacements equivalent to user cost to arrive at investment. And when you include all investment goods (that is to say, *all* commodities before they have been sold to consumers) the items constituting the gross total would be all the commodities produced, so that 'an' investment would be the production of any commodity whatever.

When you come to chapter 13 [vol. XIV pp. 465–70; *General Theory*, chapter 12], the expressions 'an investment' and 'investments' are freely used, and obviously mean the acquisition of rights in enterprises in the form of securities. In the first five sections the term 'investment' is used side by side with them, presumably (though not certainly) in its defined sense. Thereafter 'investment' is given a new definition.

Now you could, no doubt, re-write all these passages so as to conform strictly with your original definition of investment. But it seems to me that it would be much wiser to retain the use of investment in the sense of the acquisition of rights in enterprises (as in chapter 13), and to use a different term elsewhere.

Wherever you are associating 'investment' with the marginal efficiency of capital and long-term expectation, you are referring not to investment as defined but to outlay on capital goods. I think you need three separate terms, one to cover the outlay on capital goods in the narrow sense, another to cover the designed outlay on capital of all kinds (including working capital), and the third to denote the increment of wealth. The first depends on long-term expectations. The third is equal to saving, and depends on the conditions which determine saving. The second you have still to deal with.

(3) *Colin Clark*. My ground for supposing that he had discarded the figures of depreciation and maintenance which you quote, was negative. He does not use them or even adapt them in his recent memorandum on Investment in Capital Goods in Great Britain.[1]

Yours ever,
R. G. HAWTREY

To R. G. HAWTREY, *24 September 1935*

Dear Ralph,

Thank you for your letter of September 18th. The best plan will be, I think, that I should let you see the page proofs as soon as they begin to come along, which should be at no distant date. Meanwhile, there are one or two points in your letter which I would like to mention at once.

1. I have now cut out all reference to quasi-rent, having yielded to your view that my use of this term was possibly confusing and certainly unnecessary.

2. *Investment*, on the other hand, I fear I cannot materially change; though here your comments about my inconsistencies and ambiguities have been very helpful, and I will do my best to deal with them.

In the main they arise, I think, through my not infrequently omitting the adjective 'intended' or 'designed'. This is particularly noticeable to you because of the importance which you attach to the difference between the intended and the actual

---

[1] C. Clark, 'Investment in Fixed Capital in Great Britain', *London and Cambridge Economic Service Special Memorandum No. 38*, September 1934. [Ed.]

amount of new investment. Take, for example, the passage you quote from chapter 3 at the top of your page 3 [above p. 578]. The end of the passage you quote should obviously run 'for the *intended* amount of new investment will depend on what investments are expected to be profitable'. I mean that the intended investment will be governed by the marginal efficiency of capital and the rate of interest, although the actual amount will not.

Let me take your subsequent points in order. In chapter 5 (I) I mean that intended investment depends on long-term expectation, but I do not mean that long-term expectation is the only influence determining the quantity of actual investment as distinguished from intended investment. You must also remember in this context that investment includes dis-investment, i.e. investment decisions include decisions not to produce more copper until the liquid stocks are reduced.

In chapter 8 (III) I merely mean to provide for the exceptional case in which the decision to refrain from consumption may be directly connected with the decision to devote to investment, as when a bank clerk refrains from a holiday abroad in order to build a house. In any passages in which I seem to regard the adjustment of investment and saving as a process occupying time, I agree with you that I am expressing myself incorrectly and am departing from my own ideas.

In chapter 11 (II), here again it is intended investment which is immediately diminished by a rise in the rate of interest.

In the passages where I refer not to investment but to 'an' investment, I am not conscious of inconsistency. I mean by an investment on the part of an individual the acquiring by him of an asset. The aggregate of individual investment and dis-investment in this sense will always be equal to the amount of new investment in the sense of creation of new assets. Except in the case of services where production and consumption are simultaneous, I should agree that the production of any commodity whatever involves investment for a certain period of time. To the extent, however, that it is cancelled by equal dis-investment during the same period, it can be dropped out from the factors which determine aggregate investment.

On the last page of your letter [above p. 580] you say that I need three separate terms, that I have dealt with the first and the third but have not dealt with the second. This, I think, is not correct. The first concept, namely, the outlay on capital goods in the narrow sense, scarcely comes in as a separate item. But the second is what strictly speaking I call intended investment and what I often drop into calling investment without the prefix 'intended'. The third, as you say, is the thing which is equal to saving, being the sum of the intended and unintended investment.

All the above points are partly verbal, though this does not mean they are not important. But behind them, and explaining the importance you attach to them, lies, of course, the different degree of importance which you and I attach to the difference between actual and intended investment. I agree, of course, that this is a factor of some importance, inasmuch as it is one of the factors which determine the effective demand in the next period. But I do not see the same reason that you do for exclusively emphasising those changes in output which are a response to a mistake made in the previous period, as distinct from those changes in output which are not due to a past mistake but to a change in expectation due to some other cause (e.g. a change in the rate of interest). In my view, it is the intended investment and the expected consumption which are the truly operative factors. I agree that a mistake made in the previous period would have to be corrected and that in practice a process of trial and error plays an important part. But theoretically it is a mistake, in my opinion, to put *all* the emphasis on this, particularly because this would lead to a serious underestimate of the importance of changes in the rate of interest and also of changes in the marginal efficiency of capital due to other reasons than the correction of past mistakes.

Yours ever,

[copy initialled] J.M.K.

From R. G. HAWTREY, *1 October 1935*

Dear Maynard,

Thanks for your very interesting letter of the 24th September.

I am very glad you have decided to cut out quasi-rent.

On the subject of investment I have still a good deal to say.

I criticised your use of the expression 'an' investment because I found in it evidence that you do not adhere to your own definition. So long as investment retains its dictionary sense of the acquisition of rights in an enterprise, it is quite natural to regard the gross total of investment as composed of particular investments each consisting in one transaction of this type. The net total of investment is the excess of investors' purchases over their sales of such rights.

When you define investment to be the excess of production over consumption, the gross total to be split up is not investment but production. You say that by an investment on the part of an individual you mean the acquiring by him of an asset, that is to say, of any material product whatever.

The concept of 'an' investment so defined may or may not be useful, but at any rate you do not use it. The passages in which you refer to 'an' investment are all concerned either with the acquisition of a *capital* asset, or with the acquisition of rights in an enterprise. One reason which I urge for dropping your existing definition of investment is that you need some word or other to denote the acquisition of rights in an enterprise. You seem to me to have confused the two meanings in chapter 13.

In my letter of 18th September I said that you need three separate terms for:—(a) outlay on capital goods, (b) designed outlay on capital of all kinds (including working capital), (c) the increment of wealth.

You propose to call (a) 'investment' and (b) 'intended investment'. (I think intentional investment would be better, since you mean the *actual* investment carried out with intention.) It seems very necessary to find a separate term for a, if the numerous passages in which you connect investment with long-term expectation, prospective yield and marginal efficiency of capital are to stand. They are inapplicable to b. Or perhaps, when you apply them to 'investment' in the sense of b, you are making the tacit assumption that working capital, including the holding of stocks of commodities, is wholly insensitive to the terms on which money is borrowed. If you dealt explicitly with this point, you could defend your application to b of arguments which in themselves relate only to a.

I need hardly remind you that this is the main point of difference between you and me in the theory of money. You have never offered any answer at all to the arguments used on the subject in *The Art of Central Banking* (especially pp. 365–71).

You refer to the importance I attach to the difference between actual and intended investment (c and b), i.e. to the undesigned increment or decrement of unsold goods. I do attach importance to it as being the most conspicuous defect in your definition of investment and consequently a source of misunderstanding, but it is a minor point compared with the behaviour of the designed increment or decrement of working capital.

In the comments I sent you in June I suggested that, once you had established the fact that the increment of wealth is, in consequence of your definitions, identically equal to saving, you could drop all further reference to investment in this sense (c). In chapter 6 you define income in terms of output, as $A - U + B$. Saving is income, *minus* consumption, or $A - U + B - C$. Investment you likewise define in terms of output, and it is in effect $A - U + B - C$ over again. 'Saving' and 'investment' are two different names for the same thing, and their equality is a matter of the vocabulary.

The definition proves nothing. In order to arrive at a proposition with any substance in it, you ought to link up your definition of income with the individual incomes out of which savings come. In chapter 3 (I) you describe as 'indubitable' the proposition that 'the income derived in the aggregate by all the elements in the community concerned in a productive activity necessarily has a value exactly equal to the value of the output'. If you rely on that proposition to establish the conclusion that income is equal to output, you must exclude from income all the individual incomes not derived from productive activity. This is of course perfectly reasonable, but it is not self-evident. Savings arise from the unproductive incomes, such as interest on the national debt, war pensions, etc., as well as from the productive. No real difficulty is involved, but there are several alternative ways of dealing with the matter, and I think you should be more explicit.

But even when you have given a more positive content to your proposition that investment is equal to saving, it will remain a formal one. Income is equal to output because every item of output, as it accrues, is possessed by some owner, who pays the incomes of those whose productive activity has contributed towards its value, and retains the balance to form his own income. Provided the accruing value is calculated in the same way for the purposes of output and income, the identity of the two necessarily results. No *causal* relation is involved. This applies equally to the identity of saving and investment.

From the identity of saving and investment it follows that if there is a difference between saving and intended investment, there must be an equal difference between investment and intended investment. That is to say, there will be an undesigned increment or decrement of unsold goods.

As soon as that happens, a *causal* relation is put in operation, which has a tendency to bring saving and *intended* investment into equality.

You apologise for passages in which you regard the adjustment of investment and saving as a process occupying time, and say that you are expressing yourself incorrectly and departing from your own ideas. But the adjustment of *intended* investment and saving, which does occupy time, is more significant for your purposes than the purely formal equality of investment and saving, which does not.

I suggest, therefore, that you drop the use of the term investment to denote the expression $A - U + B - C$, and be content to call it saving, but that you insert an explanation of how saving in this sense is necessarily equal to the increment of wealth, how any discrepancy between it and intended investment must therefore appear in the form of an undesigned increment or decrement of unsold goods, and finally how there results a tendency for the disequilibrium to correct itself.

I feel sure that this procedure would be much closer to the ideas you are setting out to expound, and would be more intelligible to your readers.

Yours ever,
R. G. HAWTREY

To R. G. HAWTREY, *1 October 1935*

My dear Ralph,

My letter of September 4th only dealt with your notes so far as they related to the first eleven chapters. I, therefore, owe you a reply on one or two points in your notes on the later chapters.

1. Your point (on page 9 of your letter [above p. 571]) that I have been inconsistent in my terminology about profit is correct. I have tried to clean this up. I agree with the last paragraph on this page in your letter, that it is the prospective yield of each separate instrument which is relevant.

2. On page 10 [above p. 572] you say that my theory of marginal efficiency must be also applied to working capital. Certainly it must, and I intend so to apply it. But I do not see what special considerations arise. Exactly the same treatment applies. The peculiarity both of working and of liquid capital seems to me to reside in the comparative shortness of its life rather than in any other peculiarity.

3. Bottom of page 10 of your letter [above p. 572]: My

reference to 'the greatest of these marginal efficiencies' seems to me to be correct as it stands. The capital assets which have the lowest marginal efficiency will not be newly produced at all. Investment enterprise will be devoted to those which have the greatest until there is no longer any piece of new investment which can show a marginal efficiency as great as the rate of interest. Thus, in equilibrium, there will be no capital asset having a marginal efficiency greater than the rate of interest. Thus, in equilibrium the marginal efficiency of capital in general will be equal to the greatest of the marginal efficiencies of any particular asset. With reference to the last paragraph of your page 11 [above p. 572], the significance of 'marginal' lies in the fact that I am arriving at the efficiencies of those capital assets which it just on the margin pays to newly produce. That is to say, the marginal efficiency of any type of capital asset is the efficiency of one more additional unit. Isn't this the usual sense of 'marginal'?

4. Your page 12 [above p. 573]: I do not agree with your criticism on this page. If there is a tendency for the marginal efficiency of capital to exceed the rate of interest, disequilibrium will be prevented by a rise in the supply price of capital goods which will bring down the marginal efficiency of capital. That is to say, the current rate of investment will be carried on as intensively as is compatible with not driving the supply price of capital goods beyond the figure which would reduce the marginal efficiency of capital below the current rate of interest.

The classical theory assumes that the amount saved is a function of the rate of interest. This is in no sense true unless there is some assumption as to the volume of employment being given.

5. Your page 13 [above p. 573]: for many years past it has been usual for large sums to be held on deposit account at a rate of interest less than that obtainable on long-dated securities. I do not see how this is to be explained except by fear of a capital loss in the event of a long-dated security having to be realised

suddenly. What you say would only be right, in my opinion, if experience showed that no one ever kept in hand more money than is required for the convenient transaction of current business.

Doubtless it is correct that for a sufficiently long period holders of long-dated securities do not suffer a loss equal to the excess of the interest they earn over those who hold liquid securities. But it does not follow that vague anxieties are not felt by wealth owners which lead them to prefer low-yielding liquid resources to higher-yielding illiquid resources.

What are the 'other factors' to which you refer at the bottom of your page 14 [above p. 574]? You must remember 'preferring cash to investments' includes the case of 'preferring cash to a stock of goods which might fall in price'.

6. Chapter 19; your page 15 [above p. 574]: There must be some misunderstanding here. On my way of thinking, what you say at the bottom of this page is quite wrong. The last sentence of your page 16 [above p. 575] is also quite wrong. If prices are expected to rise by 2 per cent in six months and the rate of interest would otherwise be 3 per cent, it is not the case that the rate of interest will rise to 7 per cent, or, perhaps I should rather say that it is impossible that prices should be *expected* to rise by 2 per cent unless certain special conditions exist as to carrying charges. For the current state of expectation is reflected in the spot price of commodities. The expected price six months forward cannot exceed the spot price by more than the carrying charge for six months. And, if the carrying charge is such as to make possible an expected rise of 2 per cent in six months, even then there is no reason why the rate of interest should rise to 7 per cent, because no one could make money by borrowing at that rate in order to hold stocks.

Yours ever,

[copy initialled] J.M.K.

To R. G. HAWTREY, *24 October 1935*

My dear Ralph,

I expect you are much too much occupied with affairs at Geneva[1] to think of anything else just now. But, as I said I would let you have my page proofs as they became available, I now enclose the first 64 pages, and will post you further instalments as they come along.

Could you now return to me my original set of proofs? I should also like to have these back[2] in due course, since it is dangerous to have uncorrected sets in circulation.

Yours ever,
[copy initialled] J.M.K.

From R. G. HAWTREY, *29 October 1935*

Dear Maynard,

Since I have been back from Geneva, I have been able to give attention to your letter of the 1st October.

(1) You agree.

(2) You say that you intend your theory of marginal efficiency to cover working capital and 'exactly the same treatment applies'. Have you actually gone through the relevant passages with this in your mind?

Prospective yield of an investment is expressly defined in terms of long-period expectation (chapter 7), and is identified with a series of annuities (chapter 12). It is quite inapplicable to the advantages of an investment in a stock of commodities, destined for early resale. Can you have a 'series of annuities' spread over a period of six weeks?

You say that the peculiarity of working and liquid capital resides in the comparative shortness of its life. And of course, that is so. But this difference, though in itself one of degree, becomes one *of kind* in relation to your argument.

The prospective yield of an instrument is a characteristic calculable from its technical functions and its first cost. But how are you to arrive at the 'prospective yield' of a product which is purchased by a trader with a view to resale or to use as a material in production? The trader will avoid letting his stock down to so low a level as to inconvenience his operations. That consideration will determine a minimum stock. But this minimum will not

---

[1] The League of Nations' reactions to the Italian invasion of Abyssinia. [Ed.]
[2] The galley proofs were not returned and are now, thanks to Sir Ralph Hawtrey's generosity, in the Keynes Papers. The page proofs have not survived. [Ed.]

determine the amount that he will buy for stock; it will only determine the moment at which he will buy *some* additional amount. He may buy a week's supply or a month's or three months'. If he buys a relatively large quantity at a time, he has the advantages of economy in handling and of having the trouble of buying, with its calculations, negotiations and decisions, at less frequent intervals. It is these advantages (possibly with some set-off on account of any strain on his storage facilities) that constitute the 'prospective yield' for the sake of which he will pay interest if he has to borrow a part of the purchase price of the goods. This prospective yield is not a characteristic of the goods themselves, but of the buying transaction, and it varies with the quantity bought at a time.

When you come to liquidity preference in chapter 14, you found your theory on '*uncertainty* as to the future of the rate of interest, i.e. as to the complex of rates of interest for varying maturities which will rule at future dates' (p. 66 [*General Theory*, p. 168]), and your analysis is again expressed in terms of a series of annuities.

'The individual', you say, 'who believes that future rates of interest will be above the rates assumed by the market has a reason for keeping actual liquid cash.'

You now say in your letter that liquidity preference includes the case of 'preferring cash to a stock of goods which might fall in price'. But I do not think you have made that at all clear in the book. Indeed the discussion in chapter 17 seems absolutely to exclude anything of the kind. It is all in terms of 'bonds'.

(3) The question of 'the greatest of these marginal efficiencies' is only a verbal one, but surely I am right. You say that 'the capital assets which have the lowest marginal efficiency will not be newly produced at all', and that 'investment enterprise will be devoted to those which have the greatest, until there is no longer any piece of new investment which can show a marginal efficiency as great as the rate of interest'. It follows that the rate of interest is equal to (1) the lowest marginal efficiency of any capital asset which *is* produced, and likewise to (2) the highest marginal efficiency of any capital asset which *is not* produced. Since it is the lowest of those which do exist and the highest of those which do not exist, I think it better to call it the lowest than the highest.

With regard to the other verbal point, your use of the word 'marginal', you say that you are 'arriving at the efficiencies of those capital assets which it just on the margin pays to newly produce'. But that is not so. You are arriving at the efficiencies of *all* capital assets. The marginal efficiency of that which it just pays to produce is what you call the 'current' marginal efficiency of capital.

(4) With regard to the classical theory of interest, you are undoubtedly right when you say that the supply price of capital goods and with it the marginal efficiency of capital will be affected by the rate of interest. But that does not make the argument of the classical theory circular. I should say that the classical theory is *incomplete* in that it is a static theory, and takes no account of the disturbances that occur when the rate of interest departs from equilibrium. But subject to this limitation, it offers a determinate solution. The rate of interest may have to appear on both sides of the equation, but that does not make the reasoning 'circular'.

No doubt the classical economists did in fact assume full employment; that would be almost inevitable in dealing with a static problem. But it was not necessary to their argument to make any such assumption. If real wages were too high, so that unemployment resulted, the rate of interest would still tend to be equal to the marginal yield of capital. The marginal yield might be affected by causes promising a change in the price level, but that does not impair the general principle.

Nor is it, I think, inconsistent with the classical theory to allow that the volume of savings may be affected by other factors than the rate of interest (e.g. the volume of employment).

(5) *Liquidity preference*. The large deposits you refer to are important, and I think you are right when you say that it is fear of a capital loss that prevents them from being put into long-dated securities. But my impression is that you are too apt to regard the idle cash as idle *savings* arising out of *income*. I believe the large idle deposits are usually idle circulating capital accumulated not out of income but out of the proceeds of sale of goods which are not replaced. Idle circulating capital commands a high degree of liquidity preference because its *raison d'être* is to be applied to the purchase of goods at the first opportunity. Your exposition does not in terms exclude deposits of this type, but it is for the most part expressed from the point of view of the individual whose savings are the residue left after satisfying his propensity to spend, and who may be deterred from putting them in a long-term security if he fears that the security will depreciate. Since the question is one of motive and behaviour, the vital difference between the trader dealing with idle circulating capital and the individual dealing with idle savings cannot be disregarded. When I said in the comments I sent you last June that it is rare for the prices of fixed-interest securities to be driven up to such a level as to deter investors, I was thinking mainly of those who had savings to invest. In the case of idle circulating capital I should say it is probably the rule to withhold it from investment and the exception to invest it. The state of the investment market will without doubt affect in some degree the proportion of the idle circulating capital that is invested, but the primary cause de-

termining the accumulation of idle circulating capital will be simply the contraction of the business of the traders concerned, that is to say, those who ordinarily provide all or nearly all their working capital out of their own resources without resorting to temporary borrowing.

At one time I used to hold that the accumulation of idle cash was due to expectations of a fall of prices. I am now inclined to think that the mere contraction of business is a more important cause. At any rate it is a more persistent one, since sales may continue at a low level for a long time without any expectation of a fall of prices.

(6) *Interest and carrying charges.* The fundamental principle is that a prospective scarcity or plenty of any commodity tends to be reflected in the spot price, because the spot price can be raised by holding up stocks or lowered by drawing on stocks. The spot price and future price are linked together by the possibility of carrying stocks during the interval, and the future price tends to exceed the spot price by the cost of doing so.

But this principle is subject to a number of exceptions:

(1) In the case of future plenty there is a limit to the extent to which stocks can be drawn upon. If the price difference is great enough to affect materially the price charged to the consumer so that there is an expansion of demand, stocks may threaten to run short. And even quite a moderate reduction of stocks may be a source of inconvenience if at the outset they do not exceed what is required for carrying on business.

(2) The cost of carrying stocks may be prohibitive, as in the case of some perishable goods.

(3) In the case of a manufactured product it will be usual to leave forward orders to be met from current production at the time when they are becoming due for delivery. The adjustment of productive operations to actual and probable orders over the near future is often a complicated problem, but the cost of holding stocks of the finished product hardly enters into it.

(4) There may be control of stocks and output by producers and traders. This control may be guided by precise calculations as to future demand and supply and the cost of carrying stocks, and so produce just the same effect upon markets as free competition. But that is not necessarily so. Wisely or unwisely, it may establish quite different price relations. And the actual spot and forward quotations may be determined in part by intelligent anticipation of the action of the control and in part by an expectation that its policy will break down.

In the particular case of money, an anticipated scarcity or plenty takes the form of an anticipated fall or rise in the price level of commodities generally. If this tends to take effect in an immediate fall or rise in spot prices, that must be because people become in the one case less willing and in the other more willing to hold stocks of goods.

When a monetary expansion is anticipated, people become more willing to hold stocks of goods and they force up spot prices by keeping supplies off the market. But, in order to do so, they must raise money to pay for the goods; there is a pressure to borrow. If the banks are willing to lend at the pre-existing rate of interest, the result will be to transform the future monetary expansion into an immediate monetary expansion (the same result might be obtained if there were an increase in velocity of circulation, resulting from a general desire to diminish holdings of money).

If, however, the banks are unwilling to allow an immediate monetary expansion, they will meet the pressure from borrowers with a rise in the short-term rate of interest. If it is to be sufficiently deterrent, this rise must be such as to offset the anticipated rise in the price level of commodities.

Now the link between spot and forward prices is the possibility of buying spot and holding the goods for the interval of time, at the end of which the forward purchase would take effect. The trader who chooses this alternative has to bear the carrying charges and *also* the interest on the money which he pays immediately instead of at the end of the interval. Therefore the difference between spot and forward prices will be equal to carrying charges *plus* interest. If an expectation that the price level would rise 2 per cent in six months led to the short-term rate of interest rising from 3 to 7 per cent, then six months forward prices would rise 2 per cent relatively to spot prices.

Thanks for sending me the first instalment of page proofs. I should like to retain the others for a little while, if I may, as I have marked them and made references to them.

Yours ever,
R. G. HAWTREY

To R. G. HAWTREY, *30 October 1935*

Dear Ralph,

Many thanks for your further letter of October 29th. I enclose another 32 pages of page proofs.

Several of the points discussed in your letter we have, I think, now carried as far as we can. But I have a few points to add as follows (the numbers refer to your numbers):

(2) I see no difficulty in thinking of the return from an investment as consisting of a single annuity for a period which is not necessarily a year. If I buy a ton of copper today for £35 in the expectation of receiving from my investment a single lump sum of £36 in six months' time, this does not differ in principle

from buying a machine for £35, from which I hope to receive returns aggregating £50 spread over five years. Where the trader is purchasing the copper, not for re-sale, but for use as a material, his method of valuation is exactly the same as when he buys a machine, though the return may be spread over a shorter period. For example, if he lays in a stock of copper which he will use over two years, and buys some machine tools which he will wear out during the same period, there is no relevant or material distinction between the two cases. In both he will reckon by reference to the increased efficiency which each will help him to achieve.

There is a passage somewhere in my book in which I make it clear that there is one set of expectations which leads to a scale of preference between stocks of goods and debts of given maturity, and another set which determines that of the preference as between cash and a debt of a given maturity. I explained why it is important to distinguish these two cases and that the comparison between cash and a stock of goods is analysable into these two more fundamental types of preference.

(3) On my definition of the marginal efficiency of capital, there will be *no* capital asset of which the marginal efficiency exceeds the rate of interest. For equilibrium requires that the buying price of a new capital asset of the kind in question will rise until it bears a proportion to the prospective yield corresponding to the rate of interest. If its price exceeds the normal cost of production, then new production of it will continue until its price has fallen to its normal cost. Your way of approaching the question seems to imply that you are thinking of marginal efficiency of a capital asset in some sense which allows it to exceed the rate of interest.

(4) I agree that it would be more accurate to describe the classical theory as incomplete rather than as circular. But my point is that it is not incomplete in the sense that it deals with the special case rather than the general case. I maintain that as a theory it applies to no case at all. I have, however, re-written these passages, as you will see when the revised proofs reach you.

(5) I should not have created the impression that I regard the idle cash as essentially idle savings arising out of current income. For I agree with you that they are just as likely, or even more likely, to arise out of the proceeds of sales of goods which are not replaced. Here again there is a passage making it expressly clear in the revised chapter on the rate of interest of which the page proofs will be available shortly. I am thinking mainly, however, neither of savings arising out of current income nor out of idle business balances due to the contraction of business. It is the variation in the willingness to invest in long-period investment funds which I mainly have in mind, including in this resources in the hands of the banks. For example, this is the main trouble in the United States today; and, whilst it can scarcely be called a trouble in this country, it is on this factor that the price of gilt-edged securities mainly depends. E.g. a few months ago insurance companies and the like were tending to be fully or even over-invested, that is to say, buying long-term securities to cover not only the whole of their current assets but even those which they expect to receive at an early date. Today it is the other way round. Instead of anticipating the investment of prospective funds, their investment is lagging behind their receipts; and a tendency to overdraft is replaced by a tendency to carry surplus cash.

(6) My only quarrel with what you say here is that you seem to me to pay too little attention to the effect of anticipated changes in prices on the volume of current output. Also, in my opinion, equilibrium is brought about when prices are expected to rise, not mainly or necessarily by a change in the short-term rate of interest, but partly by a rise in the present spot prices of the goods, and partly by a current rate of output in excess of normal demand.

Yours ever,

[copy initialled] J.M.K.

From R. G. HAWTREY, *7 November 1935*

Dear Maynard,

I hope you will have patience with me if I pursue some of my criticisms further. (I remember your saying at Cambridge in March that we might hope to reach agreement in ten years!)

Marginal efficiency and working capital. If you want your readers to understand a 'series of annuities' to include the particular case of a payment deferred over an interval of less than one year, surely you should say so. But my criticism went beyond this. You say that the purchase of copper at £35 with a view to sale after six months at £36 does not differ in principle from buying a machine for £35 with a view to returns aggregating £50 spread over five years. But it *does*. In the first place your theory of prospective yield is based throughout on the *uncertainty* of long-period expectations. You have dropped out the express reference to long-period expectations which appeared in your former chapter 7, but the uncertainty of the future rate of interest remains at the foundation of your theory. In the case of the six months' holding of copper, uncertainty as to the rate of interest does not enter into the calculation.

Secondly, the conception of the marginal efficiencies of different types of capital assets is inapplicable to goods bought for stock. The technical contribution of materials used in manufacture consists simply in being so used. Regarded as instruments, they may be economised or replaced by substitutes, and these possibilities give some significance to their marginal efficiency for that purpose. But this marginal efficiency has not the same relation to the rate of interest as that of an instrument destined to be used for a long period. And it has nothing to do with the interest charge for holding the materials in stock in the interval between purchase and use. This affects the decision as to the amount to be bought not as to the amount to be used.

I do not think it would be possible even to modify the passages dealing with investment so as to cover the case of working capital. A totally distinct treatment is required.

Marginal efficiency and rate of interest. My previous criticisms on this point were verbal. But now I find that there is an actual fallacy at the bottom of our difference. You say that 'there is no capital asset of which the marginal efficiency exceeds the rate of interest'. Surely here you are once again confusing the prospective yield of an instrument with the prospective yield of an enterprise. The prospective yield of an enterprise depends on the proceeds of its output when sold in the market, and the market value of the enterprise is governed by the market rate of interest. But the prospective yield of an instrument depends on its cost-saving capacity. A spade may yield

595

100 per cent a day on its cost, if the additional labour needed to dig with bare hands cost a daily sum equal to the price of the spade.

If you want to calculate the contribution of the spade to the cost of potatoes dug with its help you reckon, not the 100 per cent a day that it saves in labour, but interest at the market rate (plus maintenance and depreciation). That is because all diggers of potatoes use spades, and competition keeps down the price they charge. But the cost-saving capacity of the spade remains what it is.

In the passage you quote from Marshall (p. 140) the respective yields of the different kinds of machinery, 20, 10, 6, 4, and 3 per cent, are technical characteristics which persist substantially unchanged whatever the rate of interest may be.

Classical theory of interest. I observe that you still call the argument 'circular'. But I am led to wonder whether your criticism of the classical theory does not arise out of your idea that 'the buying price of a new capital asset...will rise until it bears a proportion to the prospective yield corresponding to the rate of interest'. You say that 'the actual rate of current investment will be pushed to the point where there is no longer any class of capital asset of which the marginal efficiency exceeds the current rate of interest' (p. 136). 'Investment will be carried to the point where $\Sigma Q_r d_r$ becomes equal to the supply price' (p. 137). But that is not so. Investment in spades is only carried to the point at which there are enough spades to equip all the diggers. The difference between $\Sigma Q_r d_r$ and the price of a spade is then reflected in the cheapening of the product to the consumer.

Liquidity preference. I do not think I need say anything more.

Interest and carrying charges. You say that I 'pay too little attention to the effect of anticipated changes in prices on the volume of current output'. But variations in current output would not affect the argument at all. They may reduce the extent of the increase or decrease in stocks carried required to establish the equivalence between spot and future prices. But the fact that this increase or decrease in stocks carried is the essential link remains, and my point was that the carrying charges which determine the excess of forward prices over spot prices include *interest*. This invalidates your criticism of Irving Fisher on p. 142.

Your page proofs lead me to some further comments:—

Effective demand. If you are going to employ this concept, it is a pity to apply to it the expression 'effective demand', which has been used for so long by the economic world, including Adam Smith, Mill and Marshall, in a different sense.

But I still see grave objections to the concept itself. The footnote on p. 24, recognising that the 'expected proceeds' are a hypothetical quantity, meets only a part of my criticisms of last June. I then argued that the actual process by which the amount of employment is determined cannot be expressed in terms of a hypothetical expected demand at all. I need not elaborate what I said then, though I think it would be possible to do so.

And when you come to use your concept of effective demand, you seem to me to get involved in confusion.

On p. 27 you say that when employment increases and 'consumption is increased, but not by so much as income', employers would make a loss, unless there is 'an amount of current investment sufficient to absorb the excess of total output'. For otherwise 'the receipts of the entrepreneurs will be less than is required to induce them to offer the given amount of employment'.

This passage, as it stands, does not refer to effective demand at all. It assumes that the inducement to the entrepreneurs consists in their *actual* receipts (i.e. effective demand as understood by Adam Smith, Mill and Marshall). And the danger of loss arises from the possibility of 'investment' falling short of the excess of output over consumption (i.e. saving).

You may say that all this is to be assumed to refer to expectations. But are employers to be supposed to make all these calculations in terms of real income, current investment and the propensity to consume? Each employer's (hypothetical) expectation is presumably confined to his own product, and I do not see how you are going to aggregate these particular expectations into a total of consumption and a total of investment, nor is there any reason why these totals, if they can be formed, should be consistent with one another, or should have any relation to the propensity to consume, the marginal efficiency of capital on [? or] the rate of interest.

When you come to summarise the theory on p. 28, it is no longer what the community does spend on consumption but 'what it can be expected' so to spend that depends on the propensity to consume.

Do you mean to identify what it can be expected to spend with what it *is* expected to spend? That is what D_1 becomes under (3) on p. 29. Yet under (5) D_2 becomes 'the volume of investment' simply.

Under (8) you say 'when employment increases, D_1 will increase but not by so much as D; since, when our income increases, our consumption increases also, but not by so much'. Here D is *actual* income, and D_1 *actual* consumption.

At the top of page 30 D_1 is once again the sum which the entrepreneurs 'can expect' to get, and so the confusion persists.

In this passage the introduction of 'effective demand' is quite unnecessary. You are concerned throughout with the influence of actual sales of consumable goods and capital goods upon the activity of productive concerns. There is no reference to any other causes that may affect it.

597

I note that in chapter 5, where you examine the expectations by which employment is determined, you do not use the expression 'effective demand' at all. The passage on page 51, with the appended footnote, does something to link up 'effective demand' (in your sense) with actual sales. But I do not think it gives an accurate picture of the process by which productive activity is determined, because it does not distinguish between the retailers, whose business it is to watch sales and replenish their stocks, the manufacturers, who for the most [part] produce in response to firm forward orders, and the primary producers, whose output is to a great extent imposed upon them by natural conditions.

In chapter 8 the underlying idea seems to be that effective demand simply reflects actual demand. It seems to me that what you want to express is that if employers make a miscalculation and actual sales either outstrip or fall behind production, the result will be increased or diminished employment.

User cost. Your new definition seems to me to give us a concept which, however convenient it may be as a step towards defining investment, is of little utility in itself. 'The loss in the value of an equipment as a result of using it' was an idea of some significance, being that part of depreciation which is a prime cost. But when to this amount is added the gross total of all payments made for the purchase of goods by one entrepreneur from another, the result is a quantity which does not deserve a name of its own at all. What is the use of a calculation like this?

$$A_1 = £5,000,000,000$$
$$G - (G' - B') = £300,000,000$$
$$U = £4,700,000,000$$

How are changes in its amount to be interpreted? And what is the meaning of 'marginal user cost' when the gross total of A_1 is capable of large and fortuitous variations independent of $A - U$?

User cost cannot properly be described as 'the measure of what has been sacrificed to produce A' (p. 53). From the standpoint of the individual entrepreneur $F + U$ may be described as prime cost, but this quantity, if summed throughout the community, is deprived of all significance by endless duplications. Is not this another example of the inadvisability of trying to make the same formula fit working capital and fixed capital when they do not behave similarly?

When you say that in Marshall's *Principles* 'user cost is included as a part of prime cost under the heading of "extra wear and tear of plant"' (p. 72), is not this a survival from your previous definition of user cost?

You have not introduced any reference to unproductive incomes. Possibly you still intend to do so, for my letter of 1st October hardly reached you in time for you to introduce the necessary alterations in the page proofs. But there are some other classes of income which are not covered by your $A - U$, that is to say, (1) incomes derived from personal services rendered direct to the consumer without the intervention of an entrepreneur, (2) incomes derived from dealing in securities and credit. A and A_1 only cover purchases and sales of 'finished output', not of stocks and shares or debts.

Investment. The passage on pp. 75-6 betrays some misunderstanding of my position. I do not *myself* define investment to be the increment of wealth, *minus* any undesigned increment of unsold goods. I urged *you* to adopt this definition, because, in passages in which you use the word, that seems to me to be what you really mean by it (intended or intentional investment). That still applies to the revised version in your new proofs, e.g. pp. 27, 84, 98, 110-11.

When I stress the factor of undesigned increments of unsold goods, that is only in connection with your use of the term investment and the passages in which you suggest that forces are at work to make investment and saving equal. With your definition of investment no such forces can be at work, because investment and saving are simply two different names for the same thing.

On the other hand, when a difference develops between saving and intentional investment, the difference *invariably* takes the form of an undesigned increment or decrement of unsold goods. *For this particular phenomenon*, therefore, that is the vital factor, from which the forces tending to restore equilibrium proceed.

But I myself attach much less importance than you do to the behaviour of saving and intentional investment. I regard them as providing one out of a number of possible sources of an absorption or release of cash. I have never regarded 'the daily decisions of entrepreneurs concerning their scale of output as being varied from the scale of the previous day by reference to the changes in their stock of unsold goods' to the exclusion of other factors. Account must of course be taken of sales and prices, of unused capacity, of speculative influences, as well as of the credit position.

I have noticed one or two minor points.

Page 49, 'stocks of partly finished goods'. Surely it is the rule for manufacturers to have (or to be able promptly to obtain) sufficient stocks to enable them to meet any additional demand within their capacity without delay, so that all the different stages of manufacture may be entered upon simultaneously.

Pp. 99-100. This is Major Douglas's argument. Might you not acknowledge it?

Statistics do not support the view that the absorption of cash by sinking funds and depreciation allowances contributed to the depression in the United States. The following table shows profits of corporations assessed to income tax, dividends paid and depreciation (in $ millions):—

	Profits	Dividends	Depreciation
1929	8,740	8,356	4,430
1930	1,557	8,202	4,449
1931	−3,288	6,151	4,270
1932	−5,644	3,886	3,940

Thus even in 1930 the net provision for depreciation was *minus* 2,202 millions, and in 1932 it was *minus* 5,590 millions.

Page 103. I do not know how Kuznets gets his figures, but I suppose they include durable consumers' goods. If so, ought not the depreciation and upkeep of these goods to be deducted?

Page 113. Should not 'primary employment' be on capital goods rather than on 'investment'? All employment on the production of material commodities is on investment.

Yours ever,
R. G. HAWTREY

To R. G. HAWTREY, *8 November 1935*

My dear Ralph,

I am replying to your letter of November 7th. If this correspondence does not fatigue you, there is nothing that I like better. I was feeling that it was for me to ask forgiveness from you for pursuing it so lengthily. I do feel, however, that there are great advantages in a controversy by correspondence on issues of this kind rather than in conversation, since in talking it is so fearfully difficult not to get into misunderstandings and off on to irrelevant issues.

However, even though it is in correspondence and not in conversation, I do feel in regard to several of the points in your latest letter that we are rather at cross purposes, and that some of your criticisms really do not apply in any significant degree to the central issues I am driving at. But let me take them in turn.

Marginal efficiency and working capital. Surely there is some misunderstanding here. My definition of marginal efficiency has nothing whatever to do with the market rate of interest, except in the sense that a capital asset has to rise to a price at which its marginal efficiency is equal to a rate of interest on a debt possessing a similar degree of risk. The uncertainty of the future of the rate of interest which, as you say, lies at the foundation of my theory of liquidity preference governing interest, has no particular bearing on marginal efficiency. In the case of copper, as in the case of any other capital asset, its current price is only in equilibrium at a figure at which it offers a prospective yield equivalent to the rate of interest on a debt of corresponding maturity and corresponding risk. But whilst my theory of the rate of interest is essentially based on uncertainty, my theory of prospective yield is not. Prospective yield must take account of uncertainty, but uncertainty is merely a complication, not the essence of the matter. Your point about marginal efficiency being inapplicable to goods bought for stock is not clear to me. Is it possible that there is some confusion between aggregate efficiency and marginal efficiency? It is, of course, quite true that the rate of interest is not very important in the case of assets which are used up quickly. In your case, the rate of interest is mainly relevant as affecting the demand for the goods in which they will be embodied.

Marginal efficiency and rate of interest. Your criticisms here confirm me in the impression that you have not got my definition of marginal efficiency of capital. Investment in an instrument proceeds until either its abundance has reduced its marginal cost-saving capacity, or else its price has risen sufficiently to offset its cost-saving capacity sufficiently for its marginal efficiency, i.e. the relation of its prospective yield to its price, to have come to equilibrium with the market rate of interest. Your points here seem to have no relation at all to my particular theory, but to have a family resemblance to e.g. Hobson's criticism of Marshall's use of the marginal concept in itself, on account of some units of equipment being indivisible.

Perhaps it is I who am misunderstanding you, but I cannot here see any point at all in what you are saying.

Classical theory of the rate of interest. It is evident that exactly the same point arises here as in the matters just dealt with. I cannot see in the least what you are driving at. Naturally as investment increases Q_r diminishes, and that is one of the forces tending towards equilibrium. But this is only to say that the marginal efficiency diminishes as investment increases. I repeat that equilibrium is brought about partly by increased investment reducing prospective yield and partly by its raising the buying price of the capital asset. It comes to an end when the relation between the buying price and the prospective yield has fallen to equality with the rate of interest. I adhere, therefore, to the passage which you quote from page 137.

Interest and carrying charges. Certainly the excess of forward prices over spot prices includes interest. But I am not able to see why this invalidates my criticism of Irving Fisher.

Effective demand. In modern economics this term has gone out of use and that is part of my defence for reviving it in my own sense, but my own sense seems to me to bear an exceedingly close family resemblance to what Malthus meant by it. I am not aware that Marshall ever uses the term.[1]

The main point, however, on your page 5 [above p. 597] seems to me to affect the whole supply and demand theory and not my version of it in particular. I have the impression that you restrict the supply and demand method to market prices only, that is to say, they relate to the higgling of the market in respect of stocks which already exist. But that is not what Marshall or Pigou or most modern economists do. The demand which determines the decision as to how much plant to employ must necessarily concern itself with expectations. And I am in this respect simply trying to put more precisely what is implicit in most contemporary economics.

In the passage you quote from page 27, as in many other passages, it is not relevant to my immediate purpose for me to superimpose the complication of entrepreneurs' making mis-

---

[1] Are you thinking of 'efficient demand' which he does use occasionally?

takes. It is, of course, quite true that in this passage I mean by the receipts of the entrepreneurs the expected receipts. I am saying that in so far as employers have correct foresight, they will curtail the amount of employment they offer in accordance with the principle I state. But it really makes no difference if their foresight is momentarily incorrect, unless you are asserting a psychological law, that employers are chronically subject to a particular type of false expectation which leads them, in the contingency I am contemplating, to fail to curtail employment to the proper level and hence habitually to make a loss. I am, however, rather in despair about this comment of yours, since I cannot interpret it otherwise than as a symptom of my having wholly and absolutely failed in this section to convey to you what I am driving at. For your point, whether or not it is dialectically justified, is, in my own opinion, frightfully irrelevant to what I am trying to say.

For, it would all come to exactly the same thing if one were to suppose that the decisions of employers were not brought about by any rational attempt to foresee on the lines I indicate, but merely functioned by modifications at short intervals solely based on the method of trial and error. For, the method of trial and error would lead to exactly the same results.

If your discussion on the bottom of page 6 and the top of page 7 [above p. 597] is not intended to be more than a dialectical criticism of the actual form of my exposition, I dare say it is true that I could have written more precisely, though there is a point where an attempt to write more precisely renders one more obscure. If, however, it is directed to the essence and substance of what I am saying, then I remain deeply perplexed as to what can be in your mind.

Effective demand always reflects the current expectation of actual demand whether it is arrived at by a careful attempt at elaborate foresight on the part of the entrepreneurs, or merely by revision at short intervals on the basis of trial and error.

User cost. Your point about my footnote referring to Marshall [above p. 598] is correct. This needs modification.

I am not intending to say anything about unproductive incomes, since they are transfer incomes which have no particular importance when one is dealing with income etc. as a whole. I have not been able to see that transfer incomes involve any point relevant to my central theme.

Your point about user cost I have failed to grasp. My object has been to give a definition which would apply both to individual cases of unintegrated production and also to output as a whole. Marginal user cost is important in the first connection. In the latter connection it is $A - U$ which I am aiming at defining and A_1 drops out altogether. I am not clear what your difficulty is.

Investment. This is rather a troublesome matter. The question is, do you want me to delete the references to yourself? Substantially it seemed to me that this was your own opinion. If not, I must simply put it forward as an opinion which might be held and which is cognate to your views.

Various other minor points I will deal with. My point about the depressing effect of sinking funds is primarily, of course, a theoretical one. But I agree that it is without application to the United States if they in fact made no sinking funds during the depression period. I will look into the figures again, but I have a strong impression that I am right as to this.

Yours ever,

[copy initialled] J.M.K.

From R. G. HAWTREY, *20 November 1935*

Dear Maynard,

I am delighted to hear that, like me, you are glad to continue our correspondence.

I am afraid my last letter has given rise to a good deal of misunderstanding, and that must be my excuse for writing at rather greater length.

Marginal efficiency and working capital. What I said under this heading had reference to the statement in your letter of 1st October that 'exactly the same treatment applies' to working capital as to fixed capital. This in turn referred to a passage in my comments of June where I said, 'your theory of investment is expressed entirely in terms of long-period expectation and prospective yield'.

There are two points involved: the inapplicability to working capital (1) of the theory of prospective yield and (2) of your theory of the inducement to invest.

(1) With regard to the former, it is quite true, as you say, that it has nothing to do with uncertainty as to the rate of interest. 'In the case of copper', you say, 'as in the case of any other capital asset, its current price is only in equilibrium at a figure at which it offers a prospective yield equivalent to the rate of interest...' But to regard the 'turn' or difference between the buying and selling prices of copper as the 'prospective yield' of an asset is a mistake. It is the remuneration of the merchant for services rendered, and from the point of view of the manufacturer who actually uses the copper it is part of the cost of production of the copper. If there is an effective forward market, the carrying costs of the copper (including interest) will be covered by the difference between spot and forward prices, so that the merchant's turn will be independent of the period for which he carries his stock. If any trader (whether a merchant buying with a view to sale, or a manufacturer buying with a view to use) incurs an interest charge for carrying a stock of copper, that is for the sake of the convenience of *buying* in large quantities instead of from hand to mouth. This convenience occurs at the moment of buying, the same moment at which the charge for interest is incurred. Therefore it cannot be described as 'prospective' at all. (Irving Fisher's expression 'rate of return over cost' can be quite properly applied to it.) Nor is it a technical characteristic of the copper itself, comparable to the cost-saving capacity of an instrument. The nearest parallel, in the case of the instrument, to the interest charge incurred with a view to an advantageous buying policy, is the interest charge incurred by a manufacturer in his provision of surplus capacity of plant with a view to an anticipated future expansion of output. But the parallel is not perfect because in the former case no expectation of increased output need be involved.

(2) With regard to the inducement to invest, I find that when I referred to uncertainty of the rate of interest, I was under some misconception in regard to your argument. On a re-reading of chapters 11 and 12, I am satisfied that this is not an important factor. On the other hand, it is as clear as ever that chapters 11 and 12 are only applicable to fixed capital and not to working capital.

At the beginning of chapter 12 that part of 'expectations of prospective yields' which 'can only be forecasted with more or less confidence' is expressly identified with 'long-term expectation' (pp. 147–8).

In my comments of June I criticised this chapter on the ground that you do not distinguish adequately between the motives of the entrepreneur installing plant and those of the purchaser of shares. The purchaser of shares has to estimate the future profits of the concern. The entrepreneur, on the other hand, is already committed to his enterprise (on the assumption, which may or may not be fulfilled, that it will yield him a profit) and has to estimate what kind of equipment and how much of it will best enable him to produce the output he intends to sell.

The first flotation of the enterprise is based (like the purchase of shares) on an anticipation of profit; the promoter believes that he can *sell* the proposed new output at a price to produce a margin of profit over and above all costs, including interest on the capital equipment to be installed. The choice of plant is determined by the technical problem of how to minimise costs.

Your treatment of the inducement to invest from the point of view of the purchaser of shares entirely excludes any application to working capital. If you had treated the subject from the point of view of the entrepreneur purchasing equipment, you could have made an easy transition to the case of working capital. But you would have had to drop 'marginal efficiency' at that point.

You say: 'it is, of course, quite true that the rate of interest is not very important in the case of assets which are used up quickly'. But what I have always insisted on is that the short-term rate of interest *is* important in the case of such assets, because purchases can be so easily hastened or retarded. In the *Treatise* you argued that the short-term rate has a disproportionate effect on the long-term rate. I am not satisfied on that point (see *Art of Central Banking* pp. 378–9) and even if it were so, though the effect on long-term investment would be correspondingly accentuated, yet I think the effect on short-term investment would remain the more important, because it would be prompter and spread wider.

I suspect that you are apt to under-estimate the effect of the short-term rate of interest on traders' purchases of goods, because the *net* change in their stocks over any considerable period (e.g. a year) is usually small in comparison with the output of capital goods in the same period. But the target for the rate of interest is not the net change in stocks but the gross purchases of goods, which may be ten times the value of the output of capital goods in any interval of time. It may be that only a moderate proportion of the goods purchased is to be held with borrowed money, but a much more considerable proportion of any *additional* amount purchased will be so held (or expected to be). If the goods purchased are destined to be held only for a few weeks, the interest charge is correspondingly light. But the charge in the near future is the only *certain* part of the burden of the short-term rate of interest.

All this refers to the effect of the rate of interest on the constituent $L_1(D)$ in the notation of chapter 17 of the old proofs. It is in $L_2(r)$ that the uncertainty of the rate of interest operates. You refer in your letter of 30th October to a passage (which I have not identified) relating to the scales of preference between stocks of goods and debts of given maturity on the one hand, and between cash and debts of given maturity on the other. Does this mean that the former preference is one of the factors determining $L_2(r)$? That is hardly reconcilable with your treatment of the subject in chapter 17.

Marginal efficiency and rate of interest. I am afraid I quite failed to convey my meaning in my last letter. You write that 'investment in an instrument proceeds until either its abundance has reduced its marginal cost-saving capacity, or else its price has risen sufficiently to offset its cost-saving capacity', so that its prospective yield comes to equilibrium with the market rate of interest.

But 'abundance' may fail to reduce the cost-saving capacity of the instrument, nor will its price necessarily rise. The price of a spade need never rise appreciably above its cost of production. And its cost-saving capacity is to be measured by the amount of additional labour required to dig with bare hands, and remains always the same for any given operation.

There may, it is true, be marginal uses for a spade, e.g. where it is only used once a year, but the total addition to the demand for spades on account of such uses is negligible, and they do not impart any real elasticity to the demand for spades. And this is, I think, the usual case with instruments. They are in general designed to secure a certain calculable saving of labour, and are acquired with a view to full-time use. The demand for them depends mainly on the output of the commodities in the production of which the instruments are used, and the rate of interest on the first cost of an instrument is not likely so to affect the price of the commodity to the consumer as to influence the demand materially. The demand for the commodity puts a limit to the demand for the instrument before the instrument ever reaches a marginal use in which it yields no excess over the market rate of interest. It may even be that no such marginal use exists at all. Thus the working of the market fails to bring together the yield of the instrument in the form of cost-saving capacity on the one hand, and interest at the market rate on its first cost on the other. And the difference between the two accrues to the consumers of the final product in the form of consumers' surplus. The cost-saving capacity of the spade remains 100 per cent per diem, while its share of the cost of the potatoes it is used to dig is 5 per cent per annum on the price of the spade.

The case of durable consumers' goods is different. Your formula in fact does apply to them; investment in any line of such goods proceeds until either its abundance has reduced its prospective yield, or else its price has risen sufficiently to establish equilibrium with the market rate of interest.

That is so because a consumers' good, such as a house, is itself an 'enterprise'. The use of it per unit of time is sold to the consumer, and its prospective yield is in the form not of cost-saving but of enjoyment. The demand for houses is a function of the rent charged, and does not differ in kind from other demand functions. Moreover we are accustomed to measure the services rendered by a house to the consumer by its market value, and to disregard the consumers' surplus. We value it at the discounted value of the rent which is to be received for it.

If we treated an instrument as an 'enterprise' in the hands of a trader who lets it out on hire, we should value it in the same way by discounting the sums to be received for the hire of it. But the man who *uses* an instrument (whether he receives it on hire or owns it) makes a different calculation; he has to estimate whether its efficacy as a means of production is sufficient to make the use of it worth while. There may be a case where it is only just sufficient, that is to say, where the cost-saving capacity is just equivalent to interest at the market rate, and, if so, it has the characteristics of a marginal use. But there may be no such case. The demand for the instrument is a derived demand, depending on the output for which the instrument is required. The demand for the instrument will not expand further than the demand for the output, and has no inherent tendency to expand up to the point at which a marginal use is reached. Indeed it may be that there is no opening available for the use of the instrument in which its cost-saving capacity is not substantially above the market rate of interest, and, if that is so, no marginal use exists.

Even in a community in which the use of instruments is negligible and the capital market is concerned with nothing but durable consumers' goods, the classical theory of interest would still not be circular. The hiring value of the goods would be determined by the demand function and the available supply. If the available supply were absolutely fixed and subject neither to depreciation nor to extension, the cost of production of new capital goods would not enter into the matter, and the 'rate' of interest would have no significance at all. But if new capital goods are being produced (whether for replacements or extensions), the hiring value that they look forward to determines a rate of interest on their first cost. The new capital goods will be such as are expected to obtain among all alternatives the highest hiring value from the consumers in proportion to their cost, and will constitute a true marginal increment, the utility of which is equal to their hiring value. The utility of the durable consumers' goods corresponds to the cost-saving capacity of the instruments, and the consumers' surplus of the former

608

corresponds to the excess of cost-saving capacity of the latter over the rate of interest. Consumers' surplus, however, being a matter of hypothesis, is a much less definite thing than cost-saving capacity. A man who pays a moderate rent for good accommodation is assumed to be enjoying a consumers' surplus depending on what he would pay for each less eligible standard of accommodation down to the minimum if he could get nothing better. The calculation is very artificial and dubious, and no one would set out to derive the demand function from the consumers' surplus.

But the cost-saving capacity of an instrument is a technical matter of practical business, and does actually form the basis of the demand function. The entrepreneur who has to decide whether he will or will not buy an instrument makes the best estimate he can of its cost-saving capacity.

When you said in your letter of 30th October that 'there is no capital asset of which the marginal efficiency exceeds the rate of interest', I drew the conclusion that you were identifying the prospective yield of the capital asset with its hiring value.

It would be possible to treat the whole problem of interest on that basis, imputing to the entrepreneur a demand function for instruments without inquiring into the calculations of cost which he makes. But that would be an incomplete account of the matter, and more superficial than Marshall's analysis or Irving Fisher's. When you say that Fisher uses his 'rate of return over cost' in the same sense and for precisely the same purpose as you employ 'the marginal efficiency of capital' (p. 141), you are definitely committing yourself to the analysis which takes account of the excess of cost-saving capacity over hiring value.

When you say that 'the rate of investment will be pushed to the point on the investment demand-schedule where the marginal efficiency of capital in general is equal to the market rate of interest' (pp. 136–7), you seem to me to be identifying the marginal efficiency of the instrument with its actual hiring value. You assume that a marginal use exists for each class of capital asset in which its cost-saving capacity does not exceed the market rate of interest, and its hiring value will be equal to its cost-saving capacity in that use. This explains your use of the word 'marginal' to which I raised objection in my comments of June.

There is here a fundamental ambiguity to be cleared up. I should prefer that you should adopt the approach of Marshall and Fisher. I feel some doubt whether the other will be adequate for your purposes. But at any rate if you decide to use it you should cut out your references to the classical theory altogether.

Interest and carrying charge. Your criticism of Irving Fisher runs: 'the prices of existing goods will be forthwith so adjusted that the advantages of holding money and of holding goods are again equalised, and it will be too late for holders of money to gain or to suffer a change in the rate of interest'. I showed in my letter of 29th October that an anticipated scarcity or plenty of money will be reflected *either* in a fall or rise of spot prices, *or* in a fall or rise of the rate of interest. In the former case the anticipated scarcity or plenty of money is allowed to become actual, and it is, as you say, too late for the holders of money to gain or suffer a change in the rate of interest. But in the latter case the change in the rate of interest itself prevents the complete adjustment of spot prices, because the margin between spot and forward prices is itself modified by the change in the rate of interest.

On further consideration I am not sure that I did not go too far in my comments of June when I said that 'according to Irving Fisher the change in the value of money is only operative so far as it is foreseen'. I think he deals with both cases, and where it is not foreseen he says that expectations are falsified by a discrepancy between the rate of interest contemplated in bargains and the real rate as developed by events.

Effective demand. I find it difficult to believe that this expression has gone out of use. Marshall makes no distinction between 'efficient' and 'effective' demand, using one expression in the text and the other in a footnote. And Adam Smith uses 'effectual'. But the three can hardly be anything but synonymous.

But the verbal question is a secondary one. The important question is one of substance.

Of course it is true that 'the demand which determines the decision as to how much plant to employ must necessarily concern itself with expectations'. My objection from the beginning has been to the expression of the expectations in the form of a *numerical aggregate*. One objection, that the expectations even of an individual are not precise but lay down broad and rough limits, you have met by your footnote. But the others remain. The expectations of demand are to be found, strictly speaking, only in the minds of those, such as the retailers, who sell to the final purchasers. But it is not the retailers who give employment. That devolves on manufacturers and other producers whose expectations are concerned primarily with the orders they receive from the retailers. You may say that the orders received from retailers may be held to imply a certain corresponding demand from the consumers. But that is only approximately true. The retailers may give orders representing just a replacement of their sales without acting on any views at all about the future. They may be influenced also by views of the future, but it would be quite impossible to disentangle this factor from the rest.

I do not dispute that there are *some* instances where a definite relation can be traced between an expectation as to demand and the volume of employment given. But even then it may be very difficult to say which of a number of different and mutually inconsistent expectations in the minds of many different people contributing to a decision are to be regarded as authoritative, or over what period of the future the expectations are to be deemed to extend.

You agree that the expected demand is a hypothesis; it is that expectation of proceeds which 'if it were held with certainty' would lead to the same behaviour. And I do not think you gain anything in your exposition by interposing this hypothetical quantity between the numbers actually employed and the causes to which the decisions to employ them are due.

What I said about the passages referred to in my letter of 7th November was intended to show that the hypothetical expected demand is not really useful or material to your exposition. Practically the only cause determining employment that you deal with is the actual sales. We both agree that other causes operate, but they do not come into your exposition. And if they did there is no reason why their effect on employment should not be considered directly instead of via a hypothetical expected demand.

I referred in my letter of 7th November to employers' miscalculations, because that seemed to me the only aspect of the matter for which your hypothesis would be useful; it would enable you to express the miscalculation as a difference between two quantities, expected and actual demand.

You say that your argument leads to the same results whether miscalculations are allowed for or not. That is so, provided, as you say, that the miscalculations are corrected by a method of trial and error, so that actual sales are really the determining factor. But that is because your introduction of expected demand is in any case superfluous. The fact you have to take account of is that the state of sales leads (or does not lead) to a change in employment. No further light is thrown on it by measuring the actual amount of employment against a hypothetical expected demand.

Unproductive incomes. I think it would be wiser to mention them. Economists will be quite prepared to infer that a man with £10,000 a year from War Loan is to be regarded as having no income, but readers unfamiliar with the subject, if they happen to think of the case, may well find it a stumbling block. Even economists may find difficulties in regard to incomes derived from personal services without the intervention of an entrepreneur, and in regard to financial incomes. You also ought to take account of foreign trade.

User cost. Here I did not mean to find fault with your reasoning, but merely to criticise the application of a distinctive name to a concept which is not useful in itself.

Investment. It is hardly necessary to put in any express reference to my views. My criticisms were directed only against your phraseology. You used 'investment' in five different senses (one of which you have now dropped), and I urged you to distinguish them. The passage on pp. 75–6 attributes to me simply a different definition of investment, whereas what I want is four different definitions for four different concepts.

In your concluding paragraph you say that 'the point about the depressing effect of sinking funds is primarily, of course, a theoretical one'. But there is nothing in the passage on pp. 99–101 to show that you do not regard it as an important practical matter. To endorse Major Douglas's argument when you do not think it of any practical consequence is asking for trouble.

Yours ever,
R. G. HAWTREY

At this point Keynes passed the whole of the correspondence thus far to Joan Robinson.

To JOAN ROBINSON, *29 November 1935*

My dear Joan,

Unless it would bore you, I would be rather grateful if you would look through this voluminous correspondence with Hawtrey. I have arranged it in chronological order. By the time you have got to the end of it, you will see that we are recurring over and over again to two or three points where I am indisposed to give way. My final letter to him, with today's date on it, has not yet been dispatched. I should rather like to know whether, looking at it impartially, you feel that there are any further concessions which he can justly claim from me.

Yours ever,
J.M.K.

I also enclose a further batch of proofs.

From JOAN ROBINSON, *2 December 1935*

My dear Maynard,

I certainly don't think an archangel could have taken more trouble to be fair and to be clear. I darkly suspect that Hawtrey hasn't really taken in the theory of the rate of interest. His sudden relapse into talking about 'idle savings' seems to give him away. I think the old trouble about working capital is really due to this in an obscure way.

I think you are quite right that he is being Hobson about spades, and I certainly don't think there is anything more you can say.

Yours,

JOAN

To R. G. HAWTREY, *29 November 1935*

Dear Ralph,

After reading your letter of November 20th, I feel that we have got near to refining points of difference down to the stage when we must each go our own way. But to reduce the misunderstandings as well as the differences of opinion to a minimum, there are some points on which I should like to make another shot at expressing myself.

1. *Marginal efficiency of working capital.* My theory of prospective yield can be expressed as follows: When a man invests in a capital asset, whether it be fixed capital, working capital or a stock of liquid goods, he expects to receive as a result of this investment certain sums of money additional to what he would receive otherwise. Sometimes these sums of money will be spread in a large number of instalments over a long period. Sometimes they will be few in number and perhaps even one only, and the date may be either near or distant. But whatever the distribution of the annuities through time, the prospective yield consists of a sum or sums of money which it is expected to obtain at various dates in the future over and above what would have been obtained if the investment had not been made. I claim that this conception is equally applicable to all different kinds of capital.

I quite agree, of course, with your point on page 2 [above p. 605] that the merchant's return between the buying and the selling prices of copper has nothing to do with the prospective yield. A man who buys copper does so either because he will get an increased income through the convenience of holding copper

613

which he would not obtain otherwise, or hopes to receive eventually a sum for the copper which will reimburse him. The yield of his investment in copper consists in either or both of these returns.

My feeling is that the above is relevant in one way or another to a good many of your observations.

2. *Short-term rate of interest*. Here, of course, we are up against an old-standing difference of opinion. If we rule out the effect of the short-term rate on the long-term rate, my opinion is, as you know, that the effect is extremely small. In holding, as you do, that the short-term rate of interest has a large effect on traders' purchases of goods, I still think that you are attributing to them highly irrational behaviour without any sufficient evidence for doing so. I say it would be highly irrational, because it is easy to calculate that the change in their costs due to changes in the short-term rate of interest is extremely small as compared with the other elements in the situation. I have seen much evidence that the changes in traders' stocks are quite large enough to be an important factor, but I have never seen any to the effect that these changes are largely affected by the short-term rate of interest.

In the last paragraph of page 5 [above p. 607] of your letter, you raise the question of how the scale of preference between stocks of goods and debts of given maturity displays itself. I should say that it does so through the changes in the schedule of the marginal efficiency of capital.

3. *Marginal efficiency and rate of interest*. In the first paragraph of your page 6 [above p. 607] you quote me correctly by referring to 'marginal cost-saving capacity'. But in the second paragraph you drop out the word 'marginal'. Surely abundance must affect the *marginal* cost-saving capacity of the instrument. In paragraph 3 of this page [above p. 607] you seem to me to be saying in effect that the marginal efficiency of a spade is apt to fall with a rush. I should, of course, quite agree with your argument in this passage, that the demand for an instrument is

usually a derived demand from the demand for the commodities it is capable of producing.

4. The passage which begins at the bottom of page 8 [above p. 608] indicates that I have still failed to make clear one very fundamental aspect of my theory of the rate of interest. My point is that the rate of interest determines the *scale* on which new capital will be produced. On the basis of the second and third sentences of your page 9 [above p. 608] I do not see what is supposed to determine the amount of new capital goods which are produced. I should say, to repeat myself, that new capital goods will be produced on such a scale that their growing abundance and their rising price will, between them, bring their hiring value relatively to their first cost down to a figure which no longer exceeds the rate of interest. But this process could not determine the rate of interest, because it is only if we know the rate of interest from some other source that we can determine the scale on which the new capital goods will be produced.

5. As I think I said in my previous letter, there are a number of passages where I seem to be more in the classical tradition than you are. Several of your criticisms concerning the spades are really criticisms of the practical applicability of the marginal theory of economics. There are, of course, some qualifications to this theory and some criticisms which can be validly made. But this is not a matter which I could very well go into in this book. I am simply accepting the usual theory of the subject without attempting to refine on it.

I feel that this is also the case with the passage beginning at the bottom of page 12 [above p. 610], where you deal with the effect of expectation on demand. I am doing no more here than accept the principles which underlie supply curves other than purely market supply curves. Nevertheless, at the stage which this argument has now reached, there is, as you say, no very deep difference between us. I find it an aid to thought to introduce my numerical expression for demand in between the general state of expectation and the scale of employment which results from it. But I agree with you that it is in a sense an intermediate conception which drops out in the final analysis.

The only thing that really matters is that the given state of expectation, whatever it is, does produce by its effect on the minds of entrepreneurs and dealers a determinate level of employment. But I should find it difficult to do without my schematism as a convenient method of quantifying the state of expectation.

6. On page 14 [above p. 611] you say that practically the only cause determining employment that I deal with is the actual sales. This is not my intention, which is to take account of all possible motives and expectations influencing entrepreneurs.

7. You may very well be right that my failure to deal with unproductive income etc. may be troublesome to readers unfamiliar with the subject. But that applies equally to a great many other matters where I assume considerable knowledge of economies. It is always difficult to decide exactly on what level of abstraction one shall write. But I have tried to be strict in this matter and not to introduce discussions adequately dealt with elsewhere which are only incidental to my purpose. But I agree, of course, that this does involve assuming more knowledge on the part of the reader than all readers will have.

8. I think I can meet the question of my references to your use of investment by making it clear that you have only suggested the definition I am dealing with as *a* definition of investment.

9. When I said that my point about sinking funds was primarily theoretical, I should have said primarily 'general', my meaning being that it could not be disposed of by a particular case where it might have been unimportant. For I had in general considered that it is of great practical importance. On the other hand it is not the same as Douglas's argument. For he treats the whole of the excess of the entrepreneur's receipts over his prime cost (exclusive of user cost) as being necessarily deflationary; whereas in this passage I am making a sharp

distinction between those financial provisions which are absorbed pari passu by replacement etc. and those which are not.

Yours ever,

[copy initialled] J.M.K.

From R. G. HAWTREY, *19 December 1935*

Dear Maynard,

I think we can still make further progress with some of the points dealt with in my letter of 20th November and your reply of the 29th.

Marginal efficiency of working capital. You still do not meet my argument that the interest charge incurred on holding any stock in excess of the necessary minimum is in consideration of the convenience in buying, which is not a *prospective* but a *present* advantage.

A manufacturer using copper may estimate that he must never let his stock fall below, say, ten days' requirements. If he started with that minimum in hand, he could maintain it by buying every day the amount used on that day. If he prefers to buy relatively large quantities of copper at intervals of several weeks or months, that adds nothing either to the convenience derived from holding an adequate stock or to the proceeds of sale of his output; he does it because it saves trouble in buying and cost of delivery.

I raised this point by way of objection to your idea that exactly the same treatment applies to working capital as to fixed capital. And you have never dealt either with my further criticisms that, even if your analysis based on marginal efficiency were applicable to working capital, your actual phraseology is not. Your readers will not understand 'long-period expectations' to include 'short-period expectations', or a 'series of annuities' to include a single sum accruing after a few weeks.

Short-term rate of interest. You say that it would be 'highly irrational behaviour' on the part of a trader to be influenced in his purchase of goods by changes in the short-term rate of interest, because the resulting change in costs 'is extremely small as compared with the other elements in the situation'. But that is not so. In my letter of 1st October I mentioned that you have never offered any answer at all to the arguments used on the subject in *The Art of Central Banking* (especially pp. 365–71) and that is still so. I might add that you yourself do not regard the 'carrying charges' of stocks of commodities as by any means insignificant, and that interest forms a substantial part and usually the greater part of those charges. You argued in the *Treatise on Money* that the holding of stocks is more influenced by price prospects than by interest, and I should of course agree that *sometimes* that is so. But that does not mean that the rate of interest has no influence at all.

617

With regard to the 'scale of preference between stocks of goods and debts of given maturity', I have no difficulty in seeing how the preference displays itself. What I said in my letter of 20th November was that the inclusion of this preference among the factors determining $L_2(r)$ was not reconcilable with your treatment of the subject in chapter 17.

Marginal efficiency and rate of interest. In my original comments of June I found fault with your definition of prospective yield as being *in terms of profit*, and including not only interest but the remuneration derived by an entrepreneur from a going concern or enterprise. You agreed in your letter of 1st October that 'it is the prospective yield of each separate instrument which is relevant'. Much of my criticism of your treatment of marginal efficiency has proceeded from the assumption that it is intended to apply to instruments and not to enterprises. That assumption was fortified by your references to Marshall and Fisher, for their concepts of marginal utility and marginal rate of return over cost apply only to instruments and not to enterprises.

Most of my argument under this heading in my last two letters was directed to showing that your assumption that *each type* of capital asset has a marginal unit is not consistent with the interpretation of a capital asset to mean a separate instrument. My example of a spade illustrates this. The *total* utility or yield of a spade, even if it is used only once a year, probably exceeds 100 per cent, and is thus far above the marginal utility or yield of capital. And this is not an exception but the rule, so far as instruments are concerned. An industrial instrument is usually highly specialised, and is often only adapted to one industry. In that industry the difference between the cost of production *with* the instrument and the cost *without* it may be equivalent to scores or hundreds per cent of the first cost of the instrument. It would probably not be worth while to install the instrument at all except with a view to full-time use, and there may therefore be no instance in which its cost-saving capacity or total utility is much below the average or comes anywhere near the market rate of interest. You say that in such a case the marginal efficiency 'is apt to fall with a rush'. That is another way of saying that there is a discontinuity, and that the doctrine of marginal utility does not apply. The utility of the instrument jumps suddenly from 100 per cent per annum to *nil* without passing through any intervening values.

There will of course be *some* types of instrument of which the utility or yield will range down to the margin and beyond it, and it will be among these types that the marginal units of capital will be found. Some types, (e.g. vehicles), being adapted for a wide variety of uses and often kept for intermittent use, may have a very wide range.

Thus, so far as instruments are concerned, the doctrine of the margin is applicable only to instruments as a whole and not to each separate type of instrument. Some types of instrument will contain no marginal units.

With this reasoning in my mind, and Marshall's idea of instruments yielding 20, 10, 6, 4 or 3 per cent, I at first took your definition of the marginal efficiency of any *type* of capital on page 135 to mean the cost-saving capacity of a type of instrument, that is to say, its *total* utility or yield for the 'one more unit' might not be marginal. And I was confirmed in this interpretation when I found on page 140 that you identified the marginal efficiency of capital with Fisher's rate of return over cost and not his 'marginal' rate of return over cost. In my letter of 29th October I assumed that your 'marginal efficiency' was equivalent to the total utility or cost-saving capacity of an instrument, and that what in your first proofs you called the 'current marginal efficiency' of capital was equivalent to the marginal utility of instruments in general.

In your letter of 30th October you said that 'there will be *no* capital asset of which the marginal efficiency exceeds the rate of interest'. This seemed to rule out my previous interpretation that marginal efficiency means total utility. And I now think I was wrong all along in supposing that section 1 of chapter 11 applies to instruments at all. I believe you mean it to apply not to instruments but to enterprises.

For in the first place you define the prospective yield of an investment in terms of the returns to be obtained 'from selling its output'. It is only the output of an *enterprise* that is sold; the output of an *instrument* contributes to produce the output of the enterprise, but is not itself identifiable in the proceeds of sale. The instrument only figures in the proceeds of sale in virtue of a costing system, which shows how much of the selling price is accounted for by costs and how much goes to profit. And the costing system reckons not the total utility of the instrument but only its hiring value, which presupposes a market rate of interest.

Secondly you distinguish between the market price of a capital asset and its replacement cost. In the case of an instrument there is no such distinction. But in the case of an enterprise there is a real distinction between the market price of the enterprise itself, which includes capitalised profit or goodwill, and the market price or replacement value of its capital equipment.

Thirdly, if a capital asset means an enterprise, it is quite right to assume that every type of enterprise that is selling goods to consumers should expand up to the point at which it is yielding no more than normal profit and interest.

But if it is the case that prospective yield of an investment or capital asset means the prospective yield of an enterprise, then the marginal efficiency based on this concept cannot supply a theory of *interest*, because prospective yield includes profit. It is the dividend-yielding capacity of the enterprise. (I think it also includes economic rent, which is not covered by your term 'running expense'.)

That does not mean that you should discard the concept which you have defined as prospective yield, and substitute for it one based on the cost-saving capacity of the instrument. For the concept of dividend-yielding capacity is itself required in your reasoning, and is, I think, in some ways more important for your purpose than cost-saving capacity.

But if your readers are not to be as completely baffled and misled as I have been, it is essential to distinguish between the two concepts, and make quite clear in every context whether you are referring to the cost-saving capacity of instruments or to the dividend-yielding capacity of enterprises.

The growth of the capital equipment of the community is effected partly by widening and partly by deepening. 'Widening' means increase of output by the creation of new enterprises or the extension of existing enterprises. 'Deepening' means the substitution of capital for labour in the production of a given output.

In the long run, since the supply of labour is limited, the deepening process is the decisive one. It determines how much capital the available factors of production are to use. But over short periods (extending very likely up to several years) the motives determining flotations and extensions of enterprises may be far more important.

The marginal yield of instrumental goods only determines the rate of interest very gradually and approximately. The rate of interest, when it exceeds the marginal yield, tends to reduce the demand for capital goods by diminishing the amount of capital used in a given enterprise. But, so far as productive instruments are concerned, the reduction so effected is likely at the outset to be very small. In any new enterprise the items of capital equipment which are near the margin of yield are likely to be a very small proportion of the total. And the calculations of yield made by the entrepreneur are very approximate and probably provide a wide margin, so that a moderate change in the rate of interest does not call very urgently for their revision. Even if the rise in the rate of interest is sufficient to produce an appreciable effect on the capital equipment of new enterprises, existing enterprises will be unaffected except in so far as the items of plant that have become unremunerative fall due for replacement. In the long run a discrepancy between the rate of interest and the marginal yield of capital goods would be bound to make itself felt. But since both the rate of interest and the marginal yield are constantly varying, there might never be an uninterrupted 'long run'. There is not necessarily a predominant tendency for the marginal yield to fall. New invention is constantly supplying new openings offering a higher yield.

Probably the most important practical tendency operating to bring the marginal yield of instrumental goods and the rate of interest to equality is that the adoption of a new invention depends on its cost-saving capacity being expected to be at least equal to the rate of interest.

The case of houses and other durable consumers' goods is different from that of instrumental goods. A house is itself an 'enterprise', in that the use of the house is sold direct to the consumer. Moreover interest forms a relatively large proportion of the cost, so that a rise in the rate of interest reacts directly on demand, and affects the production of a perceptible amount of marginal units.

In the case of houses it is still possible to distinguish two different effects of a high rate of interest, the check to the number of new enterprises, and the reduction of the capital equipment of each particular new enterprise. When the rate of interest is high, there will be fewer new houses, and the standard of luxury of the houses produced will be lower.

Thus it is possible to distinguish quite generally between the causes influencing the flotation of new enterprises, and those influencing the degree of capitalisation of the particular enterprise. The flotation of new enterprises depends upon the prospect of selling their output; the degree of capitalisation of the particular enterprise depends upon the relation between the market rate of interest and the marginal yield of capital. The latter is decisive in the long run, while the former is likely to predominate in the short run, even up to several years.

Your divergence from the classical theory of interest does not really arise over the question of a circular argument at all, but over the assumption made in the classical theory that any departure of the rate of interest from the equilibrium level will correct itself. You maintain that the rate of interest is a highly psychological or conventional phenomenon, and that it may get stuck for an indefinite period above (but not below) that corresponding to equilibrium. If that occurs, designed investment will shrink to something less than savings, the excess savings will be accumulated in the form of cash, there will be a shortage of purchasing power, and a failure to sell goods, and the result will be a decline of output and unemployment.

In such conditions a reduction of wages would not be a remedy, because, as soon as costs were reduced in proportion to demand, the continuing accumulation of idle cash would cause a renewed shortage of purchasing power.

Here I find myself in a considerable measure of agreement with you. I think you are right in attributing a highly conventional character to the rate of interest. And I think it is quite *possible* that, if the rate got stuck too high, the results you describe might ensue.

I should say, however, that the reason why the rate of interest is apt to become conventionalised is that the adjustment of the marginal utility of capital to the rate of interest is so slow and approximate that people concerned in the investment market are hardly aware of it. In practice the forces which affect the long-term rate of interest are (1) any disparity between the demand for loanable funds for the purpose of new investment and the funds currently supplied (p. 165) and (2) the dividend prospects. (I use dividend prospects in a wide sense to cover the profit *plus* interest received by the entrepreneur or the shareholder.) If there is a conventional rate of interest, an excess supply of loanable funds can be checked by a reduction of the rate below the conventional level. But equally an excess *demand* for loanable funds can be checked by a *rise* of the rate above the conventional level. The convention in fact will be in the minds of borrowers as well as of lenders. So long as that is so, it seems to me that the conventionalising of the rate is unlikely in practice to lead to a deadlock.

If by marginal efficiency you mean dividend prospects, then according to your theory of interest the yield on bonds tends to be determined by a competitive comparison with the yield on shares, as measured by expected yield on new issues of shares. There is some truth in this, but you do not bring out the fact that the price of a share (even the issue price of new shares) contains an element of capitalised profit. This margin, which in the case of new issues ordinarily goes to those who have created or are relied upon to create the goodwill of the business, is very variable and disturbs the comparison between shares and bonds.

Nevertheless I think it is substantially true that a standard is set for the yield on bonds by the dividend prospects of new issues of shares, and that these latter are calculated to a great extent from the known yields of existing shares. And if this is so, are not lenders as well as borrowers likely to be led to modify their conventional rate of interest? The dealings in the market in fact are mainly carried on by lenders, for a very large proportion of the sellers of securities are intending buyers, so that it is the lenders who are conscious of the tendency of dividend prospects. The promoters of new flotations have to accept the judgment of the market as to what is a fair yield.

Nor is an estimate of yield necessarily the dominant factor in the minds of the promoters. I think you might with advantage say more in chapter 12 about the relation of market conditions to new issues. As I see it, the primary condition for a new enterprise or the extension of an existing enterprise is the *prospect of selling* the additional output. Something in the neighbourhood of normal prices and normal profits is no doubt counted on, but the new selling power or goodwill is the vital condition.

I should say therefore that depression reduces the long-term rate of interest mainly because a shrinking demand to a great extent destroys the prospects of additional selling power which would otherwise appear. The savings which would otherwise go into shares seek other outlets, and the market for fixed-interest securities is improved. The classical theory would say that the consequent fall in the rate of interest leads to the marginal yield of instrumental goods being lowered. But I believe the immediate effect in that direction is likely to be very small, and the most important result may well be the earlier issue of loans by public authorities which are more concerned with borrowing at a rate below the conventional level than with any calculation of profit. A stimulus to house-building may also follow, but this depends on the prospective demand for house room as well as on the rate of interest, and experience shows that it does not always occur.

Activity, associated with an expansion of demand, will stimulate the creation of new enterprises, but a limit will be reached when the manpower of the community is fully equipped with capital on the basis of existing productive methods. A further increase in output can then only be secured by a more intensive capitalisation. The widening process having reached its limit, further development can occur only through the deepening process. If fluctuations in activity could be eliminated, and activity and full employment could become normal and continuous, the deepening process would attract more attention. But even so it might take the form of installing more high-yielding new inventions rather than a lowering of the marginal yield of capital.

In your letter you say quite rightly that you could not go into the qualifications and criticisms of the marginal theory in your book. If you make clear the distinction to which I have referred between the cost-saving capacity of instruments and the dividend-yielding capacity of enterprises, you can rather curtail than extend your references to the marginal theory, for you can cut out this part of your criticisms of the classical theory.

Effective demand. You say you find the introduction of a numerical expression for expected demand 'an aid to thought'. But I fear that to any reader who wants to visualise your theory in relation to the facts the introduction of such an awkward fiction will be a stumbling block. The difficulties I have described to you will prevent clear thinking. I have been further impressed by these difficulties in re-reading chapter 20 on the employment function. For example, on p. 280, how can you say that D_{wr} is a unique function of the total effective demand, D_w, when each is a fortuitous aggregate of the vagaries of thousands of individual opinions which need not be consistent with one another? On page 304 surely $MV = D$ is wrong. MV is equal to the actual demand, not the expected demand.

When I said that the only cause determining employment that you deal with is the actual sales, I was referring to the passages in which you employ the idea of effective demand. I think you will find that this is so.

Unproductive incomes. Nothing more is needed than a qualifying phrase (such as I used in the second paragraph on p. 332 of *The Art of Central Banking*), but that I am quite sure would be helpful even to the trained economist. And what about the financial incomes?

Investment. How are you going to explain my suggestions without admitting that you use the word in four different senses? And are you going to introduce a definition of 'an' investment on the lines of your letter of 24th September?

Major Douglas. I did not mean to suggest that your argument on pages 99–101 was actually the same as his in all its horrors, but only that it is one arrow (and perhaps the only respectable one) in his quiver. A cross reference between this passage and p. 370 might be helpful.

Liquidity preference. In your letter of the 30th October you said you were putting in a passage to show that the idle cash accumulated through liquidity preference is not necessarily idle savings, but is 'just as likely, or even more likely, to arise out of the proceeds of sales of goods which are not replaced'. But I do not find any such passage. The passages on pp. 166–7 and p. 195 refer only to savings, current or past, and there seems nothing elsewhere to modify their effect. The distinction is important when you are considering motives, because there is a special need for liquidity in the case of idle working capital.

I am not quite satisfied as to the prominence you assign to *uncertainty* respecting the rate of interest (pp. 168–9 and 201–4). At the outset the argument is simply that if the rate of interest turns out to be higher than is expected at some time in the future, a capital loss will be incurred. What is implied, I think, is that the chance of loss will in the minds of investors outweigh the equal chance of gain. You say (p. 169), 'The actuarial profit or mathematical expectation of gain calculated in accordance with the existing probabilities... must be sufficient to compensate for the risk of disappoint-ment.' Perhaps you mean 'disappointment *as well as loss*'. If this is so, investors will ask a higher rate of interest than the prospects really justify, the 'safe' rate (pp. 201–2).

It seems to me rather far-fetched to suppose that, where there are equal chances of loss and of gain of capital value, investors will attach so much more weight to loss *plus* disappointment than to gain that they will actually forgo the income from a part of their capital altogether rather than risk it. Nor does 'disappointment' really describe the true motive, which is, I think, that in many cases a loss of £10,000 really is much more important than a gain of £10,000.

Should not your case rest rather on the existence of 'bears' who are not merely uncertain of the future rate of interest but definitely believe that the market is estimating it too low? And is it not misleading to describe the fear of a capital loss as a preference for *liquidity*? A man may be very much exercised in his mind as to whether he may suffer a capital loss on an investment of £10,000, though he may never expect to have to find cash to the amount of more than £500 at a time.

Own-rates of interest. A renewed study of chapter 17 leads me to make some further comments. I do not find your formula, '$a_1 + q_1$, $a_2 - c_2$ and l_3 will be equal' (p. 227) satisfactory. In a community in which the flow of commodities is perfectly normal, so that there are no excesses or deficiencies of spot supplies, stocks of goods are held, like cash, as working balances. The convenience of having supplies on hand, like the convenience of holding an adequate cash balance, is sufficient advantage to outweigh the gain that could be made by placing the resources in a remunerative investment. This convenience is distinct from a liquidity preference, for the liquidity preference on a stock of liquid goods is 'usually negligible' (p. 226). It therefore constitutes a *fourth* category of advantage from holding wealth. And stocks of goods will tend to be of such magnitude that the net marginal advantage (after setting off carrying costs) will be equal to the market rate of interest. Thus under the conditions assumed, that the flow of commodities is perfectly normal, all the own rates of interest will be equal to one another.

The only exception is in the case of seasonal products, where a redundant supply is normal except immediately before the next crop. People must be found to hold the redundant supply without any compensating advantage of convenience, and therefore the spot price is depressed below the forward price (up to the next crop) by the amount of carrying charges.

In general however there will be some commodities of which the spot supply is either excessive or deficient in relation either to present or future market conditions, and for which the net advantage of holding is less or greater than the rate of interest on an investment. And for them there will be an appropriate difference between spot and future prices. The excess supply of a seasonal product after the crop is merely a particular case.

In case of a present excess or a future deficiency of supplies, the premium on future supplies will rise to the level at which it will cover the carrying charges on spot supplies withheld from sale. The own rate of interest will thus be depressed below the market rate by an amount equal to the carrying charges (exclusive of interest).

In case of a present deficiency or a future excess of supplies there will be a discount on the forward price, which will be partly (but not necessarily entirely) corrected by selling off goods from stock. Traders will reduce their stocks below the level corresponding to a convenience equivalent to the market rate of interest, in order to take advantage of the temporarily high price. As their stocks get lower the marginal convenience of holding the diminished stocks gets higher. When a balance is established, the own rate of interest of the commodity is raised above the market rate by an amount equal to the discount on the forward price.

Thus the variations of the own rate of interest of a commodity are attributable to prospective changes of price arising from a present or expected excess or deficiency of supplies. This does not exclude a premium on the forward price of a commodity on which the purchasers find it convenient to hedge by buying forward. Since they could otherwise only protect themselves against changes of price by holding larger stocks, it is worth their while to pay a forward premium to avoid the carrying charges for this purpose.

Thus it is the exception for the own rate of interest of any commodity to diverge from the market rate. In the case of commodities held in stock and also in the case of money the tendency is so to adjust the amount held that the net marginal advantage of holding is equal to the market rate of interest. I will not enter upon a detailed criticism of chapter 17, but you will see at once that there is much in it which is not consistent with the foregoing reasoning.

Yours ever,

R. G. HAWTREY

P.S. 'Expected percentage appreciation (or depreciation)' (p. 227) is not the correct way of describing the difference between the forward and spot prices of a commodity. A trader who pays a premium on the forward price does not necessarily *expect* the price to rise by the amount of the premium. He is willing to pay the premium because even if the price remains unchanged he will have escaped the carrying costs.

To R. G. HAWTREY, *6 January 1936*

My dear Ralph,

My book is now in the hands of the printer, so it is now too late to make any other changes. I am afraid, indeed, that I did not make some modifications which I would have made otherwise, as I could not face the disturbance and delay of upsetting the pagination except for grave cause. All the same, I have considered very carefully your letter of December 19th, and my comments are below. This letter makes me feel that on certain points we are still further apart than you think. This is because, in my opinion, I have not yet succeeded in some aspects in conveying to you what I am driving at. So many points are still seen through your spectacles and not through mine!

1. *Marginal efficiency of working capital.* I should affirm that a purchase of excess stocks is a prospective and not a present advantage. It is not true that it saves trouble in buying and cost of delivery at the present time. It increases the trouble today with a view to diminishing it in future. No one would buy excess stocks except with a view to a future advantage.

There is a certain quantity of stocks which manufacturers and traders buy for convenience, and these bear a somewhat constant proportion to their turnover. If they buy more or less than the normal, it is practically always either because they have a view as to the relation of future prices to present prices or because they think it is going to be exceptionally easy or exceptionally difficult to obtain delivery at short notice. I still remain without evidence that changes in the rate of interest, such as ordinarily occur, play any measurable part in their decisions. There is nothing in your *Art of Central Banking* on pages 365 to 371, to which you refer me, to confute this. Your statistics contain no evidence that dealers will hold more stocks when the rate of interest falls. The fact that for certain classes of dealers their interest charges are fairly large compared with their profits proves nothing. My point is that, if there were a fall in interest charges, they would not hold larger stocks unless they expected higher prices; for the holding of larger stocks would not increase their turnover to an extent likely to cover even the reduced rate of interest.

I do speak on this matter, not merely as a theorist, but from an extremely wide practical acquaintance with commodity markets and their habits. Honestly, I really do know a great deal about this simply on the side of facts, and I am quite certain that you are wrong. In the case of non-staple articles, loss through the passage of time for reasons other than the rate of interest is of course on a scale to outweigh interest altogether. Staple articles, on the other hand, fall into two groups, those which, in recent parlance, have 'administered' prices,—e.g. cement in this country at the present time—, i.e. a price fixed monopolistically, or semi-monopolistically, and only rarely changed; and commodities produced in the full blast of competition, where there is a free market. Take lead as an example of the latter, though that has been becoming more cartelised lately. I think you would find hardly any year in the last half century in which the maximum price of lead during the year was not 50 per cent above the minimum price. The man who deals in lead must be overwhelmingly influenced, not merely by his long-period ideas of price, but by his short-period ideas. The extent to which consumers of lead hold or do not hold stocks varies enormously, since it is quite a convenient commodity to store. Some of the largest consumers of lead in the United States acquired such large stocks some two years ago that they have been virtually out of the market ever since; the same is true in the case of tin. But, if you discuss this matter with those actively concerned, you will find that changes in the rate of interest never come into their picture. On the other hand, I should agree that the state of credit does sometimes; that is, the ease or difficulty of borrowing on the advertised terms.

This is a matter which we have debated together for years. We cannot absolutely bring it to a head because it is much more a matter of fact than of theory. I can only say that I have been in constant touch for many years past with dealers in a great variety of commodities and have constantly been engaged in sizing up the significant factors from a practical point of view; and never yet have I met anyone in the practical world who shared your views as to the facts.

It is convenient to deal at this point with the postscript to your letter on page 19 [above p. 626]. I cannot here follow at all what you mean. The trader who expects the price to rise by less than the existing premium on the forward price will, of course, not buy at all. If the price remains unchanged, he will by buying forward have paid the carrying costs in the premium, whereas by postponing buying he could have avoided them altogether. It is the dealer who hedges his stock by selling it forward who escapes the carrying costs; not the one who buys forward. There is, of course, a large specialised business in carrying stocks simply in order to obtain a small arbitrage profit by selling them forward at a price which slightly exceeds the carrying costs incurred by an expert. The way in which a rise in the rate of interest acts is to widen the difference between the spot price and the forward price in the case of any commodity of which there are surplus stocks. But this will normally operate, not by raising the forward price, but by lowering the spot price. Thus there is a greater drag on current production. Thus a high rate of interest acts as an increased deterrent to present production wherever there are surplus stocks, and, at the same time, hastens the date at which the stocks will be absorbed and production can return to normal.

2. I should, of course, have mentioned stocks a great many more times, if I attached the importance to them that you do. Where, however, I am dealing with stocks, I have expressly explained that the series of annuities which makes up the expectation consists of a single term. See, e.g., page 73.

3. A good deal of your criticism is based upon alleged ambiguity as to whether I mean marginal efficiency to apply to instruments or to enterprises. My intention is to apply to both indifferently. I do not see that, at the level of abstraction in which I am writing, any different treatment is required. In a realistic study it makes, of course, a difference whether one is considering what factors lead to the increase of industries and what lead to the establishment of new ones. But the sort of considerations which are relevant to this issue are a hundred miles away from the sort of things I am discussing.

The arguments you bring forward as to the importance of

distinguishing between the two are concerned with a real subject, but not with the subject with which I am in any way concerned in this book. You are really raising the whole problem of how the marginal theory of economics deals with the problems of joint supply and joint demand. It is a subject with a substantial and respectable controversial history. But I could not possibly be expected to deal with the subject in my present book. I am simply making the same assumptions as practically every other economist makes. That is to say, I am assuming that where special difficulties of joint supply and joint demand arise, any remarks which I am making on the assumption that there are no such difficulties must be suitably modified.

Take, in this connection, the paragraph which begins at the bottom of your page 4 [above p. 619]. In this respect I am, I think, meaning exactly the same as Marshall and as every other economist means, except R.G.H.

I still see, therefore, no reason, on the level of abstraction on which I am writing, to distinguish the effect of a fall in the rate of interest on the scale of investment due to its stimulating an existing enterprise to increase its plant and its effect on stimulating the formation of new enterprises.

When you say that there is no distinction in the case of an instrument between its market price and its replacement price, do you simply mean that there is frequently no second-hand market in instruments? Of course, on the realistic plane there would be something in that; not that it would make any difference. But, of course, where the instrument is not irrevocably fixed to the ground, there generally is a second-hand market, e.g. even in cotton spindles and looms.

I hope you will prove wrong that my readers will be baffled by my not having discussed the significance to my argument, if any, of the difference between the cost-saving capacity of instruments and the dividend-yielding capacity of enterprises. No other reader of my proofs, however, up to date, and no pupil, either in lecture or in class, has ever raised the point even in the most indirect way. Moreover, if I have sinned by omission, I have sinned in the company of all other economists, since no one that I am aware has ever raised the point in theoretical discussions of the marginal efficiency of capital and the rate of interest.

4. There are a series of passages which seem to imply that you are still in the dark as to what my theory of interest is. Take, for example, the last complete paragraph of your page 6 [above pp. 619–20]. Here you appear to urge it as an argument against me that marginal efficiency based on my concept of prospective yield cannot supply a theory of interest. But, of course, it cannot. My whole point is that *no* theory of interest can be derived from marginal efficiency. My theory is that, given the marginal efficiency of capital, then the rate of interest, whatever it is, derived from quite different sources, tells us on what scale investment will take place.

The last incomplete paragraph on your page 9 [above p. 621] also seems to me extremely remote from my theory. What do you mean by the equilibrium level of the rate of interest? If you mean accurate foresight, i.e. an equality between designed investment and saving, then my theory bears no resemblance at all to what you here suggest.

Again, the second paragraph on your page 10 [above p. 621], where you refer to a reduction of wages, does not remotely resemble my argument.

In the last incomplete paragraph on the same page [above p. 622] you speak of the adjustment of the marginal utility of capital to the rate of interest being extremely slow; yet you do not appear in this passage to be aware how remote this is from my view. For my point is that the two always are adjusted, the market price of new capital instruments rising when there is a sharp demand for more capital to such a figure as will lower the marginal efficiency of that type of capital to a figure which prevents the demand from getting out of equilibrium with the supply. The point under (i) in this paragraph is as remote as anything could possibly be from my argument and I should most strongly deny it.

Again, the middle paragraph of your page 11 [above p. 622] is remote from what I am trying to say. My point is that the yield on bonds determines the *output* of new investment. In the first instance, the yield on shares has to be brought into a proper relation to the yield on bonds, but in the longer run it is affected by the output of new investment. On my theory it is the yield on bonds which determines, directly and indirectly, the yield on shares and not vice versa.

The same point arises near the bottom of page 12 [above pp. 622-3]. I should agree that the effect of a depression is to raise the market for fixed-interest securities relatively to shares. But I see no direct reason why a fall in shares should raise the price of fixed-interest securities *absolutely*. My reasons for expecting the long-term rate of interest to fall during a depression have nothing to do with the tendency of shares to fall.

5. Bottom of your page 13 [above p. 623]: Which part of my criticisms of the classical theory could I have left out if I had made clearer the distinction between instruments and enterprises?

6. *Effective demand.* The process here is exactly the same as that by which a market price is fixed for a share of which no one really knows the prospective yield accurately. I was really conceding too much in saying that it was a fiction. The market is regularly engaged in assessing in terms of an exact numeral a complex of rather vague probabilities.

$MV = D$ on page 304 should be $MV = Y$, and has been altered.

7. *Major Douglas.* I did originally put a reference to the Major in connection with my argument on pages 99-101. But, on looking into it more carefully, I felt that the resemblance was really very slight and that it would be difficult not to appear to endorse him more than I do if I were to refer to him in this context. For his point is, of course, that all provisions except for current wages unavoidably and necessarily have the deflationary effect in question.

8. *Liquidity preference.* I think I deal with this on page 194.

9. Bottom of your page 15 [above p. 624]: It is not a case of the chance of loss outweighing the *equal* chance of gain, but the *unknown* chance of gain.

10. Top of page 16 [above p. 624]: Yes, I mean 'disappointment as well as loss'.

In the second paragraph of your page 16 [above p. 624] again it is a case, not of *equal* chances but of *unknown* chances.

Why is it misleading to describe the fear of a capital loss if an asset is purchased as a reason for preferring to keep the cash and not purchase the asset?

11. Page 17 [above p. 625]: I think I have now suitably qualified my remarks so as to meet your point.

12. Page 18 [above pp. 625–6]: I am not quite clear about the argument here. As I have pointed out, the widening of the difference between spot and future prices will in general involve a fall in the former which will react on the output of the commodity in question. In the second paragraph, does 'market rate of interest' mean 'money rate of interest'? In the third paragraph, to whom do you contemplate that the goods from stock will be sold off?

I think my main point in this context is that you overlook the effect of current output.

Sorry to be so captious, but, as I said in my last letter, I think we have now got to the point of flogging old problems where we have to agree to differ.

I hope to be sending you a copy of the complete book in about a fortnight's time.

Yours ever,
[copy initialled] J.M.K.

Although most of the discussion that took place was oral or on sets of proofs that have not survived, a few fragments of the notes and letters that passed between Keynes and Richard Kahn during the summer and autumn of 1935 appear below.[1]

[1] 'Alexander' in the letters cited in full below was a nickname given to Kahn by Lydia Keynes to avoid confusion with Richard Braithwaite, another Fellow of King's. This nickname was in general use until it was dropped gradually at Lydia's prompting towards the beginning of the war.

From a letter to R. F. KAHN, *29 July 1935*

I am in the stage of not liking my book very much. It all seems very angry and much ado about a matter much simpler than I make it appear. Hawtrey's comments indicate that he hasn't the faintest idea what I'm driving at.

From a letter to R. F. KAHN, *30 July 1935*

My dear Alexander,

Thanks very much for taking so much trouble about the Mummery. Hobson never fully understood him and went off on a side-track after his death. But the book Hobson helped him to write, *The Physiology of Industry* is a wonderful work. I am giving a full account of it but old Hobson has had so much injustice done to him that I shan't say what I think about M's contribution to it being, probably, outstanding.

Yours ever,

J.M.K.

From a letter to R. F. KAHN, *27 August 1935*

I have been going in more detail into Roy's comments and have now written him an enormous letter. It is quite clear that he has not grasped what my theory of the rate of interest is, and I fancy that those chapters written a long time ago are a long way from being as clear as they might be. So I am having to face a complete re-doing.

From a letter to R. F. KAHN, *4 September 1935*

My dear Alexander,

In re-writing my note on user cost I gave some further thought to the point of yours which we discussed. It still does not appeal to my intuition. So perhaps I have not quite got your meaning even now.

It seems to me that your criterion as to when replacement takes place does not carry the question far enough. I agree that cases can easily be conceived where the marginal user cost is zero. But in the case where it is taken as greater than zero I am not, I think, assuming that the plant disintegrates suddenly. It is sufficient for me to assume that a point comes where the excess of factor cost when using old plant over the factor cost when using new plant is less than the long-period depreciation of new plant.

Furthermore, even apart from the above, are you not assuming that plant could not be used more intensively and has to be used either at a given degree of intensity or not at all? Otherwise it is sufficient for me to assume that a point comes when the excess of factor cost on bad old plant exceeds the factor cost on superior old plant plus the user cost of using the superior old plant more intensively.

I hope to have my revised note on user cost back from the printer[1] by the time I am in Cambridge, when I will show you my method of conversion to equilibration between user cost and long-period depreciation.[2]

Yours ever,

J.M.K.

Note by J.M.K. [*September 1935*]

You are assuming plant cannot be used more intensively. I do not assume it suddenly disintegrates but only that a point comes when the excess of factor cost on old plant over factor cost on new plant is less than the long-period depreciation on new plant *or* less than the user cost of using more intensively superior old plant.

From R. F. KAHN [*September 1935*]

Galley 40. Colin's gross income is to be regarded as an approximation to your $A + B$, his terms of definition being quite different.

  l. 10: omit 'user cost'.

---

[1] These galleys, which have not survived, are discussed by Kahn below.
[2] Here Keynes wrote in the margin: 'God knows what I dictated! Not this.'

Galley 27. If plant is renewed only when it is not *worthwhile* using it any longer (rather than because it cataclysmically falls to pieces), then in long-period equilibrium marginal user cost is o. (I have developed all this at great length, and am prepared, if you like, to take on the job of expounding it at some time or other.)

p. 2 of insert in galley 29. No—because marginal factor cost exceeds average factor cost. It has always been recognised that if m.f.c. = a.f.c. (under conditions of surplus capacity) there is a loss equal to the fixed costs.

Galley 29. It is the analogy with copper which is so misleading. The correct analogy is food going bad in a larder. The marginal user cost involved in depleting such a larder is o. You are assuming throughout that equipment is replaced because (*a*) it suddenly disintegrates, or (*b*) some margin of safety disappears. The opposite extreme (in which in long-period equilibrium marginal user cost is o) is that in which the factor cost of working the plant *gradually* rises with old age, until the plant yields no quasi-rent whatever—it is scrapped.

Chapter 6, galley 26 (ii). It is not made quite clear (partly because you start off with minus U and partly because A_1 has crept in) that total expected depreciation = user cost + supplementary cost.

If supplementary cost = expected depreciation of plant when not used + cost (B') involved, it would be helpful to say so. (Does this not give you your carrying cost?)

Also to point out that this is not the same as Marshall's supplementary cost.

Galley 32, bottom line. 'in both cases' belongs to an earlier epoch.

To R. F. KAHN, *7 October 1935*

My dear Alexander,

Your proposition that supplementary cost is equal to the expected depreciation of plant when not used plus the expenditure on the laid-up equipment seems to me to require the assumption that the windfall loss would be the same whether the plant is used or not.[1] If this is correct, it is difficult to bring in the point in a simple way, especially since the proof needs several symbols which I do not otherwise need.

Yours ever,

J. M. KEYNES

---

[1] Or, more simply, that the actual user cost is necessarily equal to the expected user cost. V is the excess of the *expected* total depreciation over the *actual* user cost.

TOWARDS THE GENERAL THEORY

From R. F. KAHN

I find that this all reads most beautifully. It carries with it an air of finality and inevitability which I find most convincing. I particularly like the way in which you introduce user cost at the opening of chapter 6. It is impossible now to believe that you ever intended anything different.

As you see from the attached page I have only two comments (apart from a few misprints which I have dealt with in the text).

R.F.K.

Galley slip 10, note 2 [*General Theory*, p. 19]. What about Mrs Marshall? The whole passage (p. 154 of book[1] appended) is well worth reading. The square brackets mean 'Beginners omit'.

Slip 29, opening of last paragraph [*General Theory* p. 63]. I do not like you saying that saving and investment are 'different names for the same thing'. They are *different* things (that is the whole point)—they are certainly different acts—but they are equal in *magnitude*.

I still hold that the simple-minded proof that saving = investment, appropriate for those who cannot grapple with user cost, etc. is called for— not only for the sake of the simple-minded, but to prevent the obvious retort that all your stuff depends on your peculiar definitions. What is wrong with saying that *however* income is defined,

$$\text{income} = \text{value of output} = \text{consumption} + \text{investment}$$
$$\text{also income} = \text{consumption} + \text{saving}$$
$$\therefore \text{saving} = \text{investment}$$

This truth is far too important (and far too seldom recognised) to be concealed in a mist of subtle definition.

Chapter 10, galley 120, last complete paragraph but one [vol. XIV p. 456; *General Theory*, p. 121]. The dole *causes the marginal propensity to consume* (and the *multiplier*) to be lower.

'Thus' (opening of next paragraph) is then quite wrong.

Galley 120 last line but one [vol. XIV p. 456; *General Theory*, p. 121]. Not merely 'from the incomes' but from their consumption?

Galley 122 top [vol XIV. p. 457; *General Theory*, p. 123]. You seem to omit the effects of higher prices in causing a redistribution of income to the saving classes (by way of profits).

Keynes's other constant Cambridge critic was Joan Robinson, who wrote many more notes than did Kahn. Keynes's marginal comments on her notes appear as footnotes.

---

[1] *Economics of Industry.* [Ed.]

To JOAN ROBINSON, *8 June 1935*

My dear Joan,

Here is a first instalment, namely Book I. The rest will follow shortly. Chapters 1 to 6 and 20 to 25 are in a more advanced stage of revision than the intervening chapters. I shall be extremely grateful for any criticisms of form or substance.

Could you and Austin dine with Lydia and me in King's on Thursday (June 13) at 8.0, and come with us to the Handel afterwards?

Yours ever,

J. M. KEYNES

To JOAN ROBINSON, *12 June 1935*

My dear Joan,

Here is the rest of the available proofs. I hope it isn't such a heavy bundle as it looks.

Yours ever,

J.M.K.

From JOAN ROBINSON, *16 June 1935*

My dear Maynard,

I hope it is not an impertinence for me to say that I am very much delighted with your book. It makes an impression of great power and coherence. Apart from everything else it is a great blessing to feel that the scholastic points are properly dealt with, so that we can push ahead without leaving an exposed flank. It will be extremely difficult to attack and the hostile critics will have to resort to making such silly points that they will expose themselves.

I found the chapters on the rate of interest and on money wages particularly well done, but all of it is as clear as this sort of stuff can be. The only part I found hard was the 'Essential Properties', but I suppose that can't be helped.

I should think it is the most *readable* book of its weight ever. The eloquent passages come in just at the right points to keep one going, but in spite of the differences in manner it doesn't seem scrappy as the *Treatise* did despite its severe appearance.

I have made a good number of notes. Many of them you would no doubt have dealt with in any case, for I noticed a considerable difference in the part which you said had been most recently revised.

638

I am sending them along in case you are feeling strong and would like to have a look at them before you come up.

I hope you are well recovered.

Yours always,

JOAN

If I may I will keep the proofs until you come up.

P. 8, section IV, end of second paragraph [vol. XIV p. 367; *General Theory*, p. 16]. 'Monopolistic practices on the part of employers'[1] reduce real wages for given employment and so cause 'unemployment' in just the same way as inferior technique or natural resources. Putting them in here is likely I think to give a wrong impression, many people fall into the simple error of thinking that monopoly reduces output as a whole in the same direct way as it reduces output of one commodity.

P. 10, note 2 [vol. XIV p. 369; *General Theory*, p. 21]. Rather awkward referring in the text to a footnote.[2]

P. 11, note 1 [vol. XIV p. 370, n. 1]. This use of 'price' will cause trouble.

Would aggregate $\begin{Bmatrix} \text{demand} \\ \text{supply} \end{Bmatrix}$ price be a possible phrase?[3]

Section II, paragraph 3 [vol. XIV pp. 370–71]. Would it be possible to mitigate the formalism of this passage by saying something to this effect:[4]—Under Say's Law whenever some people are set to work the income earned in respect to their product necessarily constitutes an increase in expenditure equal to the increase in output.—Your Ds make the point more mysterious than it need be. But perhaps you are doing it on purpose to get the reader into your clutches.

Later you use the convention of ′ for expectations. Do you mean it in that sense here? In one sense the distinction between D and D' *is* between reality and expectation and people might think that this is the point, but when you say that the classics assume that D and D' are necessarily equal you are saying something quite different. It might appear that you were merely suggesting that the classics neglect the possibility of disappointment.

I think you ought to make it clear that under Say's Law D will always take the value that D' happens to be. Merely saying that D and D' are *equal* obscures the fact that the causation only runs one way.

Anyway you don't use D' again at all. Could you put this bit in words and leave D' out altogether?

But see note to p. 20 below.

P. 14, 'Whatever such a community…to invest', end of 4th paragraph [vol. XIV p. 378]. Must be a misprint here or a bit missing.[5]

[1] 'I meant practices by employers corresponding to trade union closed shops.'
[2] 'Unavoidable.'   [3] 'Agreed.'   [4] 'Re-written.'   [5] 'Deleted.'

P. 17, 13th line from bottom, last word [vol. xiv p. 385; *General Theory*, p. 40]. Delete 'a' (?).

P. 19, note 2 [vol. xiv pp. 388–9; *General Theory*, pp. 42–3, footnote 2]. The unrealistic assumption is a corollary of the assumption of perfect competition. I could find you a reference to Marshall here if you would like it. But it seems hardly worthwhile.

P. 20, top [vol. xiv p. 391], D' (?) for D.

P. 25 bottom paragraph [vol. xiv p. 401]. Repeat that A includes fixed capital goods as well as consumption goods.

P. 26, top line [vol. xiv p. 402], 'the maximum extent'. Is this right?[1] B' surely ought to be the amount that the entrepreneur would in fact spend on maintenance if he had decided not to produce, not the most that he could spend. Here you are using ' in a slightly different sense. Why not have a suffix instead? (Beginning of section iii below.)

2nd paragraph. Parenthesis rather awkward—reads as tho' *balance* of outgoings was prime cost.

P. 27, 2nd paragraph [vol. xiv p. 406]. Here you are using supply price in the ordinary sense. Confirms my comment to p. 11.

P. 27, 3rd paragraph [vol. xiv p. 407]. M and A user cost would be likely to differ even if plant was all alike; e.g. wear and tear may increase more than in proportion to rate of output. (See also p. 29, note 2.)

P. 28 bottom [vol. xiv pp. 410–11]. Perhaps you could put in a footnote suggesting that the actions of business men show that they have the user-cost idea in mind altho' they do not formulate distinctly or correctly. I think some justification is required for the apparent unreality of attributing these subtle calculations to the business man.

P. 29 top [vol. xiv p. 411]. Most usual case of low user cost is a very deep slump expected to last for a long time.

P. 31 [vol. xiv p. 418]. (2) Gross quasi-rent per period of time. The word *whole* is confusing as it is not clear at first sight if it means gross for one period or net for the total of periods, i.e. difference between Q and $\Sigma Q'$ not clear.[2]

P. 32 [vol. xiv p. 422]. Ref. to *Treatise*—see chapter 8 below.[2]

P. 33 [vol. xiv p. 423]. $I - U = Y - C = S$. The paragraph of talk which now follows equation (ii) below would be better here I think. You might simply swap it for the five lines which now follow the above equation.[2]

P. 34, chapter 8, 2nd paragraph [vol. xiv p. 425]. To do the *Treatise* justice you made this clear at the time (see vol. I, p. 140 [*JMK*, vol. v, p. 126]). Obviously there you were making a wangle so that S and I were quantitatively unequal in order to emphasise that they were not the same thing. I think it would be good both for the reader and for yourself to make this clear.

[1] 'I meant "most advantageous".' [2] 'Delete.'

P. 39, 1st paragraph [vol. XIV p. 431]. 'Little, if at all, above zero' gives the impression that net investment cannot be negative.

2nd paragraph, 1st line [vol. XIV p. 431]. Word *every* seems to be wrong.

P. 43, 2nd paragraph [vol. XIV p. 444]. Sorry—you deal with this point in chapter 11, see below.

Distribution of real income. There are two separate points. (1) The institutional pattern of distribution, depending on social and legal factors. (2) The change in distribution of real income which comes about automatically as output alters.

(1) belongs in your third category with subjective factors but I wonder if it is right to put (2) in as well? The saving corresponding to a larger output is greater for two reasons: (*a*) people are richer on balance, (*b*) real income is transferred from wages to profits. This is quite a different sort of point from the fact that a more egalitarian society has a higher propensity to spend at all ranges of total real income. (Age composition of the population is an important influence on the subjective factors.)

P. 44, 5th paragraph [vol. XIV p. 447]. This gives the impression that *negative* saving when incomes decline is necessary for stability. A mere decline in rate of saving is the minimum assumption.

P. 47, last paragraph [vol. XIV pp. 451–2]. I am not at all happy about this. I am sure the calculations to which you refer, which show that the proportion of real wages is constant for all levels of employment are fishy.[1] I believe one of Alexander's young men worked some theory out showing the change in proportion of real wages in this country in recent years.

If you do not want to be bothered to go far into this point would not a better line be to dispose of it by saying that it necessarily goes in the right direction, i.e. to enhance the difference between ΔC_w and ΔY_w. It is an *a fortiori* consideration. To bring it in has the great merit of making the treatment more general as this point *must* be of great importance near full employment.

P. 48, last 7 lines [*General Theory*, p. 113]. Could you write this up a bit? Rather slight treatment of an important point.

P. 50, 3rd paragraph [vol. XIV p. 459]. 'more generally we shall mean...' You don't use it in this sense for some time, and this explanation rather obscures the next few paragraphs. See below next page.

P. 51, 1st paragraph [vol. XIV p. 460]. Not quite accurately put. M[arginal] E[fficiency] is immediately equated to rate of interest by the rise in supply prices. As capital accumulates prospective earnings fall off, the rate of investment declines, consequently supply prices fall to an extent that just offsets the

---

[1] 'Deleted.'

decline in prospective earnings. You seem to be saying that the 'two factors' reinforce each other—actually they counteract each other. The more of one the less of the other.

P. 52, section III [*General Theory*, p. 141]. Could you say here: '(using m.e. in the sense of the schedule of m.e.'s of varying amounts of investment)'? You use it in this sense thro'out the section.

P. 54, section V, first line [vol. XIV p. 464; *General Theory*, p. 145]. Here you might use the phrase schedule of m.e.'s. I think it is very important to keep the distinction before the reader all the time. When one knows the argument there is no difficulty in seeing what is meant each time, but with a puzzled or hostile reader these small verbal points cause a lot of trouble.

P. 60, line 7 [vol. XIV p. 467; *General Theory*, p. 157]. A purely literary point —I think re-iterating 'dark' here makes the passage just a little too rich. Otherwise all this is very beautiful.

Section VI [vol. XIV p. 468; *General Theory*, p. 158]. Could you find another word for *investment* here? It is often hard to get people out of the habit of meaning by 'investment' buying shares, and this will encourage a relapse.

P. 61, 3rd paragraph [vol. XIV p. 468; *General Theory*, p. 160]. The prospective yield of marriage might raise a ribald laugh.

P. 62, section VII end paragraph [vol. XIV p. 468; *General Theory*, p. 162 2nd paragraph]. 'as experience undoubtedly tells us'...something seems to be missing or transposed. Comma before 'as' (?).

P. 63, last 2 paragraphs [vol. XIV p. 470; *General Theory*, p. 164]. This is only a personal fancy—I cannot see that you gain anything by being what many people would consider over-optimistic about the behaviour of authorities. Could you say (16th line from end) 'only experience, however, *can* show'? And in last paragraph 'to see a state which is endeavouring to ensure continuous full employment, and which is in a position etc'[1] This doesn't impair the point at all, but would prevent some ill-natured mockery.

P. 64, top [vol. XIV p. 470; *General Theory*, p. 165]. Here is a passage where the schedule and the actual value of m.e. must be distinguished.

9th line: something gone wrong here.

P. 76, 5th paragraph [vol. XIV p. 485; *General Theory*, p. 191]. You are going a good deal ahead of what the reader knows by discussing relation between money wages and the rate of interest, but he has had several hints, so perhaps it does not matter.

9th line from bottom, 'zero employment'. I think you mean employment corresponding to zero rate of interest (supposing this to be less than full).[2]

P. 77, section IV, 2nd paragraph [vol. XIV p. 486]. Some confusion here between actual m.e. and schedule of m.e.'s.

[1] No.   [2] Yes. Very good point.

P. 79 [*General Theory*, pp. 195–6]. Sometimes you use roman numbers and sometimes arabic. Is there any significance in this?[1]

P. 81, section II [vol. XIV p. 488; *General Theory*, p. 200]. (i) A step in the argument seems to have been left out. When there is an increase in gold there must be an equal increase in saving (no matter whether the people who enjoy the new income themselves save or not). The question then arises whether there is an additional demand for money equal to the addition to individuals' wealth. If not the rate of interest will fall. I think two effects have got run together: (1) the temporary increase in demand for M_1 while the mining is going on, (2) the permanent increase in M_2 due to increased total of past accumulated wealth.

Each of the new gold provides income only in the weeks that it is raised, but it is a permanent addition to the stock of money, and corresponds to an equal addition to the aggregated stock of accumulated savings. Same point with deficit financed by note issue.

P. 86, 1st half of 2nd paragraph [vol. XIV p. 490]. This is true in so far as an increase in M is not offset by rise of money wages. You have exposed the absurdities of the quantity theory without mentioning one of the worst—that it does not distinguish between the kind of change in prices associated with a change in output, and the kind due to a change in money wages.[2]

P. 90 [vol. XIV p. 493; *General Theory*, p. 215, last paragraph]. 'The object of the rate of interest should be', etc. I find this very obscure. Surely the influence of prospective demand on m.e. of capital is what looks after this? You seem to be introducing a new criterion for the desirable rate of interest other than your usual one that it should be as low as possible without causing inflationary conditions. But I haven't seen what you are saying in this passage at all.[3]

The way I look at roundaboutness is this. Take a given number of men and arrange in order of the length of time taken by every known process of production. Different processes involve different amounts of time because of indivisible periods in nature (e.g. 9 months for a calf) just as different processes require different 'scales' because of technical 'lumps' (e.g. a blast furnace has to be of a certain size). When the processes are arranged in order of length it will be found that some produce more output than others (with given labour). For each length, strike out all but the most productive process (for there are no circumstances in which a less productive process will be preferred to another of the same length).

You are now left with a series of processes in ascending order of length. At

---

[1] 'None!'
[2] 'Dealt with in chapter 21, but I will mention it here.'
[3] 'I hope my slight revision here is sufficient to meet this point.'

first productivity increases with length up to the length which would prevail at zero interest. Beyond that point productivity decreases with length.

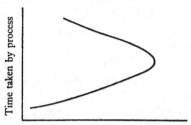

Productivity of process per unit of labour

So long as the rate of interest is positive you are on the lower part of the curve and it is true that every lengthening of process increases productivity. This seems to be the point that *B*[öhm]-*B*[awerk] was muddled about, and what Marshall meant in that footnote.

If the rate of interest is negative and if the rule is that you must employ actual capital to earn the negative interest (I think you ought to make this clear here—you mention it later) then there are two most profitable ways of producing a given output with given labour, one shorter and more productive, the other longer and less productive.

Is this what you mean? I think it is, but I found this bit much less clear than most. I think it is very important strategically.

98 (*b*) [*General Theory*, pp. 232–3]. I find this confusing. [See also reference to p. 101 below, 3rd paragraph.] The way I look at it liquidity attaches to something in which a large number of values are fixed. If wages cease to be sticky in terms of money, money is less liquid (cf. great inflation). But I don't see why wages become less sticky *because* money is liquid.

P. 100, top paragraph [vol. XIV p. 500; *General Theory*, p. 236, first paragraph]. Isn't this a rather tricky argument? If gold were in elastic supply it would cease to be money.

P. 101, 3rd paragraph [vol. XIV p. 500; *General Theory*, pp. 237–8]. Here you are dealing with my above [p. 98 (*b*) above] difficulty. But I still find it very hard. I should have said 'increasing output cannot be maintained in face of stable labour cost'. Surely stickiness depends on psychology. If it were the psychology that wages were sticky in terms of wheat, wheat would take on some of the qualities of money.[1]

But probably I am just being dense.

P. 125, last 2 paragraphs [vol. XIV p. 458; *General Theory*, pp. 130 (last paragraph)–131]. This does not seem to read quite as smoothly as your

---

[1] '*Some* but not enough.'

other eloquent passages. I think a touch here and there would make it very beautiful.

P. 129 (5) [vol. XIV p. 507; *General Theory*, p. 264 (6)]. The pessimism about m.e. of capital is surely what you want here.

P. 133 et seq. appendix [vol. XIV pp. 507–8; *General Theory*, pp. 272–9]. This sounds very convincing but I never got far enough with Pigou to be able to offer any remarks. Throughout you want to alter marginal prime cost to supply price.

P. 138, 2nd paragraph [vol. XIV p. 511; *General Theory*, p. 293 lines 31–2]. 'fixed and reliable'. Does this mean the future is known to be a repetition of the present? I think you need this condition.

P. 141, 4th paragraph [vol. XIV p. 512; *General Theory*, p. 300, first paragraph]. Supply price.

5th paragraph, 2nd line from bottom of paragraph [vol. XIV p. 512; *General Theory*, p. 300, second paragraph]. 'elastic and *their* prices have to rise.'

P. 143, section V, 4th paragraph [vol. XIV p. 512; *General Theory*, p. 304]. Same point as I remarked on in the passage about Ricardo. How does it come that zero employment is a resting place? Zero wages or zero rate of interest might be taken to give a bottom limit.

To JOAN ROBINSON, *18 June 1935*

My dear Joan,

Thank you very much indeed for the notes, which look as if they would be very useful. I have only glanced through them at this stage, since I would rather put off careful consideration until I am on the job of revising the passages to which they relate. You do not say whether the chapter on 'Essential Properties' proved fully intelligible in the long run. If it did, I should be content, since much of the stuff in this chapter, being rather unfamiliar at this stage to the author as well as to the reader, is inevitably more obscure than it will be after the passage of a little time.

I am still running a trifling temperature and not getting about. But I hope to come to Cambridge on Sunday for a couple of days.

Yours ever,

J. M. KEYNES

From JOAN ROBINSON, *19 June 1935*

My dear Maynard,

I am so very sorry to hear that you are still seedy. What a nuisance for you to be stuck in town.

I think I got the 'Essential Properties' in the end apart from particular points which I have noted. The only important one is about stickiness of wages. Here I believe you were led astray by Alexander for I have been arguing with him about it and I think he now agrees with my point of view.

You don't anywhere come right out in the open and say what liquidity *is*. I enclose a note which I take to be what you mean. If I am right about this I don't think I have any further difficulty or disagreement.

It is extraordinary to think how many tomes have been written on this subject (Knapp and all) without a grain of sense.

I hope you will be fit before Sunday. I will come around on Monday morning if I may and return the proofs.

I should very much like to be allowed to see the rest when it is done.

Yours,

JOAN

Liquidity

That asset is the most liquid which is expected to retain its value in most things. This is a multidimensional conception—two assets may have the same degree of liquidity for quite different reasons. The quality of being able to 'touch your money' at short notice (which is the everyday meaning of 'liquidity') is covered by this view of liquidity. An asset which is expected to keep its value over a long run but is subject to ups and downs is not liquid, as at any given point in the future its value is uncertain.

Money is highly liquid first because there are a very large number of debts paid in money. Second because wages and therefore all prices are more sticky in money than in anything else (the habit of thinking in terms of money reinforces this effect).

'A flight from the currency' is not really the effect of a fall in liquidity *preference* but of a fall in the liquidity of money.

In the final stages of the German inflation the mark had lost all liquidity and had lost all the characteristics of money except the least essential—'medium of exchange'.

Theoretically 'unit of account' and 'standard of deferred payments' are separable, but in practice they are closely bound together for reasons of convenience, i.e. the standard of deferred payments quickly becomes the unit of account (dollars and rye in Germany). It is the quality of being the standard of deferred payments which gives money its liquidity. In a community in which no transactions are made for more than a day ahead nothing would have much liquidity.

P. 82 top [vol. XIV p. 488; *General Theory*, p. 201]. Surely if M_1 *does* absorb the whole increase in cash there can be no fall in r, therefore no increase in M_1 (Q.E. Absurdum). This is a point that I have known to cause trouble. I think it would be worth doing it with constant money wages showing that an increase in M must lead to *some* decrease in r and increase in investment, the decrease in r being less the greater the increase in M_1 corresponding to a given increase in investment. If money wages rise as a consequence of the increased activity the rate of interest will have to go up again and the activity to fall off again. But there must be a stage at which the rate of interest falls.

(ii) V also depends on whether a given increase in D is due to an increase in N or merely to an increase in money wages.[1] I would be much happier if you kept money wages constant here.

(iii) [vol. XIV p. 488; *General Theory*, p. 202]. Numerical example hard to follow: 'rise faster than by 4 per cent per annum' reads as tho' it was 8 per cent at the end of the year. Would it be clear if you say 'rate of increase of 4 per cent a year'?. The way you have done 2 per cent is quite clear.

P. 83, lines 8–9 [vol. XIV p. 489; *General Thoery*, p. 203]. Clearer if you say 'the possible loss is low compared with the running yield'.

line 20 [vol. XIV, p. 489; *General Theory*, p. 203]. 'on account of transfer difficulties'. Isn't it stickiness of wage rates which is the trouble? The trouble really arises because capital is more mobile than labour. But in any case there is no reason to suppose that the country with a high rate is enjoying full employment.

P. 85 (3) [vol. XIV p. 489; *General Theory*, p. 207 (3)]. In a great inflation the rate of interest rises in spite of the violent fall in liquidity preference, the reason being of course the enormous absorption of cash into M_1 ∵ of rise of money incomes and prices. It is not worth going into all this, but the reader will be startled by the implication that r *falls* during inflation.

P. 92 top [vol. XIV p. 495; *General Theory*, p. 219, last full paragraph]. You mean that the community with less capital will be able to continue investing after the other has stopped. But if so it will soon become like the other community. In what sense is there 'long-period equilibrium'[2] if investment is still going on?

You have stopped rather suddenly in this section out of the short period with fixed equipment to which the rest of the book belongs. I think all you really want is to say that the greater the capital equipment in existence at any

[1] 'Why?'   [2] 'Deleted.'

moment the greater will be the propensity to save, the lower the m.e. of capital corresponding to each rate of investment, $\therefore$ the lower must be the rate of interest which will give full employment. (Assuming no inventions— you ought to make that clear.)

As a community accumulates capital it approaches the dangerous situation in which 2 per cent or even 0 per cent won't give full employment.

I think this is all you really need. I have been working out this long-period stuff and I find that to make a proper job of it one needs to bring in several considerations that are not really relevant to your main theme, e.g. I find elasticity of substitution is an important factor. I feel that this section is in a limbo between long and short period; you could make your point without bringing the long period in at all. But if you do I think a definition of 'equilibrium' is essential.

P. 91, 2nd paragraph [*General Theory*, p. 218]. During the period that the stock of capital is shrinking net saving will have to be negative. It will rise to zero when the new equilibrium with less capital is reached. M.E. of capital remains equal to rate of interest (zero) during the period of dis-investment[1] $\therefore$ price of capital goods falls below what their cost of production would be with zero rate of investment.

Last paragraph. You make m.e. of capital fall below rate of interest, which is impossible.[2]

P. 92, 2nd paragraph [vol. XIV p. 495; *General Theory*, pp. 219–20]. Here again it is not clear if you mean full employment with investment going on (a situation which cannot last) or full employment in static equilibrium.[3]

P. 92 'To dig holes in the ground' [vol. XIV p. 495; *General Theory*, p. 220]. Something has gone wrong in the next two lines.

Footnote [vol. XIV p. 496]. Here it is schedule of m.e. that is wanted.[4]

Chapter 19 [chapter 17]. Here for the first time I am finding the argument difficult. I think the reader should be given every help, e.g. p. 94, 4th paragraph [vol. XIV p. 496; *General Theory*, p. 223, bottom]. Slip in a word to say why it is likely to be '*greatest* of the own-rates. . .which rules the roost' or end of page, show how if wheat-rate were higher than money rate it would be the wheat-rate that caused the trouble.

P. 95, II, 2nd paragraph [vol. XIV p. 497]. Explain 'liquidity premium' more fully. If earnings (e.g. house-rent) are negative carrying costs it is not clear why liquidity premium and carry[ing] costs for money should be greater than for all other assets.

P. 96, 4th paragraph and p. 97 top [vol. XIV p. 498; *General Theory*, p. 229]. 'As output increases'; I was at first doubtful whether this means output of

[1] 'No.'   [2] 'No, because m.e. is relevant on *new* capital.'
[3] 'The former.'   [4] 'Deleted.'

all assets or output of the money commodity. Say *its* output. This doesn't seem quite right because one of the points about money is that it doesn't increase so fast. Perhaps output of all assets is what you want. But should it not be the stock rather than the rate of output that is increasing?

(ii) I think this condition does not hold good when there is changing uncertainty about the future exchange value of money. I think this fits in with your point of view. Money is so much the less money when future wage rates are in doubt. Could you put in a qualification here?

§§ v [*General Theory*, pp. 239–42]. I think it would be helpful if you could follow out the idea of a non-monetary economy, e.g. I take it the point is that if there is no money commodity an increase in the propensity to save lowers the rates of interest to the point at which there is a corresponding increase in investment and 'the buckets in the well case' is fulfilled.[1]

P. 106, 2nd paragraph [vol. XIV p. 502, *General Theory*, p. 245]. The degree of competition is one of your given factors.

P. 111, line 6 [vol. XIV p. 508; *General Theory*, p. 281]. The ordinary demand curve for a particular commodity. Supply curve for a particular industry.

3rd paragraph [vol. XIV p. 509; *General Theory*, p. 281]. Further, when all these conditions are given, each level of effective demand corresponds to a given distribution of income. This strengthens the presumption of given demands for particular industries.

Pp. 111–12 [vol. XIV p. 509; *General Theory*, p. 283]. You have got P'_r where I think there should be P'_{wr} in several places.

P. 112, top [*General Theory*, p. 283]. $e_{or} = O$ should be o (zero).

P. 111 [*General Theory*, p. 284]. Would it be worthwhile having a footnote to point out the relation between your 'aggregate' functions and the usual 'average' functions, e.g. your $e = 1$ corresponds to infinite E. of S. on the Marshallian convention.

P. 113, top [vol. XIV p. 509; *General Theory*, p. 285, top]. Suffixes seem to have gone wrong again.

P. 114, 2nd paragraph [*General Theory*, p. 287]. An increase in D due to increased consumption itself leads to an increase in investment $\therefore$ for a period the increase in D and in consumption is greater than it will be when the process of building up the 'higher stages' has come to an end. Is it worth while to clear up this point?[2]

P. 114 [vol. XIV p. 510; *General Theory*, p. 287]. There is a great deal about this in the *Treatise*. Indeed I think the chapter on the trade cycle is really concerned with this kind of movement.

[1] 'Yes, but I am on a different point in this particular context.'
[2] 'Dealt with elsewhere, I think.'

P. 114, 3rd paragraph [vol. XIV p. 510; *General Theory*, p. 288]. Explain 'excessive' profit stimulus.

P. 115, top (on hours of labour) [*General Theory*, p. 289]. I think it would make your treatment more watertight if you dealt with this point in defining full employment in the first place.[1] It is only slightly unrealistic to assume that a man-week corresponds to a given amount of effort.

P. 115, (1) [vol. XIV p. 510; *General Theory*, p. 290 (1)]. Could you show how this works? I don't quite see what is happening.

(2) [vol. XIV p. 510]. I think you want supply price rather than marginal cost here.[2]

Pp. 117–18, II [vol. XIV p. 455; *General Theory*, p. 116, footnote]. 'More precisely...$k = k'$.' I think this would be better in a footnote. The argument would then come on better.

P. 120 (i) [below p. 456; *General Theory*, pp. 119–20]. Also increased cost of capital goods will reduce m.e. of capital for private investment.

Hawtrey

Rate of saving determines long-term investment. Rate of discount determines investment in stocks. Rise in rate of discount causes disinvestment in stocks ∴ income declines ∴ saving declines ∴ investment in fixed capital declines.

To JOAN ROBINSON, *3 September 1935*

My dear Joan,

I now have a spare copy of the last three chapters of my book and send them herewith. The last two chapters are completely unrevised. Roy strongly objects to chapter 26 as a tendentious attempt to glorify imbeciles. I should like to know how it strikes you. Do not take chapter 27 too seriously in its present form. Somehow or other the emphasis has got quite wrong. I hope, however, to put that right without too much re-writing.

I have been occupied for several weeks in somewhat re-writing Book I and completely re-writing Book II. In the case of Book II practically not a word of the version you have read has been left standing. I will let you see this in due course, particularly since I

---

[1] 'I think I do.'　　　　　　　　　[2] 'Deleted.'

have somewhat modified my definition of user cost. I hope you will think it an improvement.

I was dismayed to hear from Austin of the pains you have been going through. I hope you are better.

Yours ever,

[copy initialled] J.M.K.

From JOAN ROBINSON, *7 September 1935*

My dear Maynard,

Thursday at 8 will be fine. It is possible Austin may have to be away, but I won't ask anyone in, in case you would like to talk about the book. I will keep my notes on these chapters until then. They are few and slight, as I find 25 and 26 very satisfactory. Of course I don't hold with 27, but you say it is to be altered anyway.

I hope you won't let Roy intimidate you about 26. I think it is very important to have it, and it is very enjoyable to read. I don't think you have overstated matters at all.

Yours,

JOAN ROBINSON

To JOAN ROBINSON, *15 September 1935*

[on the back of a note from Lydia]

The point about Marx and Ricardo is, I assume, common knowledge; and I don't think there's anything in my book you need wait for before reviewing Strachey.[1] Also the review is already very late. What about writing the review now, and then letting the editor judge?

Have you any notes on my earlier chapters? I have it in mind to begin sending them for revise in page later this week.

J.M.K.

From JOAN ROBINSON [*Autumn 1935*]

Just a few points in Book II, all of a page correction order.

I find the new definitions growing on me, but I can't pretend to be any use to you on those points because they always make me feel dizzy.

[1] J. Strachey, *The Nature of Capitalist Crisis*. Mrs Robinson's review appeared in the *Economic Journal* for June 1936. [Ed.]

P. 26, 3rd paragraph 'difficult to conceive'. Austin is very fond of cases where U is negative because $G' - G < B'$, i.e. where it does machines good to be used.[1]

Last paragraph, 2nd half. Rather obscure. Don't you mean that you have discovered what *ought* to have been meant by these propositions?

Note 2. Number of firms is assumed constant.

P. 27, last paragraph '(or, conceivably, gain)': why only conceivable? Changes in *value* can go either way equally and a rise in value may be treated as a windfall.

P. 28, footnote. Reference to Pigou wants repeating. (He will have made new definitions while people are still reading this book.)

P. 29, 28th line from bottom. 'same thing as', 'must be equal in value to'.

P. 32, last paragraph of I, 'equal intensity'. Surely what you want is that a *given* plant is used with intensity at different rates of output of the firm.

Last line of paragraph, i.e. to the increment of user cost due to an increment of rate of output.

P. 33, III. Would it be worth giving a footnote to show how this situation is dealt with under your system of definitions, i.e. by a deduction from proceeds?

P. 34, chapter 7, 3rd line. 'being, for the community as a whole, merely different aspects of the same thing.'

P. 39, 2nd paragraph, middle. 'this' seems to be referring to the wrong view.

To JOAN ROBINSON, *24 October 1935*

My dear Joan,

You kindly said that you would be willing to look through once more my page proofs on the look-out for minor points. Here are the first 64 pages. I will let you have further instalments as they come along.

I thought your paper at the [Political Economy] Club was crystal clear and extremely interesting.

Yours ever,

J.M.K.

Through these discussions the book moved towards publication date. Extracts from Keynes's letters to his mother help set the background.

[1] But it can't be. The cost of buzzing them round, if desirable, is included in B!

From a letter to FLORENCE KEYNES, *9 August 1935*

...I began the *last* chapter of my book this morning. But now again, as usual, there are interruptions.

From a letter to FLORENCE KEYNES, *26 December 1935*

...I finished my book on Tuesday—it has taken five years—all but proof-correcting the preface and index, and it ought to be published at the beginning of February. So I almost feel a man of leisure...

From a letter to FLORENCE KEYNES, *19 January 1936*

...My book is out of my hands and will be published on Feb. 4. The theatre[1] will open on Feb. 3...

---

[1] The reference is to the Arts Theatre, Cambridge. Keynes was responsible for the idea of the theatre, its execution and its finance. In 1938 he formed a trust, whose members represented King's, the University and the town, to which he made over the theatre.

THE COLLECTED WRITINGS OF JOHN MAYNARD KEYNES

Managing Editors:
Professor Sir Austin Robinson and Professor Donald Moggridge